FEDERAL INCOME TAXATION

CASES, PROBLEMS, AND MATERIALS

Fifth Edition

. . .

By

Joel S. Newman

Professor of Law
Wake Forest University

AMERICAN CASEBOOK SERIES®

WEST®

A Thomson Reuters business

Mat #41090664

© West, a Thomson business, 1997, 2002, 2005, 2008
© 2012 Thomson Reuters
    610 Opperman Drive
    St. Paul, MN 55123
    1–800–313–9378
Printed in the United States of America

ISBN: 978–0–314–27171–6

Preface to the Third Edition

Maybe this time I'll get it right.

Joel S. Newman
Winston–Salem, North Carolina
October, 2005

PREFACE TO THE SECOND EDITION

Why not?—What?—Why not?—Why should I not send it?—Why should I not dispatch it?—Why not?—Strange! I don't know why I shouldn't.

> Letter from Woldgang Amadeus Mozart to his cousin, Maria Anna Thekla Mozart, November 3, 1777.

I, too was torn about sending in this manuscript. On the one hand, the government keeps spewing forth statutes, regulations, cases, and rulings, many of which should be addressed. On the other hand, been there, done that.

Then I thought of my old barber. One summer long ago, I worked at a resort hotel. The hotel barber offered a special deal for the employees. If you would commit to getting a haircut once a week, he'd do it for a very low price. I took him up on it, and got a haircut every Monday.

The barber loved the arrangement. Ever Monday, he cut my hair. Then, for the rest of the week, as he saw me around the hotel, he could reflect upon his work. Perhaps, next Monday, he'd cut a tad closer to my left ear. Perhaps a little more off the top.

Using my own casebook in class, I felt the way that barber must have felt during the week. Perhaps this case could be replaced with a better one. Perhaps that problem could be fixed. Now, with a chance to write a new edition, it's Monday. Maybe I can finally do something about that pesky cowlick.

A word on the new legislation. How does one deal with a law which phases in and phases out at various times, and disappears completely after ten years? My solution is to address the 2001 legislation as if all of it is completely phased in, and to assume that it is here to stay. I make this latter assumption because, in many instances, failure to extend the legislation could be characterized as a tax increase. Economic and budgetary constraints notwithstanding, I am not sure that Congress has the guts. If I'm wrong, then it might be Monday all over again.

JOEL S. NEWMAN
WINSTON-SALEM, NORTH CAROLINA
August, 2001

PREFACE TO THE FIRST EDITION

I wanted to call it FEDERAL INCOME TAXATION: CASES, PROBLEMS, STUFF. Two reputable casebook publishers told me in no uncertain terms not to do that. Actually, my plan was to propose the title: MY FIRST BIG BOOK OF TAX. I figured they would be so horrified by that title that they would gratefully accede to . . . CASES, PROBLEMS, STUFF.

Didn't work.

So I'm stuck with a plain vanilla title. You probably noticed it on the front of the book. Since the title doesn't tell you a whole lot about the book, you'll just have to read on.

Sometimes, at the reception for entering first-year students (while I was still attending such things), I would meet a student who couldn't wait to get the first year drek behind her so that she could sink her teeth into the real meat of the law school curriculum—tax. It is pleasurable to teach such a student—one who arrives with a predisposition in favor of what you teach. But they are not the most fun.

I derive far more pleasure from the student who comes up at the end of the semester (preferably after the exam) and says, "I thought I would hate tax, but it really wasn't that bad. In fact, I almost like it." That's the student who, walking into class on the first day, presents the greatest challenge. That's the one who can give the instructor the greatest sense of accomplishment, if the challenge is met successfully. This casebook was written with that student in mind.

The key is that the student only *thought* she would hate tax. Therein lies your window of opportunity. Some students KNOW they will hate tax. With luck, those students can be persuaded to enroll in someone else's section.

If you can persuade your students to approach tax with an open mind, two good things will happen:

(1) The experience will be far more pleasant for all of you; and

(2) The students will learn more.

This book is designed to reach such students in two ways:

(1) by making the subject less daunting, at least toward the beginning; and

(2) by selecting materials which are interesting, and which suggest connections between tax and the rest of the students' world.

Making the subject less daunting, at least in the beginning

Learning is more pleasant, and more effective, if one begins with the simple things, and builds to the more complex. This notion has ramifications on daily assignments, chapters, and the entire book.

Daily assignments

It is important to focus upon the natural division of labor between book and instructor. At least in theory, the student reads the assignment in the book first. Only then does she go to class. Thus, the book gets the first shot at her; the instructor the second.

If follows that the materials in the book should be relatively simple—at least in the beginning. They should furnish the foundation upon which the instructor can build. Above all, it is to be hoped that the student will emerge from the reading assignment with the beginnings of knowledge, not frustration.

To emphasize the simple, however, does not suggest that the book should never titillate, annoy, or challenge the student to reach for something which may be beyond her grasp. There is risk in asking the students to stretch, but the rewards can be great. Anyway, remember that the book has only the first shot. If the book reaches too far, the instructor can always come in and clean up the mess.

Chapters and the Whole Book

In the broader sense as well, things should start simple, and only build when the foundations are solidly laid. Any tax topic can be addressed in a relatively simple way, or in a relatively complex way. In this book, I have attempted to address those topics taken up in the earlier chapters, and in the earlier parts of chapters, in a relatively simple way. Later in the chapters, and later in the book, things occasionally get more complex.

The problems are intended to work the same way. Within problem sets, the first few problems are designed to be easy, to give the student a sense of mastery and confidence. In the later problems, things can get trickier.

Selection of Materials

Here's where the "stuff" comes in. Tax casebooks should expose students to all of the sorts of materials a tax lawyer would use in her practice. Thus, this book features cases, revenue rulings, private letter rulings, committee reports, Joint Committee Prints, and a Congressional colloquy.

There are also unenacted bills, and foreign materials. The bills are there for two reasons. First, learning to read tax statutes is a major objective of the first tax course. The best way to learn to read statutes is to do it often. Bills are good reading exercises. Second, bills can add focus to policy discussions. Don't like the current law? Consider a concrete alternative.

Foreign materials also suggest concrete alternatives to the American approach. This time, however, they are alternatives with a track record.

However, the main reason to include a few foreign materials in the book is to prove that they exist. We are not alone.

There are also notes, problems, a cartoon, tables, graphs, an obituary, and some poetry. Variety is good. As to the poetry, it does irk me when my colleagues claim that us tax lawyers ain't got no culture. Then again, I did have one student who told me that she never really understood *Lucas v. Earl* until she reflected upon my haiku. Go figure.

Connections. Materials are selected, whenever possible, to connect to the students in a number of ways. First, I tried to find cases with interesting stories, or at least, stories about interesting people.

Second, materials of particular interest to students—especially law students, and their teachers, are emphasized, including:

- Students: Tax aspects of education, including taxation of scholarships, and the deductibility of education expenses and interest on students loans.

- Law students: Does a Tax LL.M. qualify the recipient for a new trade or business? Can a license to practice law be amortized?

- Budding Lawyers (especially lawyers who absolutely, positively don't want to specialize in tax): Tax aspects of divorce, tax aspects of damages.

  [In both of the latter categories, red flags are raised to alert the students that the materials will have practical value to the general practitioner.]

- Teachers: If you can't connect to the students, connecting to the teachers can be the next best thing. I have always found, for example, that talking about which travel expenses I deducted when I visited at other law schools can enliven and personalize the topic. (Was my semester as a Visiting Professor at University of Hawaii *really* a business trip?)

It is also helpful to connect to current issues. This casebook raises issues of race and gender. It also discusses AIDS, and the question of when life (and dependency exemptions) begin. Tax is the ultimate policy course.

Last but not least, questions of legal ethics are raised. There are specific references to legal ethics issues relating to conflicts problems in divorce, fraudulent charitable contribution deductions and inventory write-downs, and the penalty provisions. In addition, an excerpt from Fred Corneel's *Guidelines to Tax Practice Second* is provided as an Appendix, so that the instructor can raise other legal ethics issues as she pleases.

Editorial matters

Most citations have been deleted from the judicial opinions. Moreover, most footnotes and most concurring and dissenting opinions have been deleted. Deletions of textual matter from cases and other materials have been indicated by * * *.

Those footnotes which have not been deleted from judicial opinions retain their original numbers. Footnotes to the expository materials in the book are indicated by lower case letters.

Of course, it is assumed that the students will read the book in conjunction with the statutes and regulations. There are good, abridged versions of the tax statute and regulations available, and an attempt has been made to cite mostly to those statutes and regulations which are likely to be found in those abridged materials.

This casebook is designed to be used in either a three-semester-hour course or a four-semester-hour course. For one suggestion on how to use the book in a three-hour course, please refer to the Teacher's Manual.

JOEL S. NEWMAN
WINSTON-SALEM, NORTH CAROLINA
1998

ACKNOWLEDGMENTS

I've had a lot of help, and I'm grateful. As to faculty colleagues, I wish to thank Professors Dorothy Brown of the Emory University School of Law, Charles Davenport of Rutgers–Newark Law School, Eric Lustig of New England School of Law, Michael McIntyre of the Wayne State University Law School, and especially my Wake Forest colleague David Shores.

I also wish to thank my student assistants—Michael Schenk, Brett Hanna, and Adam King; for the Third Edition, Vincent Guglielmotti and Amanda Zimmer; for the Fourth Edition, Ryan Kinder; for the Fifth Edition, Jeffrey Kowalski.

This fifth edition, of course, would not have been possible without the benefit of my experiences, and those of my colleagues, with the first four editions. Accordingly, I would like to thank, and apologize to, all of the law students and teachers who used them. You'll be hearing from me for feedback on this one, as well.

Summary of Contents

TABLE OF CONTENTS

―――――

TABLE OF CASES

The principal cases are in bold type. Cases cited or discussed in the text are in roman type. References are to pages. Cases cited in principal cases and within other quoted materials are not included.

TABLE OF INTERNAL REVENUE CODE SECTIONS

TABLE OF REGULATIONS

TABLE OF IRS RULINGS AND ANNOUNCEMENTS

TABLE OF AUTHORITIES

References are to Pages

FEDERAL INCOME TAXATION

CASES, PROBLEMS, AND MATERIALS

Fifth Edition

CHAPTER I

INTRODUCTION

■ ■ ■

A. TAX ANXIETY

Congratulations. You cracked open the book. That's a good first step.

Many of you have dreaded this moment. Let's face your anxiety head on. You think that taxes are complex. You're right. You think that the tax course will be different from the law school courses you have taken so far. You're half right. But, if you give it a chance, you just might enjoy it.

1. WHY TAXES ARE COMPLEX

Taxes are complex for everyone, not only law students. First, all law reflects its environment. The environment of tax law is the economy, and the United States economy is about the most complex and sophisticated one in the world. It would be surprising if tax law were not equally complex.

Second, tax law involves money directly. The stakes are high, and immediate. Some of the brightest people in the country make a very good living finding ways around the tax laws. Sometimes, they do so in spite of the efforts of some pretty bright people in government who are trying to stop them. Put a bunch of bright schemers on a collision course, and who knows what will happen. But one thing is certain; it's not going to get any simpler.

Third, tax laws are used to do too many things. Arguably, tax laws ought to be used only to collect money. However, our legislators have found it impossible to resist the temptation to use them to do other things, like social engineering. If you give to charity, we'll give you a tax break. If you save the environment by filtering your smoke stack, we'll give you a tax break. Ad infinitum. Every time you add a function to a body of law, it necessarily gets more complex, and less fair. You see the result.

Finally, if you want specific villains, about two-thirds of the bulk of the tax laws can be blamed on two things—progressive rates, and capital gains. More on these later, of course. For now, progressive rates lead to taxing the same dollar of income at different rates to different people. In

1

contrast, our tax treatment of capital gains leads to taxing different dollars of income at different rates, to the same person. Put them together, and you create enormous incentives for manipulation, and complexity.

2. WHY THE TAX COURSE IS DIFFERENT, BUT NOT THAT DIFFERENT

For many law students, tax is their first numbers-oriented course, their first statutory course, and their first directly business-related course. All of these aspects can be scary to humanities majors. They were to me.

As to the numbers, we're not talking higher math. See the computations at 5, 6. Every attempt will be made in this casebook to keep the numerical examples simple. Granted, the numbers in real life aren't so easy. However, by the time you get to real life, you'll have accountants, computer programs, and other inanimate, number-crunching devices to help.

The worst thing about the statute is the way in which it deals with numbers. Expressing arithmetic functions (especially ratios) in words can be tricky. However, if you keep going back to the statute, rather than relying solely on study aids, you will get the hang of it. When digesting tax statutes, chew slowly and drink plenty of liquids.

As to the business aspects of tax, you need to learn a few business concepts anyway, if you really expect to cope in the Twenty-first Century. Actually, your parents and significant others have been waiting patiently for you to figure some of these things out.

Face it; it's time.

In the beginning, some necessary concepts will be a mite alien to humanities majors. However, they will discover that their business-oriented classmates will be more than happy to clue them in. Ironically, the humanities majors will probably end up with better grades in the course. That will be because business-oriented students often forget that the tax course is different, but it isn't that different.

Tax courses are still law school courses.[a] A significant amount of time is still spent reading and analyzing cases. What's more, tax exams often pose questions that have more than one right answer. Analysis and issue spotting are still very important. Accountants tend to forget this fact to their detriment.

---

a. As to the difference between:

　(a) tax courses and other courses, and

　(b) tax lawyers and other lawyers,

see Paul Caron, *Mamas Don't Let Your Babies Grow Up to Be Tax Lawyers*, 64 Tax Notes 379 (July 18, 1994).

3. WHY TAX CAN BE FUN

Despite the gloom and doom above, tax really can be fun. Take me. I dreaded tax, and did not understand it during law school.[b] However, after graduation, therapy, and a few square meals, things changed. When, in practice, I was actually faced with tax problems, I discovered to my surprise that I liked them. And look at me now.

You, too, might like tax. But don't be like me and wait until you get into practice to find out. If you can make this discovery while in law school, you'll be much better off.

Admittedly, some of you will never like tax. That's okay, too. But you can't practice law competently without it. At the very least, you need an alarm system, so that you can recognize a tax problem coming, and punt it off to someone who can deal with it. What's more, you will have to master the tax aspects of whatever your practice happens to be, e.g. taxation of alimony if you practice family law, or taxation of damages if you are a litigator.

And that suggests one of the aspects of tax which can be fun. It affects EVERYTHING. Whatever you do, there's a tax angle.

What's more, tax is fast. Say you're a personal injury lawyer. Say your state legislature enacts a new wrongful death statute. Would you telephone all of your clients and tell them to jump under a speeding truck to test the limits of the new law? I don't think so. However, when there is a change in tax law, you'd better believe that tax advisors all over the country are on the phone immediately, advising their clients to rearrange their affairs to take advantage.

Progress in tort law must await the happenstance of the right fact situation leading to the right case. Progress in tax law does not have to wait, because tax lawyers and their clients create the necessary facts, almost as soon as the law changes.

Like a fast game played by really talented people? Taxes are the best game in town. People pay plenty for you to play. And you don't have to be tall.

4. HOW TAX IS LEARNED

When a client walks into a tax lawyer's office and lays some facts on her, the tax lawyer asks herself the following questions, simultaneously:

Is there income?

Is there a deduction or credit?

If the answer to either of the above is yes:

    To whom?

    When?

    How is it characterized?

---

b. So much for the accuracy of the grading process.

And finally, can this client pay my fee?

In fact, many tax cases bring up lots of these issues, simultaneously. However, students can't learn all of these concepts at once. We must learn one at a time. Hence, there is a unit on income, followed by other units on deductions, who is the taxpayer, timing, etc. However, this dissonance between the way a tax lawyer looks at a fact situation and the way a student looks at a fact situation creates some learning difficulties.

First, most cases, dealing with real facts, necessarily deal with more than one issue. However, in view of the learning curve, cases are often edited so that only one issue appears. Sometimes, this editing makes the cases seem unreal.

Second, what we take apart must be put back together. To get a real sense of being a tax lawyer, the student must ultimately learn to spot and consider many issues at once. Hopefully, at some point in the course, you will take a break from analyzing and start synthesizing.

B. INTRODUCTORY NUTS AND BOLTS

1. A QUICK LOOK AT A TAX COMPUTATION: INCOME, DEDUCTIONS AND CREDITS

Add, subtract, multiply. That's all you need. In fact, in many tax computations, you don't even need that much.

Add up your income. **Subtract** your deductions. **Multiply** the net amount by the appropriate tax rate, or, even simpler, consult the Tax Table. **Subtract** your tax credits, and any tax you've already paid through withholding. If you still owe, pay it. If you've overpaid, get a refund.

Set forth below is a filled-in Form 1040EZ for Tax Year 2010:

Illustration 1

Form **1040EZ**

Department of the Treasury—Internal Revenue Service

Income Tax Return for Single and Joint Filers With No Dependents (99) **2010**

OMB No. 1545-0074

Name, Address, and SSN

See separate instructions.

PRINT CLEARLY

Your first name and initial	Last name	Your social security number
Joseph Q	Taxpayer	000 00 0000
If a joint return, spouse's first name and initial	Last name	Spouse's social security number
Home address (number and street). If you have a P.O. box, see instructions.	Apt. no.	▲ Make sure the SSN(s) above are correct. ▲
City, town or post office, state, and ZIP code. If you have a foreign address, see instructions.		Checking a box below will not change your tax or refund.

Presidential Election Campaign (see page 9) ▶ Check here if you, or your spouse if a joint return, want $3 to go to this fund . . . ▶ ☐ You ☐ Spouse

Section	Line	Description	Line	Amount
Income Attach Form(s) W-2 here. Enclose, but do not attach, any payment.	1	Wages, salaries, and tips. This should be shown in box 1 of your Form(s) W-2. Attach your Form(s) W-2.	1	10,000
	2	Taxable interest. If the total is over $1,500, you cannot use Form 1040EZ.	2	1,010
	3	Unemployment compensation and Alaska Permanent Fund dividends (see page 11).	3	
	4	Add lines 1, 2, and 3. This is your **adjusted gross income.**	4	11,010
You may be entitled to a larger deduction if you file Form 1040A or 1040. See *Before You Begin* on page 4.	5	If someone can claim you (or your spouse if a joint return) as a dependent, check the applicable box(es) below and enter the amount from the worksheet on back. ☐ You ☐ Spouse If no one can claim you (or your spouse if a joint return), enter $9,350 if **single**; $18,700 if **married filing jointly.** See back for explanation.	5	9,350
	6	Subtract line 5 from line 4. If line 5 is larger than line 4, enter -0-. This is your **taxable income.** ▶	6	1,660
Payments, Credits, and Tax	7	Federal income tax withheld from Form(s) W-2 and 1099.	7	40
	8	Making work pay credit (see worksheet on back).	8	400
	9a	**Earned income credit (EIC)** (see page 13).	9a	186
	b	Nontaxable combat pay election. 9b		
	10	Add lines 7, 8, and 9a. These are your **total payments and credits.** ▶	10	626
	11	**Tax.** Use the amount on **line 6 above** to find your tax in the tax table on pages 27 through 35 of the instructions. Then, enter the tax from the table on this line.	11	166
Refund Have it directly deposited! See page 18 and fill in 12b, 12c, and 12d or Form 8888.	12a	If line 10 is larger than line 11, subtract line 11 from line 10. This is your **refund.** If Form 8888 is attached, check here ▶ ☐	12a	
	▶ b	Routing number ☐☐☐☐☐☐☐☐☐ ▶ c Type: ☐ Checking ☐ Savings		
	▶ d	Account number		
Amount You Owe	13	If line 11 is larger than line 10, subtract line 10 from line 11. This is the **amount you owe.** For details on how to pay, see page 19. ▶	13	

Third Party Designee Do you want to allow another person to discuss this return with the IRS (see page 20)? ☐ **Yes.** Complete the following. ☐ **No**

Designee's name ▶ Phone no. ▶ Personal identification number (PIN) ▶ ☐☐☐☐☐

Sign Here Under penalties of perjury, I declare that I have examined this return, and to the best of my knowledge and belief, it is true, correct, and accurately lists all amounts and sources of income I received during the tax year. Declaration of preparer (other than the taxpayer) is based on all information of which the preparer has any knowledge.

Joint return? See page 6. Keep a copy for your records.

Your signature	Date	Your occupation	Daytime phone number
Spouse's signature. If a joint return, **both** must sign.	Date	Spouse's occupation	

Paid Preparer Use Only

Print/Type preparer's name	Preparer's signature	Date	Check ☐ if self-employed	PTIN
Firm's name ▶			Firm's EIN ▶	
Firm's address ▶			Phone no.	

For Disclosure, Privacy Act, and Paperwork Reduction Act Notice, see page 36. Cat. No. 11329W Form **1040EZ** (2010)

The wages and interest are **added** to total adjusted gross income of $11,010 on Line 4. Then, $9,350 is **subtracted** on line 5. The $9,350 represents the standard deduction of $5,700[c] and the deduction for personal exemption of $3,650[d]. What's left is net taxable income of $1,660 on line 6.

---

c. See page 547 for discussion of the standard deduction. The standard deduction is defined in § 63(c). For single taxpayers in tax year 2010, the $3,000 standard deduction listed in that section is adjusted for inflation to $5,7000, pursuant to § 63(c)(4).

d. See page 549 and Internal Revenue Code §§ 151 and 152 for discussion of the personal exemption. Come to think of it, perhaps you shouldn't. Why don't you just take my word for it for now. Chill out. Let the course come to you.

Now, **add** your federal tax withheld, your Making work pay credit, and your earned income credit on lines 7, 8, and 9a, to give you total payments of $626 on line 10.

You could take that net taxable income figure from Line 6 and **multiply** by 10%.[e] However, it is much simpler to refer to the Tax Tables that come with the Instructions to Form 1040EZ, which tell you the tax for a single taxpayer who entered between $1,650 and $1,675 on line 6 of Form 1040EZ is $166. Enter $166 on Line 10.

Now, **Subtract** the total payments of $626 from tax owed of $166. Glory be, looks like the feds owe you a refund of $460. It may not be better than sliced bread, but it's not bad.

Notice that you subtract at two different times, once before you apply the rates, and once after. Deductions are subtracted from income, **before** you apply the rates. Credits and payments are subtracted from your tax bill, **after** you apply the rates. The timing of these subtractions is important. A dollar of credit saves you more than a dollar of deduction.

What if the amount at line 5 were $1 greater? Would you ultimately pay $1 less in tax? You would not. In fact, on this simplified form, you would pay exactly the same tax[f].

What if the amount on line 8 were $1 greater. Would you ultimately pay $1 less in tax? Yes.

Line 5 items are deductions. A dollar in deductions will not save you a dollar in tax. Since it is subtracted before the rates are applied, it will only save you $1 times your marginal rate. For a 25% bracket taxpayer, a $1 deduction is worth (i.e. saves) 25 A credit of $1, however, saves (is worth) $1 to all taxpayers, provided that they owed at least $1 in tax before the credit.

This difference between deductions and credits suggests two points to ponder. First, a planning point. If deductions are worth more to some taxpayers than others, then it might be advisable to shift deductions to those who can make better use of them.

Second, a policy point. If tax breaks are proposed to achieve a given policy objective, should they be in the form of deductions or credits? If all taxpayers should be given an equal break, then credits are preferable. On the other hand, if high bracket taxpayers should be given a higher break (perhaps, for example, we want to encourage substantial contributions to art museums-something which only high-income taxpayers can do), then deductions are preferable.

As you work your way through the course, consider which items are deductions and which are credits, and why.

---

e. Code §§ 1(c) and 1(i) set the lowest rate for singles for tax years after 2000 at 10%.

f. Theoretically, if you applied the rates in § 1(c) in Tax Year 2010, you would pay 10¢ less tax. However, since the tax tables deal only in increments of $50, a $1 increase in deductions will make no difference.

2. AUTHORITIES: STATUTES, REGULATIONS, RULINGS, ETC.

Statutes

It all begins with the statute. We know about that. The statute (unless the Constitution comes into play) is the highest authority. If you can answer your question in the statute, you can stop.

Regulations

Regulations are promulgated pursuant to § 7805, by which Congress delegates authority to the Treasury Department. For the income tax matters addressed in this book, if you seek a regulation to explain a given section of the Code, simply put a "1." before the Code section, and you have the appropriate regulation. For example, for regulations which pertain to § 61, see Reg. § 1.61.

Like good wine, regulations improve with age. The longer a regulation stays on the books, the stronger it becomes. If Congress persists in leaving a given Regulation alone, the inference is that Congress is aware of the Regulation, and approves of it. Therefore, the regulation increasingly takes on the force of law.

It usually takes three years after the enactment of a statute before Treasury promulgates regulations. Therefore, take care when you read the regulations on statutes which have recently been amended. The regulations might not reflect the amendments.

When proposed regulations are promulgated, there is usually a period for written comments, followed by a formal hearing in Washington. After the formal hearing, final regulations can be promulgated. Alternatively, if the comments are too hostile, the regulations can be withdrawn, and the whole mess starts over.

Many comment letters are written by Washington insiders—lawyers and lobbyists. However, when the issue is controversial, even more comment letters are written by the general public. Often, the ones writing the comments don't understand the division of labor between the legislature and the executive branch. They complain, not about the proposed regulation (which Treasury wrote), but about the underlying statute (which Congress wrote), or, perhaps, about life in general. Comment letters can be interesting reading. See, for example, the comments of restaurant employees on the proposed tipping regulations, *infra* at 92–93.

Cases

Cases you know. Tax Court opinions are appealable to the circuit in which the taxpayer resided at the time the Tax Court petition was filed. If the taxpayer is a corporation, Tax Court opinions are appealable to the circuit in which the corporation had its principal place of business.[g] Court of Federal Claims decisions are appealable to the Federal Court of Appeal for the Federal Circuit. By now, you probably know about the Federal District Court.

Rulings

Say you are planning a major corporate transaction, and you want to be sure that you know in advance what the tax consequences will be. In some areas, if you describe the transaction to IRS, they will write back and tell you.[h] These private letter rulings are binding on the IRS, but only in the specific matter, and only if you do what you said you would do. They are now available through the Freedom of Information Act, and therefore through the tax services. They cannot be cited as precedent,[i] but they can give a feel for how the IRS views a transaction. Sometimes, they can be used to embarrass IRS, if it appears to be taking inconsistent positions.

When IRS receives a substantial number of ruling requests on a similar issue, or if IRS for other reasons thinks that a certain issue is of more general interest, it issues a public Revenue Ruling. Revenue rulings are no more than the position of one party (IRS) to a potential lawsuit. Of course, it is an important party, one which has dealt with our tax laws for a long time and has a certain amount of respect in the community. However, the most significant value of the Revenue Ruling is that it tells you what IRS will do. If you take action consistent with the ruling, you can be assured that IRS will not oppose you. If you go against the ruling, you probably have a lawsuit on your hands.

How the government communicates with the taxpayer

Consider the many ways in which the government communicates the tax laws to the people. Formally, there are the statutes and cases. Theoretically, that's all you should need. Right.

If you need more guidance, there are the regulations, rulings, and other official announcements. These often give illustrative examples, and computational help. However, most taxpayers do not consult any of these sources. Instead, government communicates with them through the tax forms, the instructions to the tax forms, and occasionally, through the IRS publications meant to explain the forms. The quickest way to access these forms and publications is through the IRS website, http://www.irs.gov.

Consider these various modes of communication, and how they differ. Have a look, for example, at the following language appearing on the inside front cover of IRS Publication 17, YOUR FEDERAL INCOME TAX:

---

g. § 7482(b).

h. Rev. Proc. 2011–1. Each year, the first Revenue Procedure sets out guidelines for obtaining rulings.

i. § 6110(k)(3).

This publication covers some subjects on which a court may have made a decision more favorable to taxpayers than the interpretation by the IRS. Until these differing interpretations are resolved by higher court decisions or in some other way, this publication will continue to present the interpretation by the IRS.

Of those who read Publication 17, how many do you suppose read that paragraph? What's more, do you suppose that Publication 17 even tells you when they are presenting an IRS position that may be controversial? In fact, Publication 17 presents all of its positions equally, as if they were all gospel. A word to the wise.

Tax students and tax professionals have many other sources of information and guidance. Of course, tax, like all other law school courses, has generated a tempting array of student aids. Consult your teacher and classmates as to which of these works best in your situation.

3. PROCEDURE

It all starts with a tax return. Generally, IRS has six years to dispute the return.[j] In the event of a false return, willful attempts to evade tax, or no return, IRS has no limitation period.[k] If they dispute the return, you will receive a 30–day letter, and will be audited by an agent. If you agree with the results of the audit, you pay, or receive your further refund, and go on your way. If you do not agree with the audit, you and IRS can resolve your differences at the conference level. If that resolution fails, you go to court.

---

j. § 6501(e).

k. § 6501(c)(1).

Illustration 2

"And if she doesn't file?"

•   •

Drawing by Shanahan; ©1991
The New Yorker Magazine, Inc.

You can pay the taxes as IRS sees them, and then sue for a refund, either in the Federal District Court or the Court of Federal Claims. Alternatively, you can litigate without paying your taxes up front by going to the U.S. Tax Court. The District Court is the only one with the option of a jury trial. The Tax Court is an expert court, better suited for complex matters. The Court of Claims is a semi-expert court, and the District Court is a generalist court.

Actual selection of a court will depend mostly on three factors. First, how do you feel about paying your taxes up front? Second, what are the actual precedents from the three courts on the subject matter in question? Third, do you wish to litigate locally, or in Washington, D.C.?

4. HISTORY

Taxes, as you probably know, go back a long way. The Rosetta Stone was a tax document. The New Testament has a few things to say about tax collectors. One of the most enduring pieces of advice about tax collecting comes from Jean Baptiste Colbert, Finance Minister to Louis XIV, who said that taxation is the art of plucking the most feathers from the goose with the least hissing. Casanova was a tax counsellor, though one wonders where he found the time.

In the United States, taxes in general, and the ensuing tea party, had something to do with the American Revolution, and the tax on whiskey had something to do with our change from the Articles of Confederation to the Constitution.

Income taxation, however, is a more recent phenomenon here. With the exception of the Civil War income taxes, the federal government funded its expenditures before 1913 largely by tariffs and excise taxes. However, the Twentieth Century changed all that.

When the 1894 Income Tax was declared unconstitutional in Pollock v. Farmers' Loan & Trust Co., 157 U.S. 429, 15 S.Ct. 673, 39 L.Ed. 759, *aff'd on rehearing,* 158 U.S. 601, 15 S.Ct. 912, 39 L.Ed. 1108 (1895), the response was to amend the Constitution. The 16th Amendment, which allowed the federal government to tax income without apportionment among the states, was ratified in 1913, followed by the 1913 Income Tax.

The income tax in the early years was not nearly as burdensome as it is today, with rates starting at 1% (albeit with surtaxes during World War I). Things muddled through for some time, with the introduction of the federal estate tax in 1916, the gift tax in 1932, and the first (and some still say the best) real codification of the tax laws in 1939.

The big change in taxation came as a result of World War II. The government needed money, so they raised the rates, at one point to a high marginal rate of 94%. Also, during the Roosevelt Administration, social security and employment taxes were introduced, which for low income taxpayers were and are more significant than the income taxes.

Rates went mostly down after the war, and the second great codification took place in 1954. After 1954, significant statutory changes took place, more or less, every seven years, to the great profit of tax lawyers and accountants. Otherwise, things remained relatively stable until 1986.

In 1986, there was the Big Deal. The liberals agreed to less progressive rates, with the highest marginal rates going down from 50% to 28%. In return, the conservatives agreed that capital gains would be taxed just like other income. This deal, and other changes, made the 1986 Tax Reform Act the most significant tax legislation in at least a generation.

After 1986, the Big Deal unraveled. Rates inched back up, and the equality of capital gains and ordinary income eroded. Further change was impeded by budget constraints, including the requirement that any further tax changes be revenue neutral—that is, that they would neither increase nor decrease total tax collections.[1]

---

1. Any tax change which raises revenue is a tax increase. No one wants to vote for a tax increase. However, any tax change that lowers revenue could lead to budget deficits. No one has been terribly excited about voting for those, either. Politically, therefore, revenue neutral tax changes have usually been the safest ones.

Clearly, more tax legislation is coming. More likely than not, it will be driven as much by the economy as by politics. The lesson to tax students is to get a good grasp of the big picture. Only then can one deal with the ever-changing details as they fly by.

5. TAX LAW AND THE CONSTITUTION

The Constitution of the United States

Article I, Section 8

* * *

The Congress shall have Power To lay and collect Taxes, Duties, Imposts and Excises, to pay the Debts and provide for the common Defence and general Welfare of the United States, but all Duties, Imposts and Excises shall be uniform throughout the United States;

* * *

No capitation, or other direct, Tax shall be laid, unless in Proportion to the Census or Enumeration herein before directed to be taken.

* * *

Amendment XVI [1913]

The Congress shall have power to lay and collect taxes on incomes, from whatever source derived, without apportionment among the several states, and without regard to any census or enumeration.

Now, the following excerpt should tell you everything you need to know about Article I, Section 8—at least for the purposes of this class.

MADISON'S NOTES OF THE DEBATES IN THE FEDERAL CONVENTION OF 1787

Mr. King asked what was the precise meaning of direct taxation?

No one answered.[m]

Constitutional issues do come up in tax, notably in two areas. First, if the government is going to take away the property of its citizens through taxation, it must do so pursuant to the due process of law. Second, the tax laws must not discriminate, lest they violate the Equal Protection Clause.[n]

Other constitutional issues occasionally arise. For example, to the extent that religious organizations can be tax-exempt, or receive tax-deductible contributions, First Amendment concerns can be raised. Criminal tax penalties raise all of the criminal law constitutional questions, including Miranda. However, there is not a heavy constitutional law dimension to the introductory tax course.

---

m. MADISON'S NOTES OF DEBATES IN THE FEDERAL CONVENTION OF 1787 (N.Y. 1987) [at 494] Monday, August 20, 1787.

n. Consider this point in light of the discussion of horizontal equity, *infra* at 23.

6. IRS AS A COLLECTION AGENCY

Taxes are, essentially, debts that taxpayers owe. Therefore, IRS is a collection agency. Consider how a debt collection agency works. First, it measures efficiency by computing how many dollars it spends per hundred dollars of collections. In this respect, IRS does rather well. Second, on the level of the individual collection agent, it measures effectiveness by adding up the number of dollars that each agent collects.

But IRS is more, and less, than a collection agency. It is an agency of the federal government, assigned the task of the fair administration of the tax laws. It is, like other agencies, a servant of the people. Measuring efficiency and amounts of collections is fine in those cases in which the debt is agreed to by both sides. However, it does not make sense in other cases. As a taxpayer, how much would you trust IRS if you knew that the agent who was auditing your taxes was being evaluated and promoted based upon the amount she collected, rather than on the fairness and accuracy of the tax result?

The Taxpayer's Bill of Rights has now made it clear that IRS employees will not be evaluated on the basis of collections. But, given the nature and function of IRS, and the continuing predilection of government to keep statistics on efficient collections, how good does that make you feel?

C. BASIC POLICY CHOICES: HOW TO FINANCE GOVERNMENT EXPENDITURE

The government is spending money. We need to come up with a way to pay for it. Three ways should come to mind:

1) Print money;

2) Borrow money; or

3) Tax.

Most countries, including the United States, do all three.

1. NON–TAX OPTIONS

Printing money will certainly do the job. However, when you print more money, you end up with more dollars chasing the same goods and services. The result is inflation.

Governmental borrowing has the same problem. When the government borrows, it drives up the interest rates for the rest of us. When interest rates go up, prices tend to follow.

So what's wrong with inflation? No one ever claimed that governmental expenditures wouldn't cost the citizens in some way. Inflation is simply the way that the cost of printing or borrowing money is passed on to the people.

The problem is that the burden of inflation does not fall equally upon all citizens. In fact, the distribution of that burden is not what many of us would consider to be fair. Retired people on fixed incomes are hurt far worse by inflation than people who are still in the work force, receiving cost of living raises.[o]

Governments tax, in addition to printing and borrowing money, because the burdens of taxation can be allocated more effectively and more fairly than the burdens of inflation. Now, consider the various forms of taxation, to see if they can distribute this burden in a fairer manner.

2. TAX OPTIONS

(a) Head Tax

The head tax is the simplest form of taxation. Say the federal government spends $750 billion each year, and there are 250 million people in the United States. What could be simpler than dividing people into dollars?

$$\frac{\$750 \text{ billion}}{250 \text{ million people}} = \$3,000 \text{ per person}$$

Tax each man, woman and child in the United States $3,000 per year, and the federal government will have $750 billion to spend.

The problem is that some people don't have the $3,000 to pay, and others could easily afford to pay much more. A head tax violates our notions of fairness.

(b) Benefits Tax

If the object is to pay for government expenditures, what could be more fair than taxing people based upon the benefit they receive from government? You get what you pay for.

A benefit tax would have many advantages. Consider the difference between a turnpike and a "free" interstate highway. On a turnpike, only those who use the road pay for the road. The further you travel on the road, the more you pay. In contrast, we all pay for the interstate highway system, whether we use it or not.[p] Perhaps those building and maintaining the roads would make more efficient decisions if the funding for the roads were directly related to their use.

---

o. "Inflation is taxation without legislation."

—Milton Friedman

p. For another example, consider the use of property taxes to fund local schools. Why should homeowners who have no children attending public schools pay for those schools? This problem has led many families to move into neighborhoods with high taxes and good schools while their children are young, only to move out of those neighborhoods when their children go off to college.

Unfortunately, not all governmental benefits can be quantified. For example, which citizens benefit from the defense budget, and how much? Is defending the life and liberty of a rich person worth more than defending the life and liberty of a poor person?

Moreover, some benefits go to citizens who, for other reasons, cannot and should not be taxed heavily. Consider welfare. The principle of benefit taxation, therefore, can only go so far in constructing a tax system.

(c) Ability to Pay: The Maharajah and the Beggar

Fairness in taxation is often discussed in terms of ability to pay. Those who are able to pay more taxes should pay more; those who are able to pay less taxes should pay less. But how do we measure ability to pay? We can measure it in three ways. We can measure income, spending, or wealth.

The rest of the book will be devoted to a study of the federal income tax. Therefore, it is unnecessary to say more about income here. Instead, what follows is a brief discussion of why income by itself might not always be a good measure of ability to pay, and how the other two measures might work.

When India became independent from the United Kingdom, the Indians asked Lord Nicholas Kaldor, a noted British economist, to advise them on creating a new system of taxation. Lord Kaldor told them to imagine a fabulously wealthy maharajah, who lived in a magnificent palace. Inside the palace were storehouses of jewels, gold, opulent clothing and wonderful foods. The maharajah relaxed in his palace day after day; everything he could ever want was close at hand.

Outside the palace gate was a beggar. He owned absolutely nothing, and lived only on the charity of passersby. Both the maharajah and the beggar, Lord Kaldor pointed out, had identical income—none! However, no one would have suggested that the maharajah and the beggar had equal ability to pay taxes.[q]

An income tax would have failed to treat the maharajah and the beggar differently. However, either a spending tax or a wealth tax would have done nicely. The maharajah both consumed [spent] much more than the beggar, and owned much more. Therefore, it is worth considering these alternative tax bases.

(d) Alternatives to the Income Tax Base

(1) Spending

A tax on spending can take many forms. Many of you are familiar with state sales taxes, and federal, state and local excise taxes (taxes the purchase or sale of a specific item). However, spending taxes can also take

---

q. Nicholas Kaldor, Indian Tax Reform (1956) in Nicholas Kaldor, Reports on Taxation II (1980).

the form of the European Value–Added Tax, or an annual consumption tax.

Spending taxes have many advocates. Most begin with Thomas Hobbes. Imagine that all goods and services used by the populace are to be found in a common pool. Those who create income are adding to the common pool. Those who spend are subtracting from the common pool. It is in the nature of taxation that whatever is taxed will be deterred, and whatever is left untaxed will be encouraged. What should we encourage, adding to the common pool or subtracting from the common pool?

Spending tax advocates also argue that, according to the generally accepted Haig–Simons economic definition of income (see p. 25 *infra*):

Income = Spending + Savings

Therefore:

Spending = Income − Savings

Accordingly, if spending were to be taxed, then taxpayers would be encouraged to save, for savings would be subtracted from the tax base. The national savings rate in the United States is comparatively low. We would all be better off if Americans were to save more.

The biggest problem with a spending tax is its alleged regressivity (*see infra* for a discussion of progressivity and regressivity). Poor people have no choice but to spend all of their income. Rich people have the discretion to spend less than all of their income. Therefore, a spending tax is necessarily a tax on all of the income of poor people, and less than all of the income of rich people.

(2) Wealth

Conceptually, taxes on wealth come in three varieties. You can tax having wealth, getting wealth, or giving wealth. The traditional local property taxes, and European annual wealth taxes, are taxes on having.

State inheritance taxes are taxes on getting, because the tax is levied on the beneficiary. In contrast, the federal estate and gift taxes are taxes on giving.

Arguably, we Americans don't own much any more. Our houses are mortgaged. We provide for our children more by paying college tuition than by willing them the family business. Instead of building up substantial estates, many of us annuitize our wealth in retirement funds, which disappear when we die. Accordingly, there is some question as to whether a wealth tax in any form could fund the government by itself.

3.   PROGRESSIVE RATES vs. FLAT RATES

When taxes are described as flat or proportional, progressive, or regressive, what is being described is the relationship between tax base and tax rates. Income taxes, spending taxes, or wealth taxes can have any of these attributes. However, for the sake of simplicity, we will assume an income tax.

A flat, or proportional tax, is one in which all taxpayers pay the same percentage of their income. A 10% tax on everyone would be a flat, or proportional tax. Graphically, it would look like this:

Illustration 3

FLAT TAX OF 10%

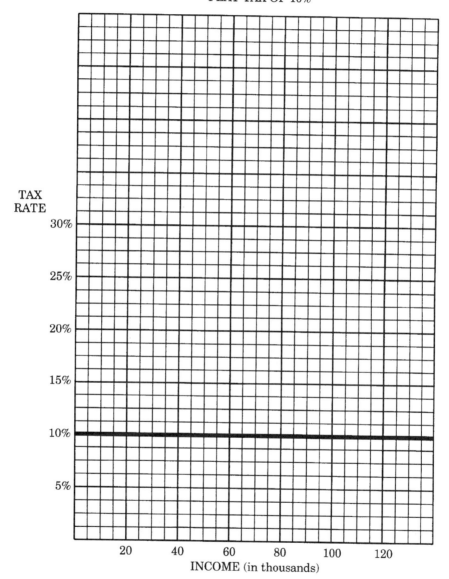

Note that a taxpayer with $100 of income would pay $10, while a taxpayer with $100,000 of income would pay $10,000. In a flat tax, those with more dollars of income pay more dollars in tax. However, everyone pays at the same rate.

In a progressive tax, those with more income pay not only more dollars, but a higher percentage. The "marginal rate"—that is, the rate on the last dollar of income, would rise with income. Graphically, the marginal rates in a progressive tax would look like this:

Illustration 4

PROGRESSIVE TAX – MARGINAL RATES

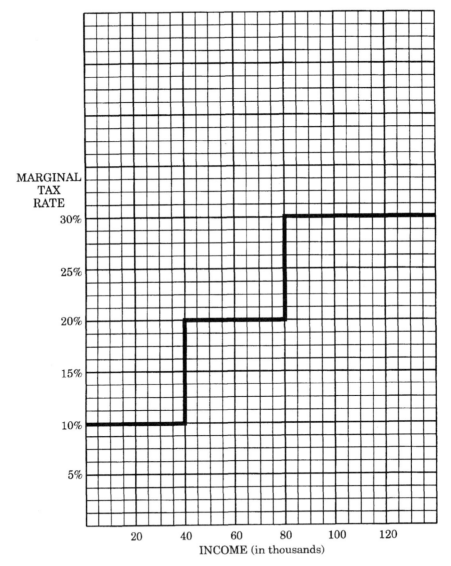

The "effective rate" is computed by dividing the tax bill by the income. Graphically, the "effective rate" of the progressive tax shown above would look like this:

Illustration 5

PROGRESSIVE TAX – EFFECTIVE RATES

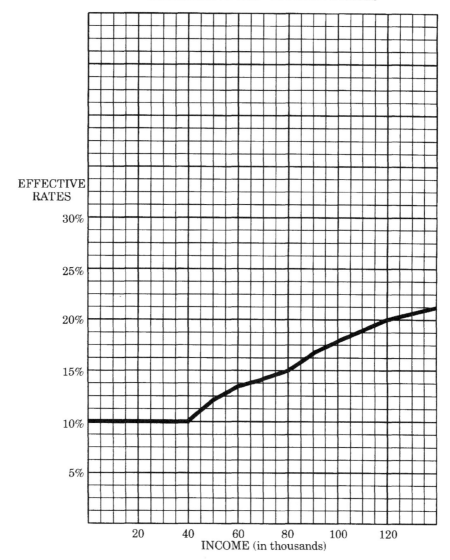

Note that the graph of the effective rates of any progressive tax will show a positive slope.

The progressive tax set forth in Tables 4 and 5 would be expressed in the statute as follows:

If taxable income is: The tax is:
Not over $40,000   10% of taxable income

Over $40,000 but not over $80,000	$4,000[r] plus 20% of the excess over $40,000
Over $80,000	$12,000[s] plus 30% of the excess over $80,000

In a regressive tax, higher income taxpayers would pay a lower rate of tax than lower income taxpayers. Graphically, the marginal rates of a regressive tax would look like this:

Illustration 6

REGRESSIVE TAX – MARGINAL RATES

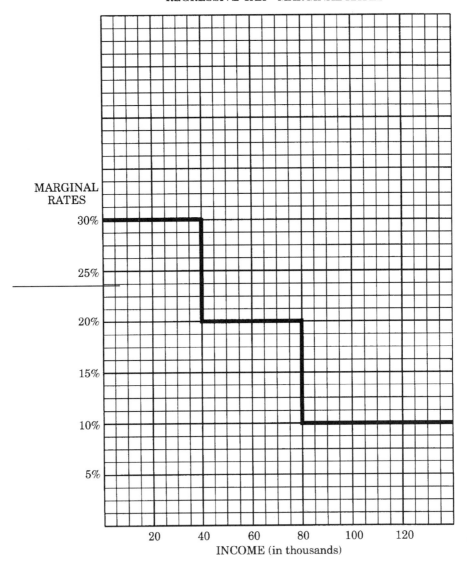

r. That's 10% of the first $40,000.

s. That's 10% of the first $40,000 ($4,000) plus 20% of the next $40,000 ($8,000).

The effective rates of that regressive tax would look like this:

Illustration 7

REGRESSIVE TAX – EFFECTIVE RATES

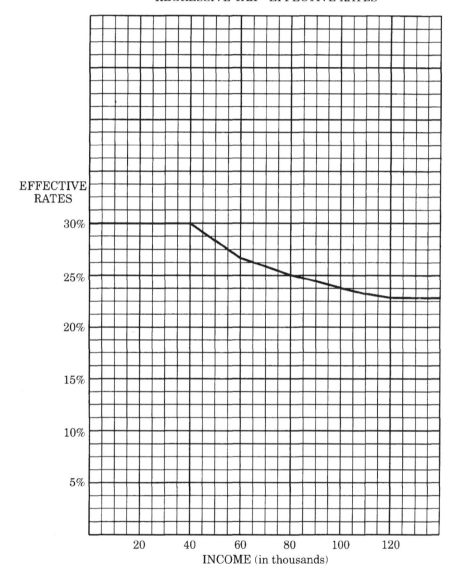

INCOME (in thousands)

Note that the slope is negative.

Everyone agrees that high income people should pay more dollars in tax than low income people. Therefore, at least a proportional tax is appropriate. The debate, then, concerns the difference between proportional and progressive, and how progressive progressive should be.

Many attempts have been made to prove how much more taxes rich people should pay on various theories. All have failed.[t] What remains is the tradeoff between efficiency and equality.[u]

Imagine that four adults, Adam, Bert, Cathy and Dalia, are marooned on a desert island. They seek a mechanism for sharing the island's bounty, and the goods and services that the four of them can produce. They begin with total equality. Each of them will get a one-fourth share, no matter what. This system works well for a few days, until it occurs to Adam that he will get exactly the same share even if he does absolutely no work. So, he stops working. Soon, the others follow suit, and the system collapses.

Next, they posit that each of the four must do at least forty hours per week of productive labor. In return, each will receive a one-fourth share. This new regime works reasonably well for a while.

Then, Bert gets sick. Before the shipwreck, Cathy was a doctor. She is asked to render medical services. "I never liked being a doctor," she says, "and I get my one-fourth share no matter what productive work I choose to do. I'll just continue pruning the coconut trees. Unless, that is, you pay me more."

There's the rub. Cathy has the ability and training to increase the welfare of the group by contributing more than her share to the common pool. However, in a regime of equal compensation, there is no incentive for her to do so. Thus, the aggregate welfare of the group remains low.

People have unequal abilities. Efficiency concerns dictate that those who are capable of producing more should produce more. However, the only way to achieve this efficiency is to give these unequally gifted people unequal incentives. Thus, efficiency destroys equality.

The only argument that really works for progressive taxation is that:

(1) the distribution of income and wealth in the country is too unequal to be tolerated; and

(2) the tax mechanism is a good way of redistributing from the haves to the have-nots.

However, any such redistribution will necessarily involve an efficiency cost. Balancing out equality gains against efficiency losses is very much a matter of individual preference.

4. HOW TO DO A POLICY ANALYSIS OF A TAX PROVISION

Now and then through the course of the term, you will be asked to consider proposed changes in the tax law, or even to consider whether or not a current provision is the best we can do. Lawyers caught up in the practice of law often have time only to consider how a current or proposed

---

t. The best description of this intellectual controversy is Walter J. Blum and Harry Kalven, Jr., THE UNEASY CASE FOR PROGRESSIVE TAXATION (1953).

u. *See generally,* Arthur Okun, EQUALITY AND EFFICIENCY: THE BIG TRADEOFF (1975).

statute relates to the particular needs of their current clients. However, law students can take a broader perspective. To one extent or another, the following questions should be posed:

a) Does it achieve horizontal equity?

b) Does it achieve vertical equity?

c) What economic impact would it have?

d) Does it make tax sense?

e) Would it complicate or simplify?

f) What other policies come into play?

Horizontal Equity

Horizontal equity stands for the proposition that people in similar circumstances should be taxed in similar ways. When analyzing an income tax provision, the most important similar circumstance is income level. Often, the horizontal equity issue is: "Which circumstances other than income level justify differential tax treatment?" For example, hair color does not justify differential tax treatment. Accordingly, a tax provision which taxed redheads more heavily than brunettes with comparable income would violate horizontal equity.

Vertical Equity

Vertical equity invites an inquiry into the impact of the tax provision on different income levels. First, the analyst must make her own judgment about the appropriate treatment of different incomes. Does she prefer her taxes to be progressive, flat, or regressive? Having thus defined her notion of vertical equity, the analyst must then consider how the tax provision in question impacts differently upon the various income levels, and determine whether or not it conforms to her notions of vertical equity.

For example, a tax credit for purchasers of personal automobiles costing more than $75,000 would be a tax break for the rich. Hence, it would violate vertical equity, for those who favor progressive taxes.

Economic Impact

Taxes deal with money. Therefore, taxes have a direct impact on the economy. One tax change with an obvious economic impact is a change in rates. A tax increase takes more money from taxpayers and puts it into government coffers. A tax decrease does the reverse. Other changes, such as liberalizing deductions or credits, are tantamount to a tax cut for some segment of the population, and should also be analyzed for economic impact.

Other, narrower provisions also affect the economy. Arguments have gone on for decades as to whether reduced capital gains rates stimulate investment. Similarly, would faster depreciation schedules prompt businesses to exchange old machines for new ones, thus becoming better able to compete internationally? These are clearly issues in which the lawyer and legislator need the help of the economist.

Does it make tax sense?

We can't all agree completely on what an ideal income tax system would look like, but we can probably agree on some fundamental points. For one, it would tax those items which most of us recognize as income. Every time an item of economic income (*see* p. 25, *infra*) is untaxed, it is appropriate to ask why.

In addition, it would tax net income. Net income means gross income minus the expenses of producing that income. Personal expenses are by definition not the expenses incurred in producing income. Therefore, they would not be deductible in an ideal income tax—at least, not without a pretty good reason. Tax sense, then, is a short-hand way of looking at departures from a net income base with a critical eye, unless they can be satisfactorily explained.

Complexity

We are all concerned with the increasing complexity of our tax laws, and with the increasing amount of time and expense it takes to comply with them. Therefore, every proposed change must be viewed with an eye toward whether it makes the whole regime more or less complex. Of course, change itself is a complicating factor. However, it must be remembered that there is often a tradeoff between fairness in individual cases and complexity. Remember, a head tax would be far simpler than what we have now, but much less fair.

Other Policy Issues

Often, it is nontax policy concerns that are at the crux of a proposed change. An increase in the tobacco tax, for example, has more to do with health policy than with tax policy. Such concerns are often the ones that hit you in the head when you consider a tax law change. However, care must be taken to evaluate the costs of such changes in tax terms, as described above, as measured against the benefits to health care, etc.

5. A FINAL PEP TALK

American taxpayers, know it or not, are staying at the Hotel California. Checking out is possible; leaving is out of the question. You like the song; you can deal with the concept. Face it—you're here for the long haul. Who knows—you might even enjoy it.

CHAPTER II

INCOME

■ ■ ■

Code: § 61

A. DEFINITIONS: ECONOMIC INCOME vs. TAX LAW INCOME

The key concept in an income tax is, of course, income. In order to understand how the tax works, and what policy choices are being made, it is helpful to start with an economist's definition of income. With that definition in place, you can think about how, and why, the tax law definition is different.

1. ECONOMIC INCOME

The Haig–Simons Definition

What do people do with their paychecks? They spend them. What do they do with anything left over? They save it. Simply put, the classic, Haig–Simons definition of income is "spending plus savings."

It might be important, however, to determine whether a given amount of income is "spending" or "savings." In this regard, one must pay attention to the particular way in which the word "spending" is used. When one buys stock, or a business machine, one is "spending," but not in the Haig–Simons sense. For this definition, "spending" means "personal spending." Buying stock or a business machine is investing, taken into account on the "savings" side, just like putting money in the bank. Moreover, "savings" includes not only what you put into savings, but the growth in what's already there. Now consider the more formal Haig–Simons definition:

Personal income may be defined as the algebraic sum of:

1) the market value of rights exercised in consumption, and

2) the change in the value of the store of property rights between the beginning and end of the period in question[a]

Note that, in the formal definition, spending, or "consumption," is described at (1). Savings, or "accumulation," is described at (2).

Haig–Simons Problems

In each case, is there income under the Haig–Simons definition? If so, how much? Is it consumption income or accumulation income?

Use of the money

    1.   John is paid $100 in wages, and

        a) He spends it on food, which he eats.

        b) He puts it in the bank.

        c) He buys a share of stock for $100.

Source of the money

    2.   Would your answers to Questions 1(a) through (c) change if, instead of earning the money as wages, he had:

        a) Found a $100 bill on the street?

        b) Stolen it?

        c) Received it as a gift from his mother?

        d) Received it as interest on his bank savings account?

Mixed Source and Use

    3.   Mary withdraws $100 from her bank savings account and spends it on food, which she eats.

    4.   Mary borrows $100 and spends it on food, which she eats.

Psychic Income

    5.   Sven wakes up in his home in Duluth, Minnesota, on a fine February morning. The sun is shining; it is a good twenty degrees warmer than usual. He says to himself, "What a lovely day! There are times when I might have gladly paid $500 in airfare and lodging expenses to fly south in February and enjoy weather like this."

    6.   In recognition of his thirty-five years of devoted service to the University, Professor Chips' students, present and past, raise $1,000. With the money, they commission a local artist to paint Professor Chips' portrait. When the portrait is completed, they give it to the University. After an appropriate unveiling ceremony, the University hangs the portrait in one of the classrooms where Professor Chips taught. Professor Chips is truly touched.

---

a. Reprinted with permission from PERSONAL INCOME TAXATION, by Henry C. Simons, p. 50. Copyright © 1938 by The University of Chicago Press, Chicago, Illinois.

2. TAX LAW INCOME

Code: §§ 61, 102

INTRODUCTORY PROBLEM

Read §§ 61, and 102. Reconsider the problems above. In which cases, if any, is tax law income different from economic income? Why? Does the tax law concern itself with source, use, both, or neither?

(a) Realization

Code: §§ 1001, 1012

Joe bought a parcel of land in 1990 for $25,000. By the end of 1994, the land was worth $100,000. Joe does nothing, other than looking smug.

Does Joe have income according to the Haig–Simons definition? Yes. The "value of the store of property rights between the beginning and end of the period in question" increased by $75,000. Therefore, he has economic income in that amount.

Does Joe have income according to the tax law? No. Pursuant to § 1001:

> The gain from the sale or other disposition of property shall be the excess of the amount **realized** therefrom over the adjusted basis ...

The amount must be "realized." "Realization" is an elusive concept. For now, however, consider that § 1001 normally doesn't contemplate that an amount can be "realized" unless there is a "sale or other disposition of the property."

Therefore, when Joe's parcel of land goes up in value, without more, he has "unrealized appreciation." Such appreciation may give rise to **economic income**, but there is no **taxable income** until there is a realization event, such as a sale of the property.

What are the advantages and disadvantages of the tax law's determination to wait until a sale of the property before levying a tax?

Suppose Joe now sells the land in 1994 for $100,000. Does this event of sale, without more, create **economic income**? No. Joe is merely converting his wealth from the form of real estate to the form of cash.

Does the event of sale create **taxable income**? It does. But how much?

Consult § 1001 again. The word "excess" means that you'll have to subtract. According to the statute:

Amount realized

– adjusted basis

gain

According to § 1001(b), "amount realized" is "the sum of any money received plus the fair market value of the property (other than money) received." In this case, only money was received. Therefore, the "amount realized" is $100,000.

According to § 1011, basis is determined under § 1012. According to § 1012, " of such property." Other sections mention certain adjustments to basis, but we have no facts to support any such adjustments. Therefore, in this case, the basis is $25,000.

Therefore, according to § 1001,

Amount Realized	$100,000
Less Adjusted Basis	− $ 25,000
Gain	$ 75,000

Therefore, when Joe sells the land in 1994, he realizes a taxable gain of $75,000.

But what if everything which cost $25,000 in 1990 was worth $100,000 in 1994?

Would that fact have any effect upon Joe's taxable gain?

(b) Bargains and Frequent Flyer Programs

PROBLEMS

1.   Broccoli costs $1.00 per bunch. Joe goes to the local grocery store to buy some. Just as he arrives, he hears an announcement over the loudspeakers that, for the next thirty minutes, broccoli will be sold for 50 cents per bunch. Delighted, Joe buys a bunch. As he walks home, he realizes that he has purchased the broccoli as planned, but he has fifty cents more in his pocket than he'd anticipated. Any taxable event?

2.   Broccoli costs $1.00 per bunch. Jack goes to the grocery store, and duly buys a bunch of broccoli for $1.00. On his way home, he notices two quarters on the sidewalk. He picks them up. Any taxable event? Can you reconcile the tax treatment of Joe with the tax treatment of Jack?

3.   The grocery across the street advertised:

"Buy a bunch of broccoli for a dollar, and get a second bunch for free!" Mary took advantage of the sale and came home with two bunches. Any taxable event?

4.   Jill, being a hardy soul, joined the Air Chance Frequent Flyer program. After paying out of her own pocket for 50,000 miles of personal flights, she was awarded a free round trip anywhere in the United States. She flew from Washington, D.C. to San Diego, on vacation. Is there a taxable event?

(a) Would it have been any different if she had flown to Atlanta to see her sister?

(b) What if Jill had accumulated the 50,000 miles by flying in the course of her business, with all of the airfare paid by her employer, and

(1) she uses the frequent flyer miles to go on her next business trip for free?

(2) she uses the frequent flyer miles to go to San Diego on vacation?

See Sheryl Stratton and Ryan Donmoyer, *Don't Ask, Don't Tell: The IRS's Frequent Flyer Policy*, 69 Tax Notes 1159 (Dec. 4, 1995); Charley v. Commissioner, 91 F.3d 72 (9th Cir.1996).

5. Jennifer, the holder of a round trip coach ticket on Air Chance, is bumped from her flight. As compensation, she is given a free round trip coach ticket on any other Air Chance flight in the domestic United States, redeemable for one year. Does she have taxable income? Does it matter if she volunteered to be bumped?

6. Jordan's Furniture, the "Official Furniture Store of the Boston Red Sox," offered to rebate the full purchase price of any furniture purchased between March 7, 2007 and April 16, 2007, and delivered before July 10, 2007, if the Red Sox won the World Series in the fall of 2007. The Red Sox did indeed win the World Series, and Jordan's rebated the full purchase price of a reported 30,000 qualifying furniture purchases. Taxable income to the rebate recipients?

(c) The Caselaw Definition of Income

COMMISSIONER v. GLENSHAW GLASS COMPANY

United States Supreme Court, 1955.
348 U.S. 426, 75 S.Ct. 473, 99 L.Ed. 483.

MR. CHIEF JUSTICE WARREN delivered the opinion of the Court.

* * * The common question is whether money received as exemplary damages for fraud or as the punitive two-thirds portion of a treble-damage antitrust recovery must be reported by a taxpayer as gross income under § 22(a) of the Internal Revenue Code of 1939 [current § 61]. * * *

The Glenshaw Glass Company, a Pennsylvania corporation, manufactures glass bottles and containers. It was engaged in protracted litigation with the Hartford–Empire Company, which manufactures machinery of a character used by Glenshaw. Among the claims advanced by Glenshaw were demands for exemplary damages for fraud and treble damages for injury to its business by reason of Hartford's violation of the federal antitrust laws. In December, 1947, the parties concluded a settlement of all pending litigation, by which Hartford paid Glenshaw approximately $800,000. Through a method of allocation which was approved by the Tax Court, and which is no longer in issue, it was ultimately determined that, of the total settlement, $324,529.94 represented payment of punitive damages for fraud and antitrust violations. Glenshaw did not report this portion of the settlement as income for the tax year involved. The Commissioner determined a deficiency claiming as taxable the entire sum less only deductible legal fees. As previously noted, the Tax Court and the Court of Appeals upheld the taxpayer. * * *

It is conceded by the respondents that there is no constitutional barrier to the imposition of a tax on punitive damages. Our question is one of statutory construction: are these payments comprehended by [§ 61]?

The sweeping scope of the controverted statute is readily apparent: Gross income "(a) General definition. 'Gross income' includes gains, profits, and income derived from salaries, wages, or compensation for personal service * * * of whatever kind and in whatever form paid, or from professions, vocations, trades, businesses, commerce, or sales, or dealings in property, whether real or personal, growing out of the owner-ship or use of or interest in such property; also from interest, rent, dividends, securities, or the transaction of any business carried on for gain or profit, or gains or profits and income derived from any source whatever. * * * "

This Court has frequently stated that this language was used by Congress to exert in this field "the full measure of its taxing power." Respondents contend that punitive damages, characterized as "windfalls" flowing from the culpable conduct of third parties, are not within the scope of the section. But Congress applied no limitations as to the source of taxable receipts, nor restrictive labels as to their nature. And the Court has given a liberal construction to this broad phraseology in recognition of the intention of Congress to tax all gains except those specifically exempt-ed. Thus, the fortuitous gain accruing to a lessor by reason of the forfeiture of a lessee's improvements on the rented property was taxed in Helvering v. Bruun, 309 U.S. 461(1940). Such decisions demonstrate that we cannot but ascribe content to the catchall provision of [§ 61], "gains or profits and income derived from any source whatever." The importance of that phrase has been too frequently recognized since its first appearance in the Revenue Act of 1913 to say now that it adds nothing to the meaning of "gross income."

Nor can we accept respondents' contention that a narrower reading of [§ 61] is required by the Court's characterization of income in Eisner v. Macomber, 252 U.S. 189, 207 (1920) as "the gain derived from capital, from labor, or from both combined." The Court was there endeavoring to determine whether the distribution of a corporate stock dividend consti-tuted a realized gain to the shareholder, or changed "only the form, not the essence," of his capital investment. It was held that the taxpayer had "received nothing out of the company's assets for his separate use and benefit." The distribution, therefore, was held not a taxable event. In that context—distinguishing gain from capital—the definition served a useful purpose. But it was not meant to provide a touchstone to all future gross income questions.

Here we have instances of undeniable accessions to wealth, clearly realized, and over which the taxpayers have complete dominion. The mere fact that the payments were extracted from the wrongdoers as punishment for unlawful conduct cannot detract from their character as taxable income to the recipients. Respondents concede, as they must, that the recoveries are taxable to the extent that they compensate for damages actually incurred. It would be an anomaly that could not be justified in the absence of clear congressional intent to say that a recovery for actual damages is taxable but not the additional amount extracted as punishment for the same conduct which caused the injury. And we find no such evidence of intent to exempt these payments.

Reversed.

Mr. Justice Douglas dissents.

Notes

1. The Glenshaw Glass Company once manufactured colored glass, including the amber glass used in Iron City beer bottles, and the green glass used in Little Kings beer bottles.

2. Note that the taxation of compensatory damages was conceded. Only the punitive damages were at issue. For further materials on the taxation of compensatory damages, *see infra* at 125.

3. Contrast the early definition of income in the *Macomber* case, cited in *Glenshaw Glass*: "the gain derived from capital, from labor, or from both combined," with the definition in *Glenshaw Glass* itself: "instances of undeniable accessions to wealth, clearly realized, and over which the taxpayers have complete dominion." How are they different?

3. IMPUTED INCOME

Notes and Problems

Imputed income is generated in two situations:

1) when a taxpayer performs services for herself; and

2) when a taxpayer enjoys the rentfree use of property which she owns.

Economists agree that there is income in both instances. The United States does not tax either one, although some countries do [*see* the Table, *infra*]. Failure to tax imputed income means that those who generate imputed [nontaxable] income have an advantage over those who generate taxable income.

Consider the following situations:

(a) Mechanic normally charges $100 for a tune-up. When she does a tune-up for someone else, the $100 she receives is taxable income, in the form of compensation for her services. When she tunes up her own car, she is performing the same service. Her compensation is that she does not have to pay anyone for the tune-up. Shouldn't she be taxed for this compensation as well?

(b) If Owner rents her house to someone else, the rental income is taxable. She has used her income-producing property to generate income. If Owner lives in her own house, the income-producing property is being used in the same way. Why shouldn't it generate taxable income to Owner, measured by the rental payments she didn't have to make?

Consider this example: Taxpayer owns Building A, and rents out all six apartments for a gross rental of $60,000 a year. She lives in Building B, in an apartment identical to the ones in her own Building A. She pays $10,000 rent per year.

What is her cash flow? What is her taxable income?

Taxpayer moves out of Building B and into one of the apartments in her own Building A. Her apartment is identical in all respects to the one where she lived before. Has her cash flow changed? Has her taxable income changed?

The anomaly in the example suggests one of the inherent tax advantages to home ownership in the United States. Others will be discussed as we reach them. Are there sound policy reasons to encourage home ownership (or condos) over apartment rental? New York City has a much higher percentage of renters, and a much lower percentage of homeowners, than the national average. Are these tax laws yet another example of anti-New York City bias?

This unfairness could be cured if homeowners were taxed on the imputed income from home ownership. Other countries do just that, including, within the last 25 years, Belgium, Denmark, Finland, Germany, the Netherlands, and Spain.

NOTE ON RACE AND GENDER ISSUES IN IMPUTED INCOME

One major item of untaxed imputed income is the value of housekeeping and child care services.

John and Jane each work outside the home, and each earns $50,000, for an aggregate family income of $100,000. However, they pay $20,000 per year to have someone clean the house and take care of the children.

Ken and Kathy live next door. Ken earns $80,000. Kathy stays home, and provides housekeeping and child care services, valued at $20,000 per year. Shouldn't the two couples be taxed the same? The household and dependent care credit [§ 21] helps somewhat, but doesn't completely solve the problem.[b]

Perhaps having one spouse stay at home to care for the house and the children is a luxury which can only be afforded by families with high incomes. If so, then isn't the failure to tax the imputed income from such services a tax break for the rich, which makes the entire income tax more regressive? In fact, minority families tend to earn less money, making it even more likely

---

b. Ken and Kathy would surely prefer not to be taxed on the value of Kathy's housekeeping and child care services. However, doesn't our failure to tax them demean their value? Moreover, does the failure to tax housework create an incentive to keep the houseworker at home, and out of the labor market? See Nancy C. Staudt, *Taxing Housework*, 84 Georgetown L.J. 1571 (1996); Katharine Silbaugh, *Turning Labor into Love: Housework and the Law*, 91 Northwestern U. L. Rev. 1 (1996).

that both spouses will have to work outside the home to make ends meet. Arguably, the failure to tax imputed income from household and child care services is a tax break which discriminates against minorities as well.

Finally, all of the tax advantages of homeownership, including the failure to tax imputed income, are available only to those who can afford to buy their own homes. Therefore, these tax breaks are available disproportionately to white, majority taxpayers. See generally, Beverly I. Moran & William Whitford, *A Black Critique of the Internal Revenue Code*, 1996 Wisc. L. Rev. 751 (1996); John A. Powell, *How Government Tax and Housing Policies Have Racially Segregated America,* in Karen B. Brown and Mary Louise Fellows, eds., TAXING AMERICA (1996).

Compliance Issues

1.   I call a plumber to fix my sink. I ask him how much he will charge. He says, "If you pay by check, $100. If you pay cash, $75." What's going on?

2.   Alphonse is a chiropractor. Daniel Patrick is a transcendental meditation therapist. Alphonse gives Daniel Patrick a one-hour chiropractic therapy session. In return, Daniel Patrick gives Alphonse a one-hour transcendental meditation therapy session. Both therapy sessions normally cost $100. However, no money changes hands. Any income? To whom? If there is income, how will the government find out about it?

3.   What if both Alphonse and Daniel Patrick are members of the same barter exchange. Alphonse gives Daniel Patrick a therapy session, and earns $100 worth of barter exchange "scrip." He then "spends" that scrip on a therapy session from Daniel Patrick. Are the tax consequences any different when the barter exchange is introduced? How will the government find out? *See* § 6045(c)(1)(B) and Revenue Ruling 79–24, 1979–1 C.B. 60.

B. BASIS AND DEBT

Code: §§ 1001, 1012, 1016

1. INTRODUCTION

Owner 1 acquires Blackacre for $100. A year later, Owner 1 sells it to Owner 2 for $200. Two years later, Owner 2 sells it to Owner 3 for $500.

The value of the land, and the ownership, are reflected in the following chart:

Illustration 8

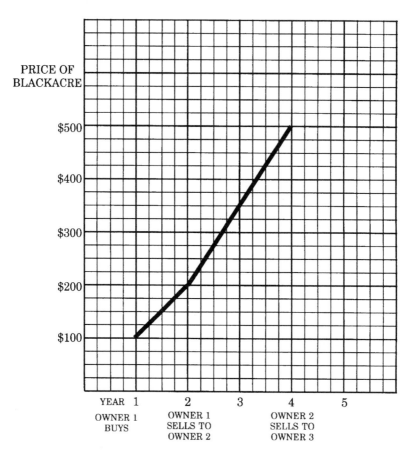

The rapacious IRS would love to tax Owner 1 on gross receipts of $200, and Owner 2 on gross receipts of $500. Total taxable income: $700. But Blackacre has only appreciated $400! What stops IRS? Section 1001, and our hero, basis. Basis must be subtracted from amount realized, so that Owner 1 is taxed only on gain of $100:

Amount Realized	$200
Basis	− $100
Gain	$100

Similarly, Owner 2 is taxed only on the gain of $300:

Amount Realized	$500
Basis	− $200
Gain	$300

Note that when Owner 2 paid $200 for Blackacre, two things happened. First, Owner 1 realized the $200 on the sale. Second, Owner 2 created a cost basis of $200 in Blackacre—the amount she paid for it. Owner 2's $200 basis reflects the realization event. It reminds the system that someone has already paid tax on the appreciation of Blackacre up to $200. That appreciation, having been taxed once, should not be taxed again.

Basis is the taxpayer's friend. The higher the basis, the lower the taxable gain.

Now consider these problems, to get a better feel for how basis works.

PROBLEMS

1. In 1990, Joe purchased vacant land for $25,000. In 1993, Joe spent an additional $35,000 to erect a building on the property.

    a) By 1994, the value of the land with improvements had increased to $150,000. Joe did nothing. What is Joe's basis?

    b) Later in 1994, Joe sold the land with the improvements for $150,000. How much taxable income?

    c) As before, Joe bought the land for $25,000 and erected the building for $35,000. This time, in 1994, Joe spent another $50,000 erecting a ten-foot-high neon sign on the roof of the building. The sign flashed the message, "If you've got it, flaunt it!" On a clear day, the sign was visible for ten miles. Joe sold the land and building (and sign) for $90,000. What result?

2. Joe began as a commercial artist, employed by a large advertising agency. His salary was $100,000 a year. There is no doubt that the market value of a year's worth of Joe's services is $100,000.

Joe quit his job at the end of the year. In the new year, he acquired canvas, brushes, and oil paint for negligible value. He spent an entire year, and produced a painting, which he sold for $100,000. How would you tax the sale? What if he could only sell it for $35,000?

3. Dick bought Blackacre (160 acres) for $1,000. Later, he sold the lower 40 acres for $7,500, and kept the remaining 120 acres. How much taxable gain does he realize? What is his basis in his remaining real estate holdings after the sale?

4. Sometimes, all parties concede that it is simply impossible to determine basis. In Inaja Land Company, Ltd. v. Commissioner, 9 T.C. 727 (1947), the Company conveyed an easement in its property in return for a cash payment. It was impossible to determine what fraction of its ownership rights in the land was represented by the easement. Accordingly, the court held that there would be no taxable event, but rather a return of capital. The entire amount realized was treated as a reduction of basis.[c]

---

    c. "Return of capital" is another way to explain why basis is subtracted from amount realized. If you purchase Blackacre for $100, you have invested $100 of your capital. If you then sell it for

When Can Basis Be Subtracted?

Subtracting basis from amount realized is certainly more pleasant than paying a tax on the gross receipts. But when is something "sold," so that basis can be subtracted?

FIRST NORTHWEST INDUSTRIES OF AMERICA, INC. v. COMMISSIONER

United States Court of Appeals, Ninth Circuit, 1981.
649 F.2d 707.

Before WRIGHT and ANDERSON, CIRCUIT JUDGES, and TAYLOR, SENIOR DISTRICT JUDGE.

WRIGHT, CIRCUIT JUDGE:

This case presents a novel issue concerning the tax treatment of a professional sports team. The Commissioner appeals the Tax Court's decision, and we reverse and remand.

I. Background

Taxpayer purchased a National Basketball Association team, the Seattle Supersonics, in 1967. It acquired 13 related rights:

1. The right to participate in a special expansion draft in which it could select 15 veteran players from ten existing teams;

2. The right to participate in the 1967 college draft;

3. The right to participate in all post–1967 annual NBA college drafts;

4. The right to participate in NBA basketball by competing against other teams, including the right to retain all home-game gate receipts;

5. The exclusive right to exhibit NBA basketball within a 75–mile radius of Seattle;

6. The right to an equal share (with other team owners) of all revenues derived from national broadcasting of NBA games;

7. The exclusive rights for local broadcasting of Sonics' games;

8. The right to an equal share of revenues derived from NBA promotional and merchandising activities;

9. The right to an equal share of revenues derived from NBA playoff and all-star games;

10. The right to enjoy the benefits of NBA reputation and goodwill;

$1,000, the first $100 of your amount realized is not taxable to you, because it is simply the return of your initial $100 capital investment.

To understand *Inaja Land*, consider a numerical example. Assume that the taxpayer bought the property for $1,000, and sold the easement for $100. There would have been no gain on the sale (return of capital). However, taxpayer's basis in the property after the sale would have been $900.

11. The rights (and obligations) of participating in a system which establishes within the NBA of priority rights to players and the bargaining rights of each team with respect to its own players;

12. The right to share equally in the proceeds from future NBA expansions;

13. Other rights, benefits, and obligations attendant to being a member of the NBA.

Taxpayer's total cost was $1,750,000. The Tax Court allocated $250,000 to the right to share in the 1968 expansion proceeds, and $500,000 to the right to participate in the special expansion draft. It found that these rights had a limited useful life and permitted taxpayer to amortize them.

These findings and conclusions are not challenged on appeal which leaves a cost of $1,000,000 for the remaining rights.

II.   Issue on Appeal and Positions of the Parties

In 1970 the NBA expanded by selling new teams in Portland, Buffalo, and Cleveland. The proceeds were distributed equally to the existing owners, including the taxpayer. The issue on appeal concerns the tax treatment of these proceeds.

A.   The Tax Court's Opinion

* * * The Tax Court reasoned * * * that taxpayer may subtract its basis * * * in computing the gain it realized from the expansion proceeds.

Taxpayer has a unique dual role. First, it is a member of the joint venture which exists to administer a professional basketball league. Second, it is an independent business entity, with full responsibility for its own profits and losses.

All team owners make small capital contributions to the joint venture. The amount paid for a new team, however, does not pay for an interest in the joint venture but for the property rights outlined above. The Tax Court labelled these rights (other than the two it permitted taxpayer to amortize) as the "basic nonterminable rights" possessed by all NBA team owners.

The Tax Court reasoned that, because there were 14 owners prior to the 1970 expansion, taxpayer had a 1/14 interest in these rights. After expansion, it had a 1/17 interest. Hence, a proportion of its original interest[3] had been transferred to the expansion teams. The Tax Court held that taxpayer could subtract from the expansion proceeds an equivalent proportion of its $1,000,000 cost (approximately $175,000).[4]

---

3. The proportion is $(1/14-1/17) / 1/14$.

4. Six judges dissented. 70 T.C. at 868.

B. The Commissioner's Position

The Commissioner argues that the rights transferred to the new owners were "created" by the existing teams. "(T)he rights obtained by the new teams were not siphoned from the existing teams but rather were entirely new rights created when the league approved the expansion plan and granted the franchises."

The Commissioner concludes that the franchise rights acquired by the taxpayer were not transferred to the new owners and, therefore, taxpayer has no basis to subtract from the amount realized in computing taxable gain.[6]

C. The Taxpayer's Position

Taxpayer makes two arguments in support of the Tax Court's decision. First, it argues that its "basic nonterminable rights" can be treated as a partnership interest, and that it sold a portion of this partnership interest to the new owners. Second, taxpayer identifies specific, valuable rights that it transferred to the new owners. * * *

D. Assets Transferred to Expansion Team Owners

We conclude that some, but not all, of the rights acquired by taxpayer in 1967 were partially transferred to the new owners. We agree with the Commissioner that taxpayer's "franchise" rights, i. e., its right to participate in the NBA and its exclusive rights to local broadcasting and to exhibit NBA basketball within a 75–mile radius of Seattle, were not transferred.[8] The Tax Court erred in including the cost of acquiring these rights in its calculation of taxpayer's basis.

A portion of the remaining "basic nonterminable rights" was transferred.[9] The Tax Court made no attempt, however, to determine the cost

---

6. The parties agree that taxpayer is entitled to subtract its basis in player contracts lost through the special draft for the 1970 expansion teams.

8. By taxpayer's right to participate in the league we refer to its right to have its team play other NBA teams, and its right to participate in the NBA draft and the system for assigning bargaining rights to players. Taxpayer argues that its right to participate in the exhibition of NBA basketball by competing against other NBA teams was diminished when expansion teams were added to the league. It retains all of the gate receipts at home games. It contends that those receipts will be reduced because it will play the "best" teams less often, and that there is greater attendance at games against the best teams. Like the Commissioner's argument with respect to broadcasting revenues, this argument confuses the impact of expansion on the value of a right with the transfer or retention of that right. Taxpayer retained the right to participate in the exhibition of NBA basketball and to retain home-game gate receipts, regardless of the post-expansion value thereof. It can be added, however, that there is no support in the record for taxpayer's argument that the value of this right was reduced by expansion. Of the expansion teams admitted since 1967, three (Milwaukee, Seattle, and Portland) have won NBA championships and, for a time at least, could have been considered the "best" teams. In addition, expansion teams can develop regional rivalries which increase attendance. The Tax Court made no findings on the effect of expansion on gate receipts. It did find that "(a)lthough NBA expansion teams have generally done poorly in an artistic and competitive sense during the first few years of the franchise's existence, they, Seattle being one, have frequently done rather well in terms of gate receipts."

9. These include the right to share in national broadcasting revenues, all-star and playoff game proceeds, expansion proceeds, and proceeds of NBA promotional and advertising activities. All of the "basic nonterminable rights" acquired by taxpayer derive value from the league's of these rights. Only if their cost can be satisfactorily ascertained may taxpayer subtract its basis in the portion transferred.[10]

On remand, the Tax Court will determine whether there is sufficient evidence to ascertain the cost of the rights which were transferred. If there is, taxpayer may subtract its basis.

REVERSED AND REMANDED.

NOTES AND QUESTIONS

1. The total cost of the Sonics in 1967 was $1.75 million. The team was sold for $350 million in 2007 and relocated to Oklahoma City. Not a bad return on the $1.75 million investment.

2. Dorothy, whose blood contains a rare antibody, goes regularly to a private laboratory, where they draw a pint of her blood. Each time, Dorothy's body replenishes the extracted blood in less than a day. In exchange, the laboratory gives Dorothy cash, and other valuable consideration. Is Dorothy selling her blood? If so, what is her basis? See United States v. Garber, 607 F.2d 92 (5th Cir.1979).

3. Derek bought a pregnant racehorse, Champagne Woman, for $60,000. In due time, Champagne Woman gave birth to a chestnut colt. When the colt was sixteen months old, Derek sold him for $125,000. How might you determine Derek's basis in the colt? See Gamble v. Commissioner, 68 T.C. 800 (1977).

2. DEBT

Code: §§ 61(a)(12); 108(a), (d)(1)

(a) Income From Discharge of Debt, Stealing

Preliminary Considerations

Archie is paid a salary of $2000 a month. Of that salary, $500 always goes to pay the mortgage, and $1,100 always goes to the grocery store. Archie pays tax on his salary, the mortgage bank pays tax on the interest, and the grocery store pays tax on its profits. Why should so many different taxes be paid on Archie's monthly salary?

Archie conjures up a plausible principle of tax law: "Whoever gets the money pays the tax." [*See,* however, Chapter 9, *infra.*] Accordingly, Archie arranges with his employer to pay $500 directly to his mortgage bank and $1,100 directly to his grocery store, every month. That way, Archie

---

goodwill, and the sale of new teams is a "portioning out" of NBA goodwill. The critical question on remand will be whether there is sufficient evidence to allocate the $1,000,000 cost between those rights which were and those which were not transferred. Recognizing that they all are related to goodwill does not resolve that question.

10. We see no error in the formula used by the Tax Court. See note 3, supra. It presumes that each existing owner transferred an equal proportion of its rights to the new owners. Taxpayer suggests it lost more than other owners. We see no support in the record for this argument. See note 8, supra.

reasons, he'll only pay tax on the net $400 per month he actually receives. Will it work? Consider in light of *Old Colony*.

OLD COLONY TRUST CO. v. COMMISSIONER

United States Supreme Court, 1929.
279 U.S. 716, 49 S.Ct. 499, 73 L.Ed. 918.

MR. CHIEF JUSTICE TAFT delivered the opinion of the Court.

[The American Woolen Company paid its officers and certain key employees salary and commissions. In addition, the corporation reimbursed these employees for the federal income tax paid on these amounts—Ed.] * * *

The decision of the Board of Tax Appeals here sought to be reviewed was that the income taxes of $681,169.88 and $351,179.27 paid by the American Woolen Company for Mr. Wood [president of the company] were additional income to him for the years 1919 and 1920.

The question certified by the Circuit Court of Appeals for answer by this Court is: "Did the payment by the employer of the income taxes assessable against the employee constitute additional taxable income to such employee?" * * *

Coming now to the merits of this case, we think the question presented is whether a taxpayer, having induced a third person to pay his income tax or having acquiesced in such payment as made in discharge of an obligation to him, may avoid the making of a return thereof [i.e. disclosure on a tax return—Ed.] and the payment of a corresponding tax. We think he may not do so. The payment of the tax by the employers was in consideration of the services rendered by the employee, and was again derived by the employee from his labor. The form of the payment is expressly declared to make no difference. It is therefore immaterial that the taxes were directly paid over to the government. The discharge by a third person of an obligation to him is equivalent to receipt by the person taxed. The certificate shows that the taxes were imposed upon the employee, that the taxes were actually paid by the employer, and that the employee entered upon his duties in the years in question under the express agreement that his income taxes would be paid by his employer. This is evidenced by the terms of the resolution passed August 3, 1916, more than one year prior to the year in which the taxes were imposed. The taxes were paid upon a valuable consideration, namely, the services rendered by the employee and as part of the compensation therefor. We think, therefore, that the payment constituted income to the employee.

* * *

Nor can it be argued that the payment of the tax * * * was a gift. The payment for services, even though entirely voluntary, was nevertheless compensation within the statute. * * *

It is next argued against the payment of this tax that, if these payments by the employer constitute income to the employee, the employee will be called upon to pay the tax imposed upon this additional income, and that the payment of the additional tax will create further income which will in turn be subject to tax, with the result that there would be a tax upon a tax. This, it is urged, is the result of the government's theory, when carried to its logical conclusion, and results in an absurdity which Congress could not have contemplated.

In the first place, no attempt has been made by the Treasury to collect further taxes, upon the theory that the payment of the additional taxes creates further income, and the question of a tax upon a tax was not before the Circuit Court of Appeals, and has not been certified to this Court. We can settle questions of that sort when an attempt to impose a tax upon a tax is undertaken, but not now. It is not, therefore, necessary to answer the argument based upon an algebraic formula to reach the amount of taxes due. The question in this case is, "Did the payment by the employer of the income taxes assessable against the employee constitute additional taxable income to such employee?" The answer must be "Yes."

Separate opinion of MR. JUSTICE MCREYNOLDS. * * *

NOTES, QUESTIONS, PROBLEMS

1.   William Wood, the key employee of note in the *Old Colony* case, made the American Woolen Company into a huge success through the sales of khaki and blue serge. He was paid salaries exceeding one million dollars—princely sums, especially in the 1920's. Later, he allegedly robbed his company, was fired by the board of directors, and ultimately committed suicide in 1926.

2.   In the winter of 2001, H & R Block offered to pay the income tax liability of any contestant who won the million dollar jackpot on "Who Wants to Be a Millionaire" during a specified period. Had H & R Block paid, how would the payment have been taxed?

3.   The Minnetonka Siblings is the last remaining family-owned major league baseball franchise, owned by the Cheapo family. There is no way that the Siblings can be competitive without a decent team manager, but the Cheapos can't afford to pay one. However, by putting together a package which combines the salary paid by the Cheapos, the revenues from a shoe contract, plus the salary paid by the local television station for the manager's weekly TV show, the Cheapos get their manager. Should the Cheapo family be taxable upon the indirect benefits they receive from the shoe company and the television station?

4.   *Old Colony* stands for the proposition that if A makes a payment for the benefit of B, then it is treated as a payment to B, and taxed accordingly. A's payment of B's debt is a payment for the benefit of B. Does it matter if A is also the creditor of B? Consider *Kirby Lumber*.

UNITED STATES v. KIRBY LUMBER CO.

United States Supreme Court, 1931.
284 U.S. 1, 52 S.Ct. 4, 76 L.Ed. 131.

MR. JUSTICE HOLMES delivered the opinion of the court.

In July, 1923, the plaintiff, the Kirby Lumber Company, issued its own bonds for $12,126,800 for which it received their par value. Later in the same year it purchased in the open market some of the same bonds at less than par, the difference of price being $137,521.30. The question is whether this difference is a taxable gain or income of the plaintiff for the year 1923. By the Revenue Act of 1921, gross income includes "gains or profits and income derived from any source whatever," and by the Treasury Regulations * * *, that have been in force through repeated re-enactments, "If the corporation purchases and retires any of such bonds at a price less than the issuing price or face value, the excess of the issuing price or face value over the purchase price is gain or income for the taxable year." We see no reason why the Regulations should not be accepted as a correct statement of the law.

In Bowers v. Kerbaugh–Empire Co., 271 U.S. 170, the defendant in error owned the stock of another company that had borrowed money repayable in marks or their equivalent for an enterprise that failed. At the time of payment the marks had fallen in value, which so far as it went was a gain for the defendant in error, and it was contended by the plaintiff in error that the gain was taxable income. But the transaction as a whole was a loss, and the contention was denied. Here there was no shrinkage of assets and the taxpayer made a clear gain. As a result of its dealings it made available $137,521.30 assets previously offset by the obligation of bonds now extinct. We see nothing to be gained by the discussion of judicial definitions. The defendant in error has realized within the year an accession to income, if we take words in their plain popular meaning, as they should be taken here.

Judgment reversed.

NOTE

To understand the Supreme Court opinion in *Kirby Lumber*, imagine that the balance sheet of the corporation before the borrowings took place was as set forth below:

Balance Sheet Prior to Transaction		
Assets		**Liabilities and Shareholder Equity**
Cash	$10,000,000	Liabilities	$ 0
		Shareholder Equity	$10,000,000
Total Assets	$10,000,000	Total Liabilities and SH Equity	$10,000,000

Right after the loan, the balance sheet looked like this:

Balance Sheet After Debt Issued			
Assets		**Liabilities and Shareholder Equity**	
Cash	$22,126,800	Liabilities	$12,126,800
		Shareholder Equity	$10,000,000
Total Assets	$22,126,800	Total Liabilities and SH Equity	$22,126,800

Note that Shareholder Equity is unchanged, as the $12,126,800 increase in assets represented by the proceeds of the loan is offset by the liability of the same amount.

After the bonds are repurchased for less than face value, the balance sheet looks like this:

Balance Sheet After Debt Repurchased and Retired			
Assets		**Liabilities and Shareholder Equity**	
Cash	$10,137,521	Liabilities	$ 0
		Shareholder Equity	$10,137,521
Total Assets	$10,137,521	Total Liabilities and SH Equity	$10,137,521

If you compare the last balance sheet with the first, you will note that shareholder equity has increased by $137,521. That increase, according to the Court, is income. But remember, not all increases in net worth (an individual's counterpart to shareholder equity) are taxable income. For example, unrealized appreciation in the value if my assets will increase my net worth, but it's still not taxable income until I sell the assets.

The Supreme Court noted:

As a result of its dealings, it [Kirby Lumber] made available $137,521.30 assets previously offset by the obligation of bonds now extinct.

Here, the Court espouses the "freeing of assets" theory—a discharge of debt "frees up" assets which were previously encumbered by the debt. With the debt gone, now those assets can be used however the taxpayer wishes. Therefore, the discharge of debt should be taxable income. But do all "freeing of assets" work that way? Suppose that I made an enforceable promise to my brother to pay him $50,000, even though he had neither performed services nor given me any cash or goods. If my brother later forgives the debt, my balance sheet looks better, and my assets are free from the debt. But do I have taxable income?

Here's a better justification for income from the discharge of debt. Why are loan proceeds not taxable income? They are not taxable income because they come with a corresponding obligation to pay them back. However, what if the debt is never repaid? In that event, the justification for not taxing the receipt of the loan proceeds turned out to be false. The only solution is to correct the error by taxing the discharged debt. See the dissenting opinion in the Third Circuit in *Zarin*.

In *Kirby Lumber*, market forces allowed the taxpayer to discharge some of its debt, by repurchasing the bonds for less than their issue price. But what if the debt is discharged for other reasons? What if the debt is legally unenforceable? What if the debtor simply doesn't have the money? Consider *Zarin*.

ZARIN v. COMMISSIONER

United States Court of Appeals, Third Circuit, 1990.
916 F.2d 110.

COWEN, CIRCUIT JUDGE.

David Zarin ("Zarin") appeals from a decision of the Tax Court holding that he recognized $2,935,000 of income from discharge of indebtedness resulting from his gambling activities, and that he should be taxed on the income. * * * After considering the issues raised by this appeal, we will reverse.

I.

Zarin was a professional engineer who participated in the development, construction, and management of various housing projects. A resident of Atlantic City, New Jersey, Zarin occasionally gambled, both in his hometown and in other places where gambling was legalized. To facilitate his gaming activities in Atlantic City, Zarin applied to Resorts International Hotel ("Resorts") for a credit line in June, 1978. Following a credit check, Resorts granted Zarin $10,000 of credit. Pursuant to this credit arrangement with Resorts, Zarin could write a check, called a marker,[2] and in return receive chips, which could then be used to gamble at the casino's tables.

Before long, Zarin developed a reputation as an extravagant "high roller" who routinely bet the house maximum while playing craps, his game of choice. Considered a "valued gaming patron" by Resorts, Zarin had his credit limit increased at regular intervals without any further credit checks, and was provided a number of complimentary services and privileges. By November, 1979, Zarin's permanent line of credit had been raised to $200,000. Between June, 1978, and December, 1979, Zarin lost $2,500,000 at the craps table, losses he paid in full.

Responding to allegations of credit abuses, the New Jersey Division of Gaming Enforcement filed with the New Jersey Casino Control Commission a complaint against Resorts. Among the 809 violations of casino regulations alleged in the complaint of October, 1979, were 100 pertaining to Zarin. Subsequently, a Casino Control Commissioner issued an Emer-

---

2. A "marker" is a negotiable draft payable to Resorts and drawn on the maker's bank.

gency Order, the effect of which was to make further extensions of credit to Zarin illegal.

Nevertheless, Resorts continued to extend Zarin's credit limit through the use of two different practices: "considered cleared" credit and "this trip only" credit.[3] Both methods effectively ignored the Emergency Order and were later found to be illegal.[4]

By January, 1980, Zarin was gambling compulsively and uncontrollably at Resorts, spending as many as sixteen hours a day at the craps table.[5] During April, 1980, Resorts again increased Zarin's credit line without further inquiries. That same month, Zarin delivered personal checks and counterchecks to Resorts which were returned as having been drawn against insufficient funds. Those dishonored checks totaled $3,435,000. In late April, Resorts cut off Zarin's credit.

Although Zarin indicated that he would repay those obligations, Resorts filed a New Jersey state court action against Zarin in November, 1980, to collect the $3,435,000. Zarin denied liability on grounds that Resort's claim was unenforceable under New Jersey regulations intended to protect compulsive gamblers. Ten months later, in September, 1981, Resorts and Zarin settled their dispute for a total of $500,000.

The Commissioner of Internal Revenue ("Commissioner") subsequently determined deficiencies in Zarin's federal income taxes for 1980 and 1981, arguing that Zarin recognized $3,435,000 of income in 1980 from larceny by trick and deception. After Zarin challenged that claim by filing a Tax Court petition, the Commissioner abandoned his 1980 claim, and argued instead that Zarin had recognized $2,935,000 of income in 1981 from the cancellation of indebtedness which resulted from the settlement with Resorts.

Agreeing with the Commissioner, the Tax Court decided, eleven judges to eight, that Zarin had indeed recognized $2,935,000 of income from the discharge of indebtedness, namely the difference between the original $3,435,000 "debt" and the $500,000 settlement. Since he was in the seventy percent tax bracket, Zarin's deficiency for 1981 was calculated to be $2,047,245. With interest to April 5, 1990, Zarin allegedly owes the Internal Revenue Service $5,209,033.96 in additional taxes. Zarin appeals the order of the Tax Court.

II.

The sole issue before this Court is whether the Tax Court correctly held that Zarin had income from discharge of indebtedness. Section 108

---

3. Under the "considered cleared" method, Resorts would treat a personal check as a cash transaction, and would therefore not apply the amount of the check in calculating the amount of credit extended Zarin. "This trip only" credit allowed Resorts to grant temporary increases of credit for a given visit, so long as the credit limit was lowered by the next visit.

4. On July 8, 1983, the New Jersey Casino Control Commission found that Resorts violated the Emergency Order at least thirteen different times, nine involving Zarin, and fined Resorts $130,000.

5. Zarin claims that at the time he was suffering from a recognized emotional disorder that caused him to gamble compulsively.

and section 61(a)(12) of the Code set forth "the general rule that gross income includes income from the discharge of indebtedness." § 108(e)(1). The Commissioner argues, and the Tax Court agreed, that pursuant to the Code, Zarin did indeed recognize income from discharge of gambling indebtedness.

Under the Commissioner's logic, Resorts advanced Zarin $3,435,000 worth of chips, chips being the functional equivalent of cash. At that time, the chips were not treated as income, since Zarin recognized an obligation of repayment. In other words, Resorts made Zarin a tax-free loan. However, a taxpayer does recognize income if a loan owed to another party is cancelled, in whole or in part. §§ 61(a)(12), 108(e). The settlement between Zarin and Resorts, claims the Commissioner, fits neatly into the cancellation of indebtedness provisions in the Code. Zarin owed $3,435,000, paid $500,000, with the difference constituting income. Although initially persuasive, the Commissioner's position is nonetheless flawed for two reasons.

III.

Initially, we find that §§ 108 and 61(a)(12) are inapplicable to the Zarin/Resorts transaction. Section 61 does not define indebtedness. On the other hand, § 108(d)(1), which repeats and further elaborates on the rule in § 61(a)(12), defines the term as any indebtedness "(A) for which the taxpayer is liable, or (B) subject to which the taxpayer holds property." In order to bring the taxpayer within the sweep of the discharge of indebtedness rules, then, the IRS must show that one of the two prongs in the § 108(d)(1) test is satisfied. It has not been demonstrated that Zarin satisfies either.

Because the debt Zarin owed to Resorts was unenforceable as a matter of New Jersey state law, it is clearly not a debt "for which the taxpayer is liable." § 108(d)(1)(A). Liability implies a legally enforceable obligation to repay, and under New Jersey law, Zarin would have no such obligation.

Moreover, Zarin did not have a debt subject to which he held property as required by section 108(d)(1)(B). Zarin's indebtedness arose out of his acquisition of gambling chips. The Tax Court held that gambling chips were not property, but rather, "a medium of exchange within the Resorts casino" and a "substitute for cash." Alternatively, the Tax Court viewed the chips as nothing more than "the opportunity to gamble and incidental services ..." We agree with the gist of these characterizations, and hold that gambling chips are merely an accounting mechanism to evidence debt.

Gaming chips in New Jersey during 1980 were regarded "solely as evidence of a debt owed to their custodian by the casino licensee and shall be considered at no time the property of anyone other than the casino licensee issuing them." Thus, under New Jersey state law, gambling chips were Resorts' property until transferred to Zarin in exchange for the markers, at which point the chips became "evidence" of indebtedness (and not the property of Zarin).

Even were there no relevant legislative pronouncement on which to rely, simple common sense would lead to the conclusion that chips were not property in Zarin's hands. Zarin could not do with the chips as he pleased, nor did the chips have any independent economic value beyond the casino. The chips themselves were of little use to Zarin, other than as a means of facilitating gambling. They could not have been used outside the casino. They could have been used to purchase services and privileges within the casino, including food, drink, entertainment, and lodging, but Zarin would not have utilized them as such, since he received those services from Resorts on a complimentary basis. In short, the chips had no economic substance.

Although the Tax Court found that theoretically, Zarin could have redeemed the chips he received on credit for cash and walked out of the casino, the reality of the situation was quite different. Realistically, before cashing in his chips, Zarin would have been required to pay his outstanding IOUs. New Jersey state law requires casinos to "request patrons to apply any chips or plaques in their possession in reduction of personal checks or Counter Checks exchanged for purposes of gaming prior to exchanging such chips or plaques for cash or prior to departing from the casino area." Since his debt at all times equalled or exceeded the number of chips he possessed, redemption would have left Zarin with no chips, no cash, and certainly nothing which could have been characterized as property.

Not only were the chips non-property in Zarin's hands, but upon transfer to Zarin, the chips also ceased to be the property of Resorts. Since the chips were in the possession of another party, Resorts could no longer do with the chips as it pleased, and could no longer control the chips' use. Generally, at the time of a transfer, the party in possession of the chips can gamble with them, use them for services, cash them in, or walk out of the casino with them as an Atlantic City souvenir. The chips therefore become nothing more than an accounting mechanism, or evidence of a debt, designed to facilitate gambling in casinos where the use of actual money was forbidden. Thus, the chips which Zarin held were not property within the meaning of § 108(d)(1)(B).

In short, because Zarin was not liable on the debt he allegedly owed Resorts, and because Zarin did not hold "property" subject to that debt, the cancellation of indebtedness provisions of the Code do not apply to the settlement between Resorts and Zarin. As such, Zarin cannot have income from the discharge of his debt.

IV.

Instead of analyzing the transaction at issue as cancelled debt, we believe the proper approach is to view it as disputed debt or contested liability. Under the contested liability doctrine, if a taxpayer, in good faith, disputed the amount of a debt, a subsequent settlement of the dispute would be treated as the amount of debt cognizable for tax purposes. The excess of the original debt over the amount determined to have been due is disregarded for both loss and debt accounting purposes. Thus, if a taxpayer took out a loan for $10,000, refused in good faith to pay the full $10,000 back, and then reached an agreement with the lendor that he would pay back only $7000 in full satisfaction of the debt, the transaction would be treated as if the initial loan was $7000. When the taxpayer tenders the $7000 payment, he will have been deemed to have paid the full amount of the initially disputed debt. Accordingly, there is no tax consequence to the taxpayer upon payment.

The seminal "contested liability" case is N. Sobel, Inc. v. Commissioner, 40 B.T.A. 1263 (1939). In Sobel, the taxpayer exchanged a $21,700 note for 100 shares of stock from a bank. In the following year, the taxpayer sued the bank for recision, arguing that the bank loan was violative of state law, and moreover, that the bank had failed to perform certain promises. The parties eventually settled the case in 1935, with the taxpayer agreeing to pay half of the face amount of the note. In the year of the settlement, the taxpayer claimed the amount paid as a loss. The Commissioner denied the loss because it had been sustained five years earlier, and further asserted that the taxpayer recognized income from the discharge of half of his indebtedness.

The Board of Tax Appeals held that since the loss was not fixed until the dispute was settled, the loss was recognized in 1935, the year of the settlement, and the deduction was appropriately taken in that year. Additionally, the Board held that the portion of the note forgiven by the bank "was not the occasion for a freeing of assets and that there was no gain ..." Therefore, the taxpayer did not have any income from cancellation of indebtedness.

There is little difference between the present case and Sobel. Zarin incurred a $3,435,000 debt while gambling at Resorts, but in court, disputed liability on the basis of unenforceability. A settlement of $500,000 was eventually agreed upon. It follows from Sobel that the settlement served only to fix the amount of debt. No income was realized or recognized. When Zarin paid the $500,000, any tax consequence dissolved.[10]

Only one other court has addressed a case factually similar to the one before us. In United States v. Hall, 307 F.2d 238 (10th Cir.1962), the taxpayer owed an unenforceable gambling debt alleged to be $225,000. Subsequently, the taxpayer and the creditor settled for $150,000. The taxpayer then transferred cattle valued at $148,110 to his creditor in satisfaction of the settlement agreement. A jury held that the parties fixed the debt at $150,000, and that the taxpayer recognized income from

---

10. Had Zarin not paid the $500,000 dollar settlement, it would be likely that he would have had income from cancellation of indebtedness. The debt at that point would have been fixed, and Zarin would have been legally obligated to pay it.

cancellation of indebtedness equal to the difference between the $150,000 and the $148,110 value affixed to the cattle. Arguing that the taxpayer recognized income equal to the difference between $225,000 and $148,000, the Commissioner appealed.

The Tenth Circuit rejected the idea that the taxpayer had any income from cancellation of indebtedness. Noting that the gambling debt was unenforceable, the Tenth Circuit said, "The cold fact is that taxpayer suffered a substantial loss from gambling, the amount of which was determined by the transfer." In effect, the Court held that because the debt was unenforceable, the amount of the loss and resulting debt cognizable for tax purposes were fixed by the settlement at $148,110. Thus, the Tenth Circuit lent its endorsement to the contested liability doctrine in a factual situation strikingly similar to the one at issue.

* * * Since Zarin contested his liability based on the unenforceability of the entire debt, and did not dispute the amount of the debt, the Commissioner would have us adopt the reasoning of the Tax Court, which found that Zarin's debt was liquidated, therefore barring the application of Sobel and the contested liability doctrine.

We reject the Tax Court's rationale. When a debt is unenforceable, it follows that the amount of the debt, and not just the liability thereon, is in dispute. Although a debt may be unenforceable, there still could be some value attached to its worth. This is especially so with regards to gambling debts. In most states, gambling debts are unenforceable, and have "but slight potential ..." Nevertheless, they are often collected, at least in part. For example, Resorts is not a charity; it would not have extended illegal credit to Zarin and others if it did not have some hope of collecting debts incurred pursuant to the grant of credit.

Moreover, the debt is frequently incurred to acquire gambling chips, and not money. Although casinos attach a dollar value to each chip, that value, unlike money's, is not beyond dispute, particularly given the illegality of gambling debts in the first place. This proposition is supported by the facts of the present case. Resorts gave Zarin $3.4 million dollars of chips in exchange for markers evidencing Zarin's debt. If indeed the only issue was the enforceability of the entire debt, there would have been no settlement. Zarin would have owed all or nothing. Instead, the parties attached a value to the debt considerably lower than its face value. In other words, the parties agreed that given the circumstances surrounding Zarin's gambling spree, the chips he acquired might not have been worth $3.4 million dollars, but were worth something. Such a debt cannot be called liquidated, since its exact amount was not fixed until settlement.

To summarize, the transaction between Zarin and Resorts can best be characterized as a disputed debt, or contested liability. Zarin owed an unenforceable debt of $3,435,000 to Resorts. After Zarin in good faith disputed his obligation to repay the debt, the parties settled for $500,000, which Zarin paid. That $500,000 settlement fixed the amount of loss and the amount of debt cognizable for tax purposes. Since Zarin was deemed to have owed $500,000, and since he paid Resorts $500,000, no adverse tax consequences attached to Zarin as a result.[12]

V.

In conclusion, we hold that Zarin did not have any income from cancellation of indebtedness for two reasons. First, the Code provisions covering discharge of debt are inapplicable since the definitional requirement in I.R.C. section 108(d)(1) was not met. Second, the settlement of Zarin's gambling debts was a contested liability. We reverse the decision of the Tax Court and remand with instructions to enter judgment that Zarin realized no income by reason of his settlement with Resorts.

STAPLETON, CIRCUIT JUDGE, dissenting.

I respectfully dissent because I agree with the Commissioner's appraisal of the economic realities of this matter.

Resorts sells for cash the exhilaration and the potential for profit inherent in games of chance. It does so by selling for cash chips that entitle the holder to gamble at its casino. Zarin, like thousands of others, wished to purchase what Resorts was offering in the marketplace. He chose to make this purchase on credit and executed notes evidencing his obligation to repay the funds that were advanced to him by Resorts. As in most purchase money transactions, Resorts skipped the step of giving Zarin cash that he would only return to it in order to pay for the opportunity to gamble. Resorts provided him instead with chips that entitled him to participate in Resorts' games of chance on the same basis as others who had paid cash for that privilege.[1] Whether viewed as a one or two-step transaction, however, Zarin received either $3.4 million in cash or an entitlement for which others would have had to pay $3.4 million.

Despite the fact that Zarin received in 1980 cash or an entitlement worth $3.4 million, he correctly reported in that year no income from his dealings with Resorts. He did so solely because he recognized, as evidenced by his notes, an offsetting obligation to repay Resorts $3.4 million in cash. In 1981, with the delivery of Zarin's promise to pay Resorts $500,000 and the execution of a release by Resorts, Resorts surrendered its claim to repayment of the remaining $2.9 million of the money Zarin had bor-

---

12. The Commissioner argues in the alternative that Zarin recognized $3,435,000 of income in 1980. This claim has no merit. Recognition of income would depend upon a finding that Zarin did not have cancellation of indebtedness income solely because his debt was unenforceable. We do not so hold. Although unenforceability is a factor in our analysis, our decision ultimately hinges upon the determination that the "disputed debt" rule applied, or alternatively, that chips are not property within the meaning of I.R.C. section 108.

1. I view as irrelevant the facts that Resorts advanced credit to Zarin solely to enable him to patronize its casino and that the chips could not be used elsewhere or for other purposes. When one buys a sofa from the furniture store on credit, the fact that the proprietor would not have advanced the credit for a different purpose does not entitle one to a tax-free gain in the event the debt to the store is extinguished for some reason.

rowed. As of that time, Zarin's assets were freed of his potential liability for that amount and he recognized gross income in that amount.[2]

The only alternatives I see to this conclusion are to hold either (1) that Zarin realized $3.4 million in income in 1980 at a time when both parties to the transaction thought there was an offsetting obligation to repay or (2) that the $3.4 million benefit sought and received by Zarin is not taxable at all. I find the latter alternative unacceptable as inconsistent with the fundamental principle of the Code that anything of commercial value received by a taxpayer is taxable unless expressly excluded from gross income.[3] Commissioner v. Glenshaw Glass Co.; United States v. Kirby Lumber Co., *supra*. I find the former alternative unacceptable as impracticable. In 1980, neither party was maintaining that the debt was unenforceable and, because of the settlement, its unenforceability was not even established in the litigation over the debt in 1981. It was not until 1989 in this litigation over the tax consequences of the transaction that the unenforceability was first judicially declared. Rather than require such tax litigation to resolve the correct treatment of a debt transaction, I regard it as far preferable to have the tax consequences turn on the manner in which the debt is treated by the parties. For present purposes, it will suffice to say that where something that would otherwise be includable in gross income is received on credit in a purchase money transaction, there should be no recognition of income so long as the debtor continues to recognize an obligation to repay the debt. On the other hand, income, if not earlier recognized, should be recognized when the debtor no longer recognizes an obligation to repay and the creditor has released the debt or acknowledged its unenforceability.

In this view, it makes no difference whether the extinguishment of the creditor's claim comes as a part of a compromise. Resorts settled for 14 cents on the dollar presumably because it viewed such a settlement as reflective of the odds that the debt would be held to be enforceable. While Zarin should be given credit for the fact that he had to pay 14 cents for a release, I see no reason why he should not realize gain in the same manner as he would have if Resorts had concluded on its own that the debt was legally unenforceable and had written it off as uncollectible.[5]

---

2. This is not a case in which parties agree subsequent to a purchase money transaction that the property purchased has a value less than thought at the time of the transaction. In such cases, the purchase price adjustment rule is applied and the agreed-upon value is accepted as the value of the benefit received by the purchaser. Nor is this a case in which the taxpayer is entitled to rescind an entire purchase money transaction, thereby to restore itself to the position it occupied before receiving anything of commercial value. In this case, the illegality was in the extension of credit by Resorts and whether one views the benefit received by Zarin as cash or the opportunity to gamble, he is no longer in a position to return that benefit.

3. As the court's opinion correctly points out, this record will not support an exclusion under § 108(a) which relates to discharge of debt in an insolvency or bankruptcy context. Section 108(e)(5) of the Code, which excludes discharged indebtedness arising from a "purchase price adjustment" is not applicable here. Among other things, § 108(e)(5) necessarily applies only to a situation in which the debtor still holds the property acquired in the purchase money transaction. Equally irrelevant is § 108(d)'s definition of "indebtedness" relied upon heavily by the court. Section 108(d) expressly defines that term solely for the purposes of § 108 and not for the purposes of § 61(a)(12).

5. A different situation exists where there is a bona fide dispute over the amount of a debt and the dispute is compromised. Rather than require tax litigation to determine the amount of

I would affirm the judgment of the Tax Court.

DISSENTING OPINION OF JUDGE TANNENWALD, BELOW (92 T.C. 1084):

TANNENWALD, J., dissenting

* * * The concept that petitioner received his money's worth from the enjoyment of using the chips (thus equating the pleasure of gambling with increase in wealth) produces the incongruous result that the more a gambler loses, the greater his pleasure and the larger the increase in his wealth. * * *

NOTES

1. Couldn't Zarin have sold the chips to another gambler? Would it matter that such a sale would have irritated Resorts International?

2. If you're wondering where Mr. Zarin got all that money in the first place, *see* Nemtin v. Zarin, 577 F.Supp. 1135 (D.N.J.1983), in which Ms. Nemtin claimed that she loaned Mr. Zarin millions of dollars to facilitate his gambling, which she wanted him to repay.

3. *Zarin* has generated considerable academic commentary. For the best of it, see Daniel Shaviro, *The Man Who Lost Too Much: Zarin v. Commissioner and the Measurement of Taxable Consumption*, 45 Tax L. Rev. 215 (1990).

4. *haiku*

In life, Zarin lost but in tax, he won. Why can't tax imitate life?

5. What is the difference between borrowing and stealing? Consider *Collins, infra.*

COLLINS v. COMMISSIONER

United States Court of Appeals, Second Circuit, 1993.
3 F.3d 625.

CARDAMONE, CIRCUIT JUDGE:

Mark D. Collins, taxpayer or appellant, appeals from a final decision of the United States Tax Court (Beghe, J.), entered October 16, 1992, determining that, as a result of unreported gross income from theft, he had an income tax deficiency for 1988 of $9,359. The theft occurred when the taxpayer, an employee of a betting parlor that accepts bets on horse races, was unable to stop himself from making wagers on his own behalf. He punched his bets on his computer without funds to pay for them. The horses Collins bet on ran like those of the bettor immortalized in Stephen C. Foster's De Camptown Races (Robbins Music Corp. 1933) (Song), some of whose horses left the racetrack, others cut across it, and one got stuck "in a big mud hole." Appellant's horses finished out of the money on most of the races he bet on and he lost heavily for the day. That which Collins

---

income received, the Commission treats the compromise figure as representing the amount of the obligation. I find this sensible and consistent with the pragmatic approach I would take.

had stolen is what he most feared to keep, as is so often the case; so he turned himself in. The theft precipitated a chain of events that led to the present appeal.

Background

A. *Theft and Racetrack Betting*

Collins was employed as a ticket vendor and computer operator at an Off–Track Betting (OTB) parlor in Auburn, New York. OTB runs a network of 298 betting parlors in New York State that permit patrons to place legal wagers on horse races without actually going to the track. Operating as a cash business, OTB does not extend credit to those making bets at its parlors. It also has a strict policy against employee betting on horse races. Collins, an apparently compulsive gambler, ignored these regulations and occasionally placed bets on his own behalf in his computer without paying for them. Until July 17, 1988 he had always managed to cover those bets without detection. On that date, appellant decided he "would like some money" and on credit punched up for himself a total of $80,280 in betting tickets.

Collins began the day by betting $20 on a horse across the board in the first race at the Finger Lakes Race Track in upstate New York, that is, he bet $20 to win, $20 to place (finish second or better), and $20 to show (finish third or better). The horse finished out of the money (not in the top three racers) and Collins lost $60. On the second race Collins again bet $40 across the board, with the same results. He was now out a total of $180. Appellant repeated this pattern, betting $600 in the third race and $1,500 in the fourth race at Finger Lakes, both of which he lost. Collins did not bet on the fifth race, but he wagered $1,500 in the sixth race, $7,500 in the seventh, and $15,000 in the eighth. Collins' luck continued to hold steady: he lost all of these races and now owed OTB $26,280.

There were only two races left that day and Collins was determined to recoup his losses. Consequently, he gambled $25,500 of OTB's money on the ninth race. This time his horse came in third, and Collins won back $8,925. He then bet $28,500 in the last or tenth race and finally picked a winner. The winning horse paid him $33,250. After this race, Collins was behind $38,105 for the day.

At the close of the races Collins put his $42,175 in winning tickets in his OTB drawer and reported his bets and his losing ticket shortfall to his supervisor, who until then had not been aware of Collins' gambling activities. She called the police, and in police custody Collins signed an affidavit admitting what he had done. On October 27, 1988 he pled guilty to one count of grand larceny in the third degree, a felony under New York law. Collins was sentenced on December 1, 1988 by the Cayuga County Court in Auburn, New York, to five years of probation, 150 hours of community service, and a $100 surcharge.

Appellant's bets not only resulted in a shortfall in his till at OTB, but also had an impact on the odds of the races on which he had made those wagers. Racetrack gambling in New York is run on a "pari-mutuel" system. Under that system all bets—on each type of wager for each race—are pooled into a single so-called mutuel fund. The odds and payoffs for the first three horses in a race depend on the total amount of money in this pool. By increasing the total sum of money in the pool, Collins' bets lowered the odds and potential payoffs on those horses on which he bet, and correspondingly increased the odds and potential payoffs on the other horses in the same race. Because Collins lost his first seven bets on July 17, his wagers increased the payout for the winners of each of those races. By contrast, Collins' last two winning bets reduced the funds available to pay off legitimate bettors who had paid cash for their winning tickets. In addition, appellant's bets increased OTB's liability to the Finger Lakes Track. Each of his bets was electronically transmitted to the racetrack via computer, and once so forwarded, OTB became liable to transfer the amount of the wager to the track.

These unauthorized actions on Collins' part resulted in OTB making a claim under its theft insurance policy with the Hartford Accident & Indemnity Co. The insurer, which paid the claim less a $5,000 deductible, sued Collins for the amount it had paid over plus costs. In December 1989 Hartford obtained a judgment against Collins for $36,601.94, and it has subsequently made attempts to enforce this judgment by garnishing Collins' wages from his new employer. The record does not reveal whether the insurer has recovered any of its money.

B. *Tax Deficiency*

* * *

[The Tax Court]-first determined that Collins' actions, rather than giving rise to gambling income, had resulted in a $38,105 gambling loss, arrived at by subtracting all the amounts he had earlier lost from his winnings on the last two races. Thus, contrary to the IRS' position, the taxpayer had not received any net income from his betting activities on July 17, 1988. The Tax Court then turned to what it deemed the more difficult question: whether the $80,280 in unpaid bets placed by Collins constituted theft or embezzlement income. It answered this query in the affirmative after undertaking a two-step inquiry that examined: (1) whether Collins realized economic value from the betting tickets he stole (the Realizable Value Test) and, if so, (2) whether Collins had sufficient control over this stolen property to derive value from it (the Control Test). The Tax Court found that Collins' larceny met both parts of the test because he had the opportunity to derive gratification and economic gain from using the stolen tickets.

Having concluded that Collins' theft resulted in income, the Tax Court calculated the amount of that income. It found a proper measure was the $80,280 value of the tickets, because Collins received from the pilfered tickets the same benefit that any legitimate purchaser would have gotten. To calculate tax liability the court then deducted from the $80,280 the $42,175 in winnings that Collins returned to his OTB till, which it characterized as a restitution payment by the taxpayer to his employer.

In sum, the Tax Court found Collins' unreported taxable income to be that amount which he stole on July 17 but did not return to his OTB till, a total that came to $38,105. As a consequence, it entered a final judgment on October 16, 1992 holding Collins liable for $9,359 in unpaid taxes for 1988. No additional penalties were assessed. The taxpayer has appealed contending, first, that the Tax Court erred by treating his illicit July 17 activities as giving rise to gross income and, second, by measuring this income by the face value of the tickets he misappropriated. We affirm.

Discussion

I.   Gross Income

A.   General Principles

* * *

Since Glenshaw Glass the term gross income has been read expansively to include all realized gains and forms of enrichment, that is, "all gains except those specifically exempted." Under this broad definition, gross income does not include all moneys a taxpayer receives. It is quite plain, for instance, that gross income does not include money acquired from borrowings. Loans do not result in realized gains or enrichment because any increase in net worth from proceeds of a loan is offset by a corresponding obligation to repay it.

This well-established principle on borrowing initially gave rise to another nettlesome question on how embezzled funds were to be treated. The Supreme Court once believed that money illegally procured from another was not gross income for tax purposes when the acquiror was legally obligated, like a legitimate borrower, to return the funds. See Commissioner v. Wilcox, 327 U.S. 404 (1946). In Rutkin v. United States, 343 U.S. 130 (1952), the Court partially and somewhat unsatisfactorily abandoned that view, holding that an extortionist, unlike an embezzler, was obligated to pay tax on his ill-gotten gains because he was unlikely to be asked to repay the money.

Rutkin left the law on embezzlement in a murky state. This condition cleared in James v. United States, 366 U.S. 213 (1961). There the Court stated unequivocally that all unlawful gains are taxable. It reasoned that embezzlers, along with others who procure money illegally, should not be able to escape taxes while honest citizens pay taxes on "every conceivable type of income." Thus, under James, a taxpayer has received income when she "acquires earnings, lawfully or unlawfully, without the consensual recognition, express or implied, of an obligation to repay and without restriction as to their disposition...." This income test includes all forms of enrichment, legal or otherwise, but explicitly excludes loans.

Distinguishing loans from unlawful taxable gains has not usually proved difficult. Loans are identified by the mutual understanding between the borrower and lender of the obligation to repay and a bona fide intent on the borrower's part to repay the acquired funds. Accordingly, in Buff v. Commissioner, 496 F.2d 847 (2d Cir.1974) we found an embezzler who confessed to his crime and within the same year signed a judgment agreeing to make repayment had received a taxable gain as opposed to a loan because he never had any intention of repaying the money. The embezzler's expressed consent to repay the loan, we determined, "was not worth the paper it was written on." The mere act of signing such a consent could not be used to escape tax liability.

It is important to note, in addition, that though an embezzler must under the James test include as taxable income all amounts illegally acquired, the taxpayer may ordinarily claim a tax deduction for payments she makes in restitution. Such a deduction is available for the tax year in which the repayments are made. See I.R.C. § 165(c).

B. Principles Applied

With this outline of the relevant legal principles in mind, we have little difficulty in holding that Collins' illegal activities gave rise to gross income. Under the expansive definitions of income advanced in Glenshaw Glass and James, larceny of any kind resulting in an unrestricted gain of moneys to a wrongdoer is a taxable event. Taxes may be assessed in the year in which the taxpayer realizes an economic benefit from his actions. In this case, Collins admitted to stealing racing tickets from OTB on July 17, 1988. This larceny resulted in the taxpayer's enrichment: he had the pleasure of betting on horses running at the Finger Lakes Race Track. Individuals purchase racing tickets from OTB because these tickets give them the pleasure of attempting to make money simply by correctly predicting the outcomes of horse races. By punching up tickets on his computer without paying for them, Collins appropriated for himself the same benefit that patrons of OTB pay money to receive. This illegally-appropriated benefit, as the tax court correctly concluded, constituted gross income to Collins in 1988.

The taxpayer raises a series of objections to this conclusion. He first insists that such a holding cannot be correct because at the end of the day he was in debt by $38,105. He asserts that a tax is being assessed on his losses rather than on any possible gain. What may seem at first glance a rather anomalous result is explained by distinguishing between Collins' theft and his gambling activities. Collins took illegally acquired assets and spent them unwisely by betting on losing horses at a racetrack.

Although the bets gave rise to gambling losses, the taxpayer gained from the misappropriation of his employer's property without its knowledge or permission. The gambling loss is not relevant to and does not offset Collins' gain in the form of opportunities to gamble that he obtained by virtue of his embezzlement. Collins' situation is quite the same as that of any other individual who embezzles money from his employer and subsequently loses it at the racetrack. Such person would properly have his illegally-acquired assets included in his gross income. Further, taxpayer would not be able to deduct gambling losses from theft income because the Internal Revenue Code only allows gambling losses to offset gambling winnings. See I.R.C. § 165(d). Collins is being treated the same way.

The taxpayer next contends his larceny resulted in no taxable gain because he recognized that he had an obligation to repay his employer for the stolen tickets. He posits that recognition of a repayment obligation transformed a wrongful appropriation into a nontaxable transaction. In effect, Collins tries to revive pre-James law under which an embezzler's gain could be found nontaxable due to the embezzler's duty to repay stolen funds. Yet, the Supreme Court has clearly abandoned the pre-James view and ruled instead that only a loan, with its attendant "consensual recognition" of the obligation to repay, is not taxable. There was no loan of funds, nor was there any "consensual recognition" here: OTB never gave Collins permission to use betting tickets. To the contrary, it has strict rules against employee betting, and Collins could not have reasonably believed that his supervisors would have approved of his transactions. His unilateral intention to pay for the stolen property did not transform a theft into a loan within the meaning of James.

The taxpayer then avers this case is analogous to Gilbert v. Commissioner, 552 F.2d 478 (2d Cir.1977), in which we found a consensual recognition of the obligation to repay despite the absence of a loan agreement. Taxpayer Edward Gilbert, as president and a director of E.L. Bruce Company, acquired on margin a substantial personal stake in the stock of a rival company, Celotex Corporation, intending to bring about a merger between Celotex and E.L. Bruce. The stock market declined after Gilbert bought these shares, and he was required to meet several margin calls. Lacking personal funds to meet these obligations, Gilbert instructed the corporate secretary of E.L. Bruce to make $1.9 million in margin payments on his behalf. A few days later, Gilbert signed secured promissory notes to repay the funds; but, the corporation's board of directors refused to ratify Gilbert's unauthorized withdrawal, demanded his resignation, and called in his notes. The board also declined to merge with Celotex, and soon thereafter the Celotex stock that Gilbert owned became essentially worthless. Gilbert could not repay his obligations to E.L. Bruce, and he eventually pled guilty to federal and state charges of unlawfully withdrawing funds from the corporation.

The IRS claimed that Gilbert's unauthorized withdrawal of funds constituted income to the taxpayer. It asserted that there was no consensual recognition of a repayment obligation because E.L. Bruce Company's board of directors was unaware of and subsequently disapproved Gilbert's actions. Citing the highly atypical nature of the case, we held that Gilbert did not realize income under the James test because (1) he not only "fully" intended but also expected "with reasonable certainty" to repay the sums taken, (2) he believed his withdrawals would be approved by the corporate board, and (3) he made prompt assignment of assets sufficient to secure the amount he owed. These facts evidenced consensual recognition and distinguished Gilbert from the more typical embezzlement case where the embezzler plans right from the beginning to abscond with the embezzled funds.

Plainly, none of the significant facts of Gilbert are present in the case at hand. Collins, unlike Gilbert, never expected to be able to repay the stolen funds. He was in no position to do so. The amount he owed OTB was three times his annual salary—a far cry from Gilbert, where the taxpayer assigned to the corporation enough assets to cover his unauthorized withdrawals. Also in contrast to Gilbert, Collins could not have believed that his employer would subsequently ratify his transactions. He knew that OTB had strict rules against employee betting. Moreover, while Gilbert was motivated by a desire to assist his corporation, Collins embezzled betting tickets because he wanted to make some money. Collins' purpose makes this a garden variety type of embezzlement case, not to be confused with a loan. Gilbert is therefore an inapposite precedent.

Finally, appellant complains of the root unfairness and harshness of the result, declaring that the imposition of a tax on his July 17 transaction is an attempt to use the income tax law to punish misconduct that has already been appropriately punished under the criminal law. Although we are not without some sympathy to the taxpayer's plight, we are unable to adopt his claim of unfairness and use it as a basis to negate the imposition of a tax on his income. The Supreme Court has repeatedly emphasized that taxing an embezzler on his illicit gains accords with the fair administration of the tax law because it removes the anomaly of having the income of an honest individual taxed while the similar gains of a criminal are not. Thus, there is no double penalty in having a taxpayer prosecuted for the crime that resulted in his obtaining ill-gotten gains and subsequently being required to pay taxes on those illegal gains. Such is not an unduly harsh result because § 165 provides that once the taxpayer makes restitution payments to OTB or its insurer, he will be able in that year to deduct the amount of those payments from his gross income.

In sum, we hold that under the expansive definition of income adopted in Glenshaw Glass and James, Collins received gross income from his theft of OTB betting tickets. There is no basis upon which we may hold that the receipt of these opportunities to gamble may be excluded from a calculation of the taxpayer's income. When and if Collins repays the stolen funds, he will be entitled to a deduction from income in the year that the funds are repaid.

II. Valuation

Having determined that the July 17 transaction resulted in a taxable gain to Collins, we next consider how that gain should be measured. It is well-settled that income received in a form other than cash is taxed at its fair market value at the time of its receipt. Fair market value is defined as "the price at which the property would change hands between a willing buyer and willing seller, neither being under any compulsion to buy or to sell and both having reasonable knowledge of relevant facts."

Based on this measure the value of Collins' tickets was the price at which they would have changed hands between legitimate bettors and OTB. This price was the retail price or face value of the tickets. Accordingly, the Tax Court properly found that the stolen tickets were worth $80,280, their retail price, and this amount was correctly included in the taxpayer's gross income, as a gain from theft. From that figure Collins was entitled to a deduction for restitution he made to OTB in 1988. Collins returned to his till on July 17 winning tickets with a face value of $42,175. Thus, the Tax Court correctly determined that Collins' total taxable theft income for the year was $38,105 ($80,280 minus $42,175).

Collins, relying upon the Third Circuit's decision in Zarin v. Commissioner, asserts the stolen tickets were essentially valueless for tax purposes. * * * [T]he Third Circuit held the gambling chips Zarin acquired with Resort's loan were not property because they had "no independent economic value." It reached this conclusion because the chips could not be used outside the casino, only having value as a means of facilitating gambling within the casino itself.

Collins seizes on this second point, insisting that like Zarin he stole opportunities to gamble and that his stolen racing tickets—like Zarin's gambling chips—had no intrinsic economic value. He thinks therefore that his taxable gain from the theft of the tickets was zero.

In disposing of that erroneous assumption, we observe that the statement in Zarin regarding the value of the casino's gambling chips was offered as part of the appellate court's interpretation of the narrow income exclusion provision of § 108(d) of the Code. Section 108(a) excludes from gross income the amount of the discharge of a taxpayer's indebtedness and § 108(d), just discussed, defines indebtedness. We are not convinced that the Third Circuit's reasoning is applicable outside the context of § 108 and the specific facts of that case where nothing was stolen and there was no embezzlement. Zarin may have been written differently had the Third Circuit been confronted with the separate question of whether to include as gross income under § 61 the face value of stolen gambling opportunities.

Zarin we think is also inapposite because it involved a consensual transaction between Resorts Casino and the taxpayer that impacted no other parties. Zarin's gambling did not cause Resorts to transfer any money from the casino to third parties, nor did it affect other players at the gaming tables. In the instant case, Collins' wagers had external consequences beyond his tax liability. His bets affected the odds of the races at the Finger Lakes Track and impacted the payouts on those races on July 17. Further, OTB had to pay the Finger Lakes Track $38,105, the face value of the losing tickets. Hence, the betting tickets here had independent and measurable economic value, and resulted in a true loss to OTB. Consequently, we regard the fair market value of the stolen gambling tickets to be the proper measure of Collins' taxable gain in 1988.

Conclusion

For the reasons stated, the decision of the tax court is accordingly affirmed.

QUESTIONS

1. Do you agree with the Court's reasoning as to why Collins' betting was properly valued at market value, while Zarin's chips had no market value, and were not property?

2. Did the cases really come out differently? Where is Mr. Collins if and when he repays all of the money?

(b) Basis and Debt

Code: §§ 61(a)(12), 1001, 1011, 1012, 1014, 7701(g)

Regulations: § 1.1001–2

Crane

It all begins with Crane v. Commissioner, 331 U.S. 1, 67 S.Ct. 1047, 91 L.Ed. 1301 (1947). In *Crane*, Mrs. Crane received a parcel of real estate as a bequest. At the time of the bequest, the fair market value of the real estate was equal to the amount of the mortgage. Let us assume that both figures were $250,000. Therefore, the equity (fair market value of the property minus mortgage debt) was zero:

Fair Market Value	$250,000
Less: Debt	– $250,000
Equals Equity	$ 0

Years later, Mrs. Crane sold the property for $2,500 cash. The new buyer assumed the mortgage. Let us stipulate that the amount of the mortgage debt was still $250,000.

The taxpayer argued that the sale created a realized gain of $2,500:

Amount Realized	$2,500
Less: Basis	– $ 0
Equals Gain	$2,500

The premises of taxpayer's argument were that:

(1) Mrs. Crane's debt was not included in her basis. Therefore, Mrs. Crane's basis was equal to her equity, which was zero.

(2) The discharge of Mrs. Crane's debt was not included in her amount realized. Therefore, the only amount which she realized upon disposition of the property was the cash received of $2,500.

The government, in contrast, argued that the debt should have been included in basis, and that the discharge of the debt should have been included in amount realized. As to basis, the government argued that her original basis was $250,000—the property's fair market value at the time of her husband's death, not reduced by the debt.

However, during the time that Mrs. Crane had held the property, she had taken deductions for depreciation. Depreciation deductions must be subtracted from basis, dollar for dollar (see discussion of § 1016 at 230).[d] As a result, Mrs. Crane's new basis was, say, $100,000

Original Basis	$250,000
Less: Depreciation Deductions	− $150,000
Equals Adjusted Basis	$100,000

The government argued that Mrs. Crane's amount realized was $252,500, or

Cash Realized	$ 2,500
PLUS: Debt Discharged	+ $250,000
Amount Realized	$252,500

Accordingly, by the government calculations,

Amount Realized	$252,500
Less: Basis	− $100,000
Equals Gain	$152,500

The government won.

For our purposes, the important issue in *Crane* is whether debt should be included in basis and amount realized.[e] Consider: A acquires Blackacre for $100. What is A's basis, if A came up with the $100 in the following ways:

a) A earned it.

b) A stole it.

c) A found it on the street.

d) A received it as a cash gift.

---

d. Depreciation adjustments should have been made on the taxpayer's theory as well. However, taxpayer argued that her basis, already at zero, could not be lowered any further. (What, if anything, is wrong with having a negative basis?) Moreover, she argued that the one who should have taken depreciation was the mortgage bank, which actually suffered the consequence of the decline in value.

e. Note that, in the case, the property was acquired by bequest. The principle, however, applies to all acquisitions.

e) A borrowed it ten years ago. It has been in A's mattress ever since.

f) A borrowed it yesterday.

g) A borrowed it today, stopping at the bank to pick up the money on the way to the real estate closing.

h) A borrowed the money at the closing, simultaneously with the purchase of the real estate. Both the bank and the seller were at the closing.

i) A borrowed the money from the seller. In effect, A paid nothing for Blackacre.

What do you conclude from your answers to these questions?

Crane was the granddaddy of all tax shelters. Consider: you can acquire Blackacre without spending a penny out of your own pocket, and yet, you can acquire a basis of $100. Basis is our friend, for two reasons. First, upon sale, we subtract basis from amount realized, thus lowering the amount of taxable gain. Second, the higher the basis, the more the depreciation deductions (trust me on this one, or if you're impatient, *see* p. 229).

However, if the good news from *Crane* concerns basis, the bad news concerns amount realized. Assume for these purposes that Seller bought Blackacre for $100,000, which he obtained by a purchase money mortgage from Bank. The property is now worth $150,000 free and clear of the mortgage. Seller's equity is therefore

Fair Market Value	$150,000
Less: Debt	− $100,000
Equals Equity	$ 50,000

Seller could sell the property to Buyer in any one of three ways. First, Buyer could pay Seller $150,000 in cash, conditioned upon Seller's promise immediately to use $100,000 of that cash to pay off Bank.

Second, Buyer could pay $50,000 directly to Seller, and another $100,000 directly to Bank:

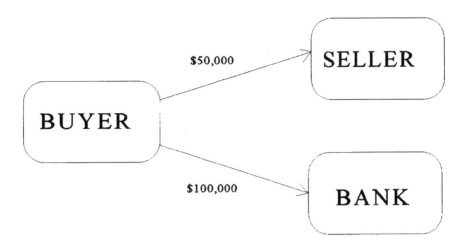

Third, Buyer could pay $50,000 directly to the Seller, and assume the mortgage:

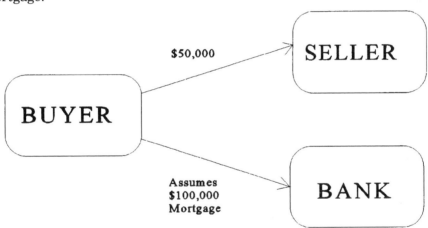

If Buyer assumes the mortgage, the present value of the principal and interest payments made over time to the Bank will be $100,000.[f]

Note that in all three transactions, everyone comes out in the same place. If the outcomes are the same, the tax consequences should be the same. Clearly, Seller has an Amount Realized of $150,000 in the first transaction. Therefore, Seller's Amount Realized must be $150,000 in all three transactions. In the second and third transaction, this result is achieved by including the debt discharged in Seller's Amount Realized.

Recourse and Nonrecourse Debt

The mortgage in *Crane* was nonrecourse (also known as "debt without personal liability"). "Nonrecourse" means that the lender has no

---

   f. *See* Appendix: Present Value Tables.

recourse against the borrower—only against the collateral. If the collateral is not sufficient to cover the debt, then the creditor is out of luck.

"Recourse debt" is also known as "debt with personal liability." If the debt is recourse, then the creditor can go after the collateral, **and** the personal assets of the debtor.

Consider two situations:

A: Fair Market Value of the Property Free of the Lien: $ 100
    Amount of the Lien: $25

B: Fair Market Value of the Property Free of the Lien: $25
    Amount of the Lien: $ 100

In which situation would it matter if the mortgage was recourse or nonrecourse?

Consider four situations:

Non–Recourse Debt	Recourse Debt
Fair Market Value [$100] > Debt [$25]	Fair Market Value [$100] > Debt [$25]
Non–Recourse Debt	Recourse Debt
Fair Market Value [$25] < Debt [$100]	Fair Market Value [$25] < Debt [$100]

In which situation might it be argued that, in practical terms, the debt owed is less than the face amount?

In the famous footnote 37 of *Crane*, the court said:

Obviously, if the value of the property is less than the amount of the mortgage, a mortgagor who is not personally liable cannot realize a benefit equal to the mortgage. Consequently, a different problem might be encountered where a mortgagor abandoned the property or transferred it subject to the mortgage without receiving boot. That is not this case.

The *Crane* Court, in the famous footnote 37, posed a question which it declined to answer. That question was answered by *Tufts*.

COMMISSIONER v. TUFTS

United States Supreme Court, 1983.
461 U.S. 300, 103 S.Ct. 1826, 75 L.Ed.2d 863.

JUSTICE BLACKMUN delivered the opinion of the Court.

Over 35 years ago, in Crane v. Commissioner, this Court ruled that a taxpayer, who sold property encumbered by a nonrecourse mortgage (the amount of the mortgage being less than the property's value), must include the unpaid balance of the mortgage in the computation of the amount the taxpayer realized on the sale. The case now before us presents the question whether the same rule applies when the unpaid amount of the nonrecourse mortgage exceeds the fair market value of the property sold.

I

On August 1, 1970, respondent Clark Pelt, a builder, and his wholly owned corporation, respondent Clark, Inc., formed a general partnership. The purpose of the partnership was to construct a 120–unit apartment complex in Duncanville, Tex., a Dallas suburb. Neither Pelt nor Clark, Inc., made any capital contribution to the partnership. Six days later, the partnership entered into a mortgage loan agreement with the Farm & Home Savings Association (F & H). Under the agreement, F & H was committed for a $1,851,500 loan for the complex. In return, the partnership executed a note and a deed of trust in favor of F & H. The partnership obtained the loan on a nonrecourse basis: neither the partnership nor its partners assumed any personal liability for repayment of the loan. Pelt later admitted four friends and relatives, respondents Tufts, Steger, Stephens, and Austin, as general partners. None of them contributed capital upon entering the partnership.

The construction of the complex was completed in August 1971. * * * Due to these contributions and deductions, the partnership's adjusted basis in the property in August 1972 was $1,455,740.

In 1971 and 1972, major employers in the Duncanville area laid off significant numbers of workers. As a result, the partnership's rental income was less than expected, and it was unable to make the payments due on the mortgage. Each partner, on August 28, 1972, sold his partnership interest to an unrelated third party, Fred Bayles. As consideration, Bayles agreed to reimburse each partner's sale expenses up to $250; he also assumed the nonrecourse mortgage.

On the date of transfer, the fair market value of the property did not exceed $1,400,000. Each partner reported the sale on his federal income tax return and indicated that a partnership loss of $55,740 had been sustained.[1] The Commissioner of Internal Revenue, on audit, determined that the sale resulted in a partnership capital gain of approximately $400,000. His theory was that the partnership had realized the full amount of the nonrecourse obligation.

* * * [T]he United States Tax Court * * * upheld the asserted deficiencies. The United States Court of Appeals for the Fifth Circuit reversed. That court * * *, in limiting Crane v. Commissioner to its facts, questioned the theoretical underpinnings of the *Crane* decision. We granted certiorari to resolve the conflict.

II

Section 752(d) of the Internal Revenue Code of 1954 specifically provides that liabilities incurred in the sale or exchange of a partnership

---

1. The loss was the difference between the adjusted basis, $1,455,740, and the fair market value of the property, $1,400,000. On their individual tax returns, the partners did not claim deductions for their respective shares of this loss. In their petitions to the Tax Court, however, the partners did claim the loss.

interest are to "be treated in the same manner as liabilities in connection with the sale or exchange of property not associated with partnerships." Section 1001 governs the determination of gains and losses on the disposition of property. Under § 1001(a), the gain or loss from a sale or other disposition of property is defined as the difference between "the amount realized" on the disposition and the property's adjusted basis. Subsection (b) of § 1001 defines "amount realized": "The amount realized from the sale or other disposition of property shall be the sum of any money received plus the fair market value of the property (other than money) received." At issue is the application of the latter provision to the disposition of property encumbered by a nonrecourse mortgage of an amount in excess of the property's fair market value.

A

In Crane v. Commissioner, *supra,* this Court took the first and controlling step toward the resolution of this issue. Beulah B. Crane was the sole beneficiary under the will of her deceased husband. At his death in January 1932, he owned an apartment building that was then mortgaged for an amount which proved to be equal to its fair market value, as determined for federal estate tax purposes. The widow, of course, was not personally liable on the mortgage. She operated the building for nearly seven years, hoping to turn it into a profitable venture; during that period, she claimed income tax deductions for depreciation, property taxes, interest, and operating expenses, but did not make payments upon the mortgage principal. In computing her basis for the depreciation deductions, she included the full amount of the mortgage debt. In November 1938, with her hopes unfulfilled and the mortgagee threatening foreclosure, Mrs. Crane sold the building. The purchaser took the property subject to the mortgage and paid Crane $3,000; of that amount, $500 went for the expenses of the sale.

Crane reported a gain of $2,500 on the transaction. She reasoned that her basis in the property was zero (despite her earlier depreciation deductions based on including the amount of the mortgage) and that the amount she realized from the sale was simply the cash she received. The Commissioner disputed this claim. He asserted that Crane's basis in the property, under [current § 1014], was the property's fair market value at the time of her husband's death, adjusted for depreciation in the interim, and that the amount realized was the net cash received plus the amount of the outstanding mortgage assumed by the purchaser.

In upholding the Commissioner's interpretation of [current § 1014],[3] the Court observed that to regard merely the taxpayer's equity in the property as her basis would lead to depreciation deductions less than the actual physical deterioration of the property, and would require the basis

---

3. Section 113(a)(5) [now section 1014] defined the basis of "property ... acquired by ... devise ... or by the decedent's estate from the decedent" as "the fair market value of such property at the time of such acquisition." The Court interpreted the term "property" to refer to the physical land and buildings owned by Crane or the aggregate of her rights to control and dispose of them.

to be recomputed with each payment on the mortgage. The Court rejected Crane's claim that any loss due to depreciation belonged to the mortgagee. The effect of the Court's ruling was that the taxpayer's basis was the value of the property undiminished by the mortgage.

The Court next proceeded to determine the amount realized under § 111(b) of the 1938 Act, [the current § 1001(b)]. In order to avoid the "absurdity," of Crane's realizing only $2,500 on the sale of property worth over a quarter of a million dollars, the Court treated the amount realized as it had treated basis, that is, by including the outstanding value of the mortgage. To do otherwise would have permitted Crane to recognize a tax loss unconnected with any actual economic loss. The Court refused to construe one section of the Revenue Act so as "to frustrate the Act as a whole."

Crane, however, insisted that the nonrecourse nature of the mortgage required different treatment. The Court, for two reasons, disagreed. First, excluding the nonrecourse debt from the amount realized would result in the same absurdity and frustration of the Code. Second, the Court concluded that Crane obtained an economic benefit from the purchaser's assumption of the mortgage identical to the benefit conferred by the cancellation of personal debt. Because the value of the property in that case exceeded the amount of the mortgage, it was in Crane's economic interest to treat the mortgage as a personal obligation; only by so doing could she realize upon sale the appreciation in her equity represented by the $2,500 boot. The purchaser's assumption of the liability thus resulted in a taxable economic benefit to her, just as if she had been given, in addition to the boot, a sum of cash sufficient to satisfy the mortgage.[4]

In a footnote [the famous Footnote 37–Ed.], pertinent to the present case, the Court observed: "Obviously, if the value of the property is less than the amount of the mortgage, a mortgagor who is not personally liable cannot realize a benefit equal to the mortgage. Consequently, a different problem might be encountered where a mortgagor abandoned the property or transferred it subject to the mortgage without receiving boot. That is not this case."

B

This case presents that unresolved issue. We are disinclined to overrule *Crane*, and we conclude that the same rule applies when the unpaid amount of the nonrecourse mortgage exceeds the value of the property transferred. *Crane* ultimately does not rest on its limited theory of economic benefit; instead, we read *Crane* to have approved the Commissioner's decision to treat a nonrecourse mortgage in this context as a true

---

4. Crane also argued that even if the statute required the inclusion of the amount of the nonrecourse debt, that amount was not Sixteenth Amendment income because the overall transaction had been "by all dictates of common sense . . . a ruinous disaster." The Court noted, however, that Crane had been entitled to and actually took depreciation deductions for nearly seven years. To allow her to exclude sums on which those deductions were based from the calculation of her taxable gain would permit her "a double deduction . . . on the same loss of assets." The Sixteenth Amendment, it was said, did not require that result.

loan. This approval underlies *Crane*'s holdings that the amount of the nonrecourse liability is to be included in calculating both the basis and the amount realized on disposition. That the amount of the loan exceeds the fair market value of the property thus becomes irrelevant.

When a taxpayer receives a loan, he incurs an obligation to repay that loan at some future date. Because of this obligation, the loan proceeds do not qualify as income to the taxpayer. When he fulfills the obligation, the repayment of the loan likewise has no effect on his tax liability.

Another consequence to the taxpayer from this obligation occurs when the taxpayer applies the loan proceeds to the purchase price of property used to secure the loan. Because of the obligation to repay, the taxpayer is entitled to include the amount of the loan in computing his basis in the property; the loan, under § 1012, is part of the taxpayer's cost of the property. Although a different approach might have been taken with respect to a nonrecourse mortgage loan,[5] the Commissioner has chosen to accord it the same treatment he gives to a recourse mortgage loan. The Court approved that choice in *Crane*, and the respondents do not challenge it here. The choice and its resultant benefits to the taxpayer are predicated on the assumption that the mortgage will be repaid in full.

When encumbered property is sold or otherwise disposed of and the purchaser assumes the mortgage, the associated extinguishment of the mortgagor's obligation to repay is accounted for in the computation of the amount realized.[6] Because no difference between recourse and nonrecourse obligations is recognized in calculating basis,[7] *Crane* teaches that the Commissioner may ignore the nonrecourse nature of the obligation in determining the amount realized upon disposition of the encumbered property. He thus may include in the amount realized the amount of the nonrecourse mortgage assumed by the purchaser. The rationale for this

---

5. The Commissioner might have adopted the theory, implicit in *Crane*'s contentions, that a nonrecourse mortgage is not true debt, but, instead, is a form of joint investment by the mortgagor and the mortgagee. On this approach, nonrecourse debt would be considered a contingent liability, under which the mortgagor's payments on the debt gradually increase his interest in the property while decreasing that of the mortgagee. Because the taxpayer's investment in the property would not include the nonrecourse debt, the taxpayer would not be permitted to include that debt in basis. We express no view as to whether such an approach would be consistent with the statutory structure and, if so, and *Crane* were not on the books, whether that approach would be preferred over Crane's analysis. We note only that the Crane Court's resolution of the basis issue presumed that when property is purchased with proceeds from a nonrecourse mortgage, the purchaser becomes the sole owner of the property. Under the *Crane* approach, the mortgagee is entitled to no portion of the basis. The nonrecourse mortgage is part of the mortgagor's investment in the property, and does not constitute a coinvestment by the mortgagee.

6. In this case, respondents received the face value of their note as loan proceeds. If respondents initially had given their note at a discount, the amount realized on the sale of the securing property might be limited to the funds actually received.

7. The Commissioner's choice in *Crane* "laid the foundation stone of most tax shelters," by permitting taxpayers who bear no risk to take deductions on depreciable property. Congress recently has acted to curb this avoidance device by forbidding a taxpayer to take depreciation deductions in excess of amounts he has at risk in the investment. Although this congressional action may foreshadow a day when nonrecourse and recourse debts will be treated differently, neither Congress nor the Commissioner has sought to alter *Crane*'s rule of including nonrecourse liability in both basis and the amount realized.

treatment is that the original inclusion of the amount of the mortgage in basis rested on the assumption that the mortgagor incurred an obligation to repay. Moreover, this treatment balances the fact that the mortgagor originally received the proceeds of the nonrecourse loan tax-free on the same assumption. Unless the outstanding amount of the mortgage is deemed to be realized, the mortgagor effectively will have received untaxed income at the time the loan was extended and will have received an unwarranted increase in the basis of his property. The Commissioner's interpretation of § 1001(b) in this fashion cannot be said to be unreasonable.

C

* * * Respondents received a mortgage loan with the concomitant obligation to repay by the year 2012. The only difference between that mortgage and one on which the borrower is personally liable is that the mortgagee's remedy is limited to foreclosing on the securing property. This difference does not alter the nature of the obligation; its only effect is to shift from the borrower to the lender any potential loss caused by devaluation of the property. If the fair market value of the property falls below the amount of the outstanding obligation, the mortgagee's ability to protect its interests is impaired, for the mortgagor is free to abandon the property to the mortgagee and be relieved of his obligation.

This, however, does not erase the fact that the mortgagor received the loan proceeds tax-free and included them in his basis on the understanding that he had an obligation to repay the full amount. When the obligation is canceled, the mortgagor is relieved of his responsibility to repay the sum he originally received and thus realizes value to that extent within the meaning of § 1001(b). From the mortgagor's point of view, when his obligation is assumed by a third party who purchases the encumbered property, it is as if the mortgagor first had been paid with cash borrowed by the third party from the mortgagee on a nonrecourse basis, and then had used the cash to satisfy his obligation to the mortgagee.

Moreover, this approach avoids the absurdity the Court recognized in *Crane*. Because of the remedy accompanying the mortgage in the nonrecourse situation, the depreciation in the fair market value of the property is relevant economically only to the mortgagee, who by lending on a nonrecourse basis remains at risk. To permit the taxpayer to limit his realization to the fair market value of the property would be to recognize a tax loss for which he has suffered no corresponding economic loss. Such a result would be to construe "one section of the Act ... so as ... to defeat the intention of another or to frustrate the Act as a whole."

In the specific circumstances of *Crane*, the economic benefit theory did support the Commissioner's treatment of the nonrecourse mortgage as a personal obligation. The footnote in Crane acknowledged the limitations of that theory when applied to a different set of facts. *Crane* also stands for the broader proposition, however, that a nonrecourse loan should be treated as a true loan. We therefore hold that a taxpayer must account for the proceeds of obligations he has received tax-free and included in basis. Nothing in either § 1001(b) or in the Court's prior decisions requires the Commissioner to permit a taxpayer to treat a sale of encumbered property asymmetrically, by including the proceeds of the nonrecourse obligation in basis but not accounting for the proceeds upon transfer of the encumbered property. * * *

IV

When a taxpayer sells or disposes of property encumbered by a nonrecourse obligation, the Commissioner properly requires him to include among the assets realized the outstanding amount of the obligation. The fair market value of the property is irrelevant to this calculation. We find this interpretation to be consistent with *Crane*.

The judgment of the Court of Appeals is therefore reversed.

It is so ordered.

JUSTICE O'CONNOR, concurring.

I concur in the opinion of the Court, accepting the view of the Commissioner. I do not, however, endorse the Commissioner's view. Indeed, were we writing on a slate clean except for the *Crane* decision, I would take quite a different approach—that urged upon us by Professor Barnett as amicus.

Crane established that a taxpayer could treat property as entirely his own, in spite of the "coinvestment" provided by his mortgagee in the form of a nonrecourse loan. That is, the full basis of the property, with all its tax consequences, belongs to the mortgagor. That rule alone, though, does not in any way tie nonrecourse debt to the cost of property or to the proceeds upon disposition. I see no reason to treat the purchase, ownership, and eventual disposition of property differently because the taxpayer also takes out a mortgage, an independent transaction. In this case, the taxpayer purchased property, using nonrecourse financing, and sold it after it declined in value to a buyer who assumed the mortgage. There is no economic difference between the events in this case and a case in which the taxpayer buys property with cash; later obtains a nonrecourse loan by pledging the property as security; still later, using cash on hand, buys off the mortgage for the market value of the devalued property; and finally sells the property to a third party for its market value.

The logical way to treat both this case and the hypothesized case is to separate the two aspects of these events and to consider, first, the ownership and sale of the property, and, second, the arrangement and retirement of the loan. Under *Crane*, the fair market value of the property on the date of acquisition—the purchase price—represents the taxpayer's basis in the property, and the fair market value on the date of disposition represents the proceeds on sale. The benefit received by the taxpayer in return for the property is the cancellation of a mortgage that is worth no more than the fair market value of the property, for that is all the mortgagee can expect to collect on the mortgage. His gain or loss on the disposition of the property equals the difference between the proceeds and the cost of acquisition. Thus, the taxation of the transaction in property reflects the economic fate of the property. If the property has declined in value, as was the case here, the taxpayer recognizes a loss on the disposition of the property. The new purchaser then takes as his basis the fair market value as of the date of the sale.

In the separate borrowing transaction, the taxpayer acquires cash from the mortgagee. He need not recognize income at that time, of course, because he also incurs an obligation to repay the money. Later, though, when he is able to satisfy the debt by surrendering property that is worth less than the face amount of the debt, we have a classic situation of cancellation of indebtedness, requiring the taxpayer to recognize income in the amount of the difference between the proceeds of the loan and the amount for which he is able to satisfy his creditor. I.R.C. § 61(a)(12). The taxation of the financing transaction then reflects the economic fate of the loan.

The reason that separation of the two aspects of the events in this case is important is, of course, that the Code treats different sorts of income differently. A gain on the sale of the property may qualify for capital gains treatment, while the cancellation of indebtedness is ordinary income, but income that the taxpayer may be able to defer. Not only does Professor Barnett's theory permit us to accord appropriate treatment to each of the two types of income or loss present in these sorts of transactions, it also restores continuity to the system by making the taxpayer-seller's proceeds on the disposition of property equal to the purchaser's basis in the property. Further, and most important, it allows us to tax the events in this case in the same way that we tax the economically identical hypothesized transaction.

Persuaded though I am by the logical coherence and internal consistency of this approach, I agree with the Court's decision not to adopt it judicially. We do not write on a slate marked only by Crane. The Commissioner's longstanding position, Rev.Rul. 76–111, 1976–1 C.B. 214, is now reflected in the regulations. Treas. Reg. § 1.1001–2. In the light of the numerous cases in the lower courts including the amount of the unrepaid proceeds of the mortgage in the proceeds on sale or disposition, it is difficult to conclude that the Commissioner's interpretation of the statute exceeds the bounds of his discretion. As the Court's opinion demonstrates, his interpretation is defensible. One can reasonably read § 1001(b)'s reference to "the amount realized from the sale or other disposition of property" to permit the Commissioner to collapse the two aspects of the transaction. As long as his view is a reasonable reading of § 1001(b), we should defer to the regulations promulgated by the agency charged with interpretation of the statute. Accordingly, I concur.

NOTES, QUESTIONS

1. How many transactions did the majority see?

2. How many transactions did the concurring opinion see?

3. What practical difference would Justice O'Connor's analysis make?

4. Remember the good news and the bad news from *Crane*? *Tufts* just makes it better, and worse. On basis, not only can you create high basis without spending any of your own money, you don't even have to be personally liable on the debt! What could be better than that?

However, on amount realized, remember that you can have a hefty amount realized, hence, taxable gain, even if you receive no cash, but only have your debt discharged. Under *Tufts*, what's even worse is that you get that amount realized even if, practically speaking, you don't really owe the money.

Be careful, however, to apply *Tufts* only to nonrecourse debt. As to recourse debt, consider the following Revenue Ruling:

REVENUE RULING 90–16

1990–1 C.B. 12.

* * *

Issue

A taxpayer transfers to a creditor a residential subdivision that has a fair market value in excess of the taxpayer's basis in satisfaction of a debt for which the taxpayer was personally liable. Is the transfer a sale or disposition resulting in the realization and recognition of gain by the taxpayer under section 1001(c) and 61(a)(3) of the Internal Revenue Code?

Facts

X was the owner and developer of a residential subdivision. To finance the development of the subdivision, X obtained a loan from an unrelated bank. X was unconditionally liable for repayment of the debt. The debt was secured by a mortgage on the subdivision.

X * * * defaulted on the debt. X negotiated an agreement with the bank whereby the subdivision was transferred to the bank and the bank released X from all liability for the amounts due on the debt. When the subdivision was transferred pursuant to the agreement, its fair market value was 10,000x dollars, X's adjusted basis in the subdivision was 8,000x dollars, and the amount due on the debt was 12,000x dollars, which did not represent any accrued but unpaid interest. * * *

Law and Analysis

* * * Section 1.1001–2(a)(1) of the regulations provides that, except as provided in section 1.1001–2(a)(2) and (3), the amount realized from a sale or other disposition of property includes the amount of liabilities from which the transferor is discharged as a result of the sale or disposition. Section 1.1001–2(a)(2) provides that the amount realized on a sale or other disposition of property that secures a recourse liability does not include amounts that are (or would be if realized and recognized) income from the discharge of indebtedness under section 61(a)(12). Example (8) under section 1.1001–2(c) illustrates these rules as follows:

> Example (8). In 1980, F transfers to a creditor an asset with a fair market value of $6,000 and the creditor discharges $7,500 of indebtedness for which F is personally liable. The amount realized on the disposition of the asset is its fair market value ($6,000). In addition, F has income from the discharge of indebtedness of $1,500 ($7,500 ! $6,000).

> In the present situation, X transferred the subdivision to the bank in satisfaction of the 12,000x dollar debt. To the extent of the fair market value of the property transferred to the creditor, the transfer of the subdivision is treated as a sale or disposition upon which gain is recognized under section 1001(c) of the Code. To the extent the fair market value of the subdivision, 10,000x dollars, exceeds its adjusted basis, 8,000x dollars, X realizes and recognizes gain on the transfer. X thus recognizes 2,000x dollars of gain.

To the extent the amount of debt, 12,000x dollars, exceeds the fair market value of the subdivision, 10,000x dollars, X realizes income from the discharge of indebtedness. * * * If the subdivision had been transferred to the bank as a result of a foreclosure proceeding in which the outstanding balance of the debt was discharged (rather than having been transferred pursuant to the settlement agreement), the result would be the same. A mortgage foreclosure, like a voluntary sale, is a "disposition" within the scope of the gain or loss provisions of section 1001 of the Code.

Holding

The transfer of the subdivision by X to the bank in satisfaction of a debt on which X was personally liable is a sale or disposition upon which gain is realized and recognized by X under sections 1001(c) and 61(a)(3) of the Code to the extent the fair market value of the subdivision transferred exceeds X's adjusted basis. Subject to the application of section 108 of the Code, to the extent the amount of debt exceeds the fair market value of the subdivision, X would also realize income from the discharge of indebtedness.

QUESTION

As to recourse financing, does *Revenue Ruling 90–16* look more like the *Tufts* majority opinion, or Justice O'Connor's concurrence?

PROBLEMS *(INCLUDING A SMIDGEN OF REVIEW)*

1. What is A's basis in each of these situations? A buys Whiteacre for $500.

    a) A pays $500 cash.

    b) (1) A pays no cash, but borrows $500 in a recourse mortgage.

    (2) Same as (b)(1), but A later pays back the mortgage loan.

    c) (1) A pays no cash, but borrows $500 in a nonrecourse mortgage.

    (2) Same as (c)(1), but A later pays back the mortgage loan.

2. A pays no cash, but borrows $500 on a recourse mortgage and buys Whiteacre. What happens to basis if, after the initial acquisition:

    a) The value of Whiteacre increases to $5,000.

    b) The value of Whiteacre increases to $5,000, and A takes out a second, recourse mortgage for an additional $3,000. A takes the $3,000 of second mortgage proceeds, and goes on a vacation. *See* Woodsam Associates, Inc. v. Commissioner, 198 F.2d 357 (2d Cir.1952).

    c) Same as (2)(b), but this time A takes the $3,000 of second mortgage proceeds, and uses it to make improvements on Whiteacre.

3. A pays no cash, but borrows $500 on a recourse mortgage to buy Whiteacre. The value of Whiteacre increases to $5,000. The amount of the mortgage debt remains at $500. What is A's amount realized if A sells:

    a) for $5,000 cash, conditioned upon A's repayment of the mortgage?

    b) for $4,500 cash, with a simultaneous payment by buyer of $500 to the mortgagee;

    c) for $4,500 cash, and an assumption of the mortgage by buyer?

    d) How do the answers to parts (a), (b), and (c) change if the mortgage had been nonrecourse?

4. A pays no cash, but borrows $500 on a recourse mortgage to buy Whiteacre. Due to depreciation deductions, A's original $500 basis is adjusted down to $25. The value of Whiteacre decreases to $100. The amount of the mortgage debt remains at $500. A quitclaims the property to the mortgagee. Mortgagee releases A from the total amount of the debt, because she knows A won't ever be able to pay it back.

    a) What are the tax consequences to A?

    b) Would your answer to (a) be any different if the debt had been nonrecourse?

5. Harry bought a house for $100,000 in 2005, at the peak of the market. He financed the purchase with a $95,000 recourse mortgage. In late 2006, Harry could no longer afford the mortgage payments, so the bank foreclosed. At the time of the foreclosure, the remaining debt was $92,000, but the fair market value of the house was only $85,000. The bank, having foreclosed on the property, declined to go after Harry for any deficiency. What are the tax consequences to Harry?

What if the foreclosure happened in 2008, after the effective date of the Mortgage Forgiveness Debt Relief Act of 2007? See §§ 108(a)(1)(E) and 108(h).

CHAPTER III

INCOME: EXCLUSIONS

■ ■ ■

We define things by what they are, and by what they are not. So far, we have discussed what is income. Now, we discuss what could have been income, but is excluded, either by statutes or caselaw. The topics include various types of gratuitous transfers, fringe benefits, scholarships, damages, and tax-exempt bonds.

A. GIFTS, BEQUESTS, AND LIFE INSURANCE

Code: §§ 101 (a), 102(a) and (c); 6053

Regulations: §§ 1.102–1(a), 1.102–1(f)(2) [proposed]

1. GIFTS

Early in the previous chapter, the Haig–Simons problems indicated that the receipt of a gift, while economic income, was not taxable income. Now, it is time to consider exactly what is a tax-free gift.

COMMISSIONER v. DUBERSTEIN

United States Supreme Court, 1960.
363 U.S. 278, 80 S.Ct. 1190, 4 L.Ed.2d 1218.

MR. JUSTICE BRENNAN delivered the opinion of the Court.

These two cases concern the provision of the Internal Revenue Code which excludes from the gross income of an income taxpayer "the value of property acquired by gift." They pose the frequently recurrent question whether a specific transfer to a taxpayer in fact amounted to a "gift" to him within the meaning of the statute. The importance to decision of the facts of the cases requires that we state them in some detail.

No. 376, Commissioner v. Duberstein. The taxpayer, Duberstein, was president of the Duberstein Iron & Metal Company, a corporation with headquarters in Dayton, Ohio. For some years the taxpayer's company had done business with Mohawk Metal Corporation, whose headquarters were in New York City. The president of Mohawk was one Berman. The taxpayer and Berman had generally used the telephone to transact their companies' business with each other, which consisted of buying and selling metals. The taxpayer testified, without elaboration, that he knew Berman "personally" and had known him for about seven years. From time to time in their telephone conversations, Berman would ask Duberstein whether the latter knew of potential customers for some of Mohawk's products in which Duberstein's company itself was not interested. Duberstein provided the names of potential customers for these items.

One day in 1951 Berman telephoned Duberstein and said that the information Duberstein had given him had proved so helpful that he wanted to give the latter a present. Duberstein stated that Berman owed him nothing. Berman said that he had a Cadillac as a gift for Duberstein, and that the latter should send to New York for it; Berman insisted that Duberstein accept the car, and the latter finally did so, protesting however that he had not intended to be compensated for the information. At the time Duberstein already had a Cadillac and an Oldsmobile, and felt that he did not need another car. Duberstein testified that he did not think Berman would have sent him the Cadillac if he had not furnished him with information about the customers. It appeared that Mohawk later deducted the value of the Cadillac as a business expense on its corporate income tax return.

Duberstein did not include the value of the Cadillac in gross income for 1951, deeming it a gift. The Commissioner asserted a deficiency for the car's value against him, and in proceedings to review the deficiency the Tax Court affirmed the Commissioner's determination. It said that "The record is significantly barren of evidence revealing any intention on the part of the payor to make a gift. * * * The only justifiable inference is that the automobile was intended by the payor to be remuneration for services rendered to it by Duberstein." The Court of Appeals for the Sixth Circuit reversed.

No. 546, Stanton v. United States. The taxpayer, Stanton, had been for approximately 10 years in the employ of Trinity Church in New York City. He was comptroller of the Church corporation, and president of a corporation, Trinity Operating Company, the church set up as a fully owned subsidiary to manage its real estate holdings, which were more extensive than simply the church property. His salary by the end of his employment there in 1942 amounted to $22,500 a year. Effective November 30, 1942, he resigned from both positions to go into business for himself. The Operating Company's directors, who seem to have included the rector and vestrymen of the church, passed the following resolution upon his resignation: "Be it resolved that in appreciation of the services rendered by Mr. Stanton * * * a gratuity is hereby awarded to him of Twenty Thousand Dollars, payable to him in equal installments of Two Thousand Dollars at the end of each and every month commencing with the month of December, 1942; provided that, with the discontinuance of his services, the Corporation of Trinity Church is released from all rights and claims to pension and retirement benefits not already accrued up to November 30, 1942.''

The Operating Company's action was later explained by one of its directors as based on the fact that, "Mr. Stanton was liked by all of the Vestry personally. He had a pleasing personality. He had come in when Trinity's affairs were in a difficult situation. He did a splendid piece of work, we felt. * * *.'' And by another: "(W)e were all unanimous in wishing to make Mr. Stanton a gift. Mr. Stanton had loyally and faithfully served Trinity in a very difficult time. We thought of him in the highest regard. We understood that he was going in business for himself. We felt that he was entitled to that evidence of good will.''

On the other hand, there was a suggestion of some ill-feeling between Stanton and the directors, arising out of the recent termination of the services of one Watkins, the Operating Company's treasurer, whose departure was evidently attended by some acrimony. At a special board meeting on October 28, 1942, Stanton had intervened on Watkins' side and asked reconsideration of the matter. The minutes reflect that "resentment was expressed as to the 'presumptuous' suggestion that the action of the Board, taken after long deliberation, should be changed.'' The Board adhered to its determination that Watkins be separated from employment, giving him an opportunity to resign rather than be discharged. At another special meeting two days later it was revealed that Watkins had not resigned; the previous resolution terminating his services was then viewed as effective; and the Board voted the payment of six months' salary to Watkins in a resolution similar to that quoted in regard to Stanton, but which did not use the term "gratuity.'' At the meeting, Stanton announced that in order to avoid any such embarrassment or question at any time as to his willingness to resign if the Board desired, he was tendering his resignation. It was tabled, though not without dissent. The next week, on November 5, at another special meeting, Stanton again tendered his resignation which this time was accepted.

The "gratuity'' was duly paid. So was a smaller one to Stanton's (and the Operating Company's) secretary, under a similar resolution, upon her resignation at the same time. The two corporations shared the expense of the payments. There was undisputed testimony that there were in fact no enforceable rights or claims to pension and retirement benefits which had not accrued at the time of the taxpayer's resignation, and that the last proviso of the resolution was inserted simply out of an abundance of caution. The taxpayer received in cash a refund of his contributions to the retirement plans, and there is no suggestion that he was entitled to more. He was required to perform no further services for Trinity after his resignation.

The Commissioner asserted a deficiency against the taxpayer after the latter had failed to include the payments in question in gross income. After payment of the deficiency and administrative rejection of a refund claim, the taxpayer sued the United States for a refund in the District

Court for the Eastern District of New York. The trial judge, sitting without a jury, made the simple finding that the payments were a "gift," and judgment was entered for the taxpayer. The Court of Appeals for the Second Circuit reversed.

The Government, urging that clarification of the problem typified by these two cases was necessary, and that the approaches taken by the Courts of Appeals for the Second and the Sixth Circuits were in conflict, petitioned for certiorari in No. 376, and acquiesced in the taxpayer's petition in No. 546. On this basis, and because of the importance of the question in the administration of the income tax laws, we granted certiorari in both cases.

The exclusion of property acquired by gift from gross income under the federal income tax laws was made in the first income tax statute passed under the authority of the Sixteenth Amendment, and has been a feature of the income tax statutes ever since. The meaning of the term "gift" as applied to particular transfers has always been a matter of contention. Specific and illuminating legislative history on the point does not appear to exist. Analogies and inferences drawn from other revenue provisions, such as the estate and gift taxes, are dubious. The meaning of the statutory term has been shaped largely by the decisional law. With this, we turn to the contentions made by the Government in these cases.

First. The Government suggests that we promulgate a new "test" in this area to serve as a standard to be applied by the lower courts and by the Tax Court in dealing with the numerous cases that arise.[6] We reject this invitation. We are of opinion that the governing principles are necessarily general and have already been spelled out in the opinions of this Court, and that the problem is one which, under the present statutory framework, does not lend itself to any more definitive statement that would produce a talisman for the solution of concrete cases. The cases at bar are fair examples of the settings in which the problem usually arises. They present situations in which payments have been made in a context with business overtones—an employer making a payment to a retiring employee; a businessman giving something of value to another businessman who has been of advantage to him in his business. In this context, we review the law as established by the prior cases here.

The course of decision here makes it plain that the statute does not use the term "gift" in the common-law sense, but in a more colloquial sense. This Court has indicated that a voluntarily executed transfer of his property by one to another, without any consideration or compensation therefor, though a common-law gift, is not necessarily a "gift" within the meaning of the statute. For the Court has shown that the mere absence of a legal or moral obligation to make such a payment does not establish that it is a gift. Old Colony Trust Co. v. Commissioner. And, importantly, if the payment proceeds primarily from "the constraining force of any moral or

---

6. The Government's proposed test is stated: "Gifts should be defined as transfers of property made for personal as distinguished from business reasons."

legal duty," or from "the incentive of anticipated benefit" of an economic nature, Bogardus v. Commissioner, 302 U.S. 34, 41, it is not a gift. And, conversely, "(w)here the payment is in return for services rendered, it is irrelevant that the donor derives no economic benefit from it." Robertson v. United States, 343 U.S. 711.[7] A gift in the statutory sense, on the other hand, proceeds from a "detached and disinterested generosity," Commissioner of Internal Revenue v. LoBue, 351 U.S. 243, 246, "out of affection, respect, admiration, charity or like impulses." Robertson v. United States. And in this regard, the most critical consideration, as the Court was agreed in the leading case here, is the transferor's "intention." Bogardus v. Commissioner, 302 U.S. 34, 43. "What controls is the intention with which payment, however voluntary, has been made." Id., 302 U.S. at page 45 (dissenting opinion).

The Government says that this "intention" of the transferor cannot mean what the cases on the common-law concept of gift call "donative intent." With that we are in agreement, for our decisions fully support this. Moreover, the Bogardus case itself makes it plain that the donor's characterization of his action is not determinative—that there must be an objective inquiry as to whether what is called a gift amounts to it in reality. It scarcely needs adding that the parties' expectations or hopes as to the tax treatment of their conduct in themselves have nothing to do with the matter. * * *

Second. The Government's proposed "test," while apparently simple and precise in its formulation, depends frankly on a set of "principles" or "presumptions" derived from the decided cases, and concededly subject to various exceptions; and it involves various corollaries, which add to its detail. Were we to promulgate this test as a matter of law, and accept with it its various presuppositions and stated consequences, we would be passing for beyond the requirements of the cases before us, and would be painting on a large canvas with indeed a broad brush. The Government derives it test from such propositions as the following: That payments by an employer to an employee, even though voluntary, ought, by and large, to be taxable; that the concept of a gift is inconsistent with a payment's being a deductible business expense; that a gift involves "personal" elements; that a business corporation cannot properly make a gift of its assets. The Government admits that there are exceptions and qualifications to these propositions. We think, to the extent they are correct, that these propositions are not principles of law but rather maxims of experience that the tribunals which have tried the facts of cases in this area have enunciated in explaining their factual determinations. Some of them simply represent truisms: it doubtless is, statistically speaking, the exceptional payment by an employer to an employee that amounts to a gift. Others are overstatements of possible evidentiary inferences relevant to a factual determination on the totality of circumstances in the case: it is doubtless relevant to the over-all inference that the transferor treats a

---

7. The cases including "tips" in gross income are classic examples of this. See, e.g., Roberts v. Commissioner, 9 Cir., 176 F.2d 221.

payment as a business deduction, or that the transferor is a corporate entity. But these inferences cannot be stated in absolute terms. Neither factor is a shibboleth. The taxing statute does not make nondeductibility by the transferor a condition on the "gift" exclusion; nor does it draw any distinction, in terms, between transfers by corporations and individuals, as to the availability of the "gift" exclusion to the transferee. The conclusion whether a transfer amounts to a "gift" is one that must be reached on consideration of all the factors.

Specifically, the trier of fact must be careful not to allow trial of the issue whether the receipt of a specific payment is a gift to turn into a trial of the tax liability, or of the propriety, as a matter of fiduciary or corporate law, attaching to the conduct of someone else. The major corollary to the Government's suggested "test" is that, as an ordinary matter, a payment by a corporation cannot be a gift, and, more specifically, there can be no such thing as a "gift" made by a corporation which would allow it to take a deduction for an ordinary and necessary business expense. As we have said, we find no basis for such a conclusion in the statute; and if it were applied as a determinative rule of "law," it would force the tribunals trying tax cases involving the donee's liability into elaborate inquiries into the local law of corporations or into the peripheral deductibility of payments as business expenses. The former issue might make the tax tribunals the most frequent investigators of an important and difficult issue of the laws of the several States, and the latter inquiry would summon one difficult and delicate problem of federal tax law as an aid to the solution of another. Or perhaps there would be required a trial of the vexed issue whether there was a "constructive" distribution of corporate property, for income tax purposes, to the corporate agents who had sponsored the transfer. These considerations, also, reinforce us in our conclusion that while the principles urged by the Government may, in nonabsolute form as crystallizations of experience, prove persuasive to the trier of facts in a particular case, neither they, nor any more detailed statement than has been made, can be laid down as a matter of law.

Third. Decision of the issue presented in these cases must be based ultimately on the application of the fact-finding tribunal's experience with the mainsprings of human conduct to the totality of the facts of each case. The nontechnical nature of the statutory standard, the close relationship of it to the date of practical human experience, and the multiplicity of relevant factual elements, with their various combinations, creating the necessity of ascribing the proper force to each, confirm us in our conclusion that primary weight in this area must be given to the conclusions of the trier of fact.

This conclusion may not satisfy an academic desire for tidiness, symmetry and precision in this area, any more than a system based on the determinations of various fact-finders ordinarily does. But we see it as implicit in the present statutory treatment of the exclusion for gifts, and in the variety of forums in which federal income tax cases can be tried. If there is fear of undue uncertainty or overmuch litigation, Congress may make more precise its treatment of the matter by singling out certain factors and making them determinative of the matters, as it has done in one field of the "gift" exclusion's former application, that of prizes and awards.[12] Doubtless diversity of result will tend to be lessened somewhat since federal income tax decisions, even those in tribunals of first instance turning on issues of fact, tend to be reported, and since there may be a natural tendency of professional triers of fact to follow one another's determinations, even as to factual matters. But the question here remains basically one of fact, for determination on a case-by-case basis.

One consequence of this is that appellate review of determinations in this field must be quite restricted. Where a jury has tried the matter upon correct instructions, the only inquiry is whether it cannot be said that reasonable men could reach differing conclusions on the issue. * * *

Fourth. A majority of the Court is in accord with the principles just outlined. And, applying them to the Duberstein case, we are in agreement, on the evidence we have set forth, that it cannot be said that the conclusion of the Tax Court was "clearly erroneous." It seems to us plain that as trier of the facts it was warranted in concluding that despite the characterization of the transfer of the Cadillac by the parties and the absence of any obligation, even of a moral nature, to make it, it was at bottom a recompense for Duberstein's past services, or an inducement for him to be of further service in the future. We cannot say with the Court of Appeals that such a conclusion was "mere suspicion" on the Tax Court's part. To us it appears based in the sort of informed experience with human affairs that fact-finding tribunals should bring to this task.

As to Stanton, we are in disagreement. To four of us, it is critical here that the District Court as trier of fact made only the simple and unelaborated finding that the transfer in question was a "gift."[14] To be sure, conciseness is to be strived for, and prolixity avoided, in findings; but, to the four of us, there comes a point where findings become so sparse and conclusory as to give no revelation of what the District Court's concept of the determining facts and legal standard may be. Such conclusory, general findings do not constitute compliance with Rule 52's direction to "find the facts specially and state separately * * * conclusions of law thereon." While the standard of law in this area is not a complex one, we four think the unelaborated finding of ultimate fact here cannot stand as a fulfillment of these requirements. It affords the reviewing court not the

---

12. § 74, which is a provision new with the 1954 Code. Previously, there had been holdings that such receipts as the "Pot O' Gold" radio giveaway and the Ross Essay Prize were "gifts." Congress intended to obviate such rulings. We imply no approval of those holdings under the general standard of the "gift" exclusion.

14. The "Findings of Fact and Conclusions of Law" were made orally, and were simply: "The resolution of the Board of Directors of the Trinity Operating Company, Incorporated, held November 19, 1942, after the resignations had been accepted of the plaintiff from his positions as controller of the corporation of the Trinity Church, and the president of the Trinity Operating Company, Incorporated, whereby a gratuity was voted to the plaintiff, Allen (sic) D. Stanton, in the amount of $20,000 payable to him in monthly installments of $2,000 each, commencing with the month of December, 1942, constituted a gift to the taxpayer, and therefore need not have been reported by him as income for the taxable years 1942, or 1943."

semblance of an indication of the legal standard with which the trier of fact has approached his task. For all that appears, the District Court may have viewed the form of the resolution or the simple absence of legal consideration as conclusive. While the judgment of the Court of Appeals cannot stand, the four of us think there must be further proceedings in the District Court looking toward new and adequate findings of fact. In this, we are joined by Mr. Justice Whittaker, who agrees that the findings were inadequate, although he does not concur generally in this opinion.

Accordingly, in No. 376, the judgment of this Court is that the judgment of the Court of Appeals is reversed, and in No. 546, that the judgment of the Court of Appeals is vacated, and the case is remanded to the District Court for further proceedings not inconsistent with this opinion. It is so ordered.

* * *

MR. JUSTICE FRANKFURTER, concurring in the judgment in No. 376 and dissenting in No. 546.

* * * Varying conceptions regarding the "mainsprings of human conduct" are derived from a variety of experiences or assumptions about the nature of man, and "experience with human affairs," is not only diverse but also often drastically conflicting. What the Court now does sets fact-finding bodies to sail on an illimitable ocean of individual beliefs and experiences. This can hardly fail to invite, if indeed not encourage, too individualized diversities in the administration of the income tax law. I am afraid that by these new phrasings the practicalities of tax administration, which should be as uniform as is possible in so vast a country as ours, will be embarrassed. By applying what has already been spelled out in the opinions of this Court, I agree with the Court in reversing the judgment in Commissioner v. Duberstein.

But I would affirm the decision of the Court of Appeals for the Second Circuit in Stanton v. United States. I would do so on the basis of the opinion of Judge Hand and more particularly because the very terms of the resolution by which the $20,000 was awarded to Stanton indicated that it was not a "gratuity" in the sense of sheer benevolence but in the nature of a generous lagniappe, something extra thrown in for services received though not legally nor morally required to be given. This careful resolution, doubtless drawn by a lawyer and adopted by some hardheaded businessmen, contained a proviso that Stanton should abandon all rights to "pension and retirement benefits." The fact that Stanton had no such claims does not lessen the significance of the clause as something "to make assurance doubly sure. The business nature of the payment is confirmed by the words of the resolution, explaining the 'gratuity' as 'in appreciation of the services rendered by Mr. Stanton as Manager of the Estate and Comptroller of the Corporation of Trinity Church throughout nearly ten years, and as President of Trinity Operating Company, Inc." The force of this document, in light of all the factors to which Judge Hand adverted in his opinion, was not in the least diminished by testimony at the trial. Thus the taxpayer has totally failed to sustain the burden I would place upon him to establish that the payment to him was wholly attributable to generosity unrelated to his performance of his secular business functions as an officer of the corporation of the Trinity Church of New York and the Trinity Operating Co. Since the record totally fails to establish taxpayer's claim, I see no need of specific findings by the trial judge.

PEEBLES v. COMMISSIONER

United States Tax Court, 2006.
T.C. Summ. Op. 2006–61.

COLVIN, JUDGE:

Background

Petitioners are married and lived in DeWitt, Arkansas, when they filed the petition. DeWitt, Arkansas, has a population of about 3,500.

In 1999, Milton D. Peebles (petitioner) was a police officer in DeWitt. Mrs. Peebles was a patient of Dr. John M. Hestir (Dr. Hestir), who had a medical practice in DeWitt. Petitioner discovered in October 1999 that Dr. Hestir and Mrs. Peebles were having an affair. Petitioner documented that fact by surreptitiously recording their phone calls. Petitioner confronted Mrs. Peebles with the evidence.

Petitioner then lured Dr. Hestir to petitioners' home on the pretext that Mrs. Peebles needed medical care. Petitioner is about 20 years younger than Dr. Hestir and is capable of being loud and garrulous when angry. One of petitioners' adult daughters was home at that time and acted appropriately to keep things under control by calling the county sheriff to their home. Petitioner was angry when Dr. Hestir arrived. At that time, petitioner confronted him with the evidence of the affair and threatened to sue him for $150,000. Dr. Hestir told petitioner that he did not have $150,000. Two days after the confrontation, petitioner made Mrs. Peebles call Dr. Hestir's wife to tell her about the affair. Petitioner then called Dr. Hestir to tell him that Dr. Hestir's wife knew about the affair. Dr. Hestir told petitioner that he did not have $150,000, but he did have $25,000. They agreed to meet 2 days later so that Dr. Hestir could pay that amount to petitioner.

Petitioner and Dr. Hestir met in the parking lot of DeWitt Bank & Trust, and Dr. Hestir gave petitioner $25,000 in cash. During the exchange, petitioner and Dr. Hestir had a conversation which petitioner taped. Dr. Hestir said he was sorry about the affair and stated that this was "free money", but that petitioner should be careful how he spent it because it could be considered income. Petitioner then said that if he and Mrs. Peebles were to divorce, he would not file on grounds of adultery or name Dr. Hestir in the proceedings. After further conversation, Dr. Hestir apologized again and said that he regretted the affair and hoped the money would help petitioner. Petitioner then stated: "Now Doc, this isn't blackmail money", to which Dr. Hestir replied: "No, I didn't say it was blackmail money; I said I hope it helps you, both of you."At the end of the meeting, petitioner warned Dr. Hestir that he should never again speak to or look at Mrs. Peebles or come to their home.

Petitioner and one of petitioners' daughters contacted the Arkansas State Medical Board (medical board) in November 1999 to report the affair between Dr. Hestir and Mrs. Peebles. In an undated letter, Dr. Hestir self-reported his misconduct to the medical board and expressed deep regret for his actions.

The medical board held a hearing on February 3, 2000. Petitioners testified at the hearing. When questioned why Dr. Hestir gave him $25,000, petitioner said: "I think it was to try to clear his conscience."

On February 8, 2000, Dr. Hestir's accountant prepared a Form 1099–MISC, Miscellaneous Income, reporting that he had paid $25,000 to petitioner. Petitioners did not report the $25,000 on their timely filed Federal income tax return for 1999.

Discussion

* * *

B.   *Whether the $25,000 Payment Was a Gift*

Petitioners contend that the $25,000 payment was a gift because it was Dr. Hestir's idea to pay it, and petitioner did not force him to pay it. Petitioner testified that he did not raise the issue of payment after the night he confronted Dr. Hestir. Petitioner threatened Dr. Hestir with a lawsuit in which he would claim $150,000 in damages. Petitioner stated that he called Dr. Hestir 2 days after the confrontation to tell him that Dr. Hestir's wife knew about the affair, and that Dr. Hestir raised the issue of money. Petitioners contend that, because Dr. Hestir raised the subject of the $25,000 payment, it was a gift. We disagree.

We believe that Dr. Hestir thought petitioner wanted a payment because of the affair. We also believe that Dr. Hestir offered the payment not because of detached generosity, but rather as a way to close the matter and avoid being sued by petitioner.

Petitioners contend that the $25,000 payment was a gift because Dr. Hestir said during the medical board hearing that it was a gift. We disagree. At that hearing, Dr. Hestir testified: (1) Petitioner took the money; and (2) petitioner said it was a gift and not blackmail, to which Dr. Hestir responded by saying: "Yes". We take this testimony only to mean that petitioner wanted it to be a gift.

Petitioners contend that Dr. Hestir paid the $25,000 out of a feeling of guilt or moral obligation. Petitioners point out that a newspaper article states that Dr. Hestir said he paid petitioner, ended the affair, and reported himself to the medical board because of his guilty conscience. A payment made because of the constraining force of moral or legal duty is not a gift.

Dr. Hestir's accountant filed the Form 1099–MISC a few days after the medical board hearing. Petitioners contend that Dr. Hestir did that to punish petitioner for reporting the matter to the medical board and to incorrectly make it appear that the $25,000 payment was not a gift. We disagree; the payment was not actually a gift.

* * *

There was trial testimony regarding the degree of physical intimidation (if any) petitioner brought to bear against Dr. Hestir when petitioner discovered the affair and received the payment of $25,000. We need not resolve those factual disputes to conclude that the payment was not a gift.

C. Conclusion

We conclude that the $25,000 payment by Dr. Hestir was not the result of detached and disinterested generosity or paid out of affection, respect, admiration, or charity. Instead it was paid to avoid a lawsuit, to avoid public and professional embarrassment, and to assuage his own feelings of guilt or moral obligation. Therefore, the $25,000 payment in 1999 is not a gift and is includable in petitioners' gross income for that year.

UNITED STATES v. CERULLO

United States District Court, S.D. Calif., 2007.
2007 WL 2683799.

Order Granting Motion to Reconsider and Granting Motion to Dismiss Indictment

* * *

Here the Defendant is a religious minister. He stands accused of failing to report to the Internal Revenue Service all of his income earned and received as a result of speaking at churches. The prosecutor takes the position that all the money received by Defendant after delivering a speech or sermon is "earned income" received in exchange for services rendered and should have been reported on his tax returns. The prosecutor's position admits no possibility that some or all of the money received by Defendant could be a gift and thus, not reportable as earned income. The Internal Revenue Code does not define a gift and offers little guidance for correctly characterizing such money received by a religious minister as either reportable earned income or excludable property acquired by gift.

However, the United States Supreme Court addressed the issue 47 years ago in *Commissioner of Internal Revenue v. Duberstein*, and that decision remains the definitive authority on how to untangle the income/gift dichotomy. *Duberstein* instructs that the "[d]ecision of the issue presented in these cases must be based ultimately on the application of the fact-finding tribunal's experience with the mainsprings of human conduct to the totality of the facts in each case." Significantly, *Duberstein* points out that the most important factor among the totality of the facts is the donor's intent. According to the Court, "what controls is the intention with which payment, however voluntary, has been made."

The prosecutor's conduct before the grand jury in Cerullo's case, when measured against this standard, fell to a level that misled the grand jury on this most critical issue. During the prosecutor's presentation, the grand jury asked at least three times about how to differentiate between earned income and gifts. Each time the prosecutor answered without mentioning the most critical factor: the donor's intent. And each time he told the grand jury to listen to the testimony of the Internal Revenue Service Agent. The revenue agent also answered the question.

During the testimony of one revenue agent, the grand jury asked, "So if I attend a sermon as a parishioner, they take up a collection which is handling the honorarium, I come up to the minister later and say, I really enjoyed your lecture, your sermon, I'd like to give you a gift, here is $500, is that considered a service, or is that considered a gift?" In answering the question the revenue agent compounded the prosecutor's error by answering the grand jury that, "I understand it's confusing, but we're not looking from the donor's standpoint; we're looking from the recipient's standpoint.". Earlier, the prosecutor asked the agent, "Does it matter that the [church offering] plate was passed, for instance?" The agent answered, "No." The prosecutor asked the agent, "Or how the money was collected that resulted in the fee being paid to the visiting minister?" The agent again answered, "No." The prosecutor continued, "As long as the evidence shows either directly or circumstantially, that the money going to the visiting minister, was [it] a fee for services?" The agent answered, "That's correct." In other words, the agent told the grand jury that donative intent was irrelevant. In contrast, the Supreme Court calls a donor' s intent *the most critical factor*. The grand jury was misled, as a result, and their ability to carry out their task impartially was destroyed.

For example, another exchange went as follows:

* * *

Grand Juror (GJ): You said we were going to get an explanation between honorarium and love gifts.

Prosecutor (P): Correct.

GJ: I'm confused if they're the same, and you're saying they're the same when it comes to income, basically?

P: I'd rather you not rely on what i have to say about it. I'd rather you rely on the revenue agent. . . . we're saying that it doesn't matter what you call it; it's what, in fact, they are. and the government's position is, these moneys were received by Morris Cerullo because he provided a service. He went to a location and spoke. He provided a service that money would not have been received if he had not done that. . . .

The grand jury kept pressing the prosecutor on how it was to evaluate the money Defendant received in terms of reportable earned income versus non-reportable gifts received. This exchange went as follows:

GJ: One other question. If a good minister solicits contributions, however, through the television or on the phone, and he receives those, as gifts from individuals or a couple of people or whatever, is that a love gift or is it—

P: Yeah, I'm going to let the revenue agent deal with that one. But I'll quickly point out, that's not what we're dealing with here. We're talking about money received for a fee for services performed.

This Court is leery of imposing upon the Government a duty to accurately instruct the grand jury on every relevant legal issue in presenting a case for indictment. Such an across-the-board rule would be as unworkable as it is unsupportable by legal precedent. Nevertheless, in this case there is one crucial over-arching legal question, the answer to which came from the Supreme Court almost half a century ago—the legal tax question of how to distinguish between reportable income and a non-reportable gift. Unfortunately, the prosecutor did not attempt to inform the grand jury of the Supreme Court's decision. Whether a prosecutor would have such a duty absent a question from the grand jury, this Court need not decide. Here, the prosecutor's duty to instruct correctly is plainly apparent. The tax statute is silent. The grand jury asked repeatedly how to distinguish a gift from earnings. It was incumbent on the prosecutor to correctly inform the grand jury as to the Supreme Court's approach on this penultimate question. Yet, the prosecutor and the revenue agent witnesses failed to tell the grand jury that the donor's intent is the most critical factor. Their failure misled the grand jury and amounts to misconduct.

The misconduct prejudiced the Defendant in this case. The money received by a clergyman from a church at which he delivers a sermon, could be adjudged to be either earned income or a gift. The judgment of the grand jury would mean the Defendant would, or would not, face a criminal trial because of his own judgment that the money he received was a gift. A grand jury might properly find probable cause to believe this Defendant committed the tax crime and issue an indictment. But it cannot properly make that judgment when instructed by the prosecutor that the donor's intent does not matter.

* * *

Therefore, the indictment against Defendant Morris Cerullo is hereby dismissed.

IT IS SO ORDERED.

2. EMPLOYEE GIFTS

Some of the most difficult applications of the *Duberstein* "definition" of "gift" arose in the context of transfers from employers to employees.

The line between "compensation for services rendered" and "gift" was increasingly hard to draw. In 1986, Congress cut the Gordian knot. Pursuant to § 102(c)(1), enacted in that year, "any amount transferred by or for an employer to, or for the benefit of, an employee" is carved out of the category of excludable gifts.

Note, however, the cross references listed in § 102(c)(2). Certain employee achievement awards [§ 74(c)] and certain de minimis fringe benefits [§ 132(e)] are treated differently.

Note also Proposed Regulation § 1.102–1(f)(2), which narrows, and somewhat muddies, the application of § 102(c).

QUESTIONS AND PROBLEMS

1. Jolly old Uncle approaches Nephew, at the reception following Nephew's graduation from medical school. "Hey Doc," says Uncle, "I have a bad cold. What should I do about it?"

"Get some rest, and drink plenty of liquids," answers Nephew. "Especially chicken soup. That will be fifty dollars."

Uncle smiles and hands over a crisp fifty dollar bill. "I'm your first patient," he says. "Congratulations."

How should the fifty dollars be treated?

2. Father tells Son, "If you can quit smoking for five years straight, I'll give you $5,000. Son quits smoking for five years, and Father duly pays. Does Son have taxable income?"

3. A member of a congregation gives $50 to her minister. What result? What if the entire congregation routinely contributed to aggregate, annual, "special occasion" payments to the minister, ranging from $5,000 to $43,000? *See* Goodwin v. United States, 67 F.3d 149 (8th Cir.1995).

4. In the fall of 2004, all 276 members of Oprah Winfey's television audience received a free Pontiac. The cars, donated to the show by Pontiac, were worth over $25,000 apiece. Taxable event?

5. During the month of February of 2005, Regis & Kelly gave away one Pontiac Montana SV6 on each of their daily TV shows. Each recipient was given the car, plus a cash award of $18,500 (to cover the income tax?) plus another cash award of up to $2,475 to cover any federal or state sales or excise taxes. What result?

6. Aunt Tilly Died. Pursuant to her will, $25,000 was left to her favorite nephew, George. How should the $25,000 be treated?

7. For the last three years of Aunt Tilly's life, a practical nurse, Wanda Smith, lived in Aunt Tilly's home, and cared for her. Pursuant to their agreement, Wanda received free room and board during these three years. In addition, Aunt Tilly promised to will $10,000 to Wanda for each year that Wanda performed services as a caretaker. Accordingly, Aunt Tilly's will left $30,000 to Wanda Smith. How should this $30,000 be treated?

8. Employer was particularly pleased with the work of Employee. Accordingly, at the end of the year, Employer gave Employee an extra $500 in addition to normal salary.

a) How should this $500 be treated?

b) Does it matter how Employer felt about it?

c) What if Employee were Employer's son?

9. Harry Winston, a famous jeweler, loaned a diamond tiara worth about two million dollars to Marla Maples, to wear on the occasion of her wedding to Donald Trump in December, 1993. Neither Ms. Maples nor Mr. Trump paid anything to Harry Winston for the use of the jewelry. However, Winston and Trump shared the security costs.

The Harry Winston firm often lends jewelry to celebrities for high profile occasions, such as the Tony Awards and the Academy Awards. There is never a charge. These events usually receive significant media coverage, with the celebrities' clothing and jewelry prominently displayed. On the other hand, Ronald Winston, son of the founder of the jewelry business, has been a friend of Donald Trump for a long time.

Assume that the fair rental value of the jewelry for the wedding would have been $1,000. How should these events have been treated by the tax laws?

See Lee A. Sheppard, *"Something Borrowed: The Tax Treatment of Marla's Tiara,"* 61 Tax Notes 1541 (Dec. 27, 1993).

What about the designer gowns "loaned" to Nancy Reagan while her husband was President?

10. In 1955, Shirley Campbell, a professional swimmer, attempted to swim across Lake Ontario. She was forced to abandon her swim with only one and one-half miles to go.

She tried again in 1956, under contract to the Toronto Daily Star. The Daily Star paid her $600 for making the attempt, and promised to pay an additional $5,000 if she succeeded. Again, she failed, this time a mere one-half mile from the finish line on the Toronto shoreline. The Daily Star paid her the $5,000 anyway.

The Canadian Tax Appeal Board ruled that the $5,000 was taxable income [Campbell v. Minister of National Revenue, 21 Tax A.B.C. 145 (1958)]. How would a United States court have ruled?

11. David Kritzik was a "wealthy widower partial to the company of young women." Over the course of several years, he paid two twin sisters, Leigh Ann Conley and Lynnette Harris, over half a million dollars, directly and indirectly. Kritzik paid federal gift taxes, but only on about half of these transfers. Consider the following additional points:[a]

• In an affidavit provided to IRS investigators before his death, Kritzik stated that he regarded both Conley and Harris as prostitutes.

• In the course of a banking transaction, Conley listed Kritzik as her "employer."

---

a. This is a tax course. Ask someone else whether these points were admissible evidence.

- In trial court testimony, Harris described her relationship with Kritzik as "a job" and "just making a living."

- Kritzik wrote a letter to an insurance company regarding the value of certain jewelry which he had "given to Ms. Lynette Harris as a gift."

- Kritzik wrote the following in letters to Ms. Harris:

  "So far as the things I give you are concerned—let me say that I get as great if not even greater pleasure in giving than you get in receiving."

  "I love giving things to you and to see you happy and enjoying them."

  "I . . . love you very much and will do all that I can to make you happy."

- Kritzik bought Harris a house, and offered to pay to remodel it. Harris overcharged him by more than $100,000 for the remodelling, and hid her excess payments in a paper corporation.

The twins were convicted of willfully evading the income tax. *See* United States v. Harris, 942 F.2d 1125 (7th Cir.1991). Which of the above points should have been relevant to the Court?

12. In an increasingly global village, the "mainsprings of human conduct" may be quite different, depending upon one's cultural perspective. How, for example, should IRS deal with older Asian–Americans who practiced guanxi? Pursuant to this time-honored tradition, items of substantial value were exchanged between business people at the beginning of a transaction. If asked, the participants might well have explained that the exchanges were not gifts, nor were they payments. They were simply the way things were done. Now what?

3. TIPPING

> . . . tips never feel like real money. Real money is 10 or 20 or 100 dollar bills, money that can be used for something important like food or rent or children's shoes. But all those single dollar bills and fistfuls of change that weigh down your purse hardly feel like real money. I have never had more pocket money than when I was a waitress. Somehow, tip money seems to disappear, and, amazingly, your purse is heavy again the next day.

> Reprinted with permission from WAITRESS: AMERICA'S UNSUNG HEROINE, by L. Elder and L. Rolens, p. 18. Copyright © 1965 by Capra Press, Santa Barbara, California.

Despite the feelings of some in the industry, tips are money. What's more, they are clearly taxable income. Whether they are given "to insure prompt service" or merely to avoid the embarrassment of being chased out of the restaurant by an angry, stiffed waiter, they clearly do not proceed out of detached and disinterested generosity. They are not gifts, and they do not fit into any other category of tax free income. Therefore, they are taxable income.

However, law and practice did not always conform. For many years, it was easy to under-report tip income. In fact, many restaurant employees felt that they had a right to under-report their tips, since they were underpaid anyway.

However, the IRS has found ways to fight back. When IRS agents audited the Seattle Space Needle restaurant, the credit card slips revealed the average percentage tip rate for all patrons who paid for their meals with plastic. The IRS assumed that those who paid cash tipped at a lower rate, because they were more likely to be using their own money, rather than using an expense account. Accordingly, IRS posited a cash tip rate a few percentage points below the plastic tip rate. They then applied their composite tip rate to the restaurant's gross sales to determine how much tip income should have been reported. When they discovered that the actual tip income reported by the restaurant staff was lower, they went after the staff, and won. Arthur J. McQuatters, ¶ 73,240 P–H Memo TC.

This scheme, of course, could only work when money was paid for restaurant services. In gambling casinos, gamblers are often given free drinks while they play. The drinks may be free, but the gamblers still commonly tip the cocktail waitresses. However, with no payment for the drinks, there was no paper trail to establish a tip rate. This time, IRS agents loitered in the gaming areas, and watched the tips change hands. Every 15 minutes or so, they retired to a phone booth to take notes on what they had seen. To keep things honest, they relied upon certain conventions. If paper money was transferred, but the denomination could not be seen, the tip was assumed to be one dollar. Similarly, if the tip was in the form of a gambling chip, then it was assumed to be the lowest value chip, unless the observer could see the chip more clearly. On this basis, IRS went after the cocktail waitresses at the Resorts International Hotel in Atlantic City, and won. Theresa Bruno, ¶ 85,168 P–H Memo TC.

Since these early forays, Congress has entered the fray. Now, pursuant to § 6053, the tip rate in a "large food or beverage establishment" is presumed to be 8 per cent. Employers in such establishments must compute 8% of their annual gross sales. If the aggregate tips reported by their employees are less than 8% of gross sales, then such employers must allocate the deficiencies among their employees as they see fit, and force them to report it as additional income. In response, some restaurants simply require their employees to report 8% in tips, whether they receive it or not. Others have simply abolished tipping, and replaced it with a mandatory service charge.

For the response of restaurant staff, consider the following comments received on the proposed regulations to § 6053:

- The IRS is always looking for ways to screw the poor people. Signed Pissed Off in Bird, Ore.

- In my opinion I don't think the Sen. or Rep. who voted on this could have SUNK ANY LOWER.

- If your act stays in effect good luck next time you dine. It will probably be cafeteria style. Who can afford to be a waitress? If it isn't a cafeteria there may be a very hot, steaming bowl of soup fall on your lap next time you do dine. That's the only kind of help that will be available.

- This is the South, people are very friendly, but they are very tight too. Sometimes I get more religious pamphlets than tips!

- If the President wouldn't have screwed the economy up so bad you wouldn't need to tax our tips. You didn't need them before. You shouldn't need them now. The whole thing sucks.

- Remember this the next time you vote to give yourself a raise or eat off of Nancy Reagan's new china ... I'll be thinking of you both next election day.

- Why don't you just take a gun and shoot us!

- I'm dehumanizing myself by working with the other hungry waitresses and hating people for their ignorance about my livelihood. The IRS loves to dehumanize—don't they?

- I have waited on one of the senators from Wyoming and didn't receive a dime let alone a percent ... I don't mind paying taxes on what I do make, but I'll be damned if I pay on something I didn't receive. It's funny all these years my word was good. Now all of a sudden it is not.

- Shame, shame, how do you sleep at night.

- I hope every one of you always gets terrible service, cold food, and may all your daughters grow up to be nothing but waitresses.

- Death to the IRS! Take your eight percent on tips and stick it up your ass.

See, Joel S. Newman, *Waiter, There's an IRS Agent In My Soup,* 40 Tax Notes 861 (Aug. 22, 1988).

4. LIFE INSURANCE. THE RELATIONSHIP OF SECTIONS 101 AND 102

Code: §§ 101(a), 102

If bequests are tax-free pursuant to § 102, it follows that life insurance proceeds should be tax-free as well. Life insurance is simply an alternative way of funding a bequest.

However, just as not all properties transferred through wills are tax-free bequests under § 102, not all life insurance proceeds are tax-free under § 101. Life insurance transactions which appear to have a commercial flavor, rather than a testamentary flavor, tend to be excepted from the exclusionary treatment. Read § 101(a), paying particular attention to the exception [§ 101(a)(2)], and the exceptions to the exception [§§ 101(a)(2)(A) and (B)], and do Problems 1 through 4.

PROBLEMS

1. John buys $100,000 of life insurance at age 25 for a single premium of $20,000. He dies at age 75. Proceeds are payable to his wife, Mary. How are those proceeds taxed?

2. Assume the same policy as in problem 1. At age 35, John, experiencing financial difficulties, sells the policy to Adam for $25,000. Adam immediately changes the beneficiary on the policy to himself. [Assume that Adam has an insurable interest in the life of John.] How is Adam taxed when he receives the $100,000 insurance proceeds upon John's death? How is John taxed on the sale of the policy at age 35?

3. Assume the same policy as in problem 1. John has AIDS. The new drugs are not working; he has less than one year to live. The insurance will pay out much sooner than one would have predicted, given the normal life expectancy of a 35–year–old. Accordingly, the policy is worth considerably more than its cash surrender value. In addition, John needs money now, to pay for his medical treatment.

    a. John cashes out his policy for much more than its normal cash surrender value, pursuant to an Accelerated Death Benefit clause in the policy. What result? See § 101(g) and Proposed Reg. § 1.101–8.

    b. John sells the policy for more than its cash surrender value, to a viatical settlement company, which specializes in buying policies from people like John. What result? See § 101(g)(2).

4. ABC Corporation is a closely held corporation. The shareholders are John, Adam, and Mary, all of whom are in their early thirties. Pursuant to a buy-sell agreement, the corporation is obligated to purchase the shares from any shareholder upon that shareholder's death. In order to fund this obligation, the corporation takes out a $100,000 policy on the life of each shareholder.

Now, John is 60. The corporation is unwilling to continue to make payments on John's policy; it prefers to purchase John's shares, when the time comes, by other means. John, however, realizes that the insurance policy, purchased when he was young and healthy, is much cheaper than any policy which he could obtain now. Therefore, he buys the policy from the corporation for $10,000. He names his wife as beneficiary. How will she be treated on the receipt of the $100,000 proceeds when John dies at age 75?

Now review § 102 and consider Problem 5.

5. Jane buys a $100,000 life insurance policy at age 25 for a single premium of $25,000. She dies at age 75, and the policy proceeds are paid to her son.

Mike puts $25,000 in a savings account at age 25. Over the course of the next 50 years, the money grows to $100,000. When Mike dies at age 75, the $100,000 is willed to his daughter.

Compare the tax treatment of Jane's investment and Mike's investment a) during their lifetimes; and b) at their deaths. Does this comparison tell you anything about the strength of the insurance lobby in America? Perhaps you'll want to reconsider this point after studying § 1014.

5. BASIS IN PROPERTY ACQUIRED BY GIFT OR BEQUEST

Code: § 1015, 101(a)(2)

Regulations: § 1.1001–1(e), 1.1015–1(a), 1.1015–4

TAFT v. BOWERS

United States Supreme Court, 1929.
278 U.S. 470, 49 S.Ct. 199, 73 L.Ed. 460.

MR. JUSTICE McREYNOLDS delivered the opinion of the Court.

* * * Abstractly stated, this is the problem:

In 1916 A purchased 100 shares of stock for $1,000, which he held until 1923 when their fair market value had become $2,000. He then gave them to B who sold them during the year 1923 for $5,000. The United States claim that under the Revenue Act of 1921, B must pay income tax upon $4,000, as realized profits. · B maintains that only $3,000—the appreciation during her ownership—can be regarded as income; that the increase during the donor's ownership is not income assessable against her within intendment of the Sixteenth Amendment.

The District Court ruled against the United States; the Circuit Court of Appeals held with them. * * *

We think the manifest purpose of Congress expressed in [current § 1015] was to require the petitioner to pay the enacted tax.

The only question subject to serious controversy is whether Congress had power to authorize the exaction.

It is said that the gift became a capital asset of the donee to the extent of its value when received and, therefore, when disposed of by her no part of that value could be treated as taxable income in her hands. * * *

If, instead of giving the stock to petitioner, the donor had sold it at market value, the excess over the capital he invested (cost) would have been income there from and subject to taxation under the Sixteenth Amendment. He would have been obliged to share the realized gain with the United States. He held the stock—the investment—subject to the right of the sovereign to take part of any increase in its value when separated through sale or conversion and reduced to his possession. Could he, contrary to the express will of Congress, by mere gift enable another to hold this stock free from such right, deprive the sovereign of the possibility of taxing the appreciation when actually severed, and convert the entire property into a capital asset of the donee, who invested nothing, as though the latter had purchased at the market price? And after a still further enhancement of the property, could the donee make a second gift with like effect, etc.? We think not.

In truth the stock represented only a single investment of capital— that made by the donor. And when through sale or conversion the increase was separated therefrom, it became income from that investment in the hands of the recipient subject to taxation according to the very words of the Sixteenth Amendment. By requiring the recipient of the entire increase to pay a part into the public treasury, Congress deprived her of no right and subjected her to no hardship. She accepted the gift with knowledge of the statute and, as to the property received, voluntarily assumed the position of her donor. When she sold the stock she actually got the original sum invested, plus the entire appreciation and out of the latter only was she called on to pay the tax demanded.

The provision of the statute under consideration seems entirely appropriate for enforcing a general scheme of lawful taxation. To accept the view urged in behalf of petitioner undoubtedly would defeat, to some extent, the purpose of Congress to take part of all gain derived from capital investments. To prevent that result and insure enforcement of its proper policy, Congress had power to require that for purposes of taxation the donee should accept the position of the donor in respect of the thing received. And in so doing, it acted neither unreasonably nor arbitrarily. * * *

There is nothing in the Constitution which lends support to the theory that gain actually resulting from the increased value of capital can be treated as taxable income in the hands of the recipient only so far as the increase occurred while he owned the property. And Irwin v. Gavit, 268 U.S. 161 (1925) is to the contrary.

The judgment below is affirmed.

The CHIEF JUSTICE took no part in the consideration or decision of these causes.

QUESTION

Shouldn't the property owner pay tax on only that appreciation which occurs during her ownership? Doesn't *Taft v. Bowers* defy this principle? How could the law be changed to correct this result, and what other problems might arise?

NOTE

Taft v. Bowers confirms that a donee will pay tax on the appreciation which occurs during her ownership of the gifted property, **and** on the appreciation which occurred during the donor's ownership. This result is obtained by the general rule of § 1015(a), which provides that the donor's basis will be carried over to the donee.

To use the numbers from *Taft v. Bowers*:

Donor's basis: $1,000
FMV on date of gift: $2,000
Donee's amount realized: $5,000

Donee's gain on sale is computed as follows:

Amount Realized	$5,000
Less [Donee's Basis	− $1,000 [§ 1015(a)]
Gain	$4,000

But what if the numbers had been reversed:

Donor's basis: $5,000
FMV on date of gift: $2,000
Donee's amount realized: $1,000

If Congress had again allowed Donor's basis to be carried over to Donee, then Donee would have realized a $4,000 loss, which may have been deductible. [Or not! *See* Chapter 4.] Congress was not willing to allow donee such a large, potential loss deduction. Therefore, § 1015(a) contains an exception. Pursuant to the exception, donee's realized loss is computed as follows:

Amount Realized	$1,000
Less Donee's Basis	− $2,000
Realized Loss [potentially deductible]	($1,000)

Read the first sentence of § 1015(a) carefully. Note the general rule: "... the basis shall be the same as it would be in the hands of the donor ..." In addition, note the two conditions for the exception:

(1) "... except that if such basis ... is greater than the fair market value of the property at the time of the gift ..." and

(2) "... for the purpose of determining loss ..."

In applying the statute to the problems below, you may find that Congress's inconsistent treatment of gains and losses will lead to some surprising results.

PROBLEMS

In all of the problems below, ignore the increase in basis for gift tax paid [§ 1015(d)].

1. Mary bought stock for $100,000. Five years later, when its value was $150,000, she gave it to John. How much gain or loss, if any, will John realize if he sells it for:

a) $175,000

b) $75,000

c) $125,000

2. Ethel bought stock for $150,000. Five years later, when its value was $120,000, she gave it to Fred. How much gain or loss, if any, will Fred realize if he sells it for:

  a) $175,000

  b) $75,000

  c) $125,000

3. Father bought stock for $25,000. When its value was $100,000, he transferred it to Son in exchange for a payment of $25,000, in a part-gift, part-sale transfer. Son resold the stock the next day for $100,000. How is Father taxed on his transfer to Son? How is Son taxed on his sale? Consult Reg. §§ 1.1001–1(e) and 1.1015–4.

4. Father bought GreenAcre for $1,000. It declined in value to $800.

  a) He sold it to Friend for $800. How is Father treated, and what is Friend's basis?

  b) He transferred it to Friend for $775, in a part-gift, part-sale transfer. Friend then sells for $800. What result?

5. Brother obtained a policy of insurance on his own life for a single premium payment of $50,000. The face amount of the policy is $200,000.

  a) Brother since transferred the policy to Sibling in exchange for a payment of $45,000 in a part gift-part sale transfer. Sibling named himself beneficiary. Brother dies. How is Sibling taxed?

  b) What if Sibling had paid $55,000?

FARID–ES–SULTANEH v. COMMISSIONER

United States Court of Appeals, Second Circuit, 1947.
160 F.2d 812.

Before SWAN, CHASE, and CLARK, CIRCUIT JUDGES.

CHASE, CIRCUIT JUDGE.

The problem presented by this petition is to fix the cost basis to be used by the petitioner in determining the taxable gain on a sale she made in 1938 of shares of corporate stock. She contends that it is the adjusted value of the shares at the date she acquired them because her acquisition was by purchase. The Commissioner's position is that she must use the adjusted cost basis of her transferor because her acquisition was by gift. The Tax Court agreed with the Commissioner and redetermined the deficiency accordingly.

* * * [In 1938, petitioner reported sales] of 12,000 shares of the common stock of the S. S. Kresge Company at varying prices per share, for the total sum of $230,802.36 which admittedly was in excess of their cost to her. How much this excess amounted to for tax purposes depends upon the legal significance of the facts now to be stated.

In December 1923 when the petitioner, then unmarried, and S. S. Kresge, then married, were contemplating their future marriage, he delivered to her 700 shares of the common stock of the S. S. Kresge Company which then had a fair market value of $290 per share. The shares were all in street form and were to be held by the petitioner "for her benefit and protection in the event that the said Kresge should die prior to the contemplated marriage between the petitioner and said Kresge." The latter was divorced from his wife on January 9, 1924, and on or about January 23, 1924 he delivered to the petitioner 1800 additional common shares of S. S. Kresge Company which were also in street form and were to be held by the petitioner for the same purposes as were the first 700 shares he had delivered to her. On April 24, 1924, and when the petitioner still retained the possession of the stock so delivered to her, she and Mr. Kresge executed a written ante-nuptial agreement wherein she acknowledged the receipt of the shares "as a gift made by the said Sebastian S. Kresge, pursuant to this indenture, and as an ante-nuptial settlement, and in consideration of said gift and said ante-nuptial settlement, in consideration of the promise of said Sebastian S. Kresge to marry her, and in further consideration of the consummation of said promised marriage" she released all dower and other marital rights, including the right to her support to which she otherwise would have been entitled as a matter of law when she became his wife. They were married in New York immediately after the ante-nuptial agreement was executed and continued to be husband and wife until the petitioner obtained a final decree of absolute divorce from him on, or about, May 18, 1928. No alimony was claimed by, or awarded to, her.

The stock so obtained by the petitioner from Mr. Kresge had a fair market value of $315 per share on April 24, 1924, and of $330 per share on, or about May 6, 1924, when it was transferred to her on the books of the corporation. She held all of it for about three years, but how much she continued to hold thereafter is not disclosed except as that may be shown by her sales in 1938. * * * Her adjusted basis for the stock she sold in 1938 was $10.66 2/3 per share computed on the basis of the fair market value of the shares which she obtained from Mr. Kresge at the time of her acquisition. His adjusted basis for the shares she sold in 1938 would have been $0.159091.

When the petitioner and Mr. Kresge were married he was 57 years old with a life expectancy of 16 1/2 years. She was then 32 years of age with a life expectancy of 33 3/4 years. He was then worth approximately $375,000,000 and owned real estate of the approximate value of $100,000,000.

The Commissioner determined the deficiency on the ground that the petitioner's stock obtained as above stated was acquired by gift within the meaning of that word as used in [the predecessor of section 1015(a)], and, as the transfer to her was after December 31, 1920, used as the basis for determining the gain on her sale of it the basis it would have had in the hands of the donor. This was correct if the just mentioned statute is applicable, and the Tax Court held it was on the authority of Wemyss v. Commissioner, and Merrill v. Fahs.

The issue here presented cannot, however, be adequately dealt with quite so summarily. The Wemyss case determined the taxability to the transferor as a gift, under [the predecessors of the federal estate and gift taxes] * * *

In our opinion the income tax provisions are not to be construed as though they were in pari materia with either the estate tax law or the gift tax statutes. * * * Because of this we think that a transfer which should be classed as a gift under the gift tax law is not necessarily to be treated as a gift income-tax-wise. Though such a consideration as this petitioner gave for the shares of stock she acquired from Mr. Kresge might not have relieved him from liability for a gift tax, had the present gift tax then been in effect, it was nevertheless a fair consideration which prevented her taking the shares as a gift under the income tax law since it precluded the existence of a donative intent.

Although the transfers of the stock made both in December 1923, and in the following January by Mr. Kresge to this taxpayer are called a gift in the ante-nuptial agreement later executed and were to be for the protection of his prospective bride if he died before the marriage was consummated, the "gift" was contingent upon his death before such marriage, an event that did not occur. Consequently, it would appear that no absolute gift was made before the ante-nuptial contract was executed and that she took title to the stock under its terms, viz: in consideration for her promise to marry him coupled with her promise to relinquish all rights in and to his property which she would otherwise acquire by the marriage. Her inchoate interest in the property of her affianced husband greatly exceeded the value of the stock transferred to her. It was a fair consideration under ordinary legal concepts of that term for the transfers of the stock by him. She performed the contract under the terms of which the stock was transferred to her and held the shares not as a donee but as a purchaser for a fair consideration.

Decision reversed.

CLARK, CIRCUIT JUDGE (dissenting).

The opinion accepts two assumptions, both necessary to the result. The first is that definitions of gift under the gift and estate tax statutes are not useful, in fact are directly opposed to, definitions of gift under the capital-gains provision of the income tax statute. The second is that the circumstances here of a transfer of the stock some months before the marriage showed, contrary to the conclusions of the Tax Court, a purchase of dower rights, rather than a gift. The first I regard as doubtful; the second, as untenable. * * *

Kresge transferred the stock to petitioner more than three months before their marriage. Part was given when Kresge was married to another woman. At these times petitioner had no dower or other rights in his property. If Kresge died before the wedding, she could never secure dower rights in his lands. Yet she would nevertheless keep the stock. Indeed the specifically stated purpose of the transfer was to protect her against his death prior to marriage. It is therefore difficult to perceive how her not yet acquired rights could be consideration for the stock. Apparently the parties themselves shared this difficulty, for in their subsequent instrument releasing dower rights they referred to the stock transfer as a gift and an antenuptial settlement.

If the transfer be thus considered a sale, as the majority hold, it would seem to follow necessarily that this valuable consideration (equivalent to one-third for life in land valued at one hundred million dollars) should have yielded sizable taxable capital gains to Kresge, as well as a capital loss to petitioner when eventually she sold. I suggest these considerations as pointing to the unreality of holding as a sale what seems clearly only intended as a stimulating cause to eventual matrimony.

Since Judge Murdock in the Tax Court found this to be a gift, not a sale, and since this decision is based in part at least upon factual considerations, it would seem binding upon us. At any rate, it should be persuasive of the result we ought to reach.

QUESTIONS

1. How would the case have come out if Mr. Kresge had died before he married Farid–es–Sultaneh?

2. Consider § 1041. Would that statute have changed the result in the case? What if the stock had been transferred after the wedding?

Tax Advice on Prenuptial Agreements

Assume that Mr. Kresge and Farid–es–Sultaneh came to your office today. They want advice on their pre-nuptial agreement. Mr. Kresge proposes to transfer a substantial amount of low basis, high value stock to his bride-to-be. What tax advice do you give? [Be sure to consider the impact of § 1041, which was not in effect in 1923.] Can you ethically advise both of them?

OBITUARY OF FARID-ES-SULTANEH

Princess Farid-es-Sultaneh, 74, Ex–Wife of S. S. Kresge, Dead.

MORRISTOWN, N.J. August 12—Princess Farid–es–Sultaneh, the thrice-divorced police captain's daughter whose last marriage was to a nephew of a former Shah of Iran, died today of leukemia in Morristown Memorial Hospital. She was 74 years old.

The princess, who actually lost that title when her three-year marriage to Prince Farid of Sadri–Azam ended in 1936, was the former Doris Mercer of Pittsburgh. While still a school girl there, she was married to a magazine publisher, Percival Harden. But there was a divorce in 1919 and Doris took a train to New York in search of an operatic singing career— which she never found—and wealth—which she gained in two subsequent marriages.

After four years of fruitless voice instruction, Doris met Sebastian S. Kresge, the millionaire founder of the five-and-dime chain stores. Their marriage ended in 1928 after a number of sensational court fights. Miss Mercer reportedly received a $3,000,000 settlement.

With that money, she sailed in luxury to Europe. An extremely attractive woman who just missed beauty, Doris resolutely returned to her singing lessons and met the prince. Soon after, in a Paris mosque, Doris became a princess.

After their divorce, the prince ran an ad in a Paris newspaper. It declared Doris could no longer call herself a "princess." But the telephone company never read the ad and Doris is listed here as one.

Doris never married again. Instead she lived a somewhat precarious life in a mansion on an 18–acre estate near the National Historical Park here. But she sold the estate in 1943 and began disposing of roomfuls of expensive belongings.

A year earlier, the former princess had been in the news when nearly $100,000 worth of her jewels were stolen from a shipment aboard a New York-to-Los Angeles airliner. With the arrest of two men, about a year later, $50,000 of the loot was recovered from a Texas junkyard.

A few years later, Constantine V. Riccardi, the "Master Swindler," was sentenced in 1948 to 10 years in prison after a Federal jury in Newark convicted him of bilking Doris of $16,000 in household belongings.

Ten years later, Doris was sued for $13,000 in bad debts, which she paid later with receipts from art and rare furniture she sold.

She has no known survivors.

Copyright ©1963 by the New York Times Co. Reprinted by permission.

6. BASIS IN PROPERTY ACQUIRED FROM DECEDENTS

Code: § 1014

NOTE

There is no earthly reason why property received gratuitously from dead people (§ 1014) should be treated differently from property received gratuitously from live people (§ 1015). However, for most of our history, it has been. Pursuant to § 1014, the basis of property acquired from decedents is the fair market value of the property on the date of decedent's death.[b] The § 1014 basis is commonly known as "stepped-up basis." This formulation derives from the fact that prices in the United States have generally been going up since 1913. However, it is certainly possible that, in a given case, basis will be "stepped-down".

---

b. In fact, the basis is often computed as the value for federal estate tax purposes pursuant to §§ 1014(a)(1) and (2).

§ 1014

Pursuant to § 1014, the basis in property acquired from a decedent will be the fair market value of the property on the date of decedent's death. Note that, in contrast to the transferred basis provision of § 1015, § 1014 applies in the same way whether the property has gone up in value or down; whether one is determining a loss or a gain.

The stepped-up basis rule of current § 1014 is yet another tax advantage given to property owners—given to homeowners over apartment renters. You have already learned that property owners don't pay tax on any appreciation until they choose to realize it. Now you know that, if they can just hold on to the property until they die, then nobody will ever pay tax on the appreciation which took place during their lifetimes.

PROBLEMS IN APPLYING § 1014

1. Reconsider problems 1 and 2, set forth after *Taft v. Bowers*. Do them again, assuming that the transfer was a bequest from decedent, rather than a gift.

2. Son had stock with a basis of $1 and a fair market value of $1,000. He transferred it to Father as a gift. Nine months later, Father died, leaving the stock to Son in his will. What is Son's basis in the stock now? See § 1014(e).

3. Sarah buys Blackacre for $25,000 when she is 25 years old. She dies at age 75. Blackacre, now worth $100,000, goes to her son by bequest. Her son sells Blackacre for $100,000. How is Sarah treated on the appreciation of Blackacre? What happens to her son when he sells it?

Reconsider problem 5 at p. 94. Compare Sarah and her son to Jane and Mike. Now do you feel better about Jane or Mike, or worse?

QUESTION

The Basic World Tax Code (drafted for use in developing countries) proposes that all property owned by decedents would be deemed sold for fair market value by the decedent on the date of death. Any deemed gain or loss would be taxed, or possibly deducted, as the case may be. The beneficiaries would then receive the same stepped-up basis that they do under our current § 1014. Certain assets, such as personal homes, would be exempted from this proposed rule. How does this proposal compare in equity terms to both current § 1014 and the new § 1022?

B. FRINGE BENEFITS

1. GENERAL

An associate in a New York law firm spends four days in Wichita, Kansas on a "corporate check"—reading over the corporate minutes of a large client to ensure that the client has complied with all of the formal requirements of state and federal law. The law firm picks up the associate's airfare, meals and lodging expenses—around $1,500. Should the associate be taxed on the $1,500?

On the first day of her vacation, a flight attendant goes to the airport to see if she can hop a free flight to San Juan. The first two flights on her airline are fully booked. However, there are some empty seats on the third, so she gets her free flight. Should the flight attendant be taxed on the value of the flight?

These are two examples of employee fringe benefits. Employee fringe benefits have always been a predominantly tax-free category of economic income. They are tax-free because:

a) They always have been. Try taxing something that has been tax-free for generations. Then, see if you get re-elected.

b) In many cases, it would be ridiculous to tax them. Should a factory worker be charged on his pro-rata share of the fair rental value of the factory?

c) They would be enormously hard to value. To get a feel for the administrative and valuation problems which might arise if all fringe benefits were taxed, consider *Turner*.

TURNER v. COMMISSIONER

United States Tax Court, 1954.
T.C. Memo. 1954–38.

Memorandum Findings of Fact and Opinion.

The Commissioner determined a deficiency of $388.96 in the income tax of the petitioners for 1948. The only question for decision is the amount which should be included in income because of the winning by Reginald of steamship tickets by answering a question on a radio program.

Findings of Fact

The petitioners are husband and wife who filed a joint return for 1948 with the collector of internal revenue for the District of North Carolina. They reported salary of $4,536.16 for 1948.

Reginald, whose name had been selected by chance from a telephone book, was called on the telephone on April 18, 1948 and was asked to name a song that was being played on a radio program. He gave the correct name of the song and then was given the opportunity to identify a second song and thus to compete for a grand prize. He correctly identified the second song and in consideration of his efforts was awarded a number of prizes, including two round trip first-class steamship tickets for a cruise between New York City and Buenos Aires. The prize was to be one ticket if the winner was unmarried, but, if he was married, his wife was to receive a ticket also. The tickets were not transferable and were good only within one year on a sailing date approved by the agent of the steamship company.

The petitioners reported income on their return of $520, representing income from the award of the two tickets. The Commissioner, in determining the deficiency, increased the income from this source to $2,220, the retail price of such tickets.

Marie was born in Brazil. The petitioners had two sons. Reginald negotiated with the agent of the steamship company, as a result of which he surrendered his rights to the two first-class tickets, and upon payment of $12.50 received four round trip tourist steamship tickets between New York City and Rio de Janeiro. The petitioners and their two sons used those tickets in making a trip from New York City to Rio de Janeiro and return during 1948.

The award of the tickets to Reginald represented income to him in the amount of $1,400.

Opinion.

MURDOCK, JUDGE:

Persons desiring to buy round trip first-class tickets between New York and Buenos Aires in April 1948, similar to those to which the petitioners were entitled, would have had to pay $2,220 for them. The petitioners, however, were not such persons. The winning of the tickets did not provide them with something which they needed in the ordinary course of their lives and for which they would have made an expenditure in any event, but merely gave them an opportunity to enjoy a luxury otherwise beyond their means. Their value to the petitioners was not equal to their retail cost. They were not transferable and not salable and there were other restrictions on their use. But even had the petitioner been permitted to sell them, his experience with other more salable articles indicates that he would have had to accept substantially less than the cost of similar tickets purchased from the steamship company and would have had selling expenses. Probably the petitioners could have refused the tickets and avoided the tax problem. Nevertheless, in order to obtain such benefits as they could from winning the tickets, they actually took a cruise accompanied by their two sons, thus obtaining free board, some savings in living expenses, and the pleasure of the trip. It seems proper that a substantial amount should be included in their income for 1948 on account of the winning of the tickets. The problem of arriving at a proper fair figure for this purpose is difficult. The evidence to assist is meager, perhaps unavoidably so. The Court, under such circumstances, must arrive at some figure and has done so.

A Limerick

Said Turner when called by the quiz show,

"I'd much rather travel to Rio.

I know that my prize is

to see Buenos Aires,

though neither trip's worth much to me-o."

QUESTION

It would appear that *Turner*, which taxes the recipient on his subjective valuation of the asset received, would make administration of the tax laws impossible. How can IRS possibly argue with a taxpayer about her subjective valuation of an asset? How come *Turner* hasn't destroyed the entire tax system?

If IRS is to survive to fight another day, *Turner* must be read narrowly. What sorts of transactions might still be covered by *Turner*, thus interpreted? Might some of these transactions be fringe benefits?

Set forth below is a pretty famous (notorious?) fringe benefit. On what grounds were the various items included and excluded from gross income? How did the Joint Committee Staff justify its recommendation to tax the taxpayer on the basis of first-class airfare, rather than on the basis of the chartered executive jets which were actually used? Do you agree?

Joint Committee on Taxation

Examination of President Nixon's Tax Returns for 1969 Through 1972

Part 6.   Personal Use of Government Aircraft
By the President's Family and Friends

1.   Scope of Examination

Since the President took office in 1969, members of his family and their friends, unaccompanied by him in many instances, have travelled extensively in the United States on Government aircraft. It appears that some of these flights were in connection with the performance of official duties, such as standing in for the President in his absence. This seems to be particularly true for many of the trips by Mrs. Nixon.

A question has been raised whether, for flights which were not primarily official business and, therefore, personal, the cost of such unreimbursed Government-furnished transportation should be considered additional income to the President.

Flights that appear to be personal are particularly those taken by Julie and Tricia to join either David Eisenhower or Edward Cox while the latter were either students or stationed in various cities other than Washington, D.C. On several occasions both Edward Cox and David

Eisenhower joined Julie and Tricia on flights to and from these same cities and to and from the President's homes in either Key Biscayne, Florida, or San Clemente, California. Occasionally, members of the President's family took along friends or guest on these flights.

Effective April 1, 1971, the President adopted a policy of reimbursing the Treasury for flights of his daughters and their husbands (or husband to be in the case of Edward Cox) when such travel was in "other than an official capacity." In doing so, the President apparently decided that there was in fact personal travel by members of his family on Government-furnished aircraft and that it was possible to make a determination as to what was personal and what was official. However, this policy was not in operation for the entire period during which members of the President's family and their friends availed themselves of Government air transportation. In addition, it does not appear that reimbursements were made for all "personal" flights after April 1, 1971. * * *

2. Analysis of Tax Treatment

Economic Benefit to the President

This aspect of the examination involves two basic questions. The first is whether the free use of Government transportation by the President's family and friends created income subject to Federal tax. If the answer to the first question is in the affirmative, it is necessary to determine to whom the income should properly be taxed. * * *

The issues presented here are to an extent unique, since there is no public record of prior determinations of tax consequences in a situation of this type. It is possible however to approach these questions in light of the employment relationship which exists between the U.S. Government and the President and to examine the authorities in the general area of benefits flowing between the employer and employee. The staff also considers the many decisions involving the corporation-shareholder relationship to have an application to this area of the examination.

* * *

It is apparent that Mrs. Nixon, the President's daughters, and the friends of the Nixon family have enjoyed the personal use of the Presidential aircraft only because of the employment relationship between the President and the United States. It is, therefore, the belief of the staff that the President has realized taxable income where members of his family or his friends had free use of Government transportation for personal excursions or where it has not been established that they were on Government business. The staff also considers this to be equally applicable where the President's family and/or friends accompanied him on trips which for him were in performance of the official duties of the President, but for which there is no evidence that the family and/or friends performed any official functions. * * *

Staff Conclusion

The staff believes that the personal use of Government airplanes by the President's family and friends should be classified as income to him for income tax purposes. * * *

One question involves the issue of whether there should be an inclusion in income of any amount with respect to the President's own use of Government aircraft. Some of his use could be classified as primarily personal since the flights take him to locations where he spends a significant part of his time on vacation. However, it is also pointed out that the President, by the nature of the office must hold himself available for work at virtually any time. In part because of this characteristic of the Presidency and in part because of the uncertain status of such items in the past, the staff is not recommending that any amounts be included in income with respect to personal transportation of the President. In making this recommendation, the staff is not suggesting that this be foreclosed as a possible issue in the future.

The staff believes, however, that the president does receive economic benefit and that an amount should be included in his income subject to tax with respect to the personal use of Government planes by his family and personal friends. * * *

* * * [I]n the case of corporate executives where a flight is considered personal the usual procedure is to charge for the cost of the flight. * * * [C]urrent charter flight rates for Jet Star executive jet aircraft are generally in the range of about $1.70 per mile or $1,000 per flight hour, or, alternatively, if based only upon the expenses involved in operating such a jet aircraft, about $1.50 per mile or $900 per flight hour. The staff, however, agrees with views which have been expressed that because of the need to safeguard the President, commercial flights for the President (and perhaps for members of his family) are an inappropriate mode of travel. Because of this the staff believes, even though the usual procedure with respect to corporate executives is to determine the value of the economic benefit on the basis of the cost of operating the aircraft, that it would be more appropriate in this case to base the value upon the charge for first class commercial fare. This is a cost of approximately 11 to 17 cents per mile.

Another issue involved is whether the income imputed to the President should include only those cases where the President was not along on the trip. It has been argued that if a trip is required by the fact that it is necessary for the President to travel, then there should be no charge for members of his family and personal friends accompanying him on the plane since they would not be on the flight but for the travel required for the President. This type of analysis has been used on occasion in determining whether income is realized in the case of airplane travel by corporate executives on business when their friends or family members accompany them. Presumably, it is on this basis that the President has refused to supply information as to the flights where the President was a passenger. However, the staff believes this type of analysis is not appropriate when all that is being treated as income is the cost of the first class fare of the individuals involved. In addition, generally where a family member accompanies an employee on a business trip, the presence of the family member must be shown to serve a business purpose for his or her expenses to be deductible. * * *

NOTES

1. *See*, § 274(m)(3), which was enacted long after the Joint Committee's Examination.

2. *See* Noyce v. Commissioner, 97 T.C. 670 (1991). Noyce, a co-founder of Intel, was allowed to deduct almost $140,000 in one year, not to mention the investment tax credit, attributable to the operation of his Cessna Citation executive jet. Although he paid considerably more than the cost of first class fares on commercial airliners, he was able to show that the considerable time savings was worth the expense.

3. Tax-free fringe benefits are a boon from government to taxpayer. They should be accepted with gratitude and humility. Or so one would have us believe. Any attempt to parlay the tax-free fringe benefit into yet additional tax exemptions and deductions is liable to wake the sleeping giant, as happened in the case below.

HAVERLY v. UNITED STATES

United States Court of Appeals, Seventh Circuit, 1975.
513 F.2d 224.

HASTINGS, SENIOR CIRCUIT JUDGE.

This case presents for resolution a single question of law which is of first impression: whether the value of unsolicited sample textbooks sent by publishers to a principal of a public elementary school, which he subsequently donated to the school's library and for which he claimed a charitable deduction, constitutes gross income to the principal within the meaning of Section 61. * * *

During the years 1967 and 1968 Charles N. Haverly was the principal of the Alice L. Barnard Elementary School in Chicago, Illinois. In each of these years publishers sent to the taxpayer unsolicited sample copies of textbooks which had a total fair market value at the time of receipt of $400. The samples were given to taxpayer for his personal retention or for whatever disposition he wished to make. The samples were provided, in the hope of receiving favorable consideration, to give taxpayer an opportunity to examine the books and determine whether they were suitable for the instructional unit for which he was responsible. The publishers did not intend that the books serve as compensation.

In 1968 taxpayer donated the books to the Alice L. Barnard Elementary School Library. The parties agreed that the donation entitled the taxpayer to a charitable deduction under § 170, in the amount of $400, the value of the books at the time of the contribution

The parties further stipulated that the textbooks received from the publishers did not constitute gifts within the meaning of § 102 since their transfer to the taxpayer did not proceed from a detached and disinterested generosity nor out of affection, respect, admiration, charity or like impulses.

Taxpayer's report of his 1968 income did not include the value of the textbooks received, but it did include a charitable deduction for the value of the books donated to the school library. The Internal Revenue Service assessed a deficiency against the taxpayer representing income taxes on the value of the textbooks received. Taxpayer paid the amount of the deficiency, filed a claim for refund and subsequently instituted this action to recover that amount. * * *

Upon agreement of the parties, the case was submitted to the district court on the uncontested facts and briefs for decision without trial. The district court issued a memorandum opinion which held that receipt of the samples did not constitute income. The court subsequently ordered, in accordance with its decision, that plaintiffs recover from the United States the sum of $120.40 plus interest. The United States appeals from that judgment. We reverse. * * *

The receipt of textbooks is unquestionably an "accession to wealth." Taxpayer recognized the value of the books when he donated them and took a $400 deduction therefor. Possession of the books increased the taxpayer's wealth. Taxpayer's receipt and possession of the books indicate that the income was "clearly realized." Taxpayer admitted that the books were given to him for his personal retention or whatever disposition he saw fit to make of them. Although the receipt of unsolicited samples may sometimes raise the question of whether the taxpayer manifested an intent to accept the property or exercised "complete dominion" over it, there is no question that this element is satisfied by the unequivocal act of taking a charitable deduction for donation of the property.

The district court recognized that the act of claiming a charitable deduction does manifest an intent to accept the property as one's own. It nevertheless declined to label receipt of the property as income because it considered such an act indistinguishable from other acts unrelated to the tax laws which also evidence an intent to accept property as one's own, such as a school principal donating his sample texts to the library without claiming a deduction. We need not resolve the question of the tax consequences of this and other hypothetical cases discussed by the district court and suggested by the taxpayer. To decide the case before us we need only hold, as we do, that when a tax deduction is taken for the donation of unsolicited samples the value of the samples received must be included in the taxpayer's gross income.

This conclusion is consistent with Revenue Ruling 70–498, 1970–2 Cum. Bull. 6, in which the Internal Revenue Service held that a newspaper's book reviewer must include in his gross income the value of unsolicited books received from publishers which are donated to a charitable organization and for which a charitable deduction is taken. This ruling was issued to supercede an earlier ruling, Rev. Rul. 70–330, 1970–1 Cum. Bull. 14, that mere retention of unsolicited books was sufficient to cause them to be gross income.[4]

The Internal Revenue Service has apparently made an administrative decision to be concerned with the taxation of unsolicited samples only when failure to tax those samples would provide taxpayers with double tax benefits. It is not for the courts to quarrel with an agency's rational allocation of its administrative resources.

In light of the foregoing, the judgment appealed from is reversed and the case is remanded to the district court with directions to enter judgment for the United States.

Reversed.

2. § 132

Code: §§ 132, 61(a)

Regulations: § 1.132, 1.61.21

Legislative History

The taxation of fringe benefits is now largely a matter of statute. To see why, read the House Ways and Means Committee Report, set forth below. Then, for some healthy cynicism about taking any Committee Report too seriously, see the Colloquy. Finally, for an overview of how § 132 works, see the Joint Committee Print.

House Ways and Means Committee Report

50TH CONGRESS   REPT. 98–432

2D SESSION   HOUSE OF REPRESENTATIVES   PART 2

TAX REFORM ACT OF 1984

---

4. The district court considered Revenue Ruling 70–498 distinguishable from the facts of the instant case on the ground that, for the book reviewer, the books were the tools of his trade. The district court did not explain why "tools of the trade" should be a significant factor in determining what is income, but even if it were, textbooks would seem to be a tool of the trade of being a school principal. The facts here indicate that it was one of taxpayer's functions as a principal to review sample textbooks to determine their suitability for his students.

SUPPLEMENTAL REPORT OF THE COMMITTEE ON WAYS AND MEANS U.S. HOUSE OF REPRESENTATIVES ON H.R. 4170

Reasons for Change

In providing statutory rules for exclusion of certain fringe benefits for income and payroll tax purposes, the committee has attempted to strike a balance between two competing objectives.

First, the committee is aware that in many industries, employees may receive, either free or at a discount, goods and services which the employer sells to the general public. In many cases, these practices are long established, and have been treated by employers, employees, and the IRS as not giving rise to taxable income. Although employees may receive an economic benefit from the availability of these free or discounted goods or services, employers often have valid business reasons, other than simply providing compensation, for encouraging employees to avail themselves of the products which they sell to the public. For example, a retail clothing business will want its salespersons to wear, when they deal with customers, the clothing which it seeks to sell to the public. In addition, the fact that the selection of goods and services usually available from a particular employer usually is restricted makes it appropriate to provide a limited exclusion, when such discounts are generally made available to employees, for the income employees realize from obtaining free or reduced-cost goods or services. The committee believes, therefore, that many present practices under which employers may provide to a broad group of employees, either free or at a discount, the products and services which the employer sells or provides to the public do not serve merely to replace cash compensation. These reasons support the committee's decision to codify the ability of employers to continue these practices without imposition of income or payroll taxes.

The second objective of the committee's bill is to set forth clear boundaries for the provision of tax-free benefits. Because of the moratorium on the issuance of fringe benefit regulations, the Treasury Department has been precluded from clarifying the tax treatment of many of the forms of noncash compensation commonly in use. As a result, the administrators of the tax law have not had clear guidelines in this area, and hence taxpayers in identical situations have been treated differently. The inequities, confusion, and administrative difficulties for businesses, employees, and the IRS resulting from this situation have increased substantially in recent years. The committee believes that it is unacceptable to allow these conditions—which have existed since 1978—to continue any longer.

In addition, the committee is concerned that without any well-defined limits on the ability of employers to compensate their employees tax-free by using a medium other than cash, new practices will emerge that could shrink the income tax base significantly, and further shift a disproportionate tax burden to those individuals whose compensation is in the form of cash. A shrinkage of the base of the social security payroll tax could also pose a threat to the viability of the social security system above and beyond the adverse projections which the Congress recently addressed in the Social Security Amendments of 1983. Finally, an unrestrained expansion of noncash compensation would increase inequities among employees in different types of businesses, and among employers as well.

The nondiscrimination rule is an important common thread among the types of fringe benefits which are excluded under the bill from income and employment taxes. Under the bill, most fringe benefits may be made available tax-free to officers, owners, or highly compensated employees only if the benefits are also provided on substantially equal terms to other employers. The committee believes that it would be fundamentally unfair to provide tax-free treatment for economic benefits that are furnished only to highly paid executives. Further, where benefits are limited to the highly paid, it is more likely that the benefit is being provided so that those who control the business can receive compensation in a nontaxable form; in that situation, the reasons stated above for allowing tax-free treatment would not be applicable. Also, if highly paid executives could receive free from taxation economic benefits that are denied to lower-paid employees, while the latter are compensated only in fully taxable cash, the committee is concerned that this situation would exacerbate problems of noncompliance among taxpayers. In this regard, some commentators argue that the current situation—in which the lack of clear rules for the tax treatment of nonstatutory fringe benefits encourages the nonreporting of many types of compensatory benefits—has led to nonreporting of types of cash income which are clearly taxable under present-law rules, such as interest and dividends.

In summary, the committee believes that by providing rules which essentially codify many present practices under which employers provide their own products and services tax-free to a broad group of employees, and by ending the uncertainties arising from a moratorium on the Treasury Department's ability to clarify the tax treatment of these benefits, the bill substantially improves the equity and administration of the tax system.

Congressional Colloquy on the Value of Committee Reports

Mr. ARMSTRONG. . . . My question, which may take [the chairman of the Committee on Finance] by surprise, is this: Is it the intention of the chairman that the Internal Revenue Service and the Tax Court and other courts take guidance as to the intention of Congress from the committee report which accompanies this bill?

Mr. DOLE. I would certainly hope so. . . .

Mr. ARMSTRONG. Mr. President, will the Senator tell me whether or not he wrote the committee report?

Mr. DOLE. Did I write the committee report?

Mr. ARMSTRONG. Yes

Mr. DOLE. No; the Senator from Kansas did not write the committee report.

Mr. ARMSTRONG. Did any Senator write the committee report?

Mr. DOLE. I have to check.

Mr. ARMSTRONG. Does the Senator know of any Senator who wrote the committee report?

Mr. DOLE. I might be able to identify one, but I would have to search. I was here all during the time it was written, I might say, and worked carefully with the staff as they worked. . . .

Mr. ARMSTRONG. Mr. President, has the Senator from Kansas, the chairman of the Finance Committee, read the committee report in its entirety?

Mr. DOLE. I am working on it. It is not a bestseller, but I am working on it.

Mr. ARMSTRONG. Mr. President, did members of the Finance Committee vote on the committee report?

Mr. DOLE. No.

Mr. ARMSTRONG. Mr. President, the reason I raise the issue is not perhaps apparent on the surface, and let me just state it: . . . . The report itself is not considered by the Committee on Finance. It was not subject to amendment by the Committee on Finance. It is not subject to amendment now by the Senate.

. . . .

. . . If there were a matter within this report which was disagreed to by the Senator from Colorado or even by a majority of all Senators, there would be no way for us to change the report. I could not offer an amendment tonight to amend the committee report.

. . . [F]or any jurist, administrator, bureaucrat, tax practitioner, or others who might chance upon the written record of this proceeding, let me just make the point that this is not the law, it was not voted on, it is not subject to amendment, and we should discipline ourselves to the task of expressing congressional intent in the statute.

128 Cong. Rec. 8659 (daily ed. July 19, 1982) as quoted in Hirschey v. F.E.R.C., 777 F.2d 1, 6, 7–8 n. 1 (D.C.Cir.1985) (Scalia, J., concurring).

Joint Committee Print

OVERVIEW OF THE TAX TREATMENT OF FRINGE BENEFITS, 1984

Prepared by the Staff of the Joint Committee on Taxation

Exclusive provisions

No-additional-cost service.—A service provided to an employee is excluded if—

(1) the employer incurs no substantial cost (including foregone revenue) in providing the service;

(2) the service is provided by the employer or another business with whom the employer has a written reciprocal agreement, and is of the same type ordinarily sold to the public in the line of business in which the employee works;

(3) the service is provided to a current or retired employee, or a spouse or dependent child of either, or a widow(er) or dependent children of a deceased employee; and

(4) for certain highly compensated employees, nondiscrimination requirements are met (see below).

Qualified employee discount.—A discount on merchandise provided to an employee is excluded to the extent it does not exceed the employer's gross profit percentage (in the relevant line of business). The exclusion does not apply to discounts on real property or to discounts on personal property of a kind commonly held for investment.

A discount on services provided to an employee is excluded to the extent it does not exceed 20 percent of the selling price of the services to nonemployee customers (with no gross profit percentage restriction).

The following conditions generally must be satisfied for the exclusion to apply:

(1) the property or service is provided by the employee and is of the same type ordinarily sold to the public in the line of business in which the employee works;

(2) the property or service is provided to a current or retired employee, a spouse or dependent child of either, or to a widow(er) or dependent children of a deceased employee; and

(3) for certain highly compensated employees, nondiscrimination requirements are met (see below).

Working condition fringe.—Property or services provided to an employee are excluded to the extent that they would be deductible as ordinary and necessary business expenses (under Code secs. 162 or 167) if the employee had paid for them.

The Act excludes, as a working condition fringe, the value of free or reduced-cost parking provided to employees on or near the employer's business premises.

De minimis fringe.—Property or services not otherwise tax-free are excluded if their fair market value is so small, taking into the account the frequency with which similar fringe benefits (otherwise excludable as de minimis fringes) are provided and other relevant factors, as to make accounting for the benefits unreasonable or administratively impracticable. For example, benefits that generally are excluded as de minimis fringes include the typing of a personal letter by a company secretary, occasional personal use of the company copying machine, monthly transit passes provided at a discount not exceeding $15, occasional company cocktail parties or picnics for employees, occasional supper money or taxi fare for employees because of overtime work, and certain holiday gifts of property with low fair market value.

Subsidized eating facilities operated by the employer also are excluded as a de minimis fringe if located on or near the employer's business premises, if revenue equals or exceeds direct operating costs, and if (for certain highly compensated employees) nondiscrimination requirements are met (see below).

Athletic facilities.—An exclusion is allowed for the value of on-premises athletic facilities provided and operated by an employer for use of its employees. Under Code section 274, the employer is not allowed a deduction for the costs of an athletic facility if the facility is not primarily for the benefit of employees (other than employees who are officers, shareholders or other owners, or highly compensated employees).

Qualified tuition reduction.—The Act provides that a reduction in tuition provided to an employee of an educational institution is excluded for income and employment tax purposes if (1) the tuition is for education below the graduate level provided by the employer or by another educational institution; (2) the education is provided to a current or retired employee, a spouse or dependent child of either, or to a widow(er) or dependent children of a deceased employee; and (3) certain nondiscrimination requirements are met (see above).

Nondiscrimination requirements.—The exclusions for non-additional-cost services, qualified employee discounts subsidized eating facilities, and qualified tuition reductions are available to officers, owners, or highly compensated employees only if the property or service is provided on substantially the same terms to each member of a group of employees defined under a reasonable classification, set up by the employer, which does not discriminate in favor of employees who are officers, owners, or highly compensated employees.

PROBLEMS

In each case, consult §§ 132 and 125, and determine whether or not taxable income is received.

1. Cheryl and Mike work as flight attendants on El Cheapo Airlines. On their days off, they fly for free on an empty seat. However, they must wait until the very last minute, to ensure that the seat remains empty, and that the airline was truly unable to sell the seat to a paying customer.

2. Pursuant to a written agreement, Cheryl travels for free, on the same terms, on another airline.

3. Mike's spouse gets a free flight.

4. Cheryl's mother and father get free flights.

5. Tom sells jewelry at the ABC Jewelry Store. When he wants to buy jewelry for himself, he gets a 25% discount. This year, the aggregate sales price of jewelry sold by the ABC Jewelry Store to customers was $1,000,000.

The cost of that jewelry was $550,000. Tom bought himself a $100 jewelry item for $75.

(a) All employees get the same discount

(b) Salespeople get a 25% discount; senior management get 35%.

(c) Tom keeps the jewelry for ten years, and then sells it to a third party for $100.

(d) On the same day that Tom purchases the jewelry from his employer, Tom resells it to a third party for $100.

(e) Tom gives the jewelry to his mother on her birthday.

6.   Tricia works as an administrative assistant for Grade A Maids, a housecleaning service. In preparation for a party, Tricia hires her employer, Grade A Maids, to clean her house. She pays $450 for housecleaning services that would normally cost $500.

7.   XYZ Corporation operates a hospital and a chain of dry cleaners. Can an employee of the XYZ Hospital enjoy a 20% taxfree discount on dry cleaning services provided by XYZ Dry Cleaners?

8.   Roger is an automobile salesman. Whenever he sells a car, he earns a 10% commission. Roger "sells himself" a car. He pays full price, and then receives a 10% commission.

9.   The dealership provides Roger with a "demo" car, which he treats as his own.

10.   Frank is a steel worker. His employer provides him, along with the other 1,000 employees, with a steel mill in which to work.

11.   Janice is a law professor. Her employer provides her with an office and a classroom, rent free.

12.   Lucy goes to a cafeteria for lunch on her business premises. The cafeteria is available to all employees. She pays for her food, but—

(a) The employer breaks even.

(b) The employer makes a profit.

(c) The employer loses money.

13.   Michelle, a low-level employee, is given a choice of $50 additional monthly cash compensation, or free parking. She takes the free parking.

14.   Rodney is a Senior Vice President of Bank. There is a gym inside the bank building, available only for Senior Vice Presidents and higher officers. Rodney pays nothing for the right to use the gym.

3. MEALS AND LODGING FURNISHED FOR THE CONVENIENCE OF THE EMPLOYER

Code: §§ 119, 107

Regulations: §§ 1.119–1, 1.107–1

UNITED STATES JUNIOR CHAMBER OF COMMERCE v. UNITED STATES

United States Court of Claims, 1964.
334 F.2d 660.

JONES, SENIOR JUDGE.

Plaintiff is a nonprofit corporation, incorporated under the laws of the State of Missouri. It was organized for "such educational and charitable purposes as will promote and foster the growth and development of young men's civic organizations in the United States." Among its activities are such programs as the promotion of interest in youth athletic programs, safe driving programs, and community and school development programs. The headquarters and principal offices of plaintiff are located in Tulsa, Oklahoma. Plaintiff owns and maintains a residential building in Tulsa, known as the "U.S. Jaycee White House" (hereinafter referred to as the House), which is the official residence and home of the president of plaintiff during his term of office.

The president of plaintiff is its chief executive officer and is elected at the annual meeting by a majority vote of plaintiff's membership. He is elected for a term of one year only, and may not succeed himself in office. During the years involved in this suit, plaintiff had three presidents who, prior to their election, lived and worked in North Carolina, Iowa, and Pennsylvania, respectively. At the expiration of their terms of office, each president returned to his respective residence and employment.

The by-laws of plaintiff provide, in pertinent part, that: "Because of the benefits and convenience accruing to the Corporation by having the President and his family, if any, reside in Tulsa in the home built by the Corporation for the President, the President and his family shall reside at the U.S. Jaycee White House in Tulsa, during his tenure of office." In accordance with the by-laws, each of the above-mentioned three presidents lived in the House during his term of office. None of the presidents paid plaintiff any rent while so residing there, and all expenses of operating and maintaining the House were paid by plaintiff. It was plaintiff's policy to recognize the building as the private residence of its president and his family during his term of office, and visits to the House by members were not approved unless a specific invitation had been extended by the president in residence. The present controversy is concerned with the question whether or not the fair rental value of the House is excludable from the gross income of plaintiff's presidents.

The Commissioner of Internal Revenue determined that the fair rental value of the House should have been included in the gross income of the various presidents, and that plaintiff should have withheld income and F.I.C.A. taxes thereon for the years 1959 and 1960. The parties agreed that the fair rental value of the House during these years was $125 per month. The Commissioner of Internal Revenue thereupon assessed such withholding and F.I.C.A. taxes against plaintiff in the amount of $705, together with interest thereon in the amount of $42.89. No part of this $747.89 in taxes and interest was actually deducted or withheld by plaintiff. After plaintiff paid these assessments and its claims for refund were disallowed, the present suit was timely filed.

It was found by our trial commissioner that plaintiff's presidents traveled extensively throughout the United States, visiting local and state organizations, in carrying out their responsibilities for supervision of all of plaintiff's affairs. During the years here in issue, roughly one-half of a president's time was spent in Tulsa actively directing plaintiff's various programs and the other half of his time was spent in traveling. While in Tulsa, plaintiff's presidents worked during both the day and night. There is an office in the House which the presidents used at night for the purpose of conducting staff meetings and briefings by subordinate officials. In addition, the presidents used the House for official entertainment connected with plaintiff's business.

The trial commissioner concluded that the evidence established that for the convenience of plaintiff, and as a condition of a president's tenure, he was, as a practical matter, required to live in the House. The trial commissioner further found that the House constituted a part of the business premises of plaintiff. Defendant disputes each and every one of these conclusions. However, we agree with the conclusions of the trial commissioner.

The Government contends that, because of the broad scope of § 61 of the 1954 Code, the fair rental value of the House constituted income to plaintiff's presidents unless such income was excludable under § 119. It is the Government's position that the fair rental value of the House was not excludable under § 119 because none of the three requirements under that section was met. Therefore, the Government concludes that the fair rental value of the House constituted income to plaintiff's presidents and that plaintiff should have withheld income and F.I.C.A. taxes thereon.

* * * [Pursuant to Section 119,] there are three conditions which must be met if the value of the lodging furnished an employee by his employer are to be excluded from the employee's gross income: The lodging must be furnished for the convenience of the employer; the employee is required to accept such lodging as a condition of his employment; and the lodging must be on the business premises of the employer. In determining the applicability of § 119, the intention of the employer (whether or not he regarded the fair rental value of the lodging furnished to be compensation) is not particularly important. Indeed, both the Senate

and House Committee Reports in discussing § 119 of the 1954 Code contain an example, which is now Example 3 in Treas. Regs. § 1.119–1(d), showing that even when the employer regarded the lodging furnished to be a part of the employee's compensation, the employee would neverthe-less be entitled to exclude the value of such lodging from his gross income if the conditions of § 119 are otherwise met. Further, § 119 itself provides that in determining whether meals or lodging are furnished for the convenience of the employer, "the provisions of an employment contract or of a State statute fixing terms of employment shall not be determina-tive of whether the meals or lodging are intended as compensation." Therefore, we conclude that the Congress intended that an objective test should be used in applying § 119.

There does not appear to be any substantial difference between the first two conditions of § 119: The "convenience of the employer" test and the "required as a condition of his employment" test. The Senate Commit-tee Report accompanying the 1954 Code defined the phrase "required as a condition of his employment" to mean "required in order for the employee to properly perform the duties of his employment." On the other hand, the Commissioner of Internal Revenue has said that:

> As a general rule, the test of "convenience of the employer" is satisfied if living quarters or meals are furnished to an employee who is required to accept such quarters and meals in order to perform properly his duties.

Although the last quoted definition was issued before the promulgation of the 1954 Code, it is at least indicative of the meaning of the phrase used by the Congress. Furthermore, the only post–1954 case cited by the Government as bearing on the "convenience of the employer" test sup-ports the above interpretation of the 1954 Code. Olkjer v. Commissioner, 32 T.C. 464 (1959).

The issue of whether or not the lodging was furnished for the convenience of the employer, or whether the employee was required to accept the lodging in order to properly perform his duties, is primarily a question of fact to be resolved by a consideration of all the facts and circumstances of the case. Under the facts of the present case we believe that the use of the House was furnished to plaintiff's presidents for the convenience of plaintiff. These presidents were elected for a term of one year each, and they may not succeed themselves in office. They came from all parts of the country. During their one year in Tulsa they were away half of the time. In these circumstances, it is not unreasonable to suppose that some of them would, for their temporary stay in Tulsa, rent living quarters not suitable for purposes of plaintiff's official activities.

Plaintiff's business is devoted primarily to organizing and promoting interest and activity on the part of young men in the affairs of their community, state and Nation. It is common knowledge that such a business requires constant staff meetings and official entertainment. Fur-thermore, plaintiff's presidents were away from Tulsa half of the time during their term in office. Consequently, when a president is back in Tulsa he must quickly catch up with his administrative duties and plan his future trips. These appear to be the reasons why the presidents frequently worked and entertained at night. Since the work and entertainment were plaintiff's business activities, plaintiff was responsible for providing suitable space for their proper execution. In light of these facts we believe that it was not unreasonable for plaintiff to permanently rid itself of the problem by furnishing its presidents with quarters where they could carry out the required work and entertainment at night.

The Government apparently does not dispute that plaintiff's official functions required access to a place such as the House. What the Government seems to be saying is that other suitable residences were available in the Tulsa area and so it was not necessary for plaintiff to furnish its presidents with the House for the proper performance of plaintiff's functions. The Government appears to be contending that § 119 does not apply unless the furnished lodging was so necessary to the performance of the duties of the employment that the absence of the specific lodging would render the performance virtually impossible.

We do not think that such a strict construction of § 119 is warranted. There are few instances in life where such an abstract concept of necessity would be met. Even in the cases cited by the Government, where the employment was at a construction jobsite 40 miles from Anchorage and so the meals and lodging furnished to the employees were allowed to be excluded, it would presumably be possible for the employer to require the employees to furnish their own housetrailers to live near the jobsite. We believe that § 119 should be given a reasonable interpretation. It seems to us that the "required as a condition of his employment" test is met if, due to the nature of the employer's business, a certain type of residence for the employee is required and that it would not be reasonable to suppose that the employee would normally have available such lodging for the use of his employer. Of course, the employee is incidentally benefited by the furnished lodging, but as the Tax Court has observed in the Olkjer and Stone cases, supra, this is true in all cases where desirable working facilities as well as living quarters are concededly furnished "for the convenience of the employer."

Finally, § 119 requires that the lodging furnished must be on the business premises of the employer. The trial commissioner found that the House constituted a part of the business premises of plaintiff because plaintiff's official functions were carried out there at night. The Government argues that the residential character of the House is not transformed by the limited use of the House for purposes connected with plaintiff's activities. We think that the business premises of § 119 means premises of the employer on which the duties of the employee are to be performed. Thus, a domestic servant who lives in the residence of this employer, and who is required to be available for duty at any time, may exclude the value of his lodging from his gross income even though the residence may or may not be the employer's "business premises." In the present case, part of plaintiff's official activities were carried out at the House which it owned. We believe that the House is part of the business premises of plaintiff within the meaning of § 119 of the 1954 Code. * * *

For the above reasons we hold that the fair rental value of the House was excludable, under § 119 of the 1954 Code, from the gross income of plaintiff's presidents. Plaintiff is therefore entitled to recover. * * *

NOTE

In Boyd Gaming Corp. v. Commissioner, 177 F.3d 1096 (9th Cir.1999), a gambling casino required its employees to stay on the business premises throughout the work shift. In view of the employees' easy access to cash and chips, there were elaborate security checkout procedures for certain employees every time they left the premises. The casino wanted to minimize these checkouts. Also, the casino wanted to prevent its employees from succumbing to the distractions and temptations of the festive Las Vegas atmosphere, which might have hampered their productivity. The Ninth Circuit deemed these, and other reasons, sufficient to satisfy the "convenience of the employer" requirement for the free lunches.

QUESTIONS

1. In 2010, the director of New York's Museum of Modern Art lived in a $6,000,000 condominium atop the Museum, both rentfree and taxfree, pursuant to § 119. On the other coast, the chief executive of the Getty Museum, north of Los Angeles, was also furnished rent free housing, courtesy of his employer. He, however, reported the housing as taxable income. Presumably, both used their residences in similar ways. Which museum got it right? *See* Kevin Flynn and Stephanie Strom, *Fine Perk for Museum Chiefs: Luxury Housing (It's Tax–Free)*, N.Y. Times (Aug. 10. 2010).

2. You are on the staff of the Joint Committee on Taxation. You have been asked to determine which people would be affected if § 107 were repealed, and "ministers of the gospel" would have to take their chances under § 119, if they wanted any tax breaks for lodgings furnished by their employers.

C. SCHOLARSHIPS AND AWARDS

Code: §§ 74, 117

Regulations: §§ 1.74–1, 1.117–1 through 1.117–4, 1.117–6

Introductory Problem

Linda, Mary, and Norma, and Olivia were law school classmates. Linda practices law with a large law firm. During the first 18 years of her daughter Laura's life, Linda averaged $150,000 in annual earnings. During that period, she annually put $5,000 of her earnings into a college fund. She invested the fund in stocks, bonds, and certificates of deposit. Over time, the fund grew to $100,000. When Laura reached college age, she applied for financial aid. However, she was not given a scholarship, because she didn't need one. Linda paid $150,000 to send her to Private University for four years.

Mary is a law partner of Linda, and earns the same amount. However, Mary spent every penny of it on her extravagant lifestyle. When her daughter, Melanie, reached college age, she applied for financial aid, and obtained $75,000 of scholarships over her four years of college. Mary paid the rest of her expenses at Private University through loans and current income.

Norma is a professor at Private University Law School. During the same period, she averaged $75,000 a year in earnings. She had no college fund. When her daughter, Nadine, reached college age, she enrolled in Private University. As a faculty member at Private University, Norma paid only $25,000 for Nadine's four years of college education.

Olivia practices law with a small firm. Over the same period, she earned an average of $85,000 a year. When her daughter, Olive, reached college age, she enrolled at State University, which everyone says is just as good as Private University (except for State's football team, which is much better). As a local resident, it cost only $50,000 for Olive's four years of college education.

How are Linda, Mary, Norma, Olivia, and their respective daughters taxed on these events? Does current tax law treat them fairly?

NOTE

Scholarships and awards have something in common with gifts, but they are not gifts (*see* the footnote discussion in *Duberstein, supra* at 82). Yet, there are policy reasons why some of these gratuitous transfers ought to be tax free. Either we approve of the conduct which merited the award, or, in the case of scholarships, we want to encourage the behavior funded by the award— education.

Prizes and Awards

Note that both prizes and awards would be difficult to tax. As to prizes, there is a question of transferability. More often than not, however, the nontransferability of a prize tends to be more a matter of good taste than law. How can you tax an athlete on the receipt of a sports trophy, such as the jewel-encrusted belt received by baseball star Maury Wills as the Outstanding Athlete of 1962, when no one but a total clod would ever try to sell it? See Wills v. Commissioner, 411 F.2d 537 (9th Cir.1969).

Wills' argument that trophies were not taxable income at all failed. However, the good news is that the taxable income from the receipt of a trophy is limited to the amount that one could get if one sold it.

An earlier version of § 74 exempted from taxation awards made for artistic, educational, or civic achievement. Presumably, Congress thought that these achievements were the most deserving of tax breaks. But why were athletic achievements left out? Do you think that they would have been left out if the issue had been raised specifically on a national referendum?

In addition, that early version of § 74 provided that awards were tax free only if the recipient had not "entered the contest." Did entering the contest suggest that the recipient had "earned" the award? Did entering the contest suggest that the recipient lacked the quality of All–American bashfulness which is the necessary hallmark of American heroes?

At any rate, the taxfree awards were severely restricted in 1986. Read the current § 74. Consider which prizes and awards are still taxfree after 1986, and why.

Scholarships

Scholarships are definitely nontransferable; they can only be used by the recipient. Therefore, there would be valuation problems, if scholarships were taxed. What is the value of a half-tuition scholarship at a private school, if there is a public school nearby which offers the same quality education at less than half the price? For that matter, if all scholarships were taxed, would it follow that all students attending public colleges and universities should be similarly taxed on the value of their subsidized education?

A major litigation issue in § 117 is the difference between a taxfree scholarship, and a taxable grant of educational benefits, transferred quid pro quo as compensation for services rendered. This issue has arisen frequently in the case of medical internships, residencies, and fellowships. For the leading case on the issue, see Bingler v. Johnson, 394 U.S. 741, 89 S.Ct. 1439, 22 L.Ed.2d 695 (1969).

What about athletic scholarships? Are they a different animal—more akin to payment for services rendered?

PROBLEMS

In each case, apply §§ 74 and 117, and determine whether or not there is taxable income.

1. Mary enters an essay contest run by a life insurance company. She writes the best essay on the subject, "Why I Wouldn't Mind Being Dead If I Had Really Good Life Insurance." For her prize, the insurance company pays full tuition at a four year college.

2. Melissa applies to college during her senior year of high school, and fills out the voluminous financial aid forms. She is awarded a full tuition scholarship to attend State University.

3. Jerry's wife teaches at State University. Jerry enrolls in the undergraduate program at State University. Jerry pays only half tuition because his wife is an employee.

(a) This benefit is available to all employees.

(b) This benefit is available only to teaching staff.

(c) What if Jerry were going for his master's degree in biology?

(d) Same as (c), except that Jerry is a teaching assistant.

4. Brutus, due to his athletic prowess, is awarded a full tuition scholarship to State University.

(a) [Let's ignore NCAA rules for a moment] He is also given a free apartment, the free use of a sports car, and his own, personal valet.

(b) The scholarship is for one year, renewable at the option of State University. Brutus's freshman athletic season is disappointing, and the scholarship is not renewed. Does this fact have any bearing on the taxation of the scholarship during his freshman year?

(c) Reconsider Melissa, from Problem 2. Her scholarship is for four years, but it is conditioned upon her maintaining a B average. During her sophomore year, her average drops below B, and the scholarship is terminated. Does this fact have any bearing?

D.   DAMAGES

Code: §§ 61, 104

Regulations: § 1.104–1

NOTE

If a court awards damages, then the payor must have done something she should not have done. Consider the damages as an attempt by the court to put the plaintiff back where she would have been had the untoward event not occurred. Generally, tax law goes through the same analysis.

Consider, for example, an employer's breach of an employment contract. Employee sues, and is awarded money damages.

Where would plaintiff have been had the bad thing not occurred? She would still be working, earning taxable wages. What, then, are the money damages? They are a substitute for the wages that plaintiff should have earned. The wages would have been taxable. Therefore, the damages, as a substitute for wages, should also be taxable.

Imagine a china shop. There is a sign, prominently displayed. It says, "You broke it, you bought it." Defendant and his pet bull stroll through the china shop, and break a vase. Storeowner points to the sign, and then goes to court. The court awards damages measured by the fair market value of the vase.

Where would storeowner have been had the defendant and his bull not shown up? Storeowner would still have an unbroken vase. Now, storeowner has cash instead. The conversion of the vase into cash looks like a sale, and will be treated like one. The damage award will be considered as an amount realized. Storeowner can subtract basis, and pay tax on the profit.

Now imagine an innocent pedestrian. Negligent automobile driver runs over pedestrian, and pedestrian's leg is amputated. Pedestrian sues, and the court awards damages.

Where would pedestrian be if the bad thing hadn't happened? She'd still have two legs. Is the condition of having two legs a taxable event? No. Therefore, the damages intended to substitute for having two legs should not be taxable.

Others have argued that the exclusion of damage awards on account of personal injury can be justified on hardship grounds—that the victim has suffered enough.

But what if the pedestrian sues for the loss of the leg, plus lost wages, now that she can no longer pursue her occupation as a figure skater? Based upon the logic above, one would think that the lost wages award would be taxable, as a substitute for taxable wages. However, here is where the logic breaks down in the face of a statute. Section 104(a)(2) exempts **any** damages (other than punitive damages) incurred as a result of personal physical injury. Therefore, once the initial event is a personal injury, then all nonpunitive damage awards which flow from that event are also taxfree.

Section 104(a)(2) has enjoyed a checkered career. In an earlier formulation, it exempted "the amount of any damages received . . . on account of personal injuries or sickness." According to the regulations, the term referred to amounts received ". . . through prosecution of a legal suit or action based upon tort or tort type rights . . ." Reg. § 1.104–1(c). The courts generally agreed, and the battle shifted to determining which rights were tort type, as opposed to contract type rights.

Clearly, all "pure" tort actions, including claims based upon physical, personal injury, personal libel, and emotional distress, gave rise to taxfree damages under this Regulation. Difficulties arose, however, in employment-related lawsuits. While the employment relationship is a matter of contract, harms can occur on the job which sound in tort. Are the resulting lawsuits contract type or tort type? Most of those lawsuits were ultimately deemed to be tort type, on various theories. However, the Supreme Court struggled mightily, and, some would say, incoherently, with the issues of sex discrimination, United States v. Burke, 504 U.S. 229, 112 S.Ct. 1867, 119 L.Ed.2d 34 (1992), and age discrimination, Commissioner v. Schleier, 515 U.S. 323, 115 S.Ct. 2159, 132 L.Ed.2d 294 (1995).

There was also the problem of the deeper meaning of the word "any." Everyone agreed that it meant that even lost wage claims, if arising out of personal injury actions, would be taxfree. But what about punitive damages? The Service originally took the position that "any" really meant "any." Rev. Rul. 75–45, 1975–1 C.B. 47. However, it later changed its mind, and argued that damages could not possibly mean "punitive damages." Punitives, of course, are noncompensatory, and therefore not intended to be a substitute for anything. As such, they are pure windfall, and therefore fully taxable under no less authority than *Glenshaw Glass*. Rev. Rul. 84–108, 1984–2 C.B.

32. The courts had similar difficulties. Compare Horton v. Commissioner, 100 T.C. 93 (1993) [punitive damages excludible], with Commissioner v. Miller, 914 F.2d 586 (4th Cir.1990) [punitive damages taxable].

Then Congress reentered the fray. In 1989, it added a sentence to § 104(a), which provided:

Paragraph (2) shall not apply to any punitive damages in connection with a case not involving physical injury or physical sickness.

Omnibus Budget Reconciliation Act of 1989, 103 Stat. 2106.

Now, it appears that Congress has had enough. In the Small Business Job Protection Act of 1996, Congress changed the operative phrase in § 104(a)(2) to "the amount of any damages **(other than punitive damages)** received . . . on account of personal **physical** injuries or **physical** sickness" [emphasis added]. Just to make sure, Congress added at the end of § 104(a):

For purposes of paragraph (2), emotional distress shall not be treated as a physical injury or physical sickness.

As a result, all punitive damages are taxable. In addition, all damages for age discrimination, sex and racial discrimination, and libel of all types are taxable.

It's simpler, but is it fair? Recall the justifications for the exclusion of damages on account of personal injury from taxation. First, the damages simply put the victim back in the position she was in before. Is this argument any less true for nonphysical injuries than for physical injuries? Second, the damages are taxfree because the victim has already suffered enough. Does this justification apply only to the victims of physical injuries? Does the new legislation give sufficient attention to the claims of human dignity which are behind many of the causes of action for nonphysical injuries?

Now, forget everything you read above, and see if you can make sense of *Murphy*.

MURPHY v. INTERNAL REVENUE SERVICE

United States Court of Appeals, District of Columbia Circuit, 2006.
460 F.3d 79.

GINSBURG: CHIEF JUDGE.

Marrita Murphy brought this suit to recover income taxes she paid on the compensatory damages for emotional distress and loss of reputation she was awarded in an administrative action she brought against her former employer. Murphy contends that under § 104(a)(2) of the Internal Revenue Code her award should have been excluded from her gross income because it was compensation received "on account of personal physical injuries or physical sickness." In the alternative, she maintains § 104(a)(2) is unconstitutional insofar as it fails to exclude from gross income revenue that is not "income" within the meaning of the Sixteenth Amendment to the Constitution of the United States.

We hold, first, that Murphy's compensation was not "received . . . on account of personal physical injuries" excludable from gross income under

§ 104(a)(2). We agree with the taxpayer, however, that § 104(a)(2) is unconstitutional as applied to her award because compensation for a non-physical personal injury is not income under the Sixteenth Amendment if, as here, it is unrelated to lost wages or earnings.

I. Background

In 1994 Marrita Leveille (now Murphy) filed a complaint with the Department of Labor alleging that her former employer, the New York Air National Guard (NYANG), in violation of various whistle-blower statutes, had "blacklisted" her and provided unfavorable references to potential employers after she had complained to state authorities of environmental hazards on a NYANG airbase. The Secretary of Labor determined the NYANG had unlawfully discriminated and retaliated against Murphy, ordered that any adverse employment references to the taxpayer in Office of Personnel Management files be withdrawn, and remanded her case to an Administrative Law Judge "for findings on compensatory damages."

On remand Murphy submitted evidence that she had suffered both mental and physical injuries as a result of the NYANG's blacklisting her. A physician testified Murphy had sustained "somatic" and "emotional" injuries. One such injury was "bruxism," or teeth grinding often associated with stress, which may cause permanent tooth damage. Upon finding Murphy had also suffered from other "physical manifestations of stress" including "anxiety attacks, shortness of breath, and dizziness," the ALJ recommended compensatory damages totaling $70,000, of which $45,000 was for "emotional distress or mental anguish," and $25,000 was for "injury to professional reputation" from having been blacklisted. None of the award was for lost wages or diminished earning capacity.

* * * Murphy included the $70,000 award in her "gross income" pursuant to § 61. As a result, she paid $20,665 in taxes on the award.

Murphy later filed an amended return in which she sought a refund of the $20,665 based upon § 104(a)(2). In support of her amended return, Murphy submitted copies of her dental and medical records. Upon deciding Murphy had failed to demonstrate the compensatory damages were attributable to "physical injury" or "physical sickness," the Internal Revenue Service denied her request for a refund. Murphy thereafter sued the IRS and the United States in the district court.

* * *Murphy now appeals the judgment of the district court with respect to her claims under § 104(a)(2) and the Sixteenth Amendment.

II. Analysis

* * *

B. Section 104(a)(2) of the IRC

* * *

Murphy * * * contends that neither § 104 of the IRC nor the regulation issued thereunder "limits the physical disability exclusion to a physical stimulus." * * *

For its part, the Government argues Murphy's exclusive focus upon the word "physical" in § 104(a)(2) is misplaced; more important is the phrase "on account of." In *O'Gilvie v. United States,* the Supreme Court read that phrase to require a "strong [ ] causal connection," thereby making § 104(a)(2) "applicable only to those personal injury lawsuit damages that were awarded by reason of, or because of, the personal injuries.". The Court specifically rejected a "but-for" formulation in favor of a "stronger causal connection." The Government therefore concludes Murphy must demonstrate she was awarded damages "because of" her physical injuries, which the Government claims she has failed to do.

* * *

In reply Murphy merely reiterates that she suffered "physical" injuries. She does not address the Government's point that she received her award "on account of" her mental distress and reputational loss, not her bruxism or other physical symptoms.

* * * Murphy no doubt suffered from certain physical manifestations of emotional distress, but the record clearly indicates the Board awarded her compensation only "for mental pain and anguish" and "for injury to professional reputation." The Board thus having left no room for doubt about the grounds for her award, we conclude Murphy's damages were not "awarded by reason of, or because of,... [physical] personal injuries," Therefore, § 104(a)(2) does not permit Murphy to exclude her award from gross income. But is that constitutional?

C. The Sixteenth Amendment

Murphy argues that, being neither a gain nor an accession to wealth, her award is not income and § 104(a)(2) is therefore unconstitutional insofar as it would make the award taxable as income. Broad though the power granted in the Sixteenth Amendment is, the Supreme Court, as Murphy points out, has long recognized "the principle that a restoration of capital [i]s not income; hence it [falls] outside the definition of 'income' upon which the law impose[s] a tax." By analogy, Murphy contends a damage award for personal injuries-including nonphysical injuries-is not income but simply a return of capital—"human capital," as it were.

According to Murphy, the Supreme Court read the concept of "human capital" into the IRC in *Glenshaw Glass*. There, in holding that punitive damages for personal injury were "gross income" under the predecessor to § 61, the Court stated:

> The long history of ... holding personal injury recoveries nontaxable on the theory that they roughly correspond to a return of capital cannot support exemption of punitive damages following injury to property.... Damages for personal injury are by definition compensa-

tory only. Punitive damages, on the other hand, cannot be considered a restoration of capital for taxation purposes.

[Glenshaw Glass, footnote 8]

In Murphy's view, the Court thereby made clear that the recovery of compensatory damages for a "personal injury"—of whatever type—is analogous to a "return of capital" and therefore is not income under the IRC or the Sixteenth Amendment.

The Government attacks Murphy's constitutional argument on all fronts. First, invoking the presumption that the Congress enacts laws within its constitutional limits, the Government asserts at the outset that § 104(a)(2) is constitutional even if, as amended in 1996, it does permit the taxation of compensatory damages. Indeed, the Government goes further, contending the Congress could, consistent with the Sixteenth Amendment, repeal § 104(a)(2) altogether and tax compensation even for physical injuries.

Noting that the power of the Congress to tax income "extends broadly to all economic gains," the Government next maintains that compensatory damages "plainly constitute economic gain, for the taxpayer unquestionably has more money after receiving the damages than she had prior to receipt of the award." On that basis, the Government contends Murphy's reliance upon footnote eight of *Glenshaw Glass* is misplaced; merely because the Congress "has historically excluded personal injury recoveries from gross income, based on the make-whole or restoration-of-human-capital theory, does not mean that such an exclusion is mandated by the Sixteenth Amendment." Because the Supreme Court in *Glenshaw Glass* was construing "gross income" with reference only to the IRC, the Government argues footnote eight addresses only a now abandoned congressional policy, not the outer limit of the Sixteenth Amendment.

* * *

In addition, the Government challenges the coherence of Murphy's analogy between a return of "human capital or well-being" and a return of "financial capital," the latter of which it acknowledges does not constitute income under the Sixteenth Amendment ... The Government first observes that financial capital, like all property, has a "basis," defined by the IRC as "the cost of such property," adjusted "for expenditures, receipts, losses, or other items, properly chargeable to [a] capital account," *id.* § 1016(a)(1); thus, when a taxpayer sells property, his income is "the excess of the amount realized therefrom over the adjusted basis." The Government then observes that "[b]ecause people do not pay cash or its equivalent to acquire their well-being, they have no basis in it for purposes of measuring a gain (or loss) upon the realization of compensatory damages." Nor is there any corresponding theory of "human depreciation," which would permit "an offsetting deduction for the exhaustion of the taxpayer's physical prowess and mental agility."

At the outset, we reject the Government's breathtakingly expansive claim of congressional power under the Sixteenth Amendment—upon which it founds the more far-reaching arguments it advances here. The Sixteenth Amendment simply does not authorize the Congress to tax as "incomes" every sort of revenue a taxpayer may receive. As the Supreme Court noted long ago, the "Congress cannot make a thing income which is not so in fact."

* * *

As we have seen, it is clear from the record that the damages were awarded to make Murphy emotionally and reputationally "whole" and not to compensate her for lost wages or taxable earnings of any kind. The emotional well-being and good reputation she enjoyed before they were diminished by her former employer were not taxable as income. Under this analysis, therefore, the compensation she received in lieu of what she lost cannot be considered income and, hence, it would appear the Sixteenth Amendment does not empower the Congress to tax her award.

* * *

In sum, every indication is that damages received solely in compensation for a personal injury are not income within the meaning of that term in the Sixteenth Amendment. First, as compensation for the loss of a personal attribute, such as well-being or a good reputation, the damages are not received in lieu of income. Second, the framers of the Sixteenth Amendment would not have understood compensation for a personal injury-including a nonphysical injury-to be income. Therefore, we hold § 104(a)(2) unconstitutional insofar as it permits the taxation of an award of damages for mental distress and loss of reputation.

III.   Conclusion

Albert Einstein may have been correct that "[t]he hardest thing in the world to understand is the income tax," but it is not hard to understand that not all receipts of money are income. Murphy's compensatory award in particular was not received "in lieu of" something normally taxed as income; nor is it within the meaning of the term "incomes" as used in the Sixteenth Amendment. Therefore, insofar as § 104(a)(2) permits the taxation of compensation for a personal injury, which compensation is unrelated to lost wages or earnings, that provision is unconstitutional. Accordingly, we remand this case to the district court to enter an order and judgment instructing the Government to refund the taxes Murphy paid on her award plus applicable interest.

ON REHEARING

493 F.3d 170, 2007.

GINSBURG, CHIEF JUDGE:

In *Murphy v. IRS,* 460 F.3d 79 (2006), we concluded Murphy's award was not exempt from taxation pursuant to § 104(a)(2), but also was not "income" within the meaning of the Sixteenth Amendment, and therefore reversed the decision of the district court. The Government petitioned for rehearing en banc, arguing for the first time that, even if Murphy's award is not income, there is no constitutional impediment to taxing it because a tax on the award is not a direct tax and is imposed uniformly. In view of the importance of the issue thus belatedly raised, the panel sua sponte vacated its judgment and reheard the case. * * * In the present opinion, we affirm the judgment of the district court based upon the newly argued ground that Murphy's award, even if it is not income within the meaning of the Sixteenth Amendment, is within the reach of the congressional power to tax under Article I, Section 8 of the Constitution.

* * *

As noted above, in 1996 the Congress amended § 104(a) to narrow the exclusion to amounts received on account of "personal physical injuries or physical sickness" from "personal injuries or sickness," and explicitly to provide that "emotional distress shall not be treated as a physical injury or physical sickness," thus making clear that an award received on account of emotional distress is not excluded from gross income under § 104(a)(2). As this amendment, which narrows the exclusion, would have no effect whatsoever if such damages were not included within the ambit of § 61, and as we must presume that "[w]hen Congress acts to amend a statute, . . . it intends its amendment to have real and substantial effect,", the 1996 amendment of § 104(a) strongly suggests § 61 should be read to include an award for damages from nonphysical harms. Although it is unclear whether § 61 covered such an award before 1996, we need not address that question here; even if the provision did not do so prior to 1996, the presumption indicates the Congress implicitly amended § 61 to cover such an award when it amended § 104(a).

* * * For the 1996 amendment of § 104(a) to "make sense," gross income in § 61(a) must, and we therefore hold it does, include an award for nonphysical damages such as Murphy received, regardless whether the award is an accession to wealth.

For the foregoing reasons, we conclude (1) Murphy's compensatory award was not received on account of personal physical injuries, and therefore is not exempt from taxation pursuant to § 104(a)(2); (2) the award is part of her "gross income," as defined by § 61 of the IRC; and (3) the tax upon the award is an excise and not a direct tax subject to the apportionment requirement of Article I, Section 9 of the Constitution. The tax is uniform throughout the United States and therefore passes constitutional muster. The judgment of the district court is accordingly

Affirmed.

A Possible Explanation of Murphy

Judge Douglas H. Ginsburg, who wrote both *Murphy* opinions, was nominated to the Supreme Court by President Reagan. In November of 1987, he asked the President to withdraw the nomination. According to a "close friend of the President," "You just can't have a law professor smoking marijuana who expects to be on the Supreme Court."[c]

NOTE FOR LITIGATORS

So you say you'll never have to think about tax again after you pass this course? Wrong. Say you represent the plaintiff, and you win. Some damages (whether pursuant to a judgment or a settlement agreement) are taxable, and some are not.[d] Sometimes, you could be suing for both taxable and taxfree damages. If you do, and if you win, then the judgment, or the settlement agreement, should specify which is which. IRS will probably accept the parties' allocation of the award, provided that they don't get too greedy. However, if you fail to allocate damages at all, you may find yourself in a second lawsuit—this time with the IRS.

AMOS v. COMMISSIONER

United States Tax Court, 2003.
T.C. Memo. 2003–329.

Memorandum Findings of Fact and Opinion

CHIECHI, J.

* * *

The only issue remaining for decision is whether the $200,000 settlement amount (settlement amount at issue) that petitioner received in 1997 in settlement of a claim is excludable under section 104(a)(2) from petitioner's gross income for that year. We hold that $120,000 is excludable and that $80,000 is not.

Findings of Fact

During 1997, petitioner was employed as a television cameraman. In that capacity, on January 15, 1997, petitioner was operating a handheld camera during a basketball game between the Minnesota Timberwolves and the Chicago Bulls. At some point during that game, Dennis Keith Rodman (Mr. Rodman), who was playing for the Chicago Bulls, landed on a group of photographers, including petitioner, and twisted his ankle. Mr. Rodman then kicked petitioner. (We shall refer to the foregoing incident involving Mr. Rodman and petitioner as the incident.)

While petitioner was seeking treatment at Hennepin County Medical Center, he contacted Gale Pearson (Ms. Pearson) about representing him with respect to the incident. Ms. Pearson was an attorney who had experience in representing plaintiffs in personal injury lawsuits. After

---

c. Steven V. Roberts, *Ginsburg Withdraws Name as Supreme Court Nominee, Citing Marijuana 'Clamor'* N.Y. Times (Nov. l8, 1987), 1.

d. Tax makes a difference to defendants as well as plaintiffs. However, since the defendants are the ones doing the paying, it is a question of deduction, not income, and is considered, along with the question of your fees, *infra* at 164 and 490.

subsequent conversations and a meeting with petitioner, Ms. Pearson agreed to represent him with respect to the incident.

On January 15, 1997, after the incident and petitioner's visit to the Hennepin County Medical Center, petitioner filed a report (police report) with the Minneapolis Police Department. In the police report, petitioner claimed that Mr. Rodman had assaulted him.

Very shortly after the incident on a date not disclosed by the record, Andrew Luger (Mr. Luger), an attorney representing Mr. Rodman with respect to the incident, contacted Ms. Pearson. Several discussions and a few meetings took place between Ms. Pearson and Mr. Luger. Petitioner accompanied Ms. Pearson to one of the meetings between her and Mr. Luger, at which time Mr. Luger noticed that petitioner was limping. Shortly after those discussions and meetings, petitioner and Mr. Rodman reached a settlement.

On January 21, 1997, Mr. Rodman and petitioner executed a document entitled "CONFIDENTIAL SETTLEMENT AGREEMENT AND RELEASE" (settlement agreement). The settlement agreement provided in pertinent part:

> For and in consideration of TWO HUNDRED THOUSAND DOL-LARS ($200,000), the mutual waiver of costs, attorneys' fees and legal expenses, if any, and other good and valuable consideration, the receipt and sufficiency of which is hereby acknowledged, Eugene Amos [petitioner], on behalf of himself, his agents, representatives, attorneys, assignees, heirs, executors and administrators, hereby releases and forever discharges Dennis Rodman, the Chicago Bulls, the National Basketball Association and all other persons, firms and corporations together with their subsidiaries, divisions and affiliates, past and present officers, directors, employees, insurers, agents, personal representatives and legal counsel, from any and all claims and causes of action of any type, known and unknown, upon and by reason of any damage, loss or injury which heretofore have been or heretoafter may be sustained by Amos arising, or which could have arisen, out of or in connection with an incident occurring between Rodman and Amos at a game between the Chicago Bulls and the Minnesota Timberwolves on January 15, 1997 during which Rodman allegedly kicked Amos ("the Incident"), including but not limited to any statements made after the Incident or subsequent conduct relating to the Incident by Amos, Rodman, the Chicago Bulls, the National Basketball Association, or any other person, firm or corporation, or any of their subsidiaries, divisions, affiliates, officers, directors, employees, insurers, agents, personal representatives and legal counsel. This Agreement and Release includes, but is not limited to claims, demands, or actions arising under the common law and under any state, federal or local statute, ordinance, regulation or order, including claims known or unknown at this time, concerning any physical,

mental or emotional injuries that may arise in the future allegedly resulting from the Incident.

* * *

It is further understood and agreed that the payment of the sum described herein is not to be construed as an admission of liability and is a compromise of a disputed claim. It is further understood that part of the consideration for this Agreement and Release includes an agreement that Rodman and Amos shall not at any time from the date of this Agreement and Release forward disparage or defame each other.

It is further understood and agreed that, as part of the consideration for this Agreement and Release, the terms of this Agreement and Release shall forever be kept confidential and not released to any news media personnel or representatives thereof or to any other person, entity, company, government agency, publication or judicial authority for any reason whatsoever except to the extent necessary to report the sum paid to appropriate taxing authorities or in response to any subpoena issued by a state or federal governmental agency or court of competent jurisdiction * * * Any court reviewing a subpoena concerning this Agreement and Release should be aware that part of the consideration for the Agreement and Release is the agreement of Amos and his attorneys not to testify regarding the existence of the Agreement and Release or any of its terms.

* * *

It is further understood and agreed that Amos and his representatives, agents, legal counsel or other advisers shall not, from the date of this Agreement and Release, disclose, disseminate, publicize or instigate or solicit any others to disclose, disseminate or publicize, any of the allegations or facts relating to the Incident, including but not limited to any allegations or facts or opinions relating to Amos' potential claims against Rodman or any allegations, facts or opinions relating to Rodman's conduct on the night of January 15, 1997 or thereafter concerning Amos. In this regard, Amos agrees not to make any further public statement relating to Rodman or the Incident or to grant any interviews relating to Rodman or the Incident. * * *

Amos further represents, promises and agrees that no administrative charge or claim or legal action of any kind has been asserted by him or on his behalf in any way relating to the Incident with the exception of a statement given by Amos to the Minneapolis Police Department. Amos further represents, promises and agrees that, as part of the consideration for this Agreement and Release, he has communicated to the Minneapolis Police Department that he does not wish to pursue a criminal charge against Rodman, and that he has communicated that he will not cooperate in any criminal investigation concerning the Incident. Amos further represents, promises and agrees that he will not pursue any criminal action against Rodman concerning the Incident, that he will not cooperate should any such action or investigation ensue, and that he will not encourage, incite or solicit others to pursue a criminal investigation or charge against Rodman concerning the Incident.

Petitioner filed a tax return (return) for his taxable year 1997. In that return, petitioner excluded from his gross income the $200,000 that he received from Mr. Rodman under the settlement agreement.

In the notice that respondent issued to petitioner with respect to 1997, respondent determined that petitioner is not entitled to exclude from his gross income the settlement amount at issue.

Opinion

Where damages are received pursuant to a settlement agreement, such as is the case here, the nature of the claim that was the actual basis for settlement controls whether such damages are excludable under section 104(a)(2). The determination of the nature of the claim is factual. Where there is a settlement agreement, that determination is usually made by reference to it. If the settlement agreement lacks express language stating what the amount paid pursuant to that agreement was to settle, the intent of the payor is critical to that determination. Although the belief of the payee is relevant to that inquiry, the character of the settlement payment hinges ultimately on the dominant reason of the payor in making the payment. Whether the settlement payment is excludable from gross income under section 104(a)(2) depends on the nature and character of the claim asserted, and not upon the validity of that claim.

The dispute between the parties in the instant case relates to how much of the settlement amount at issue Mr. Rodman paid to petitioner on account of physical injuries. It is petitioner's position that the entire $200,000 settlement amount at issue is excludable from his gross income under section 104(a)(2). In support of that position, petitioner contends that Mr. Rodman paid him the entire amount on account of the physical injuries that he claimed he sustained as a result of the incident.

Respondent counters that, except for a nominal amount (i.e., $1), the settlement amount at issue is includable in petitioner's gross income. In support of that position, respondent contends that petitioner has failed to introduce any evidence regarding, and that Mr. Rodman was skeptical about, the extent of petitioner's physical injuries as a result of the incident. Consequently, according to respondent, the Court should infer that petitioner's physical injuries were minimal. * * *

On the instant record, we reject respondent's position. With respect to respondent's contentions that petitioner has failed to introduce evidence regarding, and that Mr. Rodman was skeptical about, the extent of petitioner's physical injuries as a result of the incident, those contentions appear to ignore the well-established principle under section 104(a)(2) that it is the nature and character of the claim settled, and not its validity, that determines whether the settlement payment is excludable from gross income under section 104(a)(2). In any event, we find below that the record establishes that Mr. Rodman's dominant reason in paying the settlement amount at issue was petitioner's claimed physical injuries as a result of the incident.

On the record before us, we find that Mr. Rodman's dominant reason in paying the settlement amount at issue was to compensate petitioner for his claimed physical injuries relating to the incident. Our finding is supported by the settlement agreement, a declaration by Mr. Rodman (Mr. Rodman's declaration),[6] and Ms. Pearson's testimony.

* * *

We have found that Mr. Rodman's dominant reason in paying petitioner the settlement amount at issue was to compensate him for his claimed physical injuries relating to the incident. However, the settlement agreement expressly provided that Mr. Rodman paid petitioner a portion of the settlement amount at issue in return for petitioner's agreement not to: (1) Defame Mr. Rodman, (2) disclose the existence or the terms of the settlement agreement, (3) publicize facts relating to the incident, or (4) assist in any criminal prosecution against Mr. Rodman with respect to the incident (collectively, the nonphysical injury provisions).

The settlement agreement does not specify the portion of the settlement amount at issue that Mr. Rodman paid petitioner on account of his claimed physical injuries and the portion of such amount that Mr. Rodman paid petitioner on account of the nonphysical injury provisions in the settlement agreement. Nonetheless, based upon our review of the entire record before us, and bearing in mind that petitioner has the burden of proving the amount of the settlement amount at issue that Mr. Rodman paid him on account of physical injuries, we find that Mr. Rodman paid petitioner $120,000 of the settlement amount at issue on account of petitioner's claimed physical injuries and $80,000 of that amount on account of the nonphysical injury provisions in the settlement agreement. On that record, we further find that for the year at issue petitioner is entitled under section 104(a)(2) to exclude from his gross income $120,000 of the settlement amount at issue and is required under section 61(a) to include in his gross income $80,000 of that amount.

QUESTIONS

1. As to Mr. Rodman, was there anything else about him left to defame?

2. How well did Ms. Pearson represent Mr. Amos?

---

6. The parties introduced into evidence a declaration by Mr. Rodman, who did not appear as a witness at trial. The parties stipulated the accuracy and truthfulness of Mr. Rodman's statements in that declaration.

Limerick

By Michael Robbins, WFU Law Class of 2009

Dennis Rodman is not very small

Dennis Rodman had a great fall

He went up for the slam-a
Crashed into the camera

And kicked the poor man in the leg.

PROBLEMS

Determine the tax consequences of the judgment or settlement in each of these cases.

1. Laura is injured in an automobile accident. She sues for medical expenses, pain and suffering, emotional trauma, lost wages, and punitive damages.

a) She wins a court judgment. Which of the damages should be taxable?

b) She settles. Any difference?

2. Eric looks out the window just in time to see a drunk driver run over Eric's child. Eric suffers a heart attack, and is awarded money damages from the driver.

3. Meg and Employer sign an employment contract, which provides that Meg will work for one year for $50,000. Employer reneges, saying he's found someone better. Meg finds another job which pays $45,000. She sues Employer, and wins a court judgment for $5,000. Will she be taxed on the judgment damages?

4. After six months of intense effort, Claude finishes his oil painting, entitled, "There Is No God," and displays it for sale. Claude hopes to sell his masterpiece for $25,000. Jacques, deeply offended by the painting, breaks into the gallery and destroys it. Claude sues Jacques, and wins a judgment for $18,000.

5. Nadine rents a room from Homeowner, and pays a year's rent in advance. Homeowner's Son is a member of a rock band, and they rehearse in the room right above Nadine's. Nadine, a law student and a lover of baroque harpsichord music, finds the situation untenable. She sues for constructive eviction (essentially a claim for breach of the lease contract). What are the tax consequences to Nadine if she wins money damages, plus a promise by Homeowner to soundproof his Son's room?

6. Your client was been falsely accused of committing adultery with another man's wife. The irate husband assaulted your client, causing significant physical injuries. The irate husband also published his allegations in the local newspaper. Your client sues for $1 million for the physical injuries and the resultant lost wages, and for an additional $1 million for personal libel. Defendant, through his lawyer, has offered to settle for $100,000. Your client wants to accept. What do you advise your client about taxes?

7. Client wants to retain Trial Lawyer in a litigation matter. Trial Lawyer proposes to put language in his written retainer agreement that:

1) he will provide no tax advice whatsoever to Client; and

2) he will not take tax considerations into account at all when considering litigation strategy.

Trial Lawyer proposes to reduce his fee in exchange for limiting the scope of his representation in this manner.

Can he do it? Compare Model Rules of Professional Responsibility 1.2(c) and 1.8(h).

E.   TAX EXEMPT BONDS

Code: § 103(a)

As you will see, tax exempt bonds will be addressed here only as a vehicle for learning about tax expenditure analysis, which is a tool for evaluating tax laws in policy terms. For this purpose, you need to know only one thing. The interest paid on most bonds issued by state and local governments is not taxable by the federal government.

Tax Expenditure Analysis

The going rate of return on corporate bonds is ten per cent. Private investor is in the 35% tax bracket. She buys a $1,000 bond paying 10% interest. What will she earn on her investment in the first year, after tax?

Your state needs the use of $1,000 for one year, and would like to attract that investor to buy a state bond. What interest rate will the state have to pay to make its bond just as attractive to this investor as the private bond?

Assume that the investor in fact buys the state bond. In the first year, how much tax revenue has the federal government lost?

How much interest expense has the state government saved?

Expenditures are tested by cost/benefit analysis. They pass the test if the benefits from the expenditure are at least equal to the cost. Does this tax expenditure pass?

Do the analysis again, but now assume that the investor is in the 25% tax bracket. Is the tax expenditure still efficient?

Now, inject some reality. The state needs millions of dollars, not thousands. In order to attract the investment it needs, it must attract both 35% bracket taxpayers and 25% bracket taxpayers. What interest rate will attract both? Now is the federal tax expenditure efficient?

In the early 1970's, the average tax bracket of investors who purchased tax exempt bonds was 45%. On average, interest rates on tax exempt bonds were 30% lower than interest rates on taxable bonds. Assume a market rate of 10% on private bonds and a $1,000 bond. How much tax revenue does the federal government lose, and how much interest does the state save? Do the analysis again.

CHAPTER IV

BUSINESS DEDUCTIONS: BASIC PRINCIPLES

■ ■ ■

Often, it takes money to make money. Of course a tax on net income would allow for business deductions. How could it not?

This chapter deals with the easiest case—trade or business expenses. Admittedly, even these deductions, mostly grounded in § 162, have their complications. However, at least the deductibility of the general category is clear.

Other chapters will deal will more problematic cases for deductions, such as mixed-motive personal and business expenses (Chapter 8, *infra*), and purely personal expenses (Chapter 10, *infra*). In this chapter, the expenses are claimed to be downright, no kidding business expenses. Therefore, at least here, you know where you stand.

The expenses described here get by far the best tax treatment. Since they are "above the line," they will reduce your tax bill no matter what. Mixed-motive and personal expenses, if deductible at all, are often "below the line," and thus may or may not actually reduce your tax bill. If your interest is piqued, you might have a quick glance at the materials on the Standard Deduction and Adjusted Gross Income in Chapter X, *infra*. They will tell you what "the line" is. Otherwise, you can be content for the moment to know that the § 162 deductions get by far the best treatment.

Code: § 162(a)

A. GENERAL

A Gross Income Tax

Consider the following bill:

97TH CONGRESS S.2200 2d SESSION IN THE SENATE OF THE UNITED STATES

March 15 (legislative day, February 22), 1982.

Mr. HELMS introduced the following bill; which was read twice and referred to the Committee on Finance

---

A Bill

To amend the Internal Revenue Code of 1954 to provide that a 10–percent income tax rate shall apply to all individuals, and to repeal all deductions, credits, and exclusions for individuals other than a $2,000 deduction for each personal exemption.

Be it enacted by the Senate and House of Representatives of the United States of America in Congress assembled,

SECTION 1. SHORT TITLE.

This Act may be cited as the "Flat Rate Tax Act of 1982".

SECTION 2. 10 PERCENT INCOME TAX RATE FOR ALL INDIVIDUALS.

Section 1 of the Internal Revenue Code of 1954 (relating to tax imposed on individuals) is amended to read as follows:

"SECTION 1. TAX IMPOSED."

"There is hereby imposed on the gross income of each individual (including an estate and trust) for each taxable year a tax equal to 10 percent of such gross income."

SECTION 3. REPEAL OF ALL SPECIAL DEDUCTIONS, CREDITS, AND EXCLUSIONS FROM INCOME FOR INDIVIDUALS OTHER THAN $2,000 DEDUCTION FOR PERSONAL EXEMPTIONS.

(a) IN GENERAL.—Chapter 1 of the Internal Revenue Code of 1954 is amended by striking out all specific exclusions from gross income, all deductions, and all credits against income tax to the extent related to the computation of individual income tax liability.

(b) ALLOWANCE OF $2,000 DEDUCTION FOR PERSONAL EXEMPTIONS.—

(1) SUBSECTION (a) NOT TO APPLY.—Subsection (a) shall not apply to the deductions allowed by section 151 (relating to deductions for personal exemptions).

* * *

QUESTION

Imagine two taxpayers, Mr. Jones and Mr. Smith. Mr. Jones is the sole beneficiary of a trust. His annual income from the trust is $100,000.

Trust income	$100,000
Business expenses	− $ 0
Disposable income	$100,000

Mr. Smith owns a barber shop. His gross receipts are $100,000. However, he incurs the following expenses:

Rent	$20,000
Advertising	$ 5,000
Employee Salaries	$35,000
Total Expenses	$60,000

Therefore, his disposable income is $40,000:

Gross sales	$100,000
Business expenses	− $ 60,000
Disposable income	$ 40,000

The proposed bill would tax both Mr. Jones and Mr. Smith on $100,000. Do they have the same ability to pay taxes?

It is generally agreed that net income, not gross income, is the only fair way to measure ability to pay in an income tax. We must recognize that it is the net profits, not the gross receipts, which give us a workable measurement. Therefore, all major income taxes allow deductions for business expenses.

NOTE: BUSINESS VS. PERSONAL DEDUCTIONS

Imagine two taxpayers, Ms. White and Ms. Green. Both have income, net of business expenses, of $50,000. Ms. White lives in a cardboard box, eats only gruel, and has two outfits of clothing, one for cold weather and one for warm weather. To launder her clothes, she sneaks into a children's park after hours. She bangs her clothes on the concrete, and then rinses them in the wading pool. Her personal expenses are $500 per year. She saves $49,500 per year.

Ms. Green lives in the nicest home she can afford. She also buys the best food and clothing, and entertains herself to the very limit of her income. Her personal expenses, when she is careful, amount to $50,000 per year. She saves nothing.

If personal expenses were deductible, then Ms. White would be taxable on:

Gross Income	$50,000
Personal Expenses	− $ 500
Net Taxable Income	$49,500

Ms. Green would be taxable on:

Gross Income	$50,000
Personal Expenses	− $50,000
Net Taxable Income	$ 0

There are two problems with this result. First, most would agree that one's personal lifestyle choices should not affect one's tax bill. Second, even those who would allow personal lifestyle choices to affect taxation would hardly want to do it this way. Note that this result would encourage profligate spending, and discourage saving.

Therefore, it is in the nature of a tax on net income that business expenses are deductible, and personal expenses, subject to narrow exceptions, are not. Note that this structural tendency puts a great deal of pressure on the distinction between business expenditures and personal expenditures. This problem is discussed at Chapter 8, *infra*.

NOTE: MUST BUSINESS DEDUCTIONS BE REASONABLE?

Code: § 162(a)

Imagine that a businessperson decides to set up a frozen yogurt stand. Of course, he must rent a facility. He wants his business to have a certain class, so he rents the entire Sears Tower in Chicago. He continues to live in his modest home, and goes to the Sears Tower only to conduct his business. After one year of operation, his income statement is:

Gross Receipts from Frozen Yogurt Sales	$ 50,000
Cost of Goods Sold	− $ 10,000
Rent	− $100,000,000
Profit or Loss	($99,960,000)

He decides to terminate operations after one year.

Should his rent be deductible? Yes. First, note the presence of the word "reasonable" in § 162(a)(1) [referring to deductible compensation], the words "lavish or extravagant" in § 162(a)(2) [referring to travel expenses], and the absence of any comparable language in the general provision of § 162(a). It would appear that Congress wants to limit only those deductions described in §§ 162(a)(1) and 162(a)(2) to reasonable (nonlavish) expenses, but not the others.

Second, taxpayers should have the right to make bad business decisions. If they do so, their punishment should be that they lose money, not that they are taxed on their gross income rather than their net income. We do not need the Internal Revenue Code to police bad business decisions. The market will do that. Incurring larger business expenses than necessary will mean that the taxpayer makes less profit. Isn't that punishment enough?

Finally, a general limitation of business deductions to those which are reasonable under the circumstances would foment unnecessary litigation, and give IRS a task for which it has little competence—that of judging business behavior rather than measuring its results.

NOTE: INTRODUCTION TO MATCHING

Code: §§ 263, 167, 168

Imagine a businessman who buys a business machine for $500. The machine is used to generate income of $200 per year for five years. At the end of the fifth year, the machine abruptly crumbles into dust.

Here are three ways in which the businessman could describe what happened:

Method 1

Year	1	2	3	4	5
Income	$200	$200	$200	$200	$200
Expenses	− $500	− $ 0	− $ 0	− $ 0	− $ 0
Profits	($300)	$200	$200	$200	$200

This method reflects the flow of cash. The message: I had a rocky start, but then things improved, and I had four years of steady, handsome profits.

Method 2

Year	1	2	3	4	5
Income	$200	$200	$200	$200	$200
Expenses	− $0	− $0	− $0	− $0	− $500
Profit	$200	$200	$200	$200	($300)

This method reflects the treatment of basis which we have studied so far. Basis is subtracted only at the end, when the asset is exchanged or discarded. The message: I had four years of steady, handsome profits. Then, in the final year, I experienced a financial disaster.

Method 3

Year	1	2	3	4	5
Income	$200	$200	$200	$200	$200
Expenses	− $100	− $100	− $100	− $100	− $100
Profits	$100	$100	$100	$100	$100

This method recognizes the fact that the $500 expenditure on the machine was responsible for generating income in all five years. Therefore, the cost is spread out over the period during which the income was generated. The message: I had five pretty good years.

Method 3 applies the concept of matching. Expenses must be matched up with the income which they generate. The matching concept is a necessary tool of business accounting, and would be required even if there were no income tax. A fair net income tax, however, must apply the matching concept if it is to measure net income correctly.

The tax laws apply the matching concept in § 263. A "capital expense" is, inter alia, an expense which is likely to generate income for more than one year. Such an expense should not be deductible in full in one year. Rather, it should be spread out, and matched with the income it generates.

Section 263 ensures that a capital expense will not all be deducted in the year incurred. The task of spreading it out to the proper years is effected, or at least attempted, by depreciation deductions, set forth in §§ 167 and 168. We will revisit depreciation later.

B. WELCH AND ITS PROGENY

Code: § 162(a)

In reading the *Welch* case, you will note that Mr. Justice Cardozo considered the possibility that the expenditure in question was a capital expense. Why? Was that the only ground for his decision?

WELCH v. HELVERING

United States Supreme Court, 1933.
290 U.S. 111, 54 S.Ct. 8, 78 L.Ed. 212.

MR. JUSTICE CARDOZO delivered the opinion of the Court.

The question to be determined is whether payments by a taxpayer, who is in business as a commission agent, are allowable deductions in the computation of his income if made to the creditors of a bankrupt corporation in an endeavor to strengthen his own standing and credit.

In 1922 petitioner was the secretary of the E.L. Welch Company, a Minnesota corporation, engaged in the grain business. The company was adjudged an involuntary bankrupt, and had a discharge from its debts. Thereafter the petitioner made a contract with the Kellogg Company to purchase grain for it on a commission. In order to re-establish his relations with customers whom he had known when acting for the Welch Company and to solidify his credit and standing, he decided to pay the debts of the Welch business so far as he was able. In fulfillment of that resolve, he made payments of substantial amounts during five successive years. In 1924, the commissions were $18,028.20, the payments $3,975.97;

in 1925, the commissions $31,377.07, the payments $11,968.20; in 1926, the commissions $20,925.25, the payments $12,815.72; in 1927, the commissions $22,119.61, the payments $7,379.72; and in 1928, the commissions $26,177.56, the payments $11,068.25. The Commissioner ruled that these payments were not deductible from income as ordinary and necessary expenses, but were rather in the nature of capital expenditures, an outlay for the development of reputation and good will. The Board of Tax Appeals sustained the action of the Commissioner and the Court of Appeals for the Eighth Circuit affirmed. The case is here on certiorari.
* * *

We may assume that the payments to creditors of the Welch Company were necessary for the development of the petitioner's business, at least in the sense that they were appropriate and helpful. He certainly thought they were, and we should be slow to override his judgment. But the problem is not solved when the payments are characterized as necessary. Many necessary payments are charges upon capital. There is need to determine whether they are both necessary and ordinary. Now, what is ordinary, though there must always be a strain of constancy within it, is none the less a variable affected by time and place and circumstance. Ordinary in this context does not mean that the payments must be habitual or normal in the sense that the same taxpayer will have to make them often. A lawsuit affecting the safety of a business may happen once in a lifetime. The counsel fees may be so heavy that repetition is unlikely. None the less, the expense is an ordinary one because we know from experience that payments for such a purpose, whether the amount is large or small, are the common and accepted means of defense against attack. The situation is unique in the life of the individual affected, but not in the life of the group, the community, of which he is a part. At such times there are norms of conduct that help to stabilize our judgment, and make it certain and objective. The instance is not erratic, but is brought within a known type.

The line of demarcation is now visible between the case that is here and the one supposed for illustration. We try to classify this act as ordinary or the opposite, and the norms of conduct fail us. No longer can we have recourse to any fund of business experience, to any known business practice. Men do at times pay the debts of others without legal obligation or the lighter obligation imposed by the usages of trade or by neighborly amenities, but they do not do so ordinarily, not even though the result might be to heighten their reputation for generosity and opulence. Indeed, if language is to be read in its natural and common meaning, we should have to say that payment in such circumstances, instead of being ordinary is in a high degree extraordinary. There is nothing ordinary in the stimulus evoking it, and none in the response. Here, indeed, as so often in other branches of the law, the decisive distinctions are those of degree and not of kind. One struggles in vain for any verbal formula that will supply a ready touchstone. The standard set up by the statute is not a rule of law; it is rather a way of life. Life in all its fullness must supply the answer to the riddle.

The Commissioner of Internal Revenue resorted to that standard in assessing the petitioner's income, and found that the payments in controversy came closer to capital outlays than to ordinary and necessary expenses in the operation of a business. His ruling has the support of a presumption of correctness, and the petitioner has the burden of proving it to be wrong. Unless we can say from facts within our knowledge that these are ordinary and necessary expenses according to the ways of conduct and the forms of speech prevailing in the business world, the tax must be confirmed. But nothing told us by this record or within the sphere of our judicial notice permits us to give that extension to what is ordinary and necessary. Indeed, to do so would open the door to many bizarre analogies. One man has a family name that is clouded by thefts committed by an ancestor. To add to this own standing he repays the stolen money, wiping off, it may be, his income for the year. The payments figure in his tax return as ordinary expenses. Another man conceives the notion that he will be able to practice his vocation with greater ease and profit if he has an opportunity to enrich his culture. Forthwith the price of his education becomes an expense of the business, reducing the income subject to taxation. There is little difference between these expenses and those in controversy here. Reputation and learning are akin to capital assets, like the good will of an old partnership. For many, they are the only tools with which to hew a pathway to success. The money spent in acquiring them is well and wisely spent. It is not an ordinary expense of the operation of a business.

Many cases in the federal courts deal with phases of the problem presented in the case at bar. To attempt to harmonize them would be a futile task. They involve the appreciation of particular situations, at times with border-line conclusions. * * *

The decree should be

Affirmed.

QUESTIONS, NOTES

1. In 1872, Albert Cardozo resigned in disgrace from the New York Supreme Court, amid allegations of corruption. Sixteen years later, his son Benjamin decided that he had to become a lawyer, as it was the only way to clear his family name. Does anything sound familiar?

2. What does "necessary" mean? Does it have the same meaning as it does in the sentence, "It is necessary for humans to breathe."? If not, why not?

3. What does "ordinary" mean?

• What evidence does Justice Cardozo give that "ordinary" is the opposite of "capital"?

The Supreme Court granted certiorari due to a conflict in the circuits between *Welch* and A. Harris & Co. v. Lucas, 48 F.2d 187 (5th Cir.1931). In *A. Harris & Co.*, a retailer experienced financial difficulties, and reached a composition with creditors. After the composition, none of Harris & Co.'s suppliers would do business with it except on a cash up front basis. Harris & Co. was unable to do business that way. Upon seeking advice, Harris & Co. was told to repay its debts in full, despite the composition with creditors. Then, suppliers would grant it credit once again. It did, and they did.

In the Eighth Circuit, *Welch* distinguished *A. Harris & Co.* for two reasons. First, the composition with creditors in *A. Harris & Co.* was not the same as the bankruptcy in *Welch*. Pursuant to the law in the early 1930's, bankruptcy brought about the total extinction of the entity. In contrast, a composition with creditors did not.

Second, in *A. Harris & Co.*, the expenditures were incurred during the existence of a business. In *Welch*, by contrast, the bankruptcy had caused the end of one business, and the beginning of another. Expenditures which happen at the beginning of a business tend to be capital. Neither of these distinctions appears in Justice Cardozo's opinion.

- What evidence does he give that "ordinary" is the opposite of "extraordinary" or "bizarre"?

For authority that expenses are deductible if common to the industry, see Lilly v. Commissioner, 343 U.S. 90, 72 S.Ct. 497, 96 L.Ed. 769 (1952) [kickbacks are deductible because commonly paid in the optical industry]; United Draperies v. Commissioner, 340 F.2d 936 (7th Cir.1964) *cert. denied*, 382 U.S. 813, 86 S.Ct. 30, 15 L.Ed.2d 61 (1965) [kickbacks are nondeductible because not commonly paid in the drapery manufacturing industry].

For nondeductible, bizarre expenditures, see Goedel v. Commissioner, 39 B.T.A. 1 (1939) [taxpayer purchases insurance on the life of President Roosevelt, for fear that, if the President were to die, taxpayer's investments would decline in value] and A. Giurlani & Bro. v. Commissioner, 41 B.T.A. 403 (1940) *aff'd*, 119 F.2d 852 (9th Cir.1941) [taxpayer pays off the debts of its Italian olive oil supplier, arguing that no other olive oil would satisfy its customers].

For further thoughts on bizarre expenditures, *see Amend* and *Trebilcock*, *infra*.

- What evidence does Justice Cardozo give that "ordinary" connotes "ordinary business," to be distinguished from "ordinary personal"?

Do the facts of *Welch* satisfy any of these definitions of "ordinary"?

Code: §§ 162(a), 262

FRED W. AMEND CO. v. COMMISSIONER OF INTERNAL REVENUE

United States Court of Appeals, Seventh Circuit, 1971.
454 F.2d 399.

The petitioner-appellant, Fred W. Amend Co. (hereinafter referred to as taxpayer), prosecutes this appeal from a decision of the Tax Court which sustained the disallowance by the Commissioner of Internal Revenue, respondent-appellee, of deductions in the amounts of $5,500 and $6,200, respectively, claimed by the taxpayer on its income tax returns for its fiscal years ended October 31, 1964, and 1965. The disallowance resulted in the assessment of income tax deficiencies for those years. The deductions represent payments made by the taxpayer corporation to R. M. Halverstadt, a Christian Science practitioner, which taxpayer claimed as business expenses.

* * * Taxpayer, an Illinois corporation, manufactures and distributes jellied candies. It was organized by Fred W. Amend in 1921. He held the offices of president and treasurer until 1956 when his son-in-law became president. Amend remained as treasurer and became chairman of the board of directors. During the years in question Amend and his wife owned approximately 47 1/2 per cent of the corporation's common stock. Unrelated stockholders held but 29% of such stock. Although Amend had reached the age of 73 years he enjoyed very good health and remained active in a supervisory role with respect to the corporation's business activities.

Beginning in 1954, Amend had utilized the services of R. M. Halverstadt, a Christian Science practitioner, for consultations with respect to personal and business problems. Charges for consultations were ordinarily three dollars. The taxpayer reimbursed Amend for such consultations that related to business problems. In 1961 the taxpayer adopted a resolution authorizing Amend to arrange for the employment of a Christian Science practitioner by the company on such terms as Amend considered appropriate and in the best interests of the corporation, the practitioner to serve: "as a consultant for employees with respect to matters which so disturb them as to handicap them in performing their services for the company, and also as a consultant of the officers as to the best approach to corporate problems." Amend thereupon retained Halverstadt for the taxpayer and fixed his compensation at $400 per month. Amend increased the compensation to $5,500 per year for 1964 and then later to $6,200. None of the taxpayer's lower ranking employees were informed of the service available from Halverstadt. And, of the taxpayer's executives, only Amend availed himself of the service. * * * During the tax years in question, the business problems Amend brought to Halverstadt's attention related to personnel, office relationships, sales, production, new machinery, financing and labor relations. The practitioner offered no specific or concrete solutions. His procedure was to so interrogate Amend as to bring out the different elements involved, and thus to clarify Amend's thinking. In addition, Halverstadt relied upon the power of prayer to bring enlightenment concerning the problems to Amend and the taxpayer. He testified to daily prayerful intercession on behalf of the taxpayer's organization; that he prayed for a solution to the given problem through spiritual clarification— that Amend or the taxpayer's organization be given the right idea.

The taxpayer's secretary and general counsel testified that, in his opinion, the consultations tended to produce in Amend a more detached and calm mind, judgments less affected by emotions, a better grasp of the subject matter and generally sound decisions, all of which resulted in benefit to the taxpayer.

The Tax Court found that through the insight provided by Halverstadt's interrogation Amend was enabled to approach problems with detachment and new understanding but that Halverstadt never offered concrete solutions to any of the matters discussed. Instead, that after exploring a problem via the questioning process, Halverstadt, through prayer sought to invoke the presence of the Divine Mind—the spiritual awareness according to Christian Science teachings.

It is apparent that Halverstadt offered no business advice, as such. The Tax Court concluded that it was not Amend's skills as a businessman which Halverstadt sought to enhance. Rather, what was sought was a state of harmony in which Amend's business thinking would be brought into conformity with an ordered universe governed by the Christian Science concept of the Divine Mind. Accordingly, the court concluded that the benefits derived from Halverstadt's services were inherently personal to Amend, and thus by virtue of the proscription of Section 262 not susceptible to qualification as "business expenses" under Section 162. * * *

The taxpayer urges, in substance, that because its business problems created the occasions for and were the origin of the services performed by Halverstadt in connection with Amend's consultations with Halverstadt, this factor serves to distinguish the expense here involved[3] from a personal expense attributable to Amend and qualify it for deduction as an ordinary and necessary business expense of the corporation. But the taxpayer overlooks that "origin" alone is not the sole determinative factor. While it is a basic restriction upon the availability of a Section 162 deduction that the expense item involved must be one that has a business origin, and must be one directly connected with or proximately resulting from a business activity of the taxpayer, the inquiry does not end there. It is of equal importance that the nature of the particular expense is such that places it beyond the thrust of the bar of Section 262. United States v. Gilmore. And, with respect to this latter factor, we are of the opinion that the record herein amply supports the finding and conclusion of the Tax

---

3. The record discloses that Amend personally paid Halverstadt for those consultations during the tax years here involved which did not relate to a business problem of the corporation.

Court that the services performed by Halverstadt were by their nature inherently personal to Amend.

We have considered the additional contentions made by the taxpayer but find them equally without merit. Taxpayer's alternative argument that the expenditures are deductible as an addition to the regular compensation paid Amend is without support on the record. There is no evidence that the payments to Halverstadt were intended as compensation to Amend. And, apart from the question of whether the issue was properly raised below, taxpayer's additional argument that the payments it made to Halverstadt qualify as a "medical expense" business deduction is unpersuasive. Amend testified that he enjoyed very good health and that all of the taxpayer's personnel was covered by adequate medical and hospital insurance supplied by the taxpayer through an insurance carrier.

The decision of the Tax Court is affirmed.

Affirmed.

QUESTIONS, NOTES

1.   The court notes that the corporation reimbursed Mr. Amend only for business consultations. Mr. Amend was careful to pay for personal consultations with Rev. Halverstadt out of his own pocket [See footnote 3 of the opinion.] Yet, the court characterized the consultations for which a deduction was claimed as personal expenses.

Consider the following testimony from the trial court record:

Mr. Amend: Well, I can tell you what I was bellyaching about, but I cannot give you his (Halverstadt's) reply. We were getting about 325 cases a day out of one of those big machines and we should have been getting 700. Every time we did everything, we would just about get it up to running right and then something would happen. I don't know whether we had a jinx or not. I kept going to him on that, and I know within a short, a very short time, we were getting out 800 cases a day.

Is there anything personal about the number of cases a machine can produce?

2.   Executive is concerned about the productivity of her workforce. She hires a consultant. The consultant observes the workplace, and concludes that there is too much tension and distraction. She recommends Muzak. Is the consultant's fee deductible? Is the monthly Muzak fee deductible?

3.   Businessman gets rid of his original office furniture, all purchased second hand. In its place, he rents the most expensive office furniture he can find. In addition, he throws out the Norman Rockwell prints and rents an original Renoir to hang on the wall.

A tastefully decorated office puts him in a better frame of mind to make good business decisions, he says. What is more, when clients see his expensive office, they assume that he is successful. Therefore, they are much more inclined to respect his advice, and bring him more business.

Are these expenditures deductible?

4. In Heineman v. Commissioner, 82 T.C. 538 (1984), the CEO of a large corporation headquartered in Chicago spent some $250,000 constructing a twenty foot by twenty foot single room office suspended by a cantilevered steel frame from the side of a limestone cliff in Sister Bay, Wisconsin. The CEO used his new office every August for long range planning. He said he needed time to think. The Tax Court held the expenses of his office to be deductible.

5. In order to provide the on-line banking which its customers demand, a large bank in Charlotte, North Carolina has scrambled to recruit the requisite computer programmers. The programmers, it seems, are not quite like the other bank employees. In order to attract them, the bank has created "meditation rooms" in its bank headquarters—large, open rooms with not much furniture. Do you suppose that the banks are deducting the costs of maintaining these rooms?

6. Consider § 132(j)(4). How are Amend's expenditures different from the Muzak, the furniture, and those described in that section?

7. The court notes that Rev. Halverstadt did not provide specific answers to business questions. In fact, Christian Science ministers are not supposed to give direct advice, whether about business or personal problems, whether about medical problems or otherwise.

Have you ever been in a situation in which you paid substantial sums to discuss things with someone who asked many questions and rarely provided answers? How much tuition are you paying now? Mr. Amend didn't get concrete answers; neither do you. How dumb was he? How dumb are you?

TREBILCOCK v. COMMISSIONER

United States Tax Court, 1975.
64 T.C. 852, *aff'd*, 557 F.2d 1226 (6th Cir. 1977).

WILES, JUDGE:

Respondent determined deficiencies in petitioners' income tax of $2,658 for 1969 and $2,914 for 1970. The issue is whether Lionel Trebilcock (hereinafter petitioner), a sole proprietor, may deduct under section 162(a) $7,020 he paid in each of those years to a minister who provided spiritual advice to petitioner and his employees and performed business-related tasks.

Findings of Fact

* * * During 1969 and 1970, petitioner was sole proprietor of Litco Products (hereinafter Litco), which engaged in the brokerage of wood products. He employed five people: his father, his brother, a secretary, a traveling salesman, and the Rev. James Wardrop (hereinafter Wardrop).

Petitioner met Wardrop, an ordained minister, in the early 1950's. Before 1968, he sought Wardrop's advice but paid him no fee except reimbursement for expenses. In early 1968, however, petitioner began paying Wardrop $585 per month. In 1969 and 1970, petitioner continued paying Wardrop $585 per month, or $7,020 per year, primarily to minister spiritually to petitioner and his employees. Wardrop conducted prayer meetings, at which he tried to raise the level of spiritual awareness of the participants, and counseled petitioner and individual employees concerning their business and personal problems. When he offered advice about business problems it was not based upon his knowledge of the brokerage business for he had no such knowledge. Rather, he would receive a problem, turn to God in prayer, and then propose an answer resulting from that prayer. Wardrop was not assigned specific secular or nonreligious duties in 1969 and 1970, but he did perform certain business-related tasks. For example, he visited sawmills with petitioner, ran errands, and mailed materials for Litco.

Petitioner and his wife deducted the $7,020 paid to Wardrop in both 1969 and 1970 as an ordinary and necessary business expense under section 162(a).

Ultimate Finding of Fact

Only $1,000 of the $7,020 paid Wardrop in each year was deductible under section 162(a).

Opinion

* * *

* * * Wardrop performed four types of services; we will treat each of them in turn. When he conducted prayer meetings, this Court's opinion in *Amend* must control and therefore a portion of the deduction must be disallowed. Halverstadt tried to induce a new spiritual awareness in Amend, and Wardrop did essentially the same for petitioner and his employees. The benefits that petitioner and his employees received are personal in nature and so the proscription of section 262 must be invoked.

When Wardrop counseled petitioner and his employees about personal problems, *Amend* does not strictly apply for it did not concern personal problems. But section 262 must be invoked since the benefits derived from Wardrop's consultations were personal in nature.

When Wardrop counseled petitioner and his employees about business problems the weight of *Amend* is uncertain for in *Amend* Halverstadt offered no specific solutions to given problems while in this case Wardrop did. However, we need not decide the applicability of Amend since the deduction for this particular task is otherwise disallowed. The solutions Wardrop offered were not based upon his expertise in the brokerage of wood products; he admits he had no such expertise. Rather, his solutions came through prayer from God. A deduction under section 162(a) is allowed for all ordinary and necessary expenses paid or incurred during the taxable year in carrying on a trade or business. "Ordinary," as used in section 162(a), refers to items which arise from "transactions * * * of common or frequent occurrence in the type of business involved." "Ordinary has the connotation of normal, usual, or customary." Petitioner has offered no proof that his payments to Wardrop for solutions to business problems, considering the method Wardrop used, were "ordinary" in his type of business. We hold that petitioner has failed to carry his burden of proof. Therefore the deduction for payments attributable to this service must also be disallowed.

Although petitioner did not assign Wardrop specific secular duties, there is no dispute that Wardrop visited sawmills, ran errands, mailed materials, and performed various other business-related tasks. A deduction under section 162 is allowable for payments made to Wardrop for performing such tasks. The record provides no specific allocation between these deductible payments and those which have been disallowed. We thus apply the rule in Cohan v. Commissioner, which is essentially that certainty in determining expenses is usually impossible but that as close an approximation as possible should be made if the taxpayer had genuinely allowable expenses. Looking at the record as a whole, we think $1,000 in each year was payment for services related to business activities.

We accordingly hold that $1,000 is deductible in both 1969 and 1970 under section 162 and that the remaining $6,020 for each year is nondeductible under section 262.

NOTE, QUESTIONS

1. How is *Trebilcock* different from *Amend*?

2. Consider the following excerpt from the trial court transcript in *Trebilcock*:

Testimony of Albert Thomas [Litco salesman]:

> Q: ... In direct examination, you testified that you contacted Reverend Wardrop with respect to customers that you were concerned about. You also spoke of lost customers. What sorts of advice or help would Reverend Wardrop give you when you contacted him about those subjects?
>
> A: Well, I'd call him and I'd ask him to reach out and touch God, to look for answers, for guidance and give me through his prayer, help in answering the problem to regain that lost customer or to better do my work. To face my day with more confidence.
>
> . . . .
>
> Q: When you posed a business or a personal problem, to Reverend Wardrop, did he offer a specific solution, a course of action that you should take?
>
> A: You must understand, that when I would ask him, I would tell him about a specific problem, he would not give me an answer, he would take it to God in prayer. The next day or later on in the week, he would give an answer, advice through his prayer. He might be on his knees, several hours seeking for an answer.

Even if it is conceded that Reverend Wardrop was not, himself, an expert, didn't he consult one? Must all business consultants be certified as experts in some way for their bills to be deductible? Who is the IRS to determine who gives good advice and who doesn't?

3. In Hawaii, at one time, many construction workers refused to begin work on a job site unless the site had been blessed by a minister. If an accident later occurred on the site, the workers would refuse to return unless the site were reconsecrated. Would the minister's fees have been deductible? [Would they at least have been added to the basis of the building?]

JENKINS v. COMMISSIONER

United States Tax Court, 1983.
T.C. Memo. 1983–667.

Memorandum Findings of Fact and Opinion

Irwin, Judge:

* * *

Opinion

The sole issue presented for our decision is whether payments made by petitioner to investors in a failed corporation known as Twitty Burger, Inc., are deductible as ordinary and necessary business expenses of petitioner's business as a country music performer.

The general rule is that a shareholder may not deduct a payment made on behalf of the corporation but rather must treat it as a capital expenditure. However, the payment may be deducted if it is an ordinary and necessary expense of a trade or business of the shareholder. Lohrke v. Commissioner, 48 T.C. 679 (1967).

* * *

An exception to the general rule that one person may not deduct the expenses of another person has been recognized in those cases where the expenditures sought to be deducted were made by a taxpayer to protect or promote his own ongoing business, even though the transaction originated with another person.

In Lohrke v. Commissioner, the taxpayer was allowed a deduction for a payment made on behalf of a corporation in which he had a substantial interest. The corporation had made a shipment of defective fiber produced by a patented process owned by the taxpayer personally and from which he derived significant income. The petitioner believed that if he did not personally reimburse the customers' losses his personal business reputation would be harmed in that the corporation's involvement in the transaction might become known to the entire synthetic fiber industry. The petitioner's surname constituted a portion of the corporation's name and the taxpayer had never attempted to separate his activities as an inventor from his activities as president of the corporation to any member of the industry.

We noted in *Lohrke* that in a number of cases the courts have allowed deductions for expenditures made by a taxpayer to protect or promote his own business even though the transaction originated with another person and that the resulting expenditures would have been deductible by that other person if payment had been made by him. After a fairly exhaustive review of many of the cases dealing with this issue, the Court stated as follows:

> The tests as established by all of these cases are that we must first ascertain the purpose or motive which cause the taxpayer to pay the obligations of the other person. Once we have identified that motive, we must then judge whether it is an ordinary and necessary expense of the individual's trade or business; that is, is it an appropriate expenditure for the furtherance or promotion of that trade or business? If so, the expense is deductible by the individual paying it.

Applying this test to the facts in *Lohrke*, we found that the taxpayer was of the opinion that his failure to assume the corporate obligation would have adversely affected his licensing business because of the harm that would have resulted to his own reputation. Because we believed that the petitioner's primary motive was the protection of his personal licensing business and that the payment was proximately related to that business, the deduction was allowed as an ordinary and necessary business expense. * * *

We turn now to the case at bar. The question presented is whether one person (Conway Twitty) may deduct the expenses of another person (Twitty Burger). In order to determine whether the disallowed expenditures are deductible by petitioner under section 162 we must (1) ascertain the purpose or motive of the taxpayer in making the payments and (2) determine whether there is a sufficient connection between the expenditures and the taxpayer's trade or business. Lohrke v. Commissioner, *supra*. Petitioner bears the burden of proving that respondent's determination was in error.

The relevant facts are as follows: Petitioner Conway Twitty is a well-known country music entertainer. Most of his income is derived from his performances, songwriting, and record royalties. In 1968, Conway and several of his friends decided to form a chain of fast food restaurants and incorporated Twitty Burger under the laws of Oklahoma. During 1968 and 1969, approximately 75 of petitioner's friends and business associates invested money in Twitty Burger. Subsequently it was determined that it would be some time before the requirements of the Security and Exchange Commission could be met and a public offering of stock made. It was determined, therefore, that debentures should be issued to those persons who had invested money in the undertaking as interim evidence of their investments.

By late 1970, Twitty Burger was experiencing financial difficulties and it was determined by Twitty Burger's attorney that further attempts to obtain registration of the corporate stock would be futile. Shortly thereafter it was decided that Twitty Burger should be shut down. Except for one independently-owned franchise operating in Texas, the last Twitty Burger restaurant was closed in May 1971. Subsequently, Conway Twitty decided that the investors should be repaid the amount of their investments in the failed corporation. As Twitty Burger had no assets with which to satisfy the debentures, Conway Twitty decided he would repay the investors from his future earnings. During the years in issue, 1973 and 1974, Conway Twitty made payments to the investors of $92,892.46 and $3,600, respectively.

Respondent argues that the payments Conway Twitty made to the investors in Twitty Burger are not deductible by him as ordinary and necessary business expenses under section 162 because there was no business purpose for the payments and, additionally, there was no relationship between his involvement in Twitty Burger and his business of being a country music entertainer. Respondent argues that the payments in question here were made by Conway Twitty gratuitously in that petitioner had no personal liability to the holders of the debentures and made the payments merely out of a sense of moral obligation. Relying on Welch v. Helvering and certain of its progeny, respondent concludes that while it was "very nice" of petitioner to reimburse the investors in Twitty Burger, the required nexus between the expenditures and Conway Twitty's career as a country music entertainer does not exist and therefore the payments were not "ordinary and necessary" within the meaning of section 162.

Petitioner argues that the rule of Welch v. Helvering, *supra*, is not applicable to the case at bar because petitioner made the payments in question to protect his reputation and earning capacity in his ongoing business of being a country music entertainer whereas in Welch the Supreme Court held that the payments made there were capital expenditures of the taxpayer's new business. Petitioner maintains that under the test as formulated by this Court in Lohrke, the expenditures in issue here are deductible under section 162 if the payments were made primarily with a business motive and if there is a sufficient connection between the payments and the taxpayer's trade or business.

The question presented for our resolution is purely one of fact. While previously decided cases dealing with this issue are somewhat helpful there is, quite understandably, no case directly on point with the facts before us. * * *

There is no suggestion in the record that any of the payments were made in order to protect petitioner's investment in Twitty Burger or to revitalize the corporation. It is petitioner's contention that Conway Twitty repaid the investors in Twitty Burger from his personal funds in order to protect his personal business reputation. While it is clear from the facts that Conway was under no legal obligation to make such payments, (at least in the sense that the corporate debentures were not personally guaranteed by him), the law is clear that the absence of such an obligation is not in itself a bar to the deduction of such expenditures under section 162. In addition, the fact that the petitioner also felt a moral obligation to the people who had entrusted him with their funds does not preclude the deductibility of the payments so long as the satisfaction of the moral obligation was not the primary motivation for the expenditures.

After a thorough consideration of the record we are convinced that petitioner Conway Twitty repaid the investors in Twitty Burger with the primary motive of protecting his personal business reputation. There was the obvious similarity of the name of the corporation and petitioner's stage name. There is no doubt that the corporation's name was chosen with the idea of capitalizing on Conway Twitty's fame as a country music performer. Additionally, many of the investors were connected with the country music industry.[13] While there is no doubt that part of petitioner's motivation for making the payments involved his personal sense of morality, we do not believe that this ethical consideration was paramount.

Petitioner testified as follows concerning his motivations for repaying the Twitty Burger investors:

> I'm 99 percent entertainer. That's just about all I know. The name Conway Twitty, and the image that I work so hard for since 1955 and 56 is the foundation that I, my family, and the 30 some odd people that work for me stand on. They depend on it, and they can depend on it.

> I handle things the way I did with Shell Oil Company, with Diner's Club, with Gulf Oil Company, with a lot of other things before that and after that other than Twitty Burger. I handled them all the same way for more than one reason. First of all, because of the way I perceive myself and my image. It may not be the same as this guy over here or that one over there, but to me if Conway Twitty does some little old something, it's different than somebody else doing something because everybody has got a different relationship with whoever their fans are.

> I handled it that way because of that. Because of the image. And second and very close to it, I handled it that way because I think it is morally right, and if you owe a man something, you pay him. If a man owes you something, he pays you. And if a man is going to pay you a dollar for an hour's work, you work—you know—it sounds weird to hear myself saying those things. I know they are true. And it's the way I live, but for some reason in this day and time, I feel funny saying that. And I shouldn't because we grew up in a time when that was—that was the way it was.

> And I would love to think that that's the way it still is. But when you look around you and you deal with other people, you know it's not true 100 percent of the time anymore, but it's true with Conway

---

13. For example, Harlan Howard, Don Davis, Merle Haggard, Steve Lake, and Jimmy Loden, a/k/a/ Sonny James. Petitioner's counsel aptly remarked in his opening statement: "Imagine trying to keep a band together where somebody has stiffed the drummer's mother." We note, however, that "Pork Chop's" mother, Lucibelle Markham, was repaid in a year not at issue in this case.

Twitty and no matter which way this turns out, I'd do the same thing again tomorrow, if I had to do over. * * *

When we got the letter from Walter Beach and from Haggard's lawyer and from a couple other places, and my people said, hey, you know, we've got some letters from people saying they are going to sue you, and that you might have done something wrong as far as securities and all that stuff goes. It just scares you to death.

I mean it did me. And it would most people. I know it would. And so you—you don't want any part of that. A law suit like that with— say if Merle Haggard sued Conway Twitty or if Walter Beach sued Conway Twitty and you're in court, and they are saying it's fraud and something to do with the securities thing, and, you know, all the years I've worked for are gone. If my fans didn't give up on me, it would warp me psychologically. I couldn't function anymore because I'm the type of person I am. I remember it.

* * * I thought the country music entertainer is just as important or maybe even a little more important than a rock performer because of the longevity and because—and the reason you have that longevity is because of the fan.

The country music fan is different than the people I had dealt with back in the 50's and the kids. They will stay right with you as long as you stay within a certain boundaries. They expect a lot out of you because you—a country singer deals with—they deal with feelings and things inside of people—you know—you can listen to the words in a country song, and you're dealing with emotions and feelings that— it's kind of like a doctor, you know. I'm not comparing myself with a doctor certainly, but when a person gets to trust a doctor, that's all they need is that trust.

Petitioner presented the expert testimony of William Ivey, the Director of Country Music Foundation in Nashville, Tennessee. In his report which was introduced into evidence in lieu of direct testimony he stated as follows:

Country music is the direct, commercial descendent of the folk music carried to the Appalachian mountains by some of the early settlers of the United States. Though modern country music has developed many new characteristics which separate it from its folk roots, several important elements remain from the folk past. The emphasis on story songs, the use of many stringed instruments in performance, and the close identification of the personality of the performer with the material that is performed are all aspects of folk music which remain a part of modern country music. In the folk communities of the rural South, folk music performers were not viewed as professional entertainers, but were rather seen as friends and neighbors who happened to entertain. Thus the status of a folk musician was based not only upon performing skills but also upon those other traits of personality and character which placed a person in a good or bad light within his community. This tendency to link a performer's non-performing image with his artistry exists to some degree in all of art, but it is most noticeable and important in those musical styles which have emerged from folk roots. Country music is one of those folk-based forms.

Country entertainers go to great lengths to protect their images, for they correctly realize that both business associates and fans judge their artistic efforts in the light of perceptions of the artist's personality, professional conduct, and moral character. The business side of country music is a highly personal activity which depends heavily upon knowledge of reputation and past performance. Throughout the process of recording, touring, and composing, businesses must be established, credit extended, and payments made. The reputation of an entertainer among business associates and within the financial community can have a determinative role in that artist's ability to conduct his affairs.

Reputation can have an even greater effect upon an entertainer as it influences fans. Virtually every article written about Conway Twitty stresses the effort he makes to meet his fans. John Pugh, writing in Country Music Magazine, says "Perhaps there has never been a harder working artist than Conway Twitty.... Or an artist who cared more for his fans." Devotion to fans is a crucial part of Conway's great success, and his scrupulously maintained reputation is one element in maintaining his intense popularity. * * *

Stories abound of the problems encountered by artists who have not followed Conway's example. George Jones, Waylon Jennings, and Johnny Paycheck are all great entertainers, but each has been plagued by personal problems which have limited the extent of their success. Had, in the matter before this court, Conway Twitty allowed investors to be left dangling with heavy losses following the collapse of the Twitty Burger chain, the multiple lawsuits, unfavorable news stories and disgruntled investors would have all damaged that very reputation which was a key element in Conway's image as an artist. Though he would have continued to perform and record, there exists serious doubt that he would have achieved the unparalleled success he enjoyed during the 1970's had his reputation been so injured. In fact, his performance in the Twitty Burger matter became another ingredient in Conway's positive image. Tom Carter, writing in the Tulsa, Oklahoma, Daily World:"

> Twitty's 'character' seems a bit out of character in the entertainment world. That point was proved a few years ago when Twitty formed a restaurant chain selling 'Twitty Burgers.'

> He persuaded friends to invest $1 million. They lost it all. Twitty was determined to pay them back, rather than merely declare bankruptcy on the corporation.

As a scholar of country music and an observer of the country music scene, I am convinced that a country entertainer's character, personality, and credit reputation are part and parcel of his role as a singer. This integration of art and the individual existed in the folk communities from which country music grew, and it remains an aspect of country music today. Had Conway Twitty not maintained a flawless financial and personal reputation, he would not have become the most-successful male vocalist within the art form. Had he allowed investors to suffer as a result of Twitty Burger's failure, both his reputation and his career would thus have been damaged.

We conclude that there was a proximate relationship between the payments made to the holders of Twitty Burger debentures and petitioner's trade or business as a country music entertainer so as to render those payments an ordinary and necessary expense of that business. Although, as respondent argues, the chances of a successful lawsuit against Conway Twitty by any of the investors or the Securities and Exchange Commission was remote we agree with petitioner that the possibility of extensive adverse publicity concerning petitioner's involvement with the defunct corporation and the consequent loss of the investors' funds was very real. We do not believe it is necessary for us to find that adverse publicity emanating from Conway Twitty's failure to repay the investors in Twitty Burger would have ruined his career as a country music singer. Rather, we need only find that a proximate relationship existed between the payments and petitioner's business. We find that such relationship exists. It is not necessary that the taxpayer's trade or business be of the same type as that engaged in by the person on whose behalf the payments are made.* * *

In making these payments petitioner was furthering his business as a country music artist and protecting his business reputation for integrity. The mere fact that they were voluntary does not deprive them of their character as ordinary and necessary business expenses. Under the unique circumstances presented in this case, we hold that the payments in issue are deductible as business expenses under section 162.

IRS Nonacquiescence & the Ode to Conway Twitty
(ACTION ON DECISION)

HAROLD L. AND TEMPLE M. JENKINS
v. COMMISSIONER

United States Tax Court, 1983.
T.C. Memo. 1983–667.

Issue

Whether Conway Twitty is allowed a business expense deduction for payments to reimburse the losses of investors in a defunct restaurant known as Twitty Burger, Inc.

Discussion

The Tax Court summarized its opinion in this case with the following "Ode to Conway Twitty:"[a]

Twitty Burger went belly up

But Conway remained true

He repaid his investors, one and all

It was the moral thing to do.

His fans would not have liked it

It could have hurt his fame

Had any investors sued him

Like Merle Haggard or Sonny James.

When it was time to file taxes

Conway thought what he would do

Was deduct those payments as a business expense

Under section one-sixty-two.

In order to allow these deductions

Goes the argument of the Commissioner

The payments must be ordinary and necessary

To a business of the petitioner.

Had Conway not repaid the investors

His career would have been under cloud,

Under the unique facts of this case

Held: The deductions are allowed.

* * *

Our reaction to the Court's opinion is reflected in the following "Ode to Conway Twitty: A Reprise":

Harold Jenkins and Conway Twitty

They are both the same

But one was born

The other achieved fame.

The man is talented

And has many a friend

They opened a restaurant

His name he did lend.

They are two different things

Making burgers and song

---

a. The Tax Court's "Ode to Conway Twitty" was set forth as footnote 14 to its opinion—Ed.

The business went sour

It didn't take long.

He repaid his friends

Why did he act

Was it business or friendship

Which is fact?

Business the court held

It's deductible they feel

We disagree with the answer

But let's not appeal.

Recommendation

Nonacquiescence

NOTE, QUESTIONS

1.   Twitty also built a theme park called Twitty City in Hendersonville, Tennessee. The park was ultimately sold to a Christian cable TV company, which demolished it.

2.   What is the issue in *Jenkins*?

● Capital vs. ordinary?

● Common vs. bizarre?

● Personal vs. business?

● Which view of the case is taken by the IRS in its nonacquiescence?

3.   The judge appears to be a fan of country music. How important was that to the result? If the same facts had occurred in another industry, would the case have come out the same way?

4.   There is a blog which you find to be very useful in your work. The blog has a "tip jar," which enables blog readers to contribute to the upkeep of the blog. Concerned that, without reader contributions, the blog will terminate, you "tip" regularly. Deductible?

NOTE ON *IRS* NONACQUIESCENCES

Normally, when litigants lose, they have two choices. They can appeal, or they can go away. However, the IRS has three choices. It can appeal, it can go away, or it can nonacquiesce. When IRS nonacquiesces, it is saying that, although it will not appeal, it is not pleased with the result.

The practical effect of nonacquiescence is not terribly significant. However, when IRS nonacquiesces, it is serving notice that it disagrees with the court's resolution, and will probably continue to litigate the issue if it comes up again.

Why should IRS have an option that the rest of us don't have? Is a nonacquiescence a form of irresponsible, uh, fudging? Is it, perhaps, even bullying?

C. CAUSATION

It is not enough to show that the taxpayer's activities were ordinary and necessary business activities. One must also show that the expenses which the taxpayer seeks to deduct have the right kind of causal nexus to that business. *Gilmore*, *Kopp's*, and the *Gilliam* problem, below, all address this issue.

UNITED STATES v. GILMORE

United States Supreme Court, 1963.
372 U.S. 39, 83 S.Ct. 623, 9 L.Ed.2d 570.

MR. JUSTICE HARLAN delivered the opinion of the Court.

In 1955 the California Supreme Court confirmed the award to the respondent taxpayer of a decree of absolute divorce, without alimony, against his wife Dixie Gilmore. The case before us involves the deductibility for federal income tax purposes of that part of the husband's legal expense incurred in such proceedings as is attributable to his successful resistance of his wife's claims to certain of his assets asserted by her to be community property under California law. * * *

At the time of the divorce proceedings, instituted by the wife but in which the husband also cross-claimed for divorce, respondent's property consisted primarily of controlling stock interests in three corporations, each of which was a franchised General Motors automobile dealer. As president and principal managing officer of the three corporations, he received salaries from them aggregating about $66,800 annually, and in recent years his total annual dividends had averaged about $83,000. His total annual income derived from the corporations was thus approximately $150,000. His income from other sources was negligible.

As found by the Court of Claims, the husband's overriding concern in the divorce litigation was to protect these assets against the claims of his wife. Those claims had two aspects: first, that the earnings accumulated and retained by these three corporations during the Gilmores' marriage (representing an aggregate increase in corporate net worth of some $600,000) were the product of respondent's personal services, and not the result of accretion in capital values, thus rendering respondent's stockholdings in the enterprises pro tanto community property under California law; second, that to the extent that such stockholdings were community property, the wife, allegedly the innocent party in the divorce proceeding, was entitled under California law to more than a one-half interest in such property.

The respondent wished to defeat those claims for two important reasons. First, the loss of his controlling stock interests, particularly in the event of their transfer in substantial part to his hostile wife, might well cost him the loss of his corporate positions, his principal means of livelihood. Second, there was also danger that if he were found guilty of his wife's sensational and reputation-damaging charges of marital infidelity, General Motors Corporation might find it expedient to exercise its right to cancel these dealer franchises.

The end result of this bitterly fought divorce case was a complete victory for the husband. He, not the wife, was granted a divorce on his cross-claim; the wife's community property claims were denied in their entirety; and she was held entitled to no alimony.

Respondent's legal expenses in connection with this litigation amounted to $32,537.15 in 1953 and $8,074.21 in 1954—a total of $40,611.36 for the two taxable years in question. The Commissioner of Internal Revenue found all of these expenditures "personal" or "family" expenses and as such none of them deductible. In the ensuing refund suit, however, the Court of Claims held that 80% of such expense (some $32,500) was attributable to respondent's defense against his wife's community property claims respecting his stockholdings and hence deductible under § 23(a)(2) of the 1939 Code [current § 212] as an expense "incurred * * * for the * * * conservation * * * of property held for the production of income." In so holding the Court of Claims stated:

> Of course it is true that in every divorce case a certain amount of the legal expenses are incurred for the purpose of obtaining the divorce and a certain amount are incurred in an effort to conserve the estate and are not necessarily deductible under [§ 212], but when the facts of a particular case clearly indicate (as here) that the property, around which the controversy evolves, is held for the production of income and without this property the litigant might be denied not only the property itself but the means of earning a livelihood, then it must come under the provisions of [§ 212] * * *. The only question then is the allocation of the expenses to this phase of the proceedings.

The Government does not question the amount or formula for the expense allocation made by the Court of Claims. Its sole contention here is that the court below misconceived the test governing [§ 212] deductions, in that the deductibility of these expenses turns, so it is argued, not upon the consequences to respondent of a failure to defeat his wife's community property claims but upon the origin and nature of the claims themselves. So viewing Dixie Gilmore's claims, whether relating to the existence or division of community property, it is contended that the expense of resisting them must be deemed nondeductible "personal" or "family" expense under § 24(a)(1) [current § 262], not deductible expense under [§ 212]. For reasons given hereafter we think the Government's position is sound and that it must be sustained.

I.

For income tax purposes Congress has seen fit to regard an individual as having two personalities: "one is (as) a seeker after profit who can deduct the expenses incurred in that search; the other is (as) a creature satisfying his needs as a human and those of his family but who cannot deduct such consumption and related expenditures." The Government regards [§ 212] as embodying a category of the expenses embraced in the first of these roles. * * *

A basic restriction upon the availability of a [current § 162] deduction is that the expense item involved must be one that has a business origin. That restriction not only inheres in the language of [§ 162] itself, confining such deductions to "expenses * * * incurred * * * in carrying on any trade or business," but also follows from [§ 262], expressly rendering nondeductible "in any case * * * (p)ersonal, living, or family expenses." * * * In light of what has already been said with respect to the advent and thrust of [§ 212], it is clear that the "(p)ersonal * * * or family expenses" restriction of [§ 262] must impose the same limitation upon the reach of [§ 212]—in other words that the only kind of expenses deductible under [§ 212] are those that relate to a "business," that is, profit-seeking, purpose. The pivotal issue in this case then becomes: was this part of respondent's litigation costs a "business" rather than a "personal" or "family" expense?

The answer to this question has already been indicated in prior cases. * * *

The principle we derive from these cases is that the characterization, as "business" or "personal," of the litigation costs of resisting a claim depends on whether or not the claim arises in connection with the taxpayer's profit-seeking activities. It does not depend on the consequences that might result to a taxpayer's income-producing property from a failure to defeat the claim, for, as Lykes teaches, that "would carry us too far" and would not be compatible with the basic lines of expense deductibility drawn by Congress. Moreover, such a rule would lead to capricious results. If two taxpayers are each sued for an automobile accident while driving for pleasure, deductibility of their litigation costs would turn on the mere circumstance of the character of the assets each happened to possess, that is, whether the judgments against them stood to be satisfied out of income-or nonincome-producing property. We should be slow to attribute to Congress a purpose producing such unequal treatment among taxpayers, resting on no rational foundation.

Confirmation of these conclusions is found in the incongruities that would follow from acceptance of the Court of Claims' reasoning in this case. Had this respondent taxpayer conducted his automobile-dealer business as a sole proprietorship, rather than in corporate form, and claimed a deduction under [§ 162], the potential impact of his wife's claims would have been no different than in the present situation. Yet it cannot well be supposed that [§ 162] would have afforded him a deduction, since his expenditures, made in connection with a marital litigation, could hardly be deemed "expenses * * * incurred * * * in carrying on any trade or business." Thus, under the Court of Claims' view expenses may be even less deductible if the taxpayer is carrying on a trade or business instead of some other income-producing activity. But it was manifestly Congress' purpose with respect to deductibility to place all income-producing activities on an equal footing. And it would surely be a surprising result were it now to turn out that a change designed to achieve equality of treatment in fact had served only to reverse the inequality of treatment.

For these reasons, we resolve the conflict among the lower courts on the question before us in favor of the view that the origin and character of the claim with respect to which an expense was incurred, rather than its potential consequences upon the fortunes of the taxpayer, is the controlling basic test of whether the expense was "business" or "personal" and hence whether it is deductible or not under [§ 212]. We find the reasoning underlying the cases taking the "consequences" view unpersuasive. * * *

The judgment of the Court of Claims is reversed and the case is remanded to that court for further proceedings consistent with this opinion. It is so ordered.

Judgment of Court of Claims reversed and case remanded.

MR. JUSTICE BLACK and MR. JUSTICE DOUGLAS believe that the Court reverses this case because of an unjustifiably narrow interpretation of the 1942 amendment to § 23 of the Internal Revenue Code[§ 162] and would accordingly affirm the judgment of the Court of Claims.

QUESTION

What causal connection does the court require between the business and the expense? What problem do they seek to avoid?

NOTE ON THE GILMORES

[an earlier version of this piece appeared
in Tax Notes, Aug. 6, 2007, p. 493]

Don Gilmore was born in Wyoming, and grew up to make his fortune in the automobile business. He began selling Chevrolets in Long Beach, California, and then ran his own dealership in Phoenix, Arizona. In 1931, he was granted the first Chevrolet dealership in San Francisco. By the time of his marriage to Dixie, he owned three dealerships—Chevrolet dealerships in San Francisco and Hayward, and a Pontiac dealership in Riverside. Gilmore was the President of the Motor Car Dealers' Association of San Francisco, and served on the General Motors Dealer Council. In 1950, his baseball team—the Don Gilmore Chevrolets—had a record of 24 wins and only 3 losses.

In the 1940's, Dixie, a former actress, was married to Major Frank Clarke, a stunt pilot and actor in southern California. Don was married at the time to Barbara Briggs McMasters. Don and Dixie first met at a Beverly Hills election eve party in 1944. Some time after that first meeting, Dixie became ill. Don visited her, and pinned flowers to her pillow.

When she recovered from her illness, Dixie determined to leave southern California, and Major Clarke. She moved to Lake Tahoe, and Don visited her there. Don and Dixie were married on March 2, 1946, in Las Vegas. It was Don's fourth marriage, and Dixie's second. Don was about ten years older than Dixie.

Don borrowed $153,000 from his corporations to build a "dream house" for his new bride. The house had eleven rooms with a view in Belvedere, California. There were three master bedrooms, two servants' rooms, a swimming pool, a three-car garage and six bathrooms.

Dixie testified that, before the marriage, Don had treated her like Dresden china. After the marriage, he treated her like a hot potato. In fact, Don said of his new mansion "There are a lot of bedrooms here, and, by golly, I'm going to have all the women I want here."

Dixie and Don separated on April 8, 1952. Two days later, Dixie filed for divorce. She claimed that Don was guilty of extreme cruelty. He had made "revolting suggestions that she perform sex perversions with him and other women," which, she said, justified her refusal to sleep with him.

Don counterclaimed that Dixie was guilty of extreme cruelty to him, because she drank too much and eventually refused to sleep with him. He denied that he participated in the perversions but claimed to be a "glorified observer" thereof, and claimed that not only did plaintiff [Dixie] participate in them but that she was the instigator.

The trial took five weeks, and the court reporter's transcript covered 3,061 pages. The case was, as the California Appellate Court noted, "one of the most sordid and revolting with which courts are required to deal."

Dixie was always fashionably dressed in court. Sometimes, she would make her accusations "with a toss of her carefully coiffeured head." One day, she wore a "... black suit with a blue-gray scarf, forming a perky bow at her neck." However, the perkiness tended to wear off as the trial wore on. At least six times during the trial, she burst into tears, and left the courtroom. On another occasion, she fainted. On five of these occasions, leaving was her idea. On the sixth, her lawyer ordered her to leave, because she wouldn't stop yelling at a witness.

When Dixie left, she would sit on a bench in the hallway, sobbing. Sometimes, she managed to return, sometimes not. On one occasion, even her lawyer broke down crying:

> The dignified Christin [Dixie's lawyer] broke down in tears at the noon recess. He sobbed to his client, "I don't know how I can continue this line of questioning, Dixie. I've never seen such depths of degradation. I never heard such vulgarity, such brazenness, in all my years in the courtroom."

> Dixie said, "I know, Charles. I'd rather be tried for murder."

Each claimed that the other had thrown various objects at them. Dixie's mother testified that Don swore at Dixie, abused her, slapped her, and knocked her down. Dixie claimed that, on one occasion, in Hawaii, Don grabbed her around the waist, lifted her up, and threw her on the bed. Then, he walked out. Don claimed that Dixie threw a glass of water at him at the "swank" Meadow Club, and threw an entire plate of spaghetti at him at a drive-in. Dixie attempted suicide on at least one occasion, and Don allegedly said, "Let her die."

After they had been married for six weeks, Don announced that he was going to get himself a call girl. Dixie told him to go ahead. Soon enough, the call girl arrived in a taxi. Dixie objected strenuously, and Don sent the girl home. Then, according to Dixie, Don stuck a burning cigarette in her eye. Don denied it. Testimony from the doctor who treated Dixie was, alas, inconclusive.

There was an excursion to a "peep show" in Paris. Some of the cast members of the show were invited back to the Gilmores' suite for drinks and caviar afterward. It is unclear whether it was Don's idea or Dixie's.

Then there was the ferrying of their fifty-three foot power boat (the "Lark") from Santa Barbara back to San Francisco. Robert Sherwood, who was Don's used car manager, came along to help pilot the boat, as did the Gilmores' butler and maid. Dixie sat down on a railroad tie near the water in Santa Barbara, wearing shorts and a mink coat, and refused to board the boat. Dixie was either drunk, or concerned about a rough passage, or both. It was arranged to have her driven back to San Francisco.

With Dixie gone, Sherwood was assigned the task of procuring three other women to make the voyage with them. He found the women in a Santa Barbara night spot, and off they went. Sherwood testified that the girls all became seasick and went below, while he and Don stood watch topside all night long. However, Walter Russell, Dixie's father, was also on the cruise. He testified that Don did not stay topside all night. The party, according to Russell, was very gay, and very wet.

Finances were a major issue. Dixie claimed that she needed considerable alimony to continue the lifestyle to which she had become accustomed. A sense of that lifestyle can be gleaned from the following:

- Dixie traded in her Cadillac three times a year for a newer model
- She received a $4,000 monthly housing allowance
- She received a $250 monthly clothing allowance. Despite these allowances, Dixie had allegedly run up unpaid bills at some of San Francisco's more exclusive shops.
- She received $500 a month in spending money
- She received gifts including a sable scarf, a silver blue mink stole, a white mink stole, a silver blue full-length mink coat, a 3 carat emerald cut diamond ring, a $7,500 diamond/emerald bracelet, and a diamond watch
- Dixie and Don went on a trip to Honolulu and a four-month trip to Europe.

Accordingly, Dixie testified that she couldn't get along on less than $2,500 a month. Don lived a similarly extravagant life.

Dixie claimed that, on one occasion, Don had offered her 51% of the business, plus $2,500 a month and year-end bonuses, if she would stay married to him. But she refused. "You can't buy my soul," she said.

Judge Martinelli ultimately found for Don on all issues. He gave Dixie an hour-long, stern lecture. The Gilmore marriage, said the judge, was "surrounded by affluence, but . . . its rich participants were in fact very poor . . . They have roses, yes, but they have no petals."

Dixie was, for once, beyond tears. "I'm shocked—just shocked. The Judge doesn't like me," she said.

Ultimately, Judge Martinelli awarded Dixie no alimony. Instead, he granted her joint tenancy rights in the two homes owned by the couple, which had an aggregate equity of $158,000, plus $10,000 in attorney's fees.

After the divorce, Dixie continued to live in the Belvedere home. However, with no alimony, she couldn't afford to pay either the mortgage or the utilities. She kept the house cold and dark, except for a few candles.

On January 30, 1954, neighbors reported a disturbance. When the policeman arrived, he discovered Dixie and her father sitting in the house. Dixie was screaming.

Patrolman Williams eventually persuaded Dixie to don her platinum mink coat and get in the ambulance. She was taken to a high security room of the hospital, for violent patients. Within a few days, her father had signed papers to have her permanently committed. On February 8, she was declared legally insane, with a "schizophrenic illness of the paranoid type." Her new lawyer, James MacInnis, made arrangements to invalidate the divorce, since she had been incompetent during the trial. She was released from the hospital, to the custody of her father, on April 30.

The case was heard again. In the interim, Dixie was awarded temporary alimony of $500 per month. Don wasn't so good about paying it, but, of course, he did have obligations to various other ex-wives. Ultimately, two more courts ruled on the divorce. Both affirmed the trial court.

Meanwhile, Don was arranging to reacquire the "palatial" Belvedere home. In fact, he bought it twice. Once, he bought it from the sheriff, who sold it to satisfy unpaid bills. He bought it a second time at a mortgage foreclosure sale.

The sheriff evicted Dixie in March, 1955. She was dressed entirely in red, and wore "dime store lipstick." The entire ensemble was stunningly set off by a ranch mink stole. She also wore the diamond bracelet. "I hope I don't have to hock it," she said.

When she left the house, she brought 16 hat boxes, eight suitcases, and 50 pairs of shoes. She also brought a can of chili and six boxes of frozen vegetables. Don sent a Pinkerton guard, to make sure that she didn't take anything else. Dixie, with her luggage and her two poodles, Ciro and Cindy, moved into a motel room with a kitchenette in San Rafael.

A week later, Dixie was back in court again, asking for an increase in the $500 monthly temporary alimony. "Little girls need lots of things—cosmetics and things," she said. The court granted her $700.

In November of 1955, Don married former barber shop manicurist Sue Snelling, at the Royal Hawaiian Hotel in Honolulu. The couple flew back from Hawaii to set up housekeeping in Don's mansion in Belvedere. Ms. Snelling had actually been ready to testify at Don and Dixie's divorce trial, until Don's lawyer agreed to stipulate that Don had enjoyed "certain relationships" with Ms. Snelling and three other women.

Meanwhile, Dixie had found gainful employment as a psychiatric assistant at the Napa State Hospital—the very same facility where she, herself, had once been a patient. However, her small salary was not enough to prevent her from declaring bankruptcy in 1958. Later in that same year, she remarried—to wealthy contractor Vincent Lugli—and moved to Long Beach.

On another front, in December of 1966, after some 30 years in the courts, Don finally managed to reach a $22,000 settlement with his second wife, the former model Ladymay. By then, Don, aged 71, was married for a sixth time, and living in Novato. He was too old to go back to work, and down to his last $100,000. He was living on $127 per month in social security, plus $650 a year from other sources. Don died on February 20, 1967.

Afterward, the case went back to the Northern District of California for one last time, where the court held that Don's legal expenses had been incurred in defense of the title to his stock. As such, they could be added to his basis. On this point, the business or personal nature of the underlying dispute was irrelevant.

KOPP'S COMPANY, INC. v. UNITED STATES

United States Court of Appeals, Fourth Circuit, 1980.
636 F.2d 59.

ALBERT V. BRYAN, SENIOR CIRCUIT JUDGE:

Appellant, Kopp's Co., Inc. (the Company), contends that the trial court erred in disallowing the Company's deduction, as ordinary and necessary business expenses under Section 162(a) of the Internal Revenue Code, of the cost of settlement of a tort action and related legal fees. A refund was sought of $28,935.67, representing income taxes of $25,472.00 together with interest thereon of $3,463.67 which it had paid after the IRS rejected the deductions on its Federal income tax return for the year ending March 31, 1973. Tried non-jury in the United States District Court for the District of Maryland, final judgment with opinion denying the refund was passed and the Company appeals. We reverse.

* * * The Company is a Maryland corporation engaged in the lumber and building supply business. Its sole shareholders are Earl and Jean Kopp, who also serve as officers and directors. Their son Wayne has been employed by the Company since January, 1963, except for the period of 24 months from September, 1966, to September, 1968, spent in military service.

On November 17, 1967, while at home on leave and making personal and permissive use of a Company-owned car, Wayne was in an accident in Maryland which rendered Warren T. Danner, the driver of the other vehicle involved, a quadraplegic. In the previous five years, Wayne had been convicted of speeding 10 times and had been a party to 3 minor accidents. His license had been suspended briefly in Maryland and had been revoked in Virginia. Earl Kopp was aware of his son's driving record.

At the time of the accident, the Company and Kopp carried automobile liability policies to the face value of $100,000. Wayne and Jean, his mother, had no such insurance; Wayne had no assets. Earl's assets, aside from his interest in the Company, totalled $75,000. The Company's book value in 1970 approximated $250,000.

Danner, the victim of the accident, filed suit in 1969 against the Company, Earl, Jean and Wayne Kopp in Maryland for damages of $4.2 million. The institution of the suit led the Company's bank to freeze its credit line and to demand security upon an unsecured note; major suppliers of the Company similarly expressed concern, and the Company's financial statement thereafter carried a notation of this contingent liability.

To relieve its financial stress, the Company reached an out-of-court settlement with Danner, under the terms of which the Company's liability insurer was to pay Danner $102,000 and the Company was to pay Danner $50,000 borrowed from the Company's bank. In addition, the Company incurred $3,068 in legal fees. The compromise was effectuated in every particular prior to March 31, 1973.

In its Federal income tax return for the taxable year ending March 31, 1973, the Company deducted the $50,000 settlement and the $3,068 legal fee as ordinary and necessary business expenses under Section 162 of the Code. The IRS disallowed the deduction, assessing an income tax deficiency of $28,935.67, including interest. The Company paid the deficiency, filed for a refund and subsequently instituted this action.

Appellant argues that the payments made in satisfaction of the Danner suit and the related legal fees are properly deductible under Section 162(a) because they were made in order to protect the credit standing and financial durability of the Company. In rejecting this premise the District Court looked to United States v. Gilmore. We conclude, however, that the "origin of the claim" doctrine established there should not bar deductibility in this case. * * *

The claim with respect to which the Company incurred the expenses it seeks to deduct here, however, was not merely a personal claim only tangentially threatening to corporate assets. On the contrary, and importantly, Danner named the Company as a party defendant to his suit, thereby directly bringing the business into the litigation and jeopardizing its assets. Like the Court in Dolese v. United States, 605 F.2d 1146 (10th Cir.1979), we see the Company's direct exposure to the risk of a monetary judgment significant in distinguishing the instant litigation from that of Gilmore.

The factual stipulation before us reveals that the Company was advised by its general counsel that, at trial, it likely would be found liable for negligent entrustment of the company car to Wayne. The Company, therefore, was confronted with more than a remote threat to its assets or operations arising from a costly judgment against Wayne; it incurred the expense at issue to avert direct liability under a claim alleging that the Company itself acted negligently in permitting Wayne to operate its car. The outlay made by Kopp's Co., Inc., in resolving the Danner suit thus conforms with the guidelines for deductibility put forward in *Gilmore*.

We set aside the judgment on appeal.

Reversed.

ERVIN, CIRCUIT JUDGE, dissenting:

Because I am convinced that the amounts paid in settlement of the tort action against Kopp's Company, Inc. (hereafter "the corporation") and for legal fees incurred in connection with that litigation can in no way be characterized as business expenses within the meaning of § 162(a) of the Internal Revenue Code, I respectfully dissent.

There are two distinct inquiries to address in determining the deductibility of an expense under § 162(a). First, it must be ascertained whether the expense is personal or business related. If it is determined that the expense is business related, then the second inquiry is whether the expenditure is ordinary and necessary to the carrying on of a trade or business. Because I believe that the expenses were personal in nature, I find no need to address the second inquiry of whether the expenses were ordinary and necessary to carrying on the Kopp business.

The test for determining whether an expense qualifies as a business expenditure, as compared to a personal expense, was set forth by the Supreme Court in United States v. Gilmore. The test enunciated in *Gilmore* looks to the "origin and character of the claim with respect to which an expense was incurred," and not to the consequences that may result to a taxpayer's income producing property if the claim is not defeated. In order for litigation or settlement expenses to be deductible under the Gilmore test, they must have accrued in the defense of a suit that is connected directly with or that resulted proximately from the taxpayer's trade or business. Thus, for a deduction to be allowed under § 162(a) the transaction out of which the claim arose must have resulted from the carrying out of company business.

I am not convinced that the settlement and litigation expenses in this case constitute business expenses. The transaction out of which the claim arose was that of Mr. Kopp (hereafter "Earl") lending a car to his son for the son's personal use. The troublesome factor in this case is that Earl, who was also president and principal shareholder of a closely held corporation, Kopp's Co., Inc., lent his son a company car. If Earl had owned no corporation and had lent his own automobile to his son for the son's personal use, no litigation costs or settlement expenses would have been deductible by him, by his wife, or by his son. I cannot see how Earl's status as president of the closely held corporation transforms the entrustment of the car to the son into a corporate act. Clearly, if Earl, as president, is viewed as an agent of the corporation, he was acting outside the scope of his agency in making a personal loan of the car for purposes totally unrelated to the business. A corporation is not liable for the unauthorized acts of its agents. In conjunction with his effort to impute his own tort liability to the corporation, Earl seeks tax benefits for his wholly owned corporation which are incompatible with the purposes of § 162(a) of the Code.

The majority proceeds on the theory that, because the corporation as a party defendant incurred the litigation and settlement expenses to avert "direct liability," it met *Gilmore's* guidelines. This reliance on *Gilmore* is misplaced because *Gilmore* requires that the origin of the claim giving rise to the threat of liability must be connected with the taxpayer's profit-seeking activities. Thus, a threat to corporate assets even if real and direct, is deductible only if the origin of the threat is business related. In this case, Danner's claim against the corporation stemmed entirely from the familial relation between father and son, and not from any income producing activity of the corporation. The expenses under review were incurred as a result of Earl's personal activities rather than as a result of his business pursuits as an officer of the corporation.

The corporation seeks to distinguish *Gilmore* and to stress Dolese v. United States, 605 F.2d 1146 (10th Cir.1979) as controlling. It should be noted, however, that in *Dolese* the deductions were limited to legal fees expended in freeing the corporations from the restrictions of a restraining order. As the court points out:

> Once the corporation was inhibited from the conduct of profit-making activities by fear of violating the court order the costs of obtaining clarification and relief would seem to originate in its business activities. Therefore, to the extent a corporation incurred legal expenses in preparing pleadings required to be filed in this litigation, in obtaining permission to settle a lawsuit previously filed against it in another state or to make an investment in a rock quarry, or the like, the origin of those claims is in the profit-making activities of the corporation and the expenses are deductible.

While an argument could be made that the legal expenses for preparing pleadings required to be filed in this case on behalf of the corporation are deductible, I reject the idea that the total amount of the settlement and all of the legal costs incurred in defending Earl, his wife Jean, and their son Wayne, and the corporation are deductible as expenses incurred in carrying on any trade or business of the corporation.

I would affirm the district court's denial of the refund.

QUESTIONS, NOTE

1. How does the majority distinguish *Gilmore*? Are you convinced?

2. Imagine that the corporation had been a Fortune 500 corporation, rather than closely held. Mr. Kopp was an employee, who owned a few shares. He negligently entrusted a company car to his son, who had the same accident. Wouldn't the corporation have fired Mr. Kopp, and then sued him? Why didn't Kopp's Inc. do the same thing? What does that tell you about the corporate motivation and the business nature of the expenditure?

3. In Liberty Vending, Inc. v. Commissioner, T.C. Memo. 1998–177, John Poulus was hospitalized with heart problems. When he returned from the hospital, he discovered that his wife had filed for divorce, and obtained a court order which gave her emergency possession of his two corporations. She and her boyfriend had fired all the employees, and removed all of the cash, equipment, books and records from the business premises. On their way out, they had changed the locks. The Tax Court held that Mr. Poulus was entitled to ordinary and necessary business deductions for the legal fees incurred in regaining possession of his business assets.

4. In Capital Video Corporation v. Commissioner, 311 F.3d 458 (1st Cir.2002), the corporation was a distributor of pornographic videotapes in Cranston, Rhode Island. The corporation and its sole shareholder, Kenneth Guarino, made cash "tribute" payments totaling at least $1,700,000 to Natale Richichi, a capo in the Gambino family of La Cosa Nostra. The corporation also leased Mercedes Benz autos for Richichi and his daughter, and paid for health insurance covereage for Richichi and his wife under the Capital Video employee plan. In addition, Mr. Richichi was given a Capital Video credit card. Guarino and his bookkeeper (his former mother-in-law) made numerous arrangements to help Richichi hide these payments, and others, from the IRS. Guarino and Richichi were indicted for conspiring to defraud the IRS. Guarino ultimately entered a plea bargain, spent sixteen months in prison, and paid a $250,000 fine.

The corporation paid over $750,000 in legal fees for Mr. Guarino, and wanted to deduct them. Both sides agreed that *Lohrke* (cited in *Harold Jenkins*) controlled, when one taxpayer (Capital Video) claimed business deductions for payments made on behalf of another (Guarino). The corporation argued that the "tribute" payments were clearly deductible (presumably they were quite ordinary in this line of business in this time and place), and that the conspiracy to defraud IRS necessarily followed. The Third Circuit was not entirely sure about the origin of the expense. It noted that there was no evidence offered that Richichi would have withdrawn his "protection" had Guarino refused to help in the conspiracy to defraud IRS. Furthermore, Capital Video actually made more money while Guarino was in jail. Held: nondeductible.

PROBLEM

Consider the facts below from a Tax Court case.

Sam Gilliam was born in Tupelo, Mississippi, in 1933, and raised in Louisville, Kentucky. In 1961, he received a master of arts degree in painting from the University of Louisville.

Gilliam is, and was at all material periods, a noted artist. His works have been exhibited in numerous art galleries throughout the United States and Europe, including the Corcoran Gallery of Art, Washington, D.C.; the Philadelphia Museum of Art, Philadelphia, Pennsylvania; the Karl Solway Gallery, Cincinnati, Ohio; the Phoenix Gallery, San Francisco, California; and the University of California, Irvine, California. His works have also been exhibited and sold at the Fendrick Gallery, Washington, D.C. In addition, Gilliam is, and was at all material periods, a teacher of art. On occasion, Gilliam lectured and taught art at various institutions.

Gilliam accepted an invitation to lecture and teach for a week at the Memphis Academy of Arts in Memphis, Tennessee. On Sunday, February 23, 1975, he flew to Memphis to fulfill this business obligation.

Gilliam had a history of hospitalizations for mental and emotional disturbances and continued to be under psychiatric care until the time of his trip to Memphis. In December 1963, Gilliam was hospitalized in Louisville; Gilliam had anxieties about his work as an artist. For periods of time in both 1965 and 1966, Gilliam suffered from depression and was unable to work. In 1970, Gilliam was again hospitalized. In 1973, while Gilliam was a visiting artist at a number of university campuses in California, he found it necessary to consult an airport physician; however, when he returned to Washington, D.C., Gilliam did not require hospitalization.

* * *

On the night before his Memphis trip, Gilliam felt anxious and unable to rest. On Sunday morning, Gilliam contacted Ranville Clark (hereinafter sometimes referred to as "Clark"), a doctor Gilliam had been consulting intermittently over the years, and asked Clark to prescribe some medication to relieve his anxiety. Clark arranged for Gilliam to pick up a prescription of the drug Dalmane on the way to the airport. Gilliam had taken medication frequently during the preceding 10 years. Clark had never before prescribed Dalmane for Gilliam.

On Sunday, February 23, 1975, Gilliam got the prescription and at about 3:25 p.m., he boarded American Airlines flight 395 at Washington National Airport, Washington, D.C., bound for Memphis. Gilliam occupied a window seat. He took the Dalmane for the first time shortly after boarding the airplane.

About one and one-half hours after the airplane departed Washington National Airport, Gilliam began to act in an irrational manner. He talked of bizarre events and had difficulty in speaking. According to some witnesses, he appeared to be airsick and held his head. Gilliam began to feel trapped, anxious, disoriented, and very agitated. Gilliam said that the plane was going to crash and that he wanted a life raft. Gilliam entered the aisle and, while going from one end of the airplane to the other, he tried to exit from three different doors. Then Gilliam struck Seiji Nakamura (hereinafter sometimes referred to as "Nakamura"), another passenger, several times with a telephone receiver. Nakamura was seated toward the rear of the airplane, near one of the exits. Gilliam also threatened the navigator and a stewardess, called for help, and cried. As a result of the attack, Nakamura sustained a one-inch laceration above his left eyebrow which required four sutures. Nakamura also suffered ecchymosis of the left arm and pains in his left wrist. Nakamura was treated for these injuries at Methodist Hospital in Memphis.

On arriving in Memphis, Gilliam was arrested by Federal officials. On March 10, 1975, Gilliam was indicted. He was brought to trial in the United States District Court for the Western District of Tennessee, Western Division, on one count of violation of 49 U.S.C. section 1472(k) (relating to certain crimes aboard an aircraft in flight) and two counts of violation 49 U.S.C. section 1472(j) (relating to interference with flight crew members or flight attendants). Gilliam entered a plea of not guilty to the criminal charges. The trial began on September 8, 1975, and ended on September 10, 1975. After Gilliam presented all of his evidence, the district court granted Gilliam's motion for a judgment of acquittal by reason of temporary insanity.

Petitioners paid $8,250 and $8,600 for legal fees in 1975 and 1976, respectively, in connection with both the criminal trial and Nakamura's civil claim. In 1975, petitioners also paid $3,800 to Nakamura in settlement of the civil claim.

QUESTIONS

1. Were any of Mr. Gilliam's expenses deductible business expenses?

2. The rock band, The Who, is known for trashing their hotel rooms before/after their concerts. If the Who had been subject to US tax law, would the resulting expenses have been deductible? Would it be relevant that their fans have now come to expect them to trash their hotel rooms, and would be disappointed if they didn't?

3. In 2002, Manny Ramirez, Boston Red Sox outfielder, slid head first during a spring training game, and broke his finger. He was sent down to the Triple A Pawtucket Red Sox to rehab. On June 18, in a game against the Syracuse SkyChiefs, Ramirez, incredibly, slid head first again. This time, he didn't hurt himself, but he did lose his diamond earring, worth $15,000. Given his $15 million salary, a personal casualty loss would have been unavailable. See Chapter X, *infra*. Could Manny have taken a business loss?

4. Lamar Odom claims that the $12,000 in fines that were assessed by the NBA when he played for the Los Angeles Lakers in 2007 should be deductible. Is he right?

D. PUBLIC POLICY DOCTRINE

Code: §§ 162(c), (f) and (g)

CALIFORNIANS HELPING TO ALLEVIATE MEDICAL PROBLEMS, INC. v. COMMISSIONER

United States Tax Court, 2007.
128 T.C. 173.

LARO, JUDGE.

* * * We decide whether § 280E precludes petitioner from deducting the ordinary and necessary expenses attributable to its provision of medical marijuana pursuant to the California Compassionate Use Act of 1996, We hold that those deductions are precluded. We also decide whether § 280E precludes petitioner from deducting the ordinary and necessary expenses attributable to its provision of counseling and other caregiving services (collectively, caregiving services). We hold that those deductions are not precluded.

Findings of Fact

Petitioner's * * * articles of incorporation stated that it "is organized and operated exclusively for charitable, educational and scientific purposes" and "The property of this corporation is irrevocably dedicated to charitable purposes". Petitioner did not have Federal tax-exempt status, and it operated as an approximately break-even (i.e., the amount of its income approximated the amount of its expenses) community center for members with debilitating diseases. Approximately 47 percent of petitioner's members suffered from AIDS; the remainder suffered from cancer, multiple sclerosis, and other serious illnesses. Before joining petitioner, petitioner's executive director had 13 years of experience in health services as a coordinator of a statewide program that trained outreach workers in AIDS prevention work.

Petitioner operated with a dual purpose. Its primary purpose was to provide caregiving services to its members. Its secondary purpose was to provide its members with medical marijuana pursuant to the California Compassionate Use Act of 1996 and to instruct those individuals on how to use medical marijuana to benefit their health. Petitioner required that each member have a doctor's letter recommending marijuana as part of his or her therapy and an unexpired photo identification card from the California Department of Public Health verifying the authenticity of the doctor's letter. Petitioner required that its members not resell or redistribute the medical marijuana received from petitioner, and petitioner considered any violation of this requirement to be grounds to expel the violator from membership in petitioner's organization.

Each of petitioner's members paid petitioner a membership fee in consideration for the right to receive caregiving services and medical marijuana from petitioner. Petitioner's caregiving services were extensive. First, petitioner's staff held various weekly or biweekly support group sessions that could be attended only by petitioner's members. The "wellness group" discussed healing techniques and occasionally hosted a guest speaker; the HIV/AIDS group addressed issues of practical and emotional support; the women's group focused on women-specific issues in medical struggles; the "Phoenix" group helped elderly patients with lifelong addiction problems; the "Force" group focused on spiritual and emotional development. Second, petitioner provided its low-income members with daily lunches consisting of salads, fruit, water, soda, and hot food. Petitioner also made available to its members hygiene supplies such as toothbrushes, toothpaste, feminine hygiene products, combs, and bottles of bleach. Third, petitioner allowed its members to consult one-on-one with a counselor about benefits, health, housing, safety, and legal issues. Petitioner also provided its members with biweekly massage services. Fourth, petitioner coordinated for its members weekend social events including a Friday night movie or guest speaker and a Saturday night social with live music and a hot meal. Petitioner also coordinated for its members monthly field trips to locations such as beaches, museums, or parks. Fifth, petitioner instructed its members on yoga and on topics such as how to participate in social services at petitioner's facilities and how to follow member guidelines. Sixth, petitioner provided its members with online computer access and delivered to them informational services through its Web site. Seventh, petitioner encouraged its members to participate in political activities.

Petitioner furnished its services at its main facility in San Francisco, California, and at an office in a community church in San Francisco. The main facility was approximately 1,350 square feet and was the site of the daily lunches, distribution of hygiene supplies, benefits counseling, Friday and Saturday night social events and dinners, and computer access. This location also was the site where petitioner's members received their distribution of medical marijuana; the medical marijuana was dispensed at a counter of the main room of the facility, taking up approximately 10 percent of the main facility. The peer group meetings and yoga classes were usually held at the church, where petitioner rented space. Pursuant to the rules of the church, petitioner's members were prohibited from bringing any marijuana into the church. Petitioner also maintained a storage unit at a third location in San Francisco. Petitioner used the storage unit to store confidential medical records; no medical marijuana was distributed or used there.

Petitioner paid for the services it provided to its members by charging a membership fee that covered, and in the judgment of petitioner's management approximated, both the cost of petitioner's caregiving services and the cost of the medical marijuana that petitioner supplied to its members. Petitioner notified its members that the membership fee covered both of these costs, and petitioner charged its members no additional fee. Members received from petitioner a set amount of medical marijuana; they were not entitled to unlimited supplies.

* * *

Opinion

The parties agree that during the subject year petitioner had at least one trade or business for purposes of section 280E. According to respondent, petitioner had a single trade or business of trafficking in medical marijuana. Petitioner argues that it engaged in two trades or businesses. Petitioner asserts that its primary trade or business was the provision of caregiving services. Petitioner asserts that its secondary trade or business was the supplying of medical marijuana to its members. As to its trades or businesses, petitioner argues, the deductions for those trades or businesses are not precluded by section 280E in that the trades or businesses did not involve "trafficking" in a controlled substance. Respondent argues that section 280E precludes petitioner from benefiting from any of its deductions.

* * * Section 280E provides:

No deduction or credit shall be allowed for any amount paid or incurred during the taxable year in carrying on any trade or business if such trade or business (or the activities which comprise such trade or business) consists of trafficking in controlled substances (within the meaning of schedule I and II of the Controlled Substances Act) which is prohibited by Federal law or the law of any State in which such trade or business is conducted.

In the context of section 280E, marijuana is a schedule I controlled substance. Such is so even when the marijuana is medical marijuana recommended by a physician as appropriate to benefit the health of the user.

Respondent argues that petitioner, because it trafficked in a controlled substance, is not permitted by section 280E to deduct any of its expenses. We disagree. Our analysis begins with the text of the statute, which we must apply in accordance with its ordinary, everyday usage. We interpret that text with reference to its legislative history primarily to learn the purpose of the statute.

Congress enacted section 280E as a direct reaction to the outcome of a case in which this Court allowed a taxpayer to deduct expenses incurred in an illegal drug trade. In that case, *Edmondson v. Commissioner,* T.C. Memo.1981–623, the Court found that the taxpayer was self-employed in a trade or business of selling amphetamines, cocaine, and marijuana. The Court allowed the taxpayer to deduct his business expenses because they "were made in connection with * * * [the taxpayer's] trade or business and were both ordinary and necessary." *Id.* In discussing the case in the context of the then-current law, the Senate Finance Committee stated in its report:

Ordinary and necessary trade or business expenses are generally deductible in computing taxable income. A recent U.S. Tax Court case allowed deductions for telephone, auto, and rental expense incurred in the illegal drug trade. In that case, the Internal Revenue Service challenged the amount of the taxpayer's deduction for cost of goods (illegal drugs) sold, but did not challenge the principle that such amounts were deductible.

On public policy grounds, the Code makes certain otherwise ordinary and necessary expenses incurred in a trade or business nondeductible in computing taxable income. These nondeductible expenses include fines, illegal bribes and kickbacks, and certain other illegal payments.

The report then expressed the following reasons the committee intended to change the law: There is a sharply defined public policy against drug dealing. To allow drug dealers the benefit of business expense deductions at the same time that the U.S. and its citizens are losing billions of dollars per year to such persons is not compelled by the fact that such deductions are allowed to other, legal, enterprises. Such deductions must be disallowed on public policy grounds. [Id.]

The report explained that the enactment of section 280E has the following effect: All deductions and credits for amounts paid or incurred in the illegal trafficking in drugs listed in the Controlled Substances Act are disallowed. To preclude possible challenges on constitutional grounds, the adjustment to gross receipts with respect to effective costs of goods sold is not affected by this provision of the bill. [Id.]

Section 280E and its legislative history express a congressional intent to disallow deductions attributable to a trade or business of trafficking in controlled substances. They do not express an intent to deny the deduction of all of a taxpayer's business expenses simply because the taxpayer was involved in trafficking in a controlled substance. We hold that section 280E does not preclude petitioner from deducting expenses attributable to a trade or business other than that of illegal trafficking in controlled substances simply because petitioner also is involved in the trafficking in a controlled substance.

* * *

We now turn to analyze whether petitioner's furnishing of its caregiving services is a trade or business that is separate from its trade or business of providing medical marijuana. Taxpayers may be involved in more than one trade or business, and whether an activity is a trade or business separate from another trade or business is a question of fact that depends on (among other things) the degree of economic interrelationship between the two undertakings. The Commissioner generally accepts a taxpayer's characterization of two or more undertakings as separate activities unless the characterization is artificial or unreasonable.

We do not believe it to have been artificial or unreasonable for petitioner to have characterized as separate activities its provision of caregiving services and its provision of medical marijuana. Petitioner was regularly and extensively involved in the provision of caregiving services, and those services are substantially different from petitioner's provision of medical marijuana. By conducting its recurring discussion groups, regularly distributing food and hygiene supplies, advertising and making available the services of personal counselors, coordinating social events and field trips, hosting educational classes, and providing other social services, petitioner's caregiving business stood on its own, separate and apart from petitioner's provision of medical marijuana. On the basis of all of the facts and circumstances of this case, we hold that petitioner's provision of caregiving services was a trade or business separate and apart from its provision of medical marijuana.

Respondent argues that the "evidence indicates that petitioner's principal purpose was to provide access to marijuana, that petitioner's principal activity was providing access to marijuana, and that the principal service that petitioner provided was access to marijuana * * * and that all of petitioner's activities were merely incidental to petitioner's activity of trafficking in marijuana." We disagree. Petitioner's executive director testified credibly and without contradiction that petitioner's primary purpose was to provide caregiving services for terminally ill patients. He stated: "Right from the start we considered our primary function as being a community center for seriously ill patients in San Francisco. And only secondarily as a place where they could access their medicine." The evidence suggests that petitioner's operations were conducted with that primary function in mind, not with the principal purpose of providing marijuana to members.

* * *

Given petitioner's separate trades or businesses, we are required to apportion its overall expenses accordingly. Respondent argues that "petitioner failed to justify any particular allocation and failed to present evidence as to how * * * [petitioner's expenses] should be allocated between marijuana trafficking and other activities." We disagree. Respondent concedes that many of petitioner's activities are legal and unrelated to petitioner's provision of medical marijuana. The evidence at hand permits an allocation of expenses to those activities. Although the record may not lend itself to a perfect allocation with pinpoint accuracy, the record permits us with sufficient confidence to allocate petitioner's expenses between its two trades or businesses on the basis of the number of petitioner's employees and the portion of its facilities devoted to each business. Accordingly, in a manner that is most consistent with petitioner's breakdown of the disputed expenses, we allocate to petitioner's caregiving services 18/25 of the expenses for salaries, wages, payroll taxes, employee benefits, employee development training, meals and entertainment, and parking and tolls (18 of petitioner's 25 employees did not work directly in petitioner's provision of medical marijuana), all expenses incurred in renting facilities at the church (petitioner did not use the church to any extent to provide medical marijuana), all expenses incurred for "truck and auto" and "laundry and cleaning" (those expenses did not relate to any extent to petitioner's provision of medical marijuana), and 9/10 of the remaining expenses (90 percent of the square footage of petitioner's main facility was not used in petitioner's provision of medical marijuana).[6] We disagree with respondent that petitioner must further justify the allocation of its expenses, reluctant to substitute our judgment for the judgment of petitioner's management as to its understanding of the expenses that petitioner incurred as to each of its trades or businesses.

NOTE AND QUESTION

In *Tank Truck Rentals, Inc. v. Commissioner*, 356 U.S. 30, 78 S.Ct. 507, 2 L.Ed.2d 562 (1958), the Supreme Court held that a trucking company could not deduct the fines it paid to Pennsylvania for running overweight trucks. They reasoned that deductibility against federal taxes would alleviate the penalty, thus frustrating the clearly delineated policy of Pennsylvania of imposing maximum weight limits on trucks. Hence § 162(f). However, on the same day, the Court decided *Commissioner v. Sullivan*, 356 U.S. 27, 78 S.Ct. 512, 2 L.Ed.2d 559 (1958), which held that, even though the taxpayer's bookmaking establishment was illegal under Illinois law, the taxpayer could still deduct rental and salary expenses. The penalty for violating the criminal law should be defined by the criminal statute; it should not mean that criminals pay tax on gross income while noncriminals pay tax on net income.

How can you square what Congress did in enacting § 280E? Did the Tax Court in CHAMP finesse the statute?

E. SALARY

Code: § 162(a)(1)

Regulations: § 1.162–7

What could be a more obvious business expense than employee salaries? But if they are so obviously deductible, why must they be "reasonable"? The Court in *Exacto Spring, infra* mentions a fear of disguised dividends and sales as the rationale for the reasonableness limitation in § 162(a)(1). How would disguised dividends work?

Corporation earns $100. It distributes the $100 to Smith, who is both a shareholder and an employee.

Assume that the $100 is treated as a dividend. The corporation will be taxed on $100 income at the corporate level. There will be no deduction for the dividends paid. Dividends, generally, are viewed as a mere sharing of profits by the owners, rather than an expense of doing business. The

---

6. While we apportion most of the $212,958 in "Total deductions" to petitioner's caregiving services, we note that the costs of petitioner's medical marijuana business included the $203,661 in labor and $43,783 in other costs respondent conceded to have been properly reported on petitioner's tax return as attributable to cost of goods sold in the medical marijuana business.

receipt of the dividend by Smith, however, will be taxable. To summarize, there will be a tax at the corporate level and a second tax at the shareholder level, with no deductions.

Now assume that the $100 is treated as salary. The corporation will be taxed on the $100 income at the corporate level, just as before. However, this time, the corporation will obtain a corresponding deduction for the salary expense, wiping out the income. Smith, of course, will be taxed on $100 of salary income. To summarize, there will be only one tax—at the employee level. You can see why corporate managers, shareholders and employees would be tempted to disguise dividends as salary.

What advantages would accrue, if any, if the $100 were characterized as a loan from the corporation, or a payment by the corporation for the purchase of property from the shareholder/employee?

Lawyers should be very careful in explaining these phenomena to clients, lest they ask leading questions and end up encouraging their clients to lie.

EXACTO SPRING CORPORATION v. COMMISSIONER

United States Court of Appeals, Seventh Circuit, 1999.
196 F.3d 833.

POSNER, CHIEF JUDGE.

This appeal from a judgment by the Tax Court requires us to interpret and apply § 162(a)(1), which allows a business to deduct from its income its "ordinary and necessary business expenses, including a 'reasonable allowance for salaries or other compensation for personal services actually rendered.'" In 1993 and 1994, Exacto Spring Corporation, a closely held corporation engaged in the manufacture of precision springs, paid its cofounder, chief executive, and principal owner, William Heitz, $1.3 and $1.0 million, respectively, in salary. The Internal Revenue Service thought this amount excessive, that Heitz should not have been paid more than $381,000 in 1993 or $400,000 in 1994, with the difference added to the corporation's income, and it assessed a deficiency accordingly, which Exacto challenged in the Tax Court. That court found that the reasonable compensation for Heitz would have been $900,000 in the earlier year and $700,000 in the later one—figures roughly midway between his actual compensation and the IRS's determination—and Exacto has appealed.

In reaching its conclusion, the Tax Court applied a test that requires the consideration of seven factors, none entitled to any specified weight relative to another. The factors are, in the court's words, "(1) the type and extent of the services rendered; (2) the scarcity of qualified employees; (3) the qualifications and prior earning capacity of the employee; (4) the contributions of the employee to the business venture; (5) the net earnings of the employer; (6) the prevailing compensation paid to employees with comparable jobs; and (7) the peculiar characteristics of the employer's business." It is apparent that this test, though it or variants of it (one of which has the astonishing total of 21 factors) leaves much to be desired—being, like many other multi-factor tests, "redundant, incomplete, and unclear."

To begin with, it is nondirective. No indication is given of how the factors are to be weighed in the event they don't all line up on one side. And many of the factors, such as the type and extent of services rendered, the scarcity of qualified employees, and the peculiar characteristics of the employer's business, are vague.

Second, the factors do not bear a clear relation either to each other or to the primary purpose of § 162(a)(1), which is to prevent dividends (or in some cases gifts), which are not deductible from corporate income, from being disguised as salary, which is. Suppose that an employee who let us say was, like Heitz, a founder and the chief executive officer and principal owner of the taxpayer rendered no services at all but received a huge salary. It would be absurd to allow the whole or for that matter any part of his salary to be deducted as an ordinary and necessary business expense even if he were well qualified to be CEO of the company, the company had substantial net earnings, CEOs of similar companies were paid a lot, and it was a business in which high salaries are common. The multi-factor test would not prevent the Tax Court from allowing a deduction in such a case even though the corporation obviously was seeking to reduce its taxable income by disguising earnings as salary. The court would not allow the deduction, but not because of anything in the multi-factor test; rather because it would be apparent that the payment to the employee was not in fact for his services to the company.

Third, the seven-factor test invites the Tax Court to set itself up as a superpersonnel department for closely held corporations, a role unsuitable for courts * * *. The judges of the Tax Court are not equipped by training or experience to determine the salaries of corporate officers; no judges are.

Fourth, since the test cannot itself determine the outcome of a dispute because of its nondirective character, it invites the making of arbitrary decisions * * *. The Tax Court in this case essentially added the IRS's determination of the maximum that Mr. Heitz should have been paid in 1993 and 1994 to what he was in fact paid, and divided the sum by two. It cut the baby in half. One would have to be awfully naive to believe that the seven-factor test generated this pleasing symmetry.

Fifth, because the reaction of the Tax Court to a challenge to the deduction of executive compensation is unpredictable, corporations run unavoidable legal risks in determining a level of compensation that may be indispensable to the success of their business.

The drawbacks of the multi-factor test are well illustrated by its purported application by the Tax Court in this case. With regard to factor (1), the court found that Heitz was "indispensable to Exacto's business" and "essential to Exacto's success." Heitz is not only Exacto's CEO; he is also the company's chief salesman and marketing man plus the head of its research and development efforts and its principal inventor. The company's entire success appears to be due on the one hand to the research and development conducted by him and on the other hand to his marketing of these innovations (though he receives some additional compensation for his marketing efforts from a subsidiary of Exacto). The court decided that factor (1) favored Exacto.

Likewise factor (2), for, as the court pointed out, the design of precision springs, which is Heitz's specialty, is "an extremely specialized branch of mechanical engineering, and there are very few engineers who have made careers specializing in this area," let alone engineers like Heitz who have "the ability to identify and attract clients and to develop springs to perform a specific function for that client.... It would have been very difficult to replace Mr. Heitz." Notice how factors (1) and (2) turn out to be nearly identical.

Factors (3) and (4) also supported Exacto, the court found. "Mr Heitz is highly qualified to run Exacto as a result of his education, training, experience, and motivation. Mr. Heitz has over 40 years of highly successful experience in the field of spring design." And his "efforts were of great value to the corporation." So factor (4) duplicated (2), and so the first four factors turn out to be really only two.

* * *

Having run through the seven factors, all of which either favored the taxpayer or were neutral, the court reached a stunning conclusion: "We have considered the factors relevant in deciding reasonable compensation for Mr. Heitz. On the basis of all the evidence, we hold that reasonable compensation for Mr. Heitz" was much less than Exacto paid him. The court's only effort at explaining this result when Exacto had passed the seven-factor test with flying colors was that "we have balanced Mr. Heitz' unique selling and technical ability, his years of experience, and the difficulty of replacing Mr. Heitz with the fact that the corporate entity would have shown a reasonable return for the equity holders, after considering petitioners' concessions." But "the fact that the corporate entity would have shown a reasonable return for the equity holders" after the concessions is on the *same side* of the balance as the other factors; it does not favor the Internal Revenue Service's position. The government's lawyer was forced to concede at the argument of the appeal that she could not deny the possibility that the Tax Court had pulled its figures for Heitz's allowable compensation out of a hat.

The failure of the Tax Court's reasoning to support its result would alone require a remand. But the problem with the court's opinion goes deeper. The test it applied does not provide adequate guidance to a rational decision. We owe no deference to the Tax Court's statutory interpretations, its relation to us being that of a district court to a court of appeals, not that of an administrative agency to a court of appeals. § 7482(a)(1); David F. Shores, "Deferential Review of Tax Court Decisions: Dobson Revisited," 49 Tax Lawyer 629, 659 (1996). The federal courts of appeals, whose decisions do of course have weight as authority with us even when they are not our own decisions, have been moving toward a much simpler and more purposive test, the "independent investor" test. We applaud the trend and join it.

Because judges tend to downplay the element of judicial creativity in adapting law to fresh insights and changed circumstances, the cases we have just cited prefer to say that the "independent investor" test is the "lens" through which they view the seven (or however many) factors of the orthodox test. But that is a formality. The new test dissolves the old and returns the inquiry to basics. The Internal Revenue Code limits the amount of salary that a corporation can deduct from its income primarily in order to prevent the corporation from eluding the corporate income tax by paying dividends but calling them salary because salary is deductible and dividends are not. (Perhaps they should be, to avoid double taxation of corporate earnings, but that is not the law.) In the case of a publicly held company, where the salaries of the highest executives are fixed by a board of directors that those executives do not control, the danger of siphoning corporate earnings to executives in the form of salary is not acute. The danger is much greater in the case of a closely held corporation, in which ownership and management tend to coincide; unfortunately, as the opinion of the Tax Court in this case illustrates, judges are not competent to decide what business executives are worth.

There is, fortunately, an indirect market test, as recognized by the Internal Revenue Service's expert witness. A corporation can be conceptualized as a contract in which the owner of assets hires a person to manage them. The owner pays the manager a salary and in exchange the manager works to increase the value of the assets that have been entrusted to his management; that increase can be expressed as a rate of return to the owner's investment. The higher the rate of return (adjusted for risk) that a manager can generate, the greater the salary he can command. If the rate of return is extremely high, it will be difficult to prove that the manager is being overpaid, for it will be implausible that if he quit if his salary was cut, and he was replaced by a lower-paid manager, the owner would be better off; it would be killing the goose that lays the golden egg. The Service's expert believed that investors in a firm like Exacto would expect a 13 percent return on their investment. Presumably they would be delighted with more. They would be overjoyed to receive a return more than 50 percent greater than they expected—and 20 percent, the return that the Tax Court found that investors in Exacto had obtained, is more than 50 percent greater than the benchmark return of 13 percent.

When, notwithstanding the CEO's "exorbitant" salary (as it might appear to a judge or other modestly paid official), the investors in his company are obtaining a far higher return than they had any reason to expect, his salary is presumptively reasonable. We say "presumptively" because we can imagine cases in which the return, though very high, is not due to the CEO's exertions. Suppose Exacto had been an unprofitable company that suddenly learned that its factory was sitting on an oil field, and when oil revenues started to pour in its owner raised his salary from $50,000 a year to $1.3 million. The presumption of reasonableness would be rebutted. There is no suggestion of anything of that sort here and likewise no suggestion that Mr. Heitz was merely the titular chief executive and the company was actually run by someone else, which would be another basis for rebuttal.

The government could still have prevailed by showing that while Heitz's salary may have been no greater than would be reasonable in the circumstances, the company did not in fact intend to pay him that amount as salary, that his salary really did include a concealed dividend though it need not have. This is material (and the "independent investor" test, like the multi-factor test that it replaces, thus incomplete, though invaluable) because any business expense to be deductible must be, as we noted earlier, a bona fide expense as well as reasonable in amount. The fact that Heitz's salary was approved by the other owners of the corporation, who had no incentive to disguise a dividend as salary, goes far to rebut any inference of bad faith here, which in any event the Tax Court did not draw and the government does not ask us to draw.

The judgment is reversed with directions to enter judgment for the taxpayer.

REVERSED.

NOTE ON CORPORATE TAX INTEGRATION

Previously, we addressed the double tax on corporate earnings. Contrast this tax treatment with the tax treatment of partnerships. Partnership income flows through the partnership, and is taxed to the partners at their marginal rates—just once, not twice. Clearly, our tax laws discriminate against corporations, and in favor of partnerships.

Also, there is a significant incentive to characterize distributions from corporations as something other than dividends. No such incentives exist with respect to partnerships. Finally, since interest payments on bonds are deductible to the corporation, while dividends on stock are not, the tax laws encourage corporations to finance operations by selling bonds instead of stock. All of these factors tend to distort behavior, or at least to encourage taxpayers to mischaracterize it.

Our system of corporate taxation is called the "classical" system. Many European countries, in contrast, have a "fully integrated" system. In these countries, corporate income flows through to the shareholders, just as partnership income flows through to the partners. If there is a tax at the corporate level, it functions only as a withholding tax, to be credited against the tax owed by the shareholders on corporate source income.

Congress, in the Jobs and Growth Tax Relief Reconciliation Act of 2003, took a step away from the classical system, but they did it backwards. In a truly integrated system, the corporate level tax would be eliminated. Instead, Congress left the corporate level tax alone, and reduced the taxation of dividends at the shareholder level. Now, "qualified dividends" will be taxed to the shareholder at the lower, capital gains rate.[b] Thus, instead of double taxation, we have achieved, perhaps, taxation one and a half times.

QUESTION ON THE MILLION DOLLAR CAP

Consider § 162(m), added in 1993. What employees are really covered? How can it be avoided? What effect, if any, do you think the section will have on the market wages of high corporate officials? Does the provision make sense?

What do you think of the flat million dollar cap? Would H.R. 2888, 108th Cong., 1st. Sess. (2003) have been an improvement? It provides in part:

No deduction shall be allowed under this chapter for any excessive compensation with respect to any full-time employee.

For the purposes of this subsection, the term "excessive compensation" means, with respect to any employee, the amount by which—

(A) The compensation for services performed by such employee exceeds

(B) An amount equal to 25 times the lowest compensation for services performed by any other full-time employee during such taxable year.

Payment of Salary Obligations with Appreciated Assets

Deductible salary can be paid in cash or in kind. When salary is paid in kind, with appreciated assets, that one payment can lead to both a salary deduction and a realization of gain.

INTERNATIONAL FREIGHTING CORPORATION, INC. v. COMMISSIONER

United States Court of Appeals, Second Circuit, 1943.
135 F.2d 310.

Before L. HAND, CHASE and FRANK, CIRCUIT JUDGES.

* * * [Pursuant to a discretionary employee bonus plan, the taxpayer corporation distributed shares of DuPont stock to its employees. The corporation's basis in the stock was $16,153.35; its fair market value on the date of distribution was $24,858.75. The corporation took a deduction for $24,858.75, but the Commissioner reduced it to $16,153.35. Ed.]

By an amended answer, the Commissioner in the alternative, alleged that if it were held that taxpayer was entitled to a deduction in the amount of $24,858.75 on account of the payment of bonus in stock, then taxpayer realized a taxable profit of $8,705.39 on the disposition of the shares, and taxpayer's net taxable income otherwise determined should be increased accordingly.

The Tax Court held that taxpayer was entitled to a deduction for compensation paid in the year 1936 in the amount of $24,858.75. The Tax Court decided for the Commissioner, however, on the defense set forth in

---

b.   § 1(h)(11). See Chapter 7 generally for capital gains.

the Commissioner's amended answer, holding that taxpayer realized a gain of $8,705.39 in 1936 by paying the class B bonus in stock which had cost taxpayer $8,705.39 less than its market value when taxpayer transferred the stock to its employees. The deficiency resulting from this decision was $2,156.76. From that decision taxpayer seeks review.

FRANK, CIRCUIT JUDGE.

Up to the time in 1936 when the shares were delivered to the employees, the taxpayer retained such control of the shares that title had not passed to the employees. We think the Tax Court correctly held that the market value at the time of delivery was properly deducted by the taxpayer as an ordinary expense of the business, because that delivery was an additional reasonable compensation for past services actually rendered. The payment depleted the taxpayer's assets in an amount equal to that market value fully as much as if taxpayer had, at the time of delivery, first purchased those shares.

We turn to the question whether the transaction resulted in taxable gain to taxpayer. We think that the Tax Court correctly held that it did. The delivery of those shares was not a gift, else (1) it would have been wrongful as against taxpayer's stockholders, (2) the value of the shares could not have been deducted as an expense, and (3) the employees as donees would not be obliged to pay, as they must, an income tax on what they received. It was not a gift precisely because it was "compensation for services actually rendered," i.e., because the taxpayer received a full quid pro quo. Accordingly, cases holding that one is not liable for an income tax when he makes a gift of shares are not in point. * * *

But, as the delivery of the shares here constituted a disposition for a valid consideration, it resulted in a closed transaction with a consequent realized gain. It is of no relevance that here the taxpayer had not been legally obligated to award any shares or pay any additional compensation to the employees; bonus payments by corporations are recognized as proper even if there was no previous obligation to make them; although then not obligatory, they are regarded as made for a sufficient consideration. Since the bonuses would be invalid to the extent that what was delivered to the employees exceeded what the services of the employees were worth, it follows that the consideration received by the taxpayer from the employees must be deemed to be equal at least to the value of the shares in 1936. Here then, as there was no gift but a disposition of shares for a valid consideration equal at least to the market value of the shares when delivered, there was a taxable gain equal to the difference between the cost of the shares and that market value

[Current section 1001] provides that the gain from "the sale or other disposition of property" shall be the excess of "the amount realized therefrom" over "the adjusted basis" provided in [current section 1011] and [§ 1011]—in light of [current § 1012], makes the "basis" the cost of such property. True, [§ 1001(b)] provides that "the amount realized" is the sum of "any money received plus the fair market value of the property (other than money) received." Literally, where there is a disposition of stock for services, no "property" or "money" is received by the person who thus disposes of the stock. But, in similar circumstances, it has been held that "money's worth" is received and that such a receipt comes within [§ 1001(b)].

The taxpayer properly asks us to treat this case "as if there had been no formal bonus plan" and as if taxpayer "had simply paid outright 150 shares of duPont stock to selected employees as additional compensation." On that basis, surely there was a taxable gain. For to shift the equation once more, the case supposed is the equivalent of one in which the taxpayer in the year 1936, without entering into a previous contract fixing the amount of compensation, had employed a transposition expert for one day and, when he completed his work, had paid him 5 shares of duPont stock having market value at that time of $500 but which it had bought in a previous year for $100. There can be no doubt that, from such a transaction, taxpayer would have a taxable gain. And so here.

The order of the Tax Court is affirmed.

CHAPTER V

BUSINESS DEDUCTIONS: CAPITAL RECOVERY AND DEPRECIATION

■ ■ ■

Some business outlays can be deducted immediately, while others must be capitalized. These "capital expenses" must be added to the basis of the underlying asset. Most can be spread out over time, and deducted through either depreciation or amortization. Some, however, can only be deducted when the asset is sold—when Basis is subtracted from Amount Realized. [Remember the Introduction to Matching in Chapter IV.]

How do you distinguish an immediately deductible expense from a capital expense? In simpler times, we would have said that repairs are currently deductible, while replacements must be capitalized. Fixing a shingle is deductible now; replacing the entire roof is a capital expense. Those statements are still true, but they're not the whole truth.

In theory, any expense likely to generate income for *less than a year* should be deductible immediately. Conversely, any expense likely to generate income for *more than a year* should be capitalized. Alas, things don't quite work out that way.

The bulk of the materials below will discuss in greater detail when expenses can be deducted immediately, and when they must be capitalized. Then, depreciation and amortization will be addressed. Other situations involving spreading out capital recovery, such as annuities, will follow. Finally, there is a short note on inventory accounting, which is the way we deal with basis and amount realized when large volumes of fungible assets are sold.

A. CAPITAL EXPENSES

Code: §§ 263, 263A

Regulations: §§ 1.263(a)–1; 1.263(a)–2

REVENUE RULING 2001–4

2001–1. C.B. 295.

Issue

Are costs incurred by a taxpayer to perform work on its aircraft airframe, including the costs of a "heavy maintenance visit," deductible as ordinary and necessary business expenses under § 162 of the Internal Revenue Code, or must they be capitalized under §§ 263 and 263A?

Facts

X is a commercial airline engaged in the business of transporting passengers and freight throughout the United States and abroad. To conduct its business, X owns or leases various types of aircraft. As a condition of maintaining its operating license and airworthiness certification for these aircraft, X is required by the Federal Aviation Administration "FAA" to establish and adhere to a continuous maintenance program for each aircraft within its fleet. These programs, which are designed by X and the aircraft's manufacturer and approved by the FAA, are incorporated into each aircraft's maintenance manual. The maintenance manuals require a variety of periodic maintenance visits at various intervals during the operating lives of each aircraft. The most extensive of these for X is termed a "heavy maintenance visit" * * * which is required to be performed by X approximately every eight years of aircraft operation. The purpose of a heavy maintenance visit, according to X's maintenance manual, is to prevent deterioration of the inherent safety and reliability levels of the aircraft equipment and, if such deterioration occurs, to restore the equipment to their inherent levels.

In each of the following * * * situations, X reasonably anticipated at the time the aircraft was placed in service that the aircraft would be useful in its trade or business for up to 25 years, taking into account the repairs and maintenance necessary to keep the aircraft in an ordinarily efficient operating condition. In addition, each of the aircraft in the following * * * situations is fully depreciated for federal income tax purposes at the time of the heavy maintenance visit.

Situation 1

In 2000, X incurred $2 million for the labor and materials necessary to perform a heavy maintenance visit on the airframe of Aircraft 1, which X acquired in 1984 for $15 million (excluding the cost of engines). To perform the heavy maintenance visit, X extensively disassembled the airframe, removing items such as its engines, landing gear, cabin and passenger compartment seats, side and ceiling panels, baggage stowage bins, galleys, lavatories, floor boards, cargo loading systems, and flight control surfaces. As specified by X's maintenance manual for Aircraft 1, X then performed certain tasks on the disassembled airframe for the purpose of preventing deterioration of the inherent safety and reliability levels of the airframe. These tasks included lubrication and service; operational and visual checks; inspection and functional checks; restoration of minor parts and components; and removal, discard, and replacement of certain life-limited single cell parts, such as cartridges, canisters, cylinders, and disks.

Whenever the execution of a task revealed cracks, corrosion, excessive wear, or dysfunctional operation, X was required by the maintenance manual to restore the airframe to an acceptable condition.* * *

None of the work performed by X as part of the heavy maintenance visit * * * for Aircraft 1 resulted in a material upgrade or addition to its airframe or involved the replacement of any (or a significant portion of any) major component or substantial structural part of the airframe. This work maintained the relative value of the aircraft. The value of the aircraft declines as it ages even if the heavy maintenance work is performed.

After 45 days, the heavy maintenance visit was completed, and Aircraft 1 was reassembled, tested, and returned to X's fleet. X then continued to use Aircraft 1 for the same purposes and in the same manner that it did prior to the performance of the heavy maintenance visit. The performance of the heavy maintenance visit did not extend the useful life of the airframe beyond the 25–year useful life that X anticipated when it acquired the airframe.

Situation 2

Also in 2000, X incurred costs to perform work in conjunction with a heavy maintenance visit on the airframe of Aircraft 2. The heavy maintenance visit on Aircraft 2 involved all of the same work described in Situation 1. In addition, X found significant wear and corrosion of fuselage skins of Aircraft 2 that necessitated more extensive work than was performed on Aircraft 1. Namely, X decided to remove all of the skin panels on the belly of Aircraft 2's fuselage and replace them with new skin panels. The replaced skin panels represented a significant portion of all of the skin panels of Aircraft 2, and the work performed materially added to the value of the airframe.

Because Aircraft 2 was already out of service and its airframe disassembled for the heavy maintenance visit, X also performed certain modifications to the airframe. These modifications involved installing a cabin smoke and fire detection and suppression system, a ground proximity warning system, and an air phone system to enable passengers to send and receive voice calls, faxes, and other electronic data while in flight.

* * *

Law

* * *

Any properly performed repair, no matter how routine, could be considered to prolong the useful life and increase the value of the property if it is compared with the situation existing immediately prior to that repair. Consequently, courts have articulated a number of ways to distinguish between deductible repairs and non-deductible capital improvements. For example, in Illinois Merchants Trust Co. v. Commissioner, 4 B.T.A. 103 (1926) the court explained that repair and maintenance expenses are incurred for the purpose of keeping the property in an ordinarily efficient operating condition over its probable useful life for the uses for which the property was acquired. Capital expenditures, in contrast, are for replacements, alterations, improvements, or additions that appreciably prolong the life of the property, materially increase its value, or make it adaptable to a different use.

Even if the expenditures include the replacement of numerous parts of an asset, if the replacements are a relatively minor portion of the physical structure of the asset, or of any of its major parts, such that the asset as whole has not gained materially in value or useful life, then the costs incurred may be deducted as incidental repairs or maintenance expenses. * * *

If, however, a major component or a substantial structural part of the asset is replaced and, as a result, the asset as a whole has increased in value, life expectancy, or use then the costs of the replacement must be capitalized. * * *

In addition, although the high cost of the work performed may be considered in determining whether an expenditure is capital in nature, cost alone is not dispositive. * * *

Similarly, the fact that a taxpayer is required by a regulatory authority to make certain repairs or to perform certain maintenance on an asset in order to continue operating the asset in its business does not mean that the work performed materially increases the value of such asset, substantially prolongs its useful life, or adapts it to a new use. * * *

The characterization of any cost as a deductible repair or capital improvement depends on the context in which the cost is incurred. Specifically, where an expenditure is made as part of a general plan of rehabilitation, modernization, and improvement of the property, the expenditure must be capitalized, even though, standing alone, the item may be classified as one of repair or maintenance. * * *

Analysis

In Situation 1, the heavy maintenance * * * did not involve replacements, alterations, improvements, or additions to the airframe that appreciably prolonged its useful life, materially increased its value, or adapted it to a new or different use. Rather, the heavy maintenance visit merely kept the airframe in an ordinarily efficient operating condition over its antici-pated useful life for the uses for which the property was acquired. The fact that the taxpayer was required to perform the heavy maintenance visit to maintain its airworthiness certificate does not affect this determination.

Although the heavy maintenance visit did involve the replacement of numerous airframe parts with new parts, none of these replacements required the substitution of any (or a significant portion of any) major components or substantial structural parts of the airframe so that the airframe as a whole increased in value, life expectancy, or use. * * * In order to have a restoration under § 263(a)(2), much more extensive work would have to be done so as to substantially prolong the useful life of the airframe. Thus, the costs of the heavy maintenance visit constitute ex-penses for incidental repairs and maintenance under § 1.162–4.

Finally, the costs of the heavy maintenance visit are not required to be capitalized under §§ 263 or 263A as part of a plan of rehabilitation, modernization, or improvement to the airframe. Because the heavy main-tenance visit involved only repairs for the purpose of keeping the airframe in an ordinarily efficient operating condition, it did not include the type of substantial capital improvements necessary to trigger the plan of rehabili-tation doctrine. * * * Accordingly, the costs incurred by X for the heavy maintenance visit in Situation 1 may be deducted as ordinary and neces-sary business expenses under § 162.

In Situation 2, * * * [b]ecause the replacement of the skin panels involved replacing a significant portion of the airframe's skin panels (which in the aggregate represented a substantial structural part of the airframe) thereby materially adding to the value of and improving the airframe, the cost of replacing the skin panels must be capitalized. In addition, the additions and upgrades to Aircraft 2 in the form of the fire protection, air phone, and ground proximity warning systems must be capitalized because they materially improved the airframe. Accordingly, the costs incurred by X for labor and materials allocable to these capital improvements must be treated as capital expenditures under § 263. More-over, because the improvement of property constitutes production within the meaning of § 263A(g)(1), X is required to capitalize under § 263A the direct costs and a proper share of the allocable indirect costs associated with these improvements.

Further, the mere fact that these capital improvements were made at the same time that the work described in Situation 1 was performed on Aircraft 2 does not require capitalization of the cost of the heavy mainte-nance visit under the plan of rehabilitation doctrine. Whether a general plan of rehabilitation exists is a question of fact to be determined based on all the facts and circumstances.* * * Accordingly, the costs of the work described in Situation 1 are not part of a general plan of rehabilitation, modernization, or improvement to the airframe. The costs incurred by X for the work performed on Aircraft 2 must be allocated between capital improvements, which must be capitalized under §§ 263 and 263A, and repairs and maintenance, which may be deducted under § 162.

* * *

Holdings

Costs incurred by a taxpayer to perform work on its aircraft airframe as part of a heavy maintenance visit generally are deductible as ordinary and necessary business expenses under § 162. However, costs incurred in conjunction with a heavy maintenance visit must be capitalized to the extent they materially add to the value of, substantially prolong the useful life of, or adapt the airframe to a new or different use. In addition, costs incurred as part of a plan of rehabilitation, modernization, or improvement must be capitalized.

QUESTION

Okay, so "repairs and maintenance" are deductible immediately, while "major replacements" must be capitalized. But aren't both categories of the expenditures described in the Ruling likely to generate income for more than one year?

FALL RIVER GAS APPLIANCE COMPANY v. COMMISSIONER

United States Court of Appeals, First Circuit, 1965.
349 F.2d 515.

Lewis, Circuit Judge.

* * * Fall River Gas Company is a seller and distributor of natural gas and holds an exclusive franchise to distribute gas at retail in the Fall River, Massachusetts area. Fall River Gas Appliance Company was incorporated in 1955 as a wholly owned subsidiary. The subject expenditures were made by taxpayers in the years 1957 through 1959 and consisted of installation costs for leased gas appliances, principally water heaters and conversion burners for furnaces. The costs of installation were about $65 for each water heater and $90 for each conversion burner, consisting of labor and material charges paid out to connect the appliance to the customer's plumbing, venting and, in the case of furnace burners, varying services necessary to convert the particular furnace. Appliances were leased for an initial period of one year and conversion burners were removable at the will of the customer upon twenty-four hour notice. Upon termination of a lease, petitioners would remove the appliance, cap gas and water lines, and restore furnaces to their original condition. Labor costs upon removal prevented petitioners from recouping any appreciable amount of their original installation costs by way [of] salvage. However, it was plainly anticipated that the over-all duration of the leases would result in rental income upon the appliances and an increase in consumption of gas which would result in economic benefit to petitioners. And the record indicates that through the years 1954 to 1959 the average consumption of gas per customer more than doubled while the total number of customers did not increase appreciably. During such period petitioners installed 9,088 leased water heaters and removed 1,650 and made 962 conversion installations and removed 121. An unspecified number of installations were made after earlier removals, thus using existing connection facilities and lessening petitioners' costs.

The determination of whether a business expenditure is a capital expense is generally difficult and there is no set formula that will govern all cases. It has been held that a capital expenditure is one that secures an advantage to the taxpayer which has a life of more than one year, and that the taxpayer must acquire something of permanent use or value in his business. It is not necessary that the taxpayer acquire ownership in a new asset, but merely that he may reasonably anticipate a gain that is more or less permanent. Inquiry into the pertinency of these principles leads to the establishment of an ultimate fact, and the finding of the Tax Court must be upheld unless it is clearly erroneous.

Against this legal premise petitioners argue that the nature of the installations and their lack of permanency dictate the existence of ordinary business expense; customers could cease using gas at virtually any time, rendering the installation worthless to the petitioners and therefore not a capital asset. Although value of the installation lies in the increased amounts of gas that will be purchased, petitioners point out that they have no assured benefits because a customer may switch from gas to electricity or oil at any time. They attempt to distinguish the cases relied upon by the Tax Court and the Commissioner, holding the taxpayer need not have title to the improvement resulting from the expenditure, on the ground that in each case the taxpayer had the right to benefit from the improvement for a long period of time.

But the impact of these authorities cannot be so narrowed for in each instance the taxpayer took a considered risk in the installation of a facility upon the premises of another in anticipation of an economic benefit flowing from the existence of the facility over an indeterminable length of time. Taxpayer had no right to actual use for a period certain or at all and the rationale of the holdings is premised upon the particular advantage accorded the taxpayer. In the case at bar petitioners made many small expenditures rather than a single large one. Some installations would be, and were, poor investments; others would be, and were, very profitable. But the totality of expenditure was made in anticipation of a continuing economic benefit over a period of years and such is indicative of a capital expense. The record of gas sales and leased installations, although certainly not compelling in such regard, lends some strength to the conclusion that anticipation has become fact. * * *

Affirmed.

NOTE

In *Fall River Gas*, the expenditure was incurred in the hope that it would generate income for more than a year. What if the expenditure is incurred with the knowledge, and the intention, that it will generate both short term and long term benefits? In Dana Corp. v. United States, 174 F.3d 1344 (Fed.Cir.1999), the corporation paid a nonrefundable annual retainer to the law firm of Wachtell, Lipton, Rosen and Katz. The purpose of the retainer was to prevent the law firm from representing adverse clients in takeover situations, and to keep the law firm standing by to represent the corporation in any legal matter which might arise. If the corporation did use the law firm's services, then the annual retainer was offset against the fee charged by the law firm. In most years, the corporation deducted the retainer as an ordinary and necessary business expense. However, in 1984, the corporation offset the entire retainer against the fees charged by the law firm when the corporation acquired another company. The Federal Circuit Court held that the 1984 retainer fee had to be capitalized, even though the other annual retainers were deductible.

NORWEST CORPORATION v. COMMISSIONER

United States Tax Court, 1997.
108 T.C. 265.

JACOBS, JUDGE:

* * *

Issue I. Removal of Asbestos–Containing Materials

The first issue is whether petitioner is entitled to deduct the costs of removing asbestos-containing materials from its Douglas Street bank building. Petitioner argues that the expenditures constitute section 162(a) ordinary and necessary expenses. Respondent, on the other hand, contends that the expenditures must be capitalized pursuant to section 263(a)(1). Alternatively, respondent contends that the expenditures must be capitalized pursuant to the "general plan of rehabilitation" doctrine.

A. *The Douglas Street Building*

One of petitioner's subsidiaries, Norwest Bank Nebraska, N.A. (Norwest Nebraska), owns a building at 1919 Douglas Street in Omaha, Nebraska (the Douglas Street building or building). * * * Norwest Nebraska constructed the building in 1969 at a $4,883,232 cost. During all relevant periods, Norwest Nebraska used the Douglas Street building as an operations center as well as a branch for serving customers.

B. *Remodeling Plans*

In 1985 and 1986, Norwest Nebraska consolidated its "back room" operations at the Douglas Street building. Pursuant to that process, Norwest Nebraska undertook to determine the most efficient means for providing more space to accommodate the additional operations personnel within the building. The planning process indicated that the building needed a major remodeling. (The building had not been remodeled since its construction; Norwest Nebraska usually remodels its banks every 10 to 15 years.) Thus, by the end of 1986, petitioner and Norwest Nebraska had decided to completely remodel the Douglas Street building. In December 1986, both petitioner and Norwest Nebraska approved a preliminary budget of $2,738,000 for carpet, furniture, and improvements.

C. *Use of Asbestos–Containing Materials in the Douglas Street Building*

The Douglas Street building was constructed with asbestos-containing materials as its main fire-retardant material. (The local fire code required that buildings contain fireproofing material.) Asbestos-containing materials were sprayed on all columns, steel I-beams, and decking between floors. The health dangers of asbestos were not widely known when the Douglas Street building was constructed in 1969, and asbestos-containing materials were generally used in building construction in Omaha, Nebraska.

A commercial office building's ventilation system removes existing air from a room through a return air plenum as new air is introduced. The returned air is subsequently recycled through the building. The area between the decking and the suspended ceiling in the Douglas Street building functioned as the return air plenum. The top part of the return air plenum, the decking, was one of the components of the building where asbestos-containing materials had been sprayed during construction.

Over time, the decking, suspended ceiling tiles, and light fixtures throughout the building became contaminated. This contamination occurred because the asbestos-containing fireproofing had begun to delaminate, and pieces of this material reached the top of the suspended ceiling.

D. *Federal Asbestos Guidelines*

In the 1970's and 1980's, research confirmed that asbestos-containing materials can release fibers that cause serious diseases when inhaled or swallowed. Diseases resulting from exposure to asbestos can reach the incurable stage before detection and can cause severe disability or death. Asbestosis is a progressive and disabling lung disease caused by inhaling asbestos fibers that become lodged in the lungs. Persons exposed to asbestos may develop lung cancer or mesothelioma, an extremely rare form of cancer.

On March 29, 1971, the Environmental Protection Agency (EPA) designated asbestos a hazardous substance. The parties have stipulated that Federal, State, and local laws and regulations at all relevant times did not require asbestos-containing materials to be removed from commercial office buildings if they could be controlled in place. Nevertheless, building owners had to take precautions against the release of asbestos fibers.

The presence of asbestos in a building does not necessarily endanger the health of building occupants. The danger arises when asbestos-containing materials are damaged or disturbed, thereby releasing asbestos fibers into the air (when they can be inhaled).

The Department of Labor, Occupational Safety and Health Administration (OSHA), has established standards and guidelines for permissible levels of employee exposure to asbestos. Effective July 21, 1986, the permissible exposure limit for employees was 0.2 fiber (longer than 5 micrometers) per cubic centimeter of air, determined on the basis of an 8–hour time-weighted average. At half of the permissible exposure limit (0.1 fiber per cubic centimeter of air), employers are required to begin compliance activities such as air monitoring, employee training, and medical surveillance. Moreover, the EPA has established standards and guidelines for the general public's exposure to asbestos. The EPA-recommended guideline for general occupancy and clearance of a building after construction activities involving asbestos-containing materials is 0.01 fiber per cubic centimeter of air.

Asbestos removal must be performed by specially trained professionals wearing protective clothing and respirators. The work area must be properly contained to prevent release of fibers into other areas. Containment typically requires barriers of polyethylene plastic sheets with folded seams, complete with air locks and negative air pressure systems. Asbestos-containing materials that are removed must be wetted to reduce fiber release. Once removed, the materials must be disposed of in leak-tight containers in special landfills.

E. Testing at the Douglas Street Building and Decision to Remove Asbestos–Containing Materials

In October 1985, * * * Clayton [a consultant hired by Norwest Nebraska's insurer] conducted extensive * * * testing for airborne asbestos-fiber concentrations in the Douglas Street building. On February 25, 1987, Clayton collected air samples from the building. On April 14, 1987, it issued the results of its survey, which indicated that the airborne asbestos fiber concentrations present during normal occupancy of the Douglas Street building ranged from 0.0002 to 0.006 fiber per cubic centimeter of air. The highest level of airborne fiber concentration at the Douglas Street building (0.006 fiber per cubic centimeter of air) did not exceed either the EPA or OSHA guidelines. There was, however, the expectation that the airborne asbestos-fiber concentrations would continue to increase. Moreover, the asbestos-containing fireproofing at the Douglas Street Building had characteristics that the EPA had identified as warranting removal of the material, such as evidence of delamination, presence of debris, proximity to an air plenum, and necessity of access for maintenance.

After considering the circumstances, petitioner decided to remove the asbestos-containing materials from the Douglas Street building (other than the parking garage) in coordination with the overall remodeling project. Indeed, the remodeling could not have been undertaken without disturbing the asbestos-containing fireproofing. Thus, because petitioner and Norwest Nebraska chose to remodel, it became a matter of necessity to remove the asbestos-containing materials. Petitioner essentially decided that "managing the asbestos in place" was not a viable option, given the extent of remodeling that would disturb the asbestos.

Removing the asbestos-containing materials from the Douglas Street building at the same time as, and in connection with, the remodeling was more cost efficient than conducting the removal and renovations as two separate projects at different times. It also minimized the amount of inconvenience to building employees and customers.

* * *

F.   Contractors and Work Performed

* * *

Removing all the asbestos-containing materials from the Douglas Street building was a large project, entailing an enormous amount of work. Nearly every suspended ceiling and light fixture on all four levels of the building had to be taken down. Asbestos-containing materials were removed from the entire building.

* * *

The removal of the asbestos-containing materials from the Douglas Street building did not extend the building's useful life.

G.   Health Concerns

In addition to removing the asbestos-containing materials on account of the remodeling, petitioner also considered the health and welfare of its employees and customers. Even though the level of airborne asbestos fiber concentrations in the Douglas Street building did not exceed OSHA or EPA standards for exposure, the presence of asbestos-containing materials in the return air plenum nonetheless increased the possibility for release of asbestos fibers into the air: (1) The flow of air through the return air plenum made surface erosion of the asbestos-containing materials more likely; (2) the asbestos-containing materials had already started to delaminate or flake off, which was almost certain to become progressively worse; and (3) the necessity for working above the suspended ceiling in the return air plenum to replace light fixtures or computer cables created greater chances for disturbance of the asbestos-containing materials, and made routine maintenance more expensive.

Petitioner intended to create a safer and healthier environment for the building employees by removing the asbestos-containing materials.[5]

---

5. Before the asbestos removal and remodeling work began, John Cochran, president of Norwest Nebraska, wrote a memorandum dated Oct. 28, 1987, to the Douglas Street building employees, assuring them that Norwest Nebraska wanted their work environment to be safe.

The building indeed became safer after the asbestos-containing materials were removed.

* * *

Discussion

At issue is whether petitioner's costs of removing the asbestos-containing materials are currently deductible pursuant to section 162 or must be capitalized pursuant to section 263 or as part of a general plan of rehabilitation.

L. *Capital Expenditures vs. Current Deductions*

Section 263 requires taxpayers to capitalize costs incurred for permanent improvements, betterments, or restorations to property. In general, these costs include expenditures that add to the value or substantially prolong the life of the property or adapt such property to a new or different use. In contrast, section 162 permits taxpayers to currently deduct the costs of ordinary and necessary expenses (including incidental repairs) that neither materially add to the value of property nor appreciably prolong its life but keep the property in an ordinarily efficient operating condition.

* * *

The Court in Plainfield–Union Water Co. v. Commissioner, 39 T.C. 333, 338 (1962), articulated a test for determining whether an expenditure is capital by comparing the value, use, life expectancy, strength, or capacity of the property after the expenditure with the status of the property before the condition necessitating the expenditure arose (the Plainfield–Union test). Moreover, the Internal Revenue Code's capitalization provision envisions an inquiry into the duration and extent of the benefits realized by the taxpayer. See INDOPCO, Inc. v. Commissioner, 503 U.S. 79 (1992).

Whether an expense is deductible or must be capitalized is a factual determination. Courts have adopted a practical case-by-case approach in applying the principles of capitalization and deductibility. The decisive distinctions between current expenses and capital expenditures "are those of degree and not of kind."

M. *General Plan of Rehabilitation Doctrine*

Expenses incurred as part of a plan of rehabilitation or improvement must be capitalized even though the same expenses if incurred separately would be deductible as ordinary and necessary. Unanticipated expenses that would be deductible as business expenses if incurred in isolation must be capitalized when incurred pursuant to a plan of rehabilitation. Whether a plan of capital improvement exists is a factual question "based upon a realistic appraisal of all the surrounding facts and circumstances, including, but not limited to, the purpose, nature, extent, and value of the work done''.

An asset need not be completely out of service or in total disrepair for the general plan of rehabilitation doctrine to apply. For example, in Bank of Houston v. Commissioner, T.C. Memo. 1960–110, the taxpayer's 50–year–old building was in ''a general state of disrepair'' but still serviceable for the purposes used (before, during, and after the work) and was in good structural condition. The taxpayer hired a contractor to perform the renovation (which included nonstructural repairs to flooring, electrical wiring, plaster, window frames, patched brick, and paint, as well as plumbing repairs, demolition, and cleanup). Temporary barriers and closures were erected during work in progress. The Court recognized that each phase of the remodeling project, removed in time and context, might be considered a repair item, but stated that ''The Code, however, does not envision the fragmentation of an over-all project for deduction or capitalization purposes.'' The Court held that the expenditures were not made for incidental repairs but were part of an overall plan of rehabilitation, restoration, and improvement of the building.

N. The Parties' Arguments

Petitioner contends that the costs of removing the asbestos-containing materials are deductible as ordinary and necessary business expenses because:

(1) The asbestos removal constitutes ''repairs''[7] within the meaning of section 1.162–4, Income Tax Regs.;

(2) the asbestos removal did not increase the value of the Douglas Street building when compared to its value before it was known to contain a hazardous substance—a hazard was essentially removed and the building's value was restored to the value existing prior to the discovery of the concealed hazard;[8]

(3) although performed concurrently, the asbestos removal and remodeling were not part of a general plan of rehabilitation because they were separate and distinct projects, conceived of independently, undertaken for different purposes, and performed by separate contractors; and

(4) using the principles of section 213 (which allows individuals to deduct certain personal medical expenses that are capital in nature) and section 1.162–10, Income Tax Regs. (which allows a trade or business to

---

7. Petitioner states in its opening brief that ''The law recognizes that removing an unsafe condition is a repair rather than an improvement.''

8. Petitioner introduced the reports and testimony of two expert witnesses concerning the impact of the asbestos removal costs on the value of the Douglas Street building. These experts opined that the discovery of asbestos as a health hazard in combination with the extent of asbestos present in the building resulted in an immediate diminution in the value of the building. (One of the experts testified that the building would be appraised as if it did not contain asbestos, and then the amount it would cost to repair the condition would be deducted from the appraisal.) The expert testimony supports petitioner's argument that the asbestos removal merely restored the original value of the building (i.e., without hazardous fireproofing) but did not enhance its value.

deduct medical expenses paid to employees on account of sickness), the cost of removing a health hazard is deductible under section 162.[9]

Respondent, on the other hand, contends that the costs of removing the asbestos-containing materials must be capitalized because:

(1) The removal was neither incidental nor a repair;

(2) petitioner made permanent improvements that increased the value of the property by removing a major building component and replacing it with a new and safer component, thereby improving the original condition of the building;

(3) petitioner permanently eliminated the asbestos hazard that was present when it built the building, creating safer and more efficient operating conditions and reducing the risk of future asbestos-related damage claims and potentially higher insurance premiums;

(4) the asbestos removal and the remodeling were part of a single project to rehabilitate and improve the building;

(5) the purpose of the expenditure was not to keep the property in ordinarily efficient operating condition, but to effect a general restoration of the property as part of the remodeling; and

(6) section 213 and section 1.162–10, Income Tax Regs., are not analogous to the present case.

The parties also disagree as to whether the Plainfield–Union test is appropriate for determining whether petitioner's asbestos removal expenditures are capital. Petitioner contends that it is the appropriate test because the condition necessitating the asbestos removal was the discovery that asbestos is hazardous to human health. Accordingly, until the danger was discovered, petitioner argues that the physical presence of the asbestos had no effect on the building's value. Only after the danger was perceived could the contamination affect the building's operations and reduce its value.[12]

Petitioner points to Rev. Rul. 94–38, which cites Plainfield–Union in addressing the proper treatment of costs to remediate soil and treat groundwater that a taxpayer had contaminated with hazardous waste from its business. The ruling treats such costs (other than those attributable to the construction of groundwater treatment facilities) as currently deductible.

Respondent, on the other hand, argues that the discovery that asbestos is hazardous and that the Douglas Street building contained that substance is not a relevant or satisfactory reference point. Respondent

---

9. Petitioner also relies on Rev. Rul. 79–66, 1979–1 C.B. 114, which allows, under limited circumstances, a sec. 213 deduction for an individual taxpayer's costs of removing and covering lead-based paint in a personal residence, to the extent the costs exceed the increase in the residence's value.

12. In its reply brief, petitioner states: "While in a metaphysical sense the Douglas Street Building may have been contaminated in 1970, such contamination had no discernable impact until the hazard became known."

contends that the Plainfield–Union test does not apply herein because a comparison cannot be made between the status of the building before it contained asbestos and after the asbestos was removed; since construction, the building has always contained asbestos. In cases where the Plainfield–Union test has been applied, respondent continues, the condition necessitating the repair resulted from a physical change in the property's condition. In this case, no change occurred to the building's physical condition that necessitated the removal expenditures. The only change was in petitioner's awareness of the dangers of asbestos. Accordingly, respondent argues that the Plainfield–Union test is inapplicable, and the Court must examine other factors to determine whether an increase in the building's value occurred.

Respondent also disagrees with petitioner's reliance on Rev. Rul. 94–38, supra, arguing that the present facts are distinguishable. The remediated property addressed in the ruling was not contaminated by hazardous waste when the taxpayer acquired it. The ruling permits a deduction only for the costs of remediating soil and water whose physical condition has changed during the taxpayer's ownership of the property. Under this analysis, the taxpayer is viewed as restoring the property to the condition existing before its contamination. Thus, respondent contends, unlike Rev. Rul. 94–38, petitioner's expenditures did not return the property to the same state that existed when the property was constructed because there was never a time when the building was asbestos free. Rather, the asbestos-abatement costs improved the property beyond its original, unsafe condition.

O. Analysis

We believe that petitioner decided to remove the asbestos-containing materials from the Douglas Street building beginning in 1987 primarily because their removal was essential before the remodeling work could begin. The extent of the asbestos-containing materials in the building or the concentration of airborne asbestos fibers was not discovered until after petitioner decided to remodel the building and a budget for the remodeling had been approved. Because petitioner's extensive remodeling work would, of necessity, disturb the asbestos fireproofing, petitioner had no practical alternative but to remove the fireproofing. Performing the asbestos removal in connection with the remodeling was more cost effective than performing the same work as two separate projects at different times. (Had petitioner remodeled without removing the asbestos first, the remodeling would have been damaged by subsequent asbestos removal, thereby creating additional costs to petitioner.) We believe that petitioner's separation of the removal and remodeling work is artificial and does not properly reflect the record before us. The parties have stipulated that the asbestos removal did not increase the useful life of the Douglas Street building. We recognize (as did petitioner) that removal of the asbestos did increase the value of the building compared to its value when it was known to contain a hazard. However, we do not find, as respondent advocates, that the expenditures for asbestos removal materially increased the value of the building so as to require them to be capitalized. We find, however, that had there been no remodeling, the asbestos would have remained in place and would not have been removed until a later date. In other words, but for the remodeling, the asbestos removal would not have occurred.

The asbestos removal and remodeling were part of one intertwined project, entailing a full-blown general plan of rehabilitation, linked by logistical and economic concerns. "A remodeling project, taken as a whole, is but the result of various steps and stages." Bank of Houston v. Commissioner, T.C. Memo. 1960–110. In fact, removal of the asbestos fireproofing in the Douglas Street building was "part of the preparations for the remodeling project." Before remodeling could begin, nearly every ceiling light fixture in the building was ripped down and crews removed all the asbestos-containing materials that had been sprayed on the columns, I-beams, and decking between floors, as well as the floor tiles in the customer lobbies. Only then could the remodeling contractor perform its work. As described above, the entire project required close coordination of the asbestos removal and remodeling work.

Clearly, the purpose of removing the asbestos-containing materials was first and foremost to effectuate the remodeling and renovation of the building. Secondarily, petitioner intended to eliminate health risks posed by the presence of asbestos[15] and to minimize the potential liability for damages arising from injuries to employees and customers.

In sum, based on our analysis of all the facts and circumstances, we hold that the costs of removing the asbestos-containing materials must be capitalized because they were part of a general plan of rehabilitation and renovation that improved the Douglas Street building.

INDOPCO, INC. v. COMMISSIONER

United States Supreme Court, 1992.
503 U.S. 79, 112 S.Ct. 1039, 117 L.Ed.2d 226.

JUSTICE BLACKMUN delivered the opinion of the Court.

In this case we must decide whether certain professional expenses incurred by a target corporation in the course of a friendly takeover are deductible by that corporation as "ordinary and necessary" business expenses under § 162(a) of the federal Internal Revenue Code.

I

Most of the relevant facts are stipulated. Petitioner INDOPCO, Inc., formerly named National Starch and Chemical Corporation and hereinafter referred to as National Starch, is a Delaware corporation that manu-

---

15. We reject petitioner's argument regarding sec. 213, sec. 1.162–10, Income Tax Regs., and Rev. Rul. 79–66, 1979–1 C.B. 114. These provisions and ruling cannot convert the costs of removing the asbestos-containing materials into current deductions simply because petitioner's "concerns for the health and welfare of its employees" partially motivated the removal.

factures and sells adhesives, starches, and specialty chemical products. In October 1977, representatives of Unilever United States, Inc., also a Delaware corporation (Unilever), expressed interest in acquiring National Starch, which was one of its suppliers, through a friendly transaction. National Starch at the time had outstanding over 6,563,000 common shares held by approximately 3700 shareholders. The stock was listed on the New York Stock Exchange. Frank and Anna Greenwall were the corporation's largest shareholders and owned approximately 14.5% of the common. The Greenwalls, getting along in years and concerned about their estate plans, indicated that they would transfer their shares to Unilever only if a transaction tax-free for them could be arranged.

Lawyers representing both sides devised a "reverse subsidiary cash merger" that they felt would satisfy the Greenwalls' concerns. * * *

In November 1977, National Starch's directors were formally advised of Unilever's interest and the proposed transaction. At that time, Debevoise, Plimpton, Lyons & Gates, National Starch's counsel, told the directors that under Delaware law they had a fiduciary duty to ensure that the proposed transaction would be fair to the shareholders. National Starch thereupon engaged the investment banking firm of Morgan Stanley & Co., Inc., to evaluate its shares, to render a fairness opinion, and generally to assist in the event of the emergence of a hostile tender offer.

Although Unilever originally had suggested a price between $65 and $70 per share, negotiations resulted in a final offer of $73.50 per share, a figure Morgan Stanley found to be fair. Following approval by National Starch's board and the issuance of a favorable private ruling from the Internal Revenue Service that the transaction would be tax-free under § 351 for those National Starch shareholders who exchanged their stock for Holding preferred, the transaction was consummated in August 1978.[2]

Morgan Stanley charged National Starch a fee of $2,200,000, along with $7,586 for out-of-pocket expenses and $18,000 for legal fees. The Debevoise firm charged National Starch $490,000, along with $15,069 for out-of-pocket expenses. National Starch also incurred expenses aggregating $150,962 for miscellaneous items—such as accounting, printing, proxy solicitation, and Securities and Exchange Commission fees—in connection with the transaction. No issue is raised as to the propriety or reasonableness of these charges.

* * * [The taxpayer deducted all of the charges listed above, and the Commissioner denied them—Ed.]

The Tax Court, in an unreviewed decision, ruled that the expenditures were capital in nature and therefore not deductible under § 162(a) in the 1978 return as "ordinary and necessary expenses." The court based its holding primarily on the long-term benefits that accrued to National Starch from the Unilever acquisition. The United States Court of Appeals for the Third Circuit affirmed, upholding the Tax Court's findings that

---

2. Approximately 21% of National Starch common was exchanged for Holding preferred. The remaining 79% was exchanged for cash. App. 14.

"both Unilever's enormous resources and the possibility of synergy arising from the transaction served the long-term betterment of National Starch." In so doing, the Court of Appeals rejected National Starch's contention that, because the disputed expenses did not "create or enhance ... a separate and distinct additional asset," they could not be capitalized and therefore were deductible under § 162(a). We granted certiorari to resolve a perceived conflict on the issue among the Courts of Appeals.

II

Section 162(a) of the Internal Revenue Code allows the deduction of "all the ordinary and necessary expenses paid or incurred during the taxable year in carrying on any trade or business." In contrast, § 263 of the Code allows no deduction for a capital expenditure—an "amount paid out for new buildings or for permanent improvements or betterments made to increase the value of any property or estate." The primary effect of characterizing a payment as either a business expense or a capital expenditure concerns the timing of the taxpayer's cost recovery: While business expenses are currently deductible, a capital expenditure usually is amortized and depreciated over the life of the relevant asset, or, where no specific asset or useful life can be ascertained, is deducted upon dissolution of the enterprise. Through provisions such as these, the Code endeavors to match expenses with the revenues of the taxable period to which they are properly attributable, thereby resulting in a more accurate calculation of net income for tax purposes.

In exploring the relationship between deductions and capital expenditures, this Court has noted the "familiar rule" that "an income tax deduction is a matter of legislative grace and that the burden of clearly showing the right to the claimed deduction is on the taxpayer." The notion that deductions are exceptions to the norm of capitalization finds support in various aspects of the Code. Deductions are specifically enumerated and thus are subject to disallowance in favor of capitalization. See §§ 161 and 261. Nondeductible capital expenditures, by contrast, are not exhaustively enumerated in the Code; rather than providing a "complete list of nondeductible expenditures," § 263 serves as a general means of distinguishing capital expenditures from current expenses. For these reasons, deductions are strictly construed and allowed only "as there is a clear provision therefor."

The Court also has examined the interrelationship between the Code's business expense and capital expenditure provisions. In so doing, it has had occasion to parse § 162(a) and explore certain of its requirements. For example, in *Lincoln Savings*, we determined that, to qualify for deduction under § 162(a), "an item must (1) be 'paid or incurred during the taxable year,' (2) be for 'carrying on any trade or business,' (3) be an 'expense,' (4) be a 'necessary' expense, and (5) be an 'ordinary' expense." The Court has recognized, however, that the "decisive distinctions" between current expenses and capital expenditures "are those of degree and not of kind," and that because each case "turns on its special facts," the cases sometimes appear difficult to harmonize. *National Starch* contends that the decision in *Lincoln Savings* changed these familiar backdrops and announced an exclusive test for identifying capital expenditures, a test in which "creation or enhancement of an asset" is a prerequisite to capitalization, and deductibility under § 162(a) is the rule rather than the exception. We do not agree, for we conclude that *National Starch* has overread *Lincoln Savings*.

In *Lincoln Savings*, we were asked to decide whether certain premiums, required by federal statute to be paid by a savings and loan association to the Federal Savings and Loan Insurance Corporation (FSLIC), were ordinary and necessary expenses under § 162(a), as Lincoln Savings argued and the Court of Appeals had held, or capital expenditures under § 263, as the Commissioner contended. We found that the "additional" premiums, the purpose of which was to provide FSLIC with a secondary reserve fund in which each insured institution retained a pro rata interest recoverable in certain situations, "serv[e] to create or enhance for Lincoln what is essentially a separate and distinct additional asset." "[A]s an inevitable consequence," we concluded, "the payment is capital in nature and not an expense, let alone an ordinary expense, deductible under § 162(a)."

Lincoln Savings stands for the simple proposition that a taxpayer's expenditure that "serves to create or enhance . . . a separate and distinct" asset should be capitalized under § 263. It by no means follows, however, that only expenditures that create or enhance separate and distinct assets are to be capitalized under § 263. We had no occasion in *Lincoln Savings* to consider the tax treatment of expenditures that, unlike the additional premiums at issue there, did not create or enhance a specific asset, and thus the case cannot be read to preclude capitalization in other circumstances. In short, *Lincoln Savings* holds that the creation of a separate and distinct asset well may be a sufficient but not a necessary condition to classification as a capital expenditure.

Nor does our statement in *Lincoln Savings*, that "the presence of an ensuing benefit that may have some future aspect is not controlling" prohibit reliance on future benefit as a means of distinguishing an ordinary business expense from a capital expenditure. Although the mere presence of an incidental future benefit—"some future aspect"—may not warrant capitalization, a taxpayer's realization of benefits beyond the year in which the expenditure is incurred is undeniably important in determining whether the appropriate tax treatment is immediate deduction or capitalization. Indeed, the text of the Code's capitalization provision, § 263(a)(1), which refers to "permanent improvements or betterments," itself envisions an inquiry into the duration and extent of the benefits realized by the taxpayer.

III

In applying the foregoing principles to the specific expenditures at issue in this case, we conclude that National Starch has not demonstrated that the investment banking, legal, and other costs it incurred in connection with Unilever's acquisition of its shares are deductible as ordinary and necessary business expenses under § 162(a).

Although petitioner attempts to dismiss the benefits that accrued to National Starch from the Unilever acquisition as "entirely speculative" or "merely incidental," the Tax Court's and the Court of Appeals' findings that the transaction produced significant benefits to National Starch that extended beyond the tax year in question are amply supported by the record. For example, in commenting on the merger with Unilever, National Starch's 1978 "Progress Report" observed that the company would "benefit greatly from the availability of Unilever's enormous resources, especially in the area of basic technology." Morgan Stanley's report to the National Starch board concerning the fairness to shareholders of a possible business combination with Unilever noted that National Starch management "feels that some synergy may exist with the Unilever organization given a) the nature of the Unilever chemical, paper, plastics and packaging operations ... and b) the strong consumer products orientation of Unilever United States, Inc."

In addition to these anticipated resource-related benefits, National Starch obtained benefits through its transformation from a publicly held, freestanding corporation into a wholly owned subsidiary of Unilever. The Court of Appeals noted that National Starch management viewed the transaction as "swapping approximately 3500 shareholders for one." Following Unilever's acquisition of National Starch's outstanding shares, National Starch was no longer subject to what even it terms the "substantial" shareholder-relations expenses a publicly traded corporation incurs, including reporting and disclosure obligations, proxy battles, and derivative suits. The acquisition also allowed National Starch, in the interests of administrative convenience and simplicity, to eliminate previously authorized but unissued shares of preferred and to reduce the total number of authorized shares of common from 8,000,000 to 1,000.

Courts long have recognized that expenses such as these, "incurred for the purpose of changing the corporate structure for the benefit of future operations are not ordinary and necessary business expenses." Deductions for professional expenses thus have been disallowed in a wide variety of cases concerning changes in corporate structure. Although support for these decisions can be found in the specific terms of § 162(a), which require that deductible expenses be "ordinary and necessary" and incurred "in carrying on any trade or business," courts more frequently have characterized an expenditure as capital in nature because "the purpose for which the expenditure is made has to do with the corporation's operations and betterment, sometimes with a continuing capital asset, for the duration of its existence or for the indefinite future or for a time somewhat longer than the current taxable year." The rationale behind these decisions applies equally to the professional charges at issue in this case.

IV

The expenses that National Starch incurred in Unilever's friendly takeover do not qualify for deduction as "ordinary and necessary" business expenses under § 162(a). The fact that the expenditures do not create or enhance a separate and distinct additional asset is not controlling; the acquisition-related expenses bear the indicia of capital expenditures and are to be treated as such.

The judgment of the Court of Appeals is affirmed.

WELLS FARGO & COMPANY v. COMMISSIONER

United States Court of Appeals, Eighth Circuit, 2000.
224 F.3d 874.

[The Eighth Circuit was convinced that the Tax Court below had misconstrued *INDOPCO*. In hopes that the Tax Court, and others, would get it right in the future, the following appendix was added to the majority opinion. Did the Eighth Circuit read *INDOPCO* correctly? Ed.]

Appendix

To qualify for a deduction, "an item must (1) be 'paid or incurred during the taxable year,' (2) be for 'carrying on any trade or business,' (3) be an 'expense,' (4) be a 'necessary' expense, and (5) be an 'ordinary' expense." Assuming the first four requirements are met, the following flow chart will be helpful when determining the proper tax consequence of a business expenditure. By answering the "either or" questions in the flow chart, one can follow the chart to determine whether an expense should be capitalized or deducted. A legend is provided to assist the reader.

Illustration 9

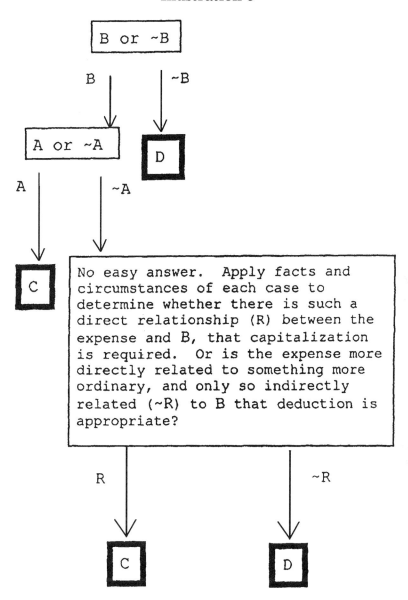

LEGEND

A = physical capital ASSET created or enhanced;

~A = NO physical capital ASSET created or enhanced;

B = BENEFIT beyond the taxable year;

~B = NO Benefit beyond the taxable year;

R = the expense is directly RELATED to B;

~R = the expense is indirectly related to B;

C = CAPITALIZE;

D = DEDUCT.

SANTA FE PACIFIC GOLD COMPANY
v. COMMISSIONER

Tax Court of the United States 2009.
132 T.C. 240.

GOEKE, JUDGE.

The issue for decision is whether Santa Fe Pacific Gold Co. (Santa Fe) is entitled to a deduction of $65 million for a payment made to Homestake Mining Co. (Homestake) as a result of the termination of a merger agreement between Santa Fe and Homestake (termination fee) for Santa Fe's 1997 tax year. For the reasons stated herein, we find that Santa Fe is entitled to a deduction pursuant to sections 162 and 165.

* * *

Initial Contact With Newmont and Homestake

On April 1, 1996, at a meeting of the Gold Institute, a mining industry association, Ron Cambre (Mr. Cambre), chief executive officer of Newmont, contacted Mr. James [President of Santa Fe] about a business combination. Mr. James was not surprised. Newmont was two to three times larger than Santa Fe and was one of the biggest companies in the mining industry. Mr. Cambre did not provide a specific proposal but informally mentioned that Newmont and Santa Fe should be looking at some sort of combination of the two companies. Newmont's interest in a combination with Santa Fe centered on Santa Fe's land position. At that time Santa Fe had a larger land position in Nevada than Newmont did. Mr. James viewed any hypothetical business combination with Newmont as a takeover of Santa Fe because of their relative sizes. Mr. James rebuffed Mr. Cambre's attempts, informing Mr. Cambre that Santa Fe wanted to continue as an independent firm.

On September 26, 1996, the Santa Fe board met again and instructed Mr. James and Mr. Batchelder [a Santa Fe director—Ed.] to approach Newmont concerning possible strategic plans. At the time, Santa Fe management was afraid of having the company put in play because that would effectively mean the company was for sale to the highest bidder. Mr. James hoped that if Santa Fe was able to remain in control during the process, it might be able to delay Newmont long enough to allow Homestake to become available. Santa Fe viewed Homestake as a possible "white knight" and hoped that an agreement with Homestake would prevent Newmont from acquiring Santa Fe. Also, an agreement and merger with Homestake would provide benefits to Santa Fe that its management viewed as absent in any merger with Newmont, including in part: (1) Shared board control; (2) shared management; (3) greater retention of Santa Fe employees; and (4) an opportunity to continue Santa Fe's business objectives.

Mr. James felt that a merger with Homestake would be much better for Santa Fe because he viewed it as an opportunity to merge two undervalued companies. The merger would also result in more Santa Fe employees keeping their jobs as a result of a fairer selection process.

* * *

December 8, 1996, Santa Fe Board Meeting

Over the next week Santa Fe and Homestake continued to work out a merger agreement. On December 8, 1996, the Santa Fe board met again to consider the Santa Fe–Homestake merger. After discussions the Santa Fe board unanimously approved the proposed agreement. As the basis for this approval the Santa Fe board resolved that an agreement between Santa Fe and Homestake was fair to and in the best interests of Santa Fe and its shareholders. The Homestake board also met that day to discuss and consider the Santa Fe–Homestake proposal. After discussions, the Homestake board decided to enter into the merger transaction with Santa Fe, finding that it was both fair and in the best interests of the corporation and its shareholders.

Santa Fe and Homestake executed a merger agreement which contained a termination fee clause. The clause provided for a payment should the agreement be terminated by either party. The termination fee clause provided in pertinent part that should Santa Fe receive an offer from a third party, and should the Santa Fe–Homestake agreement be breached because of that third party offer, then Santa Fe would be required to pay Homestake $65 million.

Termination fees are included in merger agreements for a variety of reasons, some of which may benefit the target, the acquirer, or both. From the bidder's (Homestake's) perspective, a termination fee could serve a number of purposes, including: (1) To test the seriousness of the potential target; (2) to serve as insurance for the bidder and compensate the bidder for information provided to the target and lost opportunity costs if its bid is rejected or a rival bidder emerges and wins a contest for the target; and (3) to serve to deter a competing bidder who might not be willing or able to pay the additional expense of the termination fee in order to win the contested merger. A target may benefit by the inclusion of a termination fee because the fee may: (1) Be necessary to attract a serious bidder by showing the target's willingness to enter into due diligence and negotiations; (2) allow the target's board to preserve its fiduciary duties at a known cost; and (3) protect the target by requiring a reciprocal termination fee in case the acquirer terminates the agreement.

The Santa Fe–Homestake merger agreement also contained what is known as a fiduciary-out clause. A fiduciary-out clause is a contract clause that would allow a party to the agreement to consider superior offers if not doing so would cause it to violate its fiduciary duties to its shareholders.

[Both Newmont and Homestead increased their offers, ed.]

Attempts To Obtain a Higher Offer

After Newmont increased its offer to .43 share, Santa Fe held out hope that Homestake would be able to raise its offer further. Mr. James visited Mr. Thompson, informed him that Newmont had raised its offer, and asked if Homestake could beat it. Mr. Thompson informed Mr. James that Homestake was unable to raise its offer again. At this point it became clear to Santa Fe that its agreement with Homestake would not prevent Newmont's acquisition. Delaware fiduciary duties laws required Santa Fe's board to obtain the highest value for the company's shareholders.

Newmont Wins Out

The Santa Fe board decided that Newmont's offer was superior in value to Homestake's offer. In order to fulfill the fiduciary duties imposed on directors by Delaware State law, the Santa Fe board was required to accept the offer. Accordingly, the Santa Fe board unanimously resolved to accept Newmont's offer.

* * * [Santa Fe merged with Newmont, and the $65 million termination fee was paid to Homestake—Ed.]

Santa Fe Post Merger

After the Santa Fe–Newmont agreement was executed, Newmont attempted to capitalize on the synergies of the two companies that formed the impetus for Newmont's approaching Santa Fe. Although described by Mr. Cambre as shared synergies between Santa Fe and Newmont, the synergy in reality came from Newmont's ability to mine Santa Fe's land without need of Santa Fe's executives and management. For the most part synergy was effected by cutting Santa Fe staff, shuttering all Santa Fe offices since they duplicated Newmont offices, and putting any remaining Santa Fe employees under the control of Newmont employees. Almost all of the employees terminated were employees and managers who came to Newmont from Santa Fe. All of Santa Fe's board members resigned on or before May 5, 1997. Santa Fe's headquarters was closed shortly thereafter in August 1997. Newmont also abandoned Santa Fe's 5– and 10–year plans.

On January 15, 1998, Santa Fe timely filed its Form 1120, U.S. Corporation Income Tax Return, for the short period January 1 to May 5, 1997. Santa Fe claimed a deduction of $68,660,812, of which $65 million was the termination fee paid pursuant to the merger agreement between Santa Fe and Homestake.

* * * [IRS ruled that the $65 million termination fee needed to be capitalized, not deducted, Ed.]

OPINION

* * *

III. *Origin of the Claim Doctrine*

The issue of whether expenses are deductible or must be capitalized may be resolved by the origin of the claim test. Under this test, the substance of the underlying claim or transaction out of which the expenditure in controversy arose governs whether the item is a deductible expense or a capital expenditure, regardless of the motives of the payor or the consequences that may result from the failure to defeat the claim. The origin of the claim test does not involve a "mechanical search for the first in the chain of events" but requires consideration of the issues involved, the nature and objectives of the litigation, the defenses asserted, the purpose for which the amounts claimed as deductions were expended, and all other facts relating to the litigation. The Supreme Court, in adopting the origin of the claim test, chose in favor of

> the view that the origin and character of the claim with respect to which an expense was incurred, rather than its potential consequences upon the fortunes of the taxpayer, is the controlling basic test of whether the expense was "business" or "personal" and hence whether it is deductible or not under § 23(a)(2).* * *United States v. Gilmore, supra at 49.

The origin of the claim doctrine can help determine whether the termination fee should be deducted or capitalized by determining whether it is more closely tied to the Santa Fe–Homestake deal or the Santa Fe–Newmont deal.

IV. Petitioner's Arguments

A. Significant Benefit

Petitioner argues that Santa Fe did not receive a significant benefit from payment of the termination fee. First, petitioner argues that payment of the fee reduced Santa Fe's net worth by $65 million. Second, petitioner focuses on the effects of the Santa Fe–Newmont merger on Santa Fe. Petitioner points to the removal of Santa Fe's management team, the removal of Santa Fe's board of directors, the abandonment of Santa Fe's 5– and 10–year plans, and the termination of more than half of Santa Fe's employees. Lastly, petitioner argues that Newmont closed a disproportionate number of Santa Fe facilities after the merger was consummated.

B. Origin of the Claim

Petitioner argues that the origin of the claim doctrine requires us to find that the origin of the termination fee lies with the Santa Fe–Homestake agreement, and not the Santa Fe–Newmont combination. Petitioner points to the fee's origin in the Santa Fe–Homestake agreement and to the fact that the Santa Fe–Newmont agreement also included its own separate termination fee. Petitioner also points to the fact that the obligation to pay the termination fee arose before Santa Fe's later agreement with Newmont.

* * *

Petitioner next contends that under *Wells Fargo,* the termination fee is more directly related to the Santa Fe–Homestake agreement than the Santa Fe–Newmont agreement. Therefore, because the fee is only indirectly related to the Santa Fe–Newmont deal, capitalization is not required under the origin of the claim doctrine and the termination fee is deductible.

Petitioner further argues that a finding that Newmont acted in a hostile manner supports its position. Petitioner points to language in *Staley II,* [119 F. 3d 482 (7th Cir. 1997)] and *United States v. Federated Dept. Stores, Inc.,* 171 Bankr.603 (S.D.Ohio 1994), where the courts stated that costs incurred to defend a business from attack are deductible. Petitioner contends that these cases, along with respondent's concession that costs incurred to defend a business are deductible, resolve the instant proceeding in favor of deductibility.

Lastly, petitioner argues that the termination fee should be deducted because it served to frustrate, rather than facilitate, the merger between Santa Fe and Newmont. In petitioner's view, this finding—that the fee frustrated Newmont's attempts—brings the facts of the present case out of the *INDOPCO, Inc.* line of cases and into the *Staley II* and *Federated Dept. Store* cases.

C. *Petitioner's Experts*

Petitioner put forth two experts. Petitioner's first expert, W. Eugene Seago (Mr. Seago), has worked in the accounting field for more than 30 years and is a professor of accounting at Virginia Polytechnic Institute and State University. Mr. Seago's expert report focused on the termination fee as it related to public accounting principles, including whether inclusion of the fee in Santa Fe's income would fairly represent Santa Fe's income for 1997.

Petitioner's second expert, Gilbert E. Matthews (Mr. Matthews), has more than 45 years of experience in investment banking. Mr. Matthews's report made the following conclusions: (1) That the termination fee frustrated Newmont's attempts to acquire Santa Fe; (2) that Newmont, although first acting friendly, was clearly attempting a hostile takeover; (3) that Santa Fe as an entity did not benefit from the Newmont takeover; and (4) that although short-term shareholders benefited from Newmont's takeover, that benefit did not last for more than a year (i.e., the takeover did not benefit long-term holders of Santa Fe stock).

V. *Respondent's Arguments*

A. *Significant Benefit*

It is respondent's position that the termination fee should be capitalized under section 263(a) and not deducted under section 162(a). Respondent argues that petitioner paid the termination fee in order to enter into the Newmont offer. Respondent argues that Santa Fe was not facing a hostile takeover but instead wanted to overhaul its capital structure. Respondent further argues that Santa Fe's entering into an agreement with Homestake was merely a negotiating tactic aimed at convincing Newmont to increase its offer. Respondent points to Santa Fe's contacting Newmont in September 1996 as the beginning of Santa Fe's search for a business combination. Respondent's expert argues that at that time Santa Fe was "in play" and any action taken afterwards was done to secure the highest possible value for Santa Fe's shareholders.

As evidence of this significant benefit, respondent points to the March 28, 1996, report prepared by S.G. Warburg that advised Santa Fe that Santa Fe would not become a first-tier gold company without "strategic acquisitions, mergers or alliances." Respondent also points to the Santa Fe board's decision of September 26, 1996, to investigate a possible merger with Newmont. In respondent's view this statement is indicative of a decision by Santa Fe to proceed with a merger or sale of the company. Respondent also points to statements by the Santa Fe board contained in the March 10, 1997, board minutes and in the April 4, 1997, SEC Form S–4, Joint Proxy Statement. Both documents indicated that the Santa Fe board viewed the merger with Newmont as fair and in the best interests of Santa Fe stockholders:

> In the Form S–4, the board of directors indicates that it unanimously concluded that the merger is fair and in the best interests of the Santa Fe shareholders, and accordingly, unanimously approved the merger agreement and unanimously resolve to recommend that the Santa Fe shareholders approve and adopt the merger agreement.

Respondent also points to press releases issued by Santa Fe and Newmont at the time of the merger generally touting the perceived benefits of the merger.

In respondent's view the termination fee was paid in order to enter into an agreement with Newmont and thus led to any benefits gained by entering into the agreement with Newmont. Therefore, the presence of these benefits requires that the termination fee be capitalized under section 263.

B. *Origin of the Claim*

Respondent argues that the origin of the claim doctrine requires the capitalization of the termination fee. Respondent argues that Santa Fe's payment of the termination fee was directly related to the merger with Newmont. Respondent maintains that Santa Fe was actively seeking a business merger.

Respondent points to *Acer Realty Co. v. Commissioner,* 132 F.2d 512, 513 (8th Cir.1942), affg. 45 B.T.A. 333 (1941), and similar cases. In *Acer Realty Co.,* the Court of Appeals had to determine the deductibility of large salary payments related to a capital transaction. The court found that because the large salaries were directly related to a capital transaction, the salaries were required to be capitalized as part of that transaction. In *Wells Fargo,* the Court of Appeals found that salaries paid to employees who worked on a restructuring of the corporation were deductible because they were not extraordinary like the salaries in *Acer Realty Co.* Respondent distinguishes *Wells Fargo* on the grounds that while the salaries in *Wells Fargo* would have been paid whether the subject transactions were entered into or not, the termination fee at issue in the instant case would not have been paid unless Santa Fe entered into a transaction with Newmont. Respondent points to the fact that payment of the termination fee was conditioned on a "Company Takeover Proposal" and argues that this proposal is extraordinary and thus like the salaries in *Acer Realty Co.*

Respondent also argues that petitioner's application of the origin of the claim doctrine is improper because petitioner is simply applying the doctrine in a mechanical way according to which agreement was entered into first. Respondent argues that we have previously rejected this application of the doctrine in *Boagni v. Commissioner,* 59 T.C. at 713. Respondent argues that the Santa Fe–Newmont agreement triggered the termination fee and that the termination fee was paid so Santa Fe could enter into an agreement with Newmont. Therefore, the termination fee was directly associated with and facilitated the merger, unlike the salary expenses in *Wells Fargo.*

C. *Respondent's Expert*

Respondent produced one expert witness, William H. Purcell (Mr. Purcell), a senior director at a Washington, D.C. investment banking firm. Mr. Purcell has over 40 years of experience in the investment banking business.

Mr. Purcell made a number of findings in support of respondent's arguments, including: (1) That the Santa Fe–Newmont transaction was not hostile; (2) that Santa Fe put itself into play as of October 1, 1996; and (3) that Santa Fe used the termination fee as a tool to maximize value for Santa Fe's shareholders. In Mr. Purcell's view, Santa Fe entered into an agreement with Homestake because Santa Fe wanted to send a message to Newmont that Newmont would have to raise its bid in order to acquire Santa Fe.

VI. *Analysis*

As discussed above, we must determine whether payment of the termination fee "[generated] significant benefits for * * * [Santa Fe] extending beyond the end of the taxable year." *Metrocorp. Inc. v. Commissioner,* 116 T.C. at 222. As we stated in *Metrocorp:* "Expenses must generally be capitalized when they either: (1) Create or enhance a separate and distinct asset or (2) otherwise generate significant benefits for the taxpayer extending beyond the end of the taxable year." *Id.* at 221–222. However, we must take care not to interpret every benefit received after payment of the termination fee as being caused by or related to the termination fee.

We note at the outset that this was clearly a hostile takeover of Santa Fe by Newmont. The management, board of directors, and investment bankers of Santa Fe considered Newmont hostile. Although initial contacts between the two entities were informal, Newmont went directly to Santa Fe's shareholders once it learned that Santa Fe and Homestake had entered into an agreement. The presentations Goldman Sachs made to Newmont executives clearly foresaw a hostile takeover. Mr. Cambre's letters to the Newmont board anticipated a fight and warned the board that this would lead to higher costs.

Executives of Santa Fe, Newmont, and Homestake all testified credibly that this was a hostile takeover. Further, we find credible petitioner's expert Mr. Matthews's conclusion that this was a hostile takeover. Respondent's expert's contention that this was a friendly transaction is at odds with the record as a whole and is not credible.

Although the merger was described in terms of "shared synergies", the only synergy found in the transaction benefited Newmont. By acquiring Santa Fe, Newmont was able to obtain Santa Fe's land while disregarding most of Santa Fe's annual expenses. The record makes clear that Newmont was primarily interested in obtaining Santa Fe's land position, and the only way for Newmont to acquire Santa Fe's land was to purchase the entire company. Because Newmont was ***272** primarily interested in Santa Fe's land, it quickly terminated Santa Fe's employees and discarded the business plans of Santa Fe's management. Although Santa Fe the entity continued to exist on paper, it was nothing more than a shell owning valuable land.

Santa Fe did not reap the types of benefits present in *INDOPCO*. After the merger was completed, Newmont shut down Santa Fe's headquarters and let go most of its management. The Supreme Court's decision in *INDOPCO, Inc.* to require capitalization of the fees at issue therein relied on findings of this Court and the Court of Appeals for the Second Circuit that the expenditures at issue benefited the operations of the taxpayer incurring the fees. Santa Fe's operations did not benefit from payment of the termination fee.

Santa Fe's executives testified credibly that Santa Fe did not have as a strategic goal a business merger with any other mining company. Newmont was a hostile acquirer. In attempting to avoid Newmont's overtures, Santa Fe sought a white knight: Homestake. Santa Fe was defending against an unwanted acquisition in an effort to maintain and protect its growing business. The termination fee was contracted for in an attempt to salvage its business plan and employees through a white knight combination.

The termination fee was intended to protect the Santa Fe–Homestake agreement, to deter competing bids, and to reimburse Homestake for its time and effort in the event that the deal was terminated. Although Santa Fe had structural defenses in place, its major defensive strategy was to engage in a capital transaction with a third party that would prevent Newmont's acquisition. This attempt failed. The record does not support a finding, and we do not find, that paying the termination fee produced any long-term benefit. * * *

Although the fact that National Starch became a subsidiary as a result of its merger was viewed as a benefit supporting capitalization in *INDOPCO, Inc.,* we do not find Santa Fe's becoming a subsidiary to be a significant benefit. In *INDOPCO, Inc.,* National Starch's management viewed becoming a subsidiary as a positive aspect of the acquisition because it relieved National Starch of its shareholder responsibilities. The Supreme Court relied on this change of ownership in support of its decision to require capitalization precisely because the change in ownership structure served to benefit National Starch's operations. In the instant case, Santa Fe did not become a subsidiary which functioned much as Santa Fe had before the merger. Santa Fe no longer functioned as an autonomous business after the merger. Santa Fe viewed Homestake as a potential white knight to avoid just this result. Santa Fe management sought an agreement with Homestake to avoid being absorbed by Newmont, but the results of the Newmont merger confirm the accuracy of their concerns that Santa Fe would lose its operating identity in a merger with Newmont.

As stated above, the record does not support a finding that Santa Fe had as an overarching goal a business combination. The fact that the Santa Fe board had hired investment advisers and knew the state of the industry before initiating contact with Newmont does not mean that Santa Fe had decided on a corporate restructuring. Santa Fe executives testified credibly that Santa Fe's first contact with Newmont was meant to be preventative and meant to enable Santa Fe to remain in control of any investigation and agreement. The Santa Fe–Newmont agreement was not a modified form of the Santa Fe–Homestake agreement. Payment of the termination fee and subsequent signing of the Santa Fe–Newmont agreement was not, in substance, a continuation of the Santa Fe–Homestake agreement in some modified form. The two transactions were separate: (1) A white knight transaction; and (2) a hostile takeover. See *United States v. Federated Dept. Stores Inc., supra* at 611.

Santa Fe viewed Newmont's overtures as hostile; and in an attempt to defeat Newmont's takeover, Santa Fe sought out Homestake as a white knight. Because Newmont's offer was higher than Homestake's, the Santa Fe board believed that in order to fulfill its fiduciary duties the board had to terminate its agreement with Homestake and accept Newmont's higher offer. The facts do not support respondent's contention that the termination fee was paid to restructure Santa Fe in hopes of some future benefit. See *id.* The termination fee was paid to Homestake to compensate it for whatever expenses it incurred. As the District Court concluded in *Federated Department Stores:* "in the instant case, the white knight mergers were abandoned. Any effect that this merger had on the later merger with Campeau is irrelevant."

* * *

Payment of the termination fee did not lead to significant benefits for Santa Fe extending past the year at issue. Accordingly, petitioner is entitled to deduct the amount of the termination fee pursuant to section 162. In the light of our reasoning as stated above, we do not reach petitioner's argument concerning the origin of the claim doctrine.

VII. *Conclusion*

On the basis of the foregoing, petitioner is entitled to deduct the termination fee pursuant to section 162.

ROBINSON KNIFE MANUFACTURING COMPANY, INC. v. COMMISSIONER

United States Court of Appeals, 2d Circuit, 2010.
600 F.3d 121.

CALABRESI, CIRCUIT JUDGE:

* * *

Facts

I. Robinson Knife

Robinson is a corporation whose business is the design, manufacture and marketing of kitchen tools such as spoons, soup ladles, spatulas, potato peelers, and cooking thermometers. In the process by which Robinson typically turns an idea into a saleable finished product, someone at Robinson comes up with an idea for a product. Robinson then decides which brand name would be best for that product, and if Robinson does not already have a licensing agreement that would permit it to use that trademark on the proposed product, it tries to negotiate one. Once Robinson has a licensing agreement in hand, it hires an industrial designer to design the product, and the trademark licensor is consulted "to make sure that they agree that [the designer's plans] are appropriate for the brand that's involved." Robinson next contracts out the manufacturing, usually to firms in China or Taiwan, and the products are shipped to Robinson in the United States. With the products in hand, Robinson markets them under the previously selected brand name to customers, who are generally large retailers such as Wal–Mart or Target.

Robinson's products are functionally the same as its competitors', so it largely relies on trademarks and design to differentiate its products. One particular subset of those trademarks is at issue here: famous trademarks licensed by Robinson from third parties who own the trademarks. Often Robinson makes and sells, at the same time, products that are identical, but only some of which bear the relevant trademarks, while others do not. Robinson does not advertise the Robinson name or feature it prominently on its products' packaging.

During the taxable years at issue, Robinson used, *inter alia*, two well-known licensed trademarks: Pyrex, which is owned by Corning, Inc., and

Oneida, which is owned by Oneida Ltd. The owners of these two trademarks have for many years conducted substantial and continuous advertising and marketing activities to develop trademark awareness and goodwill. As a result, it is much easier for Robinson to place a Pyrex or Oneida product at a major retailer than it is to place an otherwise identical house-brand product.

In all respects relevant to this case, the Pyrex and Oneida licensing agreements were the same. The agreements gave Robinson the exclusive right to manufacture, distribute, and sell certain types of kitchen tools using the licensed brand names. In return, Robinson agreed to pay each trademark owner a percentage of the net wholesale billing price of the kitchen tools sold under that owner's trademark. Robinson was not required to make any minimum or lump-sum royalty payment, nor did royalties for any kitchen tools accrue at any time before the tools were sold. Thus, Robinson could design and manufacture as many Pyrex or Oneida kitchen tools as it wanted without paying any royalties unless and until Robinson actually sold the products. Robinson did sell a significant volume of Pyrex- and Oneida-branded products, and during the taxable years at issue it paid royalties both to Corning and to Oneida, of $2,184,252 and $1,741,415, respectively.

II. The Tax Controversy

* * *Robinson deducted the above-mentioned payments to Corning and Oneida as ordinary and necessary business expenses under § 162. The IRS determined instead that under § 263A and the accompanying Treasury Regulations the royalty payments, rather than being immediately deductible, must be added to Robinson's capital and deducted only over time, in line with complex accounting principles. As a result, the IRS denied the deduction and issued a notice of deficiency to Robinson.

Robinson petitioned the Tax Court for a redetermination of the deficiency. Robinson there argued, as it does here, that the royalty payments were not required to be capitalized under the § 263A regulations. The Tax Court rejected Robinson's arguments. It held that, within the meaning of the Treasury Regulations, the royalties directly benefited Robinson's production activities and/or were incurred by reason of those activities. It also held that the royalties were not "marketing" costs exempt from § 263A capitalization under those regulations. Robinson timely appealed to this Court.

II. Legal Framework

A. Capitalization and Deduction

* * *As the Supreme Court has explained in the leading case on this distinction, immediate deduction of a cost is more favorable to the taxpayer than is capitalization:

> The primary effect of characterizing a payment as either a business expense or a capital expenditure concerns the timing of the taxpayer's

cost recovery: While business expenses are currently deductible, a capital expenditure usually is amortized and depreciated over the life of the relevant asset, or, where no specific asset or useful life can be ascertained, is deducted upon dissolution of the enterprise. *INDOPCO.*

The significance of the distinction is only slightly different where, as here, the expense would be capitalized to inventory. For inventory-especially inventory held for sale-the taxpayer usually does not have to rely on depreciation or wait for dissolution of the enterprise in order to obtain cost recovery. Instead, the taxpayer has to follow complex inventory accounting rules in order to get deductions over time. *See* § 1.263A–1(c)(4) These rules are designed to achieve a result that is as similar as possible to what would happen if it were administratively feasible to keep track of each individual inventory item, so that whenever an item were sold its cost basis would be known, and the taxpayer would pay income tax on the gain (or deduct the loss) from the sale of that inventory item. * * *

With ideal matching, a taxpayer would be permitted to deduct the costs of producing an inventory item no earlier, and no later, than the taxable year in which that particular inventory item is sold. Unfortunately, when a company has, say, 100,000 identical spatulas on hand at any given time and it is constantly creating and selling such spatulas (along with any number of other products), perfect matching may be difficult and the costs of producing an inventory item are sometimes recovered earlier or later than they ought to be. A distortion of income results.

B. Section 263A

As part of the most recent major revisions to the Internal Revenue Code, Congress, in the Tax Reform Act of 1986, enacted § 263A to address what it perceived as two significant problems concerning the expense/capital expenditure boundary with respect to inventory:

> First, the existing rules may allow costs that are in reality costs of producing, acquiring, or carrying property to be deducted currently, rather than capitalized into the basis of the property and recovered when the property is sold or as it is used by the taxpayer. This produces a mismatching of expenses and the related income and an unwarranted deferral of taxes. Second, different capitalization rules may apply under present law depending on the nature of the property and its intended use. These differences may create distortions in the allocation of economic resources and the manner in which certain economic activity is organized.... [I]n order to more accurately reflect income and make the income tax system more neutral, a single, comprehensive set of rules should govern the capitalization of costs of producing, acquiring, and holding property....
>
>   * * *

The statute provides that, in the case of "[r]eal or tangible personal property produced by the taxpayer," § 263A(b)(1), both "the direct costs of such property, and ... such property's proper share of those indirect costs (including taxes) part or all of which are allocable to such property," *id.* § 263A(a)(2), shall be included in inventory costs if it is inventory in the hands of the taxpayer, *id.* § 263A(a)(1)(A). Where, as here, a taxpayer does not manufacture kitchen tools itself, but instead contracts the manufacturing out, it still "produces" the kitchen tools within the statutory definition of that term. *Id.* § 263A(g)(2).

C. The § 263A Regulations

* * *

1. Whether To Capitalize

Under the regulations, "[t]axpayers subject to section 263A must capitalize all direct costs and certain indirect costs properly allocable to property produced...." § 1.263A–1(e)(1). Direct costs consist primarily of materials and labor, and the Commissioner does not claim that Robinson's royalty payments are direct costs. As to indirect costs, the regulation states the following:

> Indirect costs are defined as all costs other than direct material costs and direct labor costs (in the case of property produced).... Taxpayers subject to section 263A must capitalize all indirect costs properly allocable to property produced.... Indirect costs are properly allocable to property produced ... when the costs directly benefit or are incurred by reason of the performance of production ... activities. Indirect costs may be allocable to ... other activities that are not subject to section 263A. Taxpayers subject to section 263A must make a reasonable allocation of indirect costs between production ... and other activities.*Id.* § 1.263A–1(e)(3)(i).

Paragraphs (ii) and (iii) contain lists of "[e]xamples of indirect costs required to be capitalized," and "[i]ndirect costs not capitalized," respectively. *Id.* § 1.263A–1(e)(3). Paragraph (ii) states that the items on its list "are examples of indirect costs that must be capitalized to the extent they are properly allocable to property produced." *Id.* § 1.263A–1(e)(3)(ii). One of the items on the list is:

> (U) Licensing and franchise costs. Licensing and franchise costs include fees incurred in securing the contractual right to use a trademark, corporate plan, manufacturing procedure, special recipe, or other similar right associated with property produced.... These costs include the otherwise deductible portion (e.g., amortization) of the initial fees incurred to obtain the license or franchise and any minimum annual payments and royalties that are incurred by a licensee or a franchisee.

Id. § 1.263A–1(e)(3)(ii)(U). Conversely, paragraph (iii) states that the items on its list "are not required to be capitalized under section 263A." *Id.* § 1.263A–1(e)(3)(iii). The first item on that list is: "(A) Selling and distribution costs. These costs are marketing, selling, advertising, and distribution costs." *Id.* § 1.263A–1(e)(3)(iii)(A).

III. Deductibility of the Royalty Payments

Robinson presents three arguments that the royalty payments are not required to be capitalized under § 263A: (1) that the royalty payments are deductible as "marketing, selling, advertising, [or] distribution costs," § 1.263A–1(e)(3)(iii)(A); (2) that royalty payments which are not "incurred in securing the contractual right to use a trademark, corporate plan, manufacturing procedure, special recipe, or other similar right associated with property produced," *id.* § 1.263A–1(e)(3)(ii)(U), are always deductible; and (3) that the royalty payments were not "properly allocable to property produced," *id.* § 1.263A–1(e)(3)(i) All of these arguments present questions of first impression. We are the first court of appeals to address the treatment of intellectual property royalties under the uniform capitalization regulations.

We reject Robinson's first two arguments as addressing situations that go far beyond the case presented here, but we are persuaded that the third argument is correct. We conclude that royalty payments which are (1) calculated as a percentage of sales revenue from certain inventory, and (2) incurred only upon sale of such inventory, are not required to be capitalized under the § 263A regulations.

A. Marketing, Selling, Advertising, and Distribution Costs

According to Robinson, its royalty payments are "marketing, selling, advertising, [or] distribution costs." Although Robinson is correct that "marketing, selling, advertising, and distribution costs" are deductible, § 1.263A–1(e)(3)(iii)(A), we are not persuaded by Robinson's two arguments that all trademark royalty payments are such costs.

First, Robinson emphasizes that its object in licensing the trademarks is to entice customers to buy products that are otherwise identical to Robinson's competitors' products. But Robinson's argument proves too much. All trademarks may serve that purpose. And the regulations specifically list "fees incurred in securing the contractual right to use a *trademark*," *id.* § 1.263A–1(e)(3)(ii)(U) (emphasis added), as an "example[ ] of indirect costs that must be capitalized to the extent they are properly allocable to property produced or property acquired for resale," *id.* § 1.263A–1(e)(3)(ii). If we were to accept Robinson's view, we would effectively read the word "trademark" out of the relevant regulation.

* * *

B. Incurred in Securing the Contractual Right

Robinson next argues that its royalty payments are deductible because they are not described in § 1.263A–1(e)(3)(ii)(U), that is, because they are not "incurred in securing the contractual right to use a trademark, corporate plan, manufacturing procedure, special recipe, or other similar right associated with property produced." But Robinson's conclusion does not follow from its premise. Assuming arguendo that Robinson's royalty payments are not described in § 1.263A–1(e)(3)(ii)(U), that "description" does not include all costs, or even all trademark costs, that must be capitalized. The costs incurred by Robinson are still indirect costs, and they are, therefore, required to be capitalized to the extent they are properly allocable to property produced. * * *

C. Properly Allocable to Property Produced

Robinson's third argument is that the Tax Court's view that Robinson's royalties were "properly allocable to property produced" was based on an erroneous interpretation of § 1.263A–1(e)(3)(i). We agree.

* * *

Royalties like Robinson's in this case do not "directly benefit," and are not "incurred by reason of[,] the performance of production . . . activities." The Tax Court is clearly right that "without the license agreements, petitioner could not have legally manufactured" the Pyrex and Oneida kitchen tools. It is equally clear, however, that Robinson could have manufactured the products, and did, without paying the royalty *costs*. None of the product approval terms of the license agreements referenced by the Tax Court relates to Robinson's obligation to pay the royalty costs. Robinson could have manufactured exactly the same quantity and type of kitchen tools-that is, it could have "perform [ed]" its "production . . . activities" in exactly the same way it did—and, so long as none of this inventory was ever *sold* bearing the licensed trademarks, Robinson would have owed no royalties whatever. Robinson's royalties, therefore, were not "incurred by reason of" production activities, and did not "directly benefit" such activities. In other words, while we may agree with the Tax Court's implicit conclusion that "directly benefit or are incurred by reason of" boils down to a but-for causation test, we hold that under the plain text of the regulation it is the costs, and not the contracts pursuant to which those costs are paid, that must be a but-for cause of the taxpayer's production activities in order for the costs to be properly allocable to those activities and subject to the capitalization requirement.

IV. Conclusion

For these reasons, we hold that taxpayers subject to § 263A may deduct royalty payments that are (1) calculated as a percentage of sales revenue from certain inventory, and (2) incurred only upon sale of such inventory. Accordingly, we REVERSE the judgment of the Tax Court and REMAND with instructions to enter judgment for Robinson.

B. DEPRECIATION

Code: §§ 167(a), (c); 168(a) to (c); 263(a)

Regulations: §§ 1.167(a)–1, (a)–2, (a)–3, (b)–1, (g)–1

NOTE ON THE BASICS

Once it is decided that an expenditure is capital rather than ordinary, then depreciation is the mechanism that allows that expense to be spread out to match the stream of income. Depreciation reflects the fact that things wear out. They wear out physically, and technologically. As to the latter, consider the current wisdom that computers become obsolete in three to five years, long before they are physically incapable of performing their function.

Think of depreciation in three ways. First, it reflects the fact that business assets usually become less useful as they get older. This decline in usefulness is often accompanied by a decline in market value. However, such a market decline is not necessary to the deduction, as shown by *Fribourg Navigation, infra.*

Second, think of depreciation as a sinking fund. Business assets wear out, and, eventually, have to be replaced. A prudent businessperson might plan for this expense by making regular deposits into a bank account during the life of an asset, so that, when the asset must be replaced, the money is there to replace it. Depreciation deductions reflect the deposits that such a business-person might make.

Third, think of depreciation as a series of partial sales. Imagine, if you can, a ten foot salami, which you bought for $10. Each year, you eat one foot of salami, and sell the empty casing, for nothing.

Amount Realized	$0
Less: Allocated Basis	– $1
Loss	($1)

After ten years, you have chronic indigestion, and an aggregate $10 in losses. Depreciation represents the $10 of losses.

How is depreciation computed mechanically? Basically, you don't want to know. Leave it to the accountants. But, you should know the underlying concepts, or the lack thereof.

Originally, depreciation was computed on a straight-line basis. Imagine that you purchased a machine for $50 for use in your business. You predict that the machine will be useful to you in your business for five years, after which time you can sell it for scrap for $10.

The allowable depreciation is:

Basis	$50
Less: Salvage Value	– $10
Allowable Depreciation	$40

To compute straight-line depreciation, divide the allowable depreciation by the useful life:

$$\frac{\text{Allowable Depreciation}}{\text{Useful Life}} = \frac{\$40}{5} = \$8$$

Therefore, $8 depreciation may be deducted in each of the five years.

Now, imagine that you bought this machine as stated above, and sold it after three years for $26.

Amount Realized	$26
Less: Basis	− $50
Loss	($24)

Wait a minute. You're taking a loss of $24 now, and you took an aggregate $24 of depreciation deductions over the three years you held the machine. Isn't that double counting? Weren't the depreciation deductions meant, in part, to take into account the likelihood that the machine might be sold for less money?

This double counting is avoided by adjusting basis. Pursuant to § 1016, every time you take $1 of depreciation, you adjust basis downward by $1. Therefore, the correct calculation would be:

Amount Realized	$26
Less: Adjusted Basis	− $26 [Original Basis of $50 Less Depreciation of $24]
Gain/Loss	$0

Think about that salami. Surely, when you "sold" the first foot of salami, your basis in the remaining 9 feet of salami was no longer $10. It was $9.

This adjustment to basis also corrects for market fluctuations. Take the same facts: original acquisition price of $50, three years' aggregate depreciation deductions of $24. See what happens if the machine is then sold for $40, or $20. Note that each time, the gain or loss on sale net of the depreciation deductions equals the actual change in the market value of the machine.

Caselaw Concepts

FRIBOURG NAVIGATION COMPANY v. COMMISSIONER

United States Supreme Court, 1966.
383 U.S. 272, 86 S.Ct. 862, 15 L.Ed.2d 751.

MR. CHIEF JUSTICE WARREN delivered the opinion of the Court.

The question presented for determination is whether, as a matter of law, the sale of a depreciable asset for an amount in excess of its adjusted basis at the beginning of the year of sale bars deduction of depreciation for that year.

On December 21, 1955, the taxpayer, Fribourg Navigation Co., Inc., purchased the S. S. Joseph Feuer, a used Liberty ship, for $469,000. Prior to the acquisition, the taxpayer obtained a letter ruling from the Internal Revenue Service advising that the Service would accept straight-line depreciation of the ship over a useful economic life of three years, subject to change if warranted by subsequent experience. The letter ruling also advised that the Service would accept a salvage value on the Feuer of $5 per dead-weight ton, amounting to $54,000. Acting in accordance with the ruling the taxpayer computed allowable depreciation, and in its income tax returns for 1955 and 1956 claimed ratable depreciation deductions for the 10–day period from the date of purchase to the end of 1955 and for the full year 1956. The Internal Revenue Service audited the returns for each of these years and accepted the depreciation deductions claimed without adjustment. As a result of these depreciation deductions, the adjusted basis of the ship at the beginning of 1957 was $326,627.73.

In July of 1956, Egypt seized the Suez Canal. During the ensuing hostilities the canal became blocked by sunken vessels, thus forcing ships to take longer routes to ports otherwise reached by going through the canal. The resulting scarcity of available ships to carry cargoes caused sales prices of ships to rise sharply. In January and February of 1957, even the outmoded Liberty ships brought as much as $1,000,000 on the market. In June 1957, the taxpayer accepted an offer to sell the Feuer for $700,000. Delivery was accomplished on December 23, 1957, under modified contract terms which reduced the sale price to $695,500. * * * As it developed, the taxpayer's timing was impeccable—by December 1957, the shipping shortage had abated and Liberty ships were being scrapped for amounts nearly identical to the $54,000 which the taxpayer and the Service had originally predicted for salvage value.

On its 1957 income tax return, for information purposes only, the taxpayer reported a capital gain of $504,239.51 on the disposition of the ship, measured by the selling price less the adjusted basis after taking a depreciation allowance of $135,367.24 for 357½ days of 1957. The taxpayer's deductions from gross income for 1957 included the depreciation taken on the Feuer. Although the Commissioner did not question the original ruling as to the useful life and salvage value of the Feuer and did not reconsider the allowance of depreciation for 1955 and 1956, he disallowed the entire depreciation deduction for 1957. His position was sustained by a single judge in the Tax Court and, with one dissent, by a panel of the Court of Appeals for the Second Circuit. The taxpayer and the Commissioner agreed that the question is important, that it is currently being heavily litigated, and that there is a conflict between circuit courts of appeals on this issue. Therefore, we granted certiorari. We reverse.

I.

The Commissioner takes the position here and in a Revenue Ruling first published the day before the trial of this case in the Tax Court that the deduction for depreciation in the year of sale of a depreciable asset is limited to the amount by which the adjusted basis of the asset at the beginning of the year exceeds the amount realized from the sale. The Commissioner argues that depreciation deductions are designed to give a taxpayer deductions equal to the "actual net cost" of the asset to the taxpayer, and since the sale price of the Feuer exceeded the adjusted basis as of the first of the year, the use of the ship during 1957 "cost" the taxpayer "nothing." By tying depreciation to sale price in this manner, the Commissioner has commingled two distinct and established concepts of tax accounting—depreciation of an asset through wear and tear or gradual expiration of useful life and fluctuations in the value of that asset through changes in price levels or market values.

* * * It is, of course, undisputed that the Commissioner may require redetermination of useful life or salvage value when it becomes apparent that either of these factors has been miscalculated. The fact of sale of an asset at an amount greater than its depreciated basis may be evidence of such a miscalculation. But the fact alone of sale above adjusted basis does not establish an error in allocation. That is certainly true when, as here, the profit on sale resulted from an unexpected and shortlived, but spectacular, change in the world market. * * *

The Commissioner relies heavily on Treas.Reg. § 1.167(b)–0 providing that the reasonableness of a claim for depreciation shall be determined "upon the basis of conditions known to exist at the end of the period for which the return is made." He contends that after the sale the taxpayer "knew" that the Feuer had "cost" him "nothing" in 1957. This again ignores the distinction between depreciation and gains through market appreciation. The court below admitted that the increase in the value of the ship resulted from circumstances "normally associated with capital gain." The intended interplay of § 167 and the capital gains provisions is clearly reflected in Treas.Reg. § 1.167(a)–8(a)(1), which provides: "Where an asset is retired by sale at arm's length, recognition of gain or loss will be subject to the provisions of sections 1002, 1231, and other applicable provisions of law." * * *

V.

In light of the foregoing, we conclude that the depreciation claimed by the taxpayer for 1957 was erroneously disallowed.

Reversed.

[Dissenting opinion is omitted—Ed]

A Limerick

Fribourg Co. purchased a rusty crate.
Would it sink? It was all in the hands of fate
Then Egypt closed Suez
and gains did accruez.
However, they still could depreciate.

HARRAH'S CLUB v. UNITED STATES

United States Court of Claims, 1981.
81–1 USTC ¶ 9466, 1981 WL 15579.

PER CURIAM

Opinion

The issue in this suit for a refund of income taxes is the propriety of the deduction from gross income, as a current expense or as an allowance for depreciation, of the taxpayer's costs of restoring antique automobiles.

The taxpayer, plaintiff Harrah's Club of Reno, operates hotels and gambling casinos in Reno, Nevada. To attract patrons, taxpayer maintains a museum of antique automobiles and other vehicles, known as Harrah's Automobile Collection (HAC). Approximately 1,000 antique vehicles are exhibited, many of them restored to original or near original condition. HAC employs 150 people, and is housed in a 10–acre complex which includes showrooms, restoration workshops and an extensive research library for use in restoration planning.

The HAC is successful in its intended purpose. Almost 200,000 persons visited it during taxpayer's fiscal year 1971, the year involved. HAC vehicles, moreover, occasionally participate in antique auto races or are otherwise displayed in competitions for appearance and perfection in restoration. The 94 restored vehicles whose costs are involved in this case are often the subject of widely publicized photographs. All this brings much publicity for taxpayer's enterprises.

The restoration of antique autos seeks to replicate original appearance. The most elaborate restoration recreates the original automobile in every particular, including operational ability. The restorations whose costs are in issue are so detailed and pain-staking, taxpayer says, that the total cost of the restored vehicle is greater than its market value. The Government does not dispute this proposition, and it is accepted, although the assumed market would seem to exclude those who might believe that the publicity value of such highly restored cars and the recognized premium value of HAC-restored cars compensate for their excess of cost over market value. If there are no such buyers, it may be that there is no market for cars restored in the HAC manner.

In any event, the issue is the proper tax treatment of the excess of total restored-vehicle costs over market value. Taxpayer contends that these 'excess restoration costs' are deductible as a business expense in the year of the restoration, and if not, then they are depreciable in five, or at most ten years. * * *

Trial of the case included a viewing of the HAC premises and the vehicles on display, among them many of the cars in issue, testimony as to individual restorations and expert testimony on valuations and restorations generally. Detailed findings of fact and conclusions of law have been made, and accompany this opinion. Those relevant to the decision are stated herein. On the basis of the findings and conclusions, the taxpayer's contentions are for the reasons which follow rejected, and the complaint is dismissed. * * *

III. Depreciation of the "Excess Restoration Costs"

If not deductible, the taxpayer argues alternatively, then the "excess restoration costs" should be held depreciable over the period in which the restoration can be estimated to be useful in the business of the taxpayer.

* * * Taxpayer would separate the excess restoration costs, said to be a "separate and identifiable asset," from the remainder of the restoration costs and from the cost of the unrestored vehicle. Then, on the basis of testimony by its promotion manager, taxpayer ascribes to this identified asset an estimated useful life of five, or if not five, then ten years.

Only the first of several difficulties with this argument is that the excess restoration costs are not an asset capable of separation from the rest of the costs or the unrestored vehicle. Costs, of course, are not an asset. As for the restoration itself, it pervades the vehicle. Moreover, each restoration is different. Some restorations replace body parts or frames, some, floor boards, some, upholstery, fenders, engine covers, lights, tires, paint. Most or all replace a unique combination of these elements.

Once accomplished, a restoration cannot be severed from the vehicle. Nor can it be separately identified. In this respect, a restoration is wholly unlike an identifiable component of a building such as a plumbing or electrical system * * *.

Further, neither the restored vehicle nor its restoration has a useful life, in taxpayer's business, capable of being estimated. Under the regulation on depreciation, a useful life capable of being estimated is indispensable for the institution of a system of depreciation. Treas. Reg. § 1.167(a)–1(b) (1964). Property with an indeterminate life is nondepreciable. Restoration increases indefinitely the life of an antique car. One vehicle restored 30 years ago is on display at HAC without deterioration beyond the need for replacement of tires. No restored car in the Collection has ever needed re-restoration, been withdrawn from display because of deterioration or is likely to be so withdrawn. None has been sold, with one exception for a duplicate no longer desired. Even unrestored vehicles have without deterioration been on display at the Smithsonian Institution, in a harsher environment than HAC's showrooms, for 40 to 50 years.

Those few HAC cars occasionally entered in actual races are rarely so used and are, before and after the race, given ordinary repair and maintenance. Any damage to restored cars in connection with competitions of antique autos is a matter for repair, not depreciation. Taxpayer has stopped the occassional [sic] use of a few restored cars to transport important patrons to and from the Collection; findings cannot be made as to the duration of the practice or its effect.

The evidence establishes that there is no limit on the useful life of a restored car or other vehicle as a museum object. There is good reason to believe that the 94 restored vehicles involved in this case will, with only normal maintenance, have an indefinite life in the taxpayer's trade or business, a museum. The vehicles are kept in a humidity-controlled environment and need remarkably little repair or maintenance beyond occasional mending of a crack in a wood part.

This is not to say that the vehicles will last forever. It is to say that no limit can be put on the use of the vehicles as museum objects, and thus that the period over which the asset may reasonably be expected to be useful to the taxpayer in this trade or business is indefinite.

No credible evidence supports the assertions of ten-year and five-year estimates of useful life. The ten-year estimate is not based on any hard facts, and is contradicted by the abundant evidence as to the longer lives of restored vehicles in museums. The five-year estimate is based on no more than the remark of a promotion manager that after four or five years of intensive exposure of a car, "it can take its place in the museum and we'll take something else." The shift from one car to another for promotional use, possible because taxpayer has an abundance of choices, does not prove the loss of promotional value of the replaced car. Moreover, the witness did not mean to deny the continuing life as a museum display object, which is taxpayer's primary use of the vehicles.

Recognition of both a short promotional life and a long museum life would presumably require a division into two parts of the basis of the restored vehicle, and different periods of depreciation for the same asset as useful in taxpayer's business for different purposes. Such a bifurcation would create a phenomenon unknown in tax law. Even if conceivably valid, there is no basis in the record for an allocation as between the asset as a museum display object and as a promotional object.

A variation on the assertion of a short life is that excess restoration cost is an intangible, to be depreciated over its five-year life as a promotional asset. In taxpayer's words, "This analysis reconstitutes the restoration costs into the price not for paint, leather, wheel bearings, etc., but for a promotional display with a useful life derived from novelty, perfection and other attributes appealing to the public for offsite and periodical promotion." The value, that is, the novelty, is said to be exhausted in five years "and then [taxpayer continues] the vehicle is reduced to a shopworn but otherwise authentic representation of the original version of nuts, bolts and paint comprising an operable vehicle."

No amount of such fanciful "reconstitution" can change a restored car or a restoration into an intangible. The tangible quality of the restoration is graphically described by taxpayer itself, in its argument for an investment credit: "The restoration ... consists of placing new tangible property on old tangible property; viz., a new fender ... on an old vehicle, ..." etc. The assertion of a five-year life, even as a promotional device, has already been commented on. The vehicle is at no time, much less in five years, reduced to a shopworn condition.

Once the useful life of the vehicle as an asset used in taxpayer's business is seen to be indefinite, the asset of course cannot be given a salvage value as of the end of an estimated period of usefulness. Salvage is the amount realizable at the end of the useful life in taxpayer's business. These vehicles will have as much, if not more, value in the future as now. Without a salvage value, there can be no allowance for depreciation.

The taxpayer seeks to avoid the problem of a salvage value with the remarkable statement that "Since [the] excess restoration costs have no value when completed they can have none when exhausted ten years hence. Thus the salvage value of the excess restoration costs, constituting a separate and identifiable asset, is zero." Taxpayer has itself contradicted this assertion. Speaking of these same excess restoration costs, taxpayer says, "This is a value which [taxpayer] creates for its own use, which it does use, and which is usable particularly by itself." Again, "The value is a promotional value, of particular and unique use to a business which cannot advertise its principal source of revenue, gaming, in its principal markets."

The excess restoration costs have, indeed, a double value. As a part of the restoration costs, they matter-of-factly increase the value of the unrestored car by making it a more attractive display, better able to draw patrons to taxpayer's hotels and casinos. (The trial judge found the restored cars fascinating.) And by the very extravagance or excessiveness of their costs, the restorations add a cachet to the HAC vehicles and thereby further promote the taxpayer's business. Barnum was neither the first nor the last to exploit the drawing power of the phrase, "Brought to you at g-r-r-r-reat and untold cost."

Another contention of the taxpayer, mentioned and then seemingly withdrawn, is that the entire cost of restoration, not merely the excess restoration costs, is depreciable. The ground offered is that after five or ten years, the salvage value of the entire restored car is zero. This contention, if made, is rejected on the grounds already stated concerning the salvage value of the excess restoration costs.

Given the indefinite life of the restored vehicles, if a value at the end of the period of usefulness were to be stated, it would be the same value as at the beginning. Values of these restored vehicles, incidentally, have steadily increased to the tax year involved, 1971, and as of that time were expected by the expert witnesses to continue to increase.

For all these reasons, a depreciation allowance deduction for the excess restoration costs is out of the question.

QUESTION AND NOTE

1. The 94 antique automobiles on display at Harrah's were unique only in the perfection of their restoration. If the automobiles had been otherwise

unique, would they have been more depreciable, or less? What about, for example, the Bonnie and Clyde Death Car, now on display at Whiskey Pete's Casino in Primm, Nevada?

2. In Selig v. Commissioner, T.C. Memo. 1995–519, the taxpayer purchased the following automobiles to be exhibited for a fee at car shows:

Lotus Pantera Cost:	$63,000
Lotus Espirit Cost:	$48,000
Gemballa Ferrari Testarossa Cost:	$290,453

The Tax Court noted:

We have found that the exotic automobiles were state-of-the-art, high technology vehicles with unique design features or equipment. We have no doubt that, over time, the exotic automobiles would, because of just those factors, become obsolete in petitioner's business. The fact that petitioners have failed to show the useful lives of the exotic automobiles is irrelevant.

Depreciation deductions were allowed. Can you reconcile *Selig* and *Harrah's Club*?

NOTE: FROM STRAIGHT LINE TO *MACRS*

There were many problems with straight-line depreciation. Both useful lives and salvage values were frequently litigated. Moreover, everyone agreed that straight-line depreciation was too slow to reflect what actually happened.

The response was a series of measures to make depreciation simpler, less prone to litigation, and faster. In 1981, all of these trends reached their illogical conclusion with the Accelerated Cost Recovery System of § 168. Pursuant to ACRS, salvage value was eliminated. All business assets were placed in one of four large categories, with useful lives of 3, 5, 10 and 15 years. Depreciation for all four categories was much faster in the early years than in the later years.

Not only did this system make depreciation accomplish all of the above goals; it also arguably encouraged American business to modernize their equipment, in that it offered these large, fast, simple, juicy depreciation deductions only to assets which were placed in service after its effective date.[a]

It quickly became apparent that the 1981 changes had gone too far. As a result, in 1982, Congress replaced ACRS with MACRS—the Modified Accelerated Cost Recovery System. Same idea, only less of it.

Compare § 168 to § 167. Is it still necessary to show that an asset has a finite useful life?

---

a. The success of ACRS might be measured by the fact that the stock market went down upon its enactment. The stock market reflects the price of large, relatively old, publicly traded companies. Such companies have a great deal invested in their old capital equipment, and are not in a position to scrap all of it and buy new stuff. The companies best positioned to take advantage of the new depreciation deductions were the small companies and the new companies, who had to buy the new stuff anyway. Thus, the big, publicly traded companies were at a disadvantage, and their market price went down.

NOTE: *SIMON* AND *LIDDLE*

In 1985, Richard and Fiona Simon, both members of the first violin section of the New York Philharmonic Orchestra, purchased two violin bows, for $30,000 and $21,500, respectively. The bows were made in the nineteenth century by Francois Tourte, a French master bowmaker who was renowned for technical innovations in bow design. By 1990, the bows had appreciated in value to $45,000 and $35,000. Nonetheless, the Simons took depreciation deductions for tax year 1989 of $6,300 and $4,515.

At the trial in U.S. Tax Court,[b] the Simons demonstrated the sound qualities of several different bows by performing a number of pieces, including the Bach Double Violin Concerto. The Tax Court opinion stated:

... [o]ld violins played with old bows produce exceptional sounds that are superior to sounds produced by newer violins played with newer bows.[c]

In addition, the Tax Court found that violin bows do wear out. Eventually, a bow will become "played out," producing an inferior sound.

However, the Tax Court found that the bows had no determinable useful life, in that it was impossible to predict when they would wear out. Moreover, even a "played out" Tourte bow would command a premium price as an antique collectible. Nonetheless, the Tax Court allowed the depreciation deductions,[d] and the Second Circuit affirmed.[e]

In a related case, Brian Liddle, a professional musician in Philadelphia, bought a 17th Century Ruggeri bass violin for $28,000 in 1984. In 1987, the bass was appraised at $38,000. In 1991, believing that the Ruggeri bass had lost some of its tonal quality, Liddle traded it for an 18th Century Busan bass, appraised at $65,000. In tax year 1987, Liddle claimed a depreciation deduction on the Ruggeri bass of $3,170.

The Tax Court allowed the deduction,[f] despite the fact that the instrument had not worn out appreciably in more than a century, and had constantly appreciated in value. The Third Circuit affirmed.[g] IRS has nonacquiesced in both cases.

Both courts distinguished the case of artwork hanging on an office wall, commenting that such art work does not wear out at all.[h] The musical instruments, in contrast, were actually, physically, used. *Harrah's Club* was also distinguished in that context.

Perhaps the most interesting opinion was Judge Gerber's concurring

---

b. The litigation was closely followed, and partially funded, by the International Conference of Symphony and Opera Musicians, and Local 802 of the American Federation of Musicians.

c. 103 T.C. 247, 250

d. 103 T.C. 247 (1994).

e. 68 F.3d 41 (2d Cir.1995).

f. 103 T.C. 285 (1994).

g. 65 F.3d 329 (3d Cir.1995).

h. Associated Obstetricians and Gynecologists, P.C. v. Commissioner, 762 F.2d 38 (6th Cir.1985); Hawkins v. Commissioner, 713 F.2d 347 (8th Cir.1983); Rev. Rul. 68–232, 1968–1 C.B. 79.

opinion in Tax Court.[i] Judge Gerber posited the case of an electric guitar once owned by Elvis Presley. He suggested that such an asset has two aspects—a depreciable aspect as a musical instrument, and a nondepreciable aspect as a collectible.[j] He suggested that the bass viol and the violin bows be bifurcated, so that only the "noncollectible" portion would be depreciated. What would Judge Gerber have thought of the taxpayer's suggested bifurcation in *Harrah's Club*?

Technically, the holdings in *Simon* and *Liddle* are not relevant to the depreciability of an asset purchased today. Both the Simons' violin bows and Liddle's bass violin were placed in service between January 1, 1981 and January 1, 1987. Such assets were depreciable only if they were "recovery property," as that term was then defined by § 168. Accordingly, the precise issue in the two cases was whether or not the assets fit that definition.

In the 1986 Tax Reform Act, however, the phrase "recovery property" was deleted. Now, § 168 simply refers to "the depreciation deduction provided by section 167(a) for tangible property." Accordingly, the question of which tangible property is depreciable is now answered by § 167, not § 168.

Nonetheless, the issue addressed by the *Simon* and *Liddle* courts remains. Congress, when it enacted ACRS, simplified depreciation deductions. Salvage value was eliminated.[k] Actual useful life became irrelevant. When Congress made these changes, how much did they change the underlying nature of depreciable property? To be depreciable, must an asset wear out in some determinable way? If so, what does that mean?

Note on Amortization of Intangibles

Code: § 197

If an asset is to depreciate, it must wear out. To wear out, it must be finite.

Not everything qualifies. (See *Harrah's Club, supra*.) For example, vacant land does not depreciate. Other than land, however, for most of our tax history, tangible assets were thought to be depreciable, while intangible assets were suspect. According to our understanding of physics, everything tangible in the universe eventually wears out. Intangibles, however, are another matter.

Some intangibles clearly wear out. For example, most patents last twenty years. Therefore, they can be amortized. (For intangible assets, we use the word amortization rather than depreciation. It's the same concept.) For many years, other intangibles were thought to be clearly unamortizable, because they did not wear out in any predictable way. The clearest case was goodwill. Goodwill represents such things as the good reputation of a business, such

---

i. 103 T.C. 247, 281 (1994).

j. The 1969 Fender Stratocaster electric guitar played by Jimi Hendrix at Woodstock was sold for $320,000 at auction in 1990. Other, similar Stratocasters sell for $1,500 to $3,000.

k. If the taxpayers in *Simon* and *Liddle* had been required to subtract salvage value from basis to create allowable depreciation, then there would have been no depreciation, for everyone knew that salvage value would exceed basis.

that that business generates a higher rate of return than other businesses in the same line.

For many years, some things, like patents, were clearly amortizable. Others, like goodwill, were clearly not. Then there was a long list of things, such as customer lists, which fell in the middle. IRS would routinely argue that such items were really goodwill, and thus not amortizable. A customer list is just that—a list of customers who have patronized a business in the past. Such a list allows that firm to do more business than a new entry without such a list.

To avoid some of the litigation, Congress enacted § 197, to codify which intangibles may be amortized and which may not. Pursuant to § 197, good will may now be amortized. There are, however, some questions as to when § 197 applies, as evidenced in *Frontier Chevrolet*.

FRONTIER CHEVROLET COMPANY v. COMMISSIONER

United States Court of Appeals, 9th Circuit, 2003.
329 F.3d 1131.

TROTT, CIRCUIT JUDGE:

Frontier Chevrolet Company ("Frontier") appeals the tax court's decision that I.R.C. § 197 applied to a covenant not to compete entered into in connection with Frontier's redemption of 75% of its stock. We agree with the tax court that Frontier's redemption was an indirect acquisition of an interest in a trade or business; therefore Frontier had to amortize the covenant under § 197.

Background

A.

Frontier engaged in the trade or business of selling and servicing new and used vehicles. Roundtree Automotive Group, Inc. ("Roundtree") was a corporation engaged in the trade or business of purchasing and operating automobile dealerships and providing consulting services to those dealerships. Frank Stinson ("Stinson") was the President of Roundtree and participated in Frontier's management from 1987 to 1994.

In 1987, Roundtree purchased all of Frontier's stock. Consistent with Roundtree and Stinson's policy of management, Frontier filled the position of its executive manager with one of Stinson's long-term employees, Dennis Menholt ("Menholt"). From 1987 to 1994, Roundtree allowed Menholt to purchase 25% of Frontier's stock as part of his employment by Frontier. Before August 1, 1994, Roundtree owned 75% and Menholt owned 25% of Frontier's stock.

Frontier entered into a "Stock Sale Agreement" with Roundtree effective August 1, 1994. Pursuant to the Stock Sale Agreement, Frontier redeemed its stock owned by Roundtree using funds borrowed from General Motors Acceptance Corporation ("GMAC"). Menholt became the sole shareholder of Frontier because of the redemption.

Roundtree, Stinson, and Frontier also entered into a "Non–Competition Agreement" ("covenant") in connection with the redemption. The covenant was effective August 1, 1994, and stated in part:

> To induce [Frontier] to enter into and consummate the Stock Sale Agreement and to protect the value of the shares of stock being purchased, Roundtree and Stinson covenant, to the extent provided in Section 1 hereof, that Roundtree and Stinson shall not compete with the automobile dealership, stock of which was sold to Frontier pursuant to the Stock Sale Agreement.

Section 1 provided that Roundtree and Stinson would not compete with Frontier in the car dealership business for five years. Furthermore, in Section 1, Roundtree and Stinson acknowledged that the non-compete restrictions "are reasonable and necessary to protect the business and interest which Frontier ... is acquiring pursuant to the Stock Sale Agreement, and that any violation of these restrictions will cause substantial injury to [Frontier] or its assignees." Frontier agreed to pay Roundtree and Stinson $22,000 per month for five years as consideration for the non-compete restrictions.

Frontier's GMAC loan caused it to be leveraged with large interest expenses. During the summer of 1994, Frontier fell below the minimum working capital requirements of its franchisor and had to obtain a special waiver of working capital requirements to continue holding its franchise. In addition, Stinson and Roundtree had the ability and knowledge to compete with Frontier in the Billings, Montana automobile dealership market. Accordingly, Frontier had no known alternative to a non-compete agreement with Stinson and Roundtree to protect it from their competition. Without the covenant, Frontier may not have been able to raise capital or pay its GMAC loan.

Frontier amortized the covenant payments under § 197 on its 1994 through 1996 federal income tax returns. In 1999, Frontier filed a claim for refund for the 1995 and 1996 taxable years, asserting that the covenant should be amortized over the life of the agreement and not under § 197. Frontier and the Internal Revenue Service stipulated that the only issue for the tax court was whether Frontier must amortize the covenant not to compete under § 197.

B.

Section 197 provides, in relevant part:

(d) Section 197 intangible.—For purposes of this section—

(1) In general.—Except as otherwise provided in this section, the term "section 197 intangible" means—

* * *

(E) any covenant not to compete (or other arrangement to the extent such arrangement has substantially the same effect as a covenant not to compete) entered into in connection with an acquisition in a trade or business or substantial portion thereof. . . .

Discussion

We agree with the tax court that Frontier's redemption was an indirect acquisition of an interest in a trade or business under § 197. Frontier, however, argues that it did not acquire an interest in a trade or business pursuant to the redemption because, both before and after the redemption, Frontier was engaged in the same trade or business and it acquired no new assets. There are three problems with Frontier's arguments. First, Frontier's argument reads a requirement into § 197 that taxpayers must acquire an interest in a *new* trade or business. Frontier continued its same business, acquired no new assets, and redeemed its own stock, Frontier acquired an interest in a trade or business because it acquired possession and control over 75% of its own stock. In addition, the effect of the transaction was to transfer ownership of the company from one shareholder to another. Menholt, who previously owned only 25% of the shares, become the sole corporate shareholder.

Second, § 197's legislative history makes clear that "an interest in a trade or business includes not only the assets of a trade or business, but also stock in a corporation engaged in a trade or business." Here, Frontier acquired stock of a corporation engaged in the trade or business of selling new and used vehicles. The result does not change merely because the acquisition of stock took the form of a redemption. Indeed, the substance of the transaction was to effect a change of controlling corporate stock ownership.

Finally, before enactment of § 197, taxpayers could amortize covenants not to compete over the life of the agreement. Treas. Reg. § 1.167(a)(3). On August 10, 1993, however, Congress enacted § 197 to govern the amortization of intangibles. Congress passed § 197 to simplify amortization of intangibles by grouping certain intangibles and providing one period of amortization:

> The Federal income tax treatment of the costs of acquiring intangible assets is a source of considerable controversy between taxpayers and the Internal Revenue Service. . . .

> It is believed that much of the controversy that arises under present law with respect to acquired intangible assets could be eliminated by specifying a single method and period for recovering the cost of most acquired intangible assets. . . .

Thus, Congress' intent to simplify the treatment of intangibles indicates that § 197 treats stock acquisitions and redemptions similarly—both stock acquisitions and redemptions involve acquiring an interest in a trade or business by acquiring stock of a corporation engaged in a trade or business.

Conclusion

Because Frontier entered into the covenant in connection with the redemption of 75% of its stock, the covenant was a § 197 intangible and Frontier must amortize it over fifteen years under § 197. Accordingly, we AFFIRM the tax court.

C. ANNUITIES, AND PAYMENT OF LIFE INSURANCE PROCEEDS AT A DATE LATER THAN DEATH

Code: §§ 72(a) through (c); 101(d)

Regulations: §§ 1.72–1, 4, 5, 6; 1.101–4(a), (b), (c)

Sections 72 and 101(d) are similar to the depreciation sections, in that they allow for a taxfree recovery of the initial investment, spread out during the period of a stream of payments.

Annuities

A simple annuity is essentially a bet between the purchaser and the annuity company. Purchaser pays the annuity company $100,000 up front; the annuity company promises to pay Purchaser $5,000 a year for the rest of his life. If Purchaser lives just long enough to collect 20 payments of $5,000 each, then he gets his money back. Of course, he would have done much better if he had left the money in the bank, where it would have earned interest.

If Purchaser lives considerably more than 20 years, then he "wins." On the other hand, if he lives considerably less than 20 years, then he "loses." Section 72 is designed to characterize the annual annuity payments as either paybacks of the original investment, "winnings," or "losses."

Section 72(a) sets up the rule of **inclusion**: "Except as otherwise provided . . ." all annuity payments are included in gross income.

With that out of the way, § 72(b) sets up the **exclusion** ratio. The words set up an equation:

> Gross income does not include **that part of any amount received** . . . which bears the same ratio to **such amount** as the **investment in the contract** bears to the **expected return**.

When you read "bears the same ratio to," you know that the sentence can be expressed as an equality of ratios in the form:

$$\frac{a}{b} = \frac{c}{d}$$

In this case:

$$\frac{\text{that part of any amount received}}{\text{such amount}} = \frac{\text{investment in the contract}}{\text{expected return}}$$

Using the numbers from the example above, you know that "such amount" is $5,000.[1] "Investment in the contract" is defined at § 72(c)(1) and Reg. § 1.72–6. In this case, it is $100,000. "Expected return" is defined at § 72(c)(3) and, in this simple example, Reg. § 1.72–5(a). Assume that purchaser's life expectancy as of the annuity starting date was 25 years. In that case, the expected return would be:

annual payment	$5,000
× life expectancy	× 25 years
expected return	$125,000

"That part of any amount received" is neither known from the facts, nor defined. Let that be "x."

Therefore:

$$\frac{x}{\$5,000} = \frac{\$100,000}{\$125,000}$$

$$x = \$4,000$$

Of each $5,000 of annual annuity payment received, $4,000 will be excluded from income pursuant to § 72(b), and the remaining $1,000 will be included pursuant to § 72(a). In cases of winners and losers, however, take care to note § 72(b)(2) [exclusion limited to investment] and § 72(b)(3) [deduction where annuity payments cease before entire investment recovered], both of which are informed by the definition of "unrecovered investment" found in § 72(b)(4).

PROBLEM

Purchaser buys an annuity for $60,000. Pursuant to the annuity contract, she is to receive payments of $3,000 per year for the rest of her life. As of the annuity starting date, her life expectancy is 30 years. Read § 72 and compute how her first $3,000 payment will be treated.

Now assume that, although her life expectancy was 30 years, she actually lived:

(a) 35 years. How will her 35th payment be treated?

(b) 5 years. What happens when she dies after receiving only 5 payments?

---

[1] "such amount" refers you back to the last time you read the word "amount." Therefore, "such amount" is the "amount received as an annuity …" which, in any given year, will be $5,000.

Payment of Life Insurance Proceeds at a Date Later than Death

Beneficiaries of life insurance policies can make similar arrangements, but they are treated under § 101(d). Parse out this subsection for yourself.

PROBLEM

Assume that a life insurance beneficiary has the option of receiving a lump sum benefit of $100,000. Instead, she chooses to receive $5,000 a year for the rest of her life. Her life expectancy is 25 years. She actually lives:

(a) 25 years

(b) 30 years

(c) 5 years

How is she treated? Which treatment makes more sense, § 72 or § 101(d)?

D. INVENTORIES

NOTE

To compute gain, subtract basis from amount realized. This operation works perfectly well for the occasional sale. But it becomes cumbersome when retailers make thousands of sales per year. It makes much more sense to aggregate the computation, as follows:

Gross sales
− cost of goods sold
profit

Computing the cost of goods sold is a matter of inventory accounting. Suppose that Seller bought a vat of flour for $100,000. By year-end, she had sold every speck of the flour. Her cost of goods sold is $100,000.

What if she had one quarter of her flour left at year-end? Now, assuming that the price of flour remained constant, her cost of goods sold would be computed as follows:

beginning inventory	$100,000
− ending inventory	−$ 25,000
cost of goods sold	$ 75,000

What if she had added inventory of $50,000 during the year? In that case, cost of goods sold would be computed as follows:

beginning inventory	$100,000
+ additions to inventory	+$ 50,000
− ending inventory	−$ 25,000
= cost of goods sold	$125,000

So far, the cost of flour to Seller has been presumed to remain constant. What if the price fluctuated? Suppose, for example, that the original purchase was 100,000 pounds of flour at $1 per pound. Before any flour was sold, an additional 25,000 pounds of flour was added to inventory, which cost $2 per pound. Now, when a pound of flour is sold, which flour is it—the expensive flour, or the cheap flour? It is physically impossible to give a precise answer to this question, because the two purchases of flour are commingled in one huge vat.

To answer this question, one of two inventory accounting conventions must be used—LIFO or FIFO. LIFO stands for "last in, first out." LIFO presumes that the last inventory acquired will be the first inventory sold. In that case, the $2 per pound flour will be deemed to be sold first. The $1 per pound flour will be sold only when all 25,000 pounds of the more expensive flour have been exhausted.

FIFO stands for "first in, first out." Under FIFO, the $1 per pound flour would be deemed sold first, then the $2 per pound flour. Only after 100,000 pounds of flour had been sold would there be any deemed sales of the more expensive flour.

Example

One hundred thousand pounds of flour was purchased at $1 per pound. Subsequently, an additional 25,000 pounds of flour was purchased at $2 per pound.

Forty thousand pounds of flour are sold at $3 per pound.

(a) Under the LIFO convention, Cost of Goods Sold would be computed as follows:

Beginning Inventory	$100,000
+ Additions to Inventory	+$ 50,000
− Ending Inventory	−$ 85,000
= Cost of Goods Sold	=$ 65,000

Profit would computed as follows:

Gross Sales	$120,000
− Cost of Goods Sold	−$ 65,000
= Profit	$ 55,000

(b) Under the FIFO convention, Cost of Goods Sold would be computed as follows:

Beginning Inventory	$100,000
+ Additions to Inventory	+$ 50,000
− Ending Inventory	−$110,000

	[60,000 pounds @ $1 per pound 25,000 pounds @ $2 per pound]
= Cost of Goods Sold	=$ 40,000

Profit would computed as follows:

Gross Sales	$120,000
− Cost of Goods Sold	− $ 40,000
= Profit	$ 80,000

Imagine that you have a large storage tank of crude oil. You buy 1,000 barrels of oil at $1 per barrel in January, and put it in the tank. In February, you buy another 1,000 barrels at $2 per barrel, and put that in the tank. The $2 per barrel oil floats on top of the $1 per barrel oil. In March, you buy another 1,000 barrels for $3 per barrel. The $3 per barrel oil floats on top of the $2 per barrel oil. Now you start selling oil.

Illustration 10

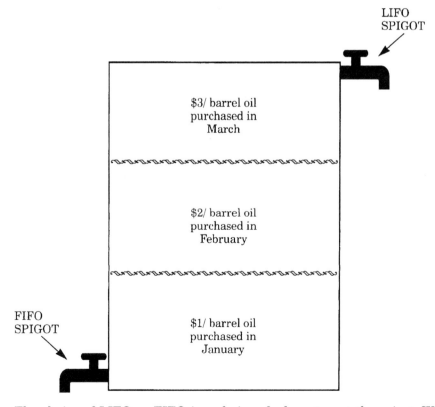

The choice of LIFO or FIFO is a choice of where to put the spigot. With LIFO, you put the spigot on top, and sell the oil purchased in March, then February, then January. With FIFO, you put the spigot on the bottom, and sell the oil purchased in January, then February, then March.

QUESTIONS

1. In the illustration above, the inventory price for oil was rising. In such a case, would you prefer LIFO or FIFO for tax accounting? Which would you prefer for financial accounting? Remember, your investors like to see profits.

2. Now assume that the inventory price for oil was falling. Would you prefer LIFO or FIFO for tax accounting? Which would you prefer for financial accounting?

Write-downs of Inventory

THOR POWER TOOL COMPANY v. COMMISSIONER

United States Supreme Court, 1979.
439 U.S. 522, 99 S.Ct. 773, 58 L.Ed.2d 785.

MR. JUSTICE BLACKMUN delivered the opinion of the Court.

* * *

I

The Inventory Issue

A.

Taxpayer is a Delaware corporation with principal place of business in Illinois. It manufactures hand-held power tools, parts and accessories, and rubber products. At its various plants and service branches, Thor maintains inventories of raw materials, work-in-process, finished parts and accessories, and completed tools. At all times relevant, Thor has used, both for financial accounting and for income tax purposes, the "lower of cost or market" method of valuing inventories.

Thor's tools typically contain from 50 to 200 parts, each of which taxpayer stocks to meet demand for replacements. Because of the difficulty, at the time of manufacture, of predicting the future demand for various parts, taxpayer produced liberal quantities of each part to avoid subsequent production runs. Additional runs entail costly retooling and result in delays in filling orders.

In 1960, Thor instituted a procedure for writing down the inventory value of replacement parts and accessories for tool models it no longer produced. It created an inventory contra-account and credited that account with 10% of each part's cost for each year since production of the parent model had ceased. The effect of the procedure was to amortize the cost of these parts over a 10–year period. For the first nine months of 1964, this produced a write-down of $22,090.

In late 1964, new management took control and promptly concluded that Thor's inventory in general was overvalued. After "a physical inventory taken at all locations" of the tool and rubber divisions, management wrote off approximately $2.75 million of obsolete parts, damaged or defective tools, demonstration or sales samples, and similar items. The Commissioner allowed this writeoff because Thor scrapped most of the articles shortly after their removal from the 1964 closing inventory.[2] Management also wrote down $245,000 of parts stocked for three unsuccessful products. The Commissioner allowed this write-down too, since Thor sold these items at reduced prices shortly after the close of 1964.

This left some 44,000 assorted items, the status of which is the inventory issue here. Management concluded that many of these articles, mostly spare parts, were "excess" inventory, that is, that they were held in excess of any reasonably foreseeable future demand. It was decided that this inventory should be written down to its "net realizable value," which, in most cases, was scrap value.

Two methods were used to ascertain the quantity of excess inventory. Where accurate data were available, Thor forecast future demand for each item on the basis of actual 1964 usage, that is, actual sales for tools and service parts, and actual usage for raw materials, work-in-process, and production parts. Management assumed that future demand for each item would be the same as it was in 1964. Thor then applied the following aging schedule: the quantity of each item corresponding to less than one year's estimated demand was kept at cost; the quantity of each item in excess of two years' estimated demand was written off entirely; and the quantity of each item corresponding to from one to two years' estimated demand was written down by 50% or 75%. Thor presented no statistical evidence to rationalize these percentages or this time frame. In the Tax Court, Thor's president justified the formula by citing general business experience, and opined that it was "somewhat in between" possible alternative solutions.[5] This first method yielded a total write-down of $744,030.

At two plants where 1964 data were inadequate to permit forecasts of future demand, Thor used its second method for valuing inventories. At these plants, the company employed flat percentage write-downs of 5%, 10% and 50% for various types of inventory. Thor presented no sales or other data to support these percentages. Its president observed that "this is not a precise way of doing it," but said that the company "felt some adjustment of this nature was in order, and these figures represented our

---

2. Both in his brief, and at oral argument, the Commissioner has maintained that the reason for the allowance of Thor's $2.75 million writeoff was that the items were scrapped soon after they were written off. The Court of Appeals accepted this explanation. Thor challenges its factual predicate, and asserts that 40% of the obsolete parts in fact remained unscrapped as late as the end of 1967. The record does not enable us to resolve this factual dispute; in any event, we must accept the Commissioner's explanation at face value.

5. "So here is where I fell back on my experience of 20 years in manufacturing of trying to determine a reasonable basis for evaluating this inventory in my previous association. We had generally written off inventory that was in excess of one year. In this case, we felt that that would be overly conservative, and it might understate the value of the inventory. On the other hand, we felt that two years ... would be too optimistic and that we would overvalue the inventory [in view of] the factors which affect inventory, such as technological change, market changes, and the like, that two years, in our opinion, was too long a period of time."

best estimate of what was required to reduce the inventory to net realizable value." This second method yielded a total write-down of $160,832.

Although Thor wrote down all its "excess" inventory at once, it did not immediately scrap the articles or sell them at reduced prices, as it had done with the $3 million of obsolete and damaged inventory, the write-down of which the Commissioner permitted. Rather, Thor retained the "excess" items physically in inventory and continued to sell them at original prices. The company found that, owing to the peculiar nature of the articles involved,[7] price reductions were of no avail in proving this "excess" inventory. As time went on, however, Thor gradually disposed of some of these items as scrap; the record is unclear as to when these dispositions took place.

Thor credited this sum to its inventory contra-account, thereby decreasing closing inventory, increasing cost of goods sold, and decreasing taxable income for the year by that amount.[9] The company contended that, by writing down excess inventory to scrap value, and by thus carrying all inventory at "net realizable value," it had reduced its inventory to "market" in accord with its "lower of cost or market" method of accounting. On audit, the Commissioner disallowed the write-down in its entirety, asserting that it did not serve clearly to reflect Thor's 1964 income for tax purposes.

The Tax Court, in upholding the Commissioner's determination, found as a fact that Thor's write-down of excess inventory did conform to "generally accepted accounting principles"; indeed, the court was "thoroughly convinced ... that such was the case." The court found that if Thor had failed to write down its inventory on some reasonable basis, its accountants would have been unable to give its financial statements the desired certification. The court held, however, that conformance with "generally accepted accounting principles" is not enough; § 446(b), and § 471 as well prescribe, as an independent requirement, that inventory accounting methods must "clearly reflect income." The Tax Court rejected Thor's argument that its write-down of "excess" inventory was authorized by Treasury Regulations, and held that the Commissioner had not abused his discretion in determining that the write-down failed to reflect 1964 income clearly.

B.

Inventory accounting is governed by §§ 446 and 471 of the Code. Section 446(a) states the general rule for methods of accounting: "Taxable

---

7. The Tax Court found that the finished tools were too specialized to attract bargain hunters; that no one would buy spare parts, regardless of price, unless they were needed to fix broken tools; that work-in-process had no value except as scrap; and that other manufacturers would not buy raw materials in the secondary market.

9. For a manufacturing concern like Thor, Gross Profit basically equals Sales minus Cost of Goods Sold. Cost of Goods Sold equals Opening Inventory, plus Cost of Inventory Acquired, minus Closing Inventory. A reduction of Closing Inventory, therefore, increases Cost of Goods Sold and decreases Gross Profit accordingly.

income shall be computed under the method of accounting on the basis of which the taxpayer regularly computes his income in keeping his books." Section 446(b) provides, however, that if the method used by the taxpayer "does not clearly reflect income, the computation of taxable income shall be made under such method as, in the opinion of the [Commissioner], does clearly reflect income." Regulations promulgated under § 446 and in effect for the taxable year 1964, state that "no method of accounting is acceptable unless, in the opinion of the Commissioner, it clearly reflects income."[10]

Section 471 prescribes the general rule for inventories. It states:

"Whenever in the opinion of the [Commissioner] the use of inventories is necessary in order clearly to determine the income of any taxpayer, inventories shall be taken by such taxpayer on such basis as the [Commissioner] may prescribe as conforming as nearly as may be to the best accounting practice in the trade or business and as most clearly reflecting the income."

As the Regulations point out, § 471 obviously establishes two distinct tests to which an inventory must conform. First, it must conform "as nearly as may be" to the "best accounting practice," a phrase that is synonymous with "generally accepted accounting principles." Second, it "must clearly reflect the income."

It is obvious that on their face, §§ 446 and 471, with their accompanying Regulations, vest the Commissioner with wide discretion in determining whether a particular method of inventory accounting should be disallowed as not clearly reflective of income. This Court's cases confirm the breadth of this discretion. * * *

As has been noted, the Tax Court found as a fact in this case that Thor's write-down of "excess" inventory conformed to "generally accepted accounting principles" and was "within the term, 'best accounting practice,' as that term is used in section 471 of the Code and the regulations promulgated under that section." Since the Commissioner has not challenged this finding, there is no dispute that Thor satisfied the first part of § 471's two-pronged test. The only question, then, is whether the Commissioner abused his discretion in determining that the write-down did not satisfy the test's second prong in that it failed to reflect Thor's 1964 income clearly. Although the Commissioner's discretion is not unbridled and may not be arbitrary we sustain his exercise of discretion here, for in this case the write-down was plainly inconsistent with the governing Regulations which the taxpayer, on its part, has not challenged.

It has been noted above that Thor at all pertinent times used the "lower of cost or market" method of inventory accounting. The rules governing this method are set out in Treas. Reg. § 1.471–4. That Regulation defines "market" to mean, ordinarily, "the current bid price prevail-

---

10. The Regulations define "method of accounting" to include "not only the over-all method of accounting of the taxpayer but also the accounting treatment of any item." Treas. Reg. § 1.446–(a)(1), 26 CFR § 1.446–1(a)(1) (1964).

ing at the date of the inventory for the particular merchandise in the volume in which usually purchased by the taxpayer." The courts have uniformly interpreted "bid price" to mean replacement cost, that is, the price the taxpayer would have to pay on the open market to purchase or reproduce the inventory items. Where no open market exists, the Regulations require the taxpayer to ascertain "bid price" by using "such evidence of a fair market price at the date or dates nearest the inventory as may be available, such as specific purchasers or sales by the taxpayer or others in reasonable volume and made in good faith, or compensation paid for cancellation of contracts for purchase commitments."

The Regulations specify two situations in which a taxpayer is permitted to value inventory below "market" as so defined. The first is where the taxpayer in the normal course of business has actually offered merchandise for sale at prices lower than replacement cost. Inventories of such merchandise may be valued at those prices less direct cost of disposition, "and the correctness of such prices will be determined by reference to the actual sales of the taxpayer for a reasonable period before and after the date of the inventory." The Regulations warn that prices "which vary materially from the actual prices so ascertained will not be accepted as reflecting the market."

The second situation in which a taxpayer may value inventory below replacement cost is where the merchandise itself is defective. If goods are "unsalable at normal prices or unusable in the normal way because of damage, imperfections, shop wear, changes of style, odd or broken lots, or other similar causes," the taxpayer is permitted to value the goods "at bona fide selling prices less direct cost of disposition." The Regulations define "bona fide selling price" to mean an "actual offering of goods during a period ending not later than 30 days after inventory date." The taxpayer bears the burden of proving that "such exceptional goods as are valued upon such selling basis come within the classifications indicated," and is required to "maintain such records of the disposition of the goods as will enable a verification of the inventory to be made."

From this language, the regulatory scheme is clear. The taxpayer must value inventory for tax purposes at cost unless the "market" is lower. "Market" is defined as "replacement cost," and the taxpayer is permitted to depart from replacement cost only in specified situations. When it makes any such departure, the taxpayer must substantiate its lower inventory valuation by providing evidence of actual offerings, actual sales, or actual contract cancellations. In the absence of objective evidence of this kind, a taxpayer's assertions as to the "market value" of its inventory are not cognizable in computing its income tax.

It is clear to us that Thor's procedures for writing down the value of its "excess" inventory were inconsistent with this regulatory scheme. Although Thor conceded that "an active market prevailed" on the inventory date, it "made no effort to determine the purchase or reproduction cost" of its "excess" inventory. Thor thus failed to ascertain "market" in accord with the general rule of the Regulations. In seeking to depart from replacement cost, Thor failed to bring itself within either of the authorized exceptions. Thor is not able to take advantage of § 1.471–4(b) since, as the Tax Court found, the company failed to sell its excess inventory or offer it for sale at prices below replacement cost. Indeed, Thor concedes that it continued to sell its "excess" inventory at original prices. Thor also is not able to take advantage of § 1.471–2(c) since, as the Tax Court and the Court of Appeals both held, it failed to bear the burden of proving that its excess inventory came within the specified classifications. Actually, Thor's "excess" inventory was normal and unexceptional, and was indistinguishable from and intermingled with the inventory that was not written down.

More importantly, Thor failed to provide any objective evidence whatever that the "excess" inventory had the "market value" management ascribed to it. The Regulations demand hard evidence of actual sales and further demand that records of actual dispositions be kept. The Tax Court found, however, that Thor made no sales and kept no records. Thor's management simply wrote down its closing inventory on the basis of a well-educated guess that some of it would never be sold. The formulae governing this write-down were derived from management's collective "business experience"; the percentages contained in those formulae seemingly were chosen for no reason other than that they were multiples of five and embodied some kind of anagogical symmetry. The Regulations do not permit this kind of evidence. If a taxpayer could write down its inventories on the basis of management's subjective estimates of the goods' ultimate salability, the taxpayer would be able, as the Tax Court observed, "to determine how much tax it wanted to pay for a given year."[13]

For these reasons, we agree with the Tax Court and with the Seventh Circuit that the Commissioner acted within his discretion in deciding that Thor's write-down of "excess" inventory failed to reflect income clearly. In the light of the well-known potential for tax avoidance that is inherent in inventory accounting, the Commissioner in his discretion may insist on a high evidentiary standard before allowing write-downs of inventory to "market." Because Thor provided no objective evidence of the reduced market value of its "excess" inventory, its write-down was plainly inconsistent with the Regulations, and the Commissioner properly disallowed it.

* * *

---

13. Thor seeks to justify its write-down by citing Space Controls, Inc. v. Commissioner, 322 F. 2d 144 (5th Cir.1963) and similar cases. In Space Controls, the taxpayer manufactured trailers under a fixed-price contract with the Government; it was stipulated that the trailers were suitable only for military use and had no value apart from the contract. The taxpayer experienced cost overruns and sought to write-down its inventory by the amount by which its cost exceeded the contract sales price. The Court of Appeals, by a divided vote, held that the write down was authorized by Treas. Reg. § 1.471–4(b), reasoning that the taxpayer in effect had offered the trailers for sale by way of the fixed-price contract. While not necessarily approving the Fifth Circuit's decision to dispense with the "actual sale" rule of § 1.471–4(b), we note that that case is distinguishable from this one. In Space Controls, the fixed-price contract offered objective evidence of reduced inventory value; the taxpayer in the present case provided no objective evidence of reduced inventory value at all. * * *

D.

Thor complains that a decision adverse to it poses a dilemma. According to the taxpayer, it would be virtually impossible for it to offer objective evidence of its "excess" inventory's lower value, since the goods cannot be sold at reduced prices; even if they could be sold, says Thor, their reduced-price sale would just "pull the rug out" from under the identical "non-excess" inventory Thor is trying to sell simultaneously. The only way Thor could establish the inventory's value by a "closed transaction" would be to scrap the articles at once. Yet immediate scrapping would be undesirable for demand for the parts ultimately might prove greater than anticipated. The taxpayer thus sees itself presented with "an unattractive Hobson's choice: either the unsalable inventory must be carried for years at its cost instead of net realizable value, thereby overstating taxable income by such overvaluation until it is scrapped, or the excess inventory must be scrapped prematurely to the detriment of the manufacturer and its customers."

If this is indeed the dilemma that confronts Thor, it is in reality the same choice that every taxpayer who has a paper loss must face. It can realize its loss now and garner its tax benefit, or it can defer realization, and its deduction, hoping for better luck later. Thor, quite simply, has suffered no present loss. It deliberately manufactured its "excess" spare parts because it judged that the marginal cost of unsalable inventory would be lower than the cost of retooling machinery should demand surpass expectations. This was a rational business judgment and, not unpredictably, Thor now has inventory it believes it cannot sell. Thor, of course, is not so confident of its prediction as to be willing to scrap the "excess" parts now; it wants to keep them on hand, just in case. This, too, is a rational judgment, but there is no reason why the Treasury should subsidize Thor's hedging of its bets. There is also no reason why Thor should be entitled, for tax purposes, to have its cake and to eat it too.

PACCAR, INC. v. COMMISSIONER

United States Court of Appeals, Ninth Circuit, 1988.
849 F.2d 393.

CARROLL, DISTRICT JUDGE:

Paccar, Inc., appeals from a decision of the United States Tax Court, upholding the determination of deficiencies assessed by the Commissioner for the tax years 1975 through 1977. The primary issue is whether Paccar may claim an inventory loss resulting from its transfer of equipment parts to a third party. We affirm.

Paccar, through its various divisions, engages in the manufacture and distribution of trucks, truck parts, mining vehicles, and rail cars. In 1976 and 1977, three divisions of Paccar (Paccar Parts, Dart, and Wagner) entered into written agreements with Sajac Company, Inc., an unrelated corporation, for the disposition of certain inventory of equipment parts.

The agreements provided: (1) Sajac would purchase "selective excess, inactive or unusable parts hereinafter referred to as scrap material" at the prevailing market price for scrap metals; (2) title, ownership and "risk of loss" would pass to Sajac, and the Paccar division would pay the costs of shipping to Sajac's warehouse; (3) Sajac was "not, in any manner, express or implied, a bailee of the scrap material, nor is Sajac in any way an agent of" the Paccar division; (4) the Paccar division retained the right to repurchase any portion of the "scrap material" sold to Sajac for at least four years after delivery of the goods to Sajac, and Sajac would advise the Paccar division of "any other disposition of the goods during this period of time;" and (5) the repurchase cost to the Paccar division would not exceed 90 percent of the Paccar division's last acquisition cost, adjusted for inflation, and the repurchase cost would be discounted if the Paccar division's repurchases exceeded certain levels. During the years at issue and in subsequent years, Paccar reacquired an average of approximately 25 percent of the inventory transferred to Sajac.

Beginning in 1976, parts were transferred to Sajac by the Paccar divisions that had entered into the above agreement with Sajac. Paccar treated the transfers of the materials to Sajac as sales for both accounting and tax purposes. Sajac likewise treated the transfers as purchases for both accounting and tax purposes. Paccar and Sajac also treated any "repurchases" as purchases and sales, respectively, for accounting and tax purposes.

The trucking industry has a policy of supplying replacement parts for trucks for seven years from the date the truck was manufactured. Paccar Parts, one of the Paccar divisions which had signed an agreement with Sajac, warehouses and distributes truck parts for the Kenworth and Peterbilt divisions of Paccar. Kenworth exceeded the industry standard and in some cases supplied replacement parts for Kenworth trucks that were more than 25 years old.

When a Kenworth or Peterbilt customer ordered a replacement part which Paccar Parts neither had in stock nor was able to obtain from other vendors, then Kenworth or Peterbilt, in order to honor its commitment to its customer, would either manufacture the part in single or small lot quantities or have the part built in one of its fabrication shops. Single or small run manufacture was disadvantageous to Paccar because it disrupted the manufacture of current production parts, involved expensive setting up of machines to manufacture the part, took from two to six weeks to complete, and resulted in the customer receiving a part at an inflated cost and after a long wait.

Paccar Parts could not accurately project the demand for slow-moving, surplus, and obsolete parts. Executives at the company knew from past experience, however, that some of the parts scrapped or disposed of as surplus and obsolete would ultimately be needed by owners of Kenworth or Peterbilt trucks. Paccar Parts wanted to keep a lifetime supply of all usable replacement parts for Kenworth and Peterbilt trucks available, even if the parts were slow-moving, surplus, or obsolete.

Paccar Parts had 64,459 part number records on its computer file. At least 26,666 of those represented parts that were not located on any of its warehouse shelves, but were available at Sajac or from another source.

In April 1976, before the Paccar agreements with Sajac were made, Jack Lemon, the owner of Sajac, provided information to the Paccar divisions, including Paccar Parts, about Sajac's "unusual service." The information stated, "[w]e are a LONG TERM DORMANT WAREHOUSE that provides manufacturers with all of [the] TAX and SPACE SAVING benefits of scrapping excess and inactive noncurrent inventory—yet they retain its availability for possible future sale." The information also stated, "our customers have generally owned our inventory 1 to 3 years before we buy it—and we keep it another 4 to 12 years." At a subsequent meeting between Lemon and Don Luther, materials manager for Paccar Parts, Sajac proposed warehousing the inventory from Paccar Parts for a period of up to 14 years; if a part in a container of inventory was "resold" to Paccar Parts within 5 years, Sajac would keep the entire container for up to 14 years.

In August 1976, Hank Uhthoff, materials disposition manager at Paccar Parts, described the Sajac program in a memorandum to the tax manager of the corporate legal department. The memorandum stated in part, "[c]ontractually we cannot maintain a semblance of control and still enjoy our arms length legal consideration of 'a sale.' However, by agreement, Sajac will scrap material at the end of a specified time, witnessed by a PACCAR Parts employee or agent ... Verbally, Sajac agrees to resell the material to us at scrap price to fulfill any future IRS disagreement of our position."

The memorandum also stated, "Sajac will not sell to anyone but PACCAR Parts. This is their current posture with existing customers. We realize that this cannot be contractually specified and still allow for an 'arms length' position." Finally, the memorandum notes "IRS regulations preclude write off of scrapped material that has not been defaced or made unusable. It is acknowledged that we are in technical violation of this rule in our current scrap program confirmed by recent Internal Audits. However, Accounting considers our risk to be minimal and insignificant contrasted to total inventory dollar figure." In another memorandum to his staff in November 1976, Uhthoff again stated, "Sajac sells only to their manufacturers."

On December 6, 1976, Uhthoff wrote in an interoffice memorandum that "[s]erious attention is being given in developing controls and monitoring devices for Sajac." Uhthoff noted, however, that, "caution must be exercised. This cannot be controlled contractually and still maintain a semblance of an arm's-length transaction. Hence, procedural controls are paramount."

In October, 1977, Paccar's accounting department issued an accounting procedure bulletin which set forth a "suggested priority" to be used in disposing of surplus and obsolete material. On the list of priorities, the seventh item was "sell to Sajac or similar inventory management company" and eighth on the list was "mutilate and scrap." Despite this stated policy, however, Paccar sent inventory to Sajac "as a matter of course in order to retain the parts for future shipment to dealers but at the same time to attempt to achieve tax benefits as if the inventory had been sold."

On its federal income tax returns, Paccar claimed inventory losses, based on the "sales" to Sajac, of $414,591 in 1976 and $336,483 in 1977. The Commissioner of Internal Revenue disallowed the losses, stating:

> It is determined that you retained such a degree of control over the use and disposition of the inventory parts as to prevent the sales from being closed and completed transactions so that the claimed losses are not allowable. In addition, it is determined disallowances of such inventory losses are necessary in order to clearly reflect income. Accordingly, your income is increased $414,591 in 1976 and $336,486 in 1977.

Paccar filed a petition for a redetermination of the deficiencies. The tax court held in favor of the Commissioner, finding that Paccar retained "the same control over the inventory that it had before shipping it to Sajac."

I

Inventory Loss

Paccar contends the tax court erred by disallowing the inventory losses claimed on the transfers to Sajac because the transfer was a bona fide sale. Because the primary issue here is whether the facts fall within the relevant legal definition, we apply the de novo standard of review. * * *

The economic substance of a transaction, rather than its form, governs whether a transaction is a bona fide sale for income tax purposes. Here, the record shows that despite the terminology used by Paccar and Sajac in their written agreement, Paccar retained control equivalent to ownership over the transferred parts. Although the sale was structured as an "arms length" transaction, the parties nevertheless: verbally agreed Sajac would not sell the parts to anyone but Paccar; developed "procedural controls" and "monitoring devices" for Sajac's management of Paccar inventory; transferred inventory to Sajac "as a matter of course ... to attempt to achieve the tax benefits as if the inventory had been sold;" described the Sajac "program" as a "warehouse" and "inventory management company;" verbally agreed to resell the material to Paccar at the scrap price if the tax benefits were disallowed; and treated the transfer as a sale/purchase for tax and accounting purchases even though Paccar admittedly knew that IRS regulations precluded write off of the material as scrap where it had not been defaced or made unusable.

In Thor Power Tool Co. v. Commissioner, the Supreme Court held that a taxpayer could not retain excess inventory items for sale at their original price and at the same time declare inventory losses resulting from lowering the inventory valuation carried on the taxpayer's records to scrap value. Here, the motivation for the transaction was, in the tax court's words, a "thinly veiled subterfuge of a 'sale'" which was "designed to circumvent our holding in Thor."[2]

Paccar argues that the transfer of title effected by the written agreements with Sajac should be "entitled to considerable weight." They cite treasury regulations stating that merchandise "should be included in inventory only if title thereto is vested in the taxpayer" and the taxpayer "should exclude from inventory goods sold ... title to which has passed to the purchaser." Any purported "sale" of inventory under this regulation, however, must be bona fide in order for ownership of the inventory to be considered to have passed from the "seller" to the "buyer." The transfer of title alone, therefore, is not determinative of a sale.

Paccar additionally contends the repurchase provisions should not prevent treatment of the agreement as a sale. In the written agreement, Paccar retained the right to repurchase and Sajac would advise Paccar of "any other disposition" of the parts. The parties verbally agreed, however, that no other disposition would be made; therefore, Paccar's right to "repurchase" the goods was exclusive. An agreement not to sell or dispose of the inventory to anyone other than the original "seller" defeats an attempt to establish a bona fide sale. The Second Circuit decision in United States v. Ingredient Technology Corp., 698 F.2d 88, is particularly appropriate here. There, the parties to the "sale" had a written agreement to sell and a separate verbal agreement to repurchase. The court stated, "it would be high irony to find that the defendants here are immune to prosecution for their scheme because they never wrote it down. The reason it was never written down ... is that such a document would prove that they had agreed to resell at the time of sale and would close the case against them." The verbal agreement for exclusive repurchase further demonstrates that Paccar retained control of the inventory, defeating the existence of a bona fide sale.

Paccar also contends the method of computing compensation for Sajac demonstrated Sajac's ownership of the inventory. Sajac received compensation based upon the amount of parts "repurchased" by Paccar, rather than a fee based upon amount and duration of storage. The record shows, however, that Sajac's compensation equaled the fair market value for storage services.[4] Although in theory, Sajac might have risked receiving compensation lower than its storage costs, "[t]ax consequences follow

---

2. Although the agreements here took place in 1976 and 1977, and the Thor opinion did not issue until 1979, the parties would presumably have been aware of the 1975 tax court decision in Thor, which was ultimately affirmed by the Supreme Court.

4. Paccar appears to misunderstand the substance of this testimony in its brief. Paccar asserts that "[t]he Commissioner's economist has agreed the repurchase price was fair market value." The testimony of the economist, however, was that the price was the fair market value for storage and not a fair market value for repurchase.

what has taken place, not what might have taken place." Even though Paccar argues that transfer of the risk of loss has been a factor in various decisions determining whether a sale occurred, no significant transfer of risk to Sajac took place here. Therefore, the method of compensation does not establish ownership of the inventory.

In its amicus brief, Sajac additionally contends that its "business plan" should be considered as a "solution" to a general economic problem. This "problem" is the same as that identified by the Court in Thor: "either the unsalable inventory must be carried for years at its cost instead of net realizable value, thereby overstating taxable income by such overvaluation until it is scrapped, or the excess inventory must be scrapped prematurely to the detriment of the manufacturer and its customers." * * *

Sajac further argues that its storage system is more economically efficient than other alternatives available to its customers. Sajac is free to sell its warehousing services on their own merits; however, the existence of efficiencies does not determine the legal issue of whether tax benefits should accrue to Sajac's customers. Because Paccar retained the same control over the inventory that it had before shipping it to Sajac, the tax court properly concluded that the transfer did not constitute a "sale," and did not err by disallowing Paccar's claimed inventory losses on the transfer.

AFFIRMED.

QUESTION

Suppose that you had prepared the returns involved in *Paccar*. Might you have been liable for the preparer penalties set forth in § 6694? You might want to consult the descriptions of those penalties, *infra* in Chapter 13.

Inventories and Imputed Income:
A British Perspective

Sharkey v. Wernher and *Mason v. Innes* are two famous British cases which reach dramatically different results. They can be reconciled, at least in part, because *Sharkey v. Wernher* involved inventory accounting, while *Mason v. Innes* did not. Consider what they say about inventories and imputed income, and consider how these situations might have been handled on this side of the pond.

SHARKEY (INSPECTOR OF TAXES) v. WERNHER

House of Lords, 1955.
Viscount Simonds, Lords Porter, Oaksey, Radcliffe and Tucker 3 All ER 493.

Reprinted with permission of LexisNexis.

[Lady Zia Wernher operated a stud farm for profit, and raced horses for pleasure. In the British system of taxation, income from the stud farm was taxable, and expenses of the stud farm were deductible. However, income and expenses of the horse racing establishment were neither taxable nor deductible.

In 1948, Lady Zia transferred five horses from the stud farm to the racing stables. To take one example, the colt Hyperion out of Doubleton had a production cost (basis) of £692, and a fair market value of £3900. The issue for the Court was, first, whether the transfer from the stud farm to the racing stables was a taxable event. Second, if it was a taxable event, was the amount realized equal to the basis (£692) or the fair market value (£3900)?

In the initial court proceeding (Vaisey, J.), it was held that £3900 had been realized. The Court of Appeals reversed, holding that £692 had been realized, leading to no gain, no loss. Opinions from the House of Lords follow—Ed.]:

VISCOUNT SIMONDS:

My Lords, I am the more puzzled by the basis on which this case has proceeded, because learned counsel for the respondent has throughout insisted on what is an elementary principle of income tax law that a man cannot be taxed on profits that he might have, but has not, made * * * The true proposition is not that a man cannot make a profit out of himself but that he cannot trade with himself. The question is whether, and how far, this general proposition must be qualified for the purposes of income tax law.

* * * I cannot escape from the obvious fact that it must be determined whether, and why, a trader, who elects to throw his stock-in-trade into the sea or dispose of it in any other way than by way of sale in the course of trade, is chargeable with any notional receipt in respect of it, before it is asked with how much he should be charged. It is, as I have said, a surprising thing that this question should remain in doubt. For unless, indeed, farming is a trade which, in this respect, differs from other trades, the same problem arises whether the owner of a stud farm diverts the produce of his farm to his own enjoyment, or a diamond merchant, neglecting profitable sales, uses his choicest jewels for the adornment of his wife or a caterer provides lavish entertainment for a daughter's wedding breakfast. Are the horses, the jewels, the cakes and ale to be treated for the purpose of income tax as disposed of for nothing, or for their market value or for the cost of their production? * * *

* * * if there are commodities which are the subject of a man's trade but may also be the subject of his use and enjoyment, I do not know how his account as a trader can properly be made up so as to ascertain his annual profits and gains unless his trading account is credited with a receipt in respect of those goods which he has diverted to his own use and enjoyment. I think, therefore, that the admission was rightly made that some sum must be brought into the stud farm account as a receipt though nothing was received, and, so far at least, the taxpayer must be regarded as having traded with himself. But still the question remains, what is that

sum to be. I suppose that, in the generality of cases in which the question arises in a farming or any other business, e.g., where the farmer supplies his own house with milk, or a market gardener with vegetables, an arbitrary or conventional sum is agreed. The House was not given any information as to the prevailing practice. Now the question precisely arises. * * * But it appears to me that, when it has been admitted or determined that an article forms part of the stock-in-trade of the trader, and that, on his parting with it so that it no longer forms part of his stock-in-trade, some sum must appear in his trading account as having been received in respect of it, the only logical way to treat it is to regard it as having been disposed of by way of trade. If so, I see no reason for ascribing to it any other sum than that which he would normally have received for it in the due course of trade, that is to say, the market value. As I have already indicated, there seems to me to be no justification for the only alternative that has been suggested, namely, the cost of production. The unreality of this alternative would be plain to the taxpayer, if, as well might happen, a very large service fee had been paid so that the cost of production was high and the market value did not equal it.

In my opinion, therefore, the judgment of the Court of Appeal was wrong and should be reversed, and the judgment of VAISEY, J., restored.

LORD PORTER: My Lords, I have had an opportunity of reading the opinion of my noble and learned friend, VISCOUNT SIMONDS, and the opinion about to be delivered by my noble and learned friend, LORD RADCLIFFE, and I agree with them both.

The Opinion of Lord Radcliffe is omitted.

NOTE, QUESTION

1. Lady Zia Wernher was the granddaughter of Czar Nicholas I. She lived at Luton Hoo, an imposing mansion on a 1,500–acre estate north of London. Luton Hoo made a brief appearance in "Four Weddings and a Funeral."

2. Imagine that Lady Wernher had an opening inventory of one horse in her stud farm—Hyperion, valued at £ 692. Now, she removes Hyperion from the stud farm, for use in her personal (nontaxable) racing activities. Having removed Hyperion from inventory, her closing inventory is zero. Therefore, her Cost of Goods Sold (opening inventory minus closing inventory) is £ 692.

But that can't be right. She didn't "sell" Hyperion; she took him. Something must be done to make the inventory accounting work. But what?

MASON (INSPECTOR OF TAXES) v. INNES
Court of Appeal, Civil Division, 1967.
2 All ER 926.

Reprinted with permission of LexisNexis.

LORD DENNING, M.R.: The taxpayer, Mr. Hammond Innes, is a writer of distinction who has for many years carried on the profession of an author. He has written many novels and travel books. He has kept his accounts on a cash basis and has submitted these to the Revenue for tax purposes. On the one side, he has included his receipts from royalties and so forth. On the other side, he has included the expenses of his travels overseas to gather material; the expenses of his study at home; and a small salary to his wife for her work for him. In this case we are concerned with one particular novel which he wrote called "The Doomed Oasis". It was based on material which he had gathered in the Persian Gulf in 1953. He started to write it in September, 1958, and worked on it up till 1959. He charged all the expenses in his accounts for those years. In 1960 he was about to publish it; but he felt that he would like to do something to support his father who had retired on modest resources. So the taxpayer decided to transfer the copyright in the book, "The Doomed Oasis", to his father as a gift. By an assignment made on Apr. 4, 1960, he assigned to his father "in consideration of natural love and affection" the copyright, performing rights and all other rights in "The Doomed Oasis". The question arises whether he is liable to tax on the value of those rights in "The Doomed Oasis". If he had sold the rights at that time in 1960 their market value would have been £15,425. The Crown says that that sum ought to be brought into his accounts and that he should be taxed on it, although he did not receive a penny for the rights because he had given them away. I may add that the taxpayer had also before publication assigned rights in two others of his novels, one to his mother and the other to his mother-in-law. So a like question may arise there.

I start with the elementary principle of income tax law that a man cannot be taxed on profits that he might have, but has not, made: see Sharkey (Inspector of Taxes) v. Wernher. At first sight that elementary principle seems to cover this case. The taxpayer did not receive anything from "The Doomed Oasis". In the case of a trader there is, however, an exception to that principle. I take for simplicity the trade of a grocer. He makes out his accounts on an "earnings basis". He brings in the value of his stock-in-trade at the beginning and end of the year: he brings in his purchases and sales; the debts owed by him and to him; and so arrives at his profit or loss. If such a trader appropriates to himself part of his stock-in-trade, such as tins of beans, and uses them for his own purposes, he must bring them into his accounts at their market value. A trader who supplies himself is accountable for the market value. That is established by Sharkey v. Wernher itself. Now, suppose that such a trader does not supply himself with tins of beans, but gives them away to a friend or relative. Again he has to bring them in at their market value. * * *

Counsel for the Crown contends that that exception is not confined to traders. It extends, he says, to professional men, such as authors, artists, barristers and many others. These professional men do not keep accounts on an "earnings basis". They keep them on a "cash basis": by which I mean that on one side of the account they enter the actual money which they expend; and on the other side they enter the actual money which they receive. They have no stock-in-trade to bring into the accounts. They do not bring in debts owing by or to them, nor work in progress. They enter only expenses on the one side and receipts on the other. Counsel for the Crown contended that liability to tax did not and should not depend on the way in which a man keeps his accounts. There is no difference in principle, he says, between a trader and a professional man. He stated his proposition quite generally in this way. The appropriation of an asset, which has been produced in the ordinary course of a trade or profession, to the trader's or professional man's own purposes, amounts to a realisation of that asset or the receipt of its value, and he must bring it into account. I cannot accept this proposition. Suppose an artist paints a picture of his mother and gives it to her. He does not receive a penny for it. Is he to pay tax on the value of it? It is unthinkable. Suppose he paints a picture which he does not like when he has finished it and destroys it. Is he liable to pay tax on the value of it? Clearly not. These instances—and they could be extended endlessly—show that the proposition in Sharkey v. Wernher does not apply to professional men. It is confined to the case of traders who keep stock-in-trade and whose accounts are, or should be, kept on an earnings basis, whereas a professional man comes within the general principle that, when nothing is received, there is nothing to be brought into account. * * *

I hold that the taxpayer is not chargeable with tax on gifts which he makes of copyright in his books. I think that GOFF, J., and the Commissioners came to a right decision. I would dismiss this appeal.

QUESTION

Does *Mason v. Innes* correctly distinguish *Sharkey v. Wernher*? How would these two cases come out in the United States?

CHAPTER VI

TIMING

■ ■ ■

So far, the focus has been on income and deductions. Now, the focus shifts to the question of "When?"

The "when" aspect of taxation should not be totally new to you. On the income side, realization, covered early in the materials, is really a timing concept: when should appreciation be recognized as taxable income—when it occurs, or only later, upon a realization event? Similarly, on the deduction side, recovery of capital issues are timing issues: when should recovery of capital deductions be taken—immediately, over the life of the asset, or at final disposition?

All else being equal, the taxpayer would prefer to **defer** income, and **accelerate** deductions. Note that neither one will necessarily affect the amount you owe, just when you owe it.[a] But the "when" can be very important. In fact, managing your affairs so that you owe $100 in taxes in 2008 instead of 2007 is tantamount to obtaining a one-year loan of $100 from the government, interest-free.

When the Tax Reform Act of 1986 shut down tax shelters, etc., (see chapter 13, *infra*), many felt that timing was the only significant device for the manipulation of taxes which remained available. Even now, when some of the 1986 changes have unraveled somewhat, the timing dimension remains one of the most significant areas available to the tax planner—far more so than was appreciated in an earlier generation.[b]

A. GENERAL ACCOUNTING PRINCIPLES

Code: §§ 446(a) through (c), 451

Regulations: §§ 1.446–1(c)(1)(i) [definition of cash method]

1.446–1(c)(1)(ii) [definition of accrual method]

---

a. However, if you can defer the income event from your peak earning years, during which you are in a relatively high bracket, to your retirement years, during which you might be in a relatively low bracket, you might have an effect on the amount of tax as well.

b. Henry Simons, in the late 1930's, characterized timing issues as "that mosquito argument."

264

1. CASH METHOD AND ACCRUAL METHOD

When must you recognize taxable income? When can you take a deduction? The cash method and the accrual method answer these questions in different ways. The cash method focuses on physical receipt and payment; the accrual method focuses on legal rights and liabilities.

PROBLEMS

Read the definitions of cash and accrual cited above, and answer the questions below.

Lawyer performed legal services for client in year one, and sent a bill. Client paid the bill in cash in year two.

1) When does lawyer recognize income if she is on:

a) the cash basis?

b) the accrual basis?

2) Assume that the legal fees are deductible by the client. When does the client take the deduction, if she is on:

a) the cash basis?

b) the accrual basis?

2. CASH EQUIVALENCY

PROBLEM

Assume the facts of Problem 1 above. Lawyer is on the cash basis. What happens in year two if:

a) Client pays by check?

b) Client pays by credit card?

c) Client gives Lawyer a live boa constrictor. It is agreed that the fair market value of the boa constrictor is equal to the amount stated in Lawyer's bill.

d) Client paints Lawyer's house. It is agreed that the fair market value of the house painting is equal to the amount stated in Lawyer's bill.

e) Client gives Lawyer a negotiable note for the full amount of Lawyer's bill.

f) Client sends Lawyer the following letter:

I am pleased with the legal services which you rendered in year one. I agree that I owe you the amount stated in your bill, which I received in year one. One of these days, I will get around to paying you.

3. CONSTRUCTIVE RECEIPT

Regulations: § 1.451–2

PROBLEM

Client offers to pay lawyer on December 31 of year one. Lawyer says, "I have a lot of income this year, and expect to have less income and more deductions next year. Could you wait and pay me on January 2 of next year?"

Client replies, "No problem. I'll just keep this check in my desk drawer over the holiday."

Lawyer is a cash basis taxpayer. When does she report the income from client?

HORNUNG v. COMMISSIONER

United States Tax Court, 1967.
47 T.C. 428.

HOYT, JUDGE:

* * *

Findings of Fact

* * *

Petitioner is a well-known professional football player who was employed by the Green Bay Packers in 1962. Prior to becoming a professional, petitioner attended the University of Notre Dame and was an All–American quarterback on the university football team.

Issue 1. The Corvette

Sport Magazine is a publication of the McFadden–Bartell Corp., with business offices in New York City. Each year Sport Magazine (hereinafter sometimes referred to as Sport or the magazine) awards a new Corvette automobile to the player selected by its editors (primarily by its editor in chief) as the outstanding player in the National Football League championship game. This award was won by John Unitas of the Baltimore Colts in 1958 and 1959 and by Norm Van Brocklin of the Philadelphia Eagles in 1960. A similar annual award is made to outstanding professional athletes in baseball, hockey, and basketball. The existence of the award is announced several days prior to the sporting event in question, and the selection and announcement of the winner is made immediately following the athletic contest. The Corvette automobiles are generally presented to the recipients at a luncheon or dinner several days subsequent to the sporting event and a photograph of the athlete receiving the car is published in the magazine, together with an article relating to his performance during the particular athletic event. The Corvette awards are intended to promote the sale of Sport Magazine and their cost is deducted by the publisher for Federal income tax purposes as promotion and advertising expense.

The Corvette which is to be awarded to the most valuable player in the National Football League championship game is generally purchased by the magazine several months prior to the date the game is played, and it is held by a New York area Chevrolet dealer until delivered to the recipient of the award. In some years when the game is played in New York the magazine has had the car on display at the stadium on the day of the game.

On December 31, 1961, petitioner played in the National Football League championship game between the Green Bay Packers and the New York Giants. The game was played in Green Bay, Wis. Petitioner scored a total of 19 points during this game and thereby established a new league record. At the end of this game petitioner was selected by the editors of Sport as the most valuable player and winner of the Corvette, and press releases were issued announcing the award. At approximately 4:30 on the afternoon of December 31, 1961, following the game, the editor in chief of Sport informed petitioner that he had been selected as the most valuable player of the game. The editor in chief did not have the key or the title to the Corvette with him in Green Bay and the petitioner did not request or demand immediate possession of the car at that time but he accepted the award.

The Corvette which was to be awarded in connection with this 1961 championship game had been purchased by Sport in September of 1961. However, since the game was played in Green Bay, Wis., the car was not on display at the stadium on the day of the game, but was in New York in the hands of a Chevrolet dealership. As far as Sport was concerned the car was "available" to petitioner on December 31, 1961, as soon as the award was announced. However, December 31, 1961, was a Sunday and the New York dealership at which the car was located was closed. Although the National Football League championship game is always played on a Sunday, Sport is prepared to make prior arrangements to have the car available in New York for the recipient of the award on that Sunday afternoon if the circumstances appear to warrant such arrangements— particularly if the game is played in New York. Such arrangements were not made in 1961 because the game was played in Green Bay, and, in the words of Sport's editor in chief, "it seemed a hundred-to-one that * * * (the recipient of the award) would want to come in (to New York) on New Year's Eve to take possession" of the prize.

On December 31, 1961, when petitioner was informed that he had won the Corvette, he was also informed that a luncheon was to be held for him in New York City on the following Wednesday by the publisher of Sport, at which luncheon his award would be presented. At that time petitioner consented to attend the luncheon in order to receive the Corvette. There was no discussion that he would obtain the car prior to the presentation ceremony previously announced. The lunch was held as scheduled on Wednesday, January 3, 1962, in a New York restaurant. Petitioner attended and was photographed during the course of the presentation of the automobile to him. A photograph of petitioner sitting in the car outside of the restaurant was published in the April 1962 issue of Sport, together with an article regarding his achievements in the championship game and the Corvette prize award. Petitioner was not required to attend the lunch or to pose for photographs or perform any other service for Sport as a condition or as consideration for his receipt of the car. * * *

Petitioner did not include the fair market value of this car in his gross income for 1962, or for any other year. McFadden–Bartell Corporation deducted its cost as a promotion and advertising expense. * * *

Opinion

Issue 1. The Corvette

Petitioner alleged in his petition that the Corvette was received by him as a gift in 1962. However, at trial and on brief, he argues that the car was constructively received in 1961, prior to the taxable year for which the deficiency is being assessed. If this contention is upheld, the question of whether the car constituted a reportable item of gross income need not be considered. This argument is based upon the assertion that the announcement and acceptance of the award occurred at approximately 4:30 on the afternoon of December 31, 1961, following the game.

It is undisputed that petitioner was selected as the most valuable player of the National Football League championship game in Green Bay on December 31, 1961. It is also undisputed that petitioner actually received the car on January 3, 1962, in New York. Petitioner relies upon the statement at the trial by the editor in chief of Sport that as far as Sport was concerned the car was 'available' to petitioner on December 31, 1961, as soon as the award was announced. It is therefore contended that the petitioner should be deemed to have received the value of the award in 1961 under the doctrine of constructive receipt.

* * * The regulations under § 451 elaborate on the meaning of constructive receipt:

> Income although not actually reduced to a taxpayer's possession is constructively received by him in the taxable year during which it is credited to his account, set apart for him, or otherwise made available so that he may draw upon it at any time, or so that he could have drawn upon it during the taxable year if notice of intention to withdraw had been given. However, income is not constructively received if the taxpayer's control of its receipt is subject to substantial limitations or restrictions. * * *

The basis of constructive receipt is essentially unfettered control by the recipient over the date of actual receipt. Petitioner has failed to convince us that he possessed such control on December 31, 1961, over the receipt of the Corvette. The evidence establishes that the Corvette which was presented to petitioner on January 3, 1962, was in the possession of a Chevrolet dealer in New York City on December 31, 1961. At the time the award was announced in Green Bay, the editor in chief of Sport had neither the title nor keys to the car, and nothing was given or presented to petitioner to evidence his ownership or right to possession of the car at that time.

Moreover, since December 31, was a Sunday, it is doubtful whether the car could have been transferred to petitioner before Monday even with the cooperation of the editor in chief of Sport. The New York dealership at which the car was located was closed. The car had not been set aside for petitioner's use and delivery was not dependent solely upon the volition of petitioner. The doctrine of constructive receipt is therefore inapplicable, and we hold that petitioner received the Corvette for income tax purposes in 1962 as he originally alleged in his petition and as he reported in his 1962 income tax return. * * *

QUESTIONS

1. Why did Hornung care whether his income was reportable in 1962 or 1961?

2. After the game, at 4:30 p.m. on December 31, 1961, in Green Bay, what was to prevent Hornung from selling the Corvette to a team-mate, delivery to take place in January? Does the outcome of the case change if Hornung had the legal right to make such a sale on December 31? Would the case had come out differently if Hornung had been given the title and keys to the car?

AMES v. COMMISSIONER

United States Tax Court, 1999.
112 T.C. 304.

GERBER, J.

Respondent determined deficiencies in petitioner's Federal income tax and section 6662(a) penalties as follows:

		Penalty
Year	Deficiency	Sec. 6662(a)
1989	$214,303.51	$42,860.70
1990	19,970.77	3,994.15
1991	27,367.39	5,473.48
1992	58,684.57	11,736.91

Findings of Fact

Petitioner is incarcerated in a Federal penitentiary for turning over state secrets to a foreign government at a time when he held a position with the Central Intelligence Agency (CIA) of the United States. * * * Petitioner's employment with the CIA spanned the years 1962 to 1994, during which he was assigned to progressively more responsible positions involving the Union of Soviet Socialist Republics (Soviet Union) and Soviet Bloc Eastern European countries. Throughout that time, petitioner held a Top Secret security clearance, and he had access to information and documents classified Secret and Top Secret.

Petitioner timely filed joint Federal income tax returns with his wife, Rosario C. Ames, for the taxable years 1989, 1990, 1991, and 1992. Petitioner's returns were filed on the cash basis for reporting income and deductions. The returns primarily reflected income from petitioner's CIA employment in the amounts of $70,337, $60,340, $62,514, and $67,578 for 1989, 1990, 1991, and 1992, respectively.

In 1984, as part of his duties as a CIA Operations officer, petitioner began meeting with officials of the Soviet Union's Embassy in Washington, D.C. These meetings were authorized by the CIA and the Federal Bureau of Investigation (FBI) and were designed to allow petitioner access to Soviet officials as possible sources for intelligence information and recruitment.

Sometime during April 1985, petitioner entered into a relationship with Soviet officials under which he betrayed his country and sold classified CIA information and information sourced in other branches of the U.S. Government to the KGB (the Soviet intelligence directorate) in return for large amounts of remuneration. Petitioner provided the KGB with classified Top Secret information relating to the penetration of the Soviet military and intelligence services by the CIA, including the identities of Soviet military and intelligence officers who were cooperating with the CIA and foreign intelligence services of governments friendly to the United States. Because of petitioner's disclosures, a number of these individuals were arrested and executed by the KGB.

In the fall of 1985, petitioner received a communication from a Soviet agent that $2 million had been set aside for him in an account that he would be able to draw upon. Petitioner was told that the money was being held by the Soviet Union, rather than in an independent or third-party bank or institution, on petitioner's behalf. Petitioner received $50,000 in cash for his initial disclosure to the KGB and additional cash payments, the specific dates of which have not been detailed in the record of this case.

Petitioner met with Soviet officials in Washington, D.C., and in 1989 he met with them in Rome. In the spring of 1989, as petitioner was preparing to return to CIA headquarters in Langley, Virginia, the KGB provided him with two written documents. The first was a financial accounting that indicated that as of May 1, 1989, approximately $1.8 million had been set aside for petitioner and that some $900,000 more had been designated for him. The second document was a nine-page letter containing a list of the types of classified U.S. Government information sought by the KGB. The second document also contained a discussion of arrangements for cash dropoff payments to petitioner upon his return to the United States, a warning to petitioner to avoid traps set by the CIA, and a detailed plan governing future communications between petitioner and the KGB.

After his return to Washington, D.C., in 1989, petitioner communicated with the Soviets primarily through a complex arrangement of signal sites (a prearranged location where an individual leaves an impersonal mark or item to convey a prearranged message) and dead drops (locations for secretly leaving packages for anonymous pickup). Petitioner personally met with the Soviets only about once a year. Throughout this period, it was typical for petitioner to make a delivery of information and receive cash by means of signal sites and dead drops. Petitioner continued his unlawful espionage activities until his arrest in 1994.

During the years 1989, 1990, 1991, and 1992, petitioner and his wife made deposits of cash received in connection with petitioner's unlawful espionage activities in the amounts of $745,000, $65,000, $91,000, and $187,000, respectively. These deposits did not represent transfers of funds from other accounts or redeposits of currency previously withdrawn from other accounts. Petitioner did not report on his income tax returns for taxable years 1989, 1990, 1991, and 1992 any of the amounts received from the KGB in connection with his illegal espionage activities. Petitioner did not report on a Federal income tax return (including his 1985 return) any amount of unlawful income he received or that had been set aside for him.

* * * Petitioner was sentenced to life imprisonment on the espionage charge and to 27 months' imprisonment on the tax charge, the two sentences to run concurrently. In addition, the plea agreement provided for the criminal forfeiture of whatever interest petitioner had in espionage-related assets. At the time of trial, petitioner was serving a life sentence in a Federal penitentiary.

Opinion

* * *

II.   When Should Petitioner Have Reported the Income From His Illegal Espionage Activities?

Petitioner contends that he constructively received most[6] of the unlawful espionage income in 1985, and, accordingly, he was not required

---

6. Petitioner contends that he constructively received almost $2 million in 1985 and, in addition, that he received $10,000 per month or $120,000 per year during each of the years at issue. Other than his constructive receipt contention, petitioner does not contend that we should modify respondent's determination. Respondent determined, on the basis of petitioner's bank deposits, that he underreported his income by $745,000, $65,000, $91,000, and $187,000 for the taxable years 1989, 1990, 1991, and 1992, respectively. Petitioner, however, does not argue that we should increase respondent's determinations for the 1990 and 1991 years, which are less than the amounts petitioner has contended that he received. Likewise, respondent did not assert an increased deficiency for the 1990 or 1991 tax years.

to report the income received and deposited during the taxable years 1989, 1990, 1991, and 1992. Respondent contends that the income was reportable in 1989 through 1992, the years petitioner actually received and deposited cash in his bank accounts. Petitioner concedes that the funds deposited during the years in issue represent cash received from the Soviet Union during the years of the deposits. Petitioner argues, however, that most of the amounts he received during the taxable years under consideration were constructively received in 1985.[7]

A taxpayer reporting income on the cash method of accounting, such as petitioner, must include an item in income for the taxable year in which the item is actually or constructively received. * * *

Following the regulatory definition, courts have held that income is recognized when a taxpayer has an unqualified, vested right to receive immediate payment. Normally, the constructive receipt doctrine precludes the taxpayer from deliberately turning his back on income otherwise available. Here, however, petitioner relies on constructive receipt as a foil to respondent's determination that the unlawful income was reportable during the years before the Court. In any event, the essence of constructive receipt is the unfettered control over the date of actual receipt. See Hornung v. Commissioner.

The determination of whether a taxpayer has constructively received income is to be made largely on a factual basis. Resolution of the controversy in petitioner's favor depends on whether he can show that he constructively received about $2 million in 1985, the year he was informed that an amount had been set aside for him. Under the circumstances here, petitioner did not possess "unfettered control" over the $2 million in 1985.

Assuming arguendo that some type of account was created and funds were segregated for petitioner, he did not have ready access to it, and certain conditions had to be met or had to occur before he could gain physical access to any funds. Petitioner had to contact the Soviets, using a complex arrangement of signal sites, to determine whether a "withdrawal" could be made. Next, the Soviets had to arrange to have the cash transferred into the United States and have it secretly left in a prearranged location for petitioner. There was no certainty that these conditions and steps could be accomplished under the existing circumstances, and the conditions represented substantial risks, limitations, and restrictions on petitioner's control of the funds, assuming they were even in existence and segregated for his exclusive benefit. See Paul v. Commissioner, T.C. Memo. 1992–582 (no constructive receipt where taxpayer would have had to travel 68 miles in order to turn in winning lottery

---

7. At trial, petitioner testified that he constructively received but fraudulently failed to report the illicit income for 1985. He explained that if he had reported the income on his Federal income tax return, his illicit and secret relationship with the Soviet Union would have been revealed. We note that petitioner's concession may have placed him at a disadvantage irrespective of our holding here. For example, if petitioner fraudulently failed to report income for 1985, the period for assessment would not have expired for 1985. See sec. 6501(c)(1).

ticket). There is no constructive receipt of income where delivery of the cash is not dependent solely upon the volition of the taxpayer. See Hornung v. Commissioner.

So long as the Soviets retained control over any funds or promised set-asides, there was no practical or legal way in which petitioner could compel payment. Constructive receipt of income has been found where a corporation offers payment or pays by check in one year, but the recipient refuses delivery or fails to cash the check until the following year. Here, no such proffer was made, and petitioner did not have a legally enforceable claim. If the KGB had questioned petitioner's loyalty at any time before payment, there is no assurance that petitioner would have continued to receive cash deliveries or payments. So long as the Soviet Union retained the ability to withhold or control the funds, there was no constructive receipt. Petitioner did not constructively receive the income before it was made physically and/or practically available to him. Accordingly, we hold that petitioner received and failed to report income in the amounts of $745,000, $65,000, $91,000, and $187,000 for the years 1989, 1990, 1991, and 1992, respectively.

4. BASIS AND DEFERRAL

In Chapter 3, you saw instances in which Congress was willing to grant a permanent exclusion of an item from taxable income. The receipt of gifts, and interest on state and local bonds, were two examples. Although Congress does occasionally grant such permanent exclusions, it is far more willing merely to defer the taxable event until a later date. More often than not, these deferrals are accomplished through the mechanism of basis.

(a) A Statutory Example

Code: §§ 109, 1019

PROBLEM

Landlord owns Apartment Building. His basis in the building is $100,000 [for the purpose of this problem, we will ignore all possible adjustments to basis, such as depreciation, other than those which might result from the soundproofing system described below]. Billy Joe Trash, an aspiring rock musician, rents an apartment from Landlord for calendar year 1995, paying the entire annual rent in advance. In February of 1995, Billy Joe asks Landlord's permission to improve the apartment by installing a built-in soundproofing system worth $5,000. Landlord enthusiastically agrees. The soundproofing system is installed in mid-March. An appraiser estimates that the soundproofing system adds $5,000 to the value of the building. Billy Joe moves out of the apartment on December 31, at the expiration of his lease. In April of 1997, Landlord sells the building for $105,000.

Billy Joe's soundproofing is clearly something of value, and it is not a gift. It must be taken into Landlord's income, but when? The three possibilities are:

1) When the soundproofing is installed in mid-March, 1995;

2) When Landlord reenters the apartment at the expiration of the lease on January 1, 1996; or

3) When Landlord sells the apartment building in April of 1997.

Consider the equities of taxing Landlord at each of these three times. Now read the statutory sections and see what Congress has wrought.

P.S. Now assume that Billy Joe hadn't prepaid the rent, and persuades Landlord to accept the soundproofing system in lieu of $5,000 of rental payment. How would your analysis change?

(b) Factoring Receivables: Cash vs. Accrual

PROBLEM

Lawyer performs services for client in year one. In year two, she sends client a bill for $100. In year three, she sells the right to collect the $100 to Frank Factor for $95. Looking only on the income side, when and what are the income events to Lawyer if she is on:

a) the cash basis?

b) the accrual basis?

(c) Bad Debts: Cash vs. Accrual

Code: § 166(b)

PROBLEM

Assume the facts of the problem above. However, this time, Lawyer does not sell the receivable to Factor in year three. Instead, in year three, Client goes bankrupt. What and when are the income and bad debt deductions if Lawyer is on:

a) the cash basis?

b) the accrual basis?

B. ANNUAL ACCOUNTING AND ITS EXCEPTIONS

Different sorts of income accrue in different ways. Employees can be paid their salaries daily, weekly, bi-weekly, monthly, or annually, before or after the work is performed. Some retailers, such as your average fast food establishment, expect recurrent, daily sales. Others, such as sellers of expensive yachts, find their sales to be comparatively few and far between. Not all income-producing ventures pan out within one year. Imagine, for example, if one were to take five years to build a privately-owned suspension bridge, in the hope that the toll revenues would eventually exceed the cost of the bridge. It might take decades before one would know if that venture had been a success.

Yet, no matter what the actual timing of the income happens to be, the government can't wait for its money. The government pays out huge amounts of money every year, so it must take in huge amounts every year. Accordingly, taxpayers must file returns at least annually, even if they don't know at the end of a given year whether or not they have really generated any income.

If one does not know, one has to make the best possible guess. However, this requirement of filing a return even when one isn't quite sure leads to two sorts of questions:

(1) How sure must you be before you are required to report uncertain income or expenses?

(2) What if you turn out to be wrong:

(a) What if you report income, and later have to give it back?

(b) What if you take a deduction for expenses paid, only to find later that the money [or property] is returned to you?

The first question is resolved by *North American Oil*. Note that its answer applies whether the taxpayer is using the cash method or the accrual method. Note, also, the court's curious use of the verb "return," by which it means "report in a tax return." The second question is resolved by §§ 1341 and 111, and the tax benefit doctrine.

1. CLAIM OF RIGHT

NORTH AMERICAN OIL CONSOLIDATED v. BURNET

United States Supreme Court, 1932.
286 U.S. 417, 52 S.Ct. 613, 76 L.Ed. 1197.

MR. JUSTICE BRANDEIS delivered the opinion of the Court.

The question for decision is whether the sum of $171,979.22, received by the North American Oil Consolidated in 1917, was taxable to it as income of that year.

The money was paid to the company under the following circumstances: Among many properties operated by it in 1916 was a section of oil land, the legal title to which stood in the name of the United States. Prior to that year, the government, claiming also the beneficial ownership, had instituted a suit to oust the company from possession; and on February 2, 1916, it secured the appointment of a receiver to operate the property, or supervise its operations, and to hold the net income thereof. The money paid to the company in 1917 represented the net profits which had been earned from that property in 1916 during the receivership. The money was paid to the receiver as earned. After entry by the District Court in 1917 of the final decree dismissing the bill, the money was paid, in that year, by the receiver to the company. The government took an appeal (without supersedeas) to the Circuit Court of Appeals. In 1920, that court affirmed the decree. In 1922, a further appeal to this Court was dismissed by stipulation. * * *

It is conceded that the net profits earned by the property during the receivership constituted income. The company contends that they should have been reported by the receiver for taxation in 1916; that, if not returnable by him, they should have been returned by the company for 1916, because they constitute income of the company accrued in that year; and that, if not taxable as income of the company for 1916, they were taxable to it as income for 1922, since the litigation was not finally terminated in its favor until 1922.

First. The income earned in 1916 and impounded by the receiver in that year was not taxable to him, because he was the receiver of only a part of the properties operated by the company. * * *

Second. The net profits were not taxable to the company as income of 1916. For the company was not required in 1916 to report as income an amount which it might never receive. There was no constructive receipt of the profits by the company in that year, because at no time during the year was there a right in the company to demand that the receiver pay over the money. Throughout 1916 it was uncertain who would be declared entitled to the profits. It was not until 1917, when the District Court entered a final decree vacating the receivership and dismissing the bill, that the company became entitled to receive the money. Nor is it material, for the purposes of this case, whether the company's return was filed on the cash receipts and disbursements basis, or on the accrual basis. In neither event was it taxable in 1916 on account of income which it had not yet received and which it might never receive.

Third. The net profits earned by the property in 1916 were not income of the year 1922—the year in which the litigation with the government was finally terminated. They became income of the company in 1917, when it first became entitled to them and when it actually received them. If a taxpayer receives earnings under a claim of right and without restriction as to its disposition, he has received income which he is required to return, even though it may still be claimed that he is not entitled to retain the money, and even though he may still be adjudged liable to restore its equivalent. If in 1922 the government had prevailed, and the company had been obliged to refund the profits received in 1917, it would have been entitled to a deduction from the profits of 1922, not from those of any earlier year.

Affirmed.

2. WHAT IF YOU RECEIVE INCOME AND LATER HAVE TO GIVE IT BACK?

Code: § 1341

UNITED STATES v. LEWIS

United States Supreme Court, 1951.
340 U.S. 590, 71 S.Ct. 522, 95 L.Ed. 560.

MR. JUSTICE BLACK delivered the opinion of the Court.

Respondent Lewis brought this action in the Court of Claims seeking a refund of an alleged overpayment of his 1944 income tax. The facts found by the Court of Claims are: In his 1944 income tax return, respondent reported about $22,000 which he had received that year as an employee's bonus. As a result of subsequent litigation in a state court, however, it was decided that respondent's bonus had been improperly computed; under compulsion of the state court's judgment he returned approximately $11,000 to his employer. Until payment of the judgment in 1946, respondent had at all times claimed and used the full $22,000 unconditionally as his own, in the good faith though "mistaken" belief that he was entitled to the whole bonus.

On the foregoing facts the Government's position is that respondent's 1944 tax should not be recomputed, but that respondent should have deducted the $11,000 as a loss in his 1946 tax return. The Court of Claims, however, * * * held that the excess bonus received "under a mistake of fact" was not income in 1944 and ordered a refund based on a recalculation of that year's tax. We granted certiorari, because this holding conflicted with many decisions of the courts of appeals, and with principles announced in North American Oil Consolidated v. Burnet.

In the North American Oil case we said: "If a taxpayer receives earnings under a claim of right and without restriction as to its disposition, he has received income which he is required to return, even though it may still be claimed that he is not entitled to retain the money, and even though he may still be adjudged liable to restore its equivalent." Nothing in this language permits an exception merely because a taxpayer is "mistaken' as to the validity of his claim." * * *

Income taxes must be paid on income received (or accrued) during an annual accounting period. The "claim of right" interpretation of the tax laws has long been used to give finality to that period, and is now deeply rooted in the federal tax system. We see no reason why the Court should depart from this well-settled interpretation merely because it results in an advantage or disadvantage to a taxpayer.[3]

---

3. It has been suggested that it would be more "equitable" to reopen respondent's 1944 tax return. While the suggestion might work to the advantage of this taxpayer, it could not be

Reversed.

MR. JUSTICE DOUGLAS (dissenting).

The question in this case is not whether the bonus had to be included in 1944 income for purposes of the tax. Plainly it should have been because the taxpayer claimed it as of right. Some years later, however, it was judicially determined that he had no claim to the bonus. The question is whether he may then get back the tax which he paid on the money.

Many inequities are inherent in the income tax. We multiply them needlessly by nice distinctions which have no place in the practical administration of the law. If the refund were allowed, the integrity of the taxable year would not be violated. The tax would be paid when due; but the government would not be permitted to maintain the unconscionable position that it can keep the tax after it is shown that payment was made on money which was not income to the taxpayer.

NOTE

The result of *United States v. Lewis* was changed by Congress when it enacted § 1341. Note the "if ... then ..." structure of § 1341(a). "If" taxpayer meets the three elements listed at § 1341(a)(1), (2) and (3), "then" taxpayer either takes a deduction in the current year [§ 1341(a)(4)] or "reopens" the prior year [§ 1341(a)(5)], depending upon which alternative gives the taxpayer a better result.

The application of § 1341, however, depends, among other things, upon whether or not "it appeared that the taxpayer had an unrestricted right" to the item which has now been returned. The bold face titles of Part V and § 1341 both paraphrase "unrestricted right" as "claim of right," the phrase made famous by *North American Oil*. But what does "claim of right" mean?

McKINNEY v. UNITED STATES

United States District Court, W.D. Texas, Austin Division, 1976.
76–2 USTC ¶ 9728, 1976 WL 1151.

ROBERTS, DISTRICT JUDGE:

* * * Plaintiff embezzled $91,702.06 from his employer, Texas Employment Commission, in 1966, culminating a plan originated in 1956, and he reported that amount as miscellaneous income on his 1966 tax return and paid the tax due on it. Subsequently, the embezzlement was discovered, Plaintiff was convicted in state court for the crime, and he repaid the embezzled money to his employer in 1969. Plaintiff claims that he is entitled to special tax treatment as a result of his repayment of the embezzled funds that had been previously included in his income and taxed. Plaintiff claims that he was engaged in the trade or business of embezzling and is therefore entitled to a deduction under § 172 of the

---

adopted as a general solution because, in many cases, the three-year statute of limitations would preclude recovery.

Internal Revenue Code for a net operating loss carryback to 1966 of the 1969 loss (caused by repayment of the embezzled funds in 1969) incurred in connection with his trade or business of embezzlement. Alternatively, Plaintiff contends that he acquired the embezzled funds under a claim of right so that the repayment of the embezzled funds in 1969 entitles him to the tax benefits of § 1341 of the Internal Revenue Code. The Government rejected these claims and allowed plaintiff to deduct the $91,702.06 on his 1969 tax return as a loss incurred in a transaction entered into for profit although not connected with a trade or business, pursuant to § 165(c)(2) of the Code. Plaintiff then instituted a claim for refund on the basis that he was entitled to a refund on either his trade or business theory or his claim of right theory. The only factual question before the Court is whether or not the Plaintiff devoted enough time to his embezzlement schemes to make them constitute a trade or business, if embezzlement can ever constitute a trade or business as a matter of law. The two legal issues before the court are: (1) whether embezzlement can as a matter of law ever constitute a trade or business and (2) whether repayment of embezzled money is sufficient as a matter of law to come within the terms of § 1341 and its tax benefits.

At the trial, Plaintiff contended that his embezzlement constituted a trade or business. Plaintiff testified that during his high school years, 1924 to 1928, he engaged in a scheme to embezzle money from a high school concession operation and in fact successfully embezzled some amount between $1,000 and $2,000. Plaintiff also testified that he successfully embezzled approximately $58,000 from his employer, Texas Employment Commission, in 1956, and that the embezzlement scheme which is the subject of the instant suit constituted his third embezzlement. Plaintiff contended that he spent approximately fifty percent of all his working time between 1956 and 1966 carrying out the embezzlement scheme that resulted in the embezzlement of the $91,702.06 in 1966. On the strength of these three embezzlements, Plaintiff contended that he was in the trade or business of being an embezzler and as such his repayment of the embezzled money in 1969 constituted an expense connected with his trade or business, and thus, was deductible under § 172 net operating loss carryback provisions. On cross examination, the Government brought out the fact that no one knew of these embezzlements prior to the discovery of the last embezzlement in 1969, and that Plaintiff had told no one of any of these schemes. The government also brought out the fact that when Plaintiff reported the embezzled funds as income in 1966, they were reported as miscellaneous income, "windfall", rather than as income from a trade or business.

* * *

Even assuming that embezzlement can theoretically be a trade or business for tax purposes, the Court does not find that Plaintiff's activities were sufficient to constitute a trade or business under § 172 of the Internal Revenue Code. Despite Plaintiff's claims, at best, Plaintiff was only an occasional embezzler, and his true trade or business was as an employee of the Texas Employment Commission. Plaintiff did not continuously engage in embezzlement as an attempt to earn a livelihood, but as an occasional lark, to see if he could successfully complete the crime. Furthermore, the Court is of the opinion that as a matter of law embezzlement is not a trade or business for § 172 purposes. There are good policy reasons for not allowing trade or business treatment of repaid embezzled funds. To allow an embezzler to get the benefits of the § 172 net operating loss carryback would place him in a much more advantageous position tax wise than he would otherwise be in, and thus it would tend to encourage the commission of this crime. Such a result would be adverse to both policy and comity considerations. See Tank Truck Rentals, Inc. v. Commissioner 356 U.S. 30 (1958). Thus, the Court holds that as a matter of law an embezzler is not entitled to the benefits of a deduction under § 172 when embezzled funds are repaid, and that even if an embezzler were entitled to the benefits of the deduction under § 172 for the repayment of the embezzled funds, the plaintiff in the instant suit has not shown that he was in the trade or business of embezzling.

Plaintiff contends that if he is not entitled to a deduction under § 172 for a loss in connection with a trade or business which would entitle him to a net operating loss carryback, then in the alternative, he is entitled to the tax benefits available under § 1341 which provide a special tax benefit rule if an item was included in gross income for a prior taxable year because it appeared that the taxpayer had an unrestricted right to such item and it is then determined in a later tax year that the taxpayer did not have an unrestricted right to the item included in income. The crucial issue, for the purpose of this case, is whether Plaintiff had an unrestricted right to the embezzled money in 1966, or as the question is otherwise stated, whether the Plaintiff had a claim of right to the money which he embezzled in 1966. If the Plaintiff held the embezzled money under a claim of right, then he would be entitled to the tax benefits of § 1341.

* * *

It seems almost too clear for argument that funds received through embezzlement and held by an embezzler are not held under a claim of right or with the appearance that the embezzler has an unrestricted right to the use of the embezzled funds. Furthermore, Plaintiff's argument that he held the embezzled funds under a claim of right and therefore is entitled to § 1341 benefits is made more doubtful by the fact that Plaintiff has previously indicated that he did not believe he held the funds in question under a claim of right. In a claim for refund filed with the Internal Revenue Service on April 14, 1970, (when Plaintiff apparently believed that it would be to his benefit to so state), the Plaintiff admitted that the embezzled funds "did not belong to me in 1966." (Defendant's exhibit "H"). Furthermore, Plaintiff admitted in a protest filed with the Internal Revenue Service on February 24, 1971, (also when he thought the argument would be to his benefit), that "the unlawful earnings acquired by me, if any, and if at any time, were not held by me without restriction as to their disposition." (Defendant's exhibit "I"). Thus, even if it were possible for embezzled funds to be held under a claim of right, the Plaintiff has previously admitted that he did not hold the embezzled funds in question under a claim of right. Plaintiff also admitted in testimony adduced at trial that he included the embezzled funds in income in 1966 not because he believed that he held them under a claim of right, but because he knew of the Supreme Court's holding in the James case and therefore included them in income because the Supreme Court had required embezzled funds to be included in income.

The Court is of the opinion that, even if Plaintiff had consistently claimed that he held the embezzled funds in question under a claim of right and had an unrestricted right to use the funds, and so believed nevertheless embezzled funds cannot, as a matter of law, be held by an embezzler under a claim of right such as to qualify for the § 1341 tax benefit provisions, if and when they are repaid. * * * [T]here is no Supreme Court case that either holds or implies that Plaintiff ought to be entitled to the benefits of § 1341 because he held the embezzled funds under a claim of right, and in fact, a careful reading of *Wilcox* and *James* seems to imply just the opposite. The Internal Revenue Service has long interpreted § 1341 as not applying to the repayment of embezzled funds. Rev. Rul. 65–254, 1965–2 Cum. Bull. 50. In addition, every court that has faced this issue has denied the embezzler the benefits of § 1341. It would also be noted that the same policy and comity considerations that militate against giving the Plaintiff the benefits of § 172 also militate against giving him the benefits of § 1341. Thus, the Court holds that as a matter of law the repayment of embezzled funds is not entitled to the § 1341 tax benefit because embezzled funds are not held under a claim of right, and that even if embezzled funds could be held under a claim of right, the Plaintiff in the instant suit did not hold the embezzled funds under a claim of right.

In conclusion, the Court can find no basis in either law or fact for giving the Plaintiff the benefits of § 172 and the net operating loss available for expenses and losses incurred in connection with a trade or business or the tax benefits of § 1341 for funds included in income because it appeared that they were held under a claim of right and then subsequently repaid because it was determined in a later tax year that the funds were not held under a claim of right and therefore were not properly includable in the taxpayer's income in the prior year. The only tax benefit to which the Plaintiff was entitled for the repayment of the embezzled funds in 1969 was a deduction under § 165(c)(2) of the Internal Revenue Code for a loss incurred in a transaction entered into for profit, although not connected with a trade or business, and the IRS gave Plaintiff this deduction. Although the Plaintiff did not receive the type of tax benefit that he desired from the § 165 deduction, it is the only deduction to which he is entitled.

[On appeal, the taxpayer abandoned the net operating loss and pursued only the § 1341 argument. He lost. 574 F.2d 1240 (5th Cir. 1978)—Ed.]

Trial Testimony in McKinney

The years and hours of planning are supported by McKinney's testimony in trial court:

McKinney: Yes sir, it was constantly on my mind. All the way from late 1940 down to 1966.

Brief for the Appellee, App. 102, *McKinney v. United States*

McKinney: I spent nearly half my time or maybe more than half my time researching, memorizing, exploring through files, records, but when I say I spent half my time, or maybe more than half my time, I'm not talking about half of a 40–hour week. I always worked about a 70–hour week, so I spent about, on the average, over the period of that whole 10 years, I spent about 30 hours a week planning, conniving, searching, researching, exploring files, collecting data that might lead to—might have led to participating with the employers in some more tax refunds.

* * *

Perhaps Mr. McKinney and the Court spoke for many of us in the following colloquy on the meaning of "claim of right":

McKinney: I now know in retrospect that the phrase "claim of right" was all fouled up in my mind and I didn't then know. I think I now know what "claim of right" means, but at that time I certainly did not know what the phrase "claim of right" means.

The Court: Would you mind telling us what it is?

McKinney: Claim of right—no, sir, Judge, please sir.

Mr. Hearne: (attorney for McKinney):   Wait a minute. Did you ask him?

The Court: Sure.

Hearne: He asked you.

The Court: He can tell us if he wants to. I haven't been able to find out what it is yet.

Brief for the Appellee, footnote 2, at App. 124–125.

Questions

If either the benefits of § 172 or § 1341 had been allowed to the taxpayer in this case, which activity would have been encouraged—embezzlement, or criminal restitution? Reconsider the Public Policy Doctrine in Chapter IV.

Section 1341 applies if "it appeared that the taxpayer had an unrestricted right to such item." Appeared to whom?

3.   WHAT IF YOU TAKE A DEDUCTION FOR EXPENSES PAID, ONLY TO FIND LATER THAT THE MONEY [OR PROPERTY] IS RETURNED TO YOU? [TAX BENEFIT DOCTRINE]

Code: § 111

Regulations: § 1.111–1

The tax benefit doctrine, and § 111, are the flip side of § 1341. In cases involving § 1341, the taxpayer has received **income** which she later gave back. In cases involving the tax benefit doctrine and § 111, the taxpayer has incurred a **deductible expense** which she later got back, either in the form of money or property. As you will see, the two situations do not work out in quite the same way.

ALICE PHELAN SULLIVAN CORPORATION v. UNITED STATES

United States Court of Claims, 1967.
381 F.2d 399.

COLLINS, JUDGE.

Plaintiff, a California corporation, brings this action to recover an alleged overpayment in its 1957 income tax. During that year, there was returned to taxpayer two parcels of realty, each of which it had previously donated and claimed as a charitable contribution deduction. The first donation had been made in 1939; the second, in 1940. Under the then applicable corporate tax rates, the deductions claimed ($4,243.49 for 1939 and $4,463.44 for 1940) yielded plaintiff an aggregate tax benefit of $1,877.49.[1]

Each conveyance had been made subject to the condition that the property be used either for a religious or for an educational purpose. In 1957, the donee decided not to use the gifts; they were therefore reconveyed to plaintiff. Upon audit of taxpayer's income tax return, it was found that the recovered property was not reflected in its 1957 gross income. The Commissioner of Internal Revenue disagreed with plaintiff's characterization of the recovery as a nontaxable return of capital. He viewed the transaction as giving rise to taxable income and therefore adjusted plaintiff's income by adding to it $8,706.93—the total of the charitable contribution deductions previously claimed and allowed. This addition to income, taxed at the 1957 corporate tax rate of 52 percent, resulted in a deficiency assessment of $4,527.60. After payment of the deficiency, plaintiff filed a claim for the refund of $2,650.11, asserting this amount as overpayment on the theory that a correct assessment could demand no more than the return of the tax benefit originally enjoyed, i.e., $1,877.49. The claim was disallowed.

---

1.   The tax rate in 1939 was 18 percent; in 1940, 24 percent.

This court has had prior occasion to consider the question which the present suit presents. In Perry v. United States, 160 F.Supp. 270, 142 Ct.Cl. 7 (1958) (Judges Madden and Laramore dissenting), it was recognized that a return to the donor of a prior charitable contribution gave rise to income to the extent of the deduction previously allowed. The court's point of division—which is likewise the division between the instant parties—was whether the 'gain' attributable to the recovery was to be taxed at the rate applicable at the time the deduction was first claimed or whether the proper rate was that in effect at the time of recovery. The majority, concluding that the Government should be entitled to recoup no more than that which it lost, held that the tax liability arising upon the return of a charitable gift should equal the tax benefit experienced at time of donation. Taxpayer urges that the *Perry* rationale dictates that a like result be reached in this case.

The Government, of course, assumes the opposite stance. * * *

A transaction which returns to a taxpayer his own property cannot be considered as giving rise to "income"—at least where that term is confined to its traditional sense of "gain derived from capital, from labor, or from both combined." Yet the principle is well engrained in our tax law that the return or recovery of property that was once the subject of an income tax deduction must be treated as income in the year of its recovery. The only limitation upon that principle is the so-called "tax-benefit rule." This rule permits exclusion of the recovered item from income so long as its initial use as a deduction did not provide a tax saving. But where full tax use of a deduction was made and a tax saving thereby obtained, then the extent of saving is considered immaterial. The recovery is viewed as income to the full extent of the deduction previously allowed.

Formerly the exclusive province of judge-made law, the tax-benefit concept now finds expression both in statute and administrative regulations. § 111 of the Internal Revenue Code of 1954 accords tax-benefit treatment to the recovery of bad debts, prior taxes, and delinquency amounts. Treasury regulations have "broadened" the rule of exclusion by extending similar treatment to "all other losses, expenditures, and accruals made the basis of deductions from gross income for prior taxable years * * *."

Drawing our attention to the broad language of this regulation, the Government insists that the present recovery must find its place within the scope of the regulation and, as such, should be taxed in a manner consistent with the treatment provided for like items of recovery, i.e., that it be taxed at the rate prevailing in the year of recovery. We are compelled to agree.

Set in historical perspective, it is clear that the cited regulation may not be regarded as an unauthorized extension of the otherwise limited congressional approval given to the tax-benefit concept. While the statute (i.e., § 111) addresses itself only to bad debts, prior taxes, and delinquency amounts, it was, as noted in Dobson v. Commissioner, 320 U.S. 489 (1943), designed not to limit the application of the judicially designed tax-benefit rule, but rather to insure against its demise. "A specific statutory exception was necessary in bad debt cases only because the courts reversed the Tax Court and established as matter of law a 'theoretically proper' rule which distorted the taxpayer's income (i.e., taxation of a recovery though no benefit may have been obtained through its earlier deduction)."

The *Dobson* decision insured the continued validity of the tax-benefit concept, and the regulation—being but the embodiment of that principle—is clearly adequate to embrace a recovered charitable contribution. But the regulation does not specify which tax rate is to be applied to the recouped deduction, and this consideration brings us to the matter here in issue.

Ever since Burnet v. Sanford & Brooks Co., 282 U.S. 359 (1931), the concept of accounting for items of income and expense on an annual basis has been accepted as the basic principle upon which our tax laws are structured. "It is the essence of any system of taxation that it should produce revenue ascertainable, and payable to the government, at regular intervals. Only by such a system is it practicable to produce a regular flow of income and apply methods of accounting, assessment, and collection capable of practical operation." To insure the vitality of the single-year concept, it is essential not only that annual income be ascertained without reference to losses experienced in an earlier accounting period, but also that income be taxed without reference to earlier tax rates. And absent specific statutory authority sanctioning a departure from this principle, it may only be said of *Perry* that it achieved a result which was more equitably just than legally correct.[5]

Since taxpayer in this case did obtain full tax benefit from its earlier deductions, those deductions were properly classified as income upon recoupment and must be taxed as such. This can mean nothing less than the application of that tax rate which is in effect during the year in which the recovered item is recognized as a factor of income. We therefore sustain the Government's position and grant its motion for summary judgment. Perry v. United States, *supra*, is hereby overruled, and plaintiff's petition is dismissed.

---

5. This opinion represents the views of the majority and complies with existing law and decisions. However, in the writer's personal opinion, it produces a harsh and inequitable result. Perhaps, it exemplifies a situation "where the latter of the law killeth; the spirit giveth life." The tax-benefit concept is an equitable doctrine which should be carried to an equitable conclusion. Since it is the declared public policy to encourage contributions to charitable and educational organizations, a donor, whose gift to such organizations is returned, should not be required to refund to the Government a greater amount than the tax benefit received when the deduction was made for the gift. Such a rule would avoid a penalty to the taxpayer and an unjust enrichment to the Government. However, the court cannot legislate and any change in the existing law rests within the wisdom and discretion of the Congress.

NOTE

The statutory language of Section 111, which at the time of Alice Phelan Sullivan was limited to bad debts, prior taxes and delinquency amounts, was broadened to its current form by the Deficit Reduction Act of 1984.

C. FUN WITH LOANS

ESTATE OF STRANAHAN v. COMMISSIONER

United States Court of Appeals, Sixth Circuit, 1973.
472 F.2d 867.

PECK, CIRCUIT JUDGE.

This appeal comes from the United States Tax Court, which partially denied appellant estate's petition for a redetermination of a deficiency in the decedent's income tax for the taxable period January 1, 1965 through November 10, 1965, the date of decedent's death.

The facts before us are briefly recounted as follows: On March 11, 1964, the decedent, Frank D. Stranahan, entered into a closing agreement with the Commissioner of Internal Revenue Service (IRS) under which it was agreed that decedent owed the IRS $754,815.72 for interest due to deficiencies in federal income, estate and gift taxes regarding several trusts created in 1932. Decedent, a cash-basis taxpayer, paid the amount during his 1964 tax year. Because his personal income for the 1964 tax year would not normally have been high enough to fully absorb the large interest deduction, decedent accelerated his future income to avoid losing the tax benefit of the interest deduction. To accelerate the income, decedent executed an agreement dated December 22, 1964, under which he assigned to his son, Duane Stranahan, $122,820 in anticipated stock dividends from decedent's Champion Spark Plug Company common stock (12,500 shares). At the time both decedent and his son were employees and shareholders of Champion. As consideration for this assignment of future stock dividends, decedent's son paid the decedent $115,000 by check dated December 22, 1964. The decedent thereafter directed the transfer agent for Champion to issue all future dividend checks to his son, Duane, until the aggregate amount of $122,820 had been paid to him. Decedent reported this $115,000 payment as ordinary income for the 1964 tax year and thus was able to deduct the full interest payment from the sum of this payment and his other income. During decedent's taxable year in question, dividends in the total amount of $40,050 were paid to and received by decedent's son. No part of the $40,050 was reported as income in the return filed by decedent's estate for this period. Decedent's son reported this dividend income on his own return as ordinary income subject to the offset of his basis of $115,000, resulting in a net amount of $7,282 of taxable income.

Subsequently, the Commissioner sent appellant (decedent's estate) a notice of deficiency claiming that the $40,050 received by the decedent's son was actually income attributable to the decedent. After making an adjustment which is not relevant here, the Tax Court upheld the deficiency in the amount of $50,916.78. The Tax Court concluded that decedent's assignment of future dividends in exchange for the present discounted cash value of those dividends "though conducted in the form of an assignment of a property right, was in reality a loan to [decedent] masquerading as a sale and so disguised lacked any business purpose; and, therefore, decedent realized taxable income in the year 1965 when the dividend was declared paid."

As pointed out by the Tax Court, several long-standing principles must be recognized. First, under § 451(a) of the Internal Revenue Code of 1954, a cash basis taxpayer ordinarily realizes income in the year of receipt rather than the year when earned. Second, a taxpayer who assigns future income for consideration in a bona fide commercial transaction will ordinarily realize ordinary income in the year of receipt. Third, a taxpayer is free to arrange his financial affairs to minimize his tax liability; thus, the presence of tax avoidance motives will not nullify an otherwise bona fide transaction. We also note there are no claims that the transaction was a sham, the purchase price was inadequate or that decedent did not actually receive the full payment of $115,000 in tax year 1964. And it is agreed decedent had the right to enter into a binding contract to sell his right to future dividends.

The Commissioner's view regards the transaction as merely a temporary shift of funds, with an appropriate interest factor, within the family unit. He argues that no change in the beneficial ownership of the stock was effected and no real risks of ownership were assumed by the son. Therefore, the Commissioner concludes, taxable income was realized not on the formal assignment but rather on the actual payment of the dividends.

It is conceded by taxpayer that the sole aim of the assignment was the acceleration of income so as to fully utilize the interest deduction. Gregory v. Helvering, 293 U.S. 465 (1935), established the landmark principle that the substance of a transaction, and not the form, determines the taxable consequences of that transaction. In the present transaction, however, it appears that both the form and the substance of the agreement assigned the right to receive future income. What was received by the decedent was the present value of that income the son could expect in the future. On the basis of the stock's past performance, the future income could have been (and was[5]) estimated with reasonable accuracy. Essentially, decedent's son paid consideration to receive future income. Of course, the fact of a family transaction does not vitiate the transaction but merely subjects it to special scrutiny.

We recognize the oft-stated principle that a taxpayer cannot escape taxation by legally assigning or giving away a portion of the income

---

5. It was determined that with the current dividend payment rate at that time of 50 cents per share per quarter, $115,000 represented the present value of the right to receive the assigned dividends of $4.60 per share discounted at the then prevailing interest rate of five percent.

derived from income producing property retained by the taxpayer. Here, however, the acceleration of income was not designed to avoid or escape recognition of the dividends but rather to reduce taxation by fully utilizing a substantial interest deduction which was available. As stated previously, tax avoidance motives alone will not serve to obviate the tax benefits of a transaction. * * *

Accordingly, we conclude the transaction to be economically realistic, with substance, and therefore should be recognized for tax purposes even though the consequences may be unfavorable to the Commissioner. The facts establish decedent did in fact receive payment. Decedent deposited his son's check for $115,000 to his personal account on December 23, 1964, the day after the agreement was signed. The agreement is unquestionably a complete and valid assignment to decedent's son of all dividends up to $122,820. The son acquired an independent right against the corporation since the latter was notified of the private agreement. Decedent completely divested himself of any interest in the dividends and vested the interest on the day of execution of the agreement with his son. * * *

The judgment is reversed and the cause remanded for further proceedings consistent with this opinion.

ABDUL JALIL AL–HAKIM v. COMMISSIONER

United States Tax Court, 1987.
T.C. Memo. 1987–136.

CLAPP, JUDGE:

* * * In 1970, petitioner Abdul Jalil al-Hakim (al-Hakim) began to negotiate contracts for professional athletes. He operated as a sole proprietor under the name "Superstar Management, the Genius of Randy Wallace" and maintained a business checking account (business account) at Lloyd's Bank in Oakland, California. * * *

Income From Lyman Bostock Findings of Fact

During 1977, al-Hakim represented Lyman Bostock (Bostock), a professional baseball player, and negotiated on his behalf with 18 teams, including the Minnesota Twins and the California Angels (Angels). al-Hakim was successful in negotiating a five-year contract for Bostock with the Angels.

Bostock and the Angels signed the contract on November 21, 1977 and the American League of Professional Baseball Clubs signed it on January 4, 1978. Under the terms of the contract, the Angels were to pay to Bostock a total of $2,250,000. Pursuant to a deferred-compensation-agreement, Bostock was to receive said $2,250,000 over 12 years— $195,000 per year for the first five years, and the remaining $1,275,000 over the next seven years.

al-Hakim's fee for negotiating Bostock's contract was $112,500, i.e., 5 percent of the $2,250,000 contract amount. Bostock was to pay the fee over ten years and in ten equal installments of $11,250 per year.

A letter from al-Hakim to Bostock stated:

Dear Lyman, As per our conversation Jan. 1, 1978, I am sending you this letter to consumate [sic] our agreement. A) Your fee of $112,500 due SUPER STAR MANAGEMENT upon league approval of your contract is to be paid at the rate of $11,250 a year for ten (10) years beggining [sic] July 1, 1978 and is to be paid each July 1st thereafter. You are aware that this is a ten year repayment schedule and that it is less than the paying term of your contract, however you desire it to be repaid as scheduled. B) You are providing SUPER STAR MANAGEMENT with an interest free loan in the amount of $112,500 by Jan. 15, 1978. This loan is to be repaid at the rate of $11,250 a year for ten (10) years beggining [sic] Dec. 30, 1978 and is to be paid each Dec. 30th thereafter.

* * *

Respectfully,

Abdul–Jalil

In January 1978, the Angels loaned to Bostock $112,500, and on January 13, 1978, Bostock loaned to al-Hakim $112,500.

In May 1978, al-Hakim billed Bostock $11,250 for the first installment of his $112,500 fee. al-Hakim, as payment for the $11,250 installment, reduced the amount, which was shown as a loan from Bostock to him, to $101,250 ($112,500 − $11,250) and reported $11,250 in income from Bostock on his 1978 Federal individual income tax return.

On May 18, 1978, al-Hakim incorporated his sole proprietorship, Superstar Management, The Genius of Randy Wallace, by transferring all its assets and liabilities, including the account receivable from, and loan payable to, Bostock, to a newly formed corporation, "The Genius of Randy Wallace, Inc." (Genius, Inc.).

In June 1978, a dispute, which concerned the terms of Bostock's contract, arose between Bostock and the Angels. As part of a settlement agreement, Bostock reported the loan from the Angels as income and deducted the balance of the fee he owed al-Hakim/Genius, Inc., as an expense. Genius, Inc., reported $101,250, the balance of the fee due al-Hakim/Genius, Inc., as income on its Federal corporate income tax return and reduced to zero the amount of the loan, which al-Hakim/Genius, Inc., owed Bostock.

Opinion

Respondent contends that petitioner was entitled to a fee from Bostock in the amount of $112,500, and al-Hakim received said amount on January 13, 1978, the date on which Bostock "loaned" al-Hakim $112,500. Petitioner contends that the $112,500, which Bostock transferred to him, was a loan. Petitioner further contends that pursuant to his arrangement with Bostock, he was entitled to only $11,250 of his fee in 1978, and pursuant to the settlement agreement, Genius, Inc., was entitled to the remaining part of his fee which was $101,250.

In the present case, petitioner testified that the $112,500, which Bostock transferred to him, was a loan, and the letter, which al-Hakim sent to Bostock, supports al-Hakim's testimony. Pursuant to the terms of the contract between al-Hakim and Bostock, Bostock was to pay al-Hakim's fee over 10 years and in 10 equal installments of $11,250 per year. Based on petitioner's testimony and its supporting documentation, we find that the $112,500, which Bostock transferred to al-Hakim on January 13, 1978, was a loan, and not the payment of his $112,500 fee.

Respondent also contends that the transfer of the $112,500 accounts receivable to Genius, Inc., was an impermissible assignment of income. al-Hakim contends that, in the context of a § 351 transfer, the assignment of income doctrine is not applicable. We agree with petitioner. * * *

QUESTION AND NOTE

(1) Assuming that the transaction had played out as intended for the full ten years, what would Bostock and Hakim have accomplished?

(2) Lyman Bostock played for the Minnesota Twins in 1975, 1976 and 1977, and for the California Angels in 1978. His lifetime batting average was .311. In September of 1978, he was shot to death near Gary, Indiana, by the husband of the woman sitting next to him. Apparently, the husband mistook Bostock for someone else.

D. ACCRUAL ACCOUNTING REVISITED

1. INCOME

TAMPA BAY DEVIL RAYS, LTD. v. COMMISSIONER

United States Tax Court, 2002.
T.C. Memo 2002–248.

MEMORANDUM FINDINGS OF FACT AND OPINION

SWIFT, J.

The primary issue for decision is whether deposits the partnership received in 1995 and 1996 on advance season tickets and on private suite reservations for major league baseball games expected to be played in 1998 are to be included in the income of the partnership when received in 1995 and 1996, or in 1998, the year to which the advance season tickets and the private suite reservations related and the first year in which the partnership's major league baseball team (the Devil Rays) played major league baseball.

Findings of Fact

On March 9, 1995, in return for commitments by the [Tampa Bay Devil Rays, Ltd.] partnership to pay a $130 million franchise fee and to meet other specified conditions, members of the American and National Leagues of major league baseball (hereinafter generally referred to simply as major league baseball) adopted a resolution under which the partnership was conditionally awarded one of major league baseball's expansion franchises. The resolution established a procedure for the eventual approval of the partnership and the Devil Rays to participate in major league baseball.

On March 24, 1995, the partnership and major league baseball entered into an agreement under which the partnership would become a full, participating member of major league baseball upon the satisfaction, no later than November 30, 1997, of the conditions specified in the above resolution and agreement.

Under the resolution and agreement, the major requirements and conditions that the partnership had to satisfy prior to receiving final approval for participation in major league baseball are described below:

(1) Obtain the funding and lines of credit sufficient to pay the $130 million franchise fee and to provide the working capital funds necessary for operation of a major league baseball team;

(2) Make full payment of the $130 million franchise fee * * *

(3) Obtain the funding for and complete renovation of the Thunderdome, the existing, domed stadium in St. Petersburg, Florida, obtain approval from the Commissioner of major league baseball of the completed renovations to the stadium, and obtain a use lease on the stadium effective January 1998;

(4) Obtain from the pre-existing minor league baseball teams located in the geographic region of St. Petersburg, Florida, the territorial or license rights to operate in the region a professional baseball team; and

(5) Establish a minor league baseball system.

As indicated, the resolution and agreement did not constitute either the partnership or the Devil Rays a final member of and participant in major league baseball. The partnership and the Devil Rays were not yet permitted to sign players to major league contracts, nor to field a major league baseball team. Rather, the resolution and agreement authorized the partnership to proceed to establish an expansion franchise that would, subject to the fulfillment of the various conditions no later than November 30, 1997, be subject to final approval by the members of major league baseball. If approved, the partnership would then be permitted to sign major league baseball players and to field a major league baseball team for participation in major league baseball beginning with the 1998 major league baseball season.

* * *

By fall 1997, the partnership had satisfied all of the conditions of the March 1995 resolution and agreement with major league baseball. Accordingly, on November 6, 1997, final agreements were entered into between the partnership and major league baseball. Thereunder, a major league baseball membership certificate was transferred to the partnership entitling the partnership to field a major league baseball team and to play in the American League at the beginning of the 1998 season.

* * *

On November 17, 1997, the partnership participated in an expansion draft of players already under contract with other major league baseball teams that was held for the benefit of the Devil Rays and the Arizona Diamondbacks, the other expansion team. In the expansion draft, the partnership drafted 35 major league baseball players for the Devil Rays. Approximately one half, or $74,725,000, of the $130 million franchise fee was allocated by the partnership to the contracts of the major league baseball players that the partnership drafted and signed in late 1997 and early 1998 for the Devil Rays' 1998 major league baseball season.

During 1995 and 1996, the partnership received funds from customers as deposits on advance season tickets (representing 25 percent of the total stated season ticket price), as deposits on reservations for private suites, and one sponsor fee in anticipation of major league baseball games to be played by the Devil Rays in St. Petersburg, Florida, during the 1998 major league baseball season.

On the application form for the advance 1998 season tickets, it was indicated that the customers' deposits were "nonrefundable". However, in spite of the reference to nonrefundability on the application forms for advance season tickets, if the partnership did not fulfill the conditions specified in the March 1995 major league baseball resolution and agreement, if the partnership and the Devil Rays were not eventually and finally approved to participate in major league baseball, and if the Devil Rays failed to play major league baseball games in 1998, the partnership would have been required to refund the deposits received from customers in 1995 and 1996 on advance season tickets and on private suite reservations relating to the 1998 major league baseball season.

With regard to the private suite reservations, if the partnership was admitted to membership in major league baseball and if the Devil Rays did play major league baseball during the 1998 season, but if five or fewer of the Devil Rays' games were canceled, due, for example, to weather, the partnership would be required to provide the holders of private suite reservations with tickets to makeup games.

If six or more of the Devil Rays' games were canceled during the 1998 season, the partnership would be required to provide holders of private suite reservations with appropriate credits toward the purchase of private suite reservations for the following season.

During 1995, the partnership adopted and followed a policy of allowing refunds to customers, upon their request, of deposits made for advance season tickets and for private suite reservations relating to expected games of the Devil Rays to be played in the 1998 major league baseball season. During 1995, the partnership made refunds to customers relating to the 1998 major league baseball season in the total amount of $260,010 from deposits received on advance season tickets and $35,000 from deposits received on private suite reservations.

Funds that the partnership received during 1995 and 1996 relating to advance season tickets, to private suite reservations, and to the sponsor fee were used by the partnership during 1995 and 1996 for general operating purposes.

Set forth below are the total funds the partnership received in 1995 and in 1996 as deposits on advance season tickets and on private suite reservations, * * * relating to the partnership's and to the Devil Rays' anticipated participation in the 1998 major league baseball season:

	Deposits On		
Year	Advance Season Tickets	Private Suites	Sponsor Fee
1995	$2,906,401	$ 449,807	—
1996	1,932,182	1,640,500	$125,000

On March 31, 1998, the Devil Rays played its first major league baseball game against the Detroit Tigers and lost the game 11 to 6. The Devil Rays apparently played all its scheduled major league baseball games for 1998 on their scheduled dates.

In 1998, the partnership began incurring significant additional expenses (that it had not incurred in prior years) relating to its first season in major league baseball. Substantially all the additional expenses relating directly to the major league baseball games the Devil Rays played in 1998 were incurred in 1998 (e.g., player salaries, stadium rental, and game-day operations).

For financial and tax purposes, the partnership maintains its books and records on the accrual method of accounting.

On its financial books and records for 1995 and 1996, taking into account yearend adjusting entries, the partnership treated the deposits it received in 1995 and in 1996 on advance season tickets and on private suite reservations as deferred revenue (i.e., as liabilities, not as income).

On its Federal partnership tax returns for 1995 and 1996, the partnership treated expenses relating to its minor league baseball activities and to general operating and overhead costs as current business expense deductions.

On its Federal partnership tax returns for 1995 and 1996, the partnership did not deduct as accrued expenses any of the anticipated expenses relating directly to the major league baseball games to be played by the Devil Rays in 1998 (e.g., major league baseball player salaries, stadium rental, and game-day operations).

Further, on its 1995 and 1996 Federal partnership tax returns, the partnership did not accrue business expense deductions of $27,753 and $8,500 incurred in 1995 and 1996, respectively, relating to the marketing and sale in 1995 and 1996 of advance season tickets and private suite reservations. Rather, those expenses were deferred and deducted on the partnership's 1998 Federal partnership tax return for 1998, the year in which the games were played.

On its Federal partnership tax returns for 1995 and 1996, the partnership did not include in income the deposits the partnership received during 1995 and 1996 (on the advance season tickets and on the private suite reservations relating to the anticipated 1998 major league baseball season). Rather, the deposits received in 1995 and 1996 on the advance season tickets and on the private suite reservations were reported by the partnership as income on the partnership's Federal partnership tax return for 1998, the year in which the Devil Rays played the games to which the advance season tickets and the suite reservations related.

* * *

The funds the partnership received in 1996 from major league baseball in connection with third-party licenses of major league baseball names, logos, and emblems were reported as income on the partnership's Federal partnership tax return for 1996.

No portion of the $130 million franchise fee (fully paid by the partnership prior to 1998) was deducted or amortized by the partnership for Federal partnership tax purposes until 1998, the year in which the Devil Rays began playing major league baseball games. In 1995, 1996, and 1997, the partnership capitalized the $130 million franchise fee. The $74,725,000 portion of the franchise fee that the partnership allocated to player contracts the partnership amortized and deducted over the lives of the player contracts, beginning in 1998, the year in which the Devil Rays played its first game. For 1998, the partnership deducted $18,764,389 as amortization on the $74,725,000 allocated to the player contracts.

On audit, respondent treated the deposits the partnership received in 1995 and in 1996 on advance season tickets and on private suite reservations as income to the partnership for 1995 and 1996. Respondent treated the $125,000 sponsor fee received in 1996 as income to the partnership for 1996.

Opinion

* * *

Specifically, under the accrual method of accounting, where funds are received by taxpayers as deposits on services to be rendered in the future the funds generally are to be included in the taxpayers' income in the year of receipt, as opposed to being deferred until the year in which taxpayers perform the related services.

In both *Auto. Club of Mich. v. Commissioner,* 353 U.S. 180 (1957) *(Auto Club),* and *AAA v. United States,* 367 U.S. 687 (1961) accrual basis taxpayers included prepaid membership dues they received in income ratably over the 12–month period covered by the membership agreements, which at times extended beyond the year in which the dues were received. The Supreme Court held in both *Auto Club* and *AAA* that the taxpayers' deferral of the prepaid membership dues did not clearly reflect the taxpayers' income and that the dues should be included in the taxpayers' income in the year of receipt. The Supreme Court noted the "artificial" nature of accruing advance dues in income on a 12–month ratable basis and over two periods where performance of the services to be rendered by the taxpayers was indefinite and uncertain (i.e., where no fixed dates for performance of the services were specified and where the specific services for which the funds were received were to be performed by the taxpayers only upon customer demand).

In *Schlude v. Commissioner,* 372 U.S. 128 (1963), a taxpayer received funds as advance payments on dance lessons to be given at unspecified times in the future to be determined by the students. In requiring the taxpayer to include the funds in income in the year of receipt, the Supreme Court relied upon its prior decisions in *Auto. Club* and *AAA,* focusing on the uncertainty as to when the dance lessons were to be given.

Artnell Co. v. Commissioner, 400 F.2d 981 (7th Cir.1968), involved facts very similar to those involved herein. Therein the Court of Appeals for the Seventh Circuit concluded that funds received by the Chicago White Sox, Inc. (White Sox) on advance ticket sales relating to major league baseball games to be played in a following year may appropriately be deferred and included in the White Sox's income in the year when the games were to be played if that deferral would clearly reflect the White Sox's income. The Court of Appeals for the Seventh Circuit remanded the case to us for analysis of whether the White Sox's deferral of reporting the funds as income until the year in which the games were played would clearly reflect income.

On remand, we concluded that the White Sox's method of accounting for the funds clearly reflected income because deferral of the funds until the year in which the games were played more clearly than respondent's method matched the income with the White Sox's major expenses that were incurred in the year when the games were played.

In subsequent opinions, we have stated that *Artnell Co.* will be limited to its facts.

We agree with petitioner that the facts before us in the instant case fall within the narrow fact pattern of *Artnell Co.*

If played, the Devil Rays' games would be played in 1998 according to a fixed and definite schedule. Had any games been postponed, the Devil

Rays would have played makeup games on fixed dates in 1998, to which makeup games the season tickets and the suite reservations would have been applicable. The partnership's major expenses of operating the Devil Rays and playing major league baseball were incurred in 1998.

If the partnership and the Devil Rays had never received final approval to participate in major league baseball for the 1998 season, the partnership never would have incurred the major expenses of operating a major league baseball team. The partnership would have been required to refund the deposits on advance season tickets and on private suite reservations. The deposits and refunds would have been a wash.

On the facts before us involving deposits received for major league baseball games to be played by the Devil Rays in 1998, with no major league baseball games played by the Devil Rays until 1998, and the related expenses incurred by the partnership in 1998,[5] the application of *Artnell Co.* is appropriate. The partnership's deferral of reporting the deposits in income until 1998, the first year in which the Devil Rays played major league baseball games, more clearly matches the partnership's related expenses that were incurred and deducted in 1998. The partnership may defer until 1998 reporting as income the deposits received in 1995 and 1996 on the advance season tickets and on the private suite reservations.

* * *

Respondent notes the partnership's deduction in 1995 and 1996 of expenses relating to its minor league baseball operation, to general operations, and to interest on the financing obtained to pay the $130 million franchise fee. We agree with petitioner that the partnership's deduction in years prior to 1998 of minor league baseball expenses, of general startup operating expenses, and of current year interest expense is not inconsistent with the deferral until 1998 of deposits relating specifically to the Devil Rays' 1998 major league baseball season.

* * *

QUESTION, PROBLEM

1. Which approach is more likely clearly to reflect income–that taken in *Auto Club of Michigan*, *AAA*, and *Schlude*, or that taken in *Artnell* and *Tampa Bay Devil Rays*? Is there any real difference in the predictability of the future events in the two groups of cases?

2. ISLOP, a chain of breakfast food restaurants, has a gift card program. Gift cards may be purchased at any ISLOP location, for $25, $50, $75, or $100. The cards are then redeemable at any ISLOP location in the United States. ISLOP is an accrual basis taxpayer.

    a. How should ISLOP be treated on the sale of the gift cards?

---

5. The $130 million franchise fee was incurred before 1998 but as indicated it was capitalized, and no amortization of the portion allocable to player salaries was begun until 1998. Respondent does not contest this treatment.

b. What if the cards are "reloadable," so that the owner can go to any ISLOP location, pay an additional amount, and walk out with an upgraded card. How should the reloads be treated?

c. ISLOP has researched the laws of all of the states, and found the best one for its purposes. ISLOP formed a subsidiary in that state for the sole purpose of handling the gift cards. Now, pursuant to the laws of that state, all ISLOP gift cards must be fully redeemed within six months of purchase. If they are not, then any value left on them is forfeited back to ISLOP. It says so in the fine print. How should this forfeiture provision change the taxation of ISLOP and its subsidiary?

See Rev. Proc. 2004–34.

2. DEDUCTIONS

CHRYSLER CORPORATION v. COMMISSIONER OF INTERNAL REVENUE

United States Court of Appeals, Sixth Circuit, 2006.
436 F.3d 644.

ALAN E. NORRIS, CIRCUIT JUDGE.

I.

Deduction for Anticipated Warranty Expenses

In its opinion, the Tax Court framed the issue in these terms:

We must decide whether for Federal income tax purposes all events necessary to determine petitioner's liability for its warranty expenses have occurred when it sells its vehicles to its dealers; in other words, has petitioner satisfied the first prong of the all events test entitling it to deduct its estimated future warranty costs on the sale of such vehicles?

In tax years 1984 and 1985, Chrysler included deductions of $567,943,243 and $297,292,155 on its federal income tax returns on the basis that it incurred those amounts as warranty expenses for motor vehicles sold in those years to its dealers. * * *

New vehicle warranties, which are at issue here, cover defects in material and manufacture. As Chrysler points out, state and federal laws regulate the entire warranty regime. * * *

Chrysler offered two kinds of express warranty: a basic warranty that applied to the first 12 months or 12,000 miles, and an extended warranty that covered certain types of repairs after the basic warranty had expired. In turn, Chrysler contracted with its dealers to repair vehicles under warranty. Typically, dealers would make repairs and then seek reimbursement from the company. However, dealers were required to comply with certain agreed upon procedures to substantiate their reimbursement requests that, if not followed, could result in non-payment. By 1984 Chrysler had installed a computer system known as the Dealer Information Access Link ("DIAL"), which an increasing number of dealers used to report warranty repairs that were subject to reimbursement. DIAL made it easier for Chrysler to track and respond to warranty claims.

Chrysler engaged consultant Arthur D. Little, Inc., to calculate the amount of warranty expenses the company incurred for tax years 1984 and 1985. Chrysler uses the accrual method of accounting and a tax year based upon the calendar year. It is undisputed that the expenses incurred by Chrysler to fix conditions covered by warranty constitute "ordinary and necessary" business expenses under § 162. During the period at issue, Chrysler accrued the entire estimated cost of its warranties in the year that it sold the vehicles to the dealers. Chrysler included this liability on its balance sheet and took it into account in the calculation of net (BOOK) income.

The Commissioner reduced Chrysler's warranty cost deduction for 1984 by $287,939,317, which had the ripple effect of increasing the company's 1985 deduction for such costs by $62,767,885.

* * *

Having set the legal stage, the [Tax Court] then examined and distinguished two Supreme Court opinions urged upon it by the parties: *United States v. Hughes Prop. Inc.*, 476 U.S. 593 (1986), and *United States v. Gen. Dynamics Corp.*, 481 U.S. 239 (1987). Because we agree that these cases are central to the resolution of this particular question, we find it useful to begin our discussion with reference to the construction given to them by the Tax Court:

> [Chrysler] places reliance on *United States v. Hughes Properties, Inc.*, for the proposition that statutory liabilities satisfy the first prong of the all events test. . . .
>
> In *Hughes Properties,* the taxpayer was a Nevada casino that was required by State statute to pay as a jackpot a certain percentage of the amounts gambled in progressive slot machines. The taxpayer was required to keep a cash reserve sufficient to pay the guaranteed jackpots when won. Hughes Properties at the conclusion of each fiscal year entered the total of the progressive jackpot amounts (shown on the payoff indicators) as an accrued liability on its books. From that total, it subtracted the corresponding figure for the preceding year to produce the current tax year's increase in accrued liability. On its Federal income tax return this net figure was asserted to be an ordinary and necessary business expense and deductible under section 162(a). The Court found that the all events test had been satisfied and the taxpayer was entitled to the deduction. The Court reasoned that the State statute made the amount shown on the payout indicators incapable of being reduced. Therefore the event creating liability was the last play of the machine before the end of the fiscal year, and that event occurred during the taxable year.
>
> We conclude that the cases cited by [Chrysler] do not strictly stand for the proposition that if a liability is fixed by statute, that fact alone

meets the first prong of the all events test. Rather we are of the opinion that the first prong of the all events test may be met when a statute has the effect of irrevocably setting aside a specific amount, as if it were to be put into an escrow account, by the close of the tax year and to be paid at a future date. In the instant case, the applicable statutes do not so provide.

[The Commissioner] relies on the analysis contained in the Supreme Court's opinion in *United States v. General Dynamics Corp.* In *General Dynamics,* the taxpayer, who self-insured its employee medical plan, deducted estimated costs of medical care under the plan. The employer's liability was determinable. The employees' medical needs had manifested themselves, employees had determined to obtain treatment, and treatment had occurred. The only events that had not occurred were the employees' filing claims for reimbursement before the end of the taxable year. The Supreme Court found that the all events test was not met until the filing of properly documented claims. The filing of the claim was the last event needed to create the liability and therefore absolutely fix the taxpayer's liability under the first prong of the all events test.

[Chrysler] focuses on the fact that the liability in *United States v. Hughes Properties, Inc., supra,* was in part fixed by operation of statute and concludes from that the first prong of the all events test is satisfied if a statute in part works to fix the liability. We do not agree. In both *Hughes Properties* and *General Dynamics* the Supreme Court focused on the last event that created the liability. In *Hughes Properties* the event creating liability was the last play of the machine before the end of the fiscal year. Because the Nevada statute fixed the amount of the irrevocable payout, that play crystalized or fixed absolutely the taxpayer's liability, thus satisfying the first prong of the all events test. In *General Dynamics,* the last event that created the liability was the employee filing the claim for reimbursement.

We are unable to find sufficient differences between the facts in *General Dynamics* and those of the instant case to justify departing from the Supreme Court's analysis. Here, as in *General Dynamics,* the last event fixing liability does not occur before the presenting of a claim, either a claim for warranty service by the customer through one of petitioner's dealers or a claim for reimbursement made on petitioner by the dealer.

As the decision of the Tax Court makes clear, the central issue on appeal is precisely what a taxpayer must do in order to establish liability with sufficient certainty to satisfy the first prong of the "all events test." We would be less than candid if we did not acknowledge a degree of sympathy with Justice O'Connor's observation in *General Dynamics* that "[t]he circumstances of this case differ little from those in *Hughes Properties.*" *Gen. Dynamics,* 481 (dissenting). However, given that the Court reached the opposite result in successive terms when faced with similar sets of facts, we must do our best to distinguish the two cases. As did the Tax Court, we see no viable way of reconciling *Hughes Properties* with *General Dynamics* other than by reading the former to stand of the proposition that "[t]he first prong of the all events test may be met when a statute has the effect of irrevocably setting aside a specific amount ... by the close of the tax year and to be paid at a future date." *Chrysler Corp. v. Comm'r, supra.* The Court in *General Dynamics* held that the "last link in the chain of events creating liability for purposes of the 'all events test' " was the actual filing of a medical claim. It based its reasoning on the fact that "General Dynamics was ... liable to pay for covered medical services *only* if properly documented claims forms were filed."

Like General Dynamics, Chrysler faces *potential* liability, which in its case is based upon the express and implied warranties that accompany the sale of its motor vehicles. However, that liability does not become firmly established until a valid warranty claim is submitted. As the Court explained, "Nor may a taxpayer deduct an estimated or an anticipated expense no matter how statistically certain, if it is based on events that have not occurred by the close of the taxable year." * * * We assume that the DIAL software made it easier for Chrysler to track and process warranty claims; it may also have assisted Arthur D. Little in calculating the cost to the company of future claims. However, even if those claims were predictable with relative accuracy, they were not actually submitted during the taxable year and therefore cannot be deducted because they remain "anticipated expenses."

In reaching this conclusion, we readily acknowledge that Chrysler has raised a number of thoughtful points. First among them is the contention that the anticipated warranty claims at issue should be analyzed with reference to the second prong of the "all events test," that is, whether "the amount of the liability can be determined with reasonable accuracy." Despite its surface appeal, this argument fails to recognize that it is not the imprecise amount of the claims that renders them non-deductible but their contingent nature. While Chrysler relies in part upon the existence of statutes, * * * to establish the "fact" of its liability, they impose legal duties with respect to warranties but do not necessarily fix liability. * * * However, simply because a manufacturer has provided a warranty to a consumer, the scope of which is defined to a some degree by statute, does not mean that liability has attached; until a claim has been filed invoking the terms of a warranty, liability remains contingent and, because of that fact, non-deductible.

* * *[L]ike the Tax Court, we conclude that this issue hinges upon our construction of *Hughes Properties* and, more importantly, *General Dynamics.* For the reasons just outlined, we detect no material distinction between *General Dynamics* and the case before us. Consequently, we affirm the judgment of the Tax Court.

* * *

Haiku

Chrysler's cars break down

You know you'll fix the Sebring

Wait until you do

FORD MOTOR COMPANY v. COMMISSIONER

United States Court of Appeals, Sixth Circuit, 1995.
71 F.3d 209.

MILBURN, CIRCUIT JUDGE.

* * *

I.

A.

Petitioner Ford Motor Company is engaged in a number of businesses, including the manufacture of cars and trucks, and it maintains its books and records and files its income taxes using the accrual method of accounting. In the years preceding 1980, some of Ford's cars and trucks were involved in automobile accidents, and in 1980, Ford entered into 20 structured settlement agreements in settlement of personal injury or accidental death claims with persons who were injured in the accidents and with survivors of persons who died as a result of the accidents. In these structured settlement agreements, Ford agreed to make periodic payments of tort damages, yearly or monthly, in exchange for a release of all claims against it. The payments were to be made over various periods of time, the longest of which was 58 years. All but three of the settlements provided for payments over a period of 40 years or more. The agreements were of three types: (I) those that required petitioner to make periodic payments for a period certain ("Type I settlements"); * * * In total, the structured settlement agreements provided for payments of $24,477,699.

To provide it with funds to cover the periodic payments, Ford purchased single premium annuity contracts at a cost of $4,424,587. The annuity contracts were structured so that the yearly annuity payments would equal the yearly amount owed to the claimants under the structured settlement agreements. None of the settlement agreements released petitioner from liability following the purchase of the annuity contract, and, in the event of a default on an annuity, petitioner would be required to pay the remaining balance owed to the tort claimants. The parties stipulated that the present value of the deferred payments that petitioner agreed to make to the claimants did not exceed the cost of the annuity contracts.

On its 1980 tax return, petitioner claimed deductions for the various types of structured settlements as follows: for the Type I settlements, it claimed the total amount of all periodic payments due; * * * These deductions totaled $10,636,994, which petitioner included as part of a product liability loss that it carried back to its 1970 taxable year pursuant to § 172(b)(1)(I). It also reported the annuity income on its 1980 federal income tax return under § 72. For financial accounting purposes, petitioner reported the 1980 structured settlements by expensing the cost of the annuity in the year of the settlement.

Respondent Commissioner determined that Ford's method of accounting for its structured settlements did not clearly reflect income under § 446(b) and disallowed the deductions petitioner claimed in excess of the cost of the annuities petitioner purchased. Respondent also excluded from petitioner's income the amounts required to be reported as income from annuity contracts, which was $323,340 in 1980. As a result, respondent determined a deficiency in petitioner's 1970 federal income tax liability of $3,300,151.

B.

Petitioner Ford challenged this deficiency determination by filing a petition in the United States Tax Court. In its amended petition, Ford claimed that it was entitled to deduct in 1980 the full amount of all payments to be made under the structured settlements, basing its valuation of the life settlements on the life expectancies of the claimants. The total deduction Ford claimed was $24,477,699.

The parties submitted the case to the United States Tax Court with all facts fully stipulated. A divided court upheld the Commissioner's position. Based on the tax court's opinion, the parties agreed on a deficiency determination of $2,833,860 under Rule 155 of the Tax Court Rules, and the tax court entered its decision in that amount. This timely appeal followed.

II.

A.

Section 446 of the Internal Revenue Code provides the general rule governing use of methods of accounting by taxpayers. Section 446(b) provides that, if the method of accounting used by the taxpayer to compute income does not clearly reflect income, "the computation of taxable income shall be made under such method as, in the opinion of the Secretary or his delegate, does clearly reflect income." The Commissioner has broad discretion under § 446(b) to determine whether a particular method of accounting clearly reflects income. "Since the Commissioner has '[m]uch latitude for discretion,' his interpretation of the statute's clear-reflection standard 'should not be interfered with unless clearly unlawful.'" Once the Commissioner has determined that a method of accounting does not clearly reflect income, she may substitute a method that, in her opinion, does clearly reflect income.

B.

There are three stages to our analysis in this case: first, we decide whether the application of § 446(b) was appropriate; second, we decide whether the tax court correctly determined that petitioner's method of accounting did not clearly reflect income; and third, we address the appropriateness of the method of accounting that the Commissioner imposed in its place.

* * *

C.

Having determined that expenses that satisfy the all events test can be disallowed when accrual would not result in a clear reflection of income, we now examine the correctness of the Commissioner's determination that Ford's method of accounting for its tort obligations did not clearly reflect income. In its opinion, the tax court used an example to "highlight the distortion [of petitioner's income] about which respondent complains." It utilized the numbers from one settlement agreement under which Ford agreed to pay the claimant $504,000 in 42 equal, annual installments of $12,000. The annuity contract that Ford purchased to fund the payments cost $141,124, demonstrating an implicit rate of return of 8.19 percent. Ford claimed a deduction in 1980 in the amount of $504,000 for this obligation. The tax court used these numbers to create three scenarios, assuming that but for the settlement agreement in question, petitioner would have had taxable income in 1980 of at least $504,000.

In the first scenario, the tax court assumed that the accident in question did not occur and that, as a result, petitioner received an additional $504,000 of currently taxable income. The tax court further assumed that petitioner would have been subject to a 40 percent marginal tax rate, leaving it with $302,400. The tax court then noted that, if the after tax proceeds were invested over 42 years at a rate of 8.19 percent, the $302,400 would grow to $8,249,751.

In the second scenario, the tax court assumed that the accident occurred but that Ford discharged its liability in full by paying and deducting $141,124 and investing the remainder over 42 years. Its current deduction of the $141,124 it paid for the annuity would leave it with $362,876 of taxable income on which it would pay tax of $145,150, leaving $217,726. If it invested the $217,726 over the 42 year period at a 8.19 percent rate of return, it would grow to $5,939,756.

In the third scenario, the tax court assumed that the events occurred as they did in the present case, with Ford deducting the full $504,000 it was required to pay the tort claimants and paying no tax. Investing the $504,000 at a rate of return of 8.19 percent and taking into account the annual payments of $12,000, the tax court found that petitioner would have $9,898,901 remaining after 42 years.

The tax court pointed out that Ford is claiming scenario three treatment and that comparing scenario three to scenario one demonstrates that petitioner is better off with the accidents than if they never occurred. The tax court held that fully deducting payments extending over a long period of time leads to a distortion of income and "the incongruous result that the greater a taxpayer's nominal liability for negligence, the more it benefits." It therefore concluded that petitioner's method of accounting did not clearly reflect income.

Petitioner challenges the tax court's approval of the Commissioner's determination that its accounting method did not clearly reflect income on several grounds. First, it argues that the tax court's numerical example was flawed by its use of a 8.19 percent rate of return. It asserts that the 8.19 percent rate of return that the tax court found implicit in one of the annuity contracts is a pre-tax rate of return because Ford is required to pay tax on amounts received as an annuity under § 72 and that the tax court instead should have used the after-tax rate of 4.91 percent. Recomputing the investment growth over 42 years using this rate of return in the three scenarios, petitioner asserts that in scenario one it would be $2,267,705; in scenario two it would be $1,632,729; and in scenario three it would be $2,192,446. Thus, petitioner argues: "Ford did not 'fare better than if the accident never occurred'; the Tax Court's apparent reason for invalidating Ford's tax treatment rests on a misconception." In her brief, respondent acknowledges the flaw in the tax court's numerical example and presents an example of her own, arguing that Ford was in a 46 percent tax bracket rather than a 40 percent tax bracket. In respondent's example, petitioner again fares better under scenario three treatment than under scenario one.

Petitioner's brief suggests that the tax court's determination that its accounting method did not clearly reflect income was based solely on the fact that, in the tax court's example, petitioner fared better with the accident than without. We conclude, however, that this factor was not determinative, and that, even viewing petitioner's numerical example as correct, the gross distortion of income that it demonstrates between the economic and tax results persuades us that the tax court's decision was not improper. Given the length of the payment periods, allowing a deduction for the full amount of liability in 1980 could lead to the result that the tax benefit from the deduction would fund the full amounts due in future years and leave petitioner with a profit. Such a result extends the accrual method of accounting beyond its inherent limitations.

Our task on appeal is to determine whether there is an adequate basis in law for the Commissioner's conclusion that Ford's method of accounting did not clearly reflect income. See RCA Corp. v. U.S., 664 F.2d. 881 (2d Cir.1981). We find several cases from other circuits that support our finding that the Commissioner's exercise of her discretion was proper.

Petitioner also argues that the tax court's decision that petitioner's method of accounting did not clearly reflect income was improper because it "[a]uthorizes [a]rbitrary and [u]nprincipled [u]se of the Commissioner's [s]ection 446(b) [p]ower.", and that, in doing so, it created an "arbitrary system ... that requires all accrual taxpayers to account for their liabilities when they become fixed, yet makes the validity of that reporting method subject to the unconstrained whim of the Commissioner."

We are not persuaded by this policy-based argument. The tax court concluded its opinion stating: Finally, we want to make clear that the mere fact that a deduction which accrues prior to the time payment is made (the timing factor) does not, by itself, cause the accrual to run afoul of the clear reflection of income requirement. Inherent in the use of an accrual method is the fact that a deduction may be allowed in advance of payment. Our holding in the instant case is not intended to draw a bright line that can be applied mechanically in other circumstances. We decide only the ultimate question of fact in the instant case; namely, whether, for tax purposes, petitioner's method of accounting for its obligations under the structured settlements clearly reflects income. We hold that it does not and that the Government did not abuse its discretion in making that determination. As the tax court observed, "[t]he issue of whether the taxpayer's method of accounting clearly reflects income is a question of fact to be determined on a case-by-case basis." We find the tax court's language sufficient to limit its holding to extreme cases such as this one in which the economic results are grossly different from the tax results and therefore conclude that the tax court's decision does not allow the Commissioner arbitrary or unprincipled discretion.

D.

Given that a change was necessary because Ford's accrual of its settlement obligations in 1980 did not clearly reflect income, Ford argues that the method of accounting that the Commissioner imposed in its place was improper. Ford asserts that the Commissioner lacked the authority to impose the method of accounting that she did because it is "inconsistent with the plain dictates of the Code and regulations and the undisputed facts of this case."

The method of accounting that the Commissioner imposed was to allow Ford a deduction for the amount that it paid for the annuities with no further deductions for the future payments that Ford will make to the claimants. To offset her disallowance of future deductions, the Commissioner will permit Ford to exclude its income from the annuity contracts. Petitioner asserts that this scheme violates established tax law for several reasons and forces Ford to use a tax treatment that it could not have adopted on its own.

First, petitioner argues that the Commissioner is imposing on it a present value method of accounting which should only be imposed in the presence of a directive by Congress to do so. Ford additionally argues that this method impermissibly allows it only to deduct the approximately $4 million it paid for the annuities without ever allowing a deduction for the additional approximately $20 million it will pay to the claimants and that the Commissioner's method is arbitrary because it is not a method that Ford could have adopted on its own.

Respondent counters that its method of accounting is a modified cash basis method that allows Ford "a dollar for dollar deduction, albeit in the form of an offset against its annuity income, for the full face amount of its future payments of approximately $24 million.'' Respondent points out that, because she allowed Ford to deduct the full cost of the annuity contracts in 1980, it has no basis in the contracts and would be fully taxable on the annuity income of $24,477,699 as it is received. However, the payments Ford is required to make to the tort claimants, which correspond exactly to the amount of its annuity income, give rise to deductions that offset the income and create a wash. Respondent argues that, because she has relieved taxpayer of the obligation to report the annuity income as it is received, she should not allow Ford any deductions for the required payments.

We find no merit in petitioner's assertion that this methodology is improper because it reduces the amount of the deductions to the present value of the payments petitioner is obligated to make. The Commissioner reduced petitioner's deduction to the cost of the annuity contracts. The stipulated facts provided only that the present value of the payments petitioner is obligated to make did not exceed this amount. There is no indication that respondent was imposing a present value method of accounting on petitioner.

Furthermore, we find no authority that prohibits the tax accounting treatment that the Commissioner and the tax court imposed here. The Commissioner's discretion to impose an alternate method of accounting under § 446(b) is not limited to methods that Ford could have adopted on its own. While we recognize that to require Ford to account for its tort obligations on the cash method might have been a more logical alternative, we cannot find that the Commissioner's exercise of her discretion was arbitrary because it resulted in an accounting treatment more favorable to Ford that a straight cash method would be. The only difference between the Commissioner's method of accounting and the cash basis method is that petitioner receives an immediate deduction for the cost of its annuities rather than recovering that cost over the terms of the annuities under § 72, and this difference inures to Ford's benefit. We therefore conclude that the tax court's decision regarding the accounting method the Commissioner imposed was proper.

III.

For the reasons stated, the judgment of the tax court is AFFIRMED.

QUESTION

The tax year in Ford Motor Company was 1980; Congress added § 461(h)(2)(C) in 1984. Read Example 1 at Reg. § 1.461–4(g)(8), and apply it to the *Ford* facts.

Chapter VII

Capital Gains

■ ■ ■

Tom bought a block of IBM stock in 1995 for $5,000. In 2003, he sold it for $8,000. As a result, he realized a gain of $3,000. That much you know. What you need to address now is why this gain was a "capital gain," and why and how such "capital gains" are treated differently.

A "capital gain" occurs when you realize a gain on the sale or exchange of a "capital asset." "Capital asset" is defined in § 1221, subject to a great deal of case-law interpretation.[a] Assuming that Tom was not a stockbroker, the IBM stock was probably a capital asset in his hands.

The real benefit comes when you have "long-term capital gains," which occur when you have held your capital asset for more than one year [§ 1222(3)] before you sold it. Recall that Tom bought the stock in 1995 and sold it in 2003. Since he held his capital asset for more than one year, the gain was "long term capital gain."

Capital assets tend to be investment property. Capital gains are supposed to occur in the relatively unusual event that such property is sold. Contrast capital gains with "ordinary income," which is all income other than capital gains. In the context of sales proceeds, the most common example of ordinary income would arise from the everyday sales of inventory by a retail store.

In this country, and many others, long term capital gains are taxed at lower rates than ordinary income. As a corollary, deductions for long term capital losses are usually not as generous as deductions for ordinary losses. This chapter will address why, and how, these capital gains and losses are treated differently.

A. POLICY, MECHANICS

1. HISTORY AND POLICY

(a) Gains

Why should Tom's gain on the sale of IBM stock be treated any differently from a grocer's gain on the sale of a bunch of broccoli? They

---

a. It is most unfortunate that the same term, "capital," is used both to define certain expenses which must be amortized rather than deducted in the year incurred [§ 263], and also to define certain assets which, if sold or exchanged, might generate special treatment on the gains or losses [§ 1221]. I wish that I could change this, but I can't.

are both surely economic income, under the Haig–Simons definition. Yet, for many years in many countries, capital gains were not recognized as taxable income at all.

The tax year in *Gray v. Darlington, infra*, was 1869, long before the adoption of either the 16th Amendment or the 1913 income tax. The case is no longer good law. Merchants' Loan & Trust Co. v. Smietanka, 255 U.S. 509, 41 S.Ct. 386, 65 L.Ed. 751 (1921) makes it quite clear that capital gains are now taxable income. Yet, the fact that the Supreme Court could have held in *Gray v. Darlington* that capital gains were not taxable income, and even could have commented that the question presented did not admit of any doubt, might help us to understand why capital gains, though taxed, are still treated differently, to this day.

GRAY v. DARLINGTON

United States Supreme Court, 1872.
82 U.S. (15 Wall.) 63, 21 L.Ed. 45.

ERROR to the Circuit Court for the Eastern District of Pennsylvania.

MR. JUSTICE FIELD delivered the opinion of the court.

In 1865 the plaintiff, being the owner of certain United States treasury notes, exchanged them for United States five-twenty bonds. In 1869 he sold these bonds at an advance of twenty thousand dollars over the cost of the treasury notes, and upon this amount the assistant assessor of the United States for the collection district in Pennsylvania, within which the plaintiff resided, assessed a tax of five per cent., alleging it to be gains, profits, and income of the plaintiff for that year. * * *

The question presented is whether the advance in the value of the bonds, during this period of four years, over their cost, realized by their sale, was subject to taxation as gains, profits, or income of the plaintiff for the year in which the bonds were sold. The answer which should be given to this question does not, in our judgment, admit of any doubt. The advance in the value of property during a series of years can, in no just sense, be considered the gains, profits, or income of any one particular year of the series, although the entire amount of the advance be at one time turned into money by a sale of the property. The statute looks, with some exceptions, for subjects of taxation only to annual gains, profits, and income. Its general language is "that there shall be levied, collected, and paid annually upon the gains, profits, and income of every person," derived from certain specified sources, a tax of five per cent., and that this tax shall be "assessed, collected, and paid upon the gains, profits, and income for the year ending the 31st of December next preceding the time for levying, collecting, and paying said tax." This language has only one meaning, and that is that the assessment, collection, and payment prescribed are to be made upon the annual products or income of one's property or labor, or such gains or profits as may be realized from a business transaction begun and completed during the preceding year. There are exceptions, as already intimated, to the general rule of assessment thus prescribed. One of these exceptions is expressed in the statute, and relates to profits upon sales of real property, requiring, in the estimation of gains, the profits of such sales to be included where the property has been purchased, not only within the preceding year, but within the two previous years. Another exception is implied from the provision of the statute which requires all gains, profits, and income derived from any source whatever, in addition to the sources enumerated, to be included in the estimation of the assessor. The estimation must, therefore, necessarily embrace gains and profits from trade and commerce, and these, for their successful prosecution, often require property to be held over a year. In the estimation of gains of any one year the trader and merchant will, in consequence, often be compelled to include the amount received upon goods sold over their cost, which were purchased in a previous year. Indeed, in the estimation of the gains and profits of a trading or commercial business for any one year, the result of many transactions have generally to be taken into account which originated previously. Except, however, in these and similar cases, and in cases of sales of real property, the statute only applies to such gains, profits, and income as are strictly acquisitions made during the year preceding that in which the assessment is levied and collected.

The mere fact that property has advanced in value between the date of its acquisition and sale does not authorize the imposition of the tax on the amount of the advance. Mere advance in value in no sense constitutes the gains, profits, or income specified by the statute. It constitutes and can be treated merely as increase of capital.

The rule adopted by the officers of the revenue in the present case would justify them in treating as gains of one year the increase in the value of property extending through any number of years, through even the entire century. The actual advance in value of property over its cost may, in fact, reach its height years before its sale; the value of the property may, in truth, be less at the time of the sale than at any previous period in ten years, yet, if the amount received exceed the actual cost of the property, the excess is to be treated, according to their views, as gains of the owner for the year in which the sale takes place. We are satisfied that no such result was intended by the statute.

JUDGMENT AFFIRMED.

Dissenting: THE CHIEF JUSTICE, and JUSTICES CLIFFORD and BRADLEY.

NOTE

As mentioned above, *Merchants' Loan & Trust* has now confirmed that capital gains are taxable income. But they are still treated differently from ordinary income. The reasons relate to bunching, inflation, and investment.

As a paradigm case, consider Investor, who purchases stock in a computer company in 1950 for $1, and sells it in 1990 for $100. The tax computation would be:

Amount Realized	$100
Less: Basis	− $ 1
Gain	$ 99

What's wrong with this picture? First, bunching. The $99 of appreciation didn't all happen in 1990; it happened over forty years. Why is forty years of appreciation bunched up into one year? Bunching is merely the flip side of realization. We could have taxed the unrealized appreciation as it happened. However, for sound reasons, we chose to wait. See the discussion of realization, *supra* at 27. As a result, we have no choice but to tax it all in 1990.

Why does bunching matter? Because it can throw the same taxable income into a higher bracket. If we had taxed Investor's unrealized appreciation as it occurred, no one year's increment would have thrown him into a different bracket. He would have paid tax at his normal rate—say, 25%. However, if we tax all of the appreciation in 1990 (add a few zeroes to the example to make it more realistic, if you like), that bunched income might push him into a higher bracket—say 35%.

Second, there is inflation. Why do you suppose that the stock went up in value so much? Surely, it went up in part because computers have become increasingly important to us. It was wise of Investor to get in on the ground floor. However, the value of the stock also went up in value because the price of everything has gone up since 1950. In short, some of that rise from one dollar to one hundred dollars is due to inflation.

Is it fair to levy a tax on "appreciation" which is caused, not by any increase in the real value of the asset, but, rather, by a decrease in the value of the dollar? Isn't it especially ironic when the folks wanting to levy the tax (the government) are the same ones who probably caused the inflation in the first place (the government)? Note that bunching gets worse, and inflation more likely, the longer you hold the asset.

Third, there is the matter of investment incentives. Think back to the moment when Investor is considering buying the stock. He reasons, "If my investment does well, I'll have to pay a tax on my gains. Perhaps I'll even be bumped up into higher rates. If my investment does poorly, I might get a deduction, but I might be in a lower bracket, so that the deduction is not worth so much. I think I'll keep my money in my mattress."

Needless to say, if we did not tax the gain, then Investor would not have had this conversation with himself. Moreover, the lower the tax on the gain, the less deterrence there is on making the investment in the first place.

Now, think ahead to 1990 again. The stock is worth $100, and Investor is pondering whether or not to sell. He reasons, "If I sell for $100, I'll have to pay tax on my gain. Then I won't have my $100 any more. I'll hold on to it longer. When it goes up some more, I'll be able to pay the tax and still have $100 left over."

This is called the "lock-in effect." Without a tax on capital gains, Investor wouldn't have quite this thought process. But wouldn't § 1014 lead him to the same place?

The lock-in effect, if it exists, is bad, because it hinders the liquidity of investment, and makes investors as a whole less willing to shift their money out of unproductive investments, like buggy whips, into more productive investments, like improved cupholders.

(b) Losses

NOTE

Imagine that Investor purchased stock for $10,000, and that it is now worth $1,000. If she sells it, she will realize a $9,000 loss. What worries Congress is that she can wait, and sell it any time she likes. Presumably, she can wait until she has a lot of income and few deductions. Then, she can realize the loss and offset some of that income.

Wait a minute. Isn't this fact simply the loss side of realization? Doesn't realization mean that you can choose the timing of either gains or losses by deciding when to sell? Anyway, is it totally a riskfree choice? Isn't it possible that, if she waits, the value of the stock will fall even further?

But, no matter. Congress was concerned about the timing of the losses. Accordingly, restrictions are placed on the ability of taxpayers to bunch too many losses in any one year.

Remember, the loss does not become deductible pursuant to these sections because it is capital. It must already be deductible under § 165. In most cases, losses on stock will be deductible under § 165(c)(2).

(c) Capital Gains and Losses: 1921 to 1986

In the United States, differential treatment of capital gains and losses began in 1921. For most of our tax history, net long term gains were taxed at about half the rates of ordinary income, while net long term losses enjoyed about half the deductions.

Conservatives have always wanted significantly lower rates for long term capital gains, and much flatter tax rates. Liberals have always wanted no differential treatment between capital transactions and ordinary income, and more progressive tax rates. In the 1986 Tax Reform Act, the two groups achieved a Great Compromise. For the conservatives, the progressivity of the tax rates was lowered considerably, with the highest marginal rates going from 50% to 28%. On the other hand, for the liberals, capital gains would be treated just like ordinary income.

(d) 1986 and Beyond

After 1986, both strands of the compromise began to unravel. On the progressivity side, the highest marginal rates on ordinary income crept back up to as much as 39.6%. On the capital gains side, however, the highest capital gains rates stayed at 28%. Therefore, Congress recreated a significant difference for high income taxpayers between ordinary income rates and capital gains rates.

Currently, after much legislation, the individual federal income tax rates on ordinary income remain mildly progressive, ranging from 10% to 35%. The rates on long term capital gains are lower, and more confusing, ranging from 10% to 15% for most transactions, and up to 28% in certain special cases.

2. MECHANICS

Code: §§ 1(h), 1211, 1212(b) 1221, 1222

As you consider the mechanics of the capital gain and loss provisions, ask yourself whether our treatment of capital gains is directly responsive to the perceived problems, or whether there were more effective solutions.

Consider § 1(h), and you will realize that, if only you had a "net capital gain," you would reach the nirvana of low tax rates. Now, what is a "net capital gain"? It is defined in § 1222(11). However, you will quickly realize when you read § 1222 that you must compute a number of intermediate numbers before you reach nirvana.

GAIN PROBLEM

Consider the following facts:

Investor bought and sold stock (all capital assets in her hands) at the following dates and prices:

Stock	Date Acquired	Basis	Date Sold	Amount Realized
Able Inc.	3/15/63	$100	2/27/96	$500
Baker Co.	6/17/96	$ 75	9/13/96	$100
Charlie Co.	7/11/91	$300	8/22/96	$150
Dog Inc.	4/21/96	$500	5/15/96	$300

What, if any, were the short-term capital gains [§ 1222(1)]?

What, if any, were the short-term capital losses [§ 1222(2)]?

What, if any, were the long-term capital gains [§ 1222(3)]?

What, if any, were the long-term capital losses [§ 1222(4)]?

Determine whether there is a net short-term capital gain [§ 1222(5)] or a net short-term capital loss [§ 1222(6)]. In what amount?

Determine whether there is a net long-term capital gain [§ 1222(7)] or a net long-term capital loss [§ 1222(8)]. In what amount?

Determine whether there is a net capital gain [§ 1222(11)] or a net capital loss [§ 1222(10)]. In what amount?

Now, what do you do with it?

Loss Example

Investor realized long term capital gains in Year 1 of $1,000, and short term capital losses of $5,000.[b] Assuming that the losses are deductible, how much can she deduct this year? Section 1211(b) provides that she can deduct the losses at least to the extent of the gains. Therefore, she can use $1,000 of her losses to wipe out the $1,000 gain.

That leaves $4,000 in losses. Section 1211(b) goes on to say that, if the losses exceed the gains, she can deduct the lower of:

(1) $3,000 (assuming that she's not married filing a separate return); or

(2) the excess of such losses over such gains.

The excess of the losses over the gains is $4,000:

Losses	$5,000
Gains	− $1,000
Excess	$4,000

The lower of $3,000 and $4,000 is $3,000. Therefore, she can deduct $3,000 in Year 1 (in addition to the $1,000 she already used to wipe out the gain).

Of the $5,000 in capital losses realized in Year 1, $4,000 have been used. That leaves $1,000 unused.

Realized capital losses	$5,000
Used to wipe out gains	− $1,000
Deductible this year [§ 1211(b)(2)]	− $3,000
Unused losses	$1,000

That unused $1,000 in capital losses constitutes a "net capital loss, pursuant to § 1222(10). Pursuant to § 1212(b), that net capital loss can be carried forward to Year 2. However, one must apply § 1212(b)(2) before applying § 1212(b)(1). Assuming that, in Year 1, Investor has adjusted taxable income [defined in § 1212(b)(2)(B)] in excess of $3,000, § 1212(b)(2)(A) provides that $3,000 [the amount Investor deducted in Year 1 pursuant to § 1211(b)] will be treated for the purpose of § 1212 as a short-term capital gain."

Now, § 1212(b)(1) can be applied. Pursuant to § 1212(b)(1)(A), the excess of the net short-term capital loss over the net long-term capital gain for Year 1 shall be a short-term capital loss in Year 2.

In Year 1, there was a short-term capital loss of $5,000 and a deemed short-term capital gain [§ 1212(b)(2)(A)] of $3,000. There were no other

---

b. Whether the gains and losses are short term or long term will be irrelevant until we consider the carryover provisions of § 1212(b).

short-term capital gains. Therefore, for the purposes of § 1212(b)(1)(A), there was a net short-term capital loss of $2,000.

In Year 1, there was a long-term capital gain of $1,000. There were no long-term capital losses. Therefore, there was a net long-term capital gain of $1,000.

Therefore, pursuant to § 1212(b)(1)(A), $1,000 will be treated as a short-term capital loss in Year 2:

Net short-term capital loss	$2,000
− Net long-term capital gain	− $1,000
Short-term capital loss in Year 2	$1,000

In Year 2, that short-term capital loss of $1,000 will be thrown in with the other capital gains and losses realized that year.

LOSS PROBLEM

Donald buys stock for investment purposes for $11,000. Three years later, he sells it for $1,000. In the year of the sale, he also realized long term capital gains of $1,500. Compute his capital loss, and determine when he can take it.

SCHEMING PROBLEMS

1. Darcia owns four blocks of stock:

Block	When Acquired	Basis	Fair Market value
A	1 month ago	$45,000	$50,000
B	3 years ago	$45,000	$50,000
C	1 month ago	$55,000	$50,000
D	3 years ago	$55,000	$50,000

(a) She is in desperate need of $50,000. The only way she can come up with the money is if she sells a block of her stock. Are there any blocks of stock which she absolutely shouldn't sell?

(b) What if she needed $100,000? Do you have any advice for her?

2. David, a calendar year taxpayer, has substantial ordinary income this year, taxable at the highest rate. He expects to have at least as much ordinary income next year. Earlier in the year, he realized a long term capital gain of $20,000.

It is now December 30. He wants to sell stock purchased last August. If he does so, he will realize a loss of $3,000 on the sale. Should he sell the stock on December 30, or should he wait until January?

Would your answer be different if the $20,000 capital gain he realized this year had been short term rather than long term?

B. WHAT IS A CAPITAL ASSET?

To determine what is a capital asset, consult § 1221. That section will tell you that everything in the universe is a capital asset, except . . .

To get a feel for capital assets, consider why inventory items should not be capital assets [§ 1221(1)]. Also, why are artistic compositions created by the taxpayer not capital assets [§ 1221(3)(A)]? When the artist sells the artistic composition to another, can it then become a capital asset?

Now see what a case law mess has been made of this definition.

RICE v. COMMISSIONER

United States Tax Court.
T.C. Memo 2009–142.

Kroupa, Judge.

* * * The first issue is whether proceeds from the sale of excess lots are properly classified as capital or ordinary under section 1221(a). Resolution of this issue depends on whether the excess lots were held primarily for sale to customers in the ordinary course of business or were held for investment purposes. We hold that the excess lots were held for investment purposes and the proceeds are capital gains and losses. * * *

FINDINGS OF FACT

Petitioners live and work in Texas, where they have a business that designs and administers 401(k) plans and manages investments for trust instruments, 401(k) plans, and individuals. Mr. Rice is a certified public accountant (CPA) and did tax planning and consulting work at accounting firms before he and his wife started their own business. Petitioners were successful in this business, reporting income in excess of a million dollars each year from their business. They provided an accountant with information regarding their finances for 2004, and he prepared the income tax return they filed.

Petitioners' Dream Home

Petitioners were looking to purchase a lot in Austin to build their dream home. Petitioners looked at two other properties before settling on the lot they purchased. The first property included half-acre lots for $200,000 each, but petitioners would have needed to buy at least two lots for their dream home. The second property they considered offered larger lots but was in an undesirable location.

Petitioners saw a sign advertising 14.4 acres of undeveloped property in a desirable location near a preserve. They took down the sign, put it in their car, and made an inquiry the same day. Petitioners purchased the property within a week for $300,000 with no financing. The property was for sale as a unit—it was not subdivided, and petitioners had no option to purchase a portion of it.

Petitioners initially wanted to keep the entire property for themselves for their dream home. Ultimately, Mrs. Rice changed her mind. Mr. Rice still wanted to keep the entire property and build a single home for them and their two children. But Mrs. Rice decided that she did not want to live on the property alone for fear of feeling isolated. Mr. Rice wanted the house to be his wife's dream home, so he relented. They decided to subdivide the property to share it with others.

Division of the Property

Petitioners had never engaged in the sale of real estate other than sales of their own personal residences before they purchased this property, nor have they engaged in it since. Petitioners first identified the portion of the property they wanted for their lot. This lot was the largest and was in a desirable place on the property.

Petitioners had to hire consultants for zoning, access, water and wastewater service, construction, and environmental issues. After they decided to subdivide the property, they hired a consultant to provide a subdivision layout. Petitioners applied for and received a zoning change to subdivide and develop the property. Petitioners divided the property into ten smaller lots, reserving eight lots for homes and two lots for environmental purposes.

Construction of Their Dream Home

Petitioners were building their dream home, and they wanted to create a certain aesthetic for their home and its surroundings. They changed the name of the subdivision from Mesa Vista to Sette Terra after seeing Cinque Terre on a trip to the Italian Riviera. They did not want just any neighbors. They wanted neighbors with money. They registered the subdivision for a homeowner's association and executed a declaration of covenants, conditions and restrictions, which applied to all the lots in the subdivision (other than Lots 9 and 10 that fell outside the subdivision).

Petitioners took two years to construct their dream home. They hired an architect to build it in an Italian style. The home has 8,000 square feet of interior space and 4,000 square feet of garages and porches. Petitioners devoted a significant amount of their spare time to building their home, and their home was the focus of their attention.

Sales and Advertising Activities

Petitioners did not devote much time to selling the excess lots. They made their first lot sale to friends in 2000. In 2002, two years after their first sale, they placed a wooden sign at the entrance to the subdivision advertising that Sette Terra had lots available for sale. This was their only advertising. Petitioners sold all their lots through word of mouth rather than the sign or other advertising.

The 2004 Lot Sales

Petitioners sold Lots 1, 9, and 10 next, the lots at issue. Lots 9 and 10 were excess lots that were sold together because only one of them was suitable for construction. These sales occurred in 2004, four years after the first sale and two years after petitioners displayed the sign.

Petitioners sold Lots 9 and 10 at a loss to Mrs. Rice's sister and her husband (related party sale). Petitioners sold another excess lot, Lot 1, to friends the same year, and they realized an $89,329.79 gain from that sale.

Remaining Lot Sales

Petitioners eventually sold the four remaining excess lots (one of which was an environmental lot attached to another property) to friends and acquaintances, reserving a lot for their daughter. These sales occurred in 2005, 2007, and 2008 but are not at issue.

* * *

OPINION

* * *

I. *Capital Gain or Ordinary Income*

This first issue is whether petitioners who purchased a property to build their dream house properly claimed capital gains treatment on their sale of Lot 1. The answer depends upon whether petitioners held the property primarily for sale to customers in the ordinary course of business or if it was held, alternatively, as a capital asset. If they held the property primarily for sale in the ordinary course, as respondent argues, the proceeds to petitioners will be treated as ordinary income and we must sustain respondent's determination with respect to that income. If the property was held as a capital asset, then we must find for petitioners on this issue.

A. *Section 1221*

The parties agree that we must look to section 1221 to determine whether the property petitioners sold was held primarily for sale to customers in the ordinary course of their trade or business, so as to be denied treatment as a capital asset. A "capital asset" is broadly defined as property held by the taxpayer, whether connected with his or her trade or business, subject to a number of exceptions. Sec. 1221(a). These exceptions include stock in trade, property of a kind that is properly included in a taxpayer's inventory, and property held primarily for sale to customers in the ordinary course of a taxpayer's trade or business. Sec. 1221(a)(1).

The United States Supreme Court has defined "primarily" as used in this context to mean "principally" or "of first importance.". The question of whether property is held primarily for sale to customers in the ordinary course of a taxpayer's business is "purely factual," and to answer it, we look to the taxpayer's intent at the time he or she disposes of the property. Generally, we examine several different factors when analyzing such a scenario, including: (1) The taxpayer's purpose in acquiring the property; (2) the purpose for which the property was subsequently held; (3) the taxpayer's everyday business and the relationship of the income from the property to total income; (4) the frequency, continuity, and substantiality of sales of property; (5) the extent of developing and improving the property to increase the sales; (6) the extent to which the taxpayer used advertising, promotion, or other activities to increase sales; (7) the use of a business office for the sale of property; (8) the character and degree of supervision or control the taxpayer exercised over any representative selling the property; and (9) the time and effort the taxpayer habitually devoted to the sales. These factors are meant only to aid the finder of fact in determining, on the entire record, the taxpayer's primary purpose for holding property. They have no independent significance, and individual comment on each factor is not necessary or required.

B. *Analysis*

We now apply these factors to the facts of this case. Petitioners purchased the property to build their dream home. The record demonstrates that they sold the excess lots to dispose of unwanted property, not that they purchased the property primarily for sale to customers in the ordinary course of business. Petitioners looked at other properties, but the one they purchased was in the school district where they wanted to live, provided them with enough space to build their dream home, and was much cheaper than the other properties they considered purchasing. Petitioners did not have the option to buy a smaller portion of the property. When petitioners initially purchased the property, they wanted to build a single-family home on it. They planned a series of improvements to the property. During this period Mrs. Rice decided that she wanted neighbors. Petitioners disposed of the excess lots after subdividing the property and creating a homeowner's association so that they could ensure a certain aesthetic and create a neighborhood. In doing so, they were protecting their home value and their investment by creating that aesthetic.

The number of lots petitioners sold in toto was small. The Court of Appeals for the Fifth Circuit, to which this case is appealable, has held that substantiality and frequency of sales is among the most important factors. *Biedenharn Realty Co. v. United States, supra* at 416–417. Petitioners did not sell an average of a lot a year. Among the eight lots suitable for construction, they sold one lot in 2000, three lots in 2004, one lot in 2005, one lot in 2007, and one lot in 2008, and they are holding one in reserve for their daughter. These sales are few and infrequent in comparison to the sales in the cases respondent cites. See, e.g., *Biedenharn Realty Co. v. United States, supra* at 411; *United States v. Winthrop, supra* at 907. The taxpayers in *Winthrop* sold 456 lots, while the taxpayers in *Biedenharn Realty Co.* sold 158 lots. This case is more consistent with

Ayling v. Commissioner, 32 T.C. 704, 706, 1959 WL 1035 (1959), cited by petitioners in which proceeds from sales of 13 lots over the course of four years were held to be eligible for capital gains treatment.

Petitioners made significant improvements to develop and sell the excess lots. We note, however, that many of those improvements would have been necessary even had they not subdivided the property. Building their own residence on the property required significant expenditures for improvements.

Solicitation and advertising efforts and brokerage activities are also significant factors in analyzing whether property sales are eligible for capital gains or ordinary treatment. Petitioners devoted very little time to the sale of the excess lots. The lots were sold primarily to friends, friends of friends, and relatives. Other than posting a sign outside the subdivision, petitioners did not advertise or promote the sale of lots. Petitioners' solicitation and advertising efforts are more characteristic of those of investors than of dealers.

Finally, petitioners had full-time jobs and devoted little time to the sale of the excess lots. Lot sales accounted for a small percentage of their income each year, and petitioners retained the proceeds rather than buying additional inventory. Petitioners were not real estate developers, had never developed land before, and have never developed land since. We conclude that petitioners purchased the property as an investment and not as property held for customers in the ordinary course of business. The gain from the sale of excess Lot 1 is entitled to capital gains treatment.

* * *

HOLLIS v. UNITED STATES

United States District Court, N.D. Ohio, Eastern Division, 1954.
121 F.Supp. 191.

MᴄNᴀᴍᴇᴇ, DɪSTRICT JUDGE.

* * * The issue presented is whether oriental art objects sold by the partnership of Hollis & Company were capital assets or property held primarily for sale to customers in the ordinary course of business within the meaning of Section 117(a)(1) of the Internal Revenue Code [current § 1221].

It is plaintiffs' position that the art objects are capital assets. The Government contends that they are property held primarily for sale in the ordinary course of business.

The facts are not in dispute but are unique and merit a somewhat extended statement. Howard Hollis was Curator of Far Eastern and Near Eastern Art at the Cleveland Museum of Art from 1929 through 1948. He is one of the leading authorities in the United States on Chinese and Japanese art. In the summer of 1946 he was granted a year's leave of absence from the Museum to take the position of Chief of the Arts and Monuments Division of the Allied Forces in Japan. His duties in that position were to make recommendations to General MacArthur for the protection, salvage, preservation or disposition of certain arts and monuments. While in Japan Hollis became aware of the opportunity to acquire unusual and unique objects of art at most attractive prices. Many wealthy Japanese who possessed rare and valuable art objects and who had suffered serious economic loss from the war were willing for the first time to dispose of these art objects. This condition, together with the favorable rate of exchange, made possible the purchase of these items at comparatively low prices. Upon his return to the United States Hollis interested a limited number of his friends in the possibilities of profit inherent in this situation. Under date of August 1, 1948 a syndicate agreement was executed by Hollis and six other persons. The name of the syndicate is Hollis & Company and its stated purpose is "acquiring as an investment a limited number of oriental art objects to be purchased by Hollis on a trip which he proposed to make to Japan, such objects to be disposed of as and when their potential increment in value appears to be fully realized and inflationary economic trends warrant."

Provision was made in the syndicate agreement for a capital investment of $33,000, to be increased by an additional $16,500 if circumstances warranted. Hollis himself was without available capital, but through advancements from the other members of the syndicate (which he agreed to repay with interest) he received a fifty per cent. interest therein. The agreement also provided that Hollis was to receive a ten per cent. commission on the gross selling price of all art objects, which was to be deducted before computation of the net profits, and provision was also made for a drawing account to Hollis of $500 per month. As of January 31, 1948 Hollis resigned his position with the Cleveland Museum of Art and left for Japan on January 3, 1949. He was in Japan about three months, during which time he purchased 157 art objects consisting of 194 individual pieces. Apparently, in order to purchase some of the more valuable objects, Hollis was required to and did buy some objects in the lower price range. All of these objects were shipped by air to the United States and arrived in this country about the same time that Hollis returned. Immediately after his arrival on the West Coast Hollis commenced selling the art objects. Sales were made to the Seattle Museum of Art, the Cleveland Museum of Art, the Toledo Museum of Art, and others. Some sales were made within three weeks of the purchase of the objects in Japan. The objects were kept at Hollis's home in Cleveland Heights, where they were displayed to prospective purchasers. There was no advertising and no published price lists. Hollis was well known to the connoisseurs of foreign art objects in the United States as well as to art collectors and art museums in this country. During the year 1949 Hollis had no other business and devoted most of his working time to the affairs of Hollis & Company. His only sources of income during that year were the commissions on sales and his share of the profits of the syndicate. He made three short trips and two long trips out of Cleveland in furtherance of the sale of the art objects. The gross sales of the syndicate for the year 1949 amounted to $65,165, which yielded a substantial profit. From his share of the profits and his commissions in 1949 Hollis received about $29,000. The number of objects sold during 1949 was twenty-five, representing fourteen separate transactions. It was understood at the time of the formation of the syndicate that it was to be a "one venture proposition," and that the disposition of all the objects purchased probably could not be made for a period of several years. A distribution of profits was made by Hollis & Company in 1949 and annually thereafter. In accordance with the syndicate agreement no additional art objects were purchased. However, on April 1, 1950 a second syndicate was formed. This was known as Howard Hollis & Company. Its purpose was to deal in oriental art objects and it differed from the original syndicate in its stated purpose and in the method of distributing profits. Hollis received a sixty per cent. interest in the second partnership and it was agreed that only fifty per cent. of the net profits of Howard Hollis & Company were to be distributed annually to the syndicate members. Unlike the first syndicate, Howard Hollis & Company could thus use part of its undivided profits for the replenishment of its inventory of art objects. The second syndicate agreement was executed by Hollis and four of the original six members of the first partnership. Under the terms of the second agreement Hollis also was to receive a ten per cent. commission on sales and a drawing account of $500 per month. Hollis made trips to Japan and purchased additional art objects on behalf of Howard Hollis & Company. Meanwhile, in the year 1950, sales were made by Hollis & Company in the amount of $51,675. In the years 1951, 1952 and 1953 sales were made on behalf of both partnerships. The inventory of each partnership was segregated and displayed at the home of Hollis, and, as was true in the case of the first partnership, there was no advertising or publication of price lists of the objects owned by the second syndicate. The accounts of both partnerships were kept by a bookkeeper in the office of the law firm representing the syndicates and were designated as "Hollis No. 1" and "Hollis No. 2."

In the first year of its operation Howard Hollis & Company sold only eight more objects than did the first syndicate. In its second year Howard Hollis & Company sold eight less objects than Hollis & Company, and in the third year both partnerships sold the same number. The ratio of gross profits to gross sales of both partnerships for a period of three years shows a slightly higher average percentage of profits for Hollis & Company, but this is accounted for largely by the more favorable rate of exchange that was in effect at the time the purchases were made for the first syndicate. * * *

It is conceded by plaintiffs that Howard Hollis & Company is a dealer in oriental art objects and that the profits realized by that partnership constituted ordinary income. However, plaintiffs contend that the art objects of Hollis & Company were held for investment and that profits derived from their sale must be treated as capital gains. Plaintiffs' argument is premised in part upon the declared purpose of the syndicate members of Hollis & Company to hold the art objects as an "investment."

But merely designating the purchase and sale of art objects as an "investment" is not decisive. While the stated purpose for which properly is acquired is entitled to some weight, "the ultimate question is the purpose for which the property is held."

Plaintiffs also rely upon the fact that Hollis & Company was a "one venture proposition" and contemplated no replenishment of inventory. In Ehrman v. C.I.R., 9 Cir., 120 F.2d 607, 610, the court said:

> "We fail to see that the reason behind a person's entering into a business—whether it is to make money or whether it is to liquidate—should be determinative of the question of whether or not the gains resulting from sales are ordinary gains or capital gains."

Hollis was impressed with the opportunities for profit in selling art objects that resulted from the post-war economic condition of the Japanese people. He enlisted the financial aid of his associates and offered them a chance to participate in what promised to be a profitable venture. The members of the syndicate knew they were entering into a new and untried business venture but were willing to finance and participate in the enterprise as an experiment. Notwithstanding the stated purpose of "acquiring an investment" it was contemplated that sales efforts were to be made immediately upon the return of Hollis from Japan. After nine months of operation it was demonstrated that Hollis's optimistic view of the possibilities of profit were fully warranted. The profits realized from the sale of but a small portion of the objects purchased indicated that the long-term prospects of such a business were most favorable. Hollis then decided that it would be advantageous to engage in the business of dealing in oriental art on a permanent basis. This was the purpose of the formation of the second syndicate. Following the organization of Howard Hollis & Company and for a period of several years, art objects purchased by both syndicates were sold, and the plans, policies and procedures followed in connection therewith were the same for each partnership. It is conceded that all of the essential criteria of a business enterprise are present in the operations of Howard Hollis & Company. I am of the opinion that the same criteria appear in the operation of Hollis & Company. The syndicate of Hollis & Company provided for a drawing account of $500 per month for Hollis, effective upon his return from Japan. Hollis was to receive a commission on sales, and his selling efforts began immediately upon his return to this country. Sales were made within a short time after his return, and the sales were regular, substantial and continuous. As is clearly shown by the evidence, there is a limited number of potential buyers of oriental art objects. Because of the restricted market and the nature of the business, it was probably considered unnecessary to advertise or to publish price lists. Both in the number of transactions and in the amounts realized from sales there was little difference in the operations or results of the two partnerships. The sales of Hollis & Company were not extraordinary. As is true with the sales of Howard Hollis & Company, they were sales in the ordinary course of business.

Plaintiffs also contend that being the first to sell oriental art objects in this country, Hollis & Company had no customers. I suppose it fair to say that the first person who in 1859 bought a pound of tea from The Great Atlantic & Pacific Tea Company was just as truly a customer as the housewife who does her weekly shopping in one of the corporation's modern chain stores. Those whose custom the taxpayer seeks are its customers. Goldsmith v. Commissioner, 143 F.2d 466 (2d Cir. 1944). Hollis & Company was a "middleman" engaged in the distribution of art objects to a class different from those from whom it bought. Although the Goldsmith case, supra, involved the wholly dissimilar subject-matter of the sale of motion picture rights by a playwright, the concurring opinion of Judge Learned Hand in that case is instructive and relevant here. Among other things, Judge Hand said:

> "Nevertheless, the business may consist of selling these goods in 'ordinary course', to those whose custom the taxpayer seeks; and these are his 'customers.' That the purpose of Congress was also not to treat such transactions as 'capital gains or losses' is patent. Although each transaction is the sale of 'property held by the taxpayer,' it is not considered as separate, but the transactions are all massed together for tax purposes as a single source of ordinary income, quite as though the taxpayer were giving his services for hire upon separate occasions. How numerous such transactions must be the statute answers only by the test that collectively they must constitute a 'trade or business.'"

* * *

I think it beyond question that Hollis & Company held the art objects for sale to its customers in the ordinary course of business.

Judgment may be entered for defendant.

PROBLEM

Your client, Tabatha Mewing, owns a large estate near Dallas, consisting of a huge manor house, outbuildings, and countless acres of vacant land. Her husband has passed away, and most of her children have moved to Atlanta. Taking care of the estate has become too much for her. She knows that the estate will bring a good price. Local real estate prices have been going up, as Dallas has expanded in size and population.

Her neighbor, who knows a bit about the local real estate market, has told her the following:

- If the estate is sold in one piece this year, it will bring $1,000,000.
- If it is subdivided into residential lots, and sold over three years, it will bring $5,000,000.
- If she spends $100,000 to advertise the new residential subdivision, it will bring $6,000,000.
- If she convinces the local authorities to make plans for sewers, parks, and schools in or near the subdivision, it will bring $7,000,000.

Which of these things should she do? What effect will they have on her tax situation?

C. CORN PRODUCTS DOCTRINE

Imagine a large bakery. It purchases substantial amounts of wheat every year, and uses it to bake bread. Clearly, its profits on bread sales are ordinary income.

Now imagine an occasional investor. In January, he acquires the right to buy 100,000 bushels of wheat at $3 per bushel. This right is to be exercised when the wheat is harvested in September. Such rights are called wheat futures.

In September, the price of wheat is $5 per bushel. Investor could exercise his wheat futures, buy 100,000 bushels for $300,000, and immediately resell the wheat for $500,000, netting a profit of $200,000. Instead, he merely sells his wheat futures for $190,000. Clearly, any gain on the sale of the wheat futures is capital gain to the occasional investor.

Now imagine that it is the bakery that purchases the wheat futures, and later sells them for a gain. Should the gain still be capital gain? Should it matter why the bakery acquired the wheat futures?

CORN PRODUCTS REFINING COMPANY
v. COMMISSIONER

United States Supreme Court, 1955.
350 U.S. 46, 76 S.Ct. 20, 100 L.Ed. 29.

MR. JUSTICE CLARK delivered the opinion of the Court.

This case concerns the tax treatment to be accorded certain transactions in commodity futures.[1] In the Tax Court, petitioner Corn Products Refining Company contended that its purchases and sales of corn futures in 1940 and 1942 were capital-asset transactions under § 117(a) of the Internal Revenue Code of 1939 [current § 1221]... [F]or the year 1942 both the Tax Court and the Court of Appeals for the Second Circuit held that the futures were not capital assets under [§ 1221]. We granted certiorari, because of an asserted conflict with holdings in the Courts of Appeals for the Third, Fifth, and Sixth Circuits. * * *

Petitioner is a nationally known manufacturer of products made from grain corn. It manufactures starch, syrup, sugar, and their byproducts, feeds and oil. Its average yearly grind of raw corn during the period 1937 through 1942 varied from thirty-five to sixty million bushels. Most of its products were sold under contracts requiring shipment in thirty days at a

---

1. A commodity future is a contract to purchase some fixed amount of a commodity at a future date for a fixed price. Corn futures, involved in the present case, are in terms of some multiple of five thousand bushels to be delivered eleven months or less after the contract.

set price or at market price on the date of delivery, whichever was lower. It permitted cancellation of such contracts, but from experience it could calculate with some accuracy future orders that would remain firm. While it also sold to a few customers on long-term contracts involving substantial orders, these had little effect on the transactions here involved.

In 1934 and again in 1936 droughts in the corn belt caused a sharp increase in the price of spot corn. With a storage capacity of only 2,300,000 bushels of corn, a bare three weeks' supply, Corn Products found itself unable to buy at a price which would permit its refined corn sugar, cerealose, to compete successfully with cane and beet sugar. To avoid a recurrence of this situation, petitioner, in 1937, began to establish a long position in corn futures "as a part of its corn buying program" and "as the most economical method of obtaining an adequate supply of raw corn" without entailing the expenditure of large sums for additional storage facilities. At harvest time each year it would buy futures when the price appeared favorable. It would take delivery on such contracts as it found necessary to its manufacturing operations and sell the remainder in early summer if no shortage was imminent. If shortages appeared, however, it sold futures only as it bought spot corn for grinding. In this manner it reached a balanced position with reference to any increase in spot corn prices. It made no effort to protect itself against a decline in prices.

In 1940 it netted a profit of $680,587.39 in corn futures, but in 1942 it suffered a loss of $109,969.38. In computing its tax liability Corn Products reported these figures as ordinary profit and loss from its manufacturing operations for the respective years. It now contends that its futures were "capital assets" under [§ 1221] and that gains and losses therefrom should have been treated as arising from the sale of a capital asset. In support of this position it claims that its futures trading was separate and apart from its manufacturing operations and that in its futures transactions it was acting as a "legitimate capitalist." It denies that its futures transactions were "hedges" or "speculative" dealings * * *.

Both the Tax Court and the Court of Appeals found petitioner's futures transactions to be an integral part of its business designed to protect its manufacturing operations against a price increase in its principal raw material and to assure a ready supply for future manufacturing requirements. Corn Products does not level a direct attack on these two-court findings but insists that its futures were "property" entitled to capital-asset treatment under [§ 1221] and as such were distinct from its manufacturing business. We cannot agree.

We find nothing in this record to support the contention that Corn Products' futures activity was separate and apart from its manufacturing operation. On the contrary, it appears that the transactions were vitally important to the company's business as a form of insurance against increases in the price of raw corn. Not only were the purchases initiated for just this reason, but the petitioner's sales policy, selling in the future at a fixed price or less, continued to leave it exceedingly vulnerable to rises in the price of corn. Further, the purchase of corn futures assured the company a source of supply which was admittedly cheaper than constructing additional storage facilities for raw corn. Under these facts it is difficult to imagine a program more closely geared to a company's manufacturing enterprise or more important to its successful operation.

Likewise the claim of Corn Products that it was dealing in the market as a "legitimate capitalist" lacks support in the record. There can be no quarrel with a manufacturer's desire to protect itself against increasing costs of raw materials. Transactions which provide such protection are considered a legitimate form of insurance. However, in labeling its activity as that of a "legitimate capitalist" exercising "good judgment" in the futures market, petitioner ignores the testimony of its own officers that in entering that market the company was "trying to protect a part of (its) manufacturing costs"; that its entry was not for the purpose of "speculating and buying and selling corn futures" but to fill an actual "need for the quantity of corn (bought) * * * in order to cover * * * what (products) we expected to market over a period of fifteen or eighteen months." It matters not whether the label be that of "legitimate capitalist" or "speculator"; this is not the talk of the capital investor but of the far-sighted manufacturer. For tax purposes petitioner's purchases have been found to "constitute an integral part of its manufacturing business" by both the Tax Court and the Court of Appeals, and on essentially factual questions the findings of two courts should not ordinarily be disturbed.

Petitioner also makes much of the conclusion by both the Tax Court and the Court of Appeals that its transactions did not constitute 'true hedging.' It is true that Corn Products did not secure complete protection from its market operations. Under its sales policy petitioner could not guard against a fall in prices. It is clear, however, that petitioner feared the possibility of a price rise more than that of a price decline. It therefore purchased partial insurance against its principal risk, and hoped to retain sufficient flexibility to avoid serious losses on a declining market.

Nor can we find support for petitioner's contention that hedging is not within the exclusions of [§ 1221]. Admittedly, petitioner's corn futures do not come within the literal language of the exclusions set out in that section. They were not stock in trade, actual inventory, property held for sale to customers or depreciable property used in a trade or business. But the capital-asset provision of [§ 1221] must not be so broadly applied as to defeat rather than further the purpose of Congress. Congress intended that profits and losses arising from the everyday operation of a business be considered as ordinary income or loss rather than capital gain or loss. The preferential treatment provided by [§ 1221] applies to transactions in property which are not the normal source of business income. It was intended "to relieve the taxpayer from * * * excessive tax burdens on gains resulting from a conversion of capital investments, and to remove the deterrent effect of those burdens on such conversions." Since this section is an exception from the normal tax requirements of the Internal Revenue Code, the definition of a capital asset must be narrowly applied and its exclusions interpreted broadly. This is necessary to effectuate the basic congressional purpose. This Court has always construed narrowly the term "capital assets" in [§ 1221].

We believe that the statute clearly refutes the contention of Corn Products. Moreover, it is significant to note that practical considerations lead to the same conclusion. To hold otherwise would permit those engaged in hedging transactions to transmute ordinary income into capital gain at will. The hedger may either sell the future and purchase in the spot market or take delivery under the future contract itself. But if a sale of the future created a capital transaction while delivery of the commodity under the same future did not, a loophole in the statute would be created and the purpose of Congress frustrated.

The judgment is affirmed.

Affirmed.

MR. JUSTICE HARLAN took no part in the consideration or decision of this case.

ARKANSAS BEST CORPORATION v. COMMISSIONER

United States Supreme Court, 1988.
485 U.S. 212, 108 S.Ct. 971, 99 L.Ed.2d 183.

JUSTICE MARSHALL delivered the opinion of the Court.

The issue presented in this case is whether capital stock held by petitioner Arkansas Best Corporation (Arkansas Best) is a "capital asset" as defined in § 1221 of the Internal Revenue Code regardless of whether the stock was purchased and held for a business purpose or for an investment purpose.

I

Arkansas Best is a diversified holding company. In 1968 it acquired approximately 65% of the stock of the National Bank of Commerce (Bank) in Dallas, Texas. Between 1969 and 1974, Arkansas Best more than tripled the number of shares it owned in the Bank, although its percentage interest in the Bank remained relatively stable. These acquisitions were prompted principally by the Bank's need for added capital. Until 1972, the Bank appeared to be prosperous and growing, and the added capital was necessary to accommodate this growth. As the Dallas real estate market declined, however, so too did the financial health of the Bank, which had a heavy concentration of loans in the local real estate industry. In 1972, federal examiners classified the Bank as a problem bank. The infusion of capital after 1972 was prompted by the loan portfolio problems of the bank.

Petitioner sold the bulk of its Bank stock on June 30, 1975, leaving it with only a 14.7% stake in the Bank. On its federal income tax return for 1975, petitioner claimed a deduction for an ordinary loss of $9,995,688 resulting from the sale of the stock. The Commissioner of Internal

Revenue disallowed the deduction, finding that the loss from the sale of stock was a capital loss, rather than an ordinary loss, and that it therefore was subject to the capital loss limitations in the Internal Revenue Code.

Arkansas Best challenged the Commissioner's determination in the United States Tax Court. The Tax Court, relying on cases interpreting Corn Products Refining Co. v. Commissioner, held that stock purchased with a substantial investment purpose is a capital asset which, when sold, gives rise to a capital gain or loss, whereas stock purchased and held for a business purpose, without any substantial investment motive, is an ordinary asset whose sale gives rise to ordinary gains or losses. The court characterized Arkansas Best's acquisitions through 1972 as occurring during the Bank's " 'growth' phase," and found that these acquisitions "were motivated primarily by investment purpose and only incidentally by some business purpose." The stock acquired during this period therefore constituted a capital asset, which gave rise to a capital loss when sold in 1975. The court determined, however, that the acquisitions after 1972 occurred during the Bank's " 'problem' phase," and, except for certain minor exceptions, "were made exclusively for business purposes and subsequently held for the same reasons." These acquisitions, the court found, were designed to preserve petitioner's business reputation, because without the added capital the Bank probably would have failed. The loss realized on the sale of this stock was thus held to be an ordinary loss.

The Court of Appeals for the Eighth Circuit reversed the Tax Court's determination that the loss realized on stock purchased after 1972 was subject to ordinary-loss treatment, holding that all of the Bank stock sold in 1975 was subject to capital-loss treatment. The court reasoned that the Bank stock clearly fell within the general definition of "capital asset" in Internal Revenue Code § 1221, and that the stock did not fall within any of the specific statutory exceptions to this definition. The court concluded that Arkansas Best's purpose in acquiring and holding the stock was irrelevant to the determination whether the stock was a capital asset. We granted certiorari, and now affirm.

II

* * * Arkansas Best acknowledges that the Bank stock falls within the literal definition of "capital asset" in § 1221, and is outside of the statutory exclusions. It asserts, however, that this determination does not end the inquiry. Petitioner argues that in Corn Products Refining Co. v. Commissioner, this Court rejected a literal reading of § 1221, and concluded that assets acquired and sold for ordinary business purposes rather than for investment purposes should be given ordinary-asset treatment. Petitioner's reading of Corn Products finds much support in the academic literature and in the courts. Unfortunately for petitioner, this broad reading finds no support in the language of § 1221.

In essence, petitioner argues that "property held by the taxpayer (whether or not connected with his trade or business)" does not include property that is acquired and held for a business purpose. In petitioner's view an asset's status as "property" thus turns on the motivation behind its acquisition. This motive test, however, is not only nowhere mentioned in § 1221, but it is also in direct conflict with the parenthetical phrase "whether or not connected with his trade or business." The broad definition of the term "capital asset" explicitly makes irrelevant any consideration of the property's connection with the taxpayer's business, whereas petitioner's rule would make this factor dispositive.

In a related argument, petitioner contends that the five exceptions listed in § 1221 for certain kinds of property are illustrative, rather than exhaustive, and that courts are therefore free to fashion additional exceptions in order to further the general purposes of the capital-asset provisions. The language of the statute refutes petitioner's construction. Section 1221 provides that "capital asset" means "property held by the taxpayer[,] . . . but does not include" the five classes of property listed as exceptions. We believe this locution signifies that the listed exceptions are exclusive. The body of § 1221 establishes a general definition of the term "capital asset," and the phrase "does not include" takes out of that broad definition only the classes of property that are specifically mentioned. The legislative history of the capital-asset definition supports this interpretation.

Petitioner's reading of the statute is also in tension with the exceptions listed in § 1221. These exclusions would be largely superfluous if assets acquired primarily or exclusively for business purposes were not capital assets. Inventory, real or depreciable property used in the taxpayer's trade or business, and accounts or notes receivable acquired in the ordinary course of business, would undoubtedly satisfy such a business-motive test. Yet these exceptions were created by Congress in separate enactments spanning 30 years. Without any express direction from Congress, we are unwilling to read § 1221 in a manner that makes surplusage of these statutory exclusions.

In the end, petitioner places all reliance on its reading of Corn Products Refining Co. v. Commissioner,—a reading we believe is too expansive.

The Court in *Corn Products* proffered the oft-quoted rule of construction that the definition of "capital asset" must be narrowly applied and its exclusions interpreted broadly, but it did not state explicitly whether the holding was based on a narrow reading of the phrase "property held by the taxpayer," or on a broad reading of the inventory exclusion of § 1221. In light of the stark language of § 1221, however, we believe that *Corn Products* is properly interpreted as involving an application of § 1221's inventory exception. Such a reading is consistent both with the Court's reasoning in that case and with § 1221. The Court stated in *Corn Products* that the company's futures transactions were "an integral part of its business designed to protect its manufacturing operations against a price increase in its principal raw material and to assure a ready supply for future manufacturing requirements." The company bought, sold, and took delivery under the futures contracts as required by the company's manufacturing needs. As Professor Bittker notes, under these circumstances, the futures can "easily be viewed as surrogates for the raw material itself." The Court of Appeals for the Second Circuit in *Corn Products* clearly took this approach. That court stated that when commodity futures are "utilized solely for the purpose of stabilizing inventory cost[,] . . . [they] cannot reasonably be separated from the inventory items," and concluded that "property used in hedging transactions properly comes within the exclusions of [§ 1221]." This Court indicated its acceptance of the Second Circuit's reasoning when it began the central paragraph of its opinion: "Nor can we find support for petitioner's contention that hedging is not within the exclusions of [§ 1221]." * * * This discussion, read in light of the Second Circuit's holding and the plain language of § 1221, convinces us that although the corn futures were not "actual inventory," their use as an integral part of the taxpayer's inventory-purchase system led the Court to treat them as substitutes for the corn inventory such that they came within a broad reading of "property of a kind which would properly be included in the inventory of the taxpayer" in § 1221.

Petitioner argues that by focusing attention on whether the asset was acquired and sold as an integral part of the taxpayer's everyday business operations, the Court in *Corn Products* intended to create a general exemption from capital-asset status for assets acquired for business purposes. We believe petitioner misunderstands the relevance of the Court's inquiry. A business connection, although irrelevant to the initial determination whether an item is a capital asset, is relevant in determining the applicability of certain of the statutory exceptions, including the inventory exception. The close connection between the futures transactions and the taxpayer's business in *Corn Products* was crucial to whether the corn futures could be considered surrogates for the stored inventory of raw corn. For if the futures dealings were not part of the company's inventory-purchase system, and instead amounted simply to speculation in corn futures, they could not be considered substitutes for the company's corn inventory, and would fall outside even a broad reading of the inventory exclusion. We conclude that *Corn Products* is properly interpreted as standing for the narrow proposition that hedging transactions that are an integral part of a business' inventory-purchase system fall within the inventory exclusion of § 1221. Arkansas Best, which is not a dealer in securities, has never suggested that the Bank stock falls within the inventory exclusion. *Corn Products* thus has no application to this case.

It is also important to note that the business-motive test advocated by petitioner is subject to the same kind of abuse that the Court condemned in *Corn Products*. The Court explained in *Corn Products* that unless hedging transactions were subject to ordinary gain and loss treatment, taxpayers engaged in such transactions could "transmute ordinary income into capital gain at will." The hedger could garner capital-asset treatment by selling the future and purchasing the commodity on the spot market, or ordinary-asset treatment by taking delivery under the future contract. In a similar vein, if capital stock purchased and held for a business purpose is an ordinary asset, whereas the same stock purchased and held with an investment motive is a capital asset, a taxpayer such as Arkansas Best could have significant influence over whether the asset would receive capital or ordinary treatment. Because stock is most naturally viewed as a capital asset, the Internal Revenue Service would be hard pressed to challenge a taxpayer's claim that stock was acquired as an investment, and that a gain arising from the sale of such stock was therefore a capital gain. Indeed, we are unaware of a single decision that has applied the business-motive test so as to require a taxpayer to report a gain from the sale of stock as an ordinary gain. If the same stock is sold at a loss, however, the taxpayer may be able to garner ordinary-loss treatment by emphasizing the business purpose behind the stock's acquisition. The potential for such abuse was evidenced in this case by the fact that as late as 1974, when Arkansas Best still hoped to sell the Bank stock at a profit, Arkansas Best apparently expected to report the gain as a capital gain.

III

We conclude that a taxpayer's motivation in purchasing an asset is irrelevant to the question whether the asset is "property held by a taxpayer (whether or not connected with his business)" and is thus within § 1221's general definition of "capital asset." Because the capital stock held by petitioner falls within the broad definition of the term "capital asset" in § 1221 and is outside the classes of property excluded from capital-asset status, the loss arising from the sale of the stock is a capital loss. Corn Products Refining Co. v. Commissioner, *supra*, which we interpret as involving a broad reading of the inventory exclusion of § 1221, has no application in the present context. Accordingly, the judgment of the Court of Appeals is affirmed.

D. ORDINARY INCOME SUBSTITUTES

An asset which has value in the marketplace can have two kinds of economic power. First, it can generate current income, in the form of rent, dividends, interest, or royalties. Second, it can generate future growth, so that it can be sold for more than its current price. Some assets have both kinds of power; some have only one. If they have neither, then they have no value.

Assume that a taxpayer holds an asset which is, in her hands, a capital asset. If she sells the whole thing for a gain, she has realized a capital gain. If she sells a piece of it—say an undivided one-half, then a gain on that sale would also be a capital gain.

Suppose that the asset is sliced up in a different way. What if the taxpayer "sells" the current income rights to the asset, but retains the rest. Can she declare a capital gain on that carve-out of income?

HORT v. COMMISSIONER

United States Supreme Court, 1941.
313 U.S. 28, 61 S.Ct. 757, 85 L.Ed. 1168.

MR. JUSTICE MURPHY delivered the opinion of the Court.

* * * Petitioner acquired the property, a lot and ten-story office building, by devise from his father in 1928. At the time he became owner, the premises were leased to a firm which had sublet the main floor to the Irving Trust Co. In 1927, five years before the head lease expired, the Irving Trust Co. and petitioner's father executed a contract in which the latter agreed to lease the main floor and basement to the former for a term of fifteen years at an annual rental of $25,000, the term to commence at the expiration of the head lease.

In 1933, the Irving Trust Co. found it unprofitable to maintain a branch in petitioner's building. After some negotiations, petitioner and the Trust Co. agreed to cancel the lease in consideration of a payment to petitioner of $140,000. Petitioner did not include this amount in gross income in his income tax return for 1933. On the contrary, he reported a loss of $21,494.75 on the theory that the amount he received as consideration for the cancellation was $21,494.75 less than the difference between the present value[c] of the unmatured rental payments and the fair rental value of the main floor and basement for the unexpired term of the lease. He did not deduct this figure, however, because he reported other losses in excess of gross income.

The Commissioner included the entire $140,000 in gross income, disallowed the asserted loss, made certain other adjustments not material here, and assessed a deficiency. The Board of Tax Appeals affirmed. The Circuit Court of Appeals affirmed per curiam * * *. [W]e granted certiorari limited to the question whether, 'in computing net gain or loss for income tax purposes, a taxpayer (can) offset the value of the lease canceled against the consideration received by him for the cancellation'.

Petitioner apparently contends that the amount received for cancellation of the lease was capital rather than ordinary income * * *. Further, he argues that even if that amount must be reported as ordinary gross income he sustained a loss which § 23(e) [current § 165] authorizes him to deduct. We cannot agree.

The amount received by petitioner for cancellation of the lease must be included in his gross income in its entirety. Section 22(a) [current § 61] * * * expressly defines gross income to include 'gains, profits, and income derived from * * * rent, * * * or gains or profits and income from any source whatever'. Plainly this definition reached the rent paid prior to cancellation just as it would have embraced subsequent payments if the lease had never been canceled. It would have included a prepayment of the discounted value of unmatured rental payments whether received at the

---

c. See the Appendix for Present Value Tables.

inception of the lease or at any time thereafter. Similarly, it would have extended to the proceeds of a suit to recover damages had the Irving Trust Co. breached the lease instead of concluding a settlement. That the amount petitioner received resulted from negotiations ending in cancellation of the lease rather than from a suit to enforce it cannot alter the fact that basically the payment was merely a substitute for the rent reserved in the lease. So far as the application of [§ 61] is concerned, it is immaterial that petitioner chose to accept an amount less than the strict present value of the unmatured rental payments rather than to engage in litigation, possibly uncertain and expensive.

The consideration received for cancellation of the lease was not a return of capital. We assume that the lease was 'property', whatever that signifies abstractly. Presumably the bond in Helvering v. Horst, [see Chapter 9—Ed.] and the lease in Helvering v. Bruun, were also 'property', but the interest coupon in Horst and the building in Bruun nevertheless were held to constitute items of gross income. Simply because the lease was 'property' the amount received for its cancellation was not a return of capital, quite apart from the fact that 'property' and 'capital' are not necessarily synonymous in the Revenue Act of 1932 or in common usage. Where, as in this case, the disputed amount was essentially a substitute for rental payments which [§ 61] expressly characterizes as gross income, it must be regarded as ordinary income, and it is immaterial that for some purposes the contract creating the right to such payments may be treated as 'property' or 'capital'.

For the same reasons, that amount was not a return of capital because petitioner acquired the lease as an incident of the realty devised to him by his father. Theoretically, it might have been possible in such a case to value realty and lease separately and to label each a capital asset. But that would not have converted into capital the amount petitioner received from the Trust Co. since § 22(b)(3) of the 1932 Act [current § 102(b)] would have required him to include in gross income the rent derived from the property, and that section, like [§ 61], does not distinguish rental payments and a payment which is clearly a substitute for rental payments.

We conclude that petitioner must report as gross income the entire amount received for cancellation of the lease without regard to the claimed disparity between that amount and the difference between the present value of the unmatured rental payments and the fair rental value of the property for the unexpired period of the lease. The cancellation of the lease involved nothing more than relinquishment of the right to future rental payments in return for a present substitute payment and possession of the leased premises. Undoubtedly it diminished the amount of gross income petitioner expected to realize, but to that extent he was relieved of the duty to pay income tax. Nothing in [§ 165] indicates that Congress intended to allow petitioner to reduce ordinary income actually received and reported by the amount of income he failed to realize. We may assume that petitioner was injured insofar as the cancellation of the lease affected the value of the realty. But that would become a deductible loss only when its extent had been fixed by a closed transaction.

The judgment of the Circuit Court of Appeals is affirmed.

QUESTION

What is the relationship of § 1241 to the result in Hort?

LATTERA v. COMMISSIONER

United States Court of Appeals, Third Circuit 2006.
437 F.3d 399.

AMBRO, CIRCUIT JUDGE.

Lottery winners, after receiving several annual installments of their lottery prize, sold for a lump sum the right to their remaining payments. They reported their sale proceeds as capital gains on their tax return, but the Internal Revenue Service (IRS) classified those proceeds as ordinary income. The substitute-for-ordinary-income doctrine holds that lump-sum consideration substituting for something that would otherwise be received at a future time as ordinary income should be taxed the same way. We agree with the Commissioner of the IRS that the lump-sum consideration paid for the right to lottery payments is ordinary income.

I. Factual Background and Procedural History

In June 1991 George and Angeline Lattera turned a one-dollar lottery ticket into $9,595,326 in the Pennsylvania Lottery. They did not then have the option to take the prize in a single lump-sum payment, so they were entitled to 26 annual installments of $369,051.

In September 1999 the Latteras sold their rights to the 17 remaining lottery payments to Singer Asset Finance Co., LLC. * * *

On their joint tax return, the Latteras reported this sale as the sale of a capital asset held for more than one year. They reported a sale price of $3,372,342, a cost or other basis of zero, and a long-term capital gain of the full sale price. The Commissioner determined that this sale price was ordinary income. In December 2002 the Latteras were sent a notice of deficiency of $660,784.

In March 2003 the Latteras petitioned the Tax Court for a redetermination of the deficiency. The Court held in favor of the Commissioner. The Latteras now appeal to our Court.

* * *

III. Discussion

The lottery payments the Latteras had a right to receive were gambling winnings, and the parties agree that the annual payments were ordinary income. But the Latteras argue that, when they sold the right to their remaining lottery payments, the sale gave rise to a long-term capital gain.

Whether the sale of a right to lottery payments by a lottery winner can be treated as a capital gain under the Internal Revenue Code is one of first impression in our Circuit. But it is not a new question. Both the Tax Court and the Ninth Circuit Court of Appeals have held that such sales deserve ordinary-income treatment. *United States v. Maginnis,* 356 F.3d 1179 (9th Cir. 2004) *Davis v. Comm'r,* 119 T.C. 1 (2002).

The Ninth Circuit's reasoning has drawn significant criticism, however. In this context, we propose a different approach. We begin with a discussion of basic concepts that underlie our reasoning.

* * *

B. The substitute-for-ordinary-income doctrine

The problem with an overly broad definition for capital assets is that it could "encompass some things Congress did not intend to be taxed as capital gains." *Maginnis,* 356 F.3d at 1181. An overly broad definition, linked with favorable capital-gains tax treatment, would encourage transactions designed to convert ordinary income into capital gains. For example, a salary is taxed as ordinary income, and the right to be paid for work is a person's property. But it is hard to conceive that Congress intends for taxpayers to get capital-gains treatment if they were to sell their rights (*i.e.,* "property held by the taxpayer") to their future paychecks.

To get around this problem, courts have created the substitute-for-ordinary-income doctrine. This doctrine says, in effect, that " 'lump sum consideration [that] seems essentially a substitute for what would otherwise be received at a future time as ordinary income' may not be taxed as a capital gain."

The seminal substitute-for-ordinary-income case is the 1941 Supreme Court decision in *Hort v. Commissioner.* * * *

The Latteras argue that the substitute-for-ordinary-income doctrine, which takes "property held by the taxpayer" outside the statutory capital-asset definition, did not survive *Arkansas Best.* * * The Tax Court has several times confirmed that *Arkansas Best* "in no way affected the viability of the principle established in the [*Hort–Lake*] line of cases." And the Ninth Circuit agrees. We follow suit, holding that the substitute-for-ordinary-income doctrine remains viable in the wake of *Arkansas Best.*

But there is a tension in the doctrine: in theory, all capital assets are substitutes for ordinary income. *See, e.g.,* William A. Klein *et al., Federal Income Taxation* 786 (12th ed. 2000) ("A fundamental principle of economics is that the value of an asset is equal to the present discounted value of all the expected net receipts from that asset over its life."); "[R]ead literally, the [substitute-for-ordinary-income] doctrine would completely swallow the concept of capital gains." Also, an "overbroad 'substitute for ordinary income' doctrine, besides being analytically unsatisfactory, would create the potential for the abuse of treating capital losses as ordinary." The doctrine must therefore be limited so as not to err on either side.

C.   The Lottery Cases

Even before the Ninth Circuit decided *Maginnis,* the Tax Court had correctly answered the question of whether sales of lottery winnings were capital gains. In *Davis v. Commissioner,* lottery winners had sold their rights to 11 of their total 14 future lottery payments for a lump sum. The Tax Court found that the lump-sum payment to the lottery winners was the "discounted value . . . of certain ordinary income which they otherwise would have received during the years 1997 through 2007." The Court held, therefore, that (1) the purchaser of the lottery payment rights paid money for "the right to receive . . . future ordinary income, and not for an increase in the value of income-producing property"; (2) the lottery winners' right to their future lottery payments was not a capital asset; and (3) the lump-sum payment was to be taxed as ordinary income.

In 2004 the Ninth Circuit decided *Maginnis,* the first (and so far only) appellate opinion to deal with this question. Maginnis won $9 million in a lottery and, after receiving five of his lottery payments, assigned all of his remaining future lottery payments to a third party for a lump-sum payment of $3,950,000. The Ninth Circuit held that Maginnis's right to future lottery payments was not a capital asset and that the lump-sum payment was to be taxed as ordinary income.

The Court relied on the substitute-for-ordinary-income doctrine, but it was concerned about taking an "approach that could potentially convert all capital gains into ordinary income [or] one that could convert all ordinary income into capital gains." The Court opted instead for "case-by-case judgments as to whether the conversion of income rights into lump-sum payments reflects the sale of a capital asset that produces a capital gain, or whether it produces ordinary income." It set out two factors, which it characterized as "crucial to [its] conclusion," but not "dispositive in all cases": "Maginnis (1) did not make any underlying investment of capital in return for the receipt of his lottery right, and (2) the sale of his right did not reflect an accretion in value over cost to any underlying asset Maginnis held."

But two commentators have criticized the analysis in *Maginnis,* especially the two factors. The first factor-underlying investment of capital-would theoretically subject all inherited and gifted property (which involves no investment at all) to ordinary-income treatment. * * *

The second factor also presents analytical problems. Not all capital assets experience an accretion in value over cost. For example, cars typically depreciate, but they are often capital assets. Levine [a commentator—Ed.] criticizes the second factor for "attempt[ing] to determine the character of a gain from its amount." The *Maginnis* Court held that there was no accretion of value over cost in lottery winnings because there was no cost, as "Maginnis did not make any capital investment in exchange for his lottery right." But if Maginnis's purchase of a lottery ticket had been a capital investment, would the second factor automatically have been satisfied? (That is, the "cost" in that scenario would have been $1, and the increase would have been $3,949,999.) Our first instinct is no. Moreover, the second factor does not seem to predict correctly the result in both *Hort* (where a building was inherited for no "cost") and *Lake* (where the working interest in the oil lease presumably had a "cost"), in both of which the taxpayer got ordinary-income treatment.

Thus, while we agree with *Maginnis'* s result, we do not simply adopt its reasoning. And it is both unsatisfying and unhelpful to future litigants to declare that we know this to be ordinary income when we see it. The problem is that, "[u]nless and until Congress establishes an arbitrary line on the otherwise seamless spectrum between *Hort–Lake* transactions and conventional capital gain transactions, the courts must locate the boundary case by case, a process that can yield few useful generalizations because there are so many relevant but imponderable criteria.

We therefore proceed to our case-by-case analysis, but in doing so we set out a method for analysis that guides our result. At the same time, however, we recognize that any rule we create could not account for every contemplated transactional variation.

D. Substitute-for-ordinary-income analysis

* * *

* * * Several types of assets we know to be capital: stocks, bonds, options, and currency contracts, for example. We could also include in this category physical assets like land and automobiles.

Similarly, there are several types of rights that we know to be ordinary income, *e.g.,* rental income and interest income. * * *

For the "family resemblance" test, we can set those two categories at the opposite poles of our analysis. For example, we presume that stock, and things that look and act like stock, will receive capital-gains treatment. For the in-between transactions that do not bear a family resemblance to the items in either category, like contracts and payment rights, we use two factors to assist in our analysis: (1) type of "carve-out" and (2) character of asset.

1. *Type of carve-out*

The notion of the carve-out, or partial sale, has significant explanatory power in the context of the *Hort–Lake* line of cases. As Marvin Chirelstein writes, the " 'substitute' language, in the view of most commentators, was merely a short-hand way of asserting that carved-out interests do not qualify as capital assets." Marvin A. Chirelstein, *Federal Income Taxation* ¶ 17.03, at 369–70 (9th ed.2002).

There are two ways of carving out interests from property: horizontally and vertically. A horizontal carve-out is one in which "temporal divisions [are made] in a property interest in which the person owning the interest disposes of part of his interest but also retains a portion of it." In lottery terms, this is what happened in *Davis, Boehme*, and *Clopton*—the lottery winners sold some of their future lottery payment rights (*e.g.,* their 2006 and 2007 payments) but retained the rights to payments further in the future (*e.g.,* their 2008 and 2009 payments). This is also what happened in *Hort* and *Lake;* portions of the total interest (a term of years carved out from a fee simple and a three-year payment right from a working interest in a oil lease, respectively) were carved out from the whole.

A vertical carve-out is one in which "a complete disposition of a person's interest in property" is made. In lottery terms, this is what happened in *Watkins* and *Maginnis*—the lottery winners sold the rights to all their remaining lottery payments.

Horizontal carve-outs typically lead to ordinary-income treatment. * * *

Vertical carve-outs are different. In *Dresser Industries,* for example, the Fifth Circuit distinguished *Lake* because the taxpayer in *Dresser* had "cut [ ] off a 'vertical slice' of its rights, rather than carv[ed] out an interest from the totality of its rights." *Dresser Indus.,* 324 F.2d at 58. But as the results in *Maginnis* and *Watkins* demonstrate, a vertical carve-out does not necessarily mean that the transaction receives capital-gains treatment.

Because a vertical carve-out could signal either capital-gains or ordinary-income treatment, we must make another determination to conclude with certainty which treatment should apply. Therefore, when we see a vertical carve-out, we proceed to the second factor—character of the asset—to determine whether the sale proceeds should be taxed as ordinary income or capital gain.

2. *Character of the asset*

The Fifth Circuit in *Dresser Industries* noted that "[t]here is, in law and fact, a vast difference between the present sale of the future right to *earn* income and the present sale of the future right to *earned* income." (emphasis in original). The taxpayer in *Dresser Industries* had assigned its right to an exclusive patent license back to the patent holder in exchange for a share of the licensing fees from third-party licensees. The Court used this "right to earn income"/"right to earned income" distinction to hold that capital-gains treatment was applicable. It noted that the asset sold was not a "right to earned income, to be paid in the future," but was "a property which would produce income." Further, it disregarded the ordinary nature of the income generated by the asset; because "all income-producing property" produces ordinary income, the sale of such property does not result in ordinary-income treatment. (This can be seen in the sale of bonds, which produce ordinary income, but the sale of which is treated as capital gain.)

Sinclair [a commentator—Ed.] explains the distinction in this way: "Earned income conveys the concept that the income has already been earned and the holder of the right to this income only has to collect it. In other words, the owner of the right to earned income is entitled to the income merely by virtue of owning the property." He gives as examples of this concept rental income, stock dividends, and rights to future lottery payments. (Of course, in the wake of dividend tax reform, stock dividends are now taxed as capital gains. I.R.C. § 1(h)(11).) For the right to earn income, on the other hand, "the holder of such right must do something further to earn the income.... [because] mere ownership of the right to earn income does not entitle the owner to income." Following *Dresser Industries,* Sinclair gives a patent as an example of this concept. *Id.*

Assets that constitute a right to earn income merit capital-gains treatment, while those that are a right to earned income merit ordinary-income treatment. Our Court implicitly made this distinction in *Tunnell v. United States,* 259 F.2d 916 (3d Cir.1958). Tunnell withdrew from a law partnership, and he assigned his rights in the law firm in exchange for $27,500. When he withdrew, the partnership had over $21,000 in uncollected accounts receivable from work that had already been done. We agreed with the District Court that "the sale of a partnership is treated as the sale of a capital asset." The sale of a partnership does not, in and of itself, confer income on the buyer; the buyer must continue to provide legal services, so it is a sale of the right to *earn* income. Consequently, as we held, the sale of a partnership receives capital-gains treatment. The accounts receivable, on the other hand, had already been earned; the buyer of the partnership only had to remain a partner to collect that income, so the sale of accounts receivable is the sale of the right to *earned* income. Thus, we held that the portion of the purchase price that reflected the sale of the accounts receivable was taxable as ordinary income.

Similarly, when an erstwhile employee is paid a termination fee for a personal-services contract, that employee still possesses the asset (the right to provide certain personal services) and the money (the termination fee) has already been "earned" and will simply be paid. The employee no longer has to perform any more services in exchange for the fee, so this is not like *Dresser Industries'* s "right to earn income." These termination fees are therefore rights to earned income and should be treated as ordinary income.

* * *

E. Application of the "family resemblance" test

Applied to this case, the "family resemblance" test draws out as follows. First, we try to determine whether an asset is like either the "capital asset" category of assets (*e.g.,* stocks, bonds, or land) or like the "income items" category (*e.g.,* rental income or interest income). If the asset does not bear a family resemblance to items in either of those categories, we move to the following factors.

We look at the nature of the sale. If the sale or assignment constitutes a horizontal carve-out, then ordinary-income treatment presumably applies. If, on the other hand, it constitutes a vertical carve-out, then we look to the character-of-the-asset factor. There, if the sale is a lump-sum payment for a future right to *earned* income, we apply ordinary-income treatment, but if it is a lump-sum payment for a future right to *earn* income, we apply capital-gains treatment.

Turning back to the Latteras, the right to receive annual lottery payments does not bear a strong family resemblance to either the "capital assets" or the "income items" listed at the polar ends of the analytical spectrum. The Latteras sold their right to all their remaining lottery payments, so this is a vertical carve-out, which could indicate either capital-gains or ordinary-income treatment. But because a right to lottery payments is a right to earned income (*i.e.*, the payments will keep arriving due simply to ownership of the asset), the lump-sum payment received by the Latteras should receive ordinary-income treatment.

This result comports with *Davis* and *Maginnis*. It also ensures that the Latteras do not "receive a tax advantage as compared to those taxpayers who would simply choose originally to accept their lottery winning in the form of a lump sum payment," something that was also important to the *Maginnis* Court.

IV. Conclusion

The lump-sum consideration paid to the Latteras in exchange for the right to their future lottery payments is ordinary income. We therefore affirm.

E. ANNUAL ACCOUNTING REVISITED

ARROWSMITH v. COMMISSIONER

United States Supreme Court, 1952.
344 U.S. 6, 73 S.Ct. 71, 97 L.Ed. 6.

MR. JUSTICE BLACK delivered the opinion of the Court.

* * * In 1937 two taxpayers, petitioners here, decided to liquidate and divide the proceeds of a corporation in which they had equal stock ownership. Partial distributions made in 1937, 1938, and 1939 were followed by a final one in 1940. Petitioners reported the profits obtained from this transaction, classifying them as capital gains. They thereby paid less income tax than would have been required had the income been attributed to ordinary business transactions for profit. About the propriety of these 1937–1940 returns, there is no dispute. But in 1944 a judgment was rendered against the old corporation and against Frederick R. Bauer, individually. The two taxpayers were required to and did pay the judgment for the corporation, of whose assets they were transferees. Classifying the loss as an ordinary business one, each took a tax deduction for 100% of the amount paid. Treatment of the loss as a capital one would have allowed deduction of a much smaller amount. The Commissioner

viewed the 1944 payment as part of the original liquidation transaction requiring classification as a capital loss, just as the taxpayers had treated the original dividends as capital gains. Disagreeing with the Commissioner the Tax Court classified the 1944 payment as an ordinary business loss. Disagreeing with the Tax Court the Court of Appeals reversed, treating the loss as "capital." This latter holding conflicts with the Third Circuit's holding in Commissioner of Internal Revenue v. Switlik, 184 F.2d 299 (3d Cir. 1950). Because of this conflict, we granted certiorari.

I.R.C. § 23(g) [current §§ 1222(2) and (4)] treats losses from sales or exchanges of capital assets as "capital losses" and I.R.C. § 115(c) [current §§ 302, 331] requires that liquidation distributions be treated as exchanges. The losses here fall squarely within the definition of "capital losses" contained in these sections. Taxpayers were required to pay the judgment because of liability imposed on them as transferees of liquidation distribution assets. And it is plain that their liability as transferees was not based on any ordinary business transaction of theirs apart from the liquidation proceedings. It is not even denied that had this judgment been paid after liquidation, but during the year 1940, the losses would have been properly treated as capital ones. For payment during 1940 would simply have reduced the amount of capital gains taxpayers received during that year.

It is contended, however, that this payment which would have been a capital transaction in 1940 was transformed into an ordinary business transaction in 1944 because of the well-established principle that each taxable year is a separate unit for tax accounting purposes. United States v. Lewis, North American Oil Consolidated v. Burnet [See Chapter 6—Ed.]. But this principle is not breached by considering all the 1937–1944 liquidation transaction events in order properly to classify the nature of the 1944 loss for tax purposes. Such an examination is not an attempt to reopen and readjust the 1937 to 1940 tax returns, an action that would be inconsistent with the annual tax accounting principle.

* * *

Affirmed.

Mr. Justice Douglas, dissenting.

I agree with Mr. Justice Jackson that these losses should be treated as ordinary, not capital, losses. There were no capital transactions in the year in which the losses were suffered. Those transactions occurred and were accounted for in earlier years in accord with the established principle that each year is a separate unit for tax accounting purposes. I have not felt, as my dissent in the Lewis case indicates, that the law made that an inexorable principle. But if it is the law, we should require observance of it—not merely by taxpayers but by the government as well. We should force each year to stand on its own footing, whoever may gain or lose from it in a particular case. We impeach that principle when we treat this year's losses as if they diminished last year's gains.

MR. JUSTICE JACKSON, whom MR. JUSTICE FRANKFURTER joins, dissenting.

This problem arises only because the judgment was rendered in a taxable year subsequent to the liquidation.

Had the liability of the transferor-corporation been reduced to judgment during the taxable year in which liquidation occurred, or prior thereto, this problem, under the tax laws, would not arise. The amount of the judgment rendered against the corporation would have decreased the amount it had available for distribution which would have reduced the liquidating dividends proportionately and diminished the capital gains taxes assessed against the stockholders. Probably it would also have decreased the corporation's own taxable income.

Congress might have allowed, under such circumstances, tax returns of the prior year to be reopened or readjusted so as to give the same tax results as would have obtained had the liability become known prior to liquidation. Such a solution is foreclosed to us and the alternatives left are to regard the judgment liability fastened by operation of law on the transferee as an ordinary loss for the year of adjudication or to regard it as a capital loss for such year.

This Court simplifies the choice to one of reading the English language, and declares that the losses here come 'squarely within' the definition of capital losses contained within two sections of the Internal Revenue Code. What seems so clear to this Court was not seen at all by the Tax Court, in this case or in earlier consideration of the same issue; nor was it grasped by the Court of Appeals for the Third Circuit.

I find little aid in the choice of alternatives from arguments based on equities. One enables the taxpayer to deduct the amount of the judgment against his ordinary income which might be taxed as high as 87%, while if the liability had been assessed against the corporation prior to liquidation it would have reduced his capital gain which was taxable at only 25% (now 26%). The consequence may readily be characterized as a windfall (regarding a windfall as anything that is left to a taxpayer after the collector has finished with him).

On the other hand, adoption of the contrary alternative may penalize the taxpayer because of two factors: (1) since capital losses are deductible only against capital gains, plus $1,000, a taxpayer having no net capital gains in the ensuing five years would have no opportunity to deduct anything beyond $5,000; and (2) had the liability been discharged by the corporation, a portion of it would probably in effect have been paid by the Government, since the corporation could have taken it as a deduction, while here the total liability comes out of the pockets of the stockholders.

Solicitude for the revenues is a plausible but treacherous basis upon which to decide a particular tax case. A victory may have implications which in future cases will cost the Treasury more than a defeat. This might be such a case, for anything I know. Suppose that subsequent to liquidation it is found that a corporation has undisclosed claims instead of liabilities and that under applicable state law they may be prosecuted for the benefit of the stockholders. The logic of the Court's decision here, if adhered to, would result in a lesser return to the Government than if the recoveries were considered ordinary income. Would it be so clear that this is a capital loss if the shoe were on the other foot?

Where the statute is so indecisive and the importance of a particular holding lies in its rational and harmonious relation to the general scheme of the tax law, I think great deference is due the twice-expressed judgment of the Tax Court.

QUESTION

Is there really a difference between reopening a prior year's return and merely peeking at it?

F.   QUASI–CAPITAL ASSETS

Code: § 1231

During World War II, the U.S. government took over all sorts of assets from private businesses for use in the war effort. These involuntary conversions were realization events. Since many of the converted assets had low bases and high current market values, the conversions threatened the owners with significant realizations of taxable gains.

Capital gains treatment was impossible under then current law, because governmental condemnation does not constitute a "sale or exchange." To mitigate the tax impact of these condemnations, Congress created what is now § 1231, to apply capital gains treatment even when assets were involuntarily converted. While they were at it, they expanded capital gains treatment to certain depreciable property.

Section 1231 extends quasi-capital gains treatment in two instances:

1) Certain § 1221 capital assets which have been involuntarily converted enjoy quasi-capital gain treatment pursuant to § 1231(a)(3)(A)(ii)(II); and

2) "Property used in the trade or business" enjoys quasi-capital gain treatment if it is either sold or exchanged [§ 1231(a)(3)(A)(i)], or involuntarily converted [§ 1231(a)(3)(A)(ii)(I). "Property used in the trade or business" is defined at § 1231(b). Read that definition, and notice how many concepts are common to both § 1221 and § 1231.

Section 1231 assets are known as quasi-capital assets, because they are not treated quite the same as § 1221 assets. In fact, all § 1231 transactions are netted out. If gains exceed losses, then all of them are treated as capital. However, if losses exceed gains, then all of them are treated as ordinary.

There is a separate netting process for certain casualties. *See* Chapter 10 *infra* for materials on the definition of "casualty." Pursuant to § 1231(a)(4)(C), if:

- there is an involuntary conversion arising from fire, storm, shipwreck or other casualty, or from theft, of any
  - property used in the trade or business, or
    - any capital asset which is held for more than 1 year and is held in connection with a trade or business or a transaction entered into for profit,

then the gains or losses from such conversions must be netted out separately. If there is a net gain on such conversions, then they are thrown in with the other § 1231 transactions. On the other hand, if there is a net loss, then such conversions are taken out of § 1231 altogether.

PROBLEM

Determine which of the transactions below are § 1231 transactions. Then, net out the § 1231 transactions and determine how they interact with the § 1221 transactions.

1. Taxpayer owned an oil painting, which he had purchased 3 years ago in a transaction entered into for profit, for $10,000. This year, when it was worth $15,000, it was stolen. Taxpayer collected the full amount of $15,000 from his insurance company.

2. Taxpayer owned vacant real estate used in his trade or business. He bought it for 5 years ago for $50,000, and sold it this year for $60,000.

3. Taxpayer owned a prize dairy cow, purchased 2 years ago for $9,000. Due to depreciation, its current basis is $7,000. He sold the cow this year for $5,000.

4. Taxpayer owned a breeder turkey, which he bought 18 months ago for $25. Its current basis is $15. He sold it this year for $20.

This year, Taxpayer's § 1221 transactions netted out to a net long-term capital loss of $8,000

G. SALE OF A BUSINESS

The case below deals with bifurcating the sold assets of a business into ordinary income and capital gain property. When the same issue arises today, § 1231 property—especially property used in the trade or business, constitutes a major portion of such assets.

WILLIAMS v. McGOWAN

United States Court of Appeals, Second Circuit, 1945.
152 F.2d 570.

Before L. HAND, SWAN, and FRANK, CIRCUIT JUDGES.

L. HAND, CIRCUIT JUDGE.

* * * [Williams and Reynolds operated a hardware business in Corning, New York, as a partnership. When Reynolds died in 1940. Williams bought out his interest—Ed.] On September 17th of the same year, Williams sold the business as a whole to the Corning Building Company for $63,926.28—its agreed value as of February 1, 1940—"plus an amount to be computed by multiplying the gross sales of the business from the first day of February, 1940 to the 28th day of September, 1940," by an agreed fraction. This value was made up of cash of about $8100, receivables of about $7000, fixtures of about $800, and a merchandise inventory of about $49,000, less some $1000 for bills payable. To this was added about $6,000 credited to Williams for profits under the language just quoted, making a total of nearly $70,000. Upon this sale Williams suffered a loss upon his original two-thirds of the business but he made a small gain upon the one-third which he had bought from Reynolds' executrix; and in his income tax return he entered both as items of "ordinary income," and not as transactions in "capital assets." This the Commissioner disallowed and recomputed the tax accordingly; Williams paid the deficiency and sued to recover it in this action. The only question is whether the business was "capital assets" under Sec. 117(a)(1) of the Internal Revenue Code [current § 1221].

* * * We have to decide only whether upon the sale of a going business it is to be comminuted into its fragments, and these are to be separately matched against the definition in [§ 1221], or whether the whole business is to be treated as if it were a single piece of property.

Our law has been sparing in the creation of juristic entities; it has never, for example, taken over the Roman "universitas facti";[1] and indeed for many years it fumbled uncertainly with the concept of a corporation.[2] One might have supposed that partnership would have been an especially promising field in which to raise "up an entity, particularly since merchants have always kept their accounts upon that basis." Yet there too our law resisted at the price of great continuing confusion; and, even when it might be thought that a statute admitted, if it did not demand, recognition of the firm as an entity, the old concepts prevailed. And so, even though we might agree that under the influence of the Uniform Partnership Act a partner's interest in the firm should be treated as indivisible, and for that reason a "capital asset" within [current § 1221], we should be chary about extending further so exotic a jural concept. Be that as it may, in this instance the section itself furnishes the answer. It starts in the broadest way by declaring that all "property" is "capital assets," and then makes three exceptions. The first is "stock in trade * * * or other property of a kind which would properly be included in the inventory"; next comes "property held * * * primarily for sale to customers"; and finally, property "used in the trade or business of a character which is subject to * * *

---

1. 'By universitas facti is meant a number of things of the same kind which are regarded as a whole; e.g. a herd, a stock of wares.'

2. "To the 'church' modern law owes its conception of a juristic person, and the clear line that it draws between 'the corporation aggregate' and the sum of its members."

allowance for depreciation." In the face of this language, although it may be true that a "stock in trade," taken by itself, should be treated as a "universitas facti," by no possibility can a whole business be so treated; and the same is true as to any property within the other exceptions. Congress plainly did mean to comminute the elements of a business; plainly it did not regard the whole as "capital assets."

As has already appeared, Williams transferred to the Corning Company "cash," "receivables," "fixtures" and a "merchandise inventory." "Fixtures" are not capital because they are subject to a depreciation allowance; the inventory, as we have just seen, is expressly excluded. So far as appears, no allowance was made for "good-will"; but, even if there had been, we held in Haberle Crystal Springs Brewing Company v. Clarke, Collector, 2 Cir., 30 F.2d 219, that "goodwill was a depreciable intangible." It is true that the Supreme Court reversed that judgment—but it based its decision only upon the fact that there could be no allowance for the depreciation of "good-will" in a brewery, a business condemned by the Eighteenth Amendment. There can of course be no gain or loss in the transfer of cash; and, although Williams does appear to have made a gain of $1072.71 upon the "receivables," the point has not been argued that they are not subject to a depreciation allowance. That we leave open for decision by the district court, if the parties cannot agree. The gain or loss upon every other item should be computed as an item in ordinary income.

Judgment reversed.

FRANK, CIRCUIT JUDGE (dissenting in part).

I agree that it is irrelevant that the business was once owned by a partnership. For when the sale to the Corning Company occurred, the partnership was dead, had become merely a memory, a ghost. To say that the sale was of the partnership's assets would, then, be to indulge in animism.

But I do not agree that we should ignore what the parties to the sale, Williams and the Corning Company, actually did. They did not arrange for a transfer to the buyer, as if in separate bundles, of the several ingredients of the business. They contracted for the sale of the entire business as a going concern. Here is what they said in their agreement: "The party of the first part agrees to sell and the party of the second part agrees to buy, all of the right, title and interest of the said party of the first part in and to the hardware business now being conducted by the said party of the first part, including cash on hand and on deposit in the First National Bank & Trust Company of Corning in the A. F. Williams Hardware Store account, in accounts receivable, bills receivable, notes receivable, merchandise and fixtures, including two G.M. trucks, good will and all other assets of every kind and description used in and about said business. * * * Said party of the first part agrees not to engage in the hardware business within a radius of twenty-five miles from the City of Corning, New York, for a period of ten years from the 1st day of October 1940."

To carve up this transaction into distinct sales-of cash, receivables, fixtures, trucks, merchandise, and good will-is to do violence to the realities. I do not think Congress intended any such artificial result. In the Senate Committee Report on the 1942 amendment to Sec. 117, it was said: 'It is believed that this Senate amendment will be of material benefit to businesses which, due to depressed conditions, have been compelled to dispose of their plant or equipment at a loss. The bill defines property used in a trade or business of a character which is subject to the allowance for depreciation, and real property held for more than six months which is not properly includible in the inventory of the taxpayer if on hand at the close of the taxable year or property held by the taxpayer primarily for sale to customers in the ordinary course of his trade or business. If a newspaper purchased the plant and equipment of a rival newspaper and later sold such plant and equipment, being subject to depreciation, would constitute property used in the trade or business within the meaning of this section.' These remarks show that what Congress contemplated was not the sale of a going business but of its dismembered part. Where a business is sold as a unit, the whole is greater than its parts. Businessmen so recognize; so, too, I think, did Congress. Interpretation of our complicated tax statutes is seldom aided by saying that taxation is an eminently practical matter (or the like). But this is one instance where, it seems to me, the practical aspects of the matter should guide our guess as to what Congress meant. I believe Congress had those aspects in mind and was not thinking of the nice distinctions between Roman and Anglo–American legal theories about legal entities.

QUESTION, NOTE

1. Your client is buying her business. Seller has agreed, pursuant to the sale, to sign a covenant not to compete. In tax terms, is your client better off if more of the monetary consideration is allocated to the covenant not to compete, or less?

2. Today, one must consult § 1060 when Williams v. McGowan issues arise.

H. SALE OF A PATENT

Code § 1235

GILSON v. COMMISSIONER

United States Tax Court.
T.C. Memo. 1984–447.

PARKER, JUDGE:

The sole issue is whether payments that petitioner Channing W. Gilson received during the years in issue constituted compensation for services, taxable as ordinary income, or payments for all substantial rights to patents, qualifying for capital gains treatment under section 1235.

FINDINGS OF FACT

Since 1951, petitioner Channing W. Gilson (hereinafter petitioner) has been a professional inventor of industrial designs, designing the external surfaces of manufactured articles so that these articles are both aesthetically pleasing and easier to use. Petitioner has won numerous awards for the excellence of his industrial designs.

During the years in issue, petitioner conducted his business as a sole proprietor under the name 'Channing Wallace Gilson, Industrial Design.' During these years, petitioner had a few large clients such as Hughes Aircraft, North American Rockwell, and Bell & Howell and many clients that were smaller manufacturing companies. During the years in issue, petitioner had 82 contracts with 53 different clients. Petitioner was an independent contractor and not an employee of any of his clients.

Typically, a potential client would contact petitioner proposing that petitioner undertake the industrial design of a new product the client had developed and hoped to manufacture and market. Next, petitioner would meet with the client's management and engineering personnel at the client's plant or office to be shown the client's new development or research work and to discuss with the client its product design requirements. Petitioner was never retained to make drawings of a design the client had already created but was always retained to create a new and original design. Petitioner would then return to his office and draw up a letter outlining the steps involved in completing an industrial design and proposing a flat fee or price for the design. Petitioner set his fees or prices on the basis of a number of factors, including the difficulty involved in completing the design, the budget of the client (if known to petitioner), petitioner's knowledge of the customer's size and ability to pay, and, occasionally, petitioner's estimate of possible bids by his competitors. Prior to the years in issue, petitioner had charged his clients by the hour. However, he abandoned that practice because he found that his customers were not interested in the number of hours he expended and instead wanted a design for a flat fee.

Typically, a client would accept petitioner's proposal through a form purchase order or form contract the client had prepared. Some of the form purchase orders or form contracts described petitioner's contractual obligation as 'industrial design work,' 'industrial design services,' 'consulting services,' or similar terms suggesting performance of services. Other contracts referred to 'Industrial Design,' 'Cost of Design,' or similar terms suggesting the sale of designs. Some of the contracts also reproduced part of petitioner's proposal letter. A few of petitioner's design contracts during these years were oral.

Following the acceptance of his proposal, petitioner would carefully research the appearance of products manufactured by the client's competitors. Petitioner maintained an extensive library of catalogs, professional and trade magazines, directories, and advertising materials regarding products and product designs that he used to ascertain competing products and prior art. Petitioner's clients also furnished him with data about their competitors' products. Petitioner would also research possible materials for use in the finished product. After completing his research, petitioner would prepare rough sketches of two or three different design proposals and would present the drawings at a meeting with the client's engineering, management, and sales personnel. The client's representatives would screen the proposals and usually discard one or more of the proposed designs.

Following this meeting, petitioner would return to his office and prepare a more detailed design proposal. Petitioner would then take the drawings of his revised proposal to another meeting with his client's representatives. The number of meetings and proposed revisions varied from client to client. These meetings with the clients, however, represented only a small part of the time required to create the design. Eventually, petitioner would prepare and present to the client the final, detailed design drawings from which the client's engineers could make production drawings. Petitioner would usually receive his fee in installments as he presented design drawings to the client. Petitioner would receive the final installment upon his completion of the project by delivery of the final design drawings to the client. Petitioner was not required to account to his clients for the time he spent on a design.

The industrial designs petitioner created for his clients were unique, innovative, attractive, and functional, and were quite different from the designs of his clients' competitors. Petitioner had many satisfied clients who returned to him for additional projects. Generally, petitioner's clients were very pleased with his designs. Each of the designs represented petitioner's own creative effort; the designers petitioner employed merely made more detailed drawings of the designs petitioner himself conceived. Many of the articles or products for which petitioner created designs were never produced or marketed by the clients for various business reasons unrelated to the quality of petitioner's designs.

Designs like those created by petitioner in this case may be patented if they are new, original, and ornamental. Determination of this question involves examination of existing design patents and of unpatented prior art more than one year old. A patent attorney advising a client on patentability would normally examine (or have an agent examine) the records of issued patents at the U.S. Patent & Trademark Office (Patent Office). Because of some uncertainty over prior art, even with a search at the Patent Office, a patent attorney would always hedge or qualify his advice to his client concerning the patentability of a design. The only way to be absolutely certain that a design is patentable is to submit a patent application and await acceptance or rejection. However, the patent attorney could examine prior art in many ways—he could examine (or have an agent examine) a library of various catalogs, professional and trade magazines, directories, and advertising materials at the Patent Office, or his own library of such materials, or rely upon the inventor-client's examination of the client's own library of such prior art reference materials. If a patent attorney or his inventor-client had an adequate library covering prior art, the attorney might qualifiedly advise that a design was patentable without a formal search at the Patent Office. A highly qualified professional inventor of industrial designs with over 30 years' experience in the field, such as petitioner, could reasonably search prior art as petitioner did in this case.

Many owners of patentable designs will make a business decision not to patent their designs, for various reasons. Between 1955 and 1978, petitioner had been issued 21 design patents, all of which he assigned. One of them was the design patent for a smoke detector that petitioner created under one of the contracts involved in this case; that smoke detector was manufactured and marketed. Petitioner has never had an application for a design patent denied. None of petitioner's designs under the contracts here in issue have ever been claimed to have infringed any patented design belonging to someone else.

 * * *

Petitioner generally would represent to each client that his design would be unique and patentable. Generally, petitioner's clients considered the patentability of the designs as an important and valuable aspect of their contracts with petitioner. Many clients would not have contracted with petitioner had he not relinquished his rights to patent his designs. The clients wanted the right to obtain the design patent because such right could become quite important in the event of business success in manufacturing and marketing the article or product. Petitioner's clients relied upon petitioner to create new and unique designs that did not imitate competitors' designs.

Out of the 82 design contracts during the years in issue, only one or two of petitioner's designs were ultimately patented. Petitioner's clients generally declined to seek patents for petitioner's designs for various business reasons unrelated to the designs themselves. These business reasons included a decision not to place the product or article into production because of the expense of tooling up for production or because of some engineering defect in the article itself, a business judgment that the small market for the product did not justify the cost, a business judgment that the minimal protection afforded by the design patent would not outweigh the cost of obtaining the patent, or a business judgment that a product's useful commercial life would be exhausted before a patent could be obtained.

OPINION

Section 1235 provides that a transfer of property consisting of all substantial rights to a patent by the person who created the property is treated as a sale or exchange of a capital asset, resulting in long-term capital gains treatment. Petitioner argues that the amounts he received under his 82 design contracts during 1971 through 1974 qualified for the special capital gains rule of section 1235. Respondent contends that the payments were merely compensation for petitioner's services, taxable as ordinary income under section 61(a)(1).

It is clear that petitioner's various contracts transferred whatever rights he possessed in the various designs. We do not accept respondent's argument that petitioner has not transferred all substantial rights to patents within the meaning of section 1235. It is largely irrelevant that out of the 82 separate contracts, only one or two of petitioner's designs were actually patented. Section 1235 does not require that a patent exist at the time of the transfer, nor even that a patent application be filed.

Although respondent seems to argue that petitioner's designs were not patentable, the record shows and the Court has found as a fact that they were. * * *

Nor do we think that petitioner's clients' nearly uniform choice not to obtain design patents indicates a lack of patentability. His clients' decisions represented their business judgments based on many factors—the fact that few of the articles were actually manufactured, the short commercial life of many of the articles that were produced, the minimal and uncertain protection afforded by design patents, and the length of time necessary to obtain a patent. These business decisions were wholly unrelated to the quality of petitioner's designs or their patentability. Respondent's implicit definition of patentability would require at least a patent application in every case, if not actual issuance of a patent. This is not the law. It is undisputed that petitioner's designs were unique, extremely attractive, and innovative. It is also notable that petitioner has never been refused a design patent and that none of his designs under the contracts here in issue has ever given rise to a claim of infringement upon another's design patent. Based on all of the facts in this case, we are convinced that petitioner's designs were patentable.

Respondent's main argument is that petitioner was merely 'hired to invent' the various designs. * * *This 'hired to invent' rule is drawn from substantive patent law rules involving the respective rights of employer and employee to patentable inventions. The consequence of finding that an employee is 'hired to invent' is that the patent rights to the invention belong to the employer, so that the employee has no patent rights to transfer for tax purposes, and the payments merely represent compensation for the services he has contracted to perform.

This rule that an employer is the equitable owner of the invention his employee has been specifically engaged to produce depends on the existence of an employment relationship. The rule does not apply outside of an employment relationship, so that an independent contractor, although specifically engaged to create a design or invention, is still the owner of the design or invention and the patent rights. Petitioner was not an employee of any of his clients but was a self-employed independent contractor. Accordingly, petitioner did not lose his patent rights in his designs simply because he contracted with his clients to create those designs.

* * *

The determinative question is whether the payments petitioner received under his design contracts constituted consideration for his transfer of all substantial rights to his patentable designs or consideration for the performance of personal services. This is a factual question. Resolving this factual issue is difficult because 'an invention is merely the fruit of the inventor's labor, and ... payment for the invention itself necessarily compensates the inventor for his services in creating the 'invention.' We are persuaded, however, and have found as a fact, that petitioner's customers paid him for his patentable designs, not for his services.

The objective of petitioner's clients in contracting with him was to obtain designs for their products. Under the terms of the design contracts, petitioner became entitled to his fees only as he produced and delivered designs. If he did not produce a design, he was NOT entitled to payment. By contrast, a person hired for his services generally gets paid whether or not his services produce anything useful.

* * *

We do not agree with respondent that petitioner's receipt of fixed lump sum fees rather than installment payments based on sales (e.g., royalties) requires a finding that petitioner's design fees represented personal service compensation. One of the goals of section 1235 was to eliminate the uncertainty over the tax consequences to inventors that flowed from different kinds of payments (e.g., lump sum, installments of a fixed sum, or royalties based on use). Although in some circumstances lump sum fees might tend to indicate compensation to employees for services, that fact has no bearing in this case. * * *

We likewise disagree with respondent's argument that capital gains treatment under section 1235 depends upon the stage of completion of the invention at the time the rights thereto are transferred. Such analysis confuses the existence of rights to be transferred with the attribution of payments received by the inventor either to those property rights or to the inventor's services. The amount of the inventor's personal labor in creating his invention is at least the same when he arranges for its sale beforehand as when he invents it before he looks for a buyer. Indeed, where as here, the inventor knew what his customer wanted, the amount of personal labor may well be LESS than when an inventor struggles to create a new product and then struggles to sell it. Also with an industrial design, there must first be an article of manufacture or product that requires a design. There is no requirement that petitioner must invent both the article and its industrial design. At most, the stage of completion is but one of many factors to consider in making our factual determination.

* * *

Underlying respondent's position seems to be a policy argument that petitioner (and others like him) should not be allowed long term capital gains treatment for income that has such a strong element of personal labor. That is a decision for Congress and not this Court. The present embodiment of Congressional policy is clear—section 1235 provides long term capital gains treatment for the transfer of a property right attributable in large part to a taxpayer's personal skill, knowledge, and labor. While the traditional lone inventor like Edison or Bell may be an endangered species, it is primarily the lone inventor for whose benefit Congress intended section 1235. This section applies only to a 'holder'—the person whose efforts created the property or a person who purchased the property from the inventor prior to its reduction to practice. Section 1235 substantially liberalized the capital gains rules for inventors by eliminating tax distinctions based on the manner of payment, by eradicating disparate treatment of amateur and professional inventors, and by repealing the holding period requirement. Part of Congress' broad remedial purpose in enacting section 1235 was to 'provide an incentive to inventors to contribute to the welfare of the Nation.' S. Rept. No. 1622, 83d Cong., 2d Sess. 439 (1954); Petitioner, a self-employed professional inventor, is precisely the sort of person for whom the benefits of section 1235 were intended. Petitioner's designs were patentable and were his to transfer. Petitioner transferred them to his clients and the payments he received were in consideration of these transfers of property. Petitioner is entitled to the benefits of section 1235.

I. RECAPTURE

Code: § 1245

Recall that the depreciation adjustments to basis ensures that the gains and losses on sale net out with the depreciation deductions to arrive at true economic appreciation or depreciation. See supra at 230. This netting process, however, only works if the income and the deductions are truly comparable. In the case of § 1231 property, it is possible for the depreciation deductions to be ordinary, with a dollar in deductions saving perhaps 35 cents in taxes, while the gain on sale is capital, taxed at perhaps 20 cents per dollar. This apples and oranges problem is addressed by the depreciation recapture rules of §§ 1245 and 1250. Section 1245, the more broadly applicable of the two, recaptures all depreciation. Section 1250 has limited application since 1986.

Problem

John purchased a machine tool for $100,000. He used it for three years, and properly took depreciation deductions of $60,000. He then sold it for $110,000. Compute his ordinary income and capital gain.

Chapter VIII

Mixed Personal and Business, Investment Deductions

■ ■ ■

A Tale of Two Macaroon Sellers

Floyd and Gerard go into the cookie business, though in very different ways. Floyd is determined to produce the world's best coconut macaroon, even though he, personally, is allergic to coconut. After diligent research, he determines that the finest coconuts in the world are located in an almost inaccessible corner of South America. He buys them, at considerable expense. Similarly, he spares no expense on the other necessary ingredients and machinery. Unfortunately, there does not appear to be a market demand for such extravagantly delicious coconut macaroons. After a year, Floyd's income statement is:

Gross Sales	$ 10,000
Less: Expenses	− $150,000
Profit/(Loss)	($140,000)

Gerard also sells coconut macaroons. He doesn't give a hoot about quality, and buys them from the cheapest supplier (day-old whenever possible). However, he cares a great deal about location (his own, that is). Gerard travels all around the world to sell his cookies. He always flies first class, and stays in the finest hotels. His decisions on where to sell his cookies are based not on where he'll make the most profit, but on where he'd like to be at that time of year. After one year of operation, his income statement looks exactly like Floyd's[a].

Okay, so both of them go bankrupt. But who had more fun?

The Moral of the Tale

In Chapter 2, it says:

We do not need the IRS to police bad business decisions. The market will do that. Incurring larger business expenses than necessary will

---

a. You might want to consider the *Dreicer* case, *infra*.

354

mean that the taxpayer makes less profit. Isn't that punishment enough?

That analysis works fine when the decision in question is whether to buy a $5,000 drill press or a $10,000 drill press for the business workshop. There is no personal pleasure in owning a glitzier drill press. The only reason to spend more on a drill press is if it will generate more profit.

Gerard's travel expenses are in a different category. They have a value to Gerard over and above their potential for increasing his profit. They, unlike the glitzier drill press, can give Gerard personal pleasure, in and of themselves.

And there's the rub. We don't have to worry about drill presses, because taxpayers have only one motive for buying them—to increase profits. We do have to worry about travel expenses, because they are in the category of mixed motive expenses. People incur mixed motive expenses for two reasons—because they will help them succeed in business, and because they are fun. If the first motive is predominant, then the expenditure should be deductible. If the second motive is predominant, then they should not be. But how can you tell?

A Caveat

In our business lives, most of us are employed by others. As employees, when we incur the types of expenditures covered in this chapter, we are often reimbursed by our employers. If we are in fact reimbursed, then there is ultimately no out-of-pocket cost, and hence no net deduction for us. Hopefully, there is no income either. Therefore, the issues raised in this Chapter will generally apply either to self-employed persons, or to employees whose expenses are unreimbursed. You might, however, want to consider the Illustrative Problem *infra* at 546 for some other scheming possibilities.

A. TRAVEL, MEALS, ENTERTAINMENT

Code: §§ 162(a)(2); 274(a), (c), (d), (e), (g), (h), (k), (*l*), (m), and especially (n); 67(a), (b)

Regulations: §§ 1.162–2; 1.274–1, 1.274–2, 1.274–4, 1.274–5T

1. TRAVEL

(a) Really Short Trips—Commuting

INTRODUCTORY PROBLEM

Winona lives right across the street from her workplace. She decides that she prefers less smog and more grass, and moves to a suburb 20 miles away. What is the proximate cause of her commuting expenses—personal or business?

Xavieria has no job, and lives in the suburbs. She takes a job downtown. What is the proximate cause of her commuting expenses—personal or business?

In Winona's case, the proximate cause of her commute was personal. In Xavieria's case, it was business. Clearly, in all cases, there are both business and personal reasons for commuting expenses. But for the job, there would be no commute. Yet, but for the decision to live some distance from the workplace, there would be no commute.

Given the mixed motive, we could have allowed deductions for commuting always, sometimes, or never. Except for some rare instances, we have chosen "never." For a different choice, consider the Commuter Aid and Relief for Suburbs (CARS) Act, proposed, but not yet adopted, in 2008. CARS would have added a new § 224:

SEC. 224.   CERTAIN COMMUTING EXPENSES.

(a) in General—In the case of an individual, there shall be allowed as a deduction an amount equal to the applicable percentage of the amount paid or incurred by the taxpayer during the table year for qualified commuting expenses of the taxpayer, his spouse, and dependents.

(b) Applicable Percentage—For purposes of this section—

(1) IN GENERAL—The term 'applicable percentage' means, with respect to the expenses of any individual in connection with a round-trip commute of a certain number of miles, the percentage determined in accordance with the following table:

In the case of a round-trip commute of:	The applicable percentage is:
Less than 10 miles	—10 percent
At least 10 miles, but not greater Than 15 miles	—30 percent
At least 15 miles, but not greater Than 25 miles	—50 percent
At least 25 miles	—75 percent.

(2) SPECIAL RULE FOR HIGH GAS MILEAGE VEHICLES AND CAR-POOLERS—Notwithstanding paragraph

(1), the applicable percentage shall be 100 percent with respect to any round-trip commute which is made—

(A) in a motor vehicle which has a gasoline equivalent fuel efficiency of more than 40 miles per gallon, or

(B) in a motor vehicle while carrying carpooling passengers.

(c) Definitions Related to Commuting—For purposes of this section—

(1) QUALIFIED COMMUTING EXPENSES—The term 'qualified commuting expenses' means reasonable expenses paid or incurred for transportation in connection with travel between an individual's residence and place of employment.

(2) ROUND–TRIP COMMUTE—The term 'round trip commute' means the reasonable driving distance from an individual's residence to such individual's place of employment and back to such residence.

* * *

Which option—current law or the CARS proposal, is more fair? Which is more consistent with government policy? Remember—it was the government that created the interstate highway system, which created suburbs and commuting in the first place.

* * *

Homes and Tax Homes

In Commissioner v. Flowers, 326 U.S. 465, 66 S.Ct. 250, 90 L.Ed. 203 (1946), the taxpayer was a lawyer for the Gulf, Mobile & Ohio Railroad in Mobile, Alabama. Mr. Flowers' office was in Mobile, but his home was in Jackson, Mississippi. He wanted to deduct the costs of transportation to and from Mobile and his meal and lodging expenses in Mobile. He lost.

The Court laid down three conditions for a traveling expense deduction under § 162(a)(2):

(1) The expense must be a reasonable and necessary traveling expense, as that term is generally understood—including such items as transportation fares and food and lodging expenses incurred while traveling.

(2) The expense must be incurred "while away from home."

(3) The expense must be incurred in pursuit of business. This means that there must be a direct connection between the expenditure and the carrying on of the trade or business of the taxpayer or of his employer. Moreover, such an expenditure must be necessary or appropriate to the development and pursuit of the business or trade.

326 U.S. at 470.

There was, and is, a dispute about the meaning of the word "home" in § 162(a)(2). The IRS thinks it means "principal place of business," often called "tax home."[b] Some circuits, however, think that "home" is where you live.[c]

Mr. Flowers would have lost under either definition. Under the IRS "tax home" concept, Flowers' home was in Mobile. Therefore, while he was in Mobile, he was not "away from home," and did not satisfy the second condition for a traveling expense deduction.

Under the "home is where you live" definition, Flowers' home was in Jackson. Therefore, when he was in Mobile, he was "away from home," and satisfied the second condition. However, he failed the third. His

---

b. *See, e.g.*, Rev. Rul. 93–86, *infra*.

c. *See, e.g.*, Six v. United States, 450 F.2d 66 (2d Cir.1971) [whether Ethel Merman moved her home from California to New York during the run of "Gypsy"].

traveling expenses were not caused by his business; rather, they were caused by his personal preference to live in Jackson, rather than Mobile.

Extreme Commuting

GREEN v. COMMISSIONER

United States Tax Court, 1980.
74 T.C. 1229.

BRUCE, JUDGE:

* * * In 1976, petitioner had income in the form of wages from Wiggins, Inc., and The Shirt Shop, both in Pensacola, Fla., in the amounts of $4,080.59 and $368.50, respectively. However, petitioner's primary source of income was from her activity as a blood plasma donor to Serologicals, Inc., of Pensacola (hereinafter the lab), an activity she has been engaged in for approximately 7 years.

By a process known as plasmapheresis, a pint of whole blood is removed from the arm of a blood plasma donor, such as petitioner. From this whole blood, the plasma is centrifugally removed and the remaining red cells are returned to the donor's body. The process is repeated. Generally, two bleeds produce one pint of plasma. Petitioner is paid for her donations by the pint.

Petitioner, who has that rare blood type known as AB negative, reported gross receipts of $7,170 from her donor activity in 1976. This amount consisted of $6,695 in donor "commissions" and $475 in travel allowances, paid at a rate of $5 per trip. Offsetting these gross receipts, petitioner claimed related business-expense deductions totaling $2,355 of which only the amount of $132 was allowed by respondent in his notice of deficiency as shown below:

Expenses	Claimed	Allowed
Legal and professional fees	$20	$20
Medical insurance	150	0
Special drugs	260	112
High protein diet foods	780	0
Travel	475	0
Depletion	670	0
Total	2,355	132

* * *

Opinion

* * * Upon the facts, we find that petitioner was in the trade or business of selling blood plasma. Therefore, to be allowable, the deductions claimed by petitioner must be substantiated as "ordinary and necessary expenses paid or incurred during the taxable year in carrying on" her activity as a seller of blood plasma. § 162. * * *

Next, petitioner claimed a deduction for "travel" in the amount of reimbursement she received from the lab for 95 trips at $5 each, or $475. Petitioner concedes that the $475 was income to her for 1976, but contends that she was transporting her product of blood plasma to the lab for sale and should be allowed to deduct the same amount. Respondent disallowed the entire amount as personal commuting expenses. Once again, the unusual situation presented by the instant set of facts requires a close examination of the distinction between business expenses, which are deductible, and personal expenses, which are not. Commuting expenses are clearly personal expenses and not deductible. Commissioner v. Flowers, 326 U.S. 465 (1946). However, petitioner did not "commute" to the lab. Instead, she made one or two trips each week to the lab to sell her product of blood plasma. The nature of her product was such that she could not transport it to market without her accompanying it. Of necessity, she had to accompany the blood plasma to the lab. Unique to this situation, petitioner was the container in which her product was transported to market. Had she been able to extract the plasma at home and transport it to the lab without her being present, such shipping expenses would have been deductible as selling expenses. Cf. § 1.61–3(a), 1.162–1(a), Income Tax Regs. Therefore, petitioner's trips to and from the lab were solely for business purposes, not for her personal comfort or convenience, and a deduction of $475 will be allowed for those trips made in 1976. * * *

Decision will be entered under Rule 155.

A Limerick

For commuting you may not deduct.

Try and you'll be out of luck.

But sell your blood fluid

While you can renew it

And claim that your body's a truck.

NOTE: OTHER EXAMPLES OF EXTREME COMMUTING

1. Weinzimer v. Commissioner, 1958 WL 796. Taxpayer was traumatized in an automobile accident, and subsequently ordered by his doctor to commute by automobile to work as emotional therapy. Held: commuting was deductible as a medical expense.

2. Revenue Ruling 75–380, 1975–2 C.B. 59, provides that if (a) transportation costs are incurred in addition to the ordinary, nondeductible commuting expenses, and (b) these costs are solely attributable to the necessity of transporting work implements to and from the job site, then those additional costs will be deductible. See the early case of Rice v. Riddell, 179 F.Supp. 576 (D.Cal.1959), in which the taxpayer could not possibly have transported either his tuba or his bass violin to work in available public transportation.

3. McCabe v. Commissioner, 688 F.2d 102 (2d Cir.1982). McCabe was a New York City policeman who lived in Suffern, New York. He was required to

carry his service revolver at all times when he was within the New York City limits. Ample public transportation was available between Suffern and New York City, provided by the Short Line Bus Company. Pursuant to New York City Regulations, Mr. McCabe would have been required to be carrying his service revolver when the bus crossed the New York City line.

The Short Line Bus took the most direct route from Suffern to New York City, which went through New Jersey. In New Jersey, passengers are not allowed to carry firearms on public transportation without a gun permit. New Jersey would not give McCabe a permit. Accordingly, McCabe commuted by personal automobile. The court held that McCabe could not deduct the additional expenses of commuting by automobile, because the expense was incurred primarily due to his personal decision to live in Suffern, New York.

4. In 1985, IRS promulgated proposed regulations to § 132, the new fringe benefits statute (see Chapter 3, *supra*). IRS decided that, when police personnel drove their squad cars home at the end of their shifts, they were commuting. Since these commuting vehicles were being provided without charge by their employers, and since commuting is nondeductible, IRS reasoned that the police would have to declare the value of each day's commute as taxable income. For the reaction of law enforcement personnel, *see* Newman, *Cops and Robbers (Which are Which?)*, 36 Tax Notes 813 (Aug. 24, 1987).

5. For more medical commuting, *see Weary v. Commissioner, infra* at Chapter 10.

(b) Medium Trips

UNITED STATES v. CORRELL

Supreme Court of the United States, 1967.
389 U.S. 299, 88 S.Ct. 445, 19 L.Ed.2d 537.

MR. JUSTICE STEWART delivered the opinion of the Court.

The Commissioner of Internal Revenue has long maintained that a taxpayer traveling on business may deduct the cost of his meals only if his trip requires him to stop for sleep or rest. The question presented here is the validity of that rule.

The respondent in this case was a traveling salesman for a wholesale grocery company in Tennessee. He customarily left home early in the morning, ate breakfast and lunch on the road, and returned home in time for dinner. In his income tax returns for 1960 and 1961, he deducted the cost of his morning and noon meals as "traveling expenses" incurred in the pursuit of his business "while away from home" under § 162(a)(2). Because the respondent's daily trips required neither sleep nor rest, the Commissioner disallowed the deductions, ruling that the cost of the respondent's meals was a "personal, living" expense under § 262 rather than a travel expense under § 162(a)(2). The respondent paid the tax, sued for a refund in the District Court, and there received a favorable jury verdict. The Court of Appeals for the Sixth Circuit affirmed, holding that the Commissioner's sleep or rest rule is not "a valid regulation under the present statute." In order to resolve a conflict among the circuits on this recurring question of federal income tax administration, we granted certiorari. * * *[6],[7]

In resolving that problem, the Commissioner has avoided the wasteful litigation and continuing uncertainty that would inevitably accompany any purely case-by-case approach to the question of whether a particular taxpayer was "away from home" on a particular day. Rather than requiring "every meal-purchasing taxpayer to take pot luck in the courts," the Commissioner has consistently construed travel "away from home" to exclude all trips requiring neither sleep nor rest, regardless of how many cities a given trip may have touched,[11] how many miles it may have covered,[12] or how many hours it may have consumed.[13] By so interpreting the statutory phrase, the Commissioner has achieved not only ease and certainty of application but also substantial fairness, for the sleep or rest rule places all one-day travelers on a similar tax footing, rather than discriminating against intracity travelers and commuters, who of course cannot deduct the cost of the meals they eat on the road.

Any rule in this area must make some rather arbitrary distinctions,[14] but at least the sleep or rest rule avoids the obvious inequity of permitting the New Yorker who makes a quick trip to Washington and back, missing neither his breakfast nor his dinner at home, to deduct the cost of his lunch merely because he covers more miles than the salesman who travels locally and must finance all his meals without the help of the Federal

---

6. Prior to the enactment in 1921 of what is now § 162(a)(2), the Commissioner had promulgated a regulation allowing a deduction for the cost of meals and lodging away from home, but only to the extent that this cost exceeded "any expenditures ordinarily required for such purposes when at home." Despite its logical appeal, the regulation proved so difficult to administer that the Treasury Department asked Congress to grant a deduction for the "entire amount" of such meal and lodging expenditures. Accordingly, § 214(a)(1) of the Revenue Act of 1921, for the first time included the language that later became § 162(a)(2). * * * The section was amended in a respect not here relevant by the Revenue Act of 1962.

7. Because § 262 makes "personal, living, or family expenses" nondeductible, * * *, the taxpayer whose business requires no travel cannot ordinarily deduct the cost of the lunch he eats away from home. But the taxpayer who can bring himself within the reach of § 162(a)(2) may deduct what he spends on his noontime meal although it costs him no more, and relates no more closely to his business, than does the lunch consumed by his less mobile counterpart.

11. The respondent lived in Fountain City, Tennessee, some 45 miles from his employer's place of business in Morristown. His territory included restaurants in the cities of Madisonville, Engelwood, Etowah, Athens, Sweetwater, Lake City, Caryville, Jacksboro, La Follette, and Jellico, all in eastern Tennessee.

12. The respondent seldom traveled farther than 55 miles from his home, but he ordinarily drove a total of 150 to 175 miles daily.

13. The respondent's employer required him to be in his sales territory at the start of the business day. To do so, he had to leave Fountain City at about 5 a.m. He usually finished his daily schedule by 4 p.m., transmitted his orders to Morristown, and returned home by 5:30 p.m.

14. The rules proposed by the respondent and by the two amici curiae filing briefs on his behalf are not exceptional in this regard. Thus, for example, the respondent suggests that § 162(a)(2) be construed to cover those taxpayers who travel outside their "own home town," or outside "the greater * * * metropolitan area" where they reside. One amicus stresses the number of "hours spent and miles traveled away from the taxpayer's principal post of duty," suggesting that some emphasis should also be placed upon the number of meals consumed by the taxpayer "outside the general area of his home."

Treasury. And the Commissioner's rule surely makes more sense than one which would allow the respondent in this case to deduct the cost of his breakfast and lunch simply because he spends a greater percentage of his time at the wheel than the commuter who eats breakfast on his way to work and lunch a block from his office.

The Court of Appeals nonetheless found in the "plain language of the statute" an insuperable obstacle to the Commissioner's construction. We disagree. The language of the statute—"meals and lodging * * * away from home"—is obviously not self-defining. And to the extent that the words chosen by Congress cut in either direction, they tend to support rather than defeat the Commissioner's position, for the statute speaks of "meals and lodging" as a unit, suggesting—at least arguably—that Congress contemplated a deduction for the cost of meals only where the travel in question involves lodging as well. Ordinarily, at least, only the taxpayer who finds it necessary to stop for sleep or rest incurs significantly higher living expenses as a direct result of his business travel,[18] and Congress might well have thought that only taxpayer in that category should be permitted to deduct their living expenses while on the road. In any event, Congress certainly recognized, when it promulgated § 162(a)(2), that the Commissioner had so understood its statutory predecessor. This case thus comes within the settled principle that "Treasury regulations and interpretations long continued without substantial change, applying to unamended or substantially reenacted statutes, are deemed to have received congressional approval and have the effect of law."

     * * *

Reversed.

MR. JUSTICE MARSHALL took no part in the consideration or decision of this case.

MR. JUSTICE DOUGLAS, with whom MR. JUSTICE BLACK and MR. JUSTICE FORTAS CONCUR, DISSENTING.

The statutory words "while away from home," may not in my view be shrunken to "overnight" by administrative construction or regulations. "Overnight" injects a time element in testing deductibility, while the statute speaks only in terms of geography. As stated by the Court of Appeals: "In an era of supersonic travel, the time factor is hardly relevant to the question of whether or not travel and meal expenses are related to the taxpayer's business and cannot be the basis of a valid regulation under the present statute."

I would affirm the judgment below.

---

18. * * * One Amicus curiae brief filed in this case asserts that "those who travel considerable distances such as (on) a one-day jet trip between New York and Chicago" spend more for "comparable meals (than) those who remain at their home base" and urges that all who travel "substantial distances" should therefore be permitted to deduct the entire cost of their meals. It may be that eating at a restaurant costs more than eating at home, but it cannot seriously be suggested that a taxpayer's bill at a restaurant mysteriously reflects the distance he has traveled to get there.

NOTE

In Bissonnette v. Commissioner, 127 T.C. 124 (2006), the taxpayer was a ferryboat captain. During the off-peak season, the ferry left Seattle at around 8:00 a.m. and arrived in Victoria, B.C. at around 11:00 a.m. It then left Victoria around 5:30 p.m. and arrived back in Seattle at around 9:00 p.m. During the six-hour layover, the passengers explored Victoria.

The employer provided a four-bedroom condominium in Victoria for Bissonnette and his crew for rest and relaxation during the layover. However, since the crew was "young and noisy," Bissonnette avoided the condo. Instead, he would typically have lunch, swim for a half hour, and then return to the ferry to sleep for four hours on a cot which he stored on board. The court held that the sleep or rest rule was satisfied. Therefore, the taxpayer was away from home while in Victoria, and his meals and incidental expenses were deductible.

(c) Really Long Trips

REVENUE RULING 93–86
1993–2 C.B. 71.

Issue

What effect does the 1–year limitation on temporary travel, as added by section 1938 of the Energy Policy Act of 1992 have on the deductibility of away from home travel expenses under section 162(a)(2) of the Internal Revenue Code?

Facts

Situation 1.   Taxpayer A is regularly employed in city CI–1. In 1993, A accepted work in city CI–2, which is 250 miles from CI–1. A realistically expected the work in CI–2 to be completed in 6 months and planned to return to CI–1 at that time. In fact, the employment lasted 10 months, after which time A returned to CI–1.

Situation 2.   The facts are the same as in Situation 1, except that Taxpayer B realistically expected the work in CI–2 to be completed in 18 months, but in fact it was completed in 10 months.

Situation 3.   The facts are the same as in Situation 1, except that Taxpayer C realistically expected the work in CI–2 to be completed in 9 months. After 8 months, however, C was asked to remain for 7 more months (for a total actual stay of 15 months).

Law and Analysis

* * *

A taxpayer's "home" for purposes of section 162(a)(2) of the Code is generally considered to be located at (1) the taxpayer's regular or principal (if more than one regular) place of business, or (2) if the taxpayer has no regular or principal place of business, then at the taxpayer's regular place of abode in a real and substantial sense. If a taxpayer comes within neither category (1) nor category (2), the taxpayer is considered to be an itinerant whose "home" is wherever the taxpayer happens to work.

Travel expenses paid or incurred in connection with an indefinite or permanent work assignment are generally nondeductible. Travel expenses paid or incurred in connection with a temporary work assignment away from home are deductible under section 162(a)(2) of the Code. The courts and the Service have held that employment is temporary for this purpose only if its termination can be foreseen within a reasonably short period of time.

Employment that is initially temporary may become indefinite due to changed circumstances. In Rev. Rul. 73–578, a citizen of a foreign country comes to the U.S. under a 6–month nonimmigrant visa to work for a U.S. employer, intending to resume regular employment in the foreign country after this period. After 4 months, however, the individual agrees to continue the employment for an additional 14 months. Rev. Rul. 73–578 holds that the individual may deduct ordinary and necessary travel expenses paid or incurred during the first 4 months of the employment. However, the individual may not deduct travel expenses paid or incurred thereafter, unless the expenses are paid or incurred in connection with temporary employment away from the location of the individual's regular employment with the U.S. employer.

Revenue Ruling 83–82, 1983–1 C.B. 45, provides that, for purposes of the deduction for travel expenses under § 162(a)(2) of the Code, if the taxpayer anticipates employment away from home to last less than 1 year, then all the facts and circumstances are considered to determine whether such employment is temporary. If the taxpayer anticipates employment to last (and it does in fact last) between 1 and 2 years, Rev. Rul. 83–82 provides a rebuttable presumption that the employment is indefinite. The taxpayer may rebut the presumption by demonstrating certain objective factors set forth in the revenue ruling. For employment with an anticipated or actual stay of 2 years or more, Rev. Rul. 83–82 holds that such employment is indefinite, regardless of any other facts or circumstances. All the factual situations in Rev. Rul. 83–82 involve employment in a single location for more than 1 year.

Section 1938 of the Energy Policy Act of 1992 amended § 162(a)(2) of the Code to provide that a taxpayer shall not be treated as being temporarily away from home during any period of employment if such period exceeds 1 year. This amendment applies to any period of employment in a single location if such period exceeds 1 year. Thus, § 162(a)(2), as amended, eliminates the rebuttable presumption category under Rev. Rul. 83–82 for employment lasting between 1 and 2 years, and shortens the 2–year limit under that ruling to 1 year. The amendment is effective for costs paid or incurred after December 31, 1992.

Accordingly, if employment away from home in a single location is realistically expected to last (and does in fact last) for 1 year or less, the employment will be treated as temporary in the absence of facts and circumstances indicating otherwise. If employment away from home in a single location is realistically expected to last for more than 1 year or there is no realistic expectation that the employment will last for 1 year or less, the employment will be treated as indefinite, regardless of whether it actually exceeds 1 year. If employment away from home in a single location initially is realistically expected to last for 1 year or less, but at some later date the employment is realistically expected to exceed 1 year that employment will be treated as temporary (in the absence of facts and circumstances indicating otherwise) until the date that the taxpayer's realistic expectation changes.

In Situation 1, A realistically expected that the work in CI–2 would last only 6 months, and it did in fact last less than 1 year. Because A had always intended to return to CI–1 at the end of A's employment in CI–2, the CI–2 employment is temporary. Thus, A's travel expenses paid or incurred in CI–2 are deductible.

In Situation 2, B's employment in CI–2 is indefinite because B realistically expected that the work in CI–2 would last longer than 1 year, even though it actually lasted less than 1 year. Thus, B's travel expenses paid or incurred in CI–2 are nondeductible.

In Situation 3, C at first realistically expected that the work in CI–2 would last only 9 months. However, due to changed circumstances occurring after 8 months, it was no longer realistic for C to expect that the employment in CI–2 would last for 1 year or less. Therefore, C's employment in CI–2 is temporary for 8 months, and indefinite for the remaining 7 months. Thus, C's travel expenses paid or incurred in CI–2 during the first 8 months are deductible, but C's travel expenses paid or incurred thereafter are nondeductible.

Holding

Under § 162(a)(2) of the Code, as amended by the Energy Policy Act of 1992, if employment away from home in a single location is realistically expected to last (and does in fact last) for 1 year or less, the employment is temporary in the absence of facts and circumstances indicating otherwise. If employment away from home in a single location is realistically expected to last for more than 1 year or there is no realistic expectation that the employment will last for 1 year or less, the employment is indefinite, regardless of whether it actually exceeds 1 year. If employment away from home in a single location initially is realistically expected to last for 1 year or less, but at some later date the employment is realistically expected to exceed 1 year, that employment will be treated as temporary (in the absence of facts and circumstances indicating otherwise) until the date that the taxpayer's realistic expectation changes.

QUESTION

Does the Revenue Ruling reflect the words of the statute?

A Short Treatise on Homelessness

Revenue Ruling 93–86 provides that, if you have no regular or principal place of business, and if you have no regular place of abode, then you are an itinerant whose home is wherever you happen to be working. In short, you have no home to be away from, so you get no deductions. Some traveling salesmen face this dilemma.

Wouldn't it be neat, though, if the traveling salesman could incur some minimal expenses—say renting a small storage shed for the entire year and staying at some fleabag motel next door for a week. He could call that home, and deduct the rest of his expenses for the year! That gambit was successful in one early case, Gustafson v. Commissioner, 3 T.C. 998 (1944). Mr. Gustafson, a salesman for a magazine headquartered in Des Moines, Iowa, was able to claim his married sister's house in Greenville, Iowa as his tax home, and deduct his travelling expenses, despite the fact that he was travelling, mostly outside the state, for 52 weeks a year.

More recent cases have been considerably less generous. Single taxpayers who claim their parents' home as their tax home are unlikely to succeed. See Holdreith v. Commissioner, T.C. Memo. 1989–449 (construction worker), Hicks v. Commissioner, 47 T.C. 71 (1966) (customer representative; paying his parents $100 a year toward their expenses didn't help, even though it addressed the duplication argument somewhat), and Henderson v. Commissioner, 143 F.3d 497 (9th Cir. 1998) (stage hand for Disney ice shows). Apparently, keeping your dog at your parents' home doesn't help much, either. See *Holdreith, Henderson, supra.*

Even without leaning on their parents, chances for single people are slim. In McNeill v. Commissioner, T.C. Memo 2003–65, a long distance trucker spent about 20 days per year at his mobile home in Missouri, mostly while reloading his truck. No dice. In Rosenspan v. United States, 438 F.2d 905 (2nd Cir. 1971), the taxpayer, a widower, drove throughout the country for some 300 days a year selling jewelry. He kept some clothing and other belongings at his brother's house in Brooklyn, New York. He spent his annual vacations in Brooklyn, in order to visit his children. However, when there, he usually stayed at a motel near JFK Airport, so as not to abuse his welcome. Held: no home; no deduction.

What if you're married? In Baugh v. Commissioner, T.C. Memo 1996–70, husband and wife were both radiation protection technicians who traveled around the country working on nuclear plants. They lived in a trailer, which they hauled with them to each jobsite. The court held that the trailer was their tax home.

If you're married with children, you're more likely to have a home, but not necessarily. In Fisher v. Commissioner, 23 T.C. 218 (1954), the taxpayer, a professional musician, brought his wife and children with him from job to job. His argument that his mother-in-law's apartment in Milwaukee was his tax home failed. In Deneke v. Commissioner, 42 T.C. 981 (1964), the taxpayer and his wife, both salespeople, spent 53 nights in the Dogwood Motel in Palestine, Texas, and were on the road the rest of the year. Their children were enrolled in boarding school in Palestine. They told the headmaster that, in case of emergency, he should contact the manager of the Motel. They lost. Not even a traveling, Pentecostal evangelist could get a break. Boyd v. Commissioner, T.C. Summ. Op. 2006–36.

Merchant seamen do somewhat better. Since they live on board ship for free, there are no lodging expenses, but there are incidental expenses. Such expenses were allowed in Johnson v. Commissioner, 115 T.C. 210 (2000), and, Zbylut v. Commissioner, T.C. Memo. 2008–44. For United States Navy personnel, however, their tax home is their ship.

Ah—the wandering life!

HANTZIS v. COMMISSIONER

United States Court of Appeals, First Circuit, 1981.
638 F.2d 248.

LEVIN H. CAMPBELL, CIRCUIT JUDGE.

* * * In the fall of 1973 Catharine Hantzis (taxpayer), formerly a candidate for an advanced degree in philosophy at the University of California at Berkeley, entered Harvard Law School in Cambridge, Massachusetts, as a full-time student. During her second year of law school she sought unsuccessfully to obtain employment for the summer of 1975 with a Boston law firm. She did, however, find a job as a legal assistant with a law firm in New York City, where she worked for ten weeks beginning in June 1975. Her husband, then a member of the faculty of Northeastern University with a teaching schedule for that summer, remained in Boston and lived at the couple's home there. At the time of the Tax Court's decision in this case, Mr. and Mrs. Hantzis still resided in Boston.

On their joint income tax return for 1975, Mr. and Mrs. Hantzis reported the earnings from taxpayer's summer employment ($3,750) and deducted the cost of transportation between Boston and New York, the cost of a small apartment rented by Mrs. Hantzis in New York and the cost of her meals in New York ($3,204). The deductions were taken under § 162(a)(2). * * *

The Commissioner disallowed the deduction on the ground that taxpayer's home for purposes of section 162(a)(2) was her place of employment and the cost of traveling to and living in New York was therefore not "incurred ... while away from home." The Commissioner also argued that the expenses were not incurred "in the pursuit of a trade or business." Both positions were rejected by the Tax Court, which found that Boston was Mrs. Hantzis' home because her employment in New York was only temporary and that her expenses in New York were "necessitated" by her employment there. The court thus held the expenses to be deductible under § 162(a)(2).

In asking this court to reverse the Tax Court's allowance of the deduction, the Commissioner has contended that the expenses were not incurred "in the pursuit of a trade or business." We do not accept this argument; nonetheless, we sustain the Commissioner and deny the deduction, on the basis that the expenses were not incurred "while away from home." * * *

III.

* * *

We begin by recognizing that the location of a person's home for purposes of section 162(a)(2) becomes problematic only when the person lives one place and works another. Where a taxpayer resides and works at a single location, he is always home, however defined; and where a taxpayer is constantly on the move due to his work, he is never "away" from home. (In the latter situation, it may be said either that he has no residence to be away from, or else that his residence is always at his place of employment.) However, in the present case, the need to determine "home" is plainly before us, since the taxpayer resided in Boston and worked, albeit briefly, in New York.

We think the critical step in defining "home" in these situations is to recognize that the "while away from home" requirement has to be construed in light of the further requirement that the expense be the result of business exigencies. The traveling expense deduction obviously is not intended to exclude from taxation every expense incurred by a taxpayer who, in the course of business, maintains two homes. Section 162(a)(2) seeks rather "to mitigate the burden of the taxpayer who, because of the exigencies of his trade or business, must maintain two places of abode and thereby incur additional and duplicate living expenses." Consciously or unconsciously, courts have effectuated this policy in part through their interpretation of the term "home" in section 162(a)(2). Whether it is held in a particular decision that a taxpayer's home is his residence or his principal place of business, the ultimate allowance or disallowance of a deduction is a function of the court's assessment of the reason for a taxpayer's maintenance of two homes. If the reason is perceived to be personal, the taxpayer's home will generally be held to be his place of employment rather than his residence and the deduction will be denied. If the reason is felt to be business exigencies, the person's home will usually be held to be his residence and the deduction will be allowed. We understand the concern of the concurrence that such an operational interpretation of the term "home" is somewhat technical and perhaps untidy, in that it will not always afford bright line answers, but we doubt the ability of either the Commissioner or the courts to invent an unyielding formula that will make sense in all cases. The line between personal and business expenses winds through infinite factual permutations; effectuation of the travel expense provision requires that any principle of decision be flexible and sensitive to statutory policy.

Construing in the manner just described the requirement that an expense be incurred "while away from home," we do not believe this requirement was satisfied in this case. Mrs. Hantzis' trade or business did not require that she maintain a home in Boston as well as one in New York. Though she returned to Boston at various times during the period of her employment in New York, her visits were all for personal reasons. It is not contended that she had a business connection in Boston that necessitated her keeping a home there; no professional interest was served by maintenance of the Boston home as would have been the case, for example, if Mrs. Hantzis had been a lawyer based in Boston with a New York client whom she was temporarily serving. The home in Boston was kept up for reasons involving Mr. Hantzis, but those reasons cannot substitute for a showing by Mrs. Hantzis that the exigencies of her trade or business required her to maintain two homes.[11] Mrs. Hantzis' decision to keep two homes must be seen as a choice dictated by personal, albeit wholly reasonable, considerations and not a business or occupational necessity. We therefore hold that her home for purposes of section 162(a)(2) was New York and that the expenses at issue in this case were not incurred "while away from home."

We are not dissuaded from this conclusion by the temporary nature of Mrs. Hantzis' employment in New York. Mrs. Hantzis argues that the brevity of her stay in New York excepts her from the business exigencies requirement of section 162(a)(2) under a doctrine supposedly enunciated by the Supreme Court in Peurifoy v. Commissioner, 358 U.S. 59 (1958) (per curiam).[12] The Tax Court here held that Boston was the taxpayer's home because it would have been unreasonable for her to move her residence to New York for only ten weeks. At first glance these contentions may seem to find support in the court decisions holding that, when a taxpayer works for a limited time away from his usual home, section 162(a)(2) allows a deduction for the expense of maintaining a second home so long as the employment is "temporary" and not "indefinite" or

---

11. In this respect, Mr. and Mrs. Hantzis' situation is analogous to cases involving spouses with careers in different locations. Each must independently satisfy the requirement that deductions taken for travel expenses incurred in the pursuit of a trade or business arise while he or she is away from home. See Chwalow v. Commissioner, 470 F.2d 475, 477–78 (3d Cir.1972) ("Where additional expenses are incurred because, for personal reasons, husband and wife maintain separate domiciles, no deduction is allowed."); Hammond v. Commissioner, 213 F.2d 43, 44 (5th Cir.1954); Foote v. Commissioner, 67 T.C. 1 (1976); Coerver v. Commissioner, 36 T.C. 252 (1961). This is true even though the spouses file a joint return. Chwalow, supra, 470 F.2d at 478.

12. In Peurifoy, the Court stated that the Tax Court had "engrafted an exception" onto the requirement that travel expenses be dictated by business exigencies, allowing "a deduction for expenditures ... when the taxpayer's employment is 'temporary' as contrasted with 'indefinite' or 'indeterminate.'" 358 U.S. at 59. Because the Commissioner did not challenge this exception, the Court did not rule on its validity. It instead upheld the circuit court's reversal of the Tax Court and disallowance of the deduction on the basis of the adequacy of the appellate court's review. The Supreme Court agreed that the Tax Court's finding as to the temporary nature of taxpayer's employment was clearly erroneous. Despite its inauspicious beginning, the exception has come to be generally accepted. Some uncertainty lingers, however, over whether the exception properly applies to the "business exigencies" or the "away from home" requirement. In fact, it is probably relevant to both. Because we treat these requirements as inextricably intertwined, we find it unnecessary to address this question: applied to either requirement, the temporary employment doctrine affects the meaning of both.

"permanent." This test is an elaboration of the requirements under section 162(a)(2) that an expense be incurred due to business exigencies and while away from home. * * * Thus it has been said,

> "Where a taxpayer reasonably expects to be employed in a location for a substantial or indefinite period of time, the reasonable inference is that his choice of a residence is a personal decision, unrelated to any business necessity. Thus, it is irrelevant how far he travels to work. The normal expectation, however, is that the taxpayer will choose to live near his place of employment. Consequently, when a taxpayer reasonable (sic) expects to be employed in a location for only a short or temporary period of time and travels a considerable distance to the location from his residence, it is unreasonable to assume that his choice of a residence is dictated by personal convenience. The reasonable inference is that he is temporarily making these travels because of a business necessity."

The temporary employment doctrine does not, however, purport to eliminate any requirement that continued maintenance of a first home have a business justification. We think the rule has no application where the taxpayer has no business connection with his usual place of residence. If no business exigency dictates the location of the taxpayer's usual residence, then the mere fact of his taking temporary employment elsewhere cannot supply a compelling business reason for continuing to maintain that residence. Only a taxpayer who lives one place, works another and has business ties to both is in the ambiguous situation that the temporary employment doctrine is designed to resolve. In such circumstances, unless his employment away from his usual home is temporary, a court can reasonably assume that the taxpayer has abandoned his business ties to that location and is left with only personal reasons for maintaining a residence there. Where only personal needs require that a travel expense be incurred, however, a taxpayer's home is defined so as to leave the expense subject to taxation. Thus, a taxpayer who pursues temporary employment away from the location of his usual residence, but has no business connection with that location, is not "away from home" for purposes of section 162(a)(2).

On this reasoning, the temporary nature of Mrs. Hantzis' employment in New York does not affect the outcome of her case. She had no business ties to Boston that would bring her within the temporary employment doctrine. By this holding, we do not adopt a rule that "home" in section 162(a)(2) is the equivalent of a taxpayer's place of business. Nor do we mean to imply that a taxpayer has a "home" for tax purposes only if he is already engaged in a trade or business at a particular location. Though both rules are alluringly determinate, we have already discussed why they offer inadequate expressions of the purposes behind the travel expense deduction. We hold merely that for a taxpayer in Mrs. Hantzis' circumstances to be "away from home in the pursuit of a trade or business," she must establish the existence of some sort of business relation both to the location she claims as "home" and to the location of her temporary employment sufficient to support a finding that her duplicative expenses are necessitated by business exigencies. This, we believe, is the meaning of the statement in Flowers that "(b)usiness trips are to be identified in relation to business demands and the traveler's business headquarters." On the uncontested facts before us, Mrs. Hantzis had no business relation to Boston; we therefore leave to cases in which the issue is squarely presented the task of elaborating what relation to a place is required under section 162(a)(2) for duplicative living expenses to be deductible.

Reversed. * * *

ANDREWS v. COMMISSIONER

United States Court of Appeals, First Circuit, 1991.
931 F.2d 132.

Levin H. Campbell, Circuit Judge.

* * *

Background

* * * Andrews was president and chief executive officer of Andrews Gunite Co., Inc. ("Andrews Gunite"), which is engaged in the swimming pool construction business in New England, a seasonal business. His salary in 1984 was $108,000. Beginning in 1964, during the off-season, Andrews, establishing a sole proprietorship known as Andrews Farms, began to race and breed horses in New England, and in 1972 moved his horse business to Pompano, Florida. Andrews' horse business proliferated and prospered.

In 1974, Andrews Gunite diversified by establishing a Florida-based division, known as Pilgrim Farms, to acquire horses to breed with two of Andrews Farms' most successful horses and to develop a racing stable similar to Andrews Farms. By 1975, Andrews Farms had 130 horses, and by 1984 Pilgrim Farms had twenty to thirty horses. Andrews was responsible, in 1984, for managing and training Pilgrim Farms horses and Andrews Farms horses, though he was compensated for his services to Pilgrim Farms only by payment of his airfare to Florida. While in Florida during racing season, Andrews worked at the racetrack from seven in the morning until noon, and he returned to the track to solicit sales of his horses and watch the races on four nights per week.

Also, in 1983, Andrews' son, who had worked for Andrews Gunite, sought to establish a pool construction business in Florida. Andrews, along with his brother and son, formed a corporation, originally known as East Coast Pools by Andrews, Inc. and renamed Pools by Andrews, Inc., to purchase the assets of a troubled pool business in Florida. Andrews owned one-third of Pools by Andrews, Inc. in 1984. Andrews assisted his son in the Florida pool business, but drew no salary for his services. By the time of trial, this pool business was one of the biggest, if not the biggest builder of pools in Florida, with offices in West Palm Beach and Orlando and plans for a third office in Tampa.

Andrews resided in Lynnfield, Massachusetts with his wife prior to and during 1984. During this period, the expansion of the horse business required Andrews to make an increasing number of trips to Florida. In order to reduce travel costs and facilitate lodging arrangements, Andrews purchased a condominium in Pompano Beach, Florida in 1976, which he used as a residence when in Florida during the racing season. The neighborhood around the condominium became unsafe, and Andrews decided to move, purchasing a single family home with a swimming pool in Lighthouse Point, Florida in 1983. The home was closer than the condominium to the Pompano Beach Raceway, where Andrews maintained, trained, and raced many of the Andrews Farms and Pilgrim Farms horses. Andrews used the Florida house as his personal residence during the racing season.

The Tax Court concluded that in 1984 Andrews worked in Florida primarily in his horse business for six months, from January through April and during November and December, and that Andrews worked primarily in his pool construction business in Massachusetts for six months, from May to October. On his 1984 amended return, Andrews claimed one hundred percent business usage on his Florida house, and claimed depreciation deductions on the furniture and house in connection with his horse racing business. He also characterized tax, mortgage interest, utilities, insurance, and other miscellaneous expenses as "lodging expenses," which he deducted in connection with the Florida pools and horse racing businesses, along with expenses for meals while he was in Florida.

Discussion

The Tax Court correctly stated: "The purpose of the section 162(a)(2) deduction is to mitigate the burden upon a taxpayer who, because of the exigencies of his trade or business, must maintain two places of abode and thereby incur additional living expenses." See Hantzis v. Commissioner. The Tax Court then stated its general rule that "a taxpayer's home for purposes of section 162(a) is the area or vicinity of his principal place of business." Responding thereafter to the Commissioner's contention that during the horse racing season Florida was Andrews' "tax home," rendering Andrews' Florida meals and lodging expenses personal and nondeductible living expenses under sections 262 and 162(a)(2), the Tax Court concluded that Andrews had two "tax homes" in 1984. The Tax Court, without further elaboration, based its decision on an observation that Andrews' business in Florida between January and mid-April and during November and December of each year was recurrent with each season, rather than temporary.

On appeal, the Commissioner who, while maintaining its ongoing position that the taxpayer's home for purposes of section 162(a)(2) is his principal place of business and that Andrews' principal place of business was in Florida, agrees with Andrews that the Tax Court erred in finding that he had more than one tax home and urges that we remand for the Tax Court to determine the location of Andrews' principal place of business. For the reasons that follow, we hold that the Tax Court erred in determining that Andrews had two "tax homes" in this case.

* * *

The issue of the reasonableness or necessity of Andrews' Florida expenses is not presented in this appeal. Rather, the Tax Court based its decision on a holding that Andrews did not satisfy the second Flowers requirement for deduction of his Florida expenses; as the Tax Court determined Andrews' home in 1984 was in both Massachusetts and Florida, he was not away from home when these expenses were incurred. We turn, then, to interpret the meaning of the "away from home" language of section 162(a)(2). The question here is whether, within the meaning of "home" in section 162(a)(2), Andrews could have had two homes in 1984. * * *

This court, in *Hantzis,* after reviewing cases addressing this issue, declined in that case to focus upon the "principal place of business" or "primary residence" definitions of "home," and suggested a "functional definition of the term." Effectuation of the travel expense provision must be guided by the policy underlying the provision that costs necessary to producing income may be deducted from taxable income. Where business necessity requires that a taxpayer maintain two places of abode, and thereby incur additional and duplicate living expenses, such duplicate expenses are a cost of producing income and should ordinarily be deductible. We believe it continues to be the case that, "[w]hether it is held in a particular decision that a taxpayer's home is his residence or his principal place of business, the ultimate allowance or disallowance of a deduction is a function of the court's assessment of the reason for a taxpayer's maintenance of two homes." "The exigencies of business rather than the personal conveniences and necessities of the traveler must be the motivating factors." The Commissioner and courts have adhered consistently to this policy that living expenses duplicated as a result of business necessity are deductible, whereas those duplicated as a result of personal choice are not.

The principle—that living expenses are deductible to the extent business necessity requires that they be duplicated—is also reflected in cases concerning temporary and itinerant workers. The courts and the Commissioner have agreed that a taxpayer cannot be expected to relocate her primary residence to a place of temporary employment. Hence, duplicate living expenses incurred at the place of temporary employment (if different from the place of usual abode), result from business exigency in satisfaction of the third prong of the Flowers test. An exception to the "principal place of business" definition of "tax home" is made where the business assignment is only temporary. Moreover, an "itinerant" worker who has no principal place of business and has no permanent place of abode ordinarily does not bear duplicate living expenses at all, and no deduction is generally allowable.

Here, we face a situation where the Tax Court found that the taxpayer, Andrews, had two businesses which apparently required that he spend a substantial amount of time in each of two widely separate places in 1984. However, the Tax Court's conclusion—that Andrews had two "tax homes"—is inconsistent with the well-settled policy underlying section 162(a)(2): that duplicated living expenses necessitated by business are deductible. We have previously said that "a taxpayer who is required to travel to get to a place of secondary employment which is sufficiently removed from his place of primary employment is just as much within the [travel expense deduction] provision as an employee who must travel at the behest of his employer." On the facts the Tax Court has found, it appears that Andrews, due to his geographically disparate horse and pool construction businesses, was required to incur duplicate living expenses. The Tax Court found that Andrews maintained at least the Massachusetts house throughout the year, and duplicate expenses were seemingly incurred by maintaining the Florida house, at least in part attributable to business exigency. If so, Andrews could have had only one "home" for purposes of section 162(a)(2) in 1984; duplicate living expenses while on business at the other house were a cost of producing income.

We do not seek to instruct the Tax Court how to determine which house in 1984, in Florida or in Massachusetts, was Andrews' "tax home," and which house gave rise to deductible duplicate living expenses while "away from home in pursuit of a trade or business," for purposes of section 162(a)(2). The guiding policy must be that the taxpayer is reasonably expected to locate his "home," for tax purposes, at his "major post of duty" so as to minimize the amount of business travel away from home that is required; a decision to do otherwise is motivated not by business necessity but by personal considerations, and should not give rise to greater business travel deductions. The length of time spent engaged in business at each location should ordinarily be determinative of which is the taxpayer's "principal place of business" or "major post of duty."[10] Defining that location as the taxpayer's "tax home" should result in allowance of deductions for duplicate living expenses incurred at the other "minor post of duty." Business necessity requires that living expenses be duplicated only for the time spent engaged in business at the "minor post of duty," whether that is the "primary residence" or not.

Vacated and remanded for further proceedings consistent with this opinion.

---

10. The Sixth Circuit has established an "objective test" to determine the situs of a taxpayer's "major post of duty," including three factors: (1) the length of time spent at the location; (2) the degree of activity in each place; and (3) the relative portion of taxpayer's income derived from each place. Markey v. Commissioner, 490 F.2d 1249 at 1255 (6th Cir. 1974). The first factor would ordinarily be the most important, since the time spent as a business necessity at the location is a reasonable proxy for the amount of living expenses that business requires be incurred in each place. We recognize, however, that other factors might be considered or even found determinative under appropriate circumstances.

WILBERT v. COMMISSIONER

United States Court of Appeals, Seventh Circuit, 2009.
553 F.3d 544.

POSNER, CIRCUIT JUDGE.

The question presented by this appeal is whether an employee who uses "bumping" rights to avoid or postpone losing his job can deduct the living expenses that he incurs when he finds himself working far from home as a result of exercising those rights. The Tax Court ruled against the taxpayer. This is one of a number of largely identical cases in the Tax Court, all brought by mechanics formerly employed by Northwest Airlines, like Wilbert, and all resolved against the taxpayer. But this seems the first case to be appealed.

Hired by Northwest in 1996, Wilbert worked for the airline at the Minneapolis airport for some years. He lived with his wife in Hudson, Wisconsin, across the Mississippi River from Minneapolis. Hudson is a suburb of Minneapolis, roughly 25 miles from the airport.

Facing financial pressures and a decline in airline traffic in the wake of the terrorist attacks of September 11, 2001, Northwest laid off many employees, including, in April 2003, Wilbert. But Northwest's mechanics each had a right to bump a more junior mechanic employed by the airline, that is, to take his job. Wilbert was able to bump a mechanic who worked for the airline in Chicago, but he worked there for only a few days before being bumped by a more senior mechanic. A few days later he was able to bump a mechanic in Anchorage, Alaska, and he worked there for three weeks before being himself bumped. He was soon able to bump a mechanic who worked in New York, at LaGuardia Airport, but he worked there for only a week before he was bumped again. At this point, he had exhausted his bumping rights. But for reasons that the parties have not explained, three weeks later the airline hired him back, outside the bumping system, to fill an interim position (maximum nine months) in Anchorage. He occupied that position for several months before being laid off again, this time for good. At no point in his hegira did he have realistic prospects of resuming work for Northwest in Minneapolis. He now lives in a Chicago suburb and works for Federal Express at O'Hare Airport. He sells real estate on the side (self-employed), as he did when he lived in Minneapolis, but his income from his real estate business there was only $2,000 in 2003, the relevant tax year, and he did not actually receive the money (a commission) until the following year.

He did not sell or rent his home in Hudson, where his wife continued to live, while working intermittently in 2003. Because he was working too far from home to be able to live there, he incurred living expenses (amounting to almost $20,000) that he would not have incurred had he remained working in Minneapolis, and those are the expenses he deducted from the taxable income shown on his 2003 return.

The Internal Revenue Code allows the deduction, as part of "the ordinary and necessary expenses ... incurred during the taxable year in carrying on any trade or business," of "traveling expenses ... *while [the taxpayer is] away from home* in the pursuit of a trade or business." § 162(a)(2) (emphasis added). There is an exception for "personal, living, or family expenses." § 262(a). The phrase we have italicized is critical. It is by an interpretation of that phrase that commuting expenses are disallowed because of "a natural reluctance ... to lighten the tax burden of people who have the good fortune to interweave work with consumption. To allow a deduction for commuting would confer a windfall on people who live in the suburbs and commute to work in the cities." *Moss v. Commissioner,* 758 F.2d 211, 212 (7th Cir.1985). The length of the commute is thus irrelevant. If Wilbert had had a permanent job in Anchorage but decided to retain his home in Minneapolis and return there on weekends and during the week live in a truck stop in Wasilla, Alaska, he could not have deducted from his taxable income the expense of traveling to and fro between Minnesota and Alaska or his room and board in Wasilla. (We ignore for the moment the possibility that Mrs. Wilbert had a job in Minneapolis, and if so its relevance.)

* * *

With our hypothetical Wilbert the long-distance commuter, compare a lawyer whose home and office are both in Minneapolis but who has an international practice and as a result spends more time on the road than he does at home. Nevertheless he can deduct his traveling expenses. His work requires him to maintain a home within normal commuting distance of Minneapolis because that is where his office is, but his work also requires him to travel, and the expenses he incurs in traveling are necessary to his work and he cannot offset them by relocating his residence to the places to which he travels because he has to maintain a home near his office. And likewise if, as in *Andrews v. Commissioner,* the taxpayer has to make such frequent trips to a particular site that it is more economical for him to rent or buy a second residence, at that site, than to live there in a hotel.

Wilbert's case falls in between our two hypothetical cases. Unlike the lawyer, he did not have to live near Minneapolis after the initial layoff because he had no work there (ignoring for the moment his real estate business). But unlike the imaginary Wilbert who has a permanent job in Alaska and so could readily relocate his home there, the real Wilbert had jobs of indefinite, unpredictable duration in Alaska (and Chicago, and New York). It would hardly have been realistic to expect him to pull up stakes and move to Anchorage and then to Chicago and then to New York and then back to Anchorage. Remember that his first stint after the initial layoff lasted only days, his second only weeks, and the third only one week. His situation was unlike that of the employee of a New York firm who, if he chooses to live in Scarsdale rather than on Fifth Avenue, is forbidden to deduct from his taxable income the commuting expense that he incurs by virtue of his choice; it is a personal choice-suburban over urban living-rather than anything necessitated by his job.

The Tax Court, with some judicial support, has tried to resolve cases such as this by asking whether the taxpayer's work away from home is "temporary" or "indefinite," and allowing the deduction of traveling expenses only if it is the former. The Internal Revenue Code does not explicitly adopt the distinction, but does provide (with an immaterial exception) that "the taxpayer shall not be treated as being temporarily away from home during any period of employment if such period exceeds 1 year."

The problem with the Tax Court's distinction is that work can be, and usually is, both temporary and indefinite, as in our lawyer example. A lawsuit he is trying in London might settle on the second day, or last a month; his sojourn away from his office will therefore be both temporary *and* indefinite. Indeed *all* work is indefinite and much "permanent" work is really temporary. An academic lawyer might accept a five-year appointment as an assistant professor with every expectation of obtaining tenure at the end of that period at that or another law school; yet one would not describe him as a "temporary" employee even if he left after six months and thus was not barred from claiming temporary status by the one-year rule. Our imaginary Wilbert who has a permanent job in Anchorage but is reluctant to move there from Minneapolis might argue (at least until he had worked a year, the statutory cutoff for "temporary" work) that no job is "permanent"—he might be fired, or he might harbor realistic hopes of getting a better job back in Minneapolis. That possibility would not permit him to deduct the expense of commuting from Minnesota to Alaska.

So "temporary versus indefinite" does not work well as a test of deductibility and neither does "personal choice versus reasonable response to the employment situation," tempting as the latter formula is because of its realism. If no reasonable person would relocate to his new place of work because of uncertainty about the duration of the new job, his choice to stay where he is, unlike a choice to commute from a suburb to the city in which one's office is located rather than live in the city, is not an optional personal choice like deciding to stay at a Four Seasons or a Ritz Carlton, but a choice forced by circumstances. Wilbert when first notified that he was being laid off could foresee a series of temporary jobs all across the country and not even limited, as we know, to the lower 48 states, and the costs of moving his home to the location of each temporary job would have been prohibitive. It would have meant moving four times in one year on a mechanic's salary to cities hundreds or (in the case of Anchorage versus Minneapolis, Chicago, or New York) thousands of miles apart.

The problem with a test that focuses on the reasonableness of the taxpayer's decision not to move is that it is bound to prove nebulous in application. For it just asks the taxpayer to give a good reason for not moving his home when he gets a job in a different place, and if he gave a good reason then his traveling expenses would be deductible as the product of a reasonable balancing of personal and business considerations. In the oft-cited case of *Hantzis v. Commissioner,* the question was whether a law student who lived in Boston with her husband during the school year could deduct her traveling expenses when she took a summer job in New York. Given the temporary nature of the job, it made perfectly good sense for her to retain her home in Boston and just camp out, as it were, in New York. What persuaded the court to reject the deduction was that she had no *business* reason to retain the house in Boston. Stated differently, she had no business reason to be living in two places at once, unlike the lawyer in our example. And so the expenses she incurred living in New York could not be thought "ordinary and *necessary* expenses ... incurred ... in carrying on any trade or business."

If this seems rather a mechanical reading of the statute, it has the support not only of the influential precedent of *Hantzis* but also of the even more influential precedent of *Commissioner v. Flowers,* where the Supreme Court said that "the exigencies of business rather than the personal conveniences and necessities of the traveler must be the motivating factors" in the decision to travel. The "business exigencies" rule, though harsh, is supported by compelling considerations of administrability. To apply a test of reasonableness the Internal Revenue Service would first have to decide whether the taxpayer should have moved to his new place of work. This might require answering such questions as whether the schools in the area of his new job were far worse than those his children currently attend, whether his elderly parents live near his existing home and require his attention, and whether his children have psychological problems that make it difficult for them to find new friends. Were it decided that it was reasonable for the taxpayer to stay put, it would then become necessary to determine whether the expenses he incurred in traveling to and from his various places of work for home visits had been reasonable-whether in other words such commutes, in point of frequency, were "ordinary and necessary" business expenses. The Internal Revenue Service would have to establish norms of reasonable home visits that presumably would vary with such things as distance and how many of the taxpayer's children were living at home and how old they were.

We are sympathetic to Wilbert's plight and recognize the artificiality of supposing that, as the government argues, he made merely a personal choice to "commute" from Minneapolis to Anchorage, and Chicago, and New York, as if Minneapolis were a suburb of those cities. But the statutory language, the precedents, and the considerations of administrability that we have emphasized persuade us to reject the test of reasonableness. The "temporary versus indefinite" test is no better, so we fall back on the rule of *Flowers* and *Hantzis* that unless the taxpayer has a business rather than a personal reason to be living in two places he cannot deduct his traveling expenses if he decides not to move. Indeed, Wilbert's situation is really no different from the common case of the construction worker who works at different sites throughout the country, never certain how long each stint will last and reluctant therefore to relocate his home. The construction worker loses, as must Wilbert.

We might well have a different case if Wilbert had had a firm, justified expectation of being restored to his job at the Minneapolis airport within a short time of his initial layoff. Suppose the airline had said to him, "We must lay you off, but you will be able to bump a less senior employee in Anchorage for a few weeks, and we are confident that by then, given your seniority, you will be able to return to Minneapolis." His situation would then be comparable to that of a Minneapolis lawyer ordered by his senior partner to spend the next month trying a case in Anchorage. But that is not this case.

Wilbert has another string to his bow, however, arguing that he had two businesses, not one, the other being the sale of real estate, and that because that business was centered in Minneapolis he had a business reason to live near there. This would be a good argument if selling real estate were his main business. *Andrews v. Commissioner, supra,* But obviously it is not, or at least was not in 2003, when his total income (and in an accrual rather than a cash sense) from selling real estate was only $2,000.

As explained in *Andrews,* "The guiding policy must be that the taxpayer is reasonably expected to locate his 'home,' for tax purposes, at his 'major post of duty' so as to minimize the amount of business travel away from home that is required; a decision to do otherwise is motivated not by business necessity but by personal considerations, and should not give rise to greater business travel deductions." If Wilbert had had to travel back to Minneapolis from his new tax "homes" from time to time in order to attend to his real estate business, the travel expense (if the business was really the reason for the travel home), and conceivably even some of his living expenses at his home (his "secondary" home, in a tax sense, since his primary home for tax purposes would follow his work), might have been deductible, just as his expenses for the office equipment that he purchased in his real estate business were. But he does not argue for such a deduction.

For completeness we note that if Wilbert's wife had a business in Minneapolis, this would make it all the more reasonable for Wilbert not to move away from Minneapolis. But it would not permit him to deduct his traveling expenses, because his decision to live with his wife (if only on occasional weekends) would (setting aside any considerations relating to his real estate sideline) be a personal rather than a business decision. ("in this respect, Mr. and Mrs. Hantzis' situation is analogous to cases involving spouses with careers in different locations. Each must independently satisfy the requirement that deductions taken for travel expenses incurred in the pursuit of a trade or business arise while he or she is away from home").

AFFIRMED.

PROBLEMS

In each case, determine whether the taxpayer has incurred deductible travel expenses, and, if appropriate, which expenses are deductible. Don't forget § 274(n).

1. Lawyer drives from home to her office in downtown Des Moines. At mid-day, she goes across the street to a restaurant for lunch.

2. She drives to Waterloo for a court appearance, has lunch in Waterloo, and returns home that evening.

3. She flies to Denver on business, has lunch in Denver, and returns home to Des Moines that same evening.

4. a. She flies to San Diego for a three day business trip. She incurs transportation, meals and lodging expenses. She flies out Sunday night and returns Wednesday night.

b. She flies to San Diego Sunday night, works Monday, Tuesday and Wednesday, spends Thursday and Friday relaxing on the beach and doing some sightseeing, and returns Friday evening.

c. Same as Problem 4(b) but, she stays until Sunday morning. Had she not stayed over a Saturday night, her airfare would have been at least double what she paid.

5. a. Lawyer accepts a two-year assignment to manage the branch office in Cedar Rapids.

b. What if things don't work out, and she returns to Des Moines after three months?

c. What if she spends six months in Cedar Rapids, then returns to Des Moines for 21 days, and then goes back to Cedar Rapids?

6. Law professor accepts a nine month visiting appointment at another law school. Three months into the fall semester, she accepts a permanent offer at the other school.

7. a. Law professor accepts a one-semester ''pure'' visitorship at the University of Hawaii. It is understood by both parties that she will definitely return to her home school at the end of the semester. During her visit, she leaves her house vacant, and rents an unfurnished apartment in Hawaii. She also rents furniture. In addition, she purchases a color television set when she arrives in Hawaii for $400, and sells it when she leaves for $250. Finally, she pays for cable TV in Hawaii, including one premium movie channel.

b. What if Law Professor didn't own a house. Instead, she rented an apartment near her home school. Her lease expired the day she left for Hawaii. Upon her return from Hawaii, she rented another apartment.

8. Would it change your answer to question 7 if she had brought her husband and three-year-old daughter with her? What about the daughter's hula lessons?

9. Section 274(n) allows only 50% of meal expenses as deductions. It used to be 100%. Now, it is 80%, for truckers, and others who are subject to

the Department of Transportation hours of service limitations. See § 274(n)(3).

Why do truckers deserve special treatment?

What if the cap were put back to 80% for everyone? Who would gain and who would lose from such a change?

2. MEALS, ENTERTAINMENT, CLOTHING

At least, in cases involving travel expenses, it all starts with a business trip.

In the three cases that follow, the taxpayers are incurring expenses which they would have incurred, at least to some extent, even if they were not engaged in business at all. One does not have to be gainfully employed to spend money on meals, entertainment, and clothing. Perhaps there should be a higher standard for obtaining business deductions for such personal items.

MOSS v. COMMISSIONER

United States Tax Court, 1983.
80 T.C. 1073.

WILBUR, JUDGE:

* * * Petitioner, an attorney, was a partner in the law firm Parrillo, Bresler, Weiss & Moss in 1976 and 1977. The firm filed a partnership return for each of the years in question. It took a deduction each year for "meetings and conferences." Petitioner has claimed his share of the firm's expense on his individual return.

Parrillo, Bresler, Weiss & Moss was a firm of six or seven lawyers who specialized in insurance defense work. Their case load was extremely heavy. Most of the lawyers spent the better part of each day participating in or preparing for depositions and trials throughout the greater Chicago area. Judges often held hearings on short notice, thus making it necessary for the firm to assign cases and plan schedules at the last minute.

Robert Parrillo, the senior partner, was responsible for all cases involving the firm's major client, the Safeway Insurance Co. His partners and associates handled the details of these cases, but no final settlements were made without his approval.

The firm had an unwritten policy of meeting every day during the noon recess at the Cafe Angelo, a small, quiet restaurant conveniently located near the courts and the office. Over lunch, the lawyers would decide who would attend various sessions;[2] discuss issues and problems that had come up in the morning; answer questions and advise each other

---

2. Petitioner introduced into evidence several examples of the firm's Daily Call Sheet. This master list, prepared by the docket secretary, showed the case name, court number, "call" (or what item was pending), location, and time of all matters scheduled. At lunch, the attorneys would decide who would handle what matters and so note on the call sheet.

on how to handle certain pending matters; update Mr. Parrillo on settlement negotiations; and, naturally, engage in a certain amount of social banter. Attorneys attended whenever possible for as long as possible; sometimes they ate, at other times they merely joined in the discussions.

The law firm paid for the meals eaten during the noontime meetings. In 1976, the total bill was $7,113.85; in 1977, they spent $7,967.85. The bill from the Cafe Angelo represents the bulk of the firm's "meeting and conference" expense.

The noon hour was the most convenient and practical time for the firm to have its daily meeting.[5] The courts were almost always in recess at this time, so most attorneys could attend. The more experienced members of the firm were available to advise and educate the fledgling litigators. Parrillo was there to discuss and approve settlements. The Cafe Angelo provided a good location, efficient service, reasonable prices, and a place where judges could locate the attorneys.

In its statutory notice of deficiency, respondent disallowed petitioner's distributive share of the Cafe Angelo expense, along with other items upon which the parties have reached an agreement.

Opinion

* * *

Petitioner contends that the luncheon meeting expenses are deductible under section 162 as ordinary and necessary business expenses. In the alternative, he claims that they qualify for deduction under section 1.162–5, Income Tax Regs., as outlays for education. Respondent, conversely, claims that the lunches are a personal and therefore nondeductible expense. We agree with respondent.[7]

* * *

The expense in question is close to that evanescent line dividing personal and business expenses. From the perspective of the partnership, the lunches were a cost incurred in earning their income. The lawyers needed to coordinate assignments and scheduling of their case load, and the noon hour was a logical, convenient time at which to do so. They considered the meeting to be part of their working day, not as an hour of reprieve from business affairs. The individuals did not feel free to make

---

5. At trial respondent suggested several other times at which the partners and associates could conceivably have met. While we agree that it would have been possible to meet at 7 a.m. or 6 p.m., we believe Mr. Parrillo's testimony that such meetings would have been less well attended and less effective.

7. Respondent has directed virtually all of his argument under sec. 162. Nevertheless, he also suggests that the deduction should be denied as petitioner has not provided adequate substantiation as required by sec. 274(d). The parties stipulated the daily "guest checks" establishing the date, place, and amount spent at the lunches; they also stipulated the corresponding checks by which each of the bills was paid. Additionally, copies of the "daily call sheets" were stipulated; there is no dispute that these call sheets introduced in evidence were a significant item discussed at the luncheons. The lawyers in the firm (with the exception of a rare guest) were the only ones eating. Respondent's sec. 274 arguments seem to reflect a decision to leave no arrow remaining in his quiver. While we have doubts that his argument has validity on the facts before us, our decision on the first issue makes it unnecessary to decide whether he is wide of the mark.

alternate plans, or to eat elsewhere. For this firm, petitioner argues, the meeting was both ordinary and necessary.

The Commissioner focuses not on the circumstances bringing the partnership together each day, but rather on the fact that the individuals were eating lunch while they were together. Rather than to section 162, he looks to section 262, and the regulations which specifically categorize meals as personal expenses. The respondent, in essence, argues that while the meeting may have been ordinary and necessary to the business, the outlay was for meals, a personal item.

The dual nature of the business lunch has long been a difficult problem for legislators and courts alike. The traditional view of the courts has been that if a personal living expense is to qualify under section 162, the taxpayer must demonstrate that it was "different from or in excess of that which would have been made for the taxpayer's personal purposes." Sutter v. Commissioner, 21 T.C. 170, 173.

Following the *Sutter* formula, numerous taxpayers have attempted to deduct the cost of meals eaten under unusual or constraining circumstances. The claims have been denied almost invariably. See, e.g., Fife v. Commissioner, 73 T.C. 621 (attorney may not deduct cost of meals eaten in restaurants due to late client meetings); Fife v. Commissioner, 73 T.C. 621 (corporation may not deduct cost of officer's locally consumed meals absent travel or compliance with section 274); Drill v. Commissioner, 8 T.C. 902 (construction worker cannot deduct cost of dinners on nights he worked overtime).[10] Daily meals are an inherently personal expense, and a taxpayer bears a heavy burden in proving they are routinely deductible.

Petitioner relies on Wells v. Commissioner, 626 F.2d 868, in support of his position. In *Wells*, we denied a deduction claimed by a public defender for the cost of occasional lunch meetings with his staff. The Court noted, however, that in a law firm, "an occasional luncheon meeting with the staff to discuss the operation of the firm would be regarded as an 'ordinary and necessary expense.'" We note, first, that this statement is dictum in a memorandum opinion, and thus not controlling. Second, that case referred to occasional lunches, a far cry from the daily sustenance involved in the case at bar. Even assuming that Wells is of any assistance to petitioner, we need not decide where the line between these two cases should be drawn, for we are convinced that outlays for meals consumed 5 days per week, 52 weeks per year would in any event fall on the nondeductible side of it.

The only recent cases where deductions were allowed for meals taken on a regular basis were Sibla v. Commissioner, 611 F.2d 1260, and Cooper v. Commissioner, 67 T.C. 870. Those cases involved Los Angeles firemen who were required to contribute to a meal fund for each day they were on duty, regardless of whether they ate or even were present at the fire

---

10. See also Hirschel v. Commissioner (Dec. 37,842(M)), T.C. Memo. 1981–189, affd. without published opinion 685 F.2d 424 (2d Cir.1982) (taxpayer-student may not deduct cost of meals on nights when class meets after work).

station. This Court allowed them to deduct the expense under section 162; a concurring opinion would have allowed the expense by analogy to section 119. On appeal, the Ninth Circuit approved of both theories, stating that because the taxpayer's situation was both unusual and unique, the expense was business rather than personal.[12]

The decision by the Ninth Circuit implies that similar considerations are involved in determining whether a meal is a business expense under section 162 and whether the value of a meal supplied by an employer should be included in gross income under section 61. Section 119 provides a limited exception to section 61 by allowing an employee to exclude such amounts if the meal is furnished on the business premises for the convenience of the employer. The cases decided under section 119 have focused on the degree to which the employee's actions are restricted by his employer's demands. Language referring to compliance with the demands of one's employer can also be found in section 162 cases decided by this Court.

Petitioner relies on this notion of restriction in contending that the cost of the lunches, like the cost of the firehouse mess in *Sibla* and *Cooper*, should be deductible. He argues that the attorneys "considered the luncheon meetings as a part of their regular work day," and that the firm incurred the expense "solely for the benefit of its practice and not for the personal convenience of its attorneys."

Petitioner has not explained, however, how this "restriction" is any different than that imposed on an attorney who must spend his lunch hour boning up on the Rules of Civil Procedure in preparation for trial or reading an evidence book to clarify a point that may arise during an afternoon session. In all these cases, the lawyer spends an extra hour at work. The mere fact that this time is given over the noon hour does not convert the cost of daily meals into a business expense to be shared by the Government.

In *Sibla* and *Cooper*, on the other hand, the firemen were required by law to contribute to the communal meals; the petitioner in Cooper was threatened with dismissal when he refused to pay for days when he was on duty but not at the station. The involuntary nature of the payment, and the taxpayer's limited ability to eat the meal for which he was paying combined to create a unique circumstance which justified allowance of the deduction. No such unique situation is presented here. On the contrary, petitioner is much like employees in all fields who find it necessary to devote their lunch hour to work-related activities.

---

12. Two cases decided after Sibla v. Commissioner (80–1 USTC par. 9143), 611 F.2d 1260 (9th Cir.1980), affg. (Dec. 34,477) 68 T.C. 422 (1977) and Cooper v. Commissioner (Dec. 34,274), 67 T.C. 870 (1977) have effectively confined that holding to its facts. In Duggan v. Commissioner, 77 T.C. 911 (1981), a Minnesota fireman was denied a deduction for contributions to the firehouse mess. The Court found that, unlike Sibla and Cooper, Duggan was not required to participate in the common mess, nor was he forced to pay for meals he did not eat. Also, the mess was organized by the employees rather than the employer. And, in Banks v. Commissioner, T.C. Memo. 1981–490, this Court again denied the deduction, stating that "the single fact that the meal was required to be eaten at the fire station did not convert the cost of such into a business expense."

In agreeing with the Commissioner on this point, we are well aware that business needs dictated the choice of the noon hour for the daily meeting. In a very real sense, these meetings contributed to the success of the partnership. But other costs contributing to the success of one's employment are treated as personal expenses. Commuting is obviously essential to one's continued employment, yet those expenses are not deductible as business expenses. As this Court stated in Amend v. Commissioner: the common thread which seems to bind the cases together is the notion that some expenses are so inherently personal that they simply cannot qualify for section 162 treatment irrespective of the role played by such expenditures in the overall scheme of the taxpayers' trade or business. * * * "A businessman's suit, a saleslady's dress, the accountant's glasses are necessary for their business but the necessity does not overcome the personal nature of these items and make them a deductible business expense.* * * "

In the instant case, we are convinced that petitioner and his partners and associates discussed business at lunch, that the meeting was a part of their working day, and that this time was the most convenient time at which to meet. We are also convinced that the partnership benefited from the exchange of information and ideas that occurred.

But this does not make his lunch deductible any more than riding to work together each morning to discuss partnership affairs would make his share of the commuting costs deductible. If only the four partners attended the luncheons, petitioner's share of the expenses (assuming they were coequal partners) would have corresponded to his share of the luncheons. This is not an occasion for the general taxpayer to share in the cost of his daily sustenance. Indeed, if petitioner is correct, only the unimaginative would dine at their own expense.

Petitioner argues, in the alternative, that the cost of the meals may be deducted under sec. 1.162–5(a), Income Tax Regs., as an educational expense. Certainly the trading of information and ideas was beneficial to younger and older attorneys alike, and in that sense the lunches were educational. However, we find no cases supporting a deduction for informal training of the type that occurred here. Nor do we think Congress intended every occasion upon which information was imparted to qualify for deduction under section 1.162–5(a), Income Tax Regs. Again, combining nourishment with enlightenment does not make the nourishment deductible.

Decision will be entered under Rule 155.

Reviewed by the Court.

STERRETT, J., concurring:

I concur in the result in this particular case, but I want to make it clear that I do not view this opinion as disallowing the cost of meals in all instances where only partners, co-workers, etc., are involved. We have here findings that the partners met at lunch because it was "convenient" and "convenient" 5 days a week, 52 weeks a year.

TANNENWALD, FAY, GOFFE, WHITAKER, KORNER, SHIELDS, HAMBLEN, and COHEN, JJ., agree with this concurring opinion.

QUESTIONS

1. What if the firm ate lunch together once a week?

2. What if the firm ate lunch in a conference room within the law offices, with the meals catered by the Cafe Angelo? What if the firm simply bought the Cafe Angelo?

DANVILLE PLYWOOD CORPORATION v. UNITED STATES

United States Court of Appeals, Federal Circuit, 1990.
899 F.2d 3.

RICHARD MILLS, DISTRICT JUDGE.

* * * Danville is a closely held Virginia corporation owned by George Buchanan, his wife, and their relatives. At all relevant times Buchanan has served as Danville's president.

Danville manufactures custom plywood for use in kitchen cabinets, store fixtures, furniture, wall panels, wall plaques, and similar items. Danville sells to wholesale distributors who in turn sell to architects, mill work houses, and cabinet shops. Each order Danville receives is filled to customer specifications and thus Danville does not maintain a fixed inventory of finished products.

* * * On its returns for 1980 and 1981 Danville claimed deductions totaling $103,444.51[2] in connection with a weekend trip for 120 persons to the Super Bowl in New Orleans, Louisiana, from January 23 through January 26, 1981.

To decide who to invite to the Super Bowl weekend, Danville looked at the current and potential income from each customer. Danville did not invite specific individuals; instead, it sent two invitations to the selected customer and instructed the customer to decide whom to send. Buchanan asserts that Danville asked the customers to send individuals with "decision making authority." The majority of the customers sent one individual who was accompanied by that individual's spouse.

Of the people attending the Super Bowl, six were employees of Danville (including Buchanan), five were spouses of the employees, one was the daughter of a shareholder, three were Buchanan's children, and

---

2. Of this amount $27,151.00 constituted payment for Super Bowl tickets; $30,721.51 for airfare for Danville's employees and guests; $45,300.00 to a tour agency for accommodations and related services; and $272.00 to General Aviation to pick up football tickets. Of the amount claimed the Commissioner disallowed $98,297.83. Of this amount $64,467.51 was disallowed on the 1980 return and $33,380.32 on the 1981 return.

four were Buchanan friends. The remaining individuals were 58 of Danville's customers, 38 spouses of those customers, two children of one of Danville's customers, and three customers of one of Danville's customers.

In making arrangements for the Super Bowl weekend, Danville sent a letter on June 5, 1980, to Abbott Tours, a New Orleans travel agency. In the letter Danville requested accommodations for three nights, Super Bowl tickets, banquet facilities for one night, and a Mississippi River cruise. Notably, Danville did not indicate that the trip was in any way business related and failed to request access to meeting rooms or other facilities appropriate for a business trip. As finalized, the weekend included accommodations at the Sheraton Hotel, a Saturday evening dinner in the hotel's dining room, and an outing to the French Quarter on Saturday night.

On January 13, 1981, Danville sent a letter to the selected customers stating that "Super Bowl weekend is just around the corner." This letter also failed to contain any reference to business meetings or discussions of any kind. Shortly before Super Bowl weekend, Buchanan distributed a memorandum to the Danville employees who would be going to New Orleans. In the memorandum, Buchanan told his employees they should promote certain types of wood, inform the customers Danville could supply 10 ft. panels, and survey the customers regarding their need for Danville to purchase a "cut-to-size" saw.

Upon arrival at the hotel, Danville's customers were met at a hospitality desk in the lobby staffed by family members of Danville's employees. Danville also displayed some of its products in an area adjacent to the lobby. During the weekend Danville's employees met informally with customers.

During the dinner on Saturday evening Danville's customers shared the dining room with other hotel guests, although the customers were segregated in one section of the dining room. There were no speakers or general announcements made at the dinner. Buchanan and Danville's other employees circulated among the tables to speak with their guests. None of the customers placed orders during the weekend although some promised to contact Danville's employees in the future. The only scheduled activity on Sunday was the Super Bowl game and by Monday the guests were preparing to leave.

     * * *

II. Statutory Scheme

* * * Prior to 1961, § 162 was the sole statutory provision regulating the deduction of entertainment expenses. In response to what was perceived as widespread abuse of expense accounts and entertainment expenses Congress enacted § 274. This provision is referred to as a "disallowance provision" and its effect is to disallow certain deductions for entertainment expenses which would otherwise be properly deductible under § 162.

Under the stricter limitations of § 274, no deduction for business expenses allowable under § 162 shall be allowed unless the taxpayer establishes that the item was "directly related to" or "associated with" the active conduct of the taxpayer's trade or business. In the case of the latter situation the item for which the deduction is claimed must directly precede or follow a substantial and bona fide business discussion.

Therefore, to be deductible, an entertainment expense must meet the requirements of both § 162 and § 274. First, the expense must be an ordinary and necessary business expense under § 162. Second, the expense must be either "directly related to" or "associated with" the active conduct of the taxpayer's business. * * *

IV.   Section 162

A.   Children and Shareholder

Three of Buchanan's children and two children of Danville's customers as well as a shareholder of Danville attended Super Bowl weekend at Danville's expense. In its brief on appeal, Danville concedes that the expenses of these six individuals were not deductible and thus we need not address this class of attendees.

B.   Employees' Spouses

Five spouses of Danville employees also attended Super Bowl weekend. Danville argues that these individuals "manned the hospitality desk all day Saturday and Sunday morning, and otherwise assisted by handling other tasks which needed attention." Danville also argues that Buchanan was aware that a significant number of the customer representatives would bring their wives and thus he "deemed it appropriate and helpful to have five wives of Danville employees" there to meet and entertain the spouses of the customer representatives.

Treasury regulations provide that when a taxpayer's wife accompanies him on a business trip, her expenses are not deductible unless the taxpayer can adequately show that her presence has a bona fide business purpose. The wife's performance of an incidental service does not meet this requirement. This regulation does not directly apply because the taxpayer here is a corporation and the deductibility involved the expenses not of the corporation president's wife, but of the wives of other employees. The principle upon which that regulation rests, however, is no less applicable to the wives of employees of a corporate taxpayer than it is to the wife of an individual taxpayer.

Under the standards of this regulation, the Claims Court concluded that the wives of Danville's employees performed at best a social function and thus their expenses were not deductible. See Weatherford v. United States, 418 F.2d 895, 897 (spouse's travel expenses not deductible because her "business function" was to be a socially gracious wife, not a professional businesswoman).

Danville cites United States v. Disney, 413 F.2d 783, 788, and Wilkins v. United States, 348 F.Supp. 1282, 1284, as examples of cases which allowed a taxpayer to deduct his wife's expenses. In Disney, the court stated that the "critical inquiries are whether the dominant purpose of the trip was to serve her husband's business purpose in making the trip and whether she actually spent a substantial amount of her time in assisting her husband in fulfilling that purpose." The court in Disney went on to state that "the result reached in an individual case is so dependent upon the peculiar facts of that case, that the decisions called to our attention are of only limited assistance."

In the case at bar, Danville simply did not present enough evidence to the Claims Court to sustain its burden of establishing that the spouses of Danville's employees performed a bona fide business purpose and not merely incidental services. See Meridian Wood Prod. Co. v. United States, 725 F.2d 1183 (expenses of corporation's president's spouse not deductible because her primary purpose was to socialize with other wives of business associates). The record leaves one with the overall impression that the wives of the employees went along for fun and merely helped out when they could.

C. Customer Representatives and Spouses

As stated previously, to qualify as an "ordinary and necessary" business expense under § 162(a) an expenditure must be both "common and accepted" in the community of which Danville is a part as well as "appropriate" for the development of Danville's business. The Claims Court found that Danville failed to carry its burden of proof to establish that the expenses for the customer representatives met these requirements. In support of this conclusion the Court cited the testimony of Will Gregory, General Manager for Central Wholesale Supply, one of Danville's customers. Mr. Gregory testified that he had attended seminars hosted by the National Building Materials Distributors Association which consisted of booths manned by vendors where the attendees could talk privately about the company's products.

Danville argues that nothing could be more "ordinary, necessary, usual, customary, common or important in a manufacturing business than efforts to promote products and increase sales." We agree that this is true as a general proposition. However, what is at issue in this case is the manner in which Danville attempted to promote its products and increase sales. The Claims Court stated that the "record inescapably demonstrates that the entertainment ... was the central focus of the excursion, with all other activities running a distant second in importance."

We cannot say the Claims Court finding is clearly erroneous. What business discussions that occurred were incidental to the main event, i.e. entertainment for Danville's customers. Similarly, expenses for the customers of one of Danville's customers who attended Super Bowl weekend are not deductible under § 162.

D. Danville's Employees

The Treasury Regulations provide that only traveling expenses which are reasonable and necessary to the conduct of the taxpayer's business and which are directly attributable to it may be deducted. The Claims Court held that Danville failed to establish that the expenses of its employees were attributable to its business, and that the trip was undertaken primarily for business purposes. The court found that none of the correspondence between Danville and Abbott Tours referred to the business nature of the trip. Furthermore, the Claims Court described the agenda distributed by Danville to its employees as little more than a "bootstrapping afterthought."

Danville argues that its employees met with customer representatives throughout the weekend and discussed business. As indicated by the Claims Court, only two of the six Danville employees who attended the Super Bowl weekend testified. Thus, the Court could not ascertain how the other four employees spent their time. In addition, the three customer representatives who testified indicated that the discussions which did occur took place "whenever we found [Buchanan] . . . and whenever we could catch him." In light of this evidence the Claims Court concluded that Danville had failed to carry its burden of proof of demonstrating that the trip was undertaken for bona fide business purposes or that the expenses were directly attributable to Danville's business.

Danville argues that these quotes of the customer representatives were taken out of context and the full quotes indicate that the representatives talked to Buchanan whenever he was not engaged in discussions with other customers. Accepting Danville's version as true, once again we must agree with the Claims Court that Danville failed to present sufficient evidence to satisfy its burden of proof. The Super Bowl weekend appears to have been little more than a group social excursion with business playing a subsidiary role.

On the narrow facts of this case, we hold that the decision of the Claims Court that Danville failed to satisfy its burden of proof that the Super Bowl expenses were "ordinary and necessary" business expenses under § 162(a) of the Code is not clearly erroneous.

In view of our holding that Danville has not met its burden relative to § 162(a), any discussion of § 274 is unnecessary.

V. Conclusion

We conclude that, on the unique facts of this case, Danville has failed to demonstrate that the findings of the Claims Court are clearly erroneous.

The judgment of the Claims Court is in all aspects

AFFIRMED.

NOTES AND QUESTIONS

1. For current law on spouses, see § 274(m)(3).

2. Is there any doubt that the expenditures on behalf of the customer representatives made it more likely that those customers would continue to buy Danville's products? Why isn't that enough?

PEVSNER v. COMMISSIONER

United States Court of Appeals, Fifth Circuit, 1980.
628 F.2d 467.

SAM D. JOHNSON, CIRCUIT JUDGE:

* * * Since June 1973 Sandra J. Pevsner, taxpayer, has been employed as the manager of the Sakowitz Yves St. Laurent Rive Gauche Boutique located in Dallas, Texas. The boutique sells only women's clothes and accessories designed by Yves St. Laurent (YSL), one of the leading designers of women's apparel. Although the clothing is ready to wear, it is highly fashionable and expensively priced. Some customers of the boutique purchase and wear the YSL apparel for their daily activities and spend as much as $20,000 per year for such apparel.

As manager of the boutique, the taxpayer is expected by her employer to wear YSL clothes while at work. In her appearance, she is expected to project the image of an exclusive lifestyle and to demonstrate to her customers that she is aware of the YSL current fashion trends as well as trends generally. Because the boutique sells YSL clothes exclusively, taxpayer must be able, when a customer compliments her on her clothes, to say that they are designed by YSL. In addition to wearing YSL apparel while at the boutique, she wears them while commuting to and from work, to fashion shows sponsored by the boutique, and to business luncheons at which she represents the boutique. During 1975, the taxpayer bought, at an employee's discount, the following items: four blouses, three skirts, one pair of slacks, one trench coat, two sweaters, one jacket, one tunic, five scarves, six belts, two pairs of shoes and four necklaces. The total cost of this apparel was $1,381.91. In addition, the sum of $240 was expended for maintenance of these items.

Although the clothing and accessories purchased by the taxpayer were the type used for general purposes by the regular customers of the boutique, the taxpayer is not a normal purchaser of these clothes. The taxpayer and her husband, who is partially disabled because of a severe heart attack suffered in 1971, lead a simple life and their social activities are very limited and informal. Although taxpayer's employer has no objection to her wearing the apparel away from work, taxpayer stated that she did not wear the clothes during off-work hours because she felt that they were too expensive for her simple everyday lifestyle. Another reason why she did not wear the YSL clothes apart from work was to make them last longer. Taxpayer did admit at trial, however, that a number of the articles were things she could have worn off the job and in which she would have looked "nice."

On her joint federal income tax return for 1975, taxpayer deducted $990 as an ordinary and necessary business expense with respect to her purchase of the YSL clothing and accessories. However, in the tax court, taxpayer claimed a deduction for the full $1381.91 cost of the apparel and for the $240 cost of maintaining the apparel. The tax court allowed the taxpayer to deduct both expenses in the total amount of $1621.91. The tax court reasoned that the apparel was not suitable to the private lifestyle maintained by the taxpayer. This appeal by the Commissioner followed.

The principal issue on appeal is whether the taxpayer is entitled to deduct as an ordinary and necessary business expense the cost of purchasing and maintaining the YSL clothes and accessories worn by the taxpayer in her employment as the manager of the boutique. This determination requires an examination of the relationship between Section 162(a) of the Internal Revenue Code of 1954, which allows a deduction for ordinary and necessary expenses incurred in the conduct of a trade or business, and Section 262 of the Code, which bars a deduction for all "personal, living, or family expenses." Although many expenses are helpful or essential to one's business activities—such as commuting expenses and the cost of meals while at work—these expenditures are considered inherently personal and are disallowed under Section 262.

The generally accepted rule governing the deductibility of clothing expenses is that the cost of clothing is deductible as a business expense only if: (1) the clothing is of a type specifically required as a condition of employment, (2) it is not adaptable to general usage as ordinary clothing, and (3) it is not so worn.

In the present case, the Commissioner stipulated that the taxpayer was required by her employer to wear YSL clothing and that she did not wear such apparel apart from work. The Commissioner maintained, however, that a deduction should be denied because the YSL clothes and accessories purchased by the taxpayer were adaptable for general usage as ordinary clothing and she was not prohibited from using them as such. The tax court, in rejecting the Commissioner's argument for the application of an objective test, recognized that the test for deductibility was whether the clothing was "suitable for general or personal wear" but determined that the matter of suitability was to be judged subjectively, in light of the taxpayer's lifestyle. Although the court recognized that the YSL apparel "might be used by some members of society for general purposes," it felt that because the "wearing of YSL apparel outside work would be inconsistent with ... (taxpayer's) lifestyle," sufficient reason was shown for allowing a deduction for the clothing expenditures.

In reaching its decision, the tax court relied heavily upon Yeomans v. Commissioner, 30 T.C. 757. In Yeomans, the taxpayer was employed as fashion coordinator for a shoe manufacturing company. Her employment necessitated her attendance at meetings of fashion experts and at fashion shows sponsored by her employer. On these occasions, she was expected to wear clothing that was new, highly styled, and such as "might be sought after and worn for personal use by women who make it a practice to dress according to the most advanced or extreme fashions." However, for her personal wear, Ms. Yeomans preferred a plainer and more conservative style of dress. As a consequence, some of the items she purchased were not suitable for her private and personal wear and were not so worn. The tax court allowed a deduction for the cost of the items that were not suitable for her personal wear. Although the basis for the decision in Yeomans is not clearly stated, the tax court in the case sub judice determined that (a) careful reading of Yeomans shows that, without a doubt, the Court based its decision on a determination of Ms. Yeomans' lifestyle and that the clothes were not suitable for her use in such lifestyle. Furthermore, the Court recognized that the clothes Ms. Yeomans purchased were suitable for wear by women who customarily wore such highly styled apparel, but such fact did not cause the court to decide the issue against her. Thus, Yeomans clearly decides the issue before us in favor of the petitioner.

Notwithstanding the tax court's decision in *Yeomans*, the Circuits that have addressed the issue have taken an objective, rather than subjective, approach. * * * Under an objective test, no reference is made to the individual taxpayer's lifestyle or personal taste. Instead, adaptability for personal or general use depends upon what is generally accepted for ordinary street wear.

The principal argument in support of an objective test is, of course, administrative necessity. The Commissioner argues that, as a practical matter, it is virtually impossible to determine at what point either price or style makes clothing inconsistent with or inappropriate to a taxpayer's lifestyle. Moreover, the Commissioner argues that the price one pays and the styles one selects are inherently personal choices governed by taste, fashion, and other unmeasurable values. Indeed, the tax court has rejected the argument that a taxpayer's personal taste can dictate whether clothing is appropriate for general use. An objective test, although not perfect, provides a practical administrative approach that allows a taxpayer or revenue agent to look only to objective facts in determining whether clothing required as a condition of employment is adaptable to general use as ordinary streetwear. Conversely, the tax court's reliance on subjective factors provides no concrete guidelines in determining the deductibility of clothing purchased as a condition of employment.

In addition to achieving a practical administrative result, an objective test also tends to promote substantial fairness among the greatest number of taxpayers. As the Commissioner suggests, it apparently would be the tax court's position that two similarly situated YSL boutique managers with identical wardrobes would be subject to disparate tax consequences depending upon the particular manager's lifestyle and "socio-economic level." This result, however, is not consonant with a reasonable interpretation of §§ 162 and 262.

For the reasons stated above, the decision of the tax court upholding the deduction for taxpayer's purchase of YSL clothing is reversed. Consequently, the portion of the tax court's decision upholding the deduction for maintenance costs for the clothing is also

REVERSED.

QUESTIONS AND NOTE

1. Remember Marla Maples' diamond tiara (*supra* at 90). Could it have been a business uniform?

2. Many law enforcement personnel are required to wear bullet-proof vests on the job. Also, they are required to be armed at all times. Most wear over-sized, ill-fitting clothing, over the vests, to conceal the heat they're packing. They claim that the clothing is not suitable for off-duty wear. IRS, however, has challenged the clothing deductions. What do you think?

3. In Morris v. Federal Commissioner of Taxation, 2002 ATC 4404, the Australian tax court allowed some ten taxpayers to deduct the costs of hats, sunscreen and sunglasses as business expenses. All ten had outdoor jobs, including farming, surveying, and charter fishing boats. They claimed that, but for their outdoor jobs, they would not have incurred the expenses. How would a United States court have ruled?

4. In tax year 1991, Stevie Nicks, who was then singing with Fleetwood Mac, deducted $43,291 paid for professional wardrobe and maintenance expenses. The IRS balked. In her Complaint, Ms. Nicks alleged:

> When performing, Petitioner is required to wear specially-designed and/or specially-purchased clothing. This clothing must be themed to each performance (including adaptation to the venue, type of music, clothing worn by others, etc.), is not suitable for ordinary wear, and is not adaptable to Petitioner's general or continued usage. In fact, much of this clothing must be discarded immediately after use because it simply cannot be reused, given the energy levels of Petitioner's performance and the heat generated on stage from lights and physical exertion. Clothing which is not discarded requires extensive repair and maintenance, including sewing, cleaning, etc.

* * *

There is no further public record available on this matter. It is assumed that it was settled.

* * *

Do you believe that it is possible sweat through a costume so badly that it is useless, after just one performance?

B. DEDUCTIONS FOR EDUCATION

1. GENERAL

Code: § 274(m)(2)

Regulations: § 1.162–5 (p 985)

In *Welch*, Mr. Justice Cardozo writes:

[A] man conceives the notion that he will be able to practice his vocation with greater ease and profit if he has an opportunity to enrich his culture. Forthwith the price of his education becomes an expense of the business, reducing the income subject to taxation. * * * The money spent in acquiring [the education] is well and wisely spent. It is not an ordinary expense of the operation of a business.

Welch was quoted in *Coughlin*, *infra*.

Of course, a stockbroker cannot deduct music appreciation classes as a business expense. However, isn't it equally obvious that a lawyer should be allowed to deduct the cost of mandatory continuing legal education? Educational expenses, then, are yet another category of expense that has both business and personal attributes. Once again, the system needs safeguards against predominantly personal expenditures trying to disguise themselves as deductible business expenditures.

With educational expenses, there is a further aspect to consider. One way of arguing for the deductibility of educational expenses is to show that they are similar to other business expenses, in that they are incurred in order to enhance the earning potential of an income-producing asset. However, in this case, the income-producing asset is a human being. This dimension suggests the concept of human capital, discussed *infra*.

COUGHLIN v. COMMISSIONER

United States Court of Appeals, Second Circuit, 1953.
203 F.2d 307.

CHASE, CIRCUIT JUDGE.

The petitioner has been a member of the bar for many years and in 1944 was admitted to practice before the Treasury Department. In 1946 he was in active practice in Binghamton, N.Y., as a member of a firm of lawyers there. The firm engaged in general practice but did considerable work which required at least one member to be skilled in matters pertaining to Federal taxation and to maintain such skill by keeping informed as to changes in the tax laws and the significance of pertinent court decisions when made. His partners relied on him to keep advised on that subject and he accepted that responsibility. One of the various ways in which he discharged it was by attending, in the above mentioned year, the Fifth Annual Institute on Federal Taxation which was conducted in New York City under the sponsorship of the Division of General Education of New York University. In so doing he incurred expenses for tuition, travel, board and lodging of $305, which he claimed as an allowable deduction under § 23(a)(1)(A) [current § 162], as ordinary and necessary expenses incurred in carrying on a trade or business and no question is raised as to their reasonableness in amount. The Commissioner disallowed the deduction and the Tax Court, four judges dissenting, upheld the disallowance on the ground that the expenses were non-business ones "because of the educational and personal nature of the object pursued by the petitioner."

The Tax Court found that the Institute on Federal Taxation was not conducted for the benefit of those unversed in the subject Federal taxation and students were warned away. In 1946, it was attended by 408 attorneys, accountants, trust officers, executives of corporations and the like. In 1947, over 1500 of such people from many states were in attendance. It was "designed by its sponsors to provide a place and atmosphere where practitioners could gather trends, thinking and developments in the field of Federal taxation from experts accomplished in that field."

Thus there is posed for solution a problem which involves no dispute as to the basic facts but is, indeed, baffling because, as is so often true of legal problems, the correct result depends upon how to give the facts the right order of importance.

We may start by noticing that the petitioner does not rely upon § 23(a)(2) [current § 212] which permits the deduction of certain non-trade or non-business expenses, but rests entirely upon his contention that the deduction he took was allowable as an ordinary and necessary expense incurred in the practice of his profession. The expenses were deductible under [§ 162(a)] if they were "directly connected with" or "proximately resulted from" the practice of his profession. And if it were usual for lawyers in practice similar to his to incur such expenses they were "ordinary." They were also "necessary" if appropriate and helpful. But this is an instance emphasizing how dim a line is drawn between expenses which are deductible because incurred in trade or business, i.e., because professional, and those which are non-deductible because personal. * * *

In Welch v. Helvering, there is a dictum that the cost of acquiring learning is a personal expense. But the issue decided in that case is far removed from the one involved here. There the taxpayer paid debts for which he was not legally liable whose payment enhanced his reputation for personal integrity and consequently the value of the good will of his business, and it was held that these payments were personal expenses. The general reference to the cost of education as a personal expense was made by way of illustrating the point then under decision, and it related to that knowledge which is obtained for its own sake as an addition to one's cultural background or for possible use in some work which might be started in the future. There is no indication that an exception is not to be made where the information acquired was needed for use in a lawyer's established practice. * * *

This situation is closely akin to that in Hill v. Commissioner, 4 Cir., 181 F.2d 906, where the expenses incurred by a teacher in attending a summer school were held deductible. The only difference is in the degree of necessity which prompted the incurrence of the expenses. The teacher couldn't retain her position unless she complied with the requirements for the renewal of her teaching certificate; and an optional way to do that, and the one she chose, was to take courses in education at a recognized institution of learning. Here the petitioner did not need a renewal of his license to practice and it may be assumed that he could have continued as a member of his firm whether or not he kept currently informed as to the law of Federal taxation. But he was morally bound to keep so informed and did so in part by means of his attendance at this session of the Institute. It was a way well adapted to fulfill his professional duty to keep sharp the tools he actually used in his going trade or business. It may be that the knowledge he thus gained incidentally increased his fund of learning in general and, in that sense, the cost of acquiring it may have been a personal expense; but we think that the immediate, over-all professional need to incur the expenses in order to perform his work with due regard to the current status of the law so overshadows the personal aspect that it is the decisive feature.

It serves also to distinguish these expenditures from those made to acquire a capital asset. Even if in its cultural aspect knowledge should for tax purposes be considered in the nature of a capital asset as was suggested in Welch v. Helvering, the rather evanescent character of that for which the petitioner spent his money deprives it of the sort of permanency such a concept embraces.

Decision reversed and cause remanded for the allowance of the deduction.

NOTES

Mr. Coughlin was maintaining or improving his skills. See Reg. § 1.162–5(c)(1). Mrs. Hill, mentioned in the *Coughlin* case, was meeting her employer's requirements. See Reg. § 1.162–5(c)(2).

In addition to these two regulations setting out when you **can** deduct educational expenses. there are two regulations which set out when you **can't**. See Reg. § 1.162–5(b)(2) [minimum educational requirements] and Reg. § 1.162–5(b)(3) [qualification for a new trade or business]. Too bad about that law school tuition.

SINGLETON–CLARKE v. COMMISSIONER

United States Tax Court.
T.C. Summ. Op. 2009–182.

LORI A. SINGLETON-CLARKE, pro se.

BRIAN S. JONES, for respondent.

GOLDBERG, SPECIAL TRIAL JUDGE:

* * *

Petitioner's Job History

Petitioner earned a bachelor of science degree in nursing (BSN) from New York University in 1984. Petitioner became a registered nurse (RN) and for the next 24 years worked in various capacities for a number of hospitals, medical centers, and long-term care facilities.

From 1984 to 1993 she worked initially as an acute bedside clinical nurse and later as a team leader supervising nurses providing acute bedside care. From 1993 to 2004 she held various nursing management positions of increasing responsibility, eventually serving as a director of nursing for a 150–bed subacute long-term care facility, responsible for "24/7" management of 110 nurses plus technicians. From 2004 to 2008 petitioner worked sequentially at three different hospitals. Though her titles were different, her tasks, activities, and responsibilities were nearly identical, concentrating in a nonsupervisory capacity as a quality control coordinator.

* * *

II. *The MBA/HCM*

Petitioner began taking courses at the University of Phoenix in March 2005, graduating in April 2008 with an MBA/HCM. She chose the University of Phoenix because the institution allowed students to complete the program via online courses, which was a major priority for petitioner.

Petitioner enrolled in the program to become more effective in her then-present duties. She realized that nursing had evolved greatly in the 24 years since she earned her bachelor's degree, and she felt disadvantaged working with highly educated doctors. Petitioner believed that although an MBA was not required for her job, the degree would give her greater credibility and the courses would make her more effective in her present and future role as a quality control coordinator.

The University of Phoenix MBA/HCM provides students "with the business management skills needed to manage successfully in today's health care delivery systems." The program features courses in "health care organizations, health care finance, quality and database management, health care infrastructure, and health care strategic management." Petitioner did well in her course work, graduating with a 3.57 grade point average.

Petitioner paid the entire cost of the program. None of her employers had a reimbursement policy for the MBA/HCM program.

III. *Application of the Law to Petitioner's Factual Situation*

A. *Petitioner's New Job at St. Mary's*

Respondent contends that without receiving the MBA/HCM in April 2008 petitioner would not have obtained her final job, the one she started in September 2008 at St. Mary's, because the St. Mary's job description, in addition to requiring an RN license, which petitioner already possessed, required at least a bachelor of science in health care administration, which petitioner had not previously earned.

Though the titles of the jobs varied, petitioner's three jobs since 2004 were nearly identical, requiring serving as a quality control coordinator at acute care hospitals and medical centers. We believe that St. Mary's would have gladly hired petitioner as a performance management coordinator even without the MBA/HCM. All three quality control positions required an RN license or a bachelor's in nursing, with clinical or risk management experience; credentials which petitioner possessed. The first two employers, Civista and Children's, had hired petitioner without the MBA/HCM. Further, petitioner was a multiple award winner, having received recognition three times from the Governor of Maryland and from three other prominent organizations. Moreover, petitioner had worked her way up to serving as a director of nursing responsible for 110 nurses plus additional technicians, clearly indicating high competence. All three quality control positions, while important, were a step down in status and pay from her former duties. For all of these reasons, we find that the MBA/HCM may have been a helpful addition to her qualifications, but was not an essential prerequisite for petitioner to secure the position at St. Mary's.

B. *Whether an MBA Qualifies Taxpayers for Any New Trade or Business*

The final remaining inquiry then is whether as an objective matter the MBA/HCM qualifies petitioner for any new trade or business, not just the particular job at St. Mary's that she acquired. Respondent contends that the MBA/HCM does qualify petitioner for a new trade or business, because in respondent's words, under the regulation "the tasks and activities she was qualified for before she obtained the degree are different than those which she is qualified to perform afterwards". We disagree.

An MBA degree is different from a degree that serves as foundational qualification to attain a professional license. For instance, this Court had denied deductions for law school expenses, because a law degree qualifies a taxpayer for the new trade or business of being a lawyer.

An MBA is a more general course of study that does not lead to a professional license or certification. This Court has had differing outcomes when deciding whether a taxpayer may deduct education expenses related to pursing an MBA, depending on the facts and circumstances of each case. The decisive factor generally is whether the taxpayer was already established in their trade or business.

For example, in the following two cases we held that the taxpayers were not entitled to deduct their MBA expenses. In *Link v. Commissioner,* 90 T.C. 460, 463–464 (1988), affd. without published opinion 869 F.2d 1491 (6th Cir.1989), the taxpayer had not established a trade or business. After graduating with an undergraduate degree in May 1981, he worked during the summer but then promptly commenced his MBA coursework in September 1981. Similarly, in *Schneider v. Commissioner,* T.C. Memo. 1983–753, the taxpayer, after graduating from West Point, served honorably in the Army for 5 years before resigning from active duty with the rank of captain and immediately starting in Harvard's MBA program. Although the taxpayer established outstanding management experience in the Army, he had never worked in business, and therefore we decided his "work as an Army officer is a different trade or business from the consulting business for which his course of study at Harvard prepared him." *Id.*

In contrast, in *Sherman v. Commissioner,* T.C. Memo.1977–301, we held that another former Army officer was entitled to deduct the expense of his Harvard MBA. The difference is that the former officer in *Sherman* had worked for 2 years as a civilian employee after resigning his Army commission and before matriculating to Harvard. Moreover, the duties of the taxpayer in *Sherman* during his 2 years of civilian work included formulating and monitoring management plans and reviewing and evaluating policies involving purchasing, inventory control, and personnel management. These were the types of subject matters taught in the MBA program.

Two other cases also illustrate situations where an MBA did not lead to a new trade or business. In *Allemeier v. Commissioner, supra,* before beginning an MBA program, the taxpayer had already worked 3 years for a pediatric orthodontic laboratory, during which time his responsibilities expanded to include designing marketing strategies for additional products, organizing informational seminars, and traveling extensively to conventions to lead seminars. This Court held that the taxpayer's trade or business did not significantly change because the MBA merely improved preexisting skills for the same general duties he was already performing before enrolling in the MBA program.

Likewise, in *Blair v. Commissioner,* T.C. Memo.1980–488, the taxpayer initially completed 1 year of undergraduate coursework. She then spent the next 13 years concentrating on raising a family while also working for small companies, gaining the equivalent of 5–1/2 years' experience in mostly clerical and secretarial duties. She also acquired some familiarity with bookkeeping, payroll, and personnel matters. Over the next 3 years the taxpayer earned a bachelor of arts degree in English, and then she was hired by a large international corporation, where she worked for a little more than 1 year as a personnel representative before commencing her MBA. The corporation promoted the taxpayer to personnel manager within 11 months after starting the 2–year MBA program. This Court held that "under any realistic interpretation" petitioner's new duties as a personnel manager did not constitute a new trade or business because she was already engaged in the same type of work, with the only major difference being that as a personnel manager she made decisions while as a personnel representative she made only recommendations. *Id.* Neither the difference in duties nor the new title was enough to constitute a new trade or business.

Analyzing petitioner's situation, her facts and circumstances far more closely resemble the cases that allowed a deduction for pursuing an MBA. Petitioner is unlike the student in *Link v. Commissioner, supra,* who went straight from his undergraduate degree into an MBA program, and the officer in *Schneider v. Commissioner, supra,* who went straight from the Army into an MBA program. Petitioner is considerably closer in circumstance to the taxpayers in *Sherman v. Commissioner, supra, Allemeier v. Commissioner,* T.C. Memo.2005–207, and *Blair v. Commissioner, supra,* who had 2 years, 3 years, and 1 year, respectively, of experience performing tasks and activities in their chosen professions before beginning their MBA programs. The facts in favor of petitioner are even stronger than those in the three cases above where the taxpayers prevailed. Petitioner worked for 1 year as a quality control coordinator and had more than 20 years of directly related work experience, gaining vast clinical and managerial knowledge in acute and subacute health care settings, before beginning the University of Phoenix MBA/HCM program.

In summary, the MBA/HCM may have improved petitioner's preexisting skill set, but objectively, she was already performing the tasks and activities of her trade or business before commencing the MBA. For all of the above reasons, we find that petitioner's MBA/HCM did not qualify her for a new trade or business, and we hold, therefore that petitioner may deduct her education expenses for 2005.

PROBLEMS

1. Doctor has been spending an increasing amount of time testifying as an expert witness in medical malpractice cases. Although she has no desire whatsoever to practice law, she decides to go to law school, in order to become a more effective expert witness. Is her law school tuition deductible?

2. Yacht salesman knows that he will sell more yachts if he can develop a rapport with his customers. In order to develop common interests with potential yacht purchasers, he takes golf lessons. Are the golf lessons deductible?

3. Lawyer has been practicing for five years in Milwaukee. Her firm gives her a one-year leave of absence to allow her to go to N.Y.U. for a tax LL.M. What expenses, if any, are deductible?

a) What if Lawyer had enrolled in N.Y.U. immediately upon graduating from law school?

b) What if Lawyer had graduated from law school, passed the Wisconsin bar, and accepted a position in the Milwaukee firm. After practising for six weeks, she takes a one-year leave of absence and goes to N.Y.U.

c) Does it change anything if tax law is a certified specialty in Wisconsin?

Compare Wassenaar v. Commissioner, 72 T.C. 1195 (1979) with Ruehmann v. Commissioner, T.C. Memo. 1971–157.

4. Alexander is a teacher of Greek. He spends his summers in Greece, soaking up Greek culture, the better to convey the essence of Greek culture to his students. Can he deduct his summer expenses?

2. HUMAN CAPITAL

Notes and Questions

1. A buys a machine for $45,000. The machine generates income of $100,000 over ten years, after which the machine is worthless and is discarded.

B, aged 57, goes to law school at night, and graduates at age 60. The law degree costs her $45,000 in tuition and books. She then practices law for 10 years, earning $10,000 per year more than she was earning before, for a total of $100,000 additional income resulting from the law degree. At age 70, she retires.

What would be proper treatment of A and B? Justify any differences in treatment.

2. Reconsider the two categories of deductible educational expenses mentioned in the regulations:

- maintaining or improving skills: Reg. § 1.162–5(c)(1)
- meeting requirements of employer: Reg. § 1.162–5(c)(2)

and the two categories of nondeductible educational expenditures:

- minimum educational requirements: Reg. § 1.162–5(b)(2)
- qualification for a new trade or business: Reg. § 1.162–5(b)(3)

Consider these categories in human capital terms, as expenditures incurred in order to improve the earnings potential of a human being as an income-producing asset. The two deductible categories look like maintenance and repair, which are generally deductible currently. In contrast, the two nondeductible categories look more like capital expenses, which are generally not currently deductible, but rather added to basis and amortized. The rub here is that human beings are not depreciable assets. Or are they? Consider *Sharon*, below.

SHARON v. COMMISSIONER

United States Tax Court, 1976.
66 T.C. 515, *aff'd per curiam*, 591 F.2d 1273 (9th Cir.1978).

Simpson, Judge:

* * *

Bar Admission Expenses

* * * [Sharon received his Bachelor's Degree from Brandeis University and his law degree from Columbia University] The petitioner expended a total of $210.20 in gaining admission to practice law in the State of New York. This amount included $175.20 for bar review courses and materials related thereto and a New York State bar examination fee of $25.

The petitioner was admitted to practice law in the State of New York on December 22, 1964. Thereafter, he was employed as an attorney by a law firm in New York City until 1967, when he accepted a position in the Office of Regional Counsel, Internal Revenue Service, and moved to California.

Although not required by his employer to be a member of the California bar, the petitioner decided to become a member of that State's bar after moving there. However, he found that the study of California law, which he undertook in preparation for the California bar examination, was helpful in his practice of law as an attorney in the Regional Counsel's office. The petitioner spent the following amounts in order to gain membership in the California bar:

Registration as law student in California	$ 20
California bar review course	$230
General bar examination fee	$150
Attorney's bar examination fee	$375
Admittance fee	$ 26
Total	$801

In 1969, the petitioner also spent a total of $11 in order to be admitted to practice before the U.S. District Court for the Northern District of California and the U.S. Court of Appeals for the Ninth Circuit. The petitioner's employer required only that he be admitted to practice before the U.S. Tax Court.

In 1970, the petitioner incurred the following expenses in connection with his admission to the U.S. Supreme Court:

Round trip air fare, San Francisco to New York	$238.35
Round trip rail fare, New York to Washington, and miscellaneous expenses	$ 75.00
Total	$313.35

The petitioner's employer did not require that he be admitted to practice before the U.S. Supreme Court but did assist him in this matter. The Chief Counsel of the IRS personally moved the admission of a group of IRS attorneys, including the petitioner. Furthermore, two of his supervisors signed his application as personal references.

During 1970, the U.S. Supreme Court rules required a personal appearance before it in Washington, D.C., to be admitted to practice.

On their return for 1969, the petitioners claimed a deduction for "Dues and Professional Expenses" of $492. The Commissioner disallowed $385 of such deduction on the grounds that the disallowed portion was not a deductible business expense, but was a nondeductible capital expenditure. On their return for 1970, the petitioners claimed a deduction of $313.35 for the cost of petitioner Joel A. Sharon's admission to practice before the U.S. Supreme Court. The Commissioner also disallowed such deduction. In addition to challenging the disallowed deductions, the petitioners alleged in their petition that they were entitled to amortize or depreciate the cost of petitioner Joel A. Sharon's education. The Commissioner denied this allegation in his answer.

* * *

Opinion

* * *

2. *Amortization of License to Practice Law in New York*

* * * The petitioner contends that he is entitled under section 167 to amortize the cost of such license over the period from the date of his admission to the bar to the date on which he reaches age 65, when he expects to retire. In his cost basis of this "intangible asset," he included the costs of obtaining his college degree ($11,125), obtaining his law degree ($6,910), a bar review course and related materials ($175.20), and the New York State bar examination fee ($25). As justification for including these education expenses in the cost of his license, he points out that, in order to take the New York bar examination, he was required to have graduated from college and an accredited law school.

The petitioners rely upon § 1.167(a)–3 of the Income Tax Regulations, which provides in part:

> If an intangible asset is known from experience or other factors to be of use in the business or in the production of income for only a limited period, the length of which can be estimated with reasonable accuracy, such an intangible asset may be the subject of a depreciation allowance. * * *

There is no merit in the petitioner's claim to an amortization deduction for the cost of his education and related expenses in qualifying himself for the legal profession. His college and law school expenses provided him with a general education which will be beneficial to him in a wide variety of ways. The costs and responsibility for obtaining such education are personal. Section 1.262–1(b)(9) of the Income Tax Regulations provides that expenditures for education are deductible only if they qualify under section 162 and section 1.162–5 of the regulations. In the words of section 1.162–5(b), all costs of "minimum educational requirements for qualification in * * * employment" are "personal expenditures or constitute an inseparable aggregate of personal and capital expenditures." There is no "rational" or workable basis for any allocation of this inseparable aggregate between the nondeductible personal component and a deductible component of the total expense. Such expenses are not made any less personal or any more separable from the aggregate by attempting to capitalize them for amortization purposes. Since the inseparable aggregate includes personal expenditures, the preeminence of section 262 over section 167 precludes any amortization deduction. The same reasoning applies to the costs of review courses and related expenses taken to qualify for the practice of a profession.

In his brief, the petitioner * * * assert[s] that he is not attempting to capitalize his educational costs, but rather, the cost of his license to practice law. Despite the label which the petitioner would apply to such costs, they nonetheless constitute the costs of his education, which are personal and nondeductible. Moreover, in his petition, he alleged that the capital asset he was seeking to amortize was his education.

There remains the $25 fee paid for the petitioner's license to practice in New York. This was not an educational expense but was a fee paid for the privilege of practicing law in New York, a nontransferable license which has value beyond the taxable years, and such fee is a capital expenditure. The Commissioner has limited his argument to the educational expenses and apparently concedes that the fee may be amortized. Since the amount of the fee is small, the petitioner might, ordinarily, be allowed to elect to deduct the full amount of the fee in the year of payment, despite its capital nature. Cf. sec. 1.162–12(a), Income Tax Regs., with respect to the treatment of inexpensive tools. However, since the fee was paid prior to the years in issue, we cannot allow a current deduction in this case. Therefore, in view of the Commissioner's concession and our conclusion with respect to the third and fourth issues, a proportionate part of such fee may be added to the amounts to be amortized in accordance with our resolution of the third issue.

3. License to Practice Law in California

The next issue to be decided is whether the petitioner may deduct or amortize the expenses he incurred in gaining admission to practice before the State and Federal courts of California. The Commissioner disallowed the amounts paid in 1969 to take the attorney's bar examination in California and the amounts paid for admission to the bar of the U.S. District Court for the Northern District of California and for admission to the U.S. Court of Appeals for the Ninth Circuit. He determined that such expenses were capital expenditures. In his brief, the petitioner argues for a current deduction only if the costs of his license to practice in California are not amortizable.

It is clear that the petitioner may not deduct under section 162(a) the fees paid to take the California attorney's bar examination and to gain admission to practice before two Federal courts in California. In Arthur E. Ryman, Jr., an associate professor of law sought to deduct as an ordinary business expense the cost of his admission to the bar of the State in which he resided. We held that since the taxpayer could reasonably expect the useful life of his license to extend beyond 1 year, the cost of such license was a capital expenditure and not a currently deductible business expense. Unlike the small fee paid to New York, the aggregate amount of such payments in 1969 is too large to disregard their capital nature and allow the petitioners to deduct them currently.

In connection with his alternative claim that he be allowed to amortize the costs of acquiring his license to practice law in California, the petitioner asserts that such costs total $801. Such amount includes the cost of a California bar review course, registration fees, and other items specified in our Findings of Fact. However, the petitioner is in error in including the cost of his bar review course, $230, in the capital cost of his license to practice in California.

It is clear that the amount the petitioner paid for the bar review course was an expenditure "made by an individual for education" within the meaning of section 1.162–5(a) of the Income Tax Regulations. Although the petitioner was authorized to practice law in some jurisdictions when he took the California bar review course, such course was nevertheless educational in the same sense as the first bar review course. The deductibility of such educational expenses is governed by the rules of section 1.162–5 of the regulations. The evidence indicates that the petitioner took the California bar examination twice, the latter time in early 1969, so that the payment for the California bar review course must have been made in a year prior to 1969. Thus, even if such payment is otherwise deductible, it may not be deducted in 1969.

Nor may the petitioner treat the payment for the California bar review course as a part of the costs of acquiring his license to practice in California. Educational expenses which are incurred to meet the minimum educational requirements for qualification in a taxpayer's trade or business or which qualify him for a new trade or business are "personal expenditures or constitute an inseparable aggregate of personal and capital expenditures." We find that the bar review course helped to qualify the petitioner for a new trade or business so that its costs are personal expenses.

We have previously adopted a "commonsense approach" in determining whether an educational expenditure qualifies a taxpayer for a "new trade or business." If the education qualified the taxpayer to perform prior to the education, then the education qualifies him for a new trade or business. Thus, we have held that a professor of social work is in a different trade or business than a social caseworker. A licensed public accountant is in a different trade or business than a certified public accountant. A registered pharmacist is in a different trade or business than an intern pharmacist, even though an intern performs many of the same tasks as a registered pharmacist, but under supervision.

Before taking the bar review course and passing the attorney's bar examination, the petitioner was an attorney licensed to practice law in New York. As an attorney for the Regional Counsel, he could represent the Commissioner in this Court. However, he could not appear in either the State courts of California, the Federal District Courts located there, nor otherwise act as an attorney outside the scope of his employment with the IRS. If he had done so, he would have been guilty of a misdemeanor. Yet, after receiving his license to practice law in California, he became a member of the State bar with all its accompanying privileges and obligations. He could appear and represent clients in all the courts of California. By comparing the tasks and activities that the petitioner was qualified to perform prior to receiving his license to practice in California with the tasks and activities he was able to perform after receiving such license, it is clear that he has qualified for a new trade or business. Consequently, the expenses of his bar review course were personal and are not includable in the cost of his license to practice law in California.

It is true that even before he became a member of the bar of California, the petitioner was engaged in the business of practicing law. However, in applying the provisions of section 1.162–5 of the regulations to determine whether educational expenses are personal or business in nature, it is not enough to find that the petitioner was already engaged in some business—we must ascertain the particular business in which he was previously engaged and whether the education qualified him to engage in a different business. Before taking the bar review course and becoming a member of the bar of California, the petitioner could not generally engage in the practice of law in that State, but the bar review course helped to qualify him to engage in such business.

The Commissioner does not argue that the capital expenditures incurred in obtaining his license to practice law in California may not be amortized. In a series of cases, the courts have held that the fees paid by physicians to acquire hospital privileges are not current business expenses but are capital expenditures amortizable over the doctor's life expectancy. We hold that the petitioner may treat the costs of acquiring his license to practice in California in a similar manner. Such costs include:

Registration fee	$ 20
General bar exam fee	$150
Attorney's bar exam fee	$375
Admittance fee	$ 26
U.S. District Court fee	$ 6
U.S. Court of Appeals fee	$ 5
Total	$582

Although the petitioner testified that he would retire at age 65 if he were financially able to do so, such testimony is not sufficient to establish the shorter useful life for which he argues.

We are aware that the petitioner's business as an employee of the Office of Regional Counsel did not require him to become a member of the California bar, and it may be argued that, within the meaning of section

167(a)(1), this intangible asset was not "used" in the petitioner's business during 1969 and 1970. However, the record does demonstrate that membership in the California bar was of some assistance to the petitioner in those years. Furthermore, when an attorney commences the practice of law, it is impossible to anticipate where his work will take him. He cannot with certainty establish what work he will receive and what bar memberships will be useful to him. Once he launches into the practice of law, he must decide what bars to join, and so long as there is some rational connection between his present or prospective work and those that he joins, we think that the expenses of joining them should be accepted as an appropriate cost of acquiring the necessary licenses to practice his profession. Since in 1969 and 1970, the petitioner was working in California, he had reason to anticipate that he might eventually leave the Government and enter into the private practice of law in that State; thus, when that possibility is considered together with the immediate benefit to be derived from membership in the California bar, there was ample reason for him to join such bar at that time. For these reasons, we are satisfied that in 1969 and 1970, the petitioner did make use of the tangible asset constituting the privilege of practicing law in California.

4. Supreme Court Admission

The fourth issue to be decided is whether the petitioner may either deduct or amortize the cost of gaining admission to practice before the U.S. Supreme Court. The petitioner deducted the travel costs he incurred in 1970 in traveling to Washington, D. C., to be personally present for the Supreme Court admission, as required by that Court's rules. The Commissioner disallowed the deduction and argued in his brief that such expenditures were capital in nature since the petitioner acquired an asset with a useful life beyond 1 year.

In his brief, the petitioner concedes that he may not deduct the costs he incurred if we find that his license to practice before the Supreme Court is an intangible asset with a useful life of more than 1 year. For the same reasons that we have concluded that the petitioner's New York and California licenses were intangible assets with a useful life of more than 1 year, we also hold that his Supreme Court license is an intangible asset with a useful life exceeding 1 year. Thus, the petitioner may not deduct under section 162 the cost of obtaining such license.

In order for such license to be amortizable pursuant to section 167, the petitioner must show that it was property used in his trade or business. There is little evidence concerning the petitioner's "use" in 1970 of his license to practice before the Supreme Court. However, he did testify that the admission to various bars was a factor used in evaluating attorneys for promotion by his employer, and the Commissioner never disputed such testimony. Furthermore, it is altogether appropriate for any attorney-at-law to become a member of the bar of the Supreme Court whenever it is convenient for him to do so. No one can know when the membership in such bar may be useful to him in the practice of law—it may bring tangible benefits today, tomorrow, or never; yet, if one holds himself out to practice law, there is ample reason for him to acquire membership in the bar of the Supreme Court. Under these circumstances, we find that the intangible asset acquired by becoming a member of such bar was used by the petitioner in 1970 and hold that he may amortize the costs of acquiring such asset over his life expectancy.

* * *

SCOTT, J., dissenting:

I respectfully disagree with the conclusion of the majority that the $25 license fee paid by petitioner to New York, the $571 paid to take the California bar examination, the $11 for admission to practice before two Federal courts in California, and the $313.35 paid for travel to Washington, via New York, to practice before the United States Supreme Court are properly amortizable over petitioner's life expectancy. I agree that these expenditures, except for transportation to Washington, via New York, the place of the home of petitioner's family, are capital expenditures. However there is nothing in this record to show the reasonable useful life of these expenditures. How long petitioner will practice law and where are so conjectural as to cause there to be no way to ascertain the reasonable useful life of the asset petitioner acquired through his capital expenditures. Although respondent apparently makes no contention that the trip to Washington, via New York, when petitioner was admitted to practice before the Supreme Court was personal, the clear inference from the fact that he did go to New York where his family lived before coming to Washington and returned there after he came to Washington is that petitioner went to New York to visit his family and incidentally came to Washington to be admitted to practice before the Supreme Court. However, if the view of the majority, that the cost of travel to Washington, via New York, was properly part of the cost of petitioner's admission to practice before the Supreme Court, were proper, then this, as the other capital expenditures, should not be amortizable since the useful life of the asset acquired is not reasonably ascertainable.

STERRETT, J., agrees with this dissent.

IRWIN, J., dissenting:

I disagree with that portion of the majority opinion which holds that petitioner may not treat the payment for the California bar review course as a part of the cost of acquiring his license to practice law in California. In the past, we have indeed adopted a "commonsense approach" in determining whether an educational expenditure qualifies a taxpayer for a new trade or business. However, I think we depart from that approach when we hold that an attorney, licensed to practice law in New York, qualifies for a new trade or business when he obtains a license to practice law in California. In Glenn v. Commissioner, 62 T.C. 270 (1974) we stated:

> We have not found a substantial case law suggesting criteria for determining when the acquisition of new titles or abilities constitutes

the entry into a new trade or business for purposes of section 1.162–5(c)(1), Income Tax Regs. What has been suggested, and we uphold such suggestion as the only commonsense approach to a classification, is that a comparison be made between the types of tasks and activities which the taxpayer was qualified to perform before the acquisition of a particular title or degree, and those which he is qualified to perform afterwards. Where we have found such activities and abilities to be significantly different, we have disallowed an educational expense deduction, based on our finding that there had been qualification for a new trade or business.

In my view there is no difference in the types of tasks and activities which petitioner was qualified to perform before and after he acquired his California license. By virtue of being licensed to practice in California, petitioner could perform the same types of tasks and activities in that state as he was already qualified to perform in New York. In this regard, respondent takes the position that once an individual is qualified to teach in State A, a college course taken in order to qualify for a teaching position in State B is neither a minimum educational requirement of his trade or business nor education qualifying him for a new trade or business. I would similarly conclude that once an individual is qualified to practice law in one State, a bar review course taken in preparation for the bar exam of another State is not education leading to qualification for a new trade or business.

STERRETT, J., dissenting:

[Opinion omitted]

QUESTIONS

- Would §§ 195 and 197 apply to these facts today?

- In 2008, David Wold offered his DePaul law degree for sale on eBay—minimum bid $100,000. Apparently, he had no further use for it. Had he sold it, how would the transaction have been taxed?

3. RECENT TAX INCENTIVES FOR EDUCATION

Code: §§ 25A, 529, 530

(a) The Hope Scholarship Credit

For each eligible student, the Hope Scholarship Credit is the sum of:

100% of the qualified tuition and fees paid by the taxpayer during the taxable year which do not exceed $1,000, and

50% of the next $1,000 of such expenses [§§ 25A(b)(1)(A) and (B) and (b)(4)].

The credit phases out for higher incomes. The threshold is modified adjusted gross income (MAGI) [§ 25A(d)(3)] of $40,000 [which is further adjusted for inflation], or $80,000 in the case of a joint return. For modified adjusted gross income in excess of the threshold, the credit is reduced pursuant to the following ratio:

$$\frac{\text{amount of reduction}}{\text{otherwise allowable credit}} = \frac{\text{Excess of MAGI over threshold}}{\$10,000 \: [\$20,000 \text{ joint return}]}$$

Example

Single taxpayer incurs over $2,000 in qualified tuition and related expenses. Her modified adjusted gross income is $45,000. Her computation is:

$$\frac{X}{\$1,500} = \frac{\$45,000 - \$40,000}{\$10,000}$$

Her Hope Scholarship Credit will be reduced from $1,500 to $750. Note that, at a modified adjusted gross income of $50,000, her credit will disappear [§ 25A(d)].

Qualified tuition and related expenses are tuition and fees paid for the taxpayer, the taxpayer's spouse, or the taxpayer's dependents, at an eligible educational institution for courses of instruction [§ 25A(f)(1)(A)]. The term does not include expenses for education involving sports, games, or hobbies, unless such education is part of an individual's degree program [§ 25A(f)(1)(B)]. Student activity fees, athletic fees, and insurance expenses do not qualify [§ 25A(f)(1)(C)].

The Hope Scholarship Credit is allowed only for the first two years of postsecondary education [§§ 25A(b)(2)(A) and (C)], and the student must be an eligible student for at least one academic period which begins during the year [§ 25A(b)(2)(B)]. To be eligible, the student must be carrying at least one half the normal full-time work load for the course of study [§ 25A(b)(3)(B)]. The credit will be denied for any student convicted of a felony drug offense [§ 25A(b)(2)(D)]. The credit amounts, and the income thresholds, are indexed for inflation [§ 25A(h)].

(b) The Lifetime Learning Credit

The Lifetime Learning Credit is equal to 20% of so much of the qualified tuition and related expenses paid by the taxpayer during the taxable year which do not exceed $10,000. Upper-income phaseouts and inflation indexing are the same as for the Hope Scholarship Credit. The eligible expenses are also the same, except that, for the Lifetime Learning Credit, they also include "expenses with respect to any course of instruction at an eligible educational institution to acquire or improve job skills of the individual" [§ 25A(c)(2)(B)]. Note that, for such expenses, the student need not be enrolled at least half-time.

The credits are coordinated with each other, with the scholarship exclusion, and with other educational benefits. Note that the Lifetime Learning Credit may be claimed for an unlimited number of years, while the Hope Scholarship Credit may only be claimed for two years.

(c) Saving for Higher Education

Section 529 allows states, and other eligible educational institutions, to establish qualified tuition programs. Pursuant to these programs, persons may purchase tuition credits, or establish accounts earmarked for the qualified higher education expenses, of a designated beneficiary. The program is itself exempt from taxation, and distributions paid toward the beneficiaries' higher education expenses will not be taxable to the beneficiary. The existence of these programs, however, may have an impact on the beneficiary's application for financial aid.

See also Section 530 on Coverdell educational savings accounts, and Section 135, which allows some redemptions of United States savings bonds for the purposes of paying higher education expenses, without triggering taxable income.

(d) Interest on Education Loans

Code: § 221

Regulations: § 1. 221–1

Interest on "qualified education loans" is deductible, up to a maximum of $2,500 per year [§ 221(b)(1)].

The deduction phases out for higher incomes. The threshold is "modified adjusted gross income" (MAGI) [§ 221(b)(2)(C)] of $50,000, or $100,000 in the case of joint returns [§ 221(b)(2)(B)(i)(II)]. These thresholds will be indexed for inflation [§ 221(g)]. For those with excess incomes, the maximum deduction will be reduced by the following ratio:

$$\frac{\text{amount of reduction}}{\text{otherwise allowable deduction}} = \frac{\text{excess of MAGI over threshold}}{\$15,000}$$

Example

Taxpayer is single in 2004. Her modified adjusted gross income is $57,500. She incurs interest on her qualified education loans in excess of $2,500. Assuming no inflation adjustments, her deduction is reduced as follows:

$$\frac{X}{\$2,500} = \frac{\$57,500 - \$50,000}{\$15,000}$$

Her deduction will be reduced from $2,500 to $1,250. Note that her deduction will disappear at a modified adjusted gross income of $65,000 [§ 221(b)].

A "qualified education loan" is any indebtedness incurred to pay qualified higher education expenses of the taxpayer, the taxpayer's spouse, or any dependent of the taxpayer at the time the indebtedness was incurred. The term includes refinancings of qualified education loans [§ 221(e)(1)]. If the taxpayer paying the interest is the dependent of another taxpayer, then no § 221 deduction will be allowed [§ 221(c)].

PROBLEMS

1. Carol attends Private Law School, where tuition is $40,000 per year. She receives a scholarship from the school of $15,000 per year. Additionally, Carol's employer pays $5,000 toward her education, which Carol can choose to receive in cash. What is Carol's Qualified Higher Education Expense, and why is it relevant?

2. Dana earned $60,000 in income this year. She paid $300 per month on her Qualified Education Loan. Of each monthly payment, $200 was for interest and $100 was for principal repayment. How much may Dana deduct?

3. Liz borrowed $40,000 at 3% to cover her total Qualified Higher Education Expense. Of the $40,000 loan proceeds, she used $30,000 for tuition, $6,000 for room and board, $1,000 for transportation to and from the school, and $3,000 on a home entertainment system. She made a voluntary payment of interest of $600. What amount may she deduct?

4. Which of these loans generate deductible interest under § 221? Assume in each case that the loan proceeds are used to pay Qualified Higher Education Expenses.

    (a) Ryan borrows $45,000 from Access, a commercial lender, at 3.5%.

    (b) Kelli borrows $20,000 from her grandmother at 1%.

    (c) Sophia borrows $30,000 at 2% from a qualified employer plan as defined in § 72(p)(4).

5. Joseph, a recent graduate, is legally obligated to pay $300 per month on his Qualified Education Loan. This year, $250 of each payment is allocated to interest, and $50 to principal. Since Joseph hasn't yet found a job, his father pays the first $300. May Joseph take a deduction? What if Joseph's father takes Joseph as a dependant?

QUESTION

Will these tax incentives for education actually reduce the costs of education to the consumers, or will they simply furnish an excuse for institutions of higher education to raise tuition? Furthermore, what is the use of these nonrefundable credits to those low income people who didn't owe any tax anyway?

C. EXPENSES FOR THE PRODUCTION OF INCOME

Code: §§ 212, 165(c)(2), 167(a)(2)

Regulations: § 1.212–1

So far, business deductions have been considered under the rubric of § 162, which requires a "trade or business." There is, however, a category of deductible expenditures which, although not "paid or incurred . . . in carrying on any trade or business," are still not purely personal. This category is described in § 212. Since § 212 is somewhat less rigid in its requirements than § 162, the "mixed motive" expenses which are the subject of this chapter will often turn out to be claimed under § 212 rather than § 162.

To understand § 212, read the *Higgins* case, which inspired it.

HIGGINS v. COMMISSIONER

United States Supreme Court, 1941.
312 U.S. 212, 61 S.Ct. 475, 85 L.Ed. 783.

Mr. Justice Reed delivered the opinion of the Court.

Petitioner, the taxpayer, with extensive investments in real estate, bonds and stocks, devoted a considerable portion of his time to the oversight of his interests and hired others to assist him in offices rented for that purpose. For the tax years in question, 1932 and 1933, he claimed the salaries and expenses incident to looking after his properties were deductible under § 23(a) of the Revenue Act of 1932 [current § 162]. The Commissioner refused the deductions. The applicable phrases are: "In computing net income there shall be allowed as deductions: (a) Expenses. * * * All the ordinary and necessary expenses paid or incurred during the taxable year in carrying on any trade or business * * *." There is no dispute over whether the claimed deductions are ordinary and necessary expenses. As the Commissioner also conceded before the Board of Tax Appeals that the real estate activities of the petitioner in renting buildings constituted a business, the Board allowed such portions of the claimed deductions as were fairly allocable to the handling of the real estate. The same offices and staffs handled both real estate and security matters. After this adjustment there remained for the year 1932 over twenty and for the year 1933 over sixteen thousand dollars expended for managing the stocks and bonds.

Petitioner's financial affairs were conducted through his New York office pursuant to his personal detailed instructions. His residence was in Paris, France, where he had a second office. By cable, telephone and mail, petitioner kept a watchful eye over his securities. While he sought permanent investments, changes, redemptions, maturities and accumulations caused limited shiftings in his portfolio. These were made under his own orders. The offices kept records, received securities, interest and dividend checks, made deposits, forwarded weekly and annual reports and undertook generally the care of the investments as instructed by the owner. Purchases were made by a financial institution. Petitioner did not participate directly or indirectly in the management of the corporations in which he held stock or bonds. The method of handling his affairs under examination had been employed by petitioner for more than thirty years. No objection to the deductions had previously been made by the Government.

The Board of Tax Appeals held that these activities did not constitute carrying on a business and that the expenses were capable of apportionment between the real estate and the investments. The Circuit Court of Appeals affirmed, and we granted certiorari, because of conflict.

Petitioner urges that the "elements of continuity, constant repetition, regularity and extent" differentiate his activities from the occasional like actions of the small investor. His activity is and the occasional action is not "carrying on business." On the other hand, the respondent urges that "mere personal investment activities never constitute carrying on a trade or business, no matter how much of one's time or of one's employees' time they may occupy." * * *

While the Commissioner has combated views similar to petitioner's in the courts, sometimes successfully and sometimes unsuccessfully, the petitioner urges that the Bureau accepted for years the doctrine that the management of one's own securities might be a business where there was sufficient extent, continuity, variety and regularity. We fail to find such a fixed administrative construction in the examples cited. It is true that the decisions are frequently put on the ground that the taxpayer's activities were sporadic but it does not follow that had those activities been continuous the Commissioner would not have used the argument advanced here, i.e., that no amount of personal investment management would turn those activities into a business. * * *

Petitioner relies strongly on the definition of business in Flint v. Stone Tracy Company, 220 U.S. 107 (1911): "Business is a very comprehensive term and embraces everything about which a person can be employed." This definition was given in considering whether certain corporations came under the Corporation Tax law which levies a tax on corporations engaged in business. The immediate issue was whether corporations engaged principally in the "holding and management of real estate" were subject to the act. A definition given for such an issue is not controlling in this dissimilar inquiry.

To determine whether the activities of a taxpayer are "carrying on a business" requires an examination of the facts in each case. As the Circuit Court of Appeals observed, all expenses of every business transaction are not deductible. Only those are deductible which relate to carrying on a business. The Bureau of Internal Revenue has this duty of determining what is carrying on a business, subject to reexamination of the facts by the Board of Tax Appeals and ultimately to review on the law by the courts on which jurisdiction is conferred. The Commissioner and the Board appraised the evidence here as insufficient to establish petitioner's activities as those of carrying on a business. The petitioner merely kept records and collected interest and dividends from his securities, through managerial attention for his investments. No matter how large the estate or how continuous or extended the work required may be, such facts are not sufficient as a matter of law to permit the courts to reverse the decision of the Board. Its conclusion is adequately supported by this record, and rests upon a conception of carrying on business similar to that expressed by this Court for an antecedent section.

The petitioner makes the point that his activities in managing his estate, both realty and personalty, were a unified business. Since it was admittedly a business in so far as the realty is concerned, he urges, there is no statutory authority to sever expenses allocable to the securities. But we see no reason why expenses not attributable, as we have just held these are not, to carrying on business cannot be apportioned. It is not unusual to allocate expenses paid for services partly personal and partly business.

Affirmed.

NOTES AND QUESTIONS

1. Congress was not pleased with *Higgins*. It thought that the expenses in that case should have been deductible. Congress could have amended § 162, to ensure that *Higgins* type expenses were deductible under that section. Instead, they enacted an entirely new provision—current § 212. Note that, in adding a new section, rather than adding language to § 162, Congress was then forced to make conforming changes to § 165 [see § 165(c)(2)] and § 167 [see § 167(a)(2)].

2. Why was the realty management in *Higgins* conceded to be a business, while the management of the taxpayer's other investments was not?

3. Section 212 also has a curious relationship with the capital gains provisions. Taxpayer sells personal (not real) property which was depreciable pursuant to § 167(a)(2) for a gain. Is the gain taxable under § 1221 or § 1231? Compare § 1221(2) with § 1231(b)(1).

HORRMANN v. COMMISSIONER

United States Tax Court, 1951.
17 T.C. 903.

Findings of Fact

* * * The property which is the basis of this case is located at 189 Howard Avenue, Grymes Hill, Staten Island, New York. The land consists of a 5–acre landscaped plot situated on the side of a hill, and on the land is a stone house and brick garage. The house was built by petitioner's father and mother in 1910 at a cost of more than $100,000. It was a replica of a castle located in Germany, and it had 17 rooms, or more. Petitioner's father lived in the house until his death sometime in the 1920's and petitioner's mother continued to live in the house as a family residence until her death in February 1940. Petitioner lived in the house until he was married in 1938. Petitioner's mother devised the property to petitioner, and for estate tax purposes the property was valued at $60,000.

The Horrmann family consisted of mother and father, four daughters, and two sons, of whom petitioner was the youngest. In addition to the devise of the property, the will also contained a wish, although not a condition, that petitioner maintain the property as a home, if possible, for the members of his mother's family. The petitioner's mother had communicated this wish to her family during her lifetime. During 1940, petitioner expended $9,000 in redecorating the house, and in November 1940, moved into the house with his wife and son. Petitioner hoped that some of his sisters or his brother would move in for the size of the house was out of proportion to the size of petitioner's immediate family, and they could share in the expense. Sixty tons of coal were required each year to heat the house, and in order to maintain the property there was required the full-time services of three or four servants for the house and a gardener for the grounds. It was an expensive residence to maintain; petitioner found that out from experience.

In October 1942, petitioner moved out of the house and rented a much smaller house at 338 Douglas Road, Emerson Hill, Staten Island, one to one and one-half miles from 189 Howard Avenue. The house leased by petitioner was smaller and was more in keeping with his income. When petitioner moved out, he did so with the intent of never returning to the property. * * *

When petitioner moved from 189 Howard Avenue the property had a reasonable market value of $45,000 allocated as follows: land, $35,000, building $10,000. In addition to stipulating these values, the parties also agreed that the buildings had a remaining useful life of 20 years.

Immediately before and after petitioner moved from the Howard Avenue property, a proposal to convert the house into separate apartments was considered. A construction company was consulted and estimated the cost of conversion would be $60,000. The plan was abandoned because of the prohibitive cost.

On or about December 19, 1942, petitioner listed the Howard Avenue property for sale with Kolff and Kaufmann, Inc., real estate brokers, with offices on Staten Island. The property was offered for sale at $75,000, which was reduced to $40,000 in November 1944, and to $30,000 in March 1945. The realtors advertised the property for sale, attempted to sell the property, and also attempted to lease the property. Offers were received from prospective tenants, but the monthly rental offered by them, $200 to $250, was inadequate. An offer of $500 per month would have been an acceptable rental from the property.

The property was offered for use as an officers' club for Halloran General Hospital which was nearby in return for payment by the Army of the taxes and maintenance costs of the property. However, nothing came of this offer. Early in 1943, the property was offered to the Coast Guard for use as accommodations for the SPARS. Because of lack of transportation facilities the Coast Guard rejected petitioner's offers to sell or lease the property. In late 1943, after petitioner entered the U.S. Maritime Service, the U.S. Army Engineers inspected the property and displayed an interest in renting the property. Petitioner's agent, however, received no offer from them. The property was also offered to the Maritime Commission and to several service organizations, but these attempts to rent or to sell the property ended in failure. At no time during the period from

October 1942 to June 5, 1945, was the Howard Avenue property or any part thereof rented, nor did it produce any income whatsoever.

On May 28, 1943, petitioner entered into a contract with a national real estate clearing house for their services in promoting the sale of the Howard Avenue property, and in accordance with that contract the clearing house prepared a listing or brochure describing the property. This brochure which was prepared under the direction and with the approval of petitioner contained the following statement: 'Not for rent.'

In January of 1945, the property at 189 Howard Avenue was broken into by vandals who inflicted heavy damage on the property by smashing furniture, decorations, fixtures, and glass, and by building fires on the floors. On June 5, 1945, the property was sold for the consideration of $23,000. Petitioner paid expenses of $2,200 incurred in connection with the sale of the property, of which $1,150 was paid to Kolff and Kaufmann, Inc., under his oral contract made with the broker in December 1942.

The expenses incurred by petitioner in the maintenance and conservation of the Howard Avenue property during the taxable years are as follows:

	1943	1944
Caretaker expenses and detective agency	$520	$700
Gas and electricity	$50	$50
Coal	$600	—
Total	$1,170	$750

Opinion

BLACK, JUDGE:

* * *

The issue which we shall first consider is whether petitioner is entitled to a deduction for depreciation on the property during the taxable years 1943, 1944, and 1945. * * *

Petitioner is entitled to a deduction for depreciation at the rate of $500 per year provided the property was held for the production of income. In determining whether the test prescribed by statute is satisfied the use made of the property and the owner's intent in respect to the future use of disposition of the property are generally controlling. Until November 1942, the property was used by petitioner solely as a personal residence, but thereafter that use was abandoned. The mere abandonment of such use does not mean that thereafter the property was held for the production of income. But when efforts are made to rent the property as were made by petitioner herein, the property is then being held for the production of income and this may be so even though no income is in fact received from the property, and even though the property is at the same time offered for sale. While an intention not to rent the house was indicated in May 1943, on the brochure of the total real estate clearing house, efforts to rent the property were made subsequent to that time. The evidence, when considered in its entirety, supports the conclusion that petitioner continuously offered to rent the property until it was sold. In the recomputation of tax for the years 1943, 1944, and 1945, petitioner is to be allowed depreciation at the rate of $500 per year until June 1945, when the property was sold.

The second issue is whether petitioner is entitled to a deduction for expenses incurred during the taxable years for the maintenance and conservation of the property. The same phrase appearing in § 23(1)(2) of the Code [current § 167(a)(2)] * * * appears also in § 23(a)(2) of the Code [current § 212(2)], the requirement being that the property be held for the production of income. The taxpayers in Mary Laughlin Robinson, claimed a deduction for depreciation on the property and expenses for services of a caretaker. Although the taxable year there was 1937, the sections of the Code applicable there contain the same standard, property held for the production of income, as is applicable here. We there held that the taxpayer was entitled to both the deductions at issue. In accordance with that Opinion, we hold that petitioner in the recomputation of tax for the years 1943 and 1944, is entitled to deductions for maintenance and conservation expenses of the property as itemized in our Findings of Fact.

The third issue is whether petitioner is entitled to a deduction for a long term capital loss arising from the sale in 1945 of the property at 189 Howard Avenue. Petitioner claims a deduction under the provisions of § 23(e)(2) of the Code [current § 165(c)(2)]* * *.

The language of the Code sections applicable in issues one and two was property held for the production of income, and the language of [§ 165(c)(2)] of the Code is different. In order for a loss to be deductible under that section it must be incurred in any transaction entered into for profit. In a situation where the use of the property as a personal residence has been abandoned, and where the owner has offered the property for sale or for rent and finally sells the property at a loss, that distinction in language may result in allowing a deduction in one case and not allowing a deduction of another type. At least the cases have distinguished between the two statutory provisions. * * * When property has been used as a personal residence, in order to convert the transaction into one entered into for profit the owner must do more than abandon the property and list it for sale or rent. * * * In [Rumsey v. Commissioner, 82 F.2d 158 (2d Cir.1936)], in denying the taxpayer any deduction for the loss so incurred, the Court said:

> The taxpayer argues with considerable persuasive force that the fact that a man first rents his house before selling it is only significant as evidentiary of his purpose to abandon it as a residence and to devote the property to business uses; that renting is not the sole criterion of such purpose, as the regulations themselves imply by the words "rented or otherwise appropriated" to income producing purposes. But we think the argument cannot prevail over counter consider-

ations. If an owner rents, his decision is irrevocable, at least for the term of the lease; and if he remodels to fit the building for business purposes, he has likewise made it impossible to resume residential uses by a mere change of mind. When, however, he only instructs an agent to sell or rent the property, its change of character remains subject to his unfettered will; he may revoke the agency at any moment. Certainly it strains the language of Article 171, Regulations 74, to find that the property is "appropriated to" and "used for" income producing purposes by merely listing it with a broker for sale or rental. * * *

We have held that an actual rental of the property is not always essential to a conversion, Estate of Maria Assmann, 16 T.C. 632, but that case is not controlling here for the taxpayer there abandoned the residence only a few days after it was inherited, and then later demolished the residence. In Mary E. Crawford, 16 T.C. 678, which involved only the question of whether the loss was a [§ 165(c)(1)] loss or a [§ 165(c)(2)] loss, the owner-taxpayer had also demolished the residence. While we held in both cases that such action constituted an appropriation or conversion, in both cases the facts indicate that from the moment the properties were inherited the taxpayers did not intend to continue to occupy the property as their personal residence.

Here the situation is different. The petitioner in the instant case soon after the death of petitioner's mother took immediate and decisive action, fixing the character of the property in their hands as residential. The surrounding circumstances point to this conclusion; their expenditure of approximately $9,000 in redecorating the house in preparation for their use of it as a home; their moving into the property within nine months after they acquired it; the sale of their former residence at Ocean Terrace shortly after they had moved into the Howard Avenue property; and finally, their occupancy of the Howard Avenue property for a period of about two years as a home and residence. They could hardly have gone further more decisively to fix the character of this property, originally neutral in their hands, as personal residential property.

As to the third issue, we think there was no conversion of the property into a transaction entered into for profit. Respondent did not err in determining that petitioner was not entitled to the benefits of a capital loss carry-over to 1946 for the loss sustained upon the sale in 1945 of the property at 189 Howard Avenue.

Decision will be entered under Rule 50.

D. BUSINESS USE OF HOMES

Code: § 280A

What could be more personal than one's home? Yet, for most Americans, their home is also their most significant financial asset. What could be more tempting than arranging one's affairs so that some of one's home expenses are deductible?

Taxpayers have been claiming deductions for the business use of their homes for a long time, with varying degrees of success. Today, in an era of tele-commuting and cyber-offices, the stakes are higher than ever. Since the Tax Reform Act of 1976, this issue has been a matter of statute.

Section 280A begins in (a) by stating that no deduction shall be allowed for personal dwelling units used by the taxpayer as a residence. Then, in (c), it carves out some narrow, deductible exceptions for the business use of the home, including the home office provisions of (c)(1), and the time-sharing rental possibilities in (c)(3). Note, however, that even these deductions are limited by (c)(5), which essentially provides that the deductions attributable to one's home will be allowable to the extent that they wipe out the income attributable to one's home, and no more.

There can be no doubt that some people have no choice but to use portions of their homes for their businesses. To deny deductions to these people would be to tax them on their gross income, rather than their net income. Yet, there are other people who really do not deserve a business deduction for any portion of their home expenses, but who would be happy to jump through whatever hoops the statute provides in order to obtain those deductions. The task for § 280A, then, is to allow the legitimate deductions, while safeguarding the system from the illegitimate deductions.

COMMISSIONER v. SOLIMAN

United States Supreme Court, 1993.
506 U.S. 168, 113 S.Ct. 701, 121 L.Ed.2d 634.

[Note: The last sentence of § 280A(c)(1) was added to the Code in 1997, as a partial response to *Soliman*. When reading the opinion, think of § 280A(c)(1) as it appeared before the Justices who decided the case—without the last sentence.]

JUSTICE KENNEDY delivered the opinion of the Court.

We address in this decision the appropriate standard for determining whether an office in the taxpayer's home qualifies as his "principal place of business" under § 280A(c)(1)(A). Because the standard followed by the Court of Appeals for the Fourth Circuit failed to undertake a comparative analysis of the various business locations of the taxpayer in deciding whether the home office was the principal place of business, we reverse.

I

Respondent Nader E. Soliman, an anesthesiologist, practiced his profession in Maryland and Virginia during 1983, the tax year in question. Soliman spent 30 to 35 hours per week with patients, dividing that time among three hospitals. About 80 percent of the hospital time was spent at Suburban Hospital in Bethesda, Maryland. At the hospitals, Soliman administered the anesthesia, cared for patients after surgery, and treated patients for pain. None of the three hospitals provided him with an office.

Soliman lived in a condominium in McLean, Virginia. His residence had a spare bedroom which he used exclusively as an office. Although he did not meet patients in the home office, Soliman spent two to three hours per day there on a variety of tasks such as contacting patients, surgeons, and hospitals by telephone; maintaining billing records and patient logs; preparing for treatments and presentations; satisfying continuing medical education requirements; and reading medical journals and books.

On his 1983 federal income tax return, Soliman claimed deductions for the portion of condominium fees, utilities, and depreciation attributable to the home office. Upon audit, the Commissioner disallowed those deductions based upon his determination that the home office was not Soliman's principal place of business. Soliman filed a petition in the Tax Court seeking review of the resulting tax deficiency.

The Tax Court, with six of its judges dissenting, ruled that Soliman's home office was his principal place of business. After noting that in its earlier decisions it identified the place where services are performed and income is generated in order to determine the principal place of business, the so-called "focal point test," the Tax Court abandoned that test, citing criticism by two Courts of Appeals. Under a new test, later summarized and adopted by the Court of Appeals, the Tax Court allowed the deduction. The dissenting opinions criticized the majority for failing to undertake a comparative analysis of Soliman's places of business to establish which one was the principal place.

The Commissioner appealed to the Court of Appeals for the Fourth Circuit. A divided panel of that court affirmed. It adopted the test used in the Tax Court and explained it as follows: "[The] test ... provides that where management or administrative activities are essential to the taxpayer's trade or business and the only available office space is in the taxpayer's home, the 'home office' can be his 'principal place of business,' with the existence of the following factors weighing heavily in favor of a finding that the taxpayer's 'home office' is his 'principal place of business:' (1) the office in the home is essential to the taxpayer's business; (2) he spends a substantial amount of time there; and (3) there is no other location available for performance of the office functions of the business." For further support, the Court of Appeals relied upon a proposed IRS regulation related to home office deductions for salespersons. Under the proposed regulation, salespersons would be entitled to home office deductions "even though they spend most of their time on the road as long as they spend 'a substantial amount of time on paperwork at home.'" While recognizing that the proposed regulation was not binding on it, the court suggested that it "evince [d] a policy to allow 'home office' deductions for taxpayers who maintain 'legitimate' home offices, even if the taxpayer does not spend a majority of his time in the office." The court concluded that the Tax Court's test would lead to identification of the "true headquarters of the business." Like the dissenters in the Tax Court, Judge Phillips in his dissent argued that the plain language of § 280A (c)(1)(A) requires a comparative analysis of the places of business to assess which one is principal, an analysis that was not undertaken by the majority.

Although other Courts of Appeals have criticized the focal point test, their approaches for determining the principal place of business differ in significant ways from the approach employed by the Court of Appeals in this case. Those other courts undertake a comparative analysis of the functions performed at each location. We granted certiorari to resolve the conflict.

II

A

Section 162(a) of the Internal Revenue Code allows a taxpayer to deduct "all the ordinary and necessary expenses paid or incurred . . . in carrying on any trade or business." That provision is qualified, however, by various limitations, including one that prohibits otherwise allowable deductions "with respect to the use of a dwelling unit which is used by the taxpayer . . . as a residence." § 280A(a). Taxpayers may nonetheless deduct expenses attributable to the business use of their homes if they qualify for one or more of the statute's exceptions to this disallowance. The exception at issue in this case is contained in § 280A(c)(1):

> Subsection (a) shall not apply to any item to the extent such item is allocable to a portion of the dwelling unit which is exclusively used on a regular basis—
>
> > (A) [as] the principal place of business for any trade or business of the taxpayer,
> >
> > (B) as a place of business which is used by patients, clients, or customers in meeting or dealing with the taxpayer in the normal course of his trade or business, or
> >
> > (C) in the case of a separate structure which is not attached to the dwelling unit, in connection with the taxpayer's trade or business.
>
> In the case of an employee, the preceding sentence shall apply only if the exclusive use referred to in the preceding sentence is for the convenience of his employer.

Congress adopted § 280A as part of the Tax Reform Act of 1976. Before its adoption, expenses attributable to the business use of a residence were deductible whenever they were "appropriate and helpful" to the taxpayer's business. This generous standard allowed many taxpayers to treat what otherwise would have been nondeductible living and family expenses as business expenses, even though the limited business tasks performed in the dwelling resulted in few, if any, additional or incremental costs to the taxpayer. Comparing the newly enacted section with the previous one, the apparent purpose of § 280A is to provide a narrower scope for the deduction, but Congress has provided no definition of "principal place of business."

In interpreting the meaning of the words in a revenue act, we look to the " 'ordinary, everyday senses' " of the words. In deciding whether a location is "the principal place of business," the common sense meaning of "principal" suggests that a comparison of locations must be undertaken. This view is confirmed by the definition of "principal," which means "most important, consequential, or influential." Courts cannot assess whether any one business location is the "most important, consequential, or influential" one without comparing it to all the other places where business is transacted.

Contrary to the Court of Appeals' suggestion, the statute does not allow for a deduction whenever a home office may be characterized as legitimate. That approach is not far removed from the "appropriate and helpful" test that led to the adoption of § 280A. Under the Court of Appeals' test, a home office may qualify as the principal place of business whenever the office is essential to the taxpayer's business, no alternative office space is available, and the taxpayer spends a substantial amount of time there. This approach ignores the question whether the home office is more significant in the taxpayer's business than every other place of business. The statute does not refer to the "principal office" of the business. If it had used that phrase, the taxpayer's deduction claim would turn on other considerations. The statute refers instead to the "principal place" of business. It follows that the most important or significant place for the business must be determined.

B

In determining the proper test for deciding whether a home office is the principal place of business, we cannot develop an objective formula that yields a clear answer in every case. The inquiry is more subtle, with the ultimate determination of the principal place of business being dependent upon the particular facts of each case. There are, however, two primary considerations in deciding whether a home office is a taxpayer's principal place of business: the relative importance of the activities performed at each business location and the time spent at each place.

Analysis of the relative importance of the functions performed at each business location depends upon an objective description of the business in question. This preliminary step is undertaken so that the decisionmaker can evaluate the activities conducted at the various business locations in light of the particular characteristics of the specific business or trade at issue. Although variations are inevitable in case-by-case determinations, any particular business is likely to have a pattern in which certain activities are of most significance. If the nature of the trade or profession requires the taxpayer to meet or confer with a client or patient or to deliver goods or services to a customer, the place where that contact occurs is often an important indicator of the principal place of business. A business location where these contacts occur has sometimes been called the "focal point" of the business and has been previously regarded by the Tax Court as conclusive in ascertaining the principal place of business. We think that phrase has a metaphorical quality that can be misleading, and, as we have said, no one test is determinative in every case. We decide, however, that the point where goods and services are delivered must be given great weight in determining the place where the most important functions are performed.

Section 280A itself recognizes that the home office gives rise to a deduction whenever the office is regularly and exclusively used "by patients, clients, or customers in meeting or dealing with the taxpayer in the normal course of his trade or business." In that circumstance, the deduction is allowed whether or not the home office is also the principal place of business. The taxpayer argues that because the point of delivery of goods and services is addressed in this provision, it follows that the availability of the principal place of business exception does not depend in any way upon whether the home office is the point of delivery. We agree with the ultimate conclusion that visits by patients, clients, and customers are not a required characteristic of a principal place of business, but we disagree with the implication that whether those visits occur is irrelevant. That Congress allowed the deduction where those visits occur in the normal course even when some other location is the principal place of business indicates their importance in determining the nature and functions of any enterprise. Though not conclusive, the point where services are rendered or goods delivered is a principal consideration in most cases. If the nature of the business requires that its services are rendered or its goods are delivered at a facility with unique or special characteristics, this is a further and weighty consideration in finding that it is the delivery point or facility, not the taxpayer's residence, where the most important functions of the business are undertaken.

Unlike the Court of Appeals, we do not regard the necessity of the functions performed at home as having much weight in determining entitlement to the deduction. In many instances, planning and initial preparation for performing a service or delivering goods are essential to the ultimate performance of the service or delivery of the goods, just as accounting and billing are often essential at the final stages of the process. But that is simply because, in integrated transactions, all steps are essential. Whether the functions performed in the home office are necessary to the business is relevant to the determination of whether a home office is the principal place of business in a particular case, but it is not controlling. Essentiality, then, is but part of the assessment of the relative importance of the functions performed at each of the competing locations.

We reject the Court of Appeals' reliance on the availability of alternative office space as an additional consideration in determining a taxpayer's principal place of business. While that factor may be relevant in deciding whether an employee taxpayer's use of a home office is "for the convenience of his employer," § 280A(c)(1), it has no bearing on the inquiry whether a home office is the principal place of business. The requirements of particular trades or professions may preclude some taxpayers from using a home office as the principal place of business. But any taxpayer's home office that meets the criteria here set forth is the principal place of business regardless of whether a different office exists or might have been established elsewhere.

In addition to measuring the relative importance of the activities undertaken at each business location, the decisionmaker should also compare the amount of time spent at home with the time spent at other places where business activities occur. This factor assumes particular significance when comparison of the importance of the functions performed at various places yields no definitive answer to the principal place of business inquiry. This may be the case when a taxpayer performs income-generating tasks at both his home office and some other location.

The comparative analysis of business locations required by the statute may not result in every case in the specification of which location is the principal place of business; the only question that must be answered is whether the home office so qualifies. There may be cases when there is no principal place of business, and the courts and the Commissioner should not strain to conclude that a home office qualifies for the deduction simply because no other location seems to be the principal place. The taxpayer's house does not become a principal place of business by default.

Justice Cardozo's observation that in difficult questions of deductibility "Life in all its fullness must supply the answer to the riddle," must not deter us from deciding upon some rules for the fair and consistent interpretation of a statute that speaks in the most general of terms. Yet we accept his implicit assertion that there are limits to the guidance from appellate courts in these cases. The consequent necessity to give considerable deference to the trier of fact is but the law's recognition that the statute is designed to accommodate myriad and ever changing forms of business enterprise.

III

Under the principles we have discussed, the taxpayer was not entitled to a deduction for home office expenses. The practice of anesthesiology requires the medical doctor to treat patients under conditions demanding immediate, personal observation. So exacting were these requirements that all of respondent's patients were treated at hospitals, facilities with special characteristics designed to accommodate the demands of the profession. The actual treatment was the essence of the professional service. We can assume that careful planning and study were required in advance of performing the treatment, and all acknowledge that this was done in the home office. But the actual treatment was the most significant event in the professional transaction. The home office activities, from an objective standpoint, must be regarded as less important to the business of the taxpayer than the tasks he performed at the hospital.

A comparison of the time spent by the taxpayer further supports a determination that the home office was not the principal place of business. The 10 to 15 hours per week spent in the home office measured against the 30 to 35 hours per week at the three hospitals are insufficient to render the home office the principal place of business in light of all of the circumstances of this case. That the office may have been essential is not controlling.

The judgment of the Court of Appeals is reversed.

It is so ordered.

[JUSTICE BLACKMUN'S concurring opinion is omitted.]

JUSTICE THOMAS, with whom JUSTICE SCALIA joins, concurring in the judgment.

Today the Court announces that "there is no one test," to determine whether a home office constitutes a taxpayer's "principal place of business" within the meaning of § 280A(c)(1)(A), and concludes that whether a taxpayer will be entitled to a home office deduction will be "dependent upon the particular facts of each case." The Court sets out two "primary considerations," to guide the analysis—the importance of the functions performed at each business location and the time spent at each location. I think this inquiry, "subtle" though it may be, will unnecessarily require the lower courts to conduct full-blown evidentiary hearings each time the Commissioner challenges a deduction under § 280A(c)(1)(A). Moreover, as structured, the Court's "test" fails to provide clear guidance as to how the two-factor inquiry should proceed. Specifically, it is unclear whether the time element and importance-of-the-functions element are of equal significance. I write separately because I believe that in the overwhelming majority of cases (including the one before us), the "focal point" test— which emphasizes the place where the taxpayer renders the services for which he is paid or sells his goods—provides a clear, reliable method for determining whether a taxpayer's home office is his "principal place of business." I would employ the totality-of-the-circumstances inquiry, guided by the two factors discussed by the Court, only in the small minority of cases where the home office is one of several locations where goods or services are delivered, and thus also one of the multiple locations where income is generated.

I certainly agree that the word "principal" connotes " 'most important,' " but I do not agree that this definition requires courts in every case to resort to a totality-of-the-circumstances analysis when determining whether the taxpayer is entitled to a home office deduction under § 280A(c)(1)(A). Rather, I think it is logical to assume that the single location where the taxpayer's business income is generated—i.e., where he provides goods or services to clients or customers—will be his principal place of business. This focal point standard was first enunciated in Baie v. Commissioner, 74 T.C. 105,[1] and has been consistently applied by the Tax

_____

1. In Baie, the taxpayer operated a hot dog stand. She prepared all the food in the kitchen at her home and transferred it daily to the stand for sale. She also used another room in her house

Court (until the present case) in determining whether a taxpayer's home office is his principal place of business.

Indeed, if one were to glance quickly through the Court's opinion today, one might think the Court was in fact adopting the focal point test. At two points in its opinion the Court hails the usefulness of the focal point inquiry: It states that the place where goods are delivered or services rendered must be given "great weight in determining the place where the most important functions are performed," and that "the point where services are rendered or goods delivered is a principal consideration in most cases." In fact, the Court's discomfort with the focal point test seems to rest on two fallacies—or perhaps one fallacy and a terminological obstinacy. First, the Court rejects the focal point test because "no one test . . . is determinative in every case." But the focal point test, as I interpret it, is not always determinative: where it provides no single principal place of business, the "totality of the circumstances" approach is invoked. Second, the Court rejects the focal point test because its name has a "metaphorical quality that can be misleading." But rechristening it the "place of sale or service test"—or whatever label the Court would find less confusing—is surely a simple matter.

The Commissioner's quarrel with the focal point test is that "it ignores management functions." To illustrate this point, the Commissioner at oral argument presented the example of a sole proprietor who runs a rental car company with many licensees around the country, and who manages the licensees from his home, advising them on how to operate the businesses. Yet the Commissioner's unease is unfounded, since the focal point inquiry easily resolves this example. The taxpayer derives his income from managing his licensees, and he performs those services at his home office. Thus, his home office would be his "principal place of business" under § 280A(c)(1)(A). On the other hand, if the taxpayer owned several car dealerships and used his home office to do the dealership's bookkeeping, he would not be entitled to deduct the expenses of his home office even if he spent the majority of his time there. This is because the focal points of that business would be the dealerships where the cars are sold—i.e., where the taxpayer sells the goods for which he is paid.

There will, of course, be the extraordinary cases where the focal point inquiry will provide no answer. One example is the sole proprietor who buys jewelry wholesale through a home office, and sells it both at various craft shows and through mail orders out of his home office. In that case, the focal point test would yield more than one location where income is generated, including the home. Where the taxpayer's business involves multiple points of sale, a court would need to fall back on a totality-of-the-circumstances analysis. That inquiry would be rationally guided, of course,

exclusively for the stand's bookkeeping. The Tax Court denied the taxpayer a home office deduction under § 280A(c)(1)(A), recognizing that although "preliminary preparation may have been beneficial to the efficient operation of petitioner's business, both the final packaging for consumption and sales occurred on the premises of the [hot dog stand]." Thus, the Court concluded that the hot dog stand was the "focal point of [the taxpayer's] activities."

by the two factors set out in the Court's opinion: an analysis of the relative importance of the functions performed at each business location and the time spent at each. The error of the Tax Court's original construction of the focal point test was the implicit view that the test allowed no escape valve. Clearly it must. Nevertheless, since in the vast majority of cases the focal point inquiry will provide a quick, objective, and reliable method of ascertaining a taxpayer's "principal place of business," I think the Court errs today in not unequivocally adopting it.

The difficulty with the Court's two-part test can be seen in its application to the facts of this case. It is uncontested that the taxpayer is paid to provide one service—anesthesiology. It is also undisputed that he performs this service at several different hospitals. At this juncture, under the focal point test, a lower court's inquiry would be complete: on these facts, the taxpayer's home office would not qualify for the § 280A(c)(1)(A) deduction. Yet under the Court's formulation, the lower court's inquiry has only just begun. It would need to hear evidence regarding the types of business activities performed at the home office and the relative amount of time the taxpayer spends there. It just so happens that in this case the taxpayer spent 30 to 35 hours per week at the hospitals where he worked. But how would a court answer the § 280A(c)(1)(A) question under the standard announced today if the facts were altered slightly, so that the taxpayer spent 30 to 35 hours at his home office and only 10 hours actually performing the service of anesthesiology at the various hospitals? Which factor would take precedence? The importance of the activities undertaken at the home compared to those at the hospitals? The number of hours spent at each location? I am at a loss, and I am afraid the taxpayer, his attorney, and a lower court would be as well.

We granted certiorari to clarify a recurring question of tax law that has been the subject of considerable disagreement. Unfortunately, this issue is no clearer today than it was before we granted certiorari. I therefore concur only in the Court's judgment.

JUSTICE STEVENS, dissenting.

* * *

II

Before 1976, home office deductions were allowed whenever the use of the office was "appropriate and helpful" to the taxpayer. That generous standard was subject to both abuse and criticism; it allowed homeowners to take deductions for personal expenses that would have been incurred even if no office were maintained at home and its vagueness made it difficult to administer. It was particularly favorable to employees who worked at home on evenings and weekends even though they had adequate office facilities at their employer's place of business.[6] In response to

---

6. Congress may have been particularly offended by the home office deductions claimed by employees of the Internal Revenue Service. See Bodzin v. Commissioner, 60 T.C. 820 (1973), rev'd, 509 F.2d 679 (CA4); Sharon v. Commissioner. The Senate Report also used a common

these criticisms, Congress enacted § 280A to prohibit deductions for business uses of dwelling units unless certain specific conditions are satisfied.

The most stringent conditions in § 280A, enacted to prevent abuse by those who wanted to deduct purely residential costs, apply to deductions claimed by employees. This provision alone prevents improper deduction for any second office located at home and used merely for the taxpayer's convenience. It thus responds to the major concern of the Commissioner identified in the legislative history.

Self-employed persons, such as respondent, must satisfy three conditions. Each is more strict and more definite than the "appropriate and helpful" standard that Congress rejected.

* * * Third, the use of the space must be as a "place of business" satisfying one of three alternative requirements. * * * Subsection (C) is obviously irrelevant in this case, as is subsection (B). The office itself is not a separate structure, and respondent does not meet his patients there. Each of the three alternatives, however, has individual significance, and it is clear that subsection (A) was included to describe places where the taxpayer does not normally meet with patients, clients, or customers. Nevertheless, the Court suggests that Soliman's failure to meet patients in his home office supports its holding. It does not. By injecting a requirement of subsection (B) into subsection (A) the Court renders the latter alternative entirely superfluous. Moreover, it sets the three subsections on unequal footing: subsection (A) will rarely apply unless it includes subsection (B); subsection (B) is preeminent; and the logic of the Court's analysis would allow a future court to discover that, under subsection (C), a separate structure is not truly "separate" (as a principal place of business is not truly "principal") unless it is also the site of meetings with patients or clients.

The meaning of "principal place of business" may not be absolutely clear, but it is absolutely clear that a taxpayer may deduct costs associated with his home office if it is his principal place of business or if it is a place of business used by patients in the normal course of his business or if it is located in a separate structure used in connection with his business. A home office could, of course, satisfy all three requirements, but to suggest that it need always satisfy subsection (B), or even that whether it satisfies (B) has anything to do with whether it satisfies (A), encourages the misapplication of a relatively simple provision of the Revenue Code.

By conflating subsections (A) and (B) the Court makes the same mistake the courts of appeal refused to make when they rejected the Tax Court's "focal point" test, which proved both unworkable and unfaithful to the statute. In this case the Tax Court itself rejected that test because it

---

example of potential abuse: "For example, if a university professor, who is provided an office by his employer, uses a den or some other room in his residence for the purpose of grading papers, preparing examinations or preparing classroom notes, an allocable portion of certain expenses . . . were incurred in order to perform these activities."

"merges the 'principal place of business' exception with the 'meeting clients' exception ... from section 280A." The Court today steps blithely into territory in which several courts of appeal and the Tax Court, whose experience in these matters is much greater than ours, have learned not to tread; in so doing it reads into the statute a limitation Congress never meant to impose.

The principal office of a self-employed person's business would seem to me to be the most typical example of a "principal place of business." It is, indeed, the precise example used in the Commissioner's proposed regulations of deductible home offices for taxpayers like respondent, who have no office space at the "focal point" of their work. Moreover, it is a mistake to focus attention entirely on the adjective "principal" and to overlook the significance of the term "place of business." When the term "principal place of business" is used in other statutes that establish the jurisdiction or venue in which a corporate defendant may be sued, it commonly identifies the headquarters of the business. The only place where a business is managed is fairly described as its "principal" place of business.

The Court suggests that Congress would have used the term "principal office" if it had intended to describe a home office like respondent's. It is probable, however, that Congress did not select the narrower term because it did not want to exclude some business uses of dwelling units that should qualify for the deduction even though they are not offices. Because some examples that do not constitute offices come readily to mind—an artist's studio, or a cabinet-maker's basement—it is easy to understand why Congress did not limit this category that narrowly.

The test applied by the Tax Court, and adopted by the Court of Appeals, is both true to the statute and practically incapable of abuse. In addition to the requirements of exclusive and regular use, those courts would require that the taxpayer's home office be essential to his business and be the only office space available to him. Respondent's home office is the only place where he can perform the administrative functions essential to his business. Because he is not employed by the hospitals where he works, and because none of those hospitals offers him an office, respondent must pay all the costs necessary for him to have any office at all. In my judgment, a principal place of business is a place maintained by or (in the rare case) for the business. As I would construe the statute in this context, respondent's office is not just the "principal" place of his trade or business; it is the only place of his trade or business.[16]

Nothing in the history of this statute provides an acceptable explanation for disallowing a deduction for the expense of maintaining an office that is used exclusively for business purposes, that is regularly so used, and that is the only place available to the taxpayer for the management of

---

16. If his tax form asked for the address of his principal place of business, respondent would certainly have given his office address (he did, of course, give that address as his business address on the relevant tax forms). It borders on the absurd to suggest that he should have identified a place over which he has no control or dominion as his place.

his business. A self-employed person's efficient use of his or her resources should be encouraged by sound tax policy. When it is clear that no risk of the kind of abuse that led to the enactment of § 280A is present, and when the taxpayer has satisfied a reasonable, even a strict, construction of each of the conditions set forth in § 280A, a deduction should be allowed for the ordinary cost of maintaining his home office.

In my judgment, the Court's contrary conclusion in this case will breed uncertainty in the law,[17] frustrate a primary purpose of the statute, and unfairly penalize deserving taxpayers. Given the growing importance of home offices, the result is most unfortunate.

I respectfully dissent.

QUESTIONS AND NOTES

1. The last sentence of § 280A(c)(1) was added by the Taxpayer Relief Act of 1997. What effect does that change have on the *Soliman* holding?

2. What was Justice Stevens' real beef? Was it with the majority, or was it with Justices Thomas and Scalia?

3. How will § 280A be applied to a painter, who paints pictures in a studio at her home, but sells them at her art gallery downtown?

4. In Popov v. Commissioner, 246 F.3d 1190 (9th Cir.2001), taxpayer, a violinist, performed regularly with two orchestras, and played for twenty-four different contractors in thirty-eight different locations, mostly for the motion picture industry. She was expected to sight read the music, and none of her employers furnished her with a practice room. Accordingly, she used the living room of her one-bedroom apartment exclusively for music, practicing four to five hours per day.

Applying *Soliman*, the Ninth Circuit found that her practicing was more important than her performing, and she spent more time practicing. Accordingly, she got her home office deduction. The Court was not terribly impressed with the Service's argument that "the point where goods and services are delivered" must control.

5. How will § 280A be applied to those who work out of their homes, connecting to co-workers, clients, and customers on their computers? Remember Revenue Ruling 99–7, *supra* at 347; Steven C. Dilley and Janet Trewin, *"Telecommuters" and Deductible Local Transportation Expenses*, 91 Tax Notes 630 (April 23, 2001).

6. § 280A(g) provides that, when a residence is rented for less than 15 days during a taxable year:

a) no deductions attributable to the rental use shall be allowed; but

b) none of the rental income will be taxable.

---

17. Most, if not all, of the uncertainty in cases debating the relative merits of the "focal point" test and the "facts and circumstances" test, as well as the uncertainty that today's opinion is sure to generate, would be eliminated by defining the term "place of business" to encompass only property that is owned or leased by the taxpayer or his employer.

If you received a home makeover from a reality TV show, could you argue that the goods and services provided in the makeover were merely in-kind rent for the use of your house during the 10–day makeover period, and thus, taxfree under this section?

INTERNATIONAL ARTISTS, LTD. v. COMMISSIONER; LIBERACE v. COMMISSIONER

United States Tax Court, 1970.
55 T.C. 94.

FAY, JUDGE:

[*International Artists* was decided before the enactment of § 280A. Moreover, in *International Artists*, the home was owned by a corporation, and used by the individual. Section 280A, in contrast, contemplates that the home will be owned by the individual who lives there.

Yet, *International Artists* presents a striking example of the business use of a home. Imagine that Liberace had owned the home, rather than International Artists, Ltd. How would § 280A, as currently drafted, have applied to these facts?]

* * *

Findings of Fact

* * * The individual petitioner herein, Walter V. Liberace (hereinafter sometimes referred to as petitioner), is a well-known musician and entertainer. Petitioner was not married during the period in question. * * *

International Artists, Ltd., the corporate petitioner herein (hereinafter sometimes referred to as the corporation), * * * derived its income during the taxable years at issue primarily from sources related to Liberace's performance as an entertainer in nightclubs and television appearances and from royalties with respect to the sale of records. * * *

The business operations of International Artists were successful during the early 1950's. The demand for Liberace performances was relatively great during this period. In addition to his appearances in nightclubs, petitioner led a weekly television show from 1952 to 1955. Partially as a result of overexposure on television, however, petitioner's popularity as an entertainer waned in the latter part of the 1950's, causing gross earnings of the corporation to fall sharply from $50,000 to $6,000 per week. The overexposure on television resulted from frequent reruns of his program following the close of the original television series in 1955.

Petitioner's public image during his period of success in the early part of the 1950's is described by him as one of "glamour and elegance." This image was conveyed to the public by means of elegant costumes, and unusual musical instruments and stage settings. It was calculated to arouse the interest of the public and draw spectators. The emphasis, in Liberace performances, had been as much upon the visible spectacle of his show as upon his musical talent. Nevertheless, in 1958, at the urging of his business manager, and prompted by his loss of popularity and reduced income, petitioner discarded the elegant image in favor of a more conservative one. His life style shifted from the spectacular to the conventional. However, this change failed to improve the deteriorating financial condition of the business and, in fact, contributed to its further decline. A second television series initiated in 1958 was forced to close after 26 weeks because of Liberace's diminished popularity.

In 1960, in an effort to revitalize the corporate business, the officers of the corporation resolved to reintroduce the previously successful "elegant" image of petitioner. Their efforts in this regard met with success. Corporate gross earnings in the ensuing 5 years steadily climbed from $300,000 per year to in excess of $1 million per year. The image of glamour accomplished by means of Liberace's unusual attire and stage settings was instrumental in capturing the public's interest. In addition, the effects of previous overexposure disappeared with the passage of time.

In 1960, to provide in part for a suitable location for the preparation of the corporate musical productions, as well as to provide a home for Liberace which would enhance his image in the eyes of the public, International Artists acquired a large house, for approximately $95,000, in a residential section of Los Angeles, overlooking the Los Angeles Basin. These premises (hereafter referred to as Harold Way), which are the subject of the controversy in the instant case, are located at 8433 Harold Way in the Hollywood Hills area of Los Angeles. The house was hereupon lavishly decorated and furnished (pursuant to the joint specifications of Liberace and other corporate officers) at a total cost to the corporation of approximately $250,000. Included in the improvements to the home were several items specifically designed to prepare the premises for its intended use in the production of musical programs, such as a soundproof music room, theatrical lighting, a projection room, and a specially designed wardrobe closet. In appearance, however, the home was simply the spectacular personal residence of Liberace. Though used to a substantial extent as a studio and home office of the corporation, as hereinafter described, Harold Way was commonly regarded as the residence of petitioner. A studio was not rented by the corporation, in part because the available studios were regarded by petitioner as ill-equipped for his purposes and because they could not provide the necessary privacy. * * *

The furniture of Harold Way was acquired by the corporation from Liberace, who in addition to his activities as a musician was the proprietor of an antique shop in Los Angeles. The house was exquisitely furnished primarily in antique-styled furniture.

The approximate size of Harold Way, according to diagrams introduced jointly into evidence, is 123 feet in length and 55–feet in width. The house is surrounded by sculptured grounds, in the rear portion of which are situated a cabana and swimming pool. The house itself is a three-story structure containing approximately 28 rooms. A brief description of the three floors of Harold Way is set forth below:

First Floor	Second Floor	Third Floor
(1) studio	(1) living room	(1) 2 bedrooms
(2) living room	(2) dining room	(2) 3 sitting rooms
(3) 3 storage closets	(3) bar and lounge	(3) 11 storage areas
(4) 2 restrooms	(4) organ equipment	(4) 3 restrooms
(5) kitchen	storage room	(5) dressing room
(6) dining room	(5) 2 restrooms	
(7) projection room	(6) 3 sitting rooms	
(8) bedroom		

The first-floor studio and living room are 33 x 21 feet and 27 x 30 feet, respectively, and together dominate the floor in both size and importance. The studio contains conference equipment, two pianos, and is soundproof. The living room is elaborately furnished and also contains two pianos. Attached to the living room is an alcove, 12 x 15 feet in size, referred to by employees of International Artists as the "stage." The second floor similarly has two prominent rooms, the living and dining rooms. The former is the largest and most exquisitely furnished room in the house. It contains, as does the first-floor living room, an elevated alcove similarly referred to as a stage, 12 x 21 feet in size.

The shows presented by International Artists required extensive preparation, particularly prior to the start of a musical season. The season generally began about the 10th of January. Preparation of the programs involved, preliminarily, the arrangement, choice, and composition of musical numbers. While this was generally done at the beginning of the season, mid-season additions of musical numbers requiring additional preparation were not uncommon. The formulation of a program was the responsibility of petitioner and Gordon Robinson, the musical director of the corporation. During this stage of preparation, Liberace and Robinson typically met in 4- to 5-hour sessions per day, with some additional time devoted to discussion of the results of the meeting.

It was necessary during the course of the season to audition, hire, and rehearse musicians and supporting casts. The corporation employed a body of musicians to provide orchestral accompaniment to Liberace. Supporting acts, generally consisting of trained singers or musicians, were included in the program in order to provide the audience with some diversion from Liberace's performance as well as to give him an opportunity to change costumes. Although the musicians engaged by International Artists were generally experienced, rehearsals were nevertheless necessary because the musicians were required, in performing for the Liberace show, to commit all musical numbers performed on the show to memory. Rehearsals were also necessary in the case of experienced supporting casts in order to integrate their acts with the balance of the performance. The numerous rehearsals thereby required were all held at Harold Way. Petitioner, whose reputation as a piano virtuoso depended upon continuous and intensive practice, similarly used Harold Way for purposes of practice and rehearsal. Auditions held at Harold Way were normally attended by Liberace, Robinson, Seymour Heller, and Ray Arnett.

* * *

Harold Way, in addition to its use as a facility for the preparation and rehearsal of the musical programs, served other important business needs. Activities in connection with the wardrobe, of major importance in the Liberace show, were conducted at Harold Way. The corporation employed two individuals to supervise the designing and maintenance of Liberace's elaborate wardrobe. Frank Acuna was primarily responsible for designing and tailoring of clothing, while Robert Fisher, a full-time employee, acted as Liberace's valet. Although Frank Acuna had a place of business of his own, he found it necessary for secrecy reasons to conduct all activities with respect to the wardrobe at Harold Way. This involved selection of fabrics, designing of costumes, and tailoring. Additional personnel were engaged to assist in embroidery work and the cleaning of costumes. The garments were hand-cleaned on the Harold Way premises. A specially designed closet held the numerous costumes used by Liberace and other entertainers on the show. Musical and stage equipment, including seven pianos, a number of violins, an organ, and candelabras used in the performance were stored at Harold Way.

Stage designing and choreography were also conducted at Harold Way. These matters were generally tended to after completion of the preliminary work, described above, with respect to musical programming. During the taxable period in question, International Artists produced six record albums. All preparatory work in connection with stage designing, choreography, and recordings took place at Harold Way.

The corporation's product, the Liberace show, was marketed primarily through the efforts of Seymour Heller, Liberace's personal manager. Heller's services to the corporation included, in addition, the coordination of job offers, negotiation of contracts, arrangement of details of travel and accommodations, and public relations. All contracts, and major decisions, were subject to the approval of petitioner as president of the corporation. Conferences between petitioner and Heller with respect to business matters were frequently held at Harold Way, usually in the second-floor dining room.

Apart from the business use of Harold Way in the production of concerts described above, Harold Way served, to some extent, a publicity and advertising function to the corporation. The home was extensively photographed. Brochures customarily distributed at Liberace performances emphasized by photograph and reference the "palatial home" of Liberace. The appearance of the home was commonly imitated on stage, including in one instance the reproduction of the circular staircase found at Harold Way. Magazine and newspaper photographers were invited and encouraged to visit the premises for publicity purposes. Press parties attended by members of the press and celebrities, calculated to generate publicity for Liberace, were sometimes, though not frequently, held at Harold Way.

As a result of the promotional efforts of International Artists, various news media often carried articles or references about Liberace. His unusual home was invariably mentioned in these articles, with description and photographs of the home figuring prominently in some instances. Petitioner is referred to in his brochure and by the press as "Mr. Showmanship." In order to maintain the continued public interest in Harold Way, the home was partially restyled every 2 or 3 years.

Prior to 1959 petitioner owned a home in Sherman Oaks. The home had been built by endorsements, i.e., through contributions of various companies for advertising purposes of their own. Because it had been built in this manner, the home, which contained among other things a piano-shaped swimming pool, became a tourist attraction and was visited extensively by the public. The Sherman Oaks home and its furnishings were the private property of Liberace. The lack of privacy at this residence influenced petitioner's decision to dispose of it in 1959. Following the disposition and prior to acquisition of Harold Way, the apartment in which petitioner resided in Los Angeles was used for general business purposes such as rehearsals, auditions, and business conferences. The apartment, because of disturbances caused to neighboring residents, was ill-suited for the business use to which it was put.

Harold Way constituted during the taxable years in question the sole business premises of International Artists. The only business purpose served by facilities other than Harold Way consisted of the maintenance of books and records at the office of Jacobs.

The extensive business use of Harold Way, described above, was for the most part restricted to specific areas of the premises. Rehearsals and auditions were primarily held on the first floor of the house. The particular rooms so utilized were the studio and living room, each containing two pianos and other necessary equipment. The former was soundproof and was heavily used as a work area. The latter, containing an alcove used as a stage, was similarly used for rehearsals. The projection room, on the first floor, was used exclusively for business purposes. The first floor was thus devoted primarily to business purposes and was used little if at all for the personal accommodation of Liberace. The wardrobe closet on the third floor was similarly used exclusively for business purposes.

Several areas of the home on the upper levels, while used sometimes for business purposes, were less frequently utilized in this manner. In this category are the living and dining rooms of the second floor. The living room, including a "stage" area and organ room, was used, although less frequently than the first-floor areas, for purposes of rehearsals. Rehearsals were normally held in this room when the production had reached a relatively complete stage. Business conferences were generally held in the dining room. In addition, activities in connection with petitioner's wardrobe were conducted in the dining room or bedroom. The kitchen and dining room facilities on the first and second floors, adjacent to the workrooms, were used occasionally for coffee breaks and discussions following work sessions.

Petitioner's personal use of Harold Way was not limited to the portion covered by the lease. While the business use of Harold Way was substantial, it was designed to and did serve during the period in question as the petitioner's principal place of residence. All parts of the home were accessible to Liberace without restriction, subject only to the overriding business use of the houses. The areas, particularly on the upper levels of the home, which were subject to occasional business use were also freely utilized by petitioner for personal purposes. Nonbusiness guests of petitioner, including family and friends, were entertained at Harold Way without restriction to the leased premises. Petitioner, who collected pianos as a hobby, spread the collection consisting primarily of miniature pianos, over the entire home. Petitioner's many automobiles were garaged at Harold Way. The gymnasium located in the garage was devoted solely to nonbusiness use. The swimming pool, cabana, and formally landscaped grounds in back of Harold Way provided petitioner with magnificent entertainment facilities. The entire home was represented to the public as the residence of Liberace, and the personal pleasure associated with such possession resided with petitioner. In short, Harold Way was purchased for the dual purpose of satisfying the business needs of the corporate petitioner while providing a home to Liberace, consistent with his life style and reputation.

Petitioner also maintained a home in Palm Springs in which he resided for approximately 15 days per year during the period in question. Petitioner resided at Harold Way whenever present in Los Angeles, whether working or not. Weekends during nonworking periods were usually spent at his home in Palm Springs.

During the taxable years in question petitioner resided in Los Angeles for approximately 95 to 130 days per year. A substantial majority of these days were devoted, in part, to preparatory work in connection with concerts produced by International Artists. * * *

NOTES AND QUESTIONS

1. 8433 Harold Way, which had previously been owned by Rudy Vallee, was sold in 1979 for a substantial profit. For a few years prior to its sale, Liberace opened the mansion to sightseeing tours at six dollars per person.

2. Should § 119 have had any bearing on this case?

3. Is it possible to view Liberace as having no personality other than his show business persona? What effect would such a view have had upon his tax situation?

E. ACTIVITIES NOT ENGAGED IN FOR PROFIT

Code: § 183

Regulations: § 1.183–1,–2

The expenses of personal hobbies are not deductible. However, if one could claim that the hobby was a profit-making venture, then one could enjoy the hobby just as much, and generate deductions as well. Notable examples of such ploys involved "hobby farms" and race horses. In the typical hobby farm, the taxpayer never had any intention of making money at farming. Rather, she wanted to shelter her other taxable income with farm losses. While she was at it, she could enjoy spending weekends on the farm, pretending to be bucolic, and getting the occasional spot of mud on her boots.

Section 183, and its predecessor, § 270, were enacted to prevent high-income taxpayers from turning their personal, nondeductible hobby expenses into deductible business expenses. The basic scheme of § 183 is to require these hobbies to be placed into separate "baskets" for tax purposes. In that way, hobby expenses would only be deductible against hobby income. For more on baskets, see Chapter 13, *infra* at 656.

The trick, of course, is to carve out the personal hobbies, which the statute calls "activities not engaged in for profit." Section 183(d) creates some helpful presumptions. If you have turned a profit for at least three of the last five years (two out of the last seven years for certain activities involving horses), then your activity is presumed to be an "activity engaged in for profit." One would think that, after five years, if you haven't made money in at least three of those years, you'll give up. Unless, that is, you never really cared about making money in the first place.

The regulations and the caselaw are also helpful in distinguishing hobbies from "for profit" activities. Generally, the thrust of the regulations is to ensure that the taxpayer is taking her profit motive seriously. As to the caselaw, consider *Dreicer*.

DREICER v. COMMISSIONER

United States Court of Appeals, District of Columbia Circuit, 1981.
665 F.2d 1292.

SPOTTSWOOD W. ROBINSON, III, CHIEF JUDGE:

Maurice C. Dreicer appeals from a decision of the United States Tax Court disallowing deductions, in computation of two years' federal income taxes, for losses incurred assertedly in professional endeavors as a multimedia personality. The Tax Court found that the particular pursuits in which Dreicer sustained the reported losses were writing and lecturing, and concluded that he had not engaged in those activities for profit, as defined by Section 183 of the Internal Revenue Code and regulations promulgated thereunder, for the stated reason that he had no bona fide expectation of realizing a profit from them.

We perceive no basis for disturbing the Tax Court's finding on the nature of the undertakings generating the losses for which deductions are sought. We do not accept, however, the legal test that the court employed in ruling on deductibility. We hold that a taxpayer engages in an activity for profit, within the meaning of Section 183 and the implementing regulations, when profit is actually and honestly his objective though the prospect of achieving it may seem dim. Because the Tax Court applied a different standard, we reverse and remand for redetermination of Dreicer's deduction claims.

I

By virtue of Section 162 of the Internal Revenue Code, a taxpayer may deduct from gross income all ordinary and necessary expenses incurred in a business, and, under Section 212, in the production or collection of income. A corollary rule, embodied in Section 165, permits deduction of losses sustained in a trade or business, or in a transaction entered into for profit. Section 183 qualifies these provisions by specifically disallowing, with limited exceptions not relevant here, deductions attributable to activities "not engaged in for profit." Thus, a taxpayer claiming a deduction under Sections 162 or 212 for an expense, or under Section 165 for a loss, must be prepared to demonstrate an associated profit motive in order to avoid the ban of Section 183. Appraising the facts salient in Dreicer's instance, which we need only summarize, the Tax Court held that he did not.

Dreicer, a citizen of the United States, maintains his residence in the Canary Islands, Spain, and engages heavily in global travel.[10] He derives a substantial income as beneficiary of a family trust, and in the early 1950's, Dreicer began to focus his professional attention on the fields of tourism and dining.[12] In 1955, he published The Diner's Companion, a compilation of his opinions on dining and on various restaurants throughout the world, but the book was a commercial failure.[14] Undaunted, Dreicer conceived the idea of some day writing another book, this one to enshrine his reminiscence on a life dedicated to epicurism and travel. In preparation for this sybaritic swan song, he spent the next twenty years traveling about the world, staying in some of the finest hotels and dining in some of the best restaurants. The material he gathered was also to be utilized in lectures before travel organizations and public appearances on radio and television. By the mid–1970s, Dreicer had completed a rough draft of the

---

10. Dreicer describes himself as a multimedia personality, under which general label he includes writing, lecturing, consulting, endorsing consumer products, hosting and appearing on radio and television talk programs.

12. Dreicer had engaged previously in origination of ideas for radio and television programs, and had been a pioneer in the television industry.

14. On $1,645 in sales of The Diner's Companion, Dreicer's total royalties were $643. After the publisher reduced the price of the book for quick sale, Dreicer purchased the remaining copies and subsequently sold 50 to 100 copies annually.

second book—parts of which originally had appeared in The Diner's Companion—and titled it My 27 Year Search for the Perfect Steak—Still Looking. Two publishing houses to which he submitted the manuscript, however, returned it, and seemingly he abandoned all hope of publishing.

When Dreicer filed his federal income tax returns for 1972 and 1973, he claimed deductible losses of $21,795.76 and $28,022.05, respectively, for travel and other related business expenses. The Commissioner of Internal Revenue thereafter issued a notice of deficiency, disallowing the deductions on the ground that the losses arose from activities not pursued for profit, and the Tax Court agreed. The court disputed Dreicer's characterization of his professional self as a multi-media personality, finding instead that he was a writer-lecturer on tourism and dining. Having so defined his activity for Section 183 analysis, the court concluded that he had not entertained a bona fide expectation of profit from writing and lecturing, and on that account denied the deductions.

Dreicer challenges the Tax Court's decision on two grounds. First, he contends that the court went amiss in finding that for purposes of Section 183 his professional activity was writing-lecturing rather than development as a public personality. He also argues that the court erred as a matter of law in confining the concept of a for-profit activity to one from which the taxpayer actually expects to make a profit. We consider each of these contentions in turn. * * *

III

Dreicer also argues that even if the activity for which he claims deductions was no more than writing and lecturing, the Tax Court applied the wrong legal standard in determining whether he engaged in it for profit, as defined by Section 183, because the court predicated its result on his profit expectation rather than to his profit objective. We agree.

Addressing the losses that Dreicer deducted for the two tax years in question, the Tax Court made a searching inquiry into Dreicer's writing and lecturing pursuits in light of various factors set forth in the Treasury regulations pertinent. The court noted Dreicer's lengthy history of substantial losses in those endeavors; his sizable independent income, which enabled him to continue writing and lecturing notwithstanding those losses;[42] the tax benefits he had obtained from deduction of such losses in earlier years; the unbusinesslike manner in which he had conducted his operations, including abandonment of efforts to get his second book published; his apparent lack of expertise on the subjects of tourism and dining; the pleasure he took in traveling and dining;[46] and his failure to achieve commercial success as a writer-lecturer.

---

42. The court found that Dreicer's income, independently of his writing and lecturing, was $130,647.14 in 1972 and $91,803.49 in 1973, derived exclusively from a family trust.

46. Dreicer claimed before the Tax Court that he derives little personal enjoyment from "living out of a suitcase." The court observed, however, that "if (Dreicer) were so adverse to this style of living, then he would have completed his 'research' long ago and have moved on to other pursuits."

We applaud the Tax Court for the thoroughness of its factual inquiry, but we cannot place the stamp of approval upon its eventual legal outcome. The court concluded that Dreicer's losses were nondeductible on the sole ground that he did not have a "bona fide expectation of profit" from writing and lecturing. The language of Section 183, its legislative history and the applicable Treasury regulation combine to demonstrate that the court's standard is erroneous as a matter of law.

Section 183 was adopted as part of the Tax Reform Act of 1969 to replace for taxable years beginning after December 31, 1969, the so-called "hobby loss" provision of former Section 270. The preexisting hobby loss feature was a limitation on deductible losses incurred in an individual's trade or business to $50,000 per year if the losses therefrom had exceeded $50,000 for five or more consecutive years—a restriction many taxpayers had proven creative enough to avoid. Both Houses of Congress however, were aware of judicial disallowances of such losses when "the activity carried on by the taxpayer from which the loss results is not a business but is merely a hobby." Each agreed, moreover, "that this basic principle provides a more effective and reasonable basis for distinguishing situations where taxpayers were not carrying on a business to realize a profit but rather were merely attempting to utilize the losses from the operation to offset their other income." The two Houses disagreed, however, over one element critical to application of this distinction.

The House bill would have replaced the old hobby loss provision with rules specifying that a taxpayer could not deduct losses arising from an activity carried on without "a reasonable expectation of realizing a profit from it." Determinations on whether the activity was conducted "with the expectation of realizing a profit" would be made on the basis of all facts and circumstances; and losses exceeding $25,000 in three out of five years would give rise to a rebuttable presumption "that the taxpayer was not operating the activity with a reasonable expectation of realizing a profit from it."

In the Senate, however, there was concern "that requiring a taxpayer to have a 'reasonable expectation' of profit may cause losses to be disallowed in situations where an activity is being carried on as a business rather than as a hobby." The Senate Committee on Finance accordingly "modified the House bill to provide that in determining whether losses from an activity are to be allowed, the focus is to be on whether the activity is engaged in for profit rather than whether it is carried on with a reasonable expectation of profit." The Committee explained:

> This will prevent the rule from being applicable to situations where many would consider that it is not reasonable to expect an activity to result in a profit even though the evidence available indicates that the activity actually is engaged in for profit. For example, it might be argued that there was not a "reasonable" expectation of profit in the case of a bona fide inventor or a person who invests in a wildcat oil well. A similar argument might be made in the case of a poor person

engaged in what appears to be an inefficient farming operation. The committee does not believe that this provision should apply to these situations or that the House intended it to so apply, if the activity actually is engaged in for profit.

In the end, the Senate prevailed. The Conference Committee, noting that "(I)n lieu of the test of 'a reasonable expectation of profit' the Senate amendment substitutes the test of 'not engaged in for profit,'" adopted the Senate version, and in that form the legislation ultimately passed both Houses. Section 183 thus emerged as the product of a congressional purpose to pivot its operation, not on whether the taxpayer expected a profit, but instead on whether the taxpayer engaged in the activity with the objective of making a profit.

The language of both Section 183 and the Treasury regulations implementing it is faithful to this legislative intent. The statutory text bars deductibility of losses emanating from "activities not engaged in for profit," not activities lacking an expectation of profit. The regulation provides relevantly:

> The determination whether an activity is engaged in for profit is to be made by reference to objective standards, taking into account all of the facts and circumstances of each case. Although a reasonable expectation of profit is not required, the facts and circumstances must indicate that the taxpayer entered into the activity or continued the activity with the objective of making a profit. . . .

In the case at bar, the Tax Court conceded that a taxpayer need not show an expectation of profit that could be deemed reasonable. It ruled that Dreicer could not deduct the losses in question because, it said, he did not have "a bona fide expectation" of profit from the action from which those losses arose:

> (T)he record in this case shows beyond a doubt that there was no possibility of (Dreicer) realizing sufficient profit from his writing and lecturing activities to recoup the very large losses sustained in the preceding years, and therefore, we are convinced that, during the years in issue, (Dreicer) could not have had a bona fide expectation of realizing a profit from such activities.

Indeed, the notion that such an expectation was a precondition to deductibility pervades the court's treatment of Dreicer's claim thereto, and became the decisive factor in its ruling:

> In conclusion, after a careful review of all the facts and circumstances of this case, we hold that (Dreicer's) activity of traveling around the world allegedly to obtain material for a transcript was an "activity . . . not engaged in for profit" within the meaning of section 183(a), since he did not have a bona fide expectation of profit. Accordingly, the losses incurred by him during 1972 and 1973 are not deductible.

By thus hinging its decision on Dreicer's profit expectations instead of his profit objectives, the Tax Court utilized the wrong test. The statute, its legislative history and the implementing Treasury regulation make explicit that the objective, not the expectation, of making a profit is to govern determinations on whether a taxpayer is engaged in a business or a hobby, and the two criteria are not the same. One may embark upon a venture for the sincere purpose of eventually reaping a profit but in the belief that the probability of financial success is small or even remote. He therefore does not really expect a profit, but nonetheless is willing to take the gamble. Under the Tax Court's test of "bona fide expectation of profit," losses incurred in the enterprise could not be deducted. Yet it cannot be gainsaid that "the activity actually is engaged in for profit"—that it was undertaken "with the objective of making a profit." We do not say that Dreicer's case is equivalent; that is for the Tax Court in the first instance, and we intimate no view on the merits. We do say that Dreicer's claims of deductibility are to be evaluated by proper legal standards.

The decision appealed from is accordingly reversed and the case is remanded to the Tax Court for further consideration in light of this opinion.

So ordered.

NOTES AND QUESTIONS

1. On remand, the Tax Court held that Mr. Dreicer did not have a "profit objective." Therefore, it reinstated its prior decision. 78 T.C. 642 (1982). The appellate court affirmed, per curiam 702 F.2d 1205 (D.C.Cir. 1983).

2. Maurice Dreicer created several innovative radio shows in New York in the late 1930's and early 1940's. His "Where Are You From?" challenged linguists to tell where members of the studio audience had been born, merely by hearing them talk. "Find the Phoney" was the radio predecessor of "To Tell the Truth," and "What's It Worth" foreshadowed "The Price is Right."

Dreicer invented a device for testing caviar. He also formed Cigar Smokers United. Perhaps his greatest commercial success was "How to Mix Them," a best-selling record on how to mix drinks.

3. *See* Irwin v. Commissioner, T.C. Memo. 1996–490. Basically, Mr. Irwin attempted to deduct all of his living expenses, including his hot tub, his daughter's college dormitory room, and traveling to Michigan for his mother's funeral. His argument was that, as a [as yet unpublished] writer of fiction, all of his life experiences had found their way into his work. He lost.

4. Anthony Ranciato also lost his Section 183 case. Ranciato v. Commissioner, T.C. Memo. 1996–67. The Court seemed to think that he kept his unprofitable pet shop going to give his mother something to do outside the home, rather than to make any money for himself.

5. High risk activities are often the ones that lead to the next business or technological breakthrough. How can we encourage inventors, wildcat oil drillers, and farmers, while discouraging people like Mr. Dreicer?

F. CHILD CARE EXPENSES

Code: § 21

Regulations: § 1.44A–1

INTRODUCTORY QUESTIONS

Husband works full-time, and Wife stays home to care for the children. Wife decides to work outside of the home. They arrange for child care. What was the proximate cause of the expense?

Husband and Wife both work outside of the home. They decide to have children. They arrange for child care. What was the proximate cause of the expense?

The questions above should show that child care expenses are mixed motive expenses. One would not incur child care expenses but for the job; one would not incur child care expenses but for the children. As has been noted earlier, in these mixed motive categories, the choice of characterizing them as predominantly business/deductible, or predominantly personal/nondeductible, is a policy choice to be made largely by Congress. Congress, and the courts, reflect prevailing social attitudes, as can be seen by contrasting the excerpt from the early *Wright Smith* decision with the later *Symes* (Canadian) and *Zoltan*, (US) cases, and the current statute.

a brief look at how things were . . .

WRIGHT SMITH v. COMMISSIONER

United States Board of Tax Appeals, 1939.
40 B.T.A. 1038, *aff'd*, 113 F.2d 114 (C.C.A.2 1940).

* * * We are told that the working wife is a new phenomenon. This is relied on to account for the apparent inconsistency that the expenses in issue are now a commonplace, yet have not been the subject of legislation, ruling, or adjudicated controversy. But if that is true it becomes all the more necessary to apply accepted principles to the novel facts. We are not prepared to say that the care of children, like similar aspects of family and household life, is other than a personal concern. The wife's services as custodian of the home and protector of its children are ordinarily rendered without monetary compensation. There results no taxable income from the performance of this service and the correlative expenditure is personal and not susceptible of deduction. Here the wife has chosen to employ others to discharge her domestic function and the services she performs are rendered outside the home. They are a source of actual income and taxable as such. But that does not deprive the same work performed by others of its personal character nor furnish a reason why its cost should be treated as an offset in the guise of a deductible item.

We are not unmindful that, as petitioners suggest, certain disbursements normally personal may become deductible by reason of their intimate connection with an occupation carried on for profit. In this category fall entertainment, and traveling expenses, and the cost of an actor's wardrobe. The line is not always an easy one to draw nor the test simple to apply. But we think its principle is clear. It may for practical purposes be said to constitute a distinction between those activities which, as a matter of common acceptance and universal experience, are "ordinary" or usual as the direct accompaniment of business pursuits, on the one hand; and those which, though they may in some indirect and tenuous degree relate to the circumstances of a profitable occupation, are nevertheless personal in their nature, of a character applicable to human beings generally, and which exist on that plane regardless of the occupation, though not necessarily of the station in life, of the individuals concerned. In the latter category, we think, fall payments made to servants or others occupied in looking to the personal wants of their employers. And we include in this group nursemaids retained to care for infant children.

... *and how they've changed* ...

Should child care expenses be treated worse than other business expenses? Consider the following excerpt from Canadian Judge Heureux–Dube's dissenting opinion, in a case in which a woman lawyer was prohibited from taking as many deductions as she would have liked for her child care expenses. *Symes* is followed by *Zoltan*, which gives a more recent US perspective.

SYMES v. CANADA

Supreme Court of Canada.
[1993] 4 S.C.R. 695, 1993 WL 1442777.

L'HEUREUX-DUBE J. (dissenting)—

* * * If we survey the experience of many men, it is apparent why it may seem intuitively obvious to some of them that child care is clearly within the personal realm. This conclusion may, in many ways, reflect many men's experience of child care responsibilities. In fact, the evidence before the Court indicates that, for most men, the responsibility of children does not impact on the number of hours they work, nor does it affect their ability to work. Further, very few men indicated that they made any work-related decisions on the basis of child-raising responsibilities. The same simply cannot currently be said for women. For women, business and family life are not so distinct and, in many ways, any such distinction is completely unreal, since a woman's ability to even participate in the work force may be completely contingent on her ability to acquire child care. The decision to retain child care is an inextricable part of the decision to work, in business or otherwise. * * * In the recently released study by the Canadian Bar Association Task Force on Gender Equality in the Legal Profession entitled Touchstones for Change: Equality, Diversity and Accountability (1993), the difficulties many women lawyers face when attempting to balance career and family were highlighted. The report states (at p. 65):

"One of the main causes of discrimination against women lawyers is the culture that surrounds work in the legal profession. That culture has been shaped by and for male lawyers. It is predicated on historical work patterns that assume that lawyers do not have significant family responsibilities. The "hidden gender" of the current arrangements for legal work manifests itself in many ways, including: the extremely long and irregular hours of work; assumptions about the availability of domestic labour to support a lawyer's activities at work; promotion within law firms which is incompatible with the child bearing and child rearing cycles of most women's lives; and the perceived conflict between allegiances owed to work and family."

* * *

[Judge Heureux–Dube quotes various Canadian sources below]

"... no one is "objective" in the sense of being without a frame of reference, yet we sometimes fail to notice the frame of reference of those who have been in a position to define the very terms and concepts in which we think."

* * *

"... as long as business has been the exclusive domain of men, the commercial needs of business have been dictated by what men (think they) need to expend in order to produce income. The fact that these expenditures also have a "personal" element was never treated as a complete bar. Thus, the courts have in the past permitted business-men to deduct club fees because men like to conduct business with each other over golf. Because some men believe expensive cars enhance their professional image, driving a Rolls Royce has been held to be an incident of a professional business."

As a consequence, one must ask whether the many business deductions available, for cars, for club dues and fees, for lavish entertainment and the wining and dining of clients and customers, and for substantial charitable donations, are so obviously business expenses rather than personal ones. Although potentially personal, each one of these expenses has been accepted as a legitimate business expense and, as each reflects a real cost incurred by certain kinds of business people to produce income from business, a deduction has been allowed. The real costs incurred by businesswomen with children are no less real, no less worthy of consideration and no less incurred in order to gain or produce income from business.

Finally, with regard to the potentially personal nature of child care expenses, the issue of "choice" has been raised as a barrier to the availability of a deduction. * * * While there is a personal component to child raising, and while the care of children may be personally rewarding, this "choice" is a choice unlike any others. This "choice" is one from which all of society benefits, yet much of the burden remains on the shoulders of women. Women "choose" to participate in an activity which is not for their benefit alone, and, in so doing, they undertake a function on behalf of all society. * * *

The decision to have children is not like any other "consumption" decision. To describe the raising of children in comparable terms to "choosing" to purchase a certain kind of automobile or live in a certain dwelling is simply untenable. As well, the many complexities surrounding child care make it inappropriate to adopt the language of voluntary assumption of costs, where those costs may, in fact, be allocated in a discriminatory fashion—the burden falling primarily on women.

ZOLTAN v. COMMISSIONER

United States Tax Court, 1982.
79 T.C. 490.

STERRETT, JUDGE:

Findings of Fact

* * * During 1977 and 1978, petitioner was employed as an accountant by a public accounting firm, where she was required to work from 8 a.m. to 5 p.m., 5 days a week. Because she lived approximately 1 hour from her place of employment, petitioner generally left her home at 7 a.m. and returned at 6 in the evening. Thus, her job required her to be away from home for approximately 55 hours per week.

Petitioner's son, Paul Zoltan, was 11 years old in 1977. It is agreed that he is a qualifying individual with respect to whom child care expenses incurred by petitioner can give rise to a credit pursuant to § 44A [current § 21].

On her 1977 income tax return, petitioner calculated that she had incurred $1,891 in employment-related expenses with respect to her son. * * * The remaining $1,180 was paid to Camp Adanac, a summer camp located in Canada where Paul Zoltan spent 8 weeks. The $1,100 summer camp expenses remaining in dispute covered various expenses incurred by Paul Zoltan, including expenses for food, lodging, and tuition. The camp program provided instruction in swimming, archery, and various other activities in an unstructured fashion.

Petitioner stated that she sent her son to summer camp so that he would be taken care of while he was out of school. Had she not sent him to camp, petitioner would have sought alternative care for her son for her 55–hour–per–week absence from home. Her alternatives included sending him to a 6–hour day camp at a cost of $400, plus hiring a housekeeper for the remaining 5 hours per day at approximately $3 per hour. Thus, her total cost under this alternative would have been approximately $1,000. As a further alternative, petitioner could have hired a full-time housekeeper to care for her child. This would have cost approximately $1,320.

* * *

Opinion

* * * Petitioner maintains that the primary reason that she sent her son away to summer camp was to assure his well-being and protection. The summer camp alternative seemed to be the most feasible one available to petitioner. She stated that it would have been difficult to find a full-time housekeeper to care for her son 55 hours a week. Furthermore, such choice would have been more expensive than the cost of summer camp. A second option would have required her to hire someone to care for her child for 5 hours each day and to send him to a day camp for the other 6. Though this alternative might have proven somewhat less expensive than summer camp, it also would have required petitioner to arrange for child care services before and after day camp and to arrange for the daily transportation of her son to and from day camp and possibly of the hired help to and from work. Moreover, "The manner of providing the care need not be the least expensive alternative available to the taxpayer."

We believe that at least part of the summer camp expense qualifies as "expenses for the care of a qualifying individual." On the facts before us, we fail to find a material distinction between the instant case and example (2) of § 1.44A–1(c)(6), Income Tax Regs., wherein the portion of a taxpayer's cost incurred to send her child to boarding school that represented care qualified as a child care expense. In the example, the taxpayer's child had to be placed in a boarding school because the taxpayer's job required her to be away from home before or after normal school hours. This portion of the regulations can be said to be twice blessed, for it qualifies as a legislative regulation, and as a beneficiary of subsequent legislative approval. Here, petitioner was forced to choose a full-time summer camp over day camp for the identical reason.

We find that petitioner's principal purpose in sending her child away to camp was to provide for his well-being and protection. Moreover, the form of care she chose was reasonable under the circumstances, especially in light of the fact that the cost of the summer camp was virtually as inexpensive as any of the various other alternatives from which she had to choose and less expensive than the most obvious alternative.

A question remains, with respect to the summer camp expense, whether an allocable portion of such expense was not incurred for the care of Paul Zoltan and therefore does not qualify under § 44A(c)(2)(A). Section 1.44A–1(c)(5), Income Tax Regs., provides that an allocation must be made between the qualifying and nonqualifying elements of an expenditure.

This issue focuses on the apparent tension between the requirement that expenses be allocated under § 1.44A–1(c)(5), Income Tax Regs., and the rule that expenses that are "incident to and inseparably a part of the care" qualify as employment-related expenses under § 1.44A–1(c)(3)(i), Income Tax Regs. We find that the summer camp provided minimal educational services (see § 1.44A–1(c)(5), Income Tax Regs.), and that the food and any recreational services provided to petitioner's son were incident to and inseparably a part of his care. Thus, no allocation is necessary, and the full $1,100 qualifies.

As a last resort, respondent contends that petitioner must prorate the expenses to reflect the fact that petitioner only was away from home for employment purposes for a total of 55 hours a week. Thus, respondent would limit qualifying expenses to 55/168, or approximately 33 percent. We disagree. Once the decision was made by petitioner to send her son to camp, she had no choice but to pay for 24–hour care, 7 days a week. Having found that the dominant motivation behind the decision was to permit petitioner to work, we conclude that the constant care of her son was inseparably part of the type of care giving rise to the qualifying expenses. We note that example (2) of § 1.44A–1(c)(6), Income Tax Regs., requires no allocation between the taxpayer's working and nonworking hours where the subject expenses are paid to send the taxpayer's son to boarding school. * * *

In holding that the entire $1,100 was properly characterized as an "employment-related expense," we are in no sense canonizing summer camp expenses for purposes of § 44A. This decision is specifically limited to the facts and circumstances before us. * * *

The second expense at issue is the $116 expense incurred by petitioner to send her son on a school trip to Washington, D.C., during the week of his Easter vacation. Again, we find that this trip was primarily undertaken for the son's well-being and protection. We note that the cost of a housekeeper for the week in question would have exceeded the cost of the trip.

Expenses incurred for transportation are subject to the disqualification provisions of § 1.44A–1(c)(3)(i), Income Tax Regs., which in pertinent part provides:

> Expenses incurred for transportation of a qualifying individual * * * between the taxpayer's household and a place outside the taxpayer's household where services for the care of the qualifying individual are provided are not incurred for the care of a qualifying individual.

We are of the opinion that the expenses incurred for the transportation of petitioner's son to Washington are not disqualified by this language. The cost of transportation from petitioner's home to the place of departure is the type of expense that this language excludes. The care of Paul Zoltan commenced at that point. The transportation by bus to Washington began after petitioner's son was placed under the care of the supervisors of the expedition. This transportation was inseparably tied to that care and does not fit within the disallowance provisions of § 1.44A–1(c)(4), Income Tax Regs.

We believe, however, that a substantial portion of the expense incurred by petitioner to send her son to Washington, D.C., constituted an educational expense of the type subject to allocation pursuant to § 1.44A–1(c)(3)(i) and § 1.44A–1(c)(5), Income Tax Regs. Petitioner has made no effort to bifurcate the cost of the D.C. trip between educational services and care services. Relying upon his assertion that petitioner was not motivated by a concern for her son's well-being and protection, respondent also failed to suggest an allocation between the competing services. Therefore, it is left to us to estimate the proper allocation. Convinced that petitioner incurred expenses attributable to care services, we apply the rule of Cohan v. Commissioner. Bearing heavily against the taxpayer, "whose inexactitude is of [her] own making," we find that petitioner incurred care-related expenses in the amount of $35 as a consequence of her son's Washington, D.C., trip. Accordingly, this amount qualifies as an "employment-related expense" within the meaning of § 44A(c)(2)(A)(ii) [see current § 21(b)(2)].

To summarize, when the characterization of an expense is challenged under [§ 21(b)(2)], the issue is resolved by reference to the specific facts at hand; the Court must ascertain the taxpayer's motive. If the disputed expense was incurred with the dominant purpose of permitting the taxpayer to be gainfully employed and to assure the child's well-being and protection while the taxpayer is so employed, it qualifies as employment-related despite the existence of other incidental benefits. A parent is not prohibited from choosing child care that carries incidental benefits so long as the moving force behind the decision is the desire to assure the protection and well-being of the child. Here, we have made a factual finding, in the case of both the summer camp and the Washington trip, that petitioner's primary concern was the care of her child. Any incidental services provided to her child at summer camp were inextricably tied to the child care services. With respect to the Washington trip, the expenses attributable to educational services must be carved out of the otherwise qualifying expense since these services were substantial and were not incidental to, or inseparably a part of, the care-related services.

The concurring and dissenting opinion is omitted.

QUESTION, PROBLEMS

1. How would *Zoltan* come out under current law? Which law do you prefer?

2. Alphonse and Hillary are married, and have two children. In 2004, Jesse is 6 years old, and Catherine is 3. Each of the children goes to dependent care center. In 2004, Alphonse and Hillary paid the dependent care center $4,000 for day care—$2,000 for Jesse and $2,000 for Catherine. The couple's adjusted gross income this year is $30,000. All of it was earned by Hillary; Alphonse does not work outside the home. However, Alphonse is a full-time student for 9 months of the year. Compute their child care credit under § 21. What if Alphonse were a student at an on-line university?

3. Clyde does volunteer work for the Red Cross. Shaquille earns $2,500 a year, which is less than the expenses of day care, commuting, and dry cleaning which he incurs in order to work. Is either one of them "gainfully employed" within the meaning of § 21(b)(2)(A)?

4. S.1253 was introduced by Senator Murkowski in the fall of 2004. It would have added some language to § 21, including the following:

§ 21(e)(11) MINIMUM CREDIT ALLOWED FOR STAY–AT–HOME PARENTS

Notwithstanding subsection (d), in the case of any taxpayer with one or more qualifying individuals described in subsection (b)(1)(A) under the age of 6 at any time during the taxable year, such taxpayer shall be deemed to have employment-related expenses with respect to such qualifying individuals in an amount equal to the greater of—

(A) the amount of employment-related expenses incurred for such qualifying individuals for the taxable year (determined under this section without regard to this paragraph), or

(B) $200 for each month in such taxable year during which such qualifying individual is under the age of 6.

Good idea?

G. INTEREST

Code: §§ 163(a), (h), 265, 221, 7872

1. BUSINESS INTEREST, PERSONAL INTEREST, AND HOME MORTGAGE INTEREST

NOTE

Whatever it costs a business to have needed business assets ought to be deductible somehow. Businesses need machines. Therefore, if a machine is rented, the rent should be deductible.

Similarly, businesses need money. Therefore, if money is "rented," then that "rent" should also be deductible. Accordingly, business interest is deductible, either now or later. If the business interest expense is properly allocated to the acquisition costs of a capital asset, then those interest costs are added to basis. See Chapter 5.

Personal interest, in contrast, should be nondeductible. A personal vacation, having no business aspects whatsoever, ought to be totally nondeductible. See Chapter 10, *infra*. It follows that the interest on a loan taken out to fund that vacation should also be totally nondeductible.

But money is fungible. Therefore, tracing which loan proceeds are used for business expenses and which are used for personal expenses can be difficult. Imagine that Taxpayer has $1,000 in savings. She plans to go on a $1,000 personal vacation, and she plans to incur a $1,000 business expense. She plans $2,000 of expenditures, but only has $1,000 in the bank, so she borrows the other $1,000.

Now she has $2,000—$1,000 in savings, and $1,000 in loan proceeds. She plans $2,000 of expenditures—$1,000 for business, and $1,000 for pleasure. Which money should she use for which purpose?

If she uses the savings for her business expense, and the loan proceeds for her vacation, then the interest on the loan would appear to be personal, and hence nondeductible. However, if she uses the savings for her vacation, and the loan proceeds for her business, then the interest on the loan would appear to be business-related, hence deductible. Of course, that is what she will claim she did. How can either the Taxpayer or the IRS trace which dollars went for which purpose, to prove what actually happened?

Until 1986, the government's general reaction to this tracing dilemma was to give up, and allow a deduction for all interest, be it personal or business. As a result, all interest, including the mortgage interest paid on a personal home, was fully deductible.

In 1984, President Reagan asked the Treasury Department to devise a plan for a complete overhaul of the entire tax code. Accordingly, Treasury gave serious consideration to a complete elimination of the deduction for personal interest, including the interest on personal home mortgages. However, any hope for such a radical change was dashed in May of 1985, when the President said, in a speech to the National Association of Realtors:

> In case there's still any doubt, I want you to know we will preserve the part of the American dream which the home-mortgage-interest deduction symbolizes.[d]

In the 1986 Tax Reform Act, Congress did eliminate the deduction for personal interest.[e] However, it retained the deduction for "qualified residence interest,"[f] which consists of "acquisition indebtedness" and "home equity indebtedness."[g] "Acquisition indebtedness must be incurred in acquiring, constructing, or substantially improving a "qualified residence," or in refinancing such debt.[h] "Home equity indebtedness," however, is merely indebtedness secured by the qualified residence, as long as it is below the relevant dollar caps.[i] Up to certain limits, then, if you are a homeowner, you can create "home equity indebtedness," and use the loan proceeds to buy a personal car, or go on vacation, paying fully deductible interest. The banks know it, and they frequently advertise their willingness to help you. Yet another discrimination in favor of homeowners and against renters.

Example

Horace bought a house a few years ago for $100,000. He took out a mortgage of $75,000. The mortgage balance is now $70,000. The house is now worth $125,000. Horace wants to buy a new luxury car for $50,000. He

---

d. Jeffrey H. Birnbaum and Alan S. Murray, SHOWDOWN AT GUCCI GULCH (N.Y. 1987) at 57.

e. Section 163(h)(1).

f. Sections 163(h)(2)(D) and 163(h)(3). For other deductible and nondeductible categories of interest, see Chapter 13, *infra*.

g. Sections 163(h)(3)(A)(i) and (ii).

h. § 163(h)(3)(B).

i. § 163(h)(3)(C).

proposes to take out a second mortgage on his house for $50,000, and use the proceeds to buy the car.

All of Horace's interest on both mortgages will be deductible as "qualified residence interest" within the meaning of § 163(h)(3). The first mortgage is "acquisition indebtedness" as defined in § 163(h)(3)(B). Horace's acquisition indebtedness is well under the $1,000,000 cap, as provided in § 163(h)(3)(B)(ii).

The second mortgage is "home equity indebtedness," as defined in § 163(h)(3)(C). The home equity indebtedness may not exceed:

fair market value of the qualified residence	[as provided in] § 163(h)(3)(C)(i)(I)	$125,000
reduced by the acquisition indebtedness with respect to such residence	§ 163(h)(3)(C)(i)(II)	− $70,000
Total		$55,000

In this case, the $50,000 home equity indebtedness is below the $55,000 limit provided above. Moreover, it is also under the $100,000 limit ($50,000 for married filing separate) as provided by § 163(h)(3)(C)(ii). Accordingly, the interest on the car loan will be fully deductible.

PROBLEM

You need a new personal car. The manufacturer (one of the American Big Three) offers new car loans for its products at a 2.9% interest rate.

You have a line of credit with your bank, secured by your home. If you used this line of credit to purchase the car, the bank would charge you 8% interest. However, the interest payments would be deductible, pursuant to § 163(h)(3).

You are in the 25% tax bracket. Which is the better deal?

The Upside Down Home Owner Subsidy

Consider the deductibility of home mortgage interest in light of tax expenditure analysis, *supra* at Chapter IIIE. Since home mortgage interest is a deduction, and not a credit, the tax break is worth more to high income taxpayers than low income taxpayers. In fact, for homeowners in the 35% tax bracket, the federal government pays a subsidy of 35¢ for every dollar of mortgage interest paid. For homeowners in the 15% tax bracket, the subsidy is only 15¢ for every dollar of mortgage interest paid. Does this make any sense?

2. INTEREST ON NEW CAR LOANS: A PROPOSED STATUTE

[S. 1957 was introduced by Senator Deconcini in November, 1991. It did not pass.]

Be it enacted by the Senate and House of Representatives of the United States of America in Congress assembled,

(a) IN GENERAL.—Paragraph (2) of section 163 (h) of the Internal Revenue Code of 1986 (defining personal interest) is amended by striking "and" at the end of sub-paragraph (D), by redesignating subparagraph (E) as sub-paragraph (F), and by inserting after subparagraph (D) the following new subparagraph:

> "(E) any interest paid or incurred on an automobile loan (as defined in paragraph (5)), and".

(b) DEFINITION.—Paragraph (5) of section 163 (h) of such Code (relating to phase-in of limitations) is amended to read as follows:

> "(5) AUTOMOBILE LOAN.—For purposes of this subsection—
>
>> "(A) IN GENERAL.—The term 'automobile loan' means any indebtedness incurred in acquiring an automobile after December 31, 1991, and before January 1, 1993, if the original use of such automobile begins with the taxpayer.
>>
>> "(B) AUTOMOBILE.—For purposes of subparagraph (A), the term 'automobile' has the meaning given to such term by section 4064(b)(1) without regard to subparagraphs (B) and (C) thereof."

For your information. § 4064(b)(1)(A) provides:

(b) DEFINITIONS.—For purposes of this section

> (1) AUTOMOBILE
>
>> (A) IN GENERAL. The term "automobile" means any 4–wheel vehicle propelled by fuel
>>
>>> (i) which is manufactured primarily for use on public streets, roads, and highways (except any vehicle operated exclusively on a rail or rails), and
>>>
>>> (ii) which is rated at 6,000 pounds unloaded gross vehicle weight or less. In the case of a limousine, the preceding sentence shall be applied without regard to clause (ii).

QUESTIONS

How would this bill have changed the law? Analyze it in terms of horizontal and vertical equity [*see* the Introduction at 25, *supra*]. Would this proposal complicate or simplify tax law? What would its effect be on the economy? Overall, would you support such a bill?

Which is more important to the United States—new car purchases or higher education? Is that a fair question?

3. LOW INTEREST AND NO INTEREST LOANS

Code: § 7872

Father has $1,000,000, earning a return of $60,000 per year, taxable at Father's marginal rate of 35%. Father spends at least $60,000 per year on his son, Shiftless. Of course, other than the dependency deduction, Father gets no tax break whatsoever for the money spent on Shiftless.

Father loans the $1,000,000 to Shiftless, at no interest. Now, Son invests the $1,000,000, and the $60,000 annual return is taxed directly to him, at his marginal rate of 15%. Father is no worse off financially, because the $60,000 is still going where it was going before, to maintain the ridiculous lifestyle of Shiftless.

Good scheme? It was, for some time. Moreover, it should serve as your first introduction to the issues of assignment of income, covered *infra* at Chapter 9. However, now low interest and no interest loans are covered by § 7872. In effect, Congress is saying, in the real world, no one loans money without interest, unless something else is going on.

Assume an interest rate of 6%. Father loans $1,000,000 to Son for one year, at no interest. The "foregone interest" [§ 7872(e)(2)] would be $60,000. Pursuant to § 7872, Father will be deemed to have transferred the $60,000 to Son [§ 7872(a)(1)(A)], whereupon Son will be deemed to have retransferred the $60,000 back to Father as interest [§ 7872(a)(1)(B)].

Illustration 11

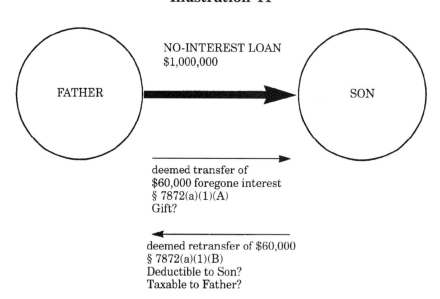

As to the deemed transfer from Father to Son, it is deductible only if it was done for a deductible reason. In this case, given the relationship of the parties, it looks like a nondeductible gift.

As to the deemed transfer from Son to Father, it would appear that the interest received is taxable to Father, while the interest paid is deductible by son, if he can show that it would have been deductible under § 163. Is it still a good scheme?

Reconsider *Al–Hakim*, *supra* at 288. Would it have worked after the enactment of § 7872?

Take the same $1,000,000 loan described above, and imagine that the lender was Employer and the borrower was his unrelated employee. Consider § 7872(c)(1)(B). How would such a transaction would be treated? See Reg. § 1.7872–4(c).

4.   ORIGINAL ISSUE DISCOUNT

[Adapted by the author from Michael J. McIntyre, *The International Income Tax Rules of the United States*, Lexis Publishing (2000, looseleaf).]

In general, original issue discount (OID) is the difference between the stated redemption price for a debt instrument at maturity and the price paid for the debt instrument at the time it was issued.[1] The redemption price is the price that the person issuing the instrument (the borrower) is obligated to pay when the instrument is mature—that is, when it becomes due and must be paid off. The OID on a bond or other debt instrument is sometimes referred to as the "premium."

> *Example.* A corporation borrows $100 in year 1 and promises to repay $150 in year 5. As evidence of its debt, it issues a debt instrument with a redemption price (sometimes called "face amount") of $150. The *original issue discount* with respect to the corporate debt instrument is $50 ($150 redemption price minus $100 price when issued).

A debt instrument may have some stated interest and also some OID. The extreme case of an OID bond is a bond issued for less than the redemption price with no stated interest at all.

OID is a substitute for periodical interest payments. When an OID bond or other debt instrument is issued, the premium due at the end of the term of the bond—that is, the OID—must compensate the holder of the bond for lending the issue price of the bond and also for lending the interest that was accruing annually on the bond.

> *Example.* A issues a bond, with a two-year term, for $100 at a time when the annual market rate of interest is 6 percent. No stated interest is payable on the bond. To make the bond attractive to prospective holders, A must agree to compensate the holder of the bond, by way of a redemption premium, not only for the $12 of interest due on the issue price but also for the delay in paying the $6 of interest that would accrue in the first year. At a 6 percent annual rate, the charge for the year's delay in making the $6 interest payment accruing in year 1 would be $.36 (6% of $6). Thus the

---

1.   IRC § 1273 (a) and (b).

redemption price of A's bond would have to be $112.36 for it to be marketable.

During periods of high interest rates, the OID for a bond with an extended term would have to be very high relative to the issue price in order to be competitive in the marketplace with a bond paying periodical interest.

> *Example.* An OID bond paying no periodical interest is issued for $100, redeemable after 25 years, at a time when the market interest rate is 15 percent. In the first year, the return on the OID bond would have to be 15 percent of the issue price, or $15, in order to be competitive with a bond paying periodical interest of 15 percent. In the second year, the return would have to be $17.30, which is 15 percent of the sum of the issue price of $100 and the deferred interest of $15. In the third year, the return would have to be $19.84 (15% of ($100 + $15 + $17.30)).

The deferred annual return in the example above would have to grow exponentially. In the 25th year, the deferred return on the issue price and the deferred interest would be $429. The sum of the accrued interest due for all 25 periods plus the issue price would amount to $3,292. That is, for an OID bond with an issue price of $100 and redeemable in 25 years to be competitive in the marketplace with a bond paying periodical interest of 15 percent, its promised redemption price would need to be almost 33 times its issue price.[2]

An investor considering the purchase of an OID bond should calculate the implicit interest rate payable on that bond. That implicit rate is called the yield, or the yield to maturity. A present worth formula can be used to compute the yield to maturity.

For a bond having no stated interest, the yield to maturity, r, expressed as an annual interest rate, can be determined by solving the following equation:

$$I = R/(1 + r) N$$

where I is the issue price, R is the redemption price, and N is the term of the bond, expressed in years. If the interest is to be compounded over some accrual period other than a year, then r would be the interest rate per accrual period and N would be the number of accrual periods over the term of the bond. A somewhat more complicated formula must be used to compute the yield to maturity for OID bonds that pay some periodical interest and also pay a premium at redemption.[3]

---

2. If the bond were redeemable after 30 years, the redemption price would have to be $6,621 for the bond to be competitive with a $100 bond paying periodical interest of 15%. See *General Explanation of the Revenue Provisions of the Tax Equity and Fiscal Responsibility Act of 1982* (1982) at 159.

3. That formula would provide that the issue price would equal the sum of the present worth of the periodical interest payments due on the bond and the present worth of the redemption price.

The United States has developed detailed rules for determining the tax consequences resulting from the issuance of debt instruments at a discount. A full discussion of those rules, contained in Code sections 1271 to 1288, is beyond the scope of this note. The OID rules provide a formula for allocating the original issue discount attributable to a bond (or other debt instrument) over the expected term of the bond. The objective of the formula is to amortize original issue discount in a manner that approximates the manner in which interest would accrue on a bond that was issued for its face amount and pays a market interest rate.

The formula for allocating original issue discount to particular taxable periods is contained in Code section 1272(a)(3) and explained in further detail in the two dozen odd pages of proposed Treasury regulations under that section. The statutory formula provides a method for spreading the total OID attributable to a bond over the term of that bond. Some portion of the OID is allocated to each day of that term. The Code refers to the OID allocated to a particular day as the "daily portion" of the OID. The OID allocated to a particular taxable year is referred to as the accrued OID for that year. The accrued OID for any year would be the sum of the daily portions for that year. With some exceptions, a holder of an OID bond is taxable each year on the OID allocated to that year, unless the holder is a related foreign person.[4] The issuer of an OID bond generally can deduct each year the accrued OID for that year.[5]

The daily portion of OID is determined by ratably spreading the OID allocated to an "accrual period" over the days in that period. An accrual period is a year or other period over which interest is being compounded. The term of a bond is divided into accrual periods, starting backwards from the redemption date. All of the accrual periods are of equal duration, except perhaps for the first accrual period. An OID bond paying some interest on an annual basis generally would have an accrual period of a year. For an OID bond paying no periodical interest, the accrual period would be 6 months.[6]

The OID allocable to the first accrual period is calculated by multiplying the issue price of the bond by the yield to maturity and subtracting the interest actually paid on the bond.

> *Example.* A bond is issued for $100. Its yield to maturity is 15 percent, its accrual period is one year, and the annual interest actually paid is $8. Under these conditions, the OID allocable to the first is $7 (15% of $100 minus $8.)[7]

---

4. IRC § 1272(a) (1).

5. Exceptions to the general rule apply for tax exempt obligations, for U.S. savings bonds, for bonds with a maturity date one year or less from the date of issuance, for obligations issued by a natural person before March 1, 1984, and for certain loans of less than $10,000 between natural persons. IRC § 1272(a)(2).

6. See Reg. § 1.1272–1(d).

7. If the first accrual period is less than a year, the yield to maturity would be adjusted to reflect the yield on the bond for that shorter period.

The OID allocable to subsequent accrual periods is calculated in a similar manner, except that the yield to maturity is multiplied by the "adjusted issue price" of the bond. The adjusted issue price is the sum of the issue price and the OID allocated to prior accrual periods. In the example above, the adjusted issue price for the bond in the second accrual period would be $107 ($100 + $7). The OID allocated to the second period would be $8.05 (15% of $107 minus $8). For the third accrual period, the adjusted issue price would be $115.05 ($100 + $7 + $8.05) and the OID allocated to that period would be $9.23 (15% of $115.05 minus $8).

In the examples above, the OID bond was issued for cash. More complicated rules apply for bonds issued for property other than cash.[8]

In some cases, the taxpayer may sell an OID bond before its maturity date. In that event, it is taxable on the OID that has accrued up to the time of the sale. The buyer is responsible for paying tax on OID accruing after the sale.

Original Issue Discount and Constructive Receipt

PRIVATE LETTER RULING 8830004 (1988)

Dear * * *

* * * An action was brought to recover damages for alleged birth defects received by X as a result of the ingestion of certain drugs prescribed while X's mother was pregnant with X. The action was settled prior to litigation and a court order was entered pursuant to the Statute providing for the deposit of certain amounts into a series of sequestered accounts. The accounts bear a legend that provides that "no withdrawal can be made from the accounts until the minor, X, attains the age of eighteen (18) years, except as authorized by a prior Order of this Court."

Pursuant to the Statute, the right to expend income and principal is dependent on the circumstances of the minor without reference to the financial ability of the parents. You state that upon proper application to the appropriate court, an order would be issued authorizing invasion of the accounts for the support, maintenance, health, medical needs and education of X. You ask whether X is in constructive receipt of the interest income on the amounts deposited in the sequestered accounts, under section 1.451–2(a) of the Income Tax Regulations.

* * * Based on the information submitted, the representations made, and the authorities cited above, we conclude that X will be taxable on the interest income paid on the amounts deposited in the sequestered accounts in the taxable year that it is earned. Additionally, if one were to conclude that the court order restricting withdrawal of the amounts deposited on behalf of X constitutes a substantial limitation or restriction within the meaning of section 1.451–2(a) of the regulations, the interest

---

8. IRC § 1273(b).

income would nevertheless be includible in X's gross income under the original issue discount provisions of section 1272 of the Code.

* * *

5. INTEREST AND INFLATION

NOTE

My associate wants to borrow $100 from me for one year. How much interest should I charge? First, there is economic rent. If I loaned my associate my house or my car for a year, I would expect to be paid for the fact that I was giving up the use of this valuable asset to someone else. Money is the same. If someone else gets to use it, he should pay rent.

Second, I must consider risk. If there is a chance that my associate will not repay the money, then I should charge more interest to compensate for that possibility.

Finally, there is inflation. Assume that 10% inflation is expected during the next year. Now, it really matters what kind of asset I loan.

If I "loaned" $100 worth of real estate to my associate, there would be no problem. Presumably, at the end of the year, the real estate that my associate returned to me would be worth $110. The buying power of the asset I loaned would be the same as the buying power of the asset returned to me. Real estate is the classic hedge against inflation.

But what if I loaned $100 cash during a year when there was 10% inflation? At the end of the year, I get my $100 back. However, its buying power will have declined by 10%.

If I had kept the money, I could have invested it in some hedge against inflation. However, this opportunity was foreclosed when I loaned the money to another. Therefore, whatever I propose to charge as interest, I should add 10% to cover inflation.

All interest has an inflation component. Should the inflation component of interest be taken into account for tax purposes, or should it be carved out? Assume that I borrow $100 for one year when the inflation rate is 20% and the interest rate is 25%. I pay $25 interest. Assuming that the interest is otherwise deductible, how many dollars of interest expense should I deduct, and how many dollars of interest income should the lender recognize? Should it be $25, or should it be $5? Current law says it should be $25.

Inflation and Interest; Inflation and Gains

As you know, there is an inflation component to gains, as well as interest. There have been many proposals to take the inflation component out of gains, so that only the appreciation in excess of inflation would be taxed. These proposals would achieve their goals by indexing basis. For example, imagine that an asset were purchased for $100 in Year 1. In Year 2, after all prices had inflated by 20% from their Year 1 levels, the asset is sold for $120. Under current law, there would be a gain of $20:

Amount Realized	$120
− Basis	− $100
Gain	$ 20

Under indexation of basis, there would be no gain:

Amount Realized	$120
− Basis indexed by inflation	− $120
Gain	0

What would happen if basis were indexed for inflation, but interest deductions were not? Imagine that, in the above example, Investor borrowed $100 at 25% interest, and used the proceeds to buy the asset. Before tax, the transaction would be a loss.

Gain on sale	$20
− Interest expense	− $25
Net Loss	($5)

The above calculation also reflects that Investor would be out of pocket $5.

However, after tax, there would be a gain.

Taxable Gain on sale	0
Deductible interest payments	$25

If Investor were in the 25% tax bracket or higher, the $25 interest deduction would save Investor at least $6.25 in taxes (25% × $25 = $6.25). That $6.25 tax saving exceeds the $5 out of pocket loss.

If both gains and interest deductions were indexed for inflation, then we could avoid the anomalous result of converting a before tax loss into an after tax gain. If the interest deduction were indexed for inflation, then only $5 of the $25 interest payment would be deductible. Therefore, the after tax computation would be:

Taxable Gain on sale	0
Deductible Interest Payments	$5

This time, the value of the interest deduction (25% × $5 = $1.25) would not exceed the out of pocket loss of $5.

Both indexation of gains and indexation of interest payments for inflation seem to be good ideas. Are they worth the complexity they would cause?

6. INTEREST AND THE ECONOMY: A COMPARATIVE APPROACH

Countries with the most generous treatment of interest deductions tend to have the lowest savings rates. The United States is such a country. It stands to reason. If the government makes it easier to borrow money, then why save? Is this a problem?

H. BAD DEBTS

Code: § 166

Reconsider Father and his son Shiftless, *supra* at 456. As we know, if Father **gave** Shiftless $60,000, there would be no deductions to Father. However, if Father **loaned** the $60,000 to Shiftless, and then Shiftless failed to pay it back, then perhaps Father would have a deductible bad debt of $60,000.

Businesses loan money for business reasons. Sometimes, the debts are not repaid. In that event, the bad debts should be a deductible business expense. However, as shown above, the presence of a bad debt deduction presents a tempting opportunity for fooling around.

The task of separating the real from the scam falls to § 166, and its caselaw. The section creates two levels of inquiry:

(1) Was there a debt at all? Often, what was claimed to be a loan was actually a gift, especially when the "borrower" was a close family member. Alternatively, the transaction might have been an equity investment, rather than a loan.

(2) If there was a debt which went bad, was it a business bad debt, or a nonbusiness bad debt? You will see that the statute gives considerably less favorable treatment to nonbusiness bad debts. Read § 166(d) and see how it relates to § 166(a).

UNITED STATES v. GENERES

United States Supreme Court, 1972.
405 U.S. 1033, 92 S.Ct. 1274, 31 L.Ed.2d 491.

MR. JUSTICE BLACKMUN delivered the opinion of the Court.

A debt a closely held corporation owed to an indemnifying shareholder-employee became worthless in 1962. The issue in this federal income tax refund suit is whether, for the shareholder-employee, that worthless obligation was a business or a nonbusiness bad debt within the meaning and reach of §§ 166(a) and (d) and of the implementing Regulations. * * *

In determining whether a bad debt is a business or a nonbusiness obligation, the Regulations focus on the relation the loss bears to the taxpayer's business. If, at the time of worthlessness, that relation is a "proximate" one, the debt qualifies as a business bad debt and the aforementioned desirable tax consequences then ensue.

The present case turns on the proper measure of the required proximate relation. Does this necessitate a "dominant" business motivation on the part of the taxpayer or is a "significant" motivation sufficient? * * *

The taxpayer as a young man in 1909 began work in the construction business. His son-in-law, William F. Kelly, later engaged independently in similar work. During World War II the two men formed a partnership in which their participation was equal. The enterprise proved successful. In 1954 Kelly–Generes Construction Co., Inc., was organized as the corporate successor to the partnership. It engaged in the heavy-construction business, primarily on public works projects.

The taxpayer and Kelly each owned 44% of the corporation's outstanding capital stock. The taxpayer's original investment in his shares was $38,900. The remaining 12% of the stock was owned by a son of the taxpayer and by another son-in-law. Mr. Generes was president of the corporation and received from it an annual salary of $12,000. Mr. Kelly was executive vice-president and received an annual salary of $15,000.

The taxpayer and Mr. Kelly performed different services for the corporation. Kelly worked full time in the field and was in charge of the day-to-day construction operations. Generes, on the other hand, devoted no more than six to eight hours a week to the enterprise. He reviewed bids and jobs, made cost estimates, sought and obtained bank financing, and assisted in securing the bid and performance bonds that are an essential part of the public-project construction business. Mr. Generes, in addition to being president of the corporation, held a full-time position as president of a savings and loan association he had founded in 1937. He received from the association an annual salary of $19,000. The taxpayer also had other sources of income. His gross income averaged about $40,000 a year during 1959–1962.

Taxpayer Generes from time to time advanced personal funds to the corporation to enable it to complete construction jobs. He also guaranteed loans made to the corporation by banks for the purchase of construction machinery and other equipment. In addition, his presence with respect to the bid and performance bonds is of particular significance. Most of these were obtained from Maryland Casualty Co. That underwriter required the taxpayer and Kelly to sign an indemnity agreement for each bond it issued for the corporation. In 1958, however, in order to eliminate the need for individual indemnity contracts, taxpayer and Kelly signed a blanket agreement with Maryland whereby they agreed to indemnify it, up to a designated amount, for any loss it suffered as surety for the corporation. Maryland then increased its line of surety credit to $2,000,000. The corporation had over $14,000,000 gross business for the period 1954 through 1962.

In 1962 the corporation seriously underbid two projects and defaulted in its performance of the project contracts. It proved necessary for Maryland to complete the work. Maryland then sought indemnity from Generes and Kelly. The taxpayer indemnified Maryland to the extent of $162,104.57. In the same year he also loaned $158,814.49 to the corporation to assist it in its financial difficulties. The corporation subsequently went into receivership and the taxpayer was unable to obtain reimbursement from it.

In his federal income tax return for 1962 the taxpayer took his loss on his direct loans to the corporation as a non-business bad debt. He claimed the indemnification loss as a business bad debt and deducted it against ordinary income. * * *

In due course the claims were made the subject of the jury trial refund suit in the United States District Court for the Eastern District of Louisiana. At the trial Mr. Generes testified that his sole motive in signing the indemnity agreement was to protect his $12,000-a-year employment with the corporation. The jury, by special interrogatory, was asked to determine whether taxpayer's signing of the indemnity agreement with Maryland "was proximately related to his trade or business of being an employee" of the corporation. The District Court charged the jury, over the Government's objection, that significant motivation satisfies the Regulations' requirement of proximate relationship. The court refused the Government's request for an instruction that the applicable standard was that of dominant rather than significant motivation.

After twice returning to the court for clarification of the instruction given, the jury found that the taxpayer's signing of the indemnity agreement was proximately related to his trade or business of being an employee of the corporation. Judgment on this verdict was then entered for the taxpayer.

The Fifth Circuit majority approved the significant-motivation standard so specified and agreed with a Second Circuit majority in Weddle v. Commissioner of Internal Revenue, 325 F.2d 849, 851, in finding comfort for so doing in the tort law's concept of proximate cause. Judge Simpson dissented. 427 F.2d, at 284. He agreed with the holding of the Seventh Circuit in Niblock v. Commissioner of Internal Revenue, 417 F.2d 1185, and with Chief Judge Lumbard, separately concurring in Weddle, 325 F.2d, at 852, that dominant and primary motivation is the standard to be applied.

II

A.   The fact responsible for the litigation is the taxpayer's dual status relative to the corporation. Generes was both a shareholder and an employee. These interests are not the same, and their differences occasion different tax consequences. in tax jargon, Generes' status as a shareholder was a nonbusiness interest. It was capital in nature and it was composed initially of tax-paid dollars. Its rewards were expectative and would flow, not from personal effort, but from investment earnings and appreciation. On the other hand, i.e., Generes' status as an employee was a business interest. Its nature centered in personal effort and labor, and salary for that endeavor would be received. The salary would consist of pre-tax dollars.

Thus, for tax purposes it becomes important and, indeed, necessary to determine the character of the debt that went bad and became uncollectible. Did the debt center on the taxpayer's business interest in the corporation or on his nonbusiness interest? If it was the former, the taxpayer deserves to prevail here. * * *

III

We conclude that in determining whether a bad debt has a "proximate" relation to the taxpayer's trade or business, as the Regulations specify, and thus qualifies as a business bad debt, the proper measure is that of dominant motivation, and that only significant motivation is not sufficient. We reach this conclusion for a number of reasons:

A. The Code itself carefully distinguishes between business and non-business items. It does so, for example, in § 165 with respect to losses, in § 166 with respect to bad debts, and in § 162 with respect to expenses. It gives particular tax benefits to business losses, business bad debts, and business expenses, and gives lesser benefits, or none at all, to nonbusiness losses, non-business bad debts, and nonbusiness expenses. It does this despite the fact that the latter are just as adverse in financial consequence to the taxpayer as are the former. But this distinction has been a policy of the income tax structure ever since the Revenue Act of 1916 provided differently for trade or business losses than it did for losses sustained in another transaction entered into for profit. And it has been the specific policy with respect to bad debts since the Revenue Act of 1942 incorporated into § 23(k) of the 1939 Code the distinction between business and non-business bad debts.

The point, however, is that the tax statutes have made the distinction, that the Congress therefore intended it to be a meaningful one, and that the distinction is not to be obliterated or blunted by an interpretation that tends to equate the business bad debt with the nonbusiness bad debt. We think that emphasis upon the significant rather than upon the dominant would have a tendency to do just that. * * *

C. The dominant-motivation standard has the attribute of workability. It provides a guideline of certainty for the trier of fact. The trier then may compare the risk against the potential reward and give proper emphasis to the objective rather than to the subjective. As has just been noted, an employee-shareholder, in making or guaranteeing a loan to his corporation, usually acts with two motivations, the one to protect his investment and the other to protect his employment. By making the dominant motivation the measure, the logical tax consequence ensues and prevents the mere presence of a business motive, however small and however insignificant, from controlling the tax result at the taxpayer's convenience. This is of particular importance in a tax system that is so largely dependent on voluntary compliance.

D.   The dominant-motivation test strengthens and is consistent with the mandate of § 262 of the Code that "no deduction shall be allowed for personal, living, or family expenses" except as otherwise provided. It prevents personal considerations from circumventing this provision. * * *

G.   The Regulations' use of the word "proximate" perhaps is not the most fortunate, for it naturally tempts one to think in tort terms. The temptation, however, is best rejected, and we reject it here. In tort law factors of duty, of foreseeability, of secondary cause, and of plural liability are under consideration, and the concept of proximate cause has been developed as an appropriate application and measure of these factors. It has little place in tax law where plural aspects are not usual, where an item either is or is not a deduction, or either is or is not a business bad debt, and where certainty is desirable.

IV

The conclusion we have reached means that the District Court's instructions, based on a standard of significant rather than dominant motivation, are erroneous and that, at least, a new trial is required. We have examined the record, however, and find nothing that would support a jury verdict in this taxpayer's favor had the dominant-motivation standard been embodied in the instructions. Judgment n.o.v. for the United States, therefore, must be ordered.

As Judge Simpson pointed out in his dissent, the only real evidence offered by the taxpayer bearing upon motivation was his own testimony that he signed the indemnity agreement "to protect my job," that "I figured in three years' time I would get my money out," and that "I never once gave it (his investment in the corporation) a thought."

The statements obviously are self-serving. In addition, standing alone, they do not bear the light of analysis. What the taxpayer was purporting to say was that his $12,000 annual salary was his sole motivation, and that his $38,900 original investment, the actual value of which prior to the misfortunes of 1962 we do not know, plus his loans to the corporation, plus his personal interest in the integrity of the corporation as a source of living for his son-in-law and as an investment for his son and his other son-in-law, were of no consequence whatever in his thinking. The comparison is strained all the more by the fact that the salary is pre-tax and the investment is taxpaid. With his total annual income about $40,000, Mr. Generes may well have reached a federal income tax bracket of 40% or more for a joint return in 1958–1962. The $12,000 salary thus would produce for him only about $7,000 net after federal tax and before any state income tax. This is the figure, and not $12,000, that has any possible significance for motivation purposes, and it is less than 1/5 of the original stock investment.

We conclude on these facts that the taxpayer's explanation falls of its own weight, and that reasonable minds could not ascribe, on this record, a dominant motivation directed to the preservation of the taxpayer's salary as president of Kelly–Generes Construction Co. Inc.

The judgment is reversed and the case is remanded with direction that judgment be entered for the United States.

It is so ordered.

Concurring and Dissenting Opinions Omitted.

PROBLEMS

Gullible loans Shady $20,000. During Year 1, Shady tells Gullible that there is no way that Shady will be able to pay back any more than $15,000. Accordingly, Gullible's debt is partially worthless in Year 1. In Year 2, Shady tells Gullible that Shady won't be able to repay any of the debt. Accordingly, in Year 2, the debt is totally worthless. Gullible had no capital gains or losses in either Year 1 or Year 2.

(a) Gullible's loan to Shady was a business debt. What deductions will Gullible have, and when?

(b) What if the debt were a nonbusiness debt?

PERRY v. COMMISSIONER

United States Tax Court, 1989.
92 T.C. 470, *aff'd without opinion,* 912 F.2d 1466 (5th Cir.1990).

CHABOT, JUDGE:

Petitioner married Richard Donald James Perry (hereinafter sometimes referred to as "Perry") on November 26, 1966. * * *

Petitioner and Perry were divorced on June 23, 1975. * * *The divorce decree granted custody of their minor children to petitioner.

Bad Debt Deduction

In paragraph 2 of the divorce decree, Perry was ordered to pay to petitioner a total of $400 per month ($200 for each child) "for the support, care, maintenance and education of the children". (The payments so ordered are hereinafter sometimes referred to as "paragraph 2 payments".) In paragraph 3 of the divorce decree, Perry was ordered to pay an additional amount of up to $400 per month, depending on the level of Perry's net income, as "alimony for petitioner's proper support and maintenance". (The payments so ordered are hereinafter sometimes referred to as "paragraph 3 payments".) * * *

In June of 1976, Perry informed petitioner that he would not make any of the payments he owed to petitioner under the divorce decree. At that time, petitioner was unemployed and attending school. Petitioner then began a long series of enforcement efforts. * * *

By the spring of 1985, Perry had become up-to-date in his paragraph 2 payments obligations. However, Perry has not made any paragraph 3 payments.

On her tax returns for 1980, 1981, and 1982, petitioner claimed dependency deductions for both Beth and Tad; respondent has not disallowed any of these dependency deductions.

On her 1980, 1981, and 1982 Federal income tax returns, petitioner claimed above-the-line deductions in the amounts of $3,000, $4,800, and $4,800, respectively, on account of the arrearages in paragraph 3 payments for those years. For 1982, petitioner reported an adjusted gross income of $29,607.

During each of the years 1980, 1981, and 1982, petitioner spent from her own funds more to support Beth and more to support Tad than she received from Perry for each of these children.

The petitions in the instant consolidated cases were filed on March 24, 1983, May 21, 1984, and May 23, 1984. On September 30, 1985, petitioner executed a document titled: "Continuing Guarantee and Agreement to Pay Support Obligations of Richard D. Perry" (hereinafter sometimes referred to as "the Guarantee") under which petitioner purported to guarantee payment to Beth and Tad of the payments due from Perry under the divorce decree. The Guarantee was to be retroactive to June 23, 1975.

Child Care Credit

During 1980 through 1982, petitioner was employed as an attorney on a full-time basis. Beth and Tad came home from school about 3 p.m., and petitioner did not usually get home from work until about 7 p.m. Because of her employment, petitioner found it necessary to secure day-care services for Beth and Tad. * * *

During 1982, petitioner paid for airfare to send Beth and Tad to stay with their grandparents in Shreveport, Louisiana, during school holidays, instead of hiring a babysitter. If petitioner had hired a babysitter for those time periods, then the babysitter would have cost more than the airfare.

Opinion

I. Bad Debt Deduction

Respondent contends that petitioner is not entitled to bad debt deductions on account of the arrearages of Perry's paragraph 3 payments because: (1) petitioner did not establish a basis in any debt; (2) petitioner did not establish the worthlessness of her right to the paragraph 3 payments; and (3) the nonpayment of the paragraph 3 payments does not fall within the definition of a capital asset to give rise to a capital loss deduction. Alternatively, respondent maintains that, if petitioner is entitled to bad debt deductions, then the amount should be less than that claimed by petitioner, in order to prevent overlapping deductions.

Petitioner maintains that she has proven all the elements necessary to show the existence, amount, basis, and worthlessness of a debt for 1980, 1981, and 1982.

We agree with respondent that petitioner does not have a basis in the debt.

In order to deduct a nonbusiness bad debt (sec. 166(a) and (d)), the taxpayer must show that a number of requirements have been satisfied. The requirement we examine in the instant case is that the debt be one in which petitioner has a basis (sec. 166(b)).

A legally enforceable divorce decree set forth Perry's obligations to make payments to petitioner. These obligations were not contingent on any expenditure by petitioner. During the years in issue, Perry was obligated to make paragraph 3 payments of $400 per month regardless of whether petitioner spent little, much, or nothing at all on child support. Similarly, petitioner's expenditures were independent of Perry's court-ordered payments, and neither created nor affected the amount of the debt that Perry owed to petitioner.

When faced with this situation in Swenson v. Commissioner, 43 T.C. 897, we held that in such a situation the taxpayer did not have a basis in the debt, and so no deduction was allowable under section 166. Petitioner has not presented any argument which would lead us to distinguish or overrule Swenson.

We conclude that petitioner had no basis in the arrearages in paragraph 3 payments, and is therefore not entitled to a bad debt deduction.

Petitioner raises several arguments to support her contention that she has a basis in the debt.

Petitioner argues that the Guarantee provides a basis in the debt from Perry. The Guarantee did not exist during any of the years in issue; it is petitioner's attempt to create post-hoc "facts". No payments could have been made during any of those years under the Guarantee. In paying for the support of Beth and Tad, petitioner was merely satisfying her own obligations to her own children.

As the mother of her children, petitioner was already effectively the guarantor of their support. Under Georgia law, "the duty of parents to support their children is joint and several, and does not cease upon separation or divorce of the parents." Under Louisiana law, the obligation to support one's children "continues after separation or divorce, and applies to both mothers and fathers." Payment made on one's own obligation does not give rise to a bad debt deduction. Petitioner acquired no basis in Perry's support obligation from (1) the mere execution of a document restating an obligation which was already hers or (2) the payment of support for her children.

* * *

We conclude that the Guarantee did not provide petitioner with a basis in the support obligations.

Petitioner also argues that her financing of Perry's education was an investment in his earning potential, that the paragraph 3 payments were intended to be the return on her investment in Perry (to the extent that they were not intended to be child support), and that when those payments became uncollectable, she incurred a capital loss. Petitioner's argument, in essence, is that by financially supporting Perry during 2–1/2 years of their 8–1/2–year marriage, she obtained a basis in the debt arising from the divorce decree. We do not agree.

Perry's obligation to make the paragraph 3 payments arose from the marital relationship and was defined by the divorce court. Petitioner's support of Perry during their marriage may well have enhanced his earning potential, but it cannot be said that petitioner supported Perry in order to acquire a right of action against him upon their subsequent divorce. The amounts that petitioner spent to help educate her husband were no more than personal expenses (see sec. 262) that do not provide her a basis in a debt.

A purported loan between family members is always subject to close scrutiny. The same is true as to a purported investment. The presumption, for tax purposes at least, is that a transfer between family members is a gift. If there ever was a written agreement between petitioner and Perry, then it would be petitioner who would be expected to produce it. If Perry ever had made payments to petitioner to evidence an obligation to repay petitioner's investment, then it would be petitioner who could show such payments. Petitioner testified and produced checks and other records. Petitioner did not testify or produce any evidence regarding Perry's obligation to repay any of the money that petitioner spent. From this we conclude that petitioner's expenditures in 1967 through 1969 did not give rise to a debt from Perry to her.

The divorce decree deals at length in paragraph 8 with "The property jointly and/or severally held by the parties" and specifies dispositions with great particularity. There is no reference in paragraph 8 to Perry's debt to petitioner. On the other hand, paragraph 9 specifically provides that Perry "will assume responsibility for all obligations and debts of the parties which accrued prior to January 1, 1975". Paragraph 3 deals, by its terms, with "payments to the wife petitioner as alimony, for her proper support and maintenance". Paragraph 3 obligations are separate from property divisions and preexisting liabilities of paragraphs 8 and 9. Paragraph 12 provides that "This Agreement constitutes the entire understanding between the parties, and there are no representations or warranties other than expressly herein set forth." From this, we conclude that the divorce decree did not embody, in the paragraph 3 payments, any obligation as to which petitioner's 1967–1969 expenditures furnished a basis.

We conclude that petitioner had no basis in Perry's support obligations for the years in issue, and consequently that petitioner is not entitled to bad debt deductions for the years in issue.

Petitioner insists that she ought to be allowed to deduct the shortfall in Perry's support payment obligations. If this were to be viewed as an appeal to public policy, i.e., the public failed to see to it that Perry satisfied his legal obligations and so the public ought to make up for this to some extent by reducing petitioner's tax obligations, then we have two responses.

Firstly, the statute for the years in issue does not embody that policy; to get that policy into the law, petitioner should go to the Congress, in which has been "vested" "All legislative Powers herein granted". United States Constitution, Art. 1, Sec. 1.

Secondly, since the tax benefit of such a deduction relates directly to the taxpayer's marginal tax bracket, it would appear that this claimed public policy would provide the greatest relief to those who have the greatest amount of other income and little or no relief to those who truly depended on the fulfillment of the support obligations. The Congress, of course, may enact any public policy it chooses (unless otherwise limited by the Constitution), but the policy that would be advanced by allowing such a deduction may fairly be viewed as topsy-turvy.

In any event, this Court will not so legislate in the guise of filling in gaps in the statute, or whatever other judicial power it is that petitioner would have us exercise.

We hold for respondent on this issue.

II.   Child Care Credit

* * *

A.   Transportation Expenses

Respondent does not dispute that the trips to Shreveport were for the dominant purpose of assuring Beth's and Tad's well-being and to permit petitioner to be gainfully employed, or that petitioner paid the amounts for which she claimed the child care credit. Rather, respondent contends that the airfare is disqualified from being an "employment-related expense", within the meaning of [§ 21(b)(2)] by section 1.44A–1(c)(3), Income Tax Regs.

Petitioner contends that she sent the children to their grandparents in Shreveport during certain school holiday periods because (1) her regular babysitter was not available at those times and (2) the airfare was less expensive than it would have been to hire babysitters for those periods. (This is because petitioner would have had to pay for care for about 11 hours per day during those periods, while on regular school days she merely had to pay for sitters for the afternoons.) Also, petitioner contends that the airline cabin attendants provided care to the children during their trips to Shreveport. Petitioner relies on our opinion in Zoltan v. Commissioner, 79 T.C. 490, as authority for treating the air travel cost as employment-related expenses.

We agree with respondent.

In pertinent part, [§ 21(b)(2)] defines "employment-related expense" as either expenses for household services, or expenses for the care of a qualifying individual. Since none of the disputed expenses constitutes household expenses within the meaning of section [§ 21(b)(2)(A)(i)], the issue for our consideration is whether the airfare expenses were incurred for the "care" of petitioner's children within the meaning of [§ 21(b)(2)(A)(ii)].

* * *

The transportation expenses in the instant cases fall on the disallowance side of the line we drew in Zoltan. Petitioner acknowledges on answering brief that the children were cared for on the flights by the cabin attendants. There is nothing in the record to indicate that the cabin attendants were under the direction of petitioner's parents (the services' providers in the instant case). Accordingly, for reasons explained in Warner v. Commissioner, 69 T.C. 995 (1978), and Zoltan, the regulation precludes us from treating the transportation expenses as employment-related expenses.

We hold for respondent on this issue.

* * *

I. LOBBYING

Code: § 162(e)

Of course business lobbying expenses should be deductible. If government threatens to regulate in a way that would hurt your business, surely you will want to do something about it. What could be more ordinary and necessary than protecting your business from governmental harm?

Of course business lobbying expenses should be nondeductible. Imagine that a business is fighting to restrict environmental regulations, while an environmental activist group is fighting to expand them. If there is to be any chance of reaching a fair result in a democracy, how can one side be allowed to fight with tax deductible dollars, while the other side must fight with taxable dollars?

Congress has compromised, as you will see in § 162(e). Does the compromise make any sense?

Chapter IX

Who Is the Taxpayer

■ ■ ■

A. SO WHO IS HE?

ARCIA v. COMMISSIONER

United States Tax Court.
T.C. Memo. 1998–178.

MEMORANDUM FINDINGS OF FACT AND OPINION

JACOBS, JUDGE:

* * *

FINDINGS OF FACT

* * *

Eduardo Macias and His Friends

Eduardo Macias, born in Cuba but living in the United States at all relevant times, served time in a U.S. prison between 1983 and 1989 for smuggling marijuana. Thereafter, he served 11 months for a parole violation. During the year in issue, Mr. Macias became an informant for the Narcotics Division of the Miami Police Department.

Prior to his imprisonment, Mr. Macias left a large quantity of money buried in plastic pipes in his backyard. He dug up the money in 1989 following his release from prison. In April 1991, Mr. Macias wanted to hide this money from his ex-wife. Accordingly, he asked a friend, Wilberto M. Morera (a self-employed construction and repair worker) to hold $115,000 for safekeeping. Mr. Morera agreed to hide Mr. Macias' money for approximately 3 months; Mr. Morera kept the money in his attic. Sometime in July 1991, Mr. Macias retrieved his money, and gave Mr. Morera $3,000 (out of the $115,000) as a gift for hiding the money.

On August 19, 1991, Mr. Macias visited another friend, Pedro Chavez. Mr. Chavez, born in Chile, was a U.S. permanent resident. He originally worked in the restaurant business (as executive chef for the Hard Rock Cafe International), and subsequently worked as a consultant in Chile, developing software for the food-service industry. Mr. Macias asked Mr.

Chavez to hide $110,000[1] for him; Mr. Chavez agreed to this request because he believed he owed Mr. Macias a favor. Mr. Macias delivered the money, and Mr. Chavez made an entry in his diary indicating the receipt of the money and the exact denominations ($90,000 in $20 bills, $16,000 in $100 bills, and $4,000 in $10 bills). Mr. Chavez kept the money in a closet in his apartment. A week later, Mr. Chavez informed Mr. Macias that he was nervous about hiding the money and asked Mr. Macias to retrieve it. When Mr. Macias retrieved the money, Mr. Chavez suggested that Mr. Macias hide the money with a mutual friend, Elio Arcia (petitioner).

Taking Mr. Chavez's advice, Mr. Macias went to visit petitioner, a childhood friend from Cuba. Petitioner agreed to hold Mr. Macias' $106,000[2] for safekeeping, concealing the money in a cooler in the garage of petitioners' home at 115 S.W. 20th Road, Miami, Florida 33129. This money was commingled with petitioner's money. Petitioner did not inform anyone about his hiding Mr. Macias' money.

The October 25, 1991, Search and Seizure

On October 25, 1991, City of Miami police officers conducted a search and seizure at petitioners' residence. This search was later determined to have been illegal. During the search, the police officers found $201,034 concealed in a cooler in petitioners' garage. The money was bound by rubber bands in stacks of mixed denominations. In addition to this money, the officers found: (1) $500 in a bedroom; (2) $1,901 on petitioner; and (3) $8,450 in a beige box in a bedroom. In total, the officers found and seized $211,886 in cash at petitioners' residence. The police officers also seized: (1) A 1990 Nissan 240SX automobile; (2) a Smith & Wesson .38–caliber 5–shot, 2″ barrel gun; (3) a Kurz 380–caliber semiautomatic gun; (4) a North America Arms .22–caliber long, 5–shot, 1″ barrel gun; (5) a North America Arms .22–caliber long 3/4″ barrel gun; (6) an Iver Johnson .30–caliber semiautomatic rifle; (7) two scales; and (8) a Glory money counter.

During the search, petitioner told one of the officers conducting the search, Detective Julio Morejon, that a portion of the money in the cooler belonged to a "friend". Petitioner did not disclose the "friend's" name.

Mrs. Arcia first learned about the money in the cooler on October 25, 1991, during the search and seizure.

[Both the City of Miami and the federal government commenced forfeiture actions against the taxpayer. Ed.]

Mr. Macias' Affidavit and Subsequent Death

On August 4, 1994, Mr. Macias signed a notarized affidavit stating that in August 1991 he "entrusted" petitioner with $110,000 for "safekeeping".

---

1. The record is silent as to what happened to the $2,000 difference between the amount remaining ($112,000) in July and the amount given to Mr. Chavez ($110,000) in August.

2. Again, the record is silent as to why Mr. Macias' funds dwindled.

On September 8, 1994, Mr. Macias met with Internal Revenue Agent Stephen Swafford in order to confirm the statements made by Mr. Macias in his affidavit. During the interview, Mr. Macias stated that he had earned the money while working as a fisherman in the Bahamas during the 1970's. He further stated that he originally buried the money in his backyard but subsequently entrusted the money to Messrs. Mendez, Chavez, and petitioner for safekeeping. After the money was seized on October 25, 1991, Mr. Macias was afraid to make a legal claim for its return because he was on parole and was concerned that if he were to claim the money, the money might be deemed to have come from an illegal source.

At the time of Mr. Macias' meeting with Agent Swafford, Mr. Macias made his living knocking coconuts off trees and selling them on a Miami street corner.

On October 19, 1994, Mr. Macias committed suicide. In his suicide note, Mr. Macias stated he was "grateful" to petitioner.

Petitioners' 1991 Federal Income Tax Return

* * *On their 1991 return, petitioners reported "other income" (line 22) of $112,000, which included $106,000 as "the Taxpayer's portion of certain funds which were seized". Petitioners claimed a constitutional privilege against self-incrimination as to the source of this income in a statement attached to their 1991 return.

* * *

Notice of Deficiency

In the notice of deficiency respondent determined that petitioners realized $212,000 of income, rather than $106,000 as reported on their 1991 return. Accordingly, respondent increased petitioners' 1991 taxable income by $106,000. Respondent also determined that petitioners were liable for a section 6651(a)(1) addition to tax and a section 6662(a) accuracy-related penalty for 1991.

OPINION

The primary issue is factual: whether petitioners had $106,000 of unreported income in 1991 arising from currency found in a cooler in petitioners' garage during the October 25, 1991, search and seizure. Petitioners claim that $106,000 of the $201,034 found in the cooler was not their money and therefore is not includable in their 1991 income. Respondent, on the other hand, contends that ownership of the funds is irrelevant; rather, the issue concerns dominion and control. Respondent posits that because petitioners had dominion and control over all of the forfeited funds, which were originally earned through an apparent illegal activity, the proceeds represent taxable income to petitioners.

The mere receipt and possession of money does not by itself constitute gross income. Gross income, as used in section 61(a), means the accrual of some gain, profit, or benefit to the taxpayer. In this regard, the Supreme

Court explained that a "gain 'constitutes taxable income when its recipient has such control over it that, as a practical matter, he derives readily realizable economic value from it.' " James v. United States. In determining what constitutes gross income, mere dominion and control over money and property, as may be exercised by a debtor or trustee, is not necessarily decisive. Rather, all relevant facts and circumstances must be considered. A taxpayer has dominion and control over cash when he or she has the freedom to use it at will, even though that freedom may be assailable by persons with better title. For instance, the use of money for personal purposes is an indication of dominion and control. Furthermore, amounts received as to which a taxpayer is acting as an agent or conduit are not required to be reported as income.

Petitioners have the burden of proof on this issue, Welch v. Helvering, and resolution of the issue depends upon our believing petitioner's explanation that he was acting as an agent for Mr. Macias—in essence, holding Mr. Macias' money for safekeeping—and that no portion thereof was used for petitioners' personal benefit. Accordingly, we must distill truth from falsehood.

Although the facts herein may seem improbable, we believe them to be true. As acknowledged by respondent, this case hinges on the credibility of the witnesses. We found Messrs. Morera, Chavez, and petitioner to be credible witnesses. We especially found Mr. Chavez to be trustworthy, along with the notations in his diary. Mr. Macias' affidavit and Agent Swaffort's testimony confirm the amazing "story" that unfolded at trial. We believe that $106,000 of the total $201,034 found in petitioner's cooler indeed belonged to Mr. Macias. By storing the money with petitioner, Mr. Macias followed a pattern: First he stored the money with Mr. Morera, then with Mr. Chavez, and finally with petitioner. Consequently, petitioner acted as a conduit or agent for Mr. Macias.

We agree with respondent that a taxpayer's forfeiture of seized currency does not prevent it from being included in his gross income. However, we disagree with respondent's contention that in this case substantive evidence exists proving that the $106,000 seized and forfeited was linked to petitioner's drug-related activities. During cross-examination, petitioner asserted his Fifth Amendment rights and refused to answer questions posed to him by respondent's counsel concerning petitioner's possible involvement in selling drugs. Although we are mindful that an individual's failure to answer questions may give rise to an inference that if he had answered, the answers would have harmed him, we do not believe this inference directly links the $106,000 at issue to an illegal activity involving petitioner.

Additionally, we disagree with respondent's argument that because petitioner was a claimant in the State and Federal actions, the $106,000 at issue must have belonged to him. "A claimant need not own the property in order to have standing to contest its forfeiture; a lesser property interest, such as a possessory interest, is sufficient for standing."

Considering all the facts and circumstances herein, we conclude that petitioners are not required to include in gross income the $106,000 of forfeited funds. Thus, we hold that petitioners are not liable for the 1991 deficiency.

NOTE

IRS made a reasonable assumption, that someone with a sizeable amount of cash probably acquired it in a taxable way. Right idea; wrong guy. Thus, the analysis shifts from "What income?" to "Whose income?"

One does not get the impression that these people were thinking about tax planning. However, most of the other people in this chapter are doing just that. The problem is, however, that to shift the tax burden to someone else, you must shift the income as well. Once you shift the income, it is no longer yours to spend. Therefore, the trick is to shift the income to someone on whom you were going to spend it anyway.

To get a feel for what is at stake, look at the single taxpayer rates, § 1(c). Ignoring deductions, exemptions, etc., compute the tax on income of $250,000. Now compute the tax on $50,000, and multiply it by five. Given our progressive rates, it should be no surprise that five taxpayers, each earning $50,000, will pay considerably less tax in the aggregate than one taxpayer earning $250,000.

So what is the taxpayer earning $250,000 to do? Assume that she has four dependents, and will be spending the money for the benefit of the household of five anyway. If she could split the income five ways among those who will benefit from it, everyone would be far better off.

These income splitting and income shifting transactions often involve family members, and especially children. However, they can also involve other taxpaying entities, such as partnerships, corporations, and trusts. Moreover, there are planning opportunities in the different taxable years of the different entities, the totally different rate schedules for corporations and trusts, and myriad other possibilities involving the shifting of deductions, credits, and the like.

QUESTIONS

In deciding who is the taxpayer, one factor is: who exercises control over the money? Consider the following situations. Is there income? To whom?

Walking down the street, I notice a $10 bill. I pick it up. Do I have taxable income?

What if I notice the $10 bill, but keep on walking?

What if I pick up the money, but immediately give it to a friend? What if I give it to a homeless man? What if I give it to the Red Cross? What if I set fire to the money?

In September, 1998, Mark McGwire hit a record-setting home run. The home run ball, which was extremely valuable as a collectible, was caught by Tim Forneris.

What if the Forneris had kept the ball. Taxable income?

What if he had sold it?

What if he had donated it to charity?

What if he could easily have caught it, but decided not to

—because he didn't want to spill his beer?

—because he saw an adorable 10–year–old boy who was sure to catch it if he didn't?

In fact, Forneris caught the ball, and gave it to McGwire, who in turn gave it to the Hall of Fame. Should Forneris have been taxed on the value of the ball?

B. ASSIGNMENT OF INCOME

1. INCOME FROM SERVICES

LUCAS v. EARL

United States Supreme Court, 1930.
281 U.S. 111, 50 S.Ct. 241, 74 L.Ed. 731.

MR. JUSTICE HOLMES delivered the opinion of the Court.

This case presents the question whether the respondent, Earl, could be taxed for the whole of the salary and attorney's fees earned by him in the years 1920 and 1921, or should be taxed for only a half of them in view of a contract with his wife which we shall mention. The Commissioner of Internal Revenue and the Board of Tax Appeals imposed a tax upon the whole, but their decision was reversed by the Circuit Court of Appeals. A writ of certiorari was granted by this court.

By the contract, made in 1901, Earl and his wife agreed "that any property either of us now has or may hereafter acquire * * * in any way, either by earnings (including salaries, fees, etc.), or any rights by contract or otherwise, during the existence of our marriage, or which we or either of us may receive by gift, bequest, devise, or inheritance, and all the proceeds, issues, and profits of any and all such property shall be treated and considered, and hereby is declared to be received, held, taken, and owned by us as joint tenants, and not otherwise, with the right of survivorship." The validity of the contract is not questioned, and we assume it to be unquestionable under the law of the State of California, in which the parties lived. Nevertheless we are of opinion that the Commissioner and Board of Tax Appeals were right.

The Revenue Act of 1918 imposes a tax upon the net income of every individual including "income derived from salaries, wages, or compensation for personal service * * * of whatever kind and in whatever form paid." * * * A very forcible argument is presented to the effect that the statute seeks to tax only income beneficially received, and that taking the question more technically the salary and fees became the joint property of

Earl and his wife on the very first instant on which they were received. We well might hesitate upon the latter proposition, because however the matter might stand between husband and wife he was the only party to the contracts by which the salary and fees were earned, and it is somewhat hard to say that the last step in the performance of those contracts could be taken by anyone but himself alone. But this case is not to be decided by attenuated subtleties. It turns on the import and reasonable construction of the taxing act. There is no doubt that the statute could tax salaries to those who earned them and provide that the tax could not be escaped by anticipatory arrangements and contracts however skillfully devised to prevent the salary when paid from vesting even for a second in the man who earned it. That seems to us the import of the statute before us and we think that no distinction can be taken according to the motives leading to the arrangement by which the fruits are attributed to a different tree from that on which they grew.

Judgment reversed.

THE CHIEF JUSTICE took no part in this case.

haiku

Trees bear many fruits.

Farmer gives fruit to his wife,

but he still owns trees.

QUESTIONS

1. Did Mr. and Mrs. Earl reach their agreement in order to lower their income tax? How do you know?

2. I have $100 in the bank. Who pays tax on the 2011 interest income (posted on December 31, 2011)—me, or my assignee, if:

   a. I keep the $100 and assign the right to the 2011 interest on January 2, 2012?

   b. I keep the $100 and assign the right to the 2011 interest on January 1, 2011?

   c. I assign all of my rights to the bank account, including the original $100 and all interest on January 2, 2012?

   d. I assign all of my rights to the bank account, including the original $100 and all interest on January 1, 2011?

3. I own an apartment building, worth $100,000. It generates net rental income of $10,000 a year. Who pays tax on the 2011 rent (payable all on December 31, 2011)—me, or my assignee, if:

   a. I keep the building and assign the 2011 rent on January 2, 2012?

   b. I keep the building and assign the 2011 rent on January 1, 2011?

   c. I transfer the building, plus the 2011 rent, on January 2, 2012?

   d. I transfer the building, plus the 2011 rent, on January 1, 2011?

4. Mr. Earl, as a lawyer, can be seen as an income-producing asset. Forget the Thirteenth Amendment. By valid contract, he assigns himself, and all future income to be earned by him, to his wife. Who pays the tax on his future earnings? How is Mr. Earl different from the bank account and the apartment building?

2. INCOME FROM PROPERTY

BLAIR v. COMMISSIONER

United States Supreme Court, 1937.
300 U.S. 5, 57 S.Ct. 330, 81 L.Ed. 465.

Mr. Chief Justice Hughes delivered the opinion of the Court.

This case presents the question of the liability of a beneficiary of a testamentary trust for a tax upon the income which he had assigned to his children prior to the tax years and which the trustees had paid to them accordingly.

The trust was created by the will of William Blair, a resident of Illinois who died in 1899, and was of property located in that State. One-half of the net income was to be paid to the donor's widow during her life. His son, the petitioner Edward Tyler Blair, was to receive the other one-half and, after the death of the widow, the whole of the net income during his life. In 1923, after the widow's death, petitioner assigned to his daughter, Lucy Blair Linn, an interest amounting to $6,000 for the remainder of that calendar year, and to $9,000 in each calendar year thereafter, in the net income which the petitioner was then or might thereafter be entitled to receive during his life. At about the same time, he made like assignments of interests, amounting to $9,000 in each calendar year, in the net income of the trust to his daughter Edith Blair and to his son, Edward Seymour Blair, respectively. In later years, by similar instruments, he assigned to these children additional interests, and to his son William McCormick Blair other specified interests, in the net income. The trustees accepted the assignments and distributed the income directly to the assignees. * * *

Third. The question remains whether, treating the assignments as valid, the assignor was still taxable upon the income under the federal income tax act. That is a federal question.

Our decisions in Lucas v. Earl and Burnet v. Leininger, 285 U.S. 136 (1932) are cited. In the Lucas Case the question was whether an attorney was taxable for the whole of his salary and fees earned by him in the tax years or only upon one-half by reason of an agreement with his wife by which his earnings were to be received and owned by them jointly. We were of the opinion that the case turned upon the construction of the taxing act. We said that "the statute could tax salaries to those who earned them and provide that the tax could not be escaped by anticipatory arrangements and contracts however skillfully devised to prevent the salary when paid from vesting even for a second in the man who earned it." That was deemed to be the meaning of the statute as to compensation for personal service and the one who earned the income was held to be subject to the tax. In Burnet v. Leininger, supra, a husband, a member of a firm, assigned future partnership income to his wife. We found that the revenue act dealt explicitly with the liability of partners as such. The wife did not become a member of the firm; the act specifically taxed the distributive share of each partner in the net income of the firm; and the husband by the fair import of the act remained taxable upon his distributive share. These cases are not in point. The tax here is not upon earnings which are taxed to the one who earns them. Nor is it a case of income attributable to a taxpayer by reason of the application of the income to the discharge of his obligation. Old Colony Trust Company v. Commissioner. There is here no question of evasion or of giving effect to statutory provisions designed to forestall evasion; or of the taxpayer's retention of control.

In the instant case, the tax is upon income as to which, in the general application of the revenue acts, the tax liability attaches to ownership.

The Government points to the provisions of the revenue acts imposing upon the beneficiary of a trust the liability for the tax upon the income distributable to the beneficiary. But the term is merely descriptive of the one entitled to the beneficial interest. These provisions cannot be taken to preclude valid assignments of the beneficial interest, or to affect the duty of the trustee to distribute income to the owner of the beneficial interest, whether he was such initially or becomes such by valid assignment. The one who is to receive the income as the owner of the beneficial interest is to pay the tax. If under the law governing the trust the beneficial interest is assignable, and if it has been assigned without reservation, the assignee thus becomes the beneficiary and is entitled to rights and remedies accordingly. We find nothing in the revenue acts which denies him that status.

The decision of the Circuit Court of Appeals turned upon the effect to be ascribed to the assignments. The court held that the petitioner had no interest in the corpus of the estate and could not dispose of the income until he received it. Hence it was said that "the income was his" and his assignment was merely a direction to pay over to others what was due to himself. The question was considered to involve "the date when the income became transferable." The Government refers to the terms of the assignment—that it was of the interest in the income "which the said party of the first part now is, or may hereafter be, entitled to receive during his life from the trustees." From this it is urged that the assignments "dealt only with a right to receive the income" and that "no attempt was made to assign any equitable right, title or interest in the trust itself." This construction seems to us to be a strained one. We think it apparent that the conveyancer was not seeking to limit the assignment so as to make it anything less than a complete transfer of the specified interest of the petitioner as the life beneficiary of the trust, but that with ample caution he was using words to effect such a transfer. That the state court so construed the assignments appears from the final decree which described them as voluntary assignments of interests of the petitioner "in said trust estate," and it was in that aspect that petitioner's right to make the assignments was sustained.

The will creating the trust entitled the petitioner during his life to the net income of the property held in trust. He thus became the owner of an equitable interest in the corpus of the property. By virtue of that interest he was entitled to enforce the trust, to have a breach of trust enjoined and to obtain redress in case of breach. The interest was present property alienable like any other, in the absence of a valid restraint upon alienation. The beneficiary may thus transfer a part of his interest as well as the whole. The assignment of the beneficial interest is not the assignment of a chose in action but of the "right, title, and estate in and to property."

We conclude that the assignments were valid, that the assignees thereby became the owners of the specified beneficial interests in the income, and that as to these interests they and not the petitioner were taxable for the tax years in question. The judgment of the Circuit Court of Appeals is reversed and the cause is remanded with direction to affirm the decision of the Board of Tax Appeals.

QUESTION

In light of Justice Holmes' metaphor in *Lucas v. Earl*, what is the fruit, and what is the tree in the *Blair* case? You might find it easier to consider this question if you first assume that the $6,000 and $9,000 annual assignments represented all of the income generated by the trust. Then, assume that they did not.

HELVERING v. HORST

United States Supreme Court, 1940.
311 U.S. 112, 61 S.Ct. 144, 85 L.Ed. 75.

Mr. Justice Stone delivered the opinion of the Court.

The sole question for decision is whether the gift, during the donor's taxable year, of interest coupons detached from the bonds, delivered to the donee and later in the year paid at maturity, is the realization of income taxable to the donor.

In 1934 and 1935 respondent, the owner of negotiable bonds, detached from them negotiable interest coupons shortly before their due date and delivered them as a gift to his son who in the same year collected them at maturity. The Commissioner ruled that under the applicable § 22 of the Revenue Act of 1934 [current § 61], the interest payments were taxable, in the years when paid, to the respondent donor who reported his income on the cash receipts basis. The circuit court of appeals reversed the order of the Board of Tax Appeals sustaining the tax. We granted certiorari, because of the importance of the question in the administration of the revenue laws and because of an asserted conflict in principle of the decision below with that of Lucas v. Earl, and with that of decisions by other circuit courts of appeals.

The court below thought that as the consideration for the coupons had passed to the obligor, the donor had, by the gift, parted with all control over them and their payment, and for that reason the case was distinguishable from Lucas v. Earl, and Burnet v. Leininger, 285 U.S. 136 (1932) where the assignment of compensation for services had preceded the rendition of the services, and where the income was held taxable to the donor.

The holder of a coupon bond is the owner of two independent and separable kinds of right. One is the right to demand and receive at maturity the principal amount of the bond representing capital investment. The other is the right to demand and receive interim payments of interest on the investment in the amounts and on the dates specified by the coupons. Together they are an obligation to pay principal and interest given in exchange for money or property which was presumably the consideration for the obligation of the bond. Here respondent, as owner of the bonds, had acquired the legal right to demand payment at maturity of the interest specified by the coupons and the power to command its payment to others which constituted an economic gain to him.

Admittedly not all economic gain of the taxpayer is taxable income. From the beginning the revenue laws have been interpreted as defining "realization" of income as the taxable event rather than the acquisition of the right to receive it. And "realization" is not deemed to occur until the income is paid. But the decisions and regulations have consistently recognized that receipt in cash or property is not the only characteristic of realization of income to a taxpayer on the cash receipts basis. Where the taxpayer does not receive payment of income in money or property realization may occur when the last step is taken by which he obtains the fruition of the economic gain which has already accrued to him.

In the ordinary case the taxpayer who acquires the right to receive income is taxed when he receives it, regardless of the time when his right to receive payment accrued. But the rule that income is not taxable until realized has never been taken to mean that the taxpayer, even on the cash receipts basis, who has fully enjoyed the benefit of the economic gain represented by his right to receive income, can escape taxation because he has not himself received payment of it from his obligor. The rule, founded on administrative convenience, is only one of postponement of the tax to the final event of enjoyment of the income, usually the receipt of it by the taxpayer, and not one of exemption from taxation where the enjoyment is consummated by some event other than the taxpayer's personal receipt of money or property. This may occur when he has made such use or disposition of his power to receive or control the income as to procure in its place other satisfactions which are of economic worth. The question here is, whether because one who in fact receives payment for services or interest payments is taxable only on his receipt of the payments, he can escape all tax by giving away his right to income in advance of payment. If the taxpayer procures payment directly to his creditors of the items of interest or earnings due him, or if he sets up a revocable trust with income payable to the objects of his bounty, he does not escape taxation because he did not actually receive the money.

Underlying the reasoning in these cases is the thought that income is "realized" by the assignor because he, who owns or controls the source of the income, also controls the disposition of that which he could have received himself and diverts the payment from himself to others as the means of procuring the satisfaction of his wants. The taxpayer has equally enjoyed the fruits of his labor or investment and obtained the satisfaction of his desires whether he collects and uses the income to procure those satisfactions, or whether he disposes of his right to collect it as the means of procuring them.

Although the donor here, by the transfer of the coupons, has precluded any possibility of his collecting them himself he has nevertheless, by his act, procured payment of the interest, as a valuable gift to a member of his family. Such a use of his economic gain, the right to receive income, to procure a satisfaction which can be obtained only by the expenditure of money or property, would seem to be the enjoyment of the income whether the satisfaction is the purchase of goods at the corner grocery, the payment of his debt there, or such non-material satisfactions as may result from the payment of a campaign or community chest contribution, or a gift to his favorite son. Even though he never receives the money he derives money's worth from the disposition of the coupons which he has used as money or money's worth in the procuring of a satisfaction which is procurable only by the expenditure of money or money's worth. The enjoyment of the economic benefit accruing to him by virtue of his acquisition of the coupons is realized as completely as it would have been if he had collected the interest in dollars and expended them for any of the purposes named.

In a real sense he has enjoyed compensation for money loaned or services rendered and not any the less so because it is his only reward for them. To say that one who has made a gift thus derived from interest or earnings paid to his donee has never enjoyed or realized the fruits of his investment or labor because he has assigned them instead of collecting them himself and then paying them over to the donee, is to affront common understanding and to deny the facts of common experience. Common understanding and experience are the touchstones for the interpretation of the revenue laws.

The power to dispose of income is the equivalent of ownership of it. The exercise of that power to procure the payment of income to another is the enjoyment and hence the realization of the income by him who exercises it. We have had no difficulty in applying that proposition where the assignment preceded the rendition of the services, for it was recognized in the Leininger case that in such a case the rendition of the service by the assignor was the means by which the income was controlled by the donor and of making his assignment effective. But it is the assignment by which the disposition of income is controlled when the service precedes the assignment and in both cases it is the exercise of the power of disposition of the interest or compensation with the resulting payment to the donee which is the enjoyment by the donor of income derived from them.

This was emphasized in Blair v. Commissioner, on which respondent relies, where the distinction was taken between a gift of income derived from an obligation to pay compensation and a gift of income-producing property. In the circumstances of that case the right to income from the trust property was thought to be so identified with the equitable ownership of the property from which alone the beneficiary derived his right to receive the income and his power to command disposition of it that a gift of the income by the beneficiary became effective only as a gift of his ownership of the property producing it. Since the gift was deemed to be a gift of the property the income from it was held to be the income of the owner of the property, who was the donee, not the donor, a refinement which was unnecessary if respondent's contention here is right, but one clearly inapplicable to gifts of interest or wages. Unlike income thus derived from an obligation to pay interest or compensation, the income of the trust was regarded as no more the income of the donor than would be the rent from a lease or a crop raised on a farm after the leasehold or the farm had been given away. We have held without deviation that where the donor retains control of the trust property the income is taxable to him although paid to the donee. The dominant purpose of the revenue laws is the taxation of income to those who earn or otherwise create the right to receive it and enjoy the benefit of it when paid. The tax laid by the 1934 Revenue Act upon income "derived from * * * wages, or compensation for personal service, of whatever kind and in whatever form paid * * *; also from interest * * * " therefore cannot fairly be interpreted as not applying to income derived from interest or compensation when he who is entitled to receive it makes use of his power to dispose of it in procuring satisfactions which he would otherwise procure only by the use of the money when received.

It is the statute which taxes the income to the donor although paid to his donee. True, in those cases the service which created the right to income followed the assignment and it was arguable that in point of legal theory the right to the compensation vested instantaneously in the assignor when paid although he never received it; while here the right of the assignor to receive the income antedated the assignment which transferred the right and thus precluded such an instantaneous vesting. But the statute affords no basis for such "attenuated subtleties." The distinction was explicitly rejected as the basis of decision in Lucas v. Earl. It should be rejected here, for no more than in the Earl case can the purpose of the statute to tax the income to him who earns, or creates and enjoys it be escaped by "anticipatory arrangements * * * however skillfully devised" to prevent the income from vesting even for a second in the donor.

Nor is it perceived that there is any adequate basis for distinguishing between the gift of interest coupons here and a gift of salary or commissions. The owner of a negotiable bond and of the investment which it represents, if not the lender, stands in the place of the lender. When, by the gift of the coupons, he has separated his right to interest payments from his investment and procured the payment of the interest to his donee, he has enjoyed the economic benefits of the income in the same manner and to the same extent as though the transfer were of earnings and in both cases the import of the statute is that the fruit is not to be attributed to a different tree from that on which it grew.

Reversed.

The separate opinion of MR. JUSTICE MCREYNOLDS.

* * * The unmatured coupons given to the son were independent negotiable instruments, complete in themselves. Through the gift they became at once the absolute property of the donee, free from the donor's control and in no way dependent upon ownership of the bonds. No question of actual fraud or purpose to defraud the revenue is presented.
* * *

QUESTIONS

1. Compare *Horst* to *Mason v. Innes* case, *supra*, Chapter 5.

2. What is left of *Horst* after the enactment of § 1286?

MEISNER v. UNITED STATES

United States Court of Appeals, Eighth Circuit, 1998.
133 F.3d 654.

HANSEN, CIRCUIT JUDGE.

Jennifer Meisner appeals from the district court's denial of her motion for judgment as a matter of law (JMOL) in this federal income tax refund suit, contending that there was insufficient evidence to support a jury verdict for the United States. She also takes issue with several of the jury instructions and with the verdict form. We affirm.

I.

Jennifer Meisner was married to Randall Meisner from 1963 to 1981. Randall held certain pieces of intellectual property, consisting of licenses and copyrights related to songs performed by the Eagles, a singing group to which he at one time belonged. In 1978, Randall entered into a termination agreement with the Eagles. In this agreement, Randall ceded all of this intellectual property to the Eagles in return for a royalties contract entitling him to a portion of proceeds from the sales of certain of the Eagles' recordings. He has not been a shareholder, director, or member of the Eagles since that time.

In 1981, the Meisners divorced. At divorce, the couple entered into a property settlement agreement (PSA), pursuant to which Jennifer acquired an undivided forty percent interest in the royalty contract. Paragraph nine of the PSA provides:

> [Jennifer] shall have as her separate property and the title to the same shall be quieted in her the following items:
>
> * * *
>
> c. Forty percent (40%) of all earnings, copyrights, and recording rights [Randall] owns as a performer and/or composer as set forth in paragraph 5b.

Paragraph five of the PSA clarifies that the rights ceded to Jennifer include royalties, and provides, inter alia, that Jennifer's rights to an undivided forty percent interest in the royalty contract was not subject to any reversionary or contingent interests, but would survive her own death as well as that of her ex-husband. It also provides that Jennifer's 40 percent would be paid directly from the Eagles to Jennifer. The jury found, and both parties now agree, that after the divorce, Randall had no power to affect Jennifer's rights to the royalty payments.

Jennifer has received royalties consistent with her forty percent interest every year since 1982. In 1994, she requested a refund of the federal income taxes she had paid on these royalties, claiming that the royalties were properly taxable to her ex-husband rather than to her. A jury trial was held regarding her claims for 1987, 1988, 1990, and 1993. At the close of the evidence, Jennifer moved for JMOL. The judge denied her motion, finding that a question of material fact still existed. The judge sent the case to the jury with a special verdict form limited to the issue of whether Randall had exercised power or control over Jennifer's royalty rights. The jury found that Randall had not exerted power or control over Jennifer's rights—a verdict for the government. Jennifer appeals the denial of her motion for judgment as a matter of law and contests the instructions and verdict form given to the jury.

* * *

When a taxpayer is firmly entitled to receive income but anticipatorily assigns this income to another, the donor will be taxed on it just as though he had actually received it. This is true even if the income will not accrue until some future date. See Helvering v. Horst. However, if the taxpayer instead assigns an income-producing asset, the result is different. All income that is thereafter produced by the asset is taxed to the assignee. See, e.g., Blair v. Commissioner. This distinction between income and income-producing assets is generally discussed in terms of "fruits" and "trees," and the rule is that fruits may not, for tax purposes, be attributed "to a different tree from that on which they grew." Lucas v. Earl.

In deciding whether the rights assigned by Randall to Jennifer constituted a tree or merely fruits, we are mindful of the Supreme Court's decision in another assignment of royalties case, Commissioner v. Sunnen, 333 U.S. 591 (1948), which both parties cite as the controlling authority. There the Court wrote:

It is not enough to trace income to the property which is its true source, a matter which may become more metaphysical than legal. Nor is the tax problem with which we are concerned necessarily answered by the fact that such property, if it can be properly identified, has been assigned. The crucial question remains whether the assignor retains sufficient power and control over the assigned property or over receipt of the income to make it reasonable to treat him as the recipient of the income for tax purposes. As was said in Corliss v. Bowers, "taxation is not so much concerned with the refinements of title as it is with actual command over the property taxed—the actual benefit for which the tax is being paid."

The district court rightly determined that this case, like *Sunnen*, turns on the amount of "power and control" retained by Randall after the transfer.

Our review of the record reveals no evidence of retained control by Randall. Randall unconditionally assigned Jennifer an undivided forty percent interest. He carved out no reversionary interest for either himself or his estate and retained no direct or indirect ability to affect the value of the rights transferred. Nor did he retain power over Jennifer's receipt of royalty payments—the checks did not come through him, but went directly to Jennifer. * * *

It is also significant that the transfer of rights occurred pursuant to a divorce settlement. In the context of a gift to a loved one (usually one within the donor's nuclear family), it can be argued that "[t]he exercise of that power to procure the payment of income to another is the enjoyment and hence the realization of the income by him who exercises it." The same cannot be said in the context of a divorce settlement. Nor can it be argued that a transfer pursuant to a divorce fails to "effect any substantial change in the taxpayer's economic status." Divorce transfers are much more akin to negotiated arms-length transactions between adversaries than to displays of generosity.

Because there is no evidence of retained control over Jennifer's rights by Randall and because this transfer of rights occurred pursuant to a divorce, we cannot say that the evidence is "susceptible of no reasonable inference sustaining the position of [the government]." We therefore affirm the district court's denial of Jennifer's motion for JMOL.

* * *

Accordingly, we affirm the judgment of the district court.

NOTES, QUESTION

1. Randy Meisner, born in Scotts Bluff, Nebraska, is the best selling recording artist in Nebraska history. One wonders who came in second.

2. *Compare* Kochansky v. Commissioner, 92 F.3d 957 (9th Cir. 1996). Kochansky, a lawyer, brought a medical malpractice lawsuit on behalf of the McNarys. Kochansky was to be paid on a contingent fee basis. After the suit was filed, but before it settled, Kochansky divorced his wife. The divorce agreement provided that he would split any contingent fee earned on the McNary lawsuit with his wife. Mr. Kochansky's fee was "undisputed compensation for Kochansky's personal services." As such, the entire contingent fee was taxable to him.

3. What about contingent fee awards in general? Is the proportion of the contingent fee payable to the lawyer taxable to the lawyer, the client, or both?

Why should it matter? Suppose that the client wins a judgment of $100,000, but must pay one third, or $33,333, to the lawyer, pursuant to the contingent fee agreement. If the client is taxed only upon her net damage proceeds and the lawyer is taxed on her contingent fees, then the client is taxed on $66,667 and the lawyer is taxed on $33,333. However, if the client must first take the $100,000 judgment damages into taxable income, then surely the legal fees are an expense of producing income, and therefore deductible. As such, the client should be taxed on

Income	$100,000
–legal fees	– $ 33,333
Net income	$ 66,667

So what's the difference? There are two differences, and they both relate to the fact that the legal fees, though deductible, would be a "miscellaneous itemized deduction," as defined in § 67(b). First, pursuant to § 67(a) miscellaneous itemized deductions are allowed only to the extent that, in the aggregate, they exceed two per cent of adjusted gross income. See *infra* at 546 for more coverage of miscellaneous itemized deductions, and at 545 for coverage of adjusted gross income. For now, however, consider that, if adjusted gross income were, say, $50,000, then 2% of adjusted gross income would be $1,000. Therefore, the first $1,000 of the legal fees would be disallowed as a deduction.

Second, you need to consider the impact of the Alternative Minimum Tax (AMT). See *infra* at 653 for fuller coverage. For now, suffice it to say that Congress is concerned that some taxpayers take too many deductions, and thus pay taxes at too low a rate. To alleviate these concerns, some taxpayers are required to compute their taxes a second time, eliminating many of the deductions, to make sure that they are paying taxes equal to at least 26% of this higher income figure. When AMT is computed, the legal fee deduction is eliminated.

Thus, the legal fees are technically deductible, but, at the end of the day, they may not be. Therefore, the client/taxpayer would be far better off if the contingent legal fee portion of her damage award were never taken into account in her taxable income. Accordingly, there was enough at stake to take this issue to litigation in many circuits, and finally to the Supreme Court.

COMMISSIONER v. BANKS

United States Supreme Court, 2005.
543 U.S. 426, 125 S.Ct. 826, 160 L.Ed.2d 859.

JUSTICE KENNEDY delivered the opinion of the Court.

The question in these consolidated cases is whether the portion of a money judgment or settlement paid to a plaintiff's attorney under a contingent-fee agreement is income to the plaintiff under the Internal Revenue Code. The issue divides the courts of appeals. In one of the instant cases, *Banks v. Commissioner,* the Court of Appeals for the Sixth Circuit held the contingent-fee portion of a litigation recovery is not included in the plaintiff's gross income. The Courts of Appeals for the Fifth and Eleventh Circuits also adhere to this view. In the other case under review, *Banaitis v. Commissioner*, the Court of Appeals for the Ninth Circuit held that the portion of the recovery paid to the attorney as a contingent fee is excluded from the plaintiff's gross income if state law gives the plaintiff's attorney a special property interest in the fee, but not otherwise. Six Courts of Appeals have held the entire litigation recovery, including the portion paid to an attorney as a contingent fee, is income to the plaintiff. Some of these Courts of Appeals discuss state law, but little of their analysis appears to turn on this factor. Other Courts of Appeals have been explicit that the fee portion of the recovery is always income to the plaintiff regardless of the nuances of state law. We granted certiorari to resolve the conflict.

We hold that, as a general rule, when a litigant's recovery constitutes income, the litigant's income includes the portion of the recovery paid to the attorney as a contingent fee. We reverse the decisions of the Courts of Appeals for the Sixth and Ninth Circuits.

I

A. Commissioner v. Banks

In 1986, respondent John W. Banks, II, was fired from his job as an educational consultant with the California Department of Education. He retained an attorney on a contingent-fee basis and filed a civil suit against the employer in a United States District Court. The complaint alleged employment discrimination. The original complaint asserted various additional claims under state law, but Banks later abandoned these. After trial commenced in 1990, the parties settled for $464,000. Banks paid $150,000 of this amount to his attorney pursuant to the fee agreement.

Banks did not include any of the $464,000 in settlement proceeds as gross income in his 1990 federal income tax return. In 1997 the Commissioner of Internal Revenue issued Banks a notice of deficiency for the 1990 tax year. The Tax Court upheld the Commissioner's determination, finding that all the settlement proceeds, including the $150,000 Banks had paid to his attorney, must be included in Banks' gross income.

The Court of Appeals for the Sixth Circuit reversed in part. It agreed the net amount received by Banks was included in gross income but not the amount paid to the attorney. * * * [T]he court held the contingent-fee agreement was not an anticipatory assignment of Banks' income because the litigation recovery was not already earned, vested, or even relatively certain to be paid when the contingent-fee contract was made. A contingent-fee arrangement, the court reasoned, is more like a partial assignment of income-producing property than an assignment of income. The attorney is not the mere beneficiary of the client's largess, but rather earns his fee through skill and diligence. This reasoning, the court held, applies whether or not state law grants the attorney any special property interest (*e.g.,* a superior lien) in part of the judgment or settlement proceeds.

B. Commissioner v. Banaitis

After leaving his job as a vice president and loan officer at the Bank of California in 1987, Sigitas J. Banaitis retained an attorney on a contingent-fee basis and brought suit in Oregon state court against the Bank of California and its successor in ownership, the Mitsubishi Bank. The complaint alleged that Mitsubishi Bank willfully interfered with Banaitis' employment contract, and that the Bank of California attempted to induce Banaitis to breach his fiduciary duties to customers and discharged him when he refused. The jury awarded Banaitis compensatory and punitive damages. After resolution of all appeals and post-trial motions, the parties settled. The defendants paid $4,864,547 to Banaitis; and, following the formula set forth in the contingent-fee contract, the defendants paid an additional $3,864,012 directly to Banaitis' attorney.

Banaitis did not include the amount paid to his attorney in gross income on his federal income tax return, and the Commissioner issued a notice of deficiency. The Tax Court upheld the Commissioner's determination, but the Court of Appeals for the Ninth Circuit reversed. In contrast to the Court of Appeals for the Sixth Circuit, the *Banaitis* court viewed state law as pivotal. Where state law confers on the attorney no special property rights in his fee, the court said, the whole amount of the judgment or settlement ordinarily is included in the plaintiff's gross income. Oregon state law, however, like the law of some other States, grants attorneys a superior lien in the contingent-fee portion of any recovery. As a result, the court held, contingent-fee agreements under Oregon law operate not as an anticipatory assignment of the client's income but as a partial transfer to the attorney of some of the client's property in the lawsuit.

II

To clarify why the issue here is of any consequence for tax purposes, two preliminary observations are useful. The first concerns the general issue of deductibility. For the tax years in question the legal expenses in these cases could have been taken as miscellaneous itemized deductions subject to the ordinary requirements, [§ 67] but doing so would have been of no help to respondents because of the operation of the Alternative Minimum Tax (AMT). For noncorporate individual taxpayers, the AMT establishes a tax liability floor equal to 26 percent of the taxpayer's "alternative minimum taxable income" (minus specified exemptions) up to $175,000, plus 28 percent of alternative minimum taxable income over $175,000. §§ 55(a), (b). Alternative minimum taxable income, unlike ordinary gross income, does not allow any miscellaneous itemized deductions. §§ 56(b)(1)(A)(i).

Second, after these cases arose Congress enacted the American Jobs Creation Act of 2004,. Section 703 of the Act amended the Code by adding § 62(a)(19). The amendment allows a taxpayer, in computing adjusted gross income, to deduct "attorney fees and court costs paid by, or on behalf of, the taxpayer in connection with any action involving a claim of unlawful discrimination." The Act defines "unlawful discrimination" to include a number of specific federal statutes, §§ 62(e)(1) to (16), any federal whistle-blower statute, § 62(e)(17), and any federal, state, or local law "providing for the enforcement of civil rights" or "regulating any aspect of the employment relationship . . . or prohibiting the discharge of an employee, the discrimination against an employee, or any other form of retaliation or reprisal against an employee for asserting rights or taking other actions permitted by law," § 62(e)(18). *Id.* These deductions are permissible even when the AMT applies. Had the Act been in force for the transactions now under review, these cases likely would not have arisen. The Act is not retroactive, however, so while it may cover future taxpayers in respondents' position, it does not pertain here.

III

* * *

Respondents argue that the anticipatory assignment doctrine is a judge-made antifraud rule with no relevance to contingent-fee contracts of the sort at issue here. The Commissioner maintains that a contingent-fee agreement should be viewed as an anticipatory assignment to the attorney of a portion of the client's income from any litigation recovery. We agree with the Commissioner.

In an ordinary case attribution of income is resolved by asking whether a taxpayer exercises complete dominion over the income in question. In the context of anticipatory assignments, however, the assignor often does not have dominion over the income at the moment of receipt. In that instance the question becomes whether the assignor retains dominion over the income-generating asset, because the taxpayer "who owns or controls the source of the income, also controls the disposition of that which he could have received himself and diverts the payment from himself to others as the means of procuring the satisfaction of his wants."

Looking to control over the income-generating asset, then, preserves the principle that income should be taxed to the party who earns the income and enjoys the consequent benefits.

In the case of a litigation recovery the income-generating asset is the cause of action that derives from the plaintiff's legal injury. The plaintiff retains dominion over this asset throughout the litigation. We do not understand respondents to argue otherwise. Rather, respondents advance two counterarguments. First, they say that, in contrast to the bond coupons assigned in *Horst,* the value of a legal claim is speculative at the moment of assignment, and may be worth nothing at all. Second, respondents insist that the claimant's legal injury is not the only source of the ultimate recovery. The attorney, according to respondents, also contributes income-generating assets—effort and expertise—without which the claimant likely could not prevail. On these premises respondents urge us to treat a contingent-fee agreement as establishing, for tax purposes, something like a joint venture or partnership in which the client and attorney combine their respective assets—the client's claim and the attorney's skill—and apportion any resulting profits.

We reject respondents' arguments. Though the value of the plaintiff's claim may be speculative at the moment the fee agreement is signed, the anticipatory assignment doctrine is not limited to instances when the precise dollar value of the assigned income is known in advance. Though *Horst* involved an anticipatory assignment of a predetermined sum to be paid on a specific date, the holding in that case did not depend on ascertaining a liquidated amount at the time of assignment. In the cases before us, as in *Horst,* the taxpayer retained control over the income-generating asset, diverted some of the income produced to another party, and realized a benefit by doing so. As Judge Wesley correctly concluded in a recent case, the rationale of *Horst* applies fully to a contingent-fee contract. That the amount of income the asset would produce was uncertain at the moment of assignment is of no consequence.

We further reject the suggestion to treat the attorney-client relationship as a sort of business partnership or joint venture for tax purposes. The relationship between client and attorney, regardless of the variations in particular compensation agreements or the amount of skill and effort the attorney contributes, is a quintessential principal-agent relationship. The client may rely on the attorney's expertise and special skills to achieve a result the client could not achieve alone. That, however, is true of most principal-agent relationships, and it does not alter the fact that the client retains ultimate dominion and control over the underlying claim. The control is evident when it is noted that, although the attorney can make tactical decisions without consulting the client, the plaintiff still must determine whether to settle or proceed to judgment and make, as well, other critical decisions. Even where the attorney exercises independent judgment without supervision by, or consultation with, the client, the attorney, as an agent, is obligated to act solely on behalf of, and for the exclusive benefit of, the client-principal, rather than for the benefit of the attorney or any other party.

The attorney is an agent who is duty bound to act only in the interests of the principal, and so it is appropriate to treat the full amount of the recovery as income to the principal. In this respect Judge Posner's observation is apt: "[T]he contingent-fee lawyer [is not] a joint owner of his client's claim in the legal sense any more than the commission salesman is a joint owner of his employer's accounts receivable." In both cases a principal relies on an agent to realize an economic gain, and the gain realized by the agent's efforts is income to the principal. The portion paid to the agent may be deductible, but absent some other provision of law it is not excludable from the principal's gross income.

This rule applies whether or not the attorney-client contract or state law confers any special rights or protections on the attorney, so long as these protections do not alter the fundamental principal-agent character of the relationship. State laws vary with respect to the strength of an attorney's security interest in a contingent fee and the remedies available to an attorney should the client discharge or attempt to defraud the attorney. No state laws of which we are aware, however, even those that purport to give attorneys an "ownership" interest in their fees, * * * convert the attorney from an agent to a partner.

Respondents and their *amici* propose other theories to exclude fees from income or permit deductibility. These suggestions include: (1) The contingent-fee agreement establishes a Subchapter K partnership; (2) litigation recoveries are proceeds from disposition of property, so the attorney's fee should be subtracted as a capital expense pursuant to §§ 1001, 1012, and 1016, and (3) the fees are deductible reimbursed employee business expenses under § 62(a)(2)(A). These arguments, it appears, are being presented for the first time to this Court. We are especially reluctant to entertain novel propositions of law with broad implications for the tax system that were not advanced in earlier stages of the litigation and not examined by the Courts of Appeals. We decline comment on these supplementary theories. * * *

IV

The foregoing suffices to dispose of Banaitis' case. Banks' case, however, involves a further consideration. Banks brought his claims under federal statutes that authorize fee awards to prevailing plaintiffs' attorneys. He contends that application of the anticipatory assignment principle would be inconsistent with the purpose of statutory fee shifting provisions. In the federal system statutory fees are typically awarded by the court under the lodestar approach, and the plaintiff usually has little control over the amount awarded. Sometimes, as when the plaintiff seeks only injunctive relief, or when the statute caps plaintiffs' recoveries, or when for other reasons damages are substantially less than attorney's fees, court-awarded attorney's fees can exceed a plaintiff's monetary recovery. Treating the fee award as income to the plaintiff in such cases, it is argued, can lead to the perverse result that the plaintiff loses money by winning the suit. Furthermore, it is urged that treating statutory fee awards as income to plaintiffs would undermine the effectiveness of fee-shifting statutes in deputizing plaintiffs and their lawyers to act as private attorneys general.

We need not address these claims. After Banks settled his case, the fee paid to his attorney was calculated solely on the basis of the private contingent-fee contract. There was no court-ordered fee award, nor was there any indication in Banks' contract with his attorney, or in the settlement agreement with the defendant, that the contingent fee paid to Banks' attorney was in lieu of statutory fees Banks might otherwise have been entitled to recover. Also, the amendment added by the American Jobs Creation Act redresses the concern for many, perhaps most, claims governed by fee-shifting statutes.

* * *

For the reasons stated, the judgments of the Courts of Appeals for the Sixth and Ninth Circuits are reversed, and the cases are remanded for further proceedings consistent with this opinion.

It is so ordered.

The Chief Justice took no part in the decision of these cases.

PRIVATE LETTER RULING 201015016

Dear * * *:

FACTS

In Year 1, Taxpayer was one of several named plaintiffs who brought Lawsuit against Defendants alleging that Defendants engaged in improper practices under the Act. Lawsuit was not a class action. Taxpayer was represented on a *pro bono* basis by Legal Aid Organization 1, Legal Aid Organization 2, and Law Firm. These organizations took the case to ensure that businesses like Defendants' comply with the Act.

Taxpayer entered into a Retainer Agreement with Legal Aid Organization 1. In the "Fees and Costs" section, the Retainer Agreement states that, "[Legal Aid Organization 1] will not charge [Taxpayer] a fee for its services." Law Firm joined Legal Aid Organization 1 as co-counsel and agreed to represent Taxpayer and the other plaintiffs at no charge. Legal Aid Organization 2 also represented the plaintiffs at no charge. Taxpayer did not enter into a retainer agreement or other contract for services with Legal Aid Organization 2 or Law Firm. Taxpayer has no obligation, contractual or otherwise, to pay any fees or other costs to Legal Aid Organization 1, Legal Aid Organization 2 or Law Firm.

Taxpayer and the co-plaintiffs prevailed in Lawsuit. In year 2, the court entered judgment and awarded Taxpayer $x, the maximum recovery under the Act. Under Section X of Act, plaintiffs are entitled to recover "the costs of the action, together with reasonable attorneys' fees and costs." In Year 2, Legal Aid Organization 1 and Law Firm filed a motion for attorneys' fees and costs. In Year 3, the court issued Order, awarding $z attorneys' fees and other costs to co-counsel, Legal Aid Organization 1 and Law Firm. The portion of the $z attorneys' fees attributable to Taxpayer's claim was $y.

LAW AND ANALYSIS

Taxpayer concedes that the $x award is taxable income but contends that the award of $y in attorneys' fees is not includible in Taxpayer's gross income under § 61.

* * *

Attorneys' fees awarded to a successful litigant are generally includible in the litigant's gross income under either the anticipatory assignment of income doctrine of *Banks* and *Lucas v. Earl* or under the payment of a liability doctrine enunciated in *Old Colony Trust*. Under both analyses, the litigant has an obligation, by express or implied agreement, to pay attorneys fees. Taxpayer's case is distinguishable because Taxpayer had no obligation to pay attorneys' fees. In fact, Taxpayer's agreement (retainer contract) expressly provided that Legal Aid Organization 1 would not charge Taxpayer any fee for legal services. In addition, Taxpayer had no retainer contract with (and did not otherwise agree to pay any fees to) Legal Aid Organization 2 or Law Firm for their legal services. Rather, Legal Aid Organization 1 and Law Firm requested attorneys' fees directly under the provisions of Section X of Act; they did not seek attorneys' fees on behalf of Taxpayer or in lieu of Taxpayer's contingency fee obligation.

We therefore conclude that the award of $y in attorneys' fees is not includible in Taxpayer's gross income under § 61.

C. CHILDREN

1. EARNED INCOME OF CHILDREN

Code: § 73

ALLEN v. COMMISSIONER

United States Tax Court, 1968.
50 T.C. 466.

Findings of Fact

* * *

Petitioner was born on March 8, 1942. In the spring of 1960 petitioner, then age 18, was living with his mother, Mrs. Era Allen, in Wampum,

Pa., and was a senior at a local high school. Mrs. Allen had been separated from her husband since 1957. She had eight children, of whom three, including petitioner, were dependent upon her for support during 1960. She received no funds from her husband, and supported her family by doing housework, sewing, or laundry work.

In the course of his high school years, petitioner acquired a reputation as an outstanding baseball and basketball player. He was anxious to play professional baseball, and had even expressed a desire to leave high school for that purpose before graduation, but was not permitted to do so by his mother. During petitioner's junior year in high school, word of his athletic talents reached John Ogden (hereinafter "Ogden"), a baseball "scout" for the Philadelphia National League Club, commonly known and hereinafter referred to as the Phillies. * * *.

* * *

* * * Ogden became very friendly with petitioner's family. He hired Coy Allen, petitioner's older brother of about 36 or 37 who had played some semiprofessional baseball in the past, as a scout for the Phillies. He also signed Harold Allen, another brother of petitioner, to a contract to play baseball in the Phillies organization. He visited the Allen home often, and talked to petitioner about playing baseball. He did not, however, attempt immediately to sign petitioner to a contract because of a rule adhered to by the Phillies and other baseball teams prohibiting the signing of any boy attending high school to a baseball contract until after his graduation.

Ogden, as well as representatives of a dozen or more other baseball teams that also desired petitioner's services, discussed petitioner's prospects with his mother, Era Allen. She was the head of the family, and she made all the family decisions. Although petitioner discussed baseball with the various scouts, he referred them to his mother in connection with any proposed financial arrangements, and he felt "bound" to play for which ever club his mother might select.

Era Allen conducted all negotiations with Ogden in respect of the financial arrangements that might be made for petitioner if it should be determined that he would play for the Phillies. However, she knew nothing about baseball, particularly the financial aspects of baseball, and she relied almost entirely upon advice from her son Coy Allen. After petitioner had entered into a contract to play for the Phillies organization, as hereinafter more fully set forth, Era Allen paid Coy $2,000 in 1960 for his services out of the funds which she received under that contract, and she deducted that amount from her gross income on her 1960 individual income tax return.

One of the principal items of negotiation with Ogden was the amount of "bonus" to be paid for petitioner's agreement to play for the Phillies organization. Such bonus was in addition to the monthly or periodic compensation to be paid petitioner for services actually rendered as a ballplayer. The purpose of the bonus was to assure the Phillies of the right to the player's services, if he were to play at all, and to prevent him from playing for any other club except with permission of the Phillies. Scouts for other teams had made offers of a bonus of at least $20,000 or $25,000. During the course of the negotiations Ogden made successive offers of a bonus in the amounts of $35,000, $50,000, and finally $70,000. The $70,000 offer was satisfactory to petitioner's mother, but she wanted $40,000 of that amount paid to her and $30,000 to petitioner. She thought that she was entitled to a portion of the bonus because she was responsible for his coming into baseball by her hard work, perseverance, taking care of petitioner, and seeing that he "did the right thing." Although it had been informally agreed prior to petitioner's graduation that he would go with the Phillies, the contract was presented to and signed by petitioner some 30 or 40 minutes after he had received his high school diploma on June 2, 1960.

The contract was formally between petitioner and the Williamsport Baseball Club, one of six or seven minor league teams affiliated with the Phillies. * * * The contract was on the standard form prescribed by the National Association of Professional Baseball Leagues. Since petitioner was a minor, his mother gave her consent to his execution of the contract by signing her name under a printed paragraph at the end of the form contract entitled "Consent of Parent or Guardian." Such consent was given explicitly "to the execution of this contract by the minor player party hereto," and was stated to be effective as to any assignment or renewal of the contract as therein specified. She was not a party to the contract. The Phillies, in accordance with their usual practice, would not have entered into any such contract, through the Williamsport Club or otherwise, without having obtained the consent of a parent or guardian of the minor player.

In addition to providing for a salary of $850 per month for petitioner's services as a ballplayer, the contract provided for the $70,000 bonus, payable over a 5–year period, of which $40,000 was to be paid directly to petitioner's mother and $30,000 to petitioner.

It was generally the practice in baseball to have the signature of a parent or guardian when signing a player under the age of 21 to a contract, and a contract lacking such signature would probably not have been approved by the president of the National Association of Professional Baseball Leagues.

* * * [I]n light of petitioner's future potential and ability, Ogden, who negotiated petitioner's bonus, and Quinn [VP and general manager of the Phillies, Ed.], who had the final say in these matters, felt that $70,000 was a fair price to pay to "get" the right to petitioner's services as a professional baseball player. It was a matter of indifference to them as to whom the bonus was paid or what division was made of the money. * * *

Following the execution of the foregoing contract in June 1960 with the Williamsport Club, petitioner performed services as a professional baseball player under annual contracts for various minor league teams affiliated with the Phillies until sometime in 1963. From that time, he has performed his services directly for the Phillies, and in 1967 his annual salary as a baseball player was approximately $65,000.

In his notice of deficiency to petitioner in respect of the taxable years 1961 and 1962, and his notice of deficiency to petitioner Richard and his wife Barbara Allen in respect of the taxable year 1963, the Commissioner determined that the bonus payments received by petitioner's mother in 1961, 1962, and 1963 represented amounts received in respect of a minor child and were taxable to petitioner under sections 61 and 73 of the Internal Revenue Code of 1954; he increased petitioner's taxable income in each of those years accordingly.

Opinion

RAUM, JUDGE:

1. Inclusion of Bonus in Petitioner's Gross Income.—(a) Petitioner was only 18 years old when the events giving rise to the bonus payments in controversy took place. Accordingly, if the payments made during the years in issue (1961–63) by the Phillies to Era Allen, petitioner's mother, constitute "amounts received in respect of the services" of petitioner within the meaning of section 73(a) I.R.C. 1954, then plainly they must be included in petitioner's gross income rather than in that of his mother. Although petitioner contends that the statute does not cover the present situation, we hold that the payments made to his mother during the years in issue were received solely in respect of petitioner's services, and that all such amounts were therefore includable in his income.

Petitioner argues that the payments received by his mother, totaling $40,000 over a 5–year period, were not part of his bonus for signing a contract to play baseball for the Phillies organization, but rather represented compensation for her, paid by the Phillies in return for her influencing petitioner to sign the contract and giving her written consent thereto. But there was no evidence of any written or oral agreement between the Phillies and Era Allen in which she agreed to further the Phillies' interests in this manner, and we shall not lightly infer the existence of an agreement by a mother dealing on behalf of her minor child which would or could have the effect of consigning her child's interests to a secondary position so that she might act for her own profit. Moreover, we think the evidence in the record consistently points to the conclusion that the payments received from the Phillies by Era Allen were considered and treated by the parties as part of petitioner's total bonus of $70,000. This sum was paid by the Phillies solely to obtain the exclusive right to petitioner's services as a professional baseball player; no portion thereof was in fact paid for his mother's consent.

We note, first of all, that there was no separate written agreement between the Phillies and Era Allen concerning the payment of $40,000 to her * * * Moreover, if further proof be needed that the Phillies did not consider any part of the $70,000 bonus as compensation for Era Allen's services it is provided by the testimony of John Ogden, the baseball scout responsible for petitioner's signing a contract with the Phillies' organization. Although Ogden resisted being pinned down, the clear import of his testimony was that the total bonus paid was determined solely by petitioner's ability to play baseball and his future prospects as a player, that the Phillies considered $70,000 a fair price to pay for the right to petitioner's services, and that it made little difference to them whether petitioner's mother received any part of the bonus so determined.

Era Allen herself did not claim to be entitled to $40,000 by virtue of any services performed for or on behalf of the Phillies, and in fact made clear in her testimony that she bargained, as one would expect, "for whatever was best for my son." Rather, she insisted upon a large portion of petitioner's bonus because she felt that petitioner would never have reached the point at which he was able to sign a lucrative contract with a professional baseball team had it not been for her hard work and perseverance in supporting him. And indeed, as the mother of a minor child, one who by the fruits of her own labor had contributed to the support of her minor child without the help of the child's father, she appears to have been entitled to all of petitioner's earnings under Pennsylvania law.

Prior to 1944, the Commissioner's rulings and regulations "required a parent to report in his (or her) return the earnings of a minor child, if under the laws of the state where they resided, the parent had a right to such earnings," even if none or only part of the child's earnings were actually appropriated by the parent. Because parents were not entitled to the earnings of their minor children in all States, and because even in those States following this common-law doctrine the parents' right to the earnings of, a minor child could be lost if it was found that the child had been emancipated, the result of the Commissioner's policy was that:

> for Federal income tax purposes, opposite results * * * obtained(ed) under the same set of facts depending upon the applicable State law. In addition, such variations in the facts as make applicable to the exceptions to the general rule in each jurisdiction tend(ed) to produce additional uncertainty with respect to the tax treatment of the earnings of minor children.

To remedy these defects, Congress in 1944 enacted the substantially identical predecessor of section 73 of the Internal Revenue Code of 1954, providing the easily determinable and uniform rule that all amounts received "in respect of the services of a child" shall be included in his income. "Thus, even though the contract of employment is made directly by the parent and the parent receives the compensation for the services, for the purposes of the Federal income tax the amounts would be considered to be taxable to the child because earned by him." We think section 73 reverses what would have been the likely result in this case under pre–1944 law wholly apart from the contract, and that the $70,000 bonus is taxable in full to petitioner.

Petitioner stresses the fact that the $70,000 bonus paid by the Phillies did not constitute a direct payment for his "services" as a professional baseball player, which were to be compensated at an agreed salary of $850 per month, for the $70,000 was to be paid in all events, whether or not petitioner ever performed any services for the Phillies organization. Therefore, it is argued, the bonus payments could not have constituted compensation for services which alone are taxed to a minor child under section 73. This argument misreads the statute, which speaks in terms of "amounts received in respect of the services of a child," and not merely of compensation for services performed. True, petitioner performed no services in the usual sense for his $70,000 bonus, unless his act of signing the contract be considered such, but the bonus payments here were paid by the Phillies as an inducement to obtain his services as a professional baseball player and to preclude him from rendering those services to other professional baseball teams; they thus certainly constituted amounts received "in respect of" his services.

This is not merely a technically correct interpretation of the statute; it is consistent with and necessary to the achievement of its purposes. Although a bonus such as that involved here is admittedly an indirect rather than a direct payment for services, there can be little doubt that it would be considered part of a child's "earnings" for the purpose of the common-law rule giving a father the right to the services and earnings of his minor children, and for the purpose of statutes such as that in Pennsylvania, extending this right to the mother. So, if the uniform rule of section 73 be held inapplicable to such bonuses, their treatment for tax purposes when earned by a minor would then be subject once again to the peculiarities of local law and to the factual imbroglio precipitated by the common-law rules in respect of the earnings of a minor child, the very problems which led to the enactment of section 73. To be sure, the committee reports on the predecessor of section 73 refer at one point to the need for uniformity in the taxation of "compensation for services performed by a minor child," but it seems likely that the bonus situation which we have here was at most overlooked, not intentionally omitted. Certainly the legislators took no chances with the statute itself, which speaks in the much broader terms of any "amounts received in respect of the services" of a child. There is no readily apparent reason why the narrow construction urged by petitioner should have been intended by Congress, and the language of the committee reports, though not necessarily inconsistent with the result we reach, must in any event yield in the interpretation of section 73 to the clear legislative purposes which prompted its enactment.

(b) Even if the amounts in issue were not received "in respect of the services" of a child under section 73, we think that the bonus installments paid to the petitioner's mother during the tax years 1961–63 are nevertheless chargeable to him under the general provisions of section 61. It has long been established that one who becomes entitled to receive income may not avoid tax thereon by causing it to be paid to another through "anticipatory arrangements however skillfully devised."

* * *

Accordingly, even if the bonus payments may not be considered as amounts received in respect of services so as to be covered by section 73(a), they nevertheless represent income of petitioner, taxable to him, notwithstanding the arrangement to have a portion thereof paid to his mother.

2. Petitioner's Alternative Contention—Deduction of Bonus Payments From His Gross Income.—Finally, petitioner argues alternatively that if his entire $70,000 bonus is includable in his income, he should be allowed to deduct the bonus payments received by his mother as an ordinary and necessary expense incurred in carrying on his trade or business as a professional baseball player. He places great reliance in this argument upon Hundley v. Commissioner, 48 T.C. 339 (1967), a case recently decided by this Court in which a professional baseball player was allowed to deduct that portion of his bonus for signing a baseball contract which was paid directly to his father, the result of an agreement entered into some 2 years before the contract was signed as a means of compensating the father for his services as a baseball coach and business agent. However, the special facts in *Hundley*, which supported a finding of reasonableness for the amount of the deduction claimed and warranted the conclusion that the amounts paid there in fact represented a bona fide expense incurred in carrying on the taxpayer's trade or business of being a professional baseball player, are almost entirely absent here.[7]

It is unnecessary to determine the exact sum which would have constituted a reasonable payment to Era Allen for her services, though we note that only $2,000 was paid to her son Coy Allen for the advice she so greatly relied on, for we are certain that in any case it could not have exceeded the $16,000 received by her in 1960. Although the year 1960 is not before us in these proceedings, we can and do take into account the

---

7. In Hundley, the player's father was a former semiprofessional baseball player and baseball coach who spent many hours coaching his son, at the expense of his own construction business, teaching him a "unique one-handed catching technique" and making him into a baseball player of professional caliber; he traveled for 2 years at his own expense to keep in close touch and on friendly terms with all the baseball scouts; and when his son graduated from high school he conducted the final negotiations in an "unusual and skillful" manner whereby all the representatives of the various baseball teams were allowed to make secret offers during a 2-week period following his son's graduation from high school. Here, on the other hand, petitioner's mother had nothing whatever to do with her son's development as a baseball player, and in fact knew nothing about baseball or financial matters and had to rely upon her son Coy Allen in her negotiations with the scouts. Moreover, in Hundley, the large sum payable to the father was received under a contingent compensation agreement entered into some 2 years earlier which entitled him to receive 50 percent of any bonus which his son might receive for signing a baseball contract. Since the agreement had been reached at a time when it was uncertain whether the son would develop into a player of professional baseball caliber and, even if he did, whether he would receive any bonus whatever, and when bonuses that were paid by professional baseball teams were usually small, the Court held that the agreement was reasonable when made and that the compensation received thereunder was therefore reasonable in amount. There was no preexisting agreement between petitioner and his mother in this case, however, and no persuasive explanation as to why her services were thought to be worth $40,000.

payment made to her in that year in determining whether the deductions now claimed by petitioner for payments made to her in the years 1961, 1962, and 1963 are reasonable in amount and deductible as "ordinary and necessary" business expenses. We think that clearly are not, and hold that petitioner is not entitled to deductions in any amount for payments made to his mother in those years.

Decisions will be entered for the respondent.

NOTE

Richie Allen was National League Rookie of the Year (for the Phillies) in 1964. In 1972, he was the American League Most Valuable Player (for the White Sox). Some of his more memorable quotes are:

- If a horse won't eat it, I don't want to play on it; and
- I'll play first, third, left, I'll play anywhere, except Philadelphia.

2.   THE KIDDIE TAX—UNEARNED INCOME OF CHILDREN

Code: § 1(g)

Allen and § 73 deal with the earned income of children, usually a rare commodity when you consider what sorts of families engage in income shifting. "Unearned income," such as interest and dividends, is much more common. With respect to such income, one must deal with § 1(g).

PROBLEM

Junior is Parents' 17–year–old only child. Parents are in the 35% bracket. They transfer a one hundred thousand dollar bond, earning 10% interest, to Junior. Junior earns $10,000 taxable interest this year, and no other income. How will the interest be taxed? How will next year's $10,000 of interest be taxed, when Junior is 18 years old?

3.   UNIFORM GIFTS TO MINORS ACT

In the Kiddie Tax problem above, Parents transferred the bond outright to Junior. Most parents are loath to cede all control. However, if the parents retain control, then the transfer is not effective, and the parents will be taxed as if they still owned the income producing assets, regardless of the application of the Kiddie Tax.

Congress, however, and the state legislatures, have sided with the parents on this issue. In order to encourage transfers of income producing assets to children, the income generated by transfers pursuant to the Uniform Gifts to Minors Acts (enacted in most states) will be taxed to the children and not the parents (subject, of course, to the Kiddie Tax), despite the fact that, under those Acts, the parents retain substantial control of the assets until the children reach their majority.

D. INCOME PRODUCING ENTITIES

1. PARTNERSHIPS

Want to split your cattle business income five ways? Form a partnership with your four sons. Stated that way, it sounds like a scam.

Yet, many legitimate businesses are conducted in the partnership form. Moreover, as sole entrepreneurs get along in years, it makes sense for them to pass their businesses on to the next generation. Partnerships are excellent vehicles for such transfers, for a host of non-tax reasons.

In the case below, how did the Tax Court determine which family partnerships should be recognized for tax purposes? How did the Fifth Circuit and the Supreme Court make their determinations?

COMMISSIONER v. CULBERTSON

United States Supreme Court, 1949.
337 U.S. 733, 69 S.Ct. 1210, 93 L.Ed. 1659.

MR. CHIEF JUSTICE VINSON delivered the opinion of the Court.

This case requires our further consideration of the family partnership problem. The Commissioner of Internal Revenue ruled that the entire income from a partnership allegedly entered into by respondent and his four sons must be taxed to respondent, and the Tax Court sustained that determination. The Court of Appeals for the Fifth Circuit reversed. We granted certiorari to consider the Commissioner's claim that the principles of Commissioner v. Tower, 327 U.S. 280, and Lusthaus v. Commissioner, 327 U.S. 293, have been departed from in this and other courts of appeals decisions.

Respondent taxpayer is a rancher. From 1915 until October 1939, he had operated a cattle business in partnership with R. S. Coon. Coon, who had numerous business interests in the Southwest and had largely financed the partnership, was 79 years old in 1939 and desired to dissolve the partnership because of ill health. To that end, the bulk of the partnership herd was sold until, in October of that year, only about 1,500 head remained. These cattle were all registered Herefords, the brood or foundation herd. Culbertson wished to keep these cattle and approached Coon with an offer of $65 a head. Coon agreed to sell at that price, but only upon condition that Culbertson would sell an undivided one-half interest in the herd to his four sons at the same price. His reasons for imposing this condition were his intense interest in maintaining the Hereford strain which he and Culbertson had developed, his conviction that Culbertson was too old to carry on the work alone, and his personal interest in the Culbertson boys. Culbertson's sons were enthusiastic about the proposition, so respondent thereupon bought the remaining cattle from the Coon and Culbertson partnership for $99,440. Two days later Culbertson sold an undivided one-half interest to the four boys, and the following day they gave their father a note for $49,720 at 4 per cent interest due one year from date. Several months later a new note for $57,674 was executed by the boys to replace the earlier note. The increase in amount covered the purchase by Culbertson and his sons of other properties formerly owned by Coon and Culbertson. This note was paid by the boys in the following manner:

Credit for overcharge	$ 5,930
Gifts from respondent	21,744
One-half of a loan procured by Culbertson & Sons partnership	30,000

The loan was repaid from the proceeds from operation of the ranch.

The partnership agreement between taxpayer and his sons was oral. The local paper announced the dissolution of the Coon and Culbertson partnership and the continuation of the business by respondent and his boys under the name of Culbertson & Sons. A bank account was opened in this name, upon which taxpayer, his four sons and a bookkeeper could check. At the time of formation of the new partnership, Culbertson's oldest son was 24 years old, married, and living on the ranch, of which he had for two years been foreman under the Coon and Culbertson partnership. He was a college graduate and received $100 a month plus board and lodging for himself and his wife both before and after formation of Culbertson & Sons and until entering the Army. The second son was 22 years old, was married and finished college in 1940, the first year during which the new partnership operated. He went directly into the Army following graduation and rendered no services to the partnership. The two younger sons, who were 18 and 16 years old respectively in 1940, went to school during the winter and worked on the ranch during the summer.

The tax years here involved are 1940 and 1941. A partnership return was filed for both years indicating a division of income approximating the capital attributed to each partner. It is the disallowance of this division of the income from the ranch that brings this case into the courts.

First. The Tax Court read our decisions in Commissioner v. Tower, *supra*, and Lusthaus v. Commissioner, *supra*, as setting out two essential tests of partnership for income-tax purposes: that each partner contribute to the partnership either vital services or capital originating with him. Its decision was based upon a finding that none of respondent's sons had satisfied those requirements during the tax years in question. Sanction for the use of these "tests" of partnership is sought in this paragraph from our opinion in the *Tower* case:

"There can be no question that a wife and a husband may, under certain circumstances, becomes partners for tax, as for other, purposes. If she either invests capital originating with her or substantially contributes to the control and management of the business, or otherwise performs vital additional services, or does all of these things she may be a partner as contemplated by §§ 181 and 182 [current §§ 701 and 702]. The Tax Court has recognized that under such circumstances the income belongs to the wife. A wife may become a general or a limited partner with her husband. But when she does not share in the management and control of the business, contributes no vital additional service, and where the husband purports in some way to have given her a partnership interest, the Tax Court may properly take these circumstances into consideration in determining whether the partnership is real within the meaning of the federal revenue laws."

It is the Commissioner's contention that the Tax Court's decision can and should be reinstated upon the mere reaffirmation of the quoted paragraph.

The Court of Appeals, on the other hand, was of the opinion that a family partnership entered into without thought of tax avoidance should be given recognition taxwise whether or not it was intended that some of the partners contribute either capital or services during the tax year and whether or not they actually made such contributions, since it was formed "with the full expectation and purpose that the boys would, in the future, contribute their time and services to the partnership." We must consider, therefore, whether an intention to contribute capital or services sometime in the future is sufficient to satisfy ordinary concepts of partnership, as required by the *Tower* case. * * *

In the *Tower* case we held that despite the claimed partnership, the evidence fully justified the Tax Court's holding that the husband, through his ownership of the capital and his management of the business, actually created the right to receive and enjoy the benefit of the income and was thus taxable upon that entire income under [current §§ 1 and 61]. In such case, other members of the partnership cannot be considered "Individuals carrying on business in partnership" and thus "liable for income tax * * * in their individual capacity" within the meaning of [current § 701]. If it is conceded that some of the partners contributed neither capital nor services to the partnership during the tax years in question, as the Court of Appeals was apparently willing to do in the present case, it can hardly be contended that they are in any way responsible for the production of income during those years. The partnership sections of the Code are, of course, geared to the sections relating to taxation of individual income, since no tax is imposed upon partnership income as such. To hold that "Individuals carrying on business in partnership" include persons who contribute nothing during the tax period would violate the first principle of income taxation: that income must be taxed to him who earns it. Lucas v. Earl; Helvering v. Clifford; National Carbide Corp. v. Commissioner.

Furthermore, our decision in Commissioner v. Tower, *supra,* clearly indicates the importance of participation in the business by the partners during the tax year. We there said that a partnership is created "when persons join together their money, goods, labor, or skill for the purpose of carrying on a trade, profession, or business and when there is community of interest in the profits and losses." This is, after all, but the application of an often iterated definition of income—the gain derived from capital, from labor, or from both combined—to a particular form of business organization. A partnership is, in other words, an organization for the production of income to which each partner contributes one or both of the ingredients of income—capital or services. The intent to provide money, goods, labor, or skill sometime in the future cannot meet the demands of [current §§ 1 and 61] of the Code that he who presently earns the income through his own labor and skill and the utilization of his own capital be taxed therefor. The vagaries of human experience preclude reliance upon even good faith intent as to future conduct as a basis for the present taxation of income.[8]

Second. We turn next to a consideration of the Tax Court's approach to the family partnership problem. It treated as essential to membership in a family partnership for tax purposes the contribution of either "vital services" or "original capital." Use of these "tests" of partnership indicates, at best, an error in emphasis. It ignores what we said is the ultimate question for decision, namely, "whether the partnership is real within the meaning of the federal revenue laws" and makes decisive what we described as "circumstances (to be taken) into consideration" in making that determination.

The *Tower* case thus provides no support for such an approach. We there said that the question whether the family partnership is real for income-tax purposes depends upon "whether the partners really and truly intended to join together for the purpose of carrying on the business and sharing in the profits and losses or both. And their intention in this respect is a question of fact, to be determined from testimony disclosed by their 'agreement, considered as a whole, and by their conduct in execution of its provisions.' We see no reason why this general rule should not apply in tax cases where the Government challenges the existence of a partnership for tax purposes."

The question is not whether the services or capital contributed by a partner are of sufficient importance to meet some objective standard supposedly established by the *Tower* case, but whether, considering all the facts—the agreement, the conduct of the parties in execution of its provisions, their statements, the testimony of disinterested persons, the relationship of the parties, their respective abilities and capital contributions, the actual control of income and the purposes for which it is used,

---

8. The reductio ad absurdum of the theory that children may be partners with their parents before they are capable of being entrusted with the disposition of partnership funds or of contributing substantial services occurred in Tinkoff v. Commissioner, 120 F.2d 564, where a taxpayer made his son a partner in his accounting firm the day the son was born.

and any other facts throwing light on their true intent—the parties in good faith and acting with a business purpose intended to join together in the present conduct of the enterprise. There is nothing new or particularly difficult about such a test. Triers of fact are constantly called upon to determine the intent with which a person acted. * * *

But the Tax Court did not view the question as one concerning the bona fide intent of the parties to join together as partners. Not once in its opinion is there even an oblique reference to any lack of intent on the part of respondent and his sons to combine their capital and services "for the purpose of carrying on the business." Instead the court, focusing entirely upon concepts of "vital services" and "original capital," simply decided that the alleged partners had not satisfied those tests when the facts were compared with those in the Tower case. The court's opinion is replete with such statements as "we discern nothing constituting what we think is a requisite contribution to a real partnership. * * * We find no son adding 'vital additional service' which would take the place of capital contributed because of formation of a partnership * * * it is clear that the sons made no capital contribution within the meaning of the Tower case."[13]

Unquestionably a court's determination that the services contributed by a partner are not "vital" and that he has not participated in "management and control of the business" or contributed "original capital" has the effect of placing a heavy burden on the taxpayer to show the bona fide intent of the parties to join together as partners. But such a determination is not conclusive, and that is the vice in the "tests" adopted by the Tax Court. It assumes that there is no room for an honest difference of opinion as to whether the services or capital furnished by the alleged partner are of sufficient importance to justify his inclusion in the partnership. If, upon a consideration of all the facts, it is found that the partners joined together in good faith to conduct a business, having agreed that the services or capital to be contributed presently by each is of such value to the partnership that the contributor should participate in the distribution of profits, that is sufficient. The Tower case did not purport to authorize the Tax Court to substitute its judgment for that of the parties; it simply furnished some guides to the determination of their true intent. Even though it was admitted in the *Tower* case that the wife contributed no original capital, management of the business, or other vital services, this Court did not say as a matter of law that there was no valid partnership. We said, instead, that "There was, thus, more than ample evidence to support the Tax Court's finding that no genuine union for partnership purposes was ever intended, and that the husband earned the income."

Third. The Tax Court's isolation of "original capital" as an essential of membership in a family partnership also indicates an erroneous reading

---

13. In the Tower case the taxpayer argued that he had a right to reduce his taxes by any legal means, to which this Court agreed. We said, however, that existence of a tax avoidance motive gives some indication that there was no bona fide intent to carry on business as a partnership. If Tower had set up objective requirements of membership in a family partnership, such as "vital services" and "original capital," the motives behind adoption of the partnership form would have been irrelevant.

of the *Tower* opinion. We did not say that the donee of an intra-family gift could never become a partner through investment of the capital in the family partnership, any more than we said that all family trusts are invalid for tax purposes in Helvering v. Clifford, supra. The facts may indicate, on the contrary, that the amount thus contributed and the income therefrom should be considered the property of the donee for tax, as well as general law, purposes. In the *Tower* and *Lusthaus* cases this Court, applying the principles of Lucas v. Earl, *supra*; Helvering v. Clifford, *supra*; and Helvering v. Horst, *supra*; found that the purported gift, whether or not technically complete, had made no substantial change in the economic relation of members of the family to the income. In each case the husband continued to manage and control the business as before, and income from the property given to the wife and invested by her in the partnership continued to be used in the business or expended for family purposes. We characterized the results of the transactions entered into between husband and wife as "a mere paper reallocation among the family members," noting that "The actualities of their relation to the income did not change." This, we thought, provided ample grounds for the finding that no true partnership was intended; that the husband was still the true earner of the income.

But application of the Clifford–Horst principle does not follow automatically upon a gift to a member of one's family, followed by its investment in the family partnership. If it did, it would be necessary to define "family" and to set precise limits of membership therein. We have not done so for the obvious reason that existence of the family relationship does not create a status which itself determines tax questions, but is simply a warning that things may not be what they seem. It is frequently stated that transactions between members of a family will be carefully scrutinized. But more particularly, the family relationship often makes it possible for one to shift tax incidence by surface changes of ownership without disturbing in the least his dominion and control over the subject of the gift or the purposes for which the income from the property is used. He is able, in other words, to retain "the substance of full enjoyment of all the rights which previously he had in the property."

The fact that transfers to members of the family group may be mere camouflage does not, however, mean that they invariably are. The *Tower* case recognized that one's participation in control and management of the business is a circumstance indicating an intent to be a bona fide partner despite the fact that the capital contributed originated elsewhere in the family. If the donee of property who then invests it in the family partnership exercises dominion and control over that property—and through that control influences the conduct of the partnership and the disposition of its income—he may well be a true partner. Whether he is free to, and does, enjoy the fruits of the partnership is strongly indicative of the reality of his participation in the enterprise. In the *Tower* and *Lusthaus* cases we distinguished between active participation in the affairs of the business by a donee of a share in the partnership on the one hand,

and his passive acquiescence to the will of the donor on the other. This distinction is of obvious importance to a determination of the true intent of the parties. It is meaningless if "original capital" is an essential test of membership in a family partnership.

The cause must therefore be remanded to the Tax Court for a decision as to which, if any, of respondent's sons were partners with him in the operation of the ranch during 1940 and 1941. As to which of them, in other words, was there a bona fide intent that they be partners in the conduct of the cattle business, either because of services to be performed during those years, or because of contributions of capital of which they were the true owners, as we have defined that term in the Clifford, Horst, and Tower cases? No question as to the allocation of income between capital and services is presented in this case, and we intimate no opinion on that subject.

The decision of the Court of Appeals is reversed with directions to remand the cause to the Tax Court for further proceedings in conformity with this opinion.

[Other opinions have been omitted.]

2. CORPORATIONS

The scheme here is for a high-income athlete to insert a corporation between himself and his real employer. Ideally, though not in the case below, the real employer contracts with the corporation, which in turn contracts with the athlete. The athlete's salary is thus split between himself and the corporation.

The corporation pays a relatively small amount to the athlete now as compensation. It will pay him the rest later. In the interim, the corporation pays little or no tax, because the corporation is incorporated in a tax haven, which doesn't levy income taxes.

In the case below, note the primacy of *Lucas v. Earl*, and of the question of control.

JOHNSON v. COMMISSIONER

United States Tax Court, 1982.
78 T.C. 882, *aff'd without opinion*, 734 F.2d 20 (9th Cir. 1984).

FAY, JUDGE:

Findings of Fact

* * * [Petitioner Charles Johnson played professional basketball for the San Francisco Warriors, and later the Washington Bullets, from 1972 through 1979. He signed a contract] on August 16, 1974, with Presentaciones Musicales, S.A. (PMSA), a Panamanian corporation. In very general terms, that agreement (hereinafter the PMSA-petitioner agreement) gave PMSA the right to petitioner's services in professional sports for 6 years

beginning August 16, 1974, gave PMSA the right to control petitioner's services with respect to professional sports, and obligated PMSA to pay petitioner $1,500 per month. On August 20, 1974, PMSA licensed its rights and obligations under the PMSA-petitioner agreement to EST International Ltd. (EST), a British Virgin Islands limited liability company. Under that licensing arrangement, EST was obligated to pay any expenses and to make the payments to petitioner required under the PMSA-petitioner agreement. EST was to remit to PMSA 95 percent of the "net revenue" collected by EST under the PMSA-petitioner agreement.

* * * [The NBA teams refused to have any contractual relationship with PMSA or EST, and instead dealt only with Johnson. However, all payments due from the teams under the NBA Uniform Players Contracts which they had executed with Johnson were remitted to EST.]

The PMSA-petitioner agreement gave PMSA the right to require petitioner to perform services but acknowledged that any regulations of any professional association would control. That agreement provided both that "Basic commercial and economic control of [petitioner's] services is intended to reside in PMSA at all times," and that petitioner "shall not undertake to perform personal athletic services of any kind for the duration of this agreement without the prior written approval of PMSA." Neither PMSA nor EST in any way actively participated in negotiations with the Warriors or in petitioner's playing of basketball. At trial, petitioner acknowledged that no change with respect to his working relationship with the Warriors occurred after the PMSA-petitioner agreement was executed.

* * * [T]he PMSA-petitioner agreement gave PMSA the right to petitioner's services in professional sports for 6 years and obligated PMSA to pay petitioner $1,500 per month. The $1,500 per month was listed as "compensation for initial term [6 years]" and was made payable to petitioner for his life. However, the agreement provided further: Should JOHNSON [petitioner] fail to perform services under any license arrangement [unless he is incapacitated] to any professional athletic team or related athletic endeavor for any consecutive twenty-four (24) month period, * * * PMSA may bring this Agreement to an end and shall retain without the necessity of making any further payment of any kind to JOHNSON all the rights held by PMSA under this agreement. Thus, if petitioner, for 24 consecutive months, failed to perform under any athletic license to a professional team, PMSA was relieved of its obligation to pay petitioner. * * *

On his Federal income tax returns for 1975, 1976, and 1977, petitioner reported no wages or salary, but did report the payments he received from EST as business income. He attached to those returns Forms W-2 issued by the Warriors with respect to his services. Petitioner received refunds of Federal income taxes with respect to 1975, 1976, and 1977. Those refund checks, as well as checks representing refunds of State income taxes, were specially endorsed by petitioner to EST. By a statement attached to an application for an extension to file for 1975, petitioner disclosed his reporting position with respect to personal service income.

In his statutory notices of deficiency, respondent determined all amounts paid by the Warriors in 1975, 1976, and 1977 with respect to petitioner's services were income to petitioner. Thus, he increased petitioner's income by $60,894, $67,060, and $70,327 for 1975, 1976, and 1977, respectively. These increases reflect the excess of the amounts paid by the Warriors with respect to petitioner's services over the amount paid petitioner by EST with respect to those services.

Opinion

At issue is whether amounts paid by the Warriors with respect to petitioner's services as a basketball player are income to petitioner or to the corporation to which the amounts were remitted. Respondent, relying on the rule of Lucas v. Earl, that income must be taxed to its earner, contends petitioner was the true earner. Petitioner maintains this is a "loan-out" case like Fox v. Commissioner, 37 B.T.A. 271 (B.T.A. 1938) and that Lucas v. Earl is inapplicable.[11] We find Lucas v. Earl indistinguishable in any meaningful sense and hold for respondent.[12]

In Lucas v. Earl, the taxpayer executed an agreement with his wife that any property acquired by either of them, including wages and salary, would be considered joint property. The U.S. Supreme Court accepted the validity of that contract, but held the taxpayer earned the salary in issue therein and must be taxed on it. In so holding, the Court noted: It [the case] turns on the import and reasonable construction of the taxing act. There is no doubt that the statute could tax salaries to those who earned them and provide that the tax could not be escaped by anticipatory arrangements and contracts however skillfully devised to prevent the salary when paid from vesting even for a second in the man who earned it.* * * From that quote is derived the oft-cited "first principle of income taxation: That income must be taxed to him who earns it." However, the realities of the business world prevent an overly simplistic application of the Lucas v. Earl rule whereby the true earner may be identified by merely pointing to the one actually turning the spade or dribbling the ball. Recognition must be given to corporations as taxable entities which, to a great extent, rely upon the personal services of their employees to produce corporate income. When a corporate employee performs labors which give rise to income, it solves little merely to identify the actual laborer. Thus, a

---

11. Petitioner makes no contention, given the payments required to be made to him by EST, that his contractual rights with the Warriors were sold. The parties debate this case solely on the "who" aspect of the assignment of income doctrine, and make no arguments concerning the "when" aspect of that doctrine. See generally Estate of Stranahan v. Commissioner. Thus, we do not decide whether petitioner received adequate consideration in his dealings with PMSA and EST. * * *

12. Given our holding, we need not address respondent's alternate contention that the arrangement between petitioner and the various entities, other than the Warriors, was a sham. * * *

tension has evolved between the basic tenets of Lucas v. Earl and recognition of the nature of the corporate business form.[13]

While the generally accepted test for resolving the "who is taxed" tension is who actually earns the income, that test may easily become sheer sophistry when the "who" choices are a corporation or its employee. Whether a one-person professional service corporation or a multi-faceted corporation is presented, there are many cases in which, in a practical sense, the key employee is responsible for the influx of moneys. Nor may a workable test be couched in terms of for whose services the payor of the income intends to pay. In numerous instances, a corporation is hired solely in order to obtain the services of a specific corporate employee.[14]

Given the inherent impossibility of logical application of a per se actual earner test, a more refined inquiry has arisen in the form of who controls the earning of the income. An examination of the case law from Lucas v. Earl hence reveals two necessary elements before the corporation, rather than its service-performer employee, may be considered the controller of the income. First, the service-performer employee must be just that—an employee of the corporation whom the corporation has the right to direct or control in some meaningful sense. Second, there must exist between the corporation and the person or entity using the services a contract or similar indicium recognizing the corporation's controlling position.

In the case before us, we accept arguendo that the PMSA-petitioner agreement was a valid contract which required the payments with respect to petitioner's performance as a basketball player ultimately to be made to PMSA or EST. We also accept arguendo that the PMSA-petitioner agreement gave PMSA a right of control over petitioner's services, although respondent maintains the agreement's control provisions systematically were ignored. Thus, the first element is satisfied. However, the second element is lacking, and that is what brings this case within Lucas v. Earl rather than the cases relied on by petitioner.

In Fox v. Commissioner, the taxpayer was a cartoonist who formed a corporation. He transferred to the corporation cash and property and assigned to the corporation copyrights and his exclusive services for a number of years. The corporation executed a contract with a syndicate giving the syndicate the right to use the taxpayer's cartoons in return for a percentage of gross sales. The amount the corporation thus received greatly exceeded the amount the corporation paid the taxpayer for his services. The Court held the excess amounts were not the taxpayer's income. Lucas v. Earl was inapplicable because the employment relationships existed between the corporation and the syndicate and between the

---

13. That tension is most acute when a corporation operates a personal service business and has as its sole or principal employee its sole or principal shareholder. In those cases where sec. 482 applies, resort to general sec. 61 principles usually is not necessary since sec. 482 provides a smoother route to the same "who is taxed" result.

14. Such instances are commonplace in personal service businesses such as law, medicine, accounting, and entertainment.

corporation and the taxpayer and not between the taxpayer and the syndicate.

In Laughton v. Commissioner, 40 B.T.A. 101 (B.T.A. 1939), the taxpayer, an actor, formed a corporation. He contracted with the corporation to receive a weekly payment and certain expense payments in return for his exclusive services. The corporation executed contracts with two film studios whereby the taxpayer's services were loaned to the film studios. The Court held the taxpayer was not taxable on the amounts paid to the corporation by the studios because those amounts were paid "under contracts between it [the corporation] and the studios" and there simply was no assignment of income by the taxpayer.

Petitioner herein stands upon vastly different ground than did the taxpayers in *Fox* and *Laughton*. While petitioner had a contract with PMSA, and by assignment, EST, he also had an employment contract with the Warriors. Crucial is the fact that there was no contract or agreement between the Warriors and PMSA or EST. Nor can any oral contract between those entities be implied. The Warriors adamantly refused to sign any contract or agreement with any person or entity other than petitioner. Thus, the existing employment relationships were between petitioner and PMSA/EST and between petitioner and the Warriors. The relationship between PMSA/EST and the Warriors necessary for PMSA/EST to be considered actually in control of the earnings was not present. As with Mr. Earl, petitioner "was the only party to the contracts by which the salary * * * [was] earned."[10]

Nor may the assignments of earnings executed by petitioner suffice to make PMSA/EST the taxable party. Such assignments merely demonstrate petitioner's control over the earnings such as would an ordinary assignment of wages to a bank. Nor is it important that petitioner contractually was obligated to pay his earnings to PMSA/EST. The U.S. Supreme Court in Lucas v. Earl accepted the validity of the contract involved therein requiring transmission of one-half to Mrs. Earl, but nevertheless held Mr. Earl taxable as the true earner.

In summary, we find petitioner, rather than PMSA or EST, actually controlled the earning of the amounts paid by the Warriors with respect to petitioner's services. Thus, those amounts were income to petitioner under section 61(a)(1).

NOTE

1. Johnson was a guard. His NBA career averages were:

Points per game	8.1
Rebounds per game	2.5
Assists per game	1.9

---

10. We do not mean to imply this case necessarily would have been decided in petitioner's favor had a contract been executed between the Warriors and PMSA or EST. See note 12 supra.

2. *See also*, Leavell v. Commissioner, 104 T.C. 140 (1995).

3. As you can see, there are difficult issues regarding whether income and/or deductions are attributable to an individual, or to the corporation or partnership which she created. Furthermore, it is not always so easy to tell whether the entity in question is indeed a corporation, or a partnership. The stakes can be quite high, and litigation can be costly. To alleviate at least the latter concern, IRS has promulgated the "check-the-box" regulations. Pursuant to these regulations, in many instances, the taxpayer decides whether she wants the entity to be a partnership or a corporation. Then, she simply checks the appropriate box on the form, electing the treatment she desires. *See* Regulation § 301.7701–3.

3. TRUSTS

When one creates a trust, there are three possible taxpayer groups—the settlors, the trusts themselves, and the trust beneficiaries. If the trust is a grantor trust, then the trust entity is essentially ignored, and income earned by trust assets (and corresponding deductions) is taxed to the grantor, as if the trust had never been created. On the other hand, if the trust is a nongrantor trust, then the grantor will not be taxed on trust income. Instead, the income will be taxed either to the trust or its beneficiaries.

Grantor Trusts

If the grantor has retained so much dominion and control over trust assets that it is as if she has never really transferred them, then she will be taxed as if she still owns them. This doctrine was originally expressed in Helvering v. Clifford, 309 U.S. 331, 60 S.Ct. 554, 84 L.Ed. 788 (1940), but is now almost entirely a matter of statute. Thus, if the grantor conveys assets into a trust, but retains too much of a reversionary interest (§ 673), too much power to designate beneficiaries (§ 674), too much administrative power (§ 675), a power to revoke (§ 676), or a power to enjoy trust income (§ 677), then the grantor trust rules will apply.

Nongrantor Trusts

If the trust does not run afoul of the grantor trust rules, then the nongrantor trust rules of Subchapter J apply. The issue then becomes whether the trust or the beneficiaries will be taxed.

Uncle owns $100,000 in bonds, which generate taxable interest of $12,000 per year. If Uncle gives the bonds to Nephew, the receipt of the bonds will be taxfree pursuant to § 102. Interest income subsequent to the gift will be taxable to Nephew.

What if Uncle makes two gifts simultaneously—a gift of the bonds themselves to Nephew, and a gift of the future interest income to Niece? Are both gifts taxfree under § 102? No. Pursuant to § 102(b) and Irwin v.

Gavit, 268 U.S. 161, 45 S.Ct. 475, 69 L.Ed. 897, the gift of the bonds is taxfree, but the gift of the interest is still taxable. Nice try.

Uncle conveys the bonds to a trust. The income beneficiaries of the trust are Nephew and Niece. The trust is in a relatively low tax bracket; Nephew and Niece are in high brackets.[a] Uncle instructs the trustee to accumulate the interest in the trust, and to distribute $12,000 worth of the bonds themselves to Nephew and Niece. Uncle reasons that, pursuant to the analysis set forth above, a distribution of principal will be taxfree to the beneficiaries. Therefore, the interest will be taxable to the trust, even if the beneficiaries receive a like amount in principal.

Nice try. Since the enactment of the current version of Subchapter J, we no longer accept the trustee's characterization of the distributions. Instead, through the mechanism of distributable net income ("DNI"), we use a "last in, first out" principle (*see* materials on "last in, first out" in the discussion of inventories in Chapter 5). All distributions will be deemed distributions of income, and therefore taxable to the beneficiaries, until the income has been used up. Therefore, in this case, distributions of up to $12,000 (DNI) will be taxable to Nephew and Niece. Any distributions in excess of $12,000 this year will be treated as taxfree distributions of trust corpus.

That, in a simplistic nutshell, is how Subchapter J works.

E. TAXATION OF THE FAMILY

In the U.S. tax system, the taxpayer is the individual human being. However, the economic unit is often a larger group. More often than not, family members pool their income and resources, and then make expenditures for the benefit of the group. Therefore, the relevant unit for inflow and outflow is the family, or some other communal living arrangement larger than one person.

This dissonance between the taxable unit and the economic unit causes problems throughout the tax laws. Normally, when one taxpayer provides something of value to another, there is a taxable event. What about the provision of food, clothing, and shelter (not to mention tuition) from parents to children? Perhaps that's what § 102 is all about.

It has been proposed that the family unit be recognized as the taxable unit, and that all income earned by the family be allocated and taxed to the family members who enjoy it. So far, at least in the United States, that idea has not flown. We do allow deductions and credits for some of the expenses of raising children. *See*, for example, Chapter 8, *supra* for discussion of the child care credit, and Chapter 10, *infra*, for the depen-

---

a. Subchapter J. was enacted when typical trust beneficiaries were in higher brackets than the trusts themselves. Now, with bracket compression pursuant to § 1(e), the relative tax brackets of trusts and beneficiaries are often reversed.

dency exemption and the child tax credit. However, allocating some fraction of family income to the children who benefit from it is another matter. At any rate, questions of the allocation of income among family members persist. This section will consider allocation of income between husband and wife, both while married, and afterward.

1. THE JOINT RETURN

Code: Compare § 1(a) with §§ 1(c) and 1(d)

Shortly after *Lucas v. Earl* came Poe v. Seaborn, 282 U.S. 101, 51 S.Ct. 58, 75 L.Ed. 239 (1930). *Poe v. Seaborn* held that the income of husbands and wives in community property states would be split for tax purposes. It turned out that what could not be done by contract in *Lucas v. Earl* could be accomplished by community property statutes. This decision created a huge tax advantage for married couples in community property states. As a result, other states rushed to become community property states, or at least quasi-community property states.

In order to ameliorate the differences among the states, Congress created the joint return in 1948. To see how it works, compare the "Married Filing Separate Returns" rates in § 1(d) with the "Married Filing Joint Returns" rates in § 1(a). Compute the tax under both rates for a married couple in which each spouse earns $18,450, for an aggregate income of $36,900. Now compute the tax under both rates for a married couple in which each spouse earns $44,575, for an aggregate income of $89,150. You will note that the rates in § 1(a) were derived by halving the income, applying the rates in § 1(d), and multiplying the result by two.

2. THE MARRIAGE PENALTY

By creating a tax break for married couples in 1948, Congress created a tax penalty for singles. In some cases, singles paid 40% more tax than a married couple with the same aggregate income. To ameliorate this penalty, the single taxpayer rates, which are lower than the married filing separately rates, were created in 1969. To see how much lower, simply consider how much more quickly the taxable incomes in § 1(d) reach the higher rates, compared to the unmarried rates of § 1(c).

Now, single taxpayers have the advantage of the singles rates, and the disadvantage of the lack of access to the joint return. Married couples whose income is already pretty evenly split don't need the joint return, and suffer from the higher rates. Therefore, they suffer the marriage penalty. Married couples whose income is not evenly split get an advantage from the joint return that outweighs the penalty of the higher rates.

Can the tax rates be structured so that neither marriage penalties nor singles penalties exist? Imagine a tax system in which income up to $10,000 is taxed at 10%, while income in excess of $10,000 is taxed at 20%.

Assume the following taxpayers, income, and tax:

Taxpayer	Income	Tax
Alex	$10,000	$1,000
Becky	$10,000	$1,000
Charles	$0	$0
Deborah	$20,000	$3,000

Now imagine that Alex marries Becky, and Charles marries Deborah. If income remains constant, and they each pay tax at the same rates as when they were single, Alex and Becky will pay an aggregate tax of $2,000 on their combined $20,000 of income. Charles and Deborah, however, will pay an aggregate tax of $3,000 on their identical combined income of $20,000. This result violates "marriage neutrality"—the principle that married couples with the same combined income have the same ability to pay, and ought to pay the same tax.

The obvious choices are either to have both couples pay $2,000, or to have both couples pay $3,000. However, if both couples pay $2,000, then Evangeline, a single taxpayer with income of $20,000, will want to know why she is paying tax of $3,000 while married couples with the same income of $20,000 are paying tax of $2,000.

On the other hand, if both couples pay tax of $3,000, then Becky and Alex will ask why each of them paid a tax of $1,000 on $10,000 of income when they were single, while they are now each paying a tax of $1,500 (half of $3,000) on the same $10,000 of income, when they are married.

In fact, there are three goals which an income tax system might have:

1) Progressive rates

2) Marriage neutrality—treating married couples with the same aggregate income the same; and

3) Fairness as between marrieds and singles.

It is impossible for one tax system to accomplish more than two of the three goals. Has our system made the right choices? Is marriage neutrality even a laudable goal? Perhaps we should tax Charles and Deborah at higher rates to mitigate the unfairness of not taxing the imputed income from the household services which Charles is providing. For that matter, who deserves a tax break—marrieds or singles? Should singles get the break because they don't enjoy the same economies of scale in living expenses that marrieds do?

When the income of a married couple is split 100%–0%, the tax advantages of marriage are at their highest. Conversely, when the income is split 50–50, the tax disadvantages of being married are at their highest. The break-even point is around 80%–20%. If the spouse earning the lesser income earns less than 20% of the total, then there is a marriage bonus. If the spouse earning the lesser income earns more than 20% of the total, then there is a marriage penalty.

Note that only higher income couples can afford for one of the two spouses not to earn income outside the home. Therefore, higher income couples tend to get a marriage bonus. Lower income couples tend to get a marriage penalty.

There is a racial/ethnic dimension as well. In 1990, the average white married woman earned 29.3% of the household income. The average black married woman earned 39.7%. United States Commission on Civil Rights, THE ECONOMIC STATUS OF BLACK WOMEN: AN EXPLORATORY INVESTIGATION Table 8.6 (1990). See also, Dorothy Brown, *Race, Class, and Gender Essentialism in Tax Literature: The Joint Return,* 54 WASH. & LEE L. REV. 1469 (1997). Therefore, black married couples were more likely to face a marriage penalty than white married couples. For a similar analysis with respect to Asian–American couples, see Mylinh Uy, *Tax and Race: The Impact on Asian Americans*, 11 ASIAN L. J. 117, 138 (2004). Is this fair? Was it intended?

Look at this phenomenon in a different way. When the husband and the wife each earns more or less the same amount of money, there is a tax penalty on getting married. Therefore, for such couples, there is a tax incentive to stay single. In effect, couples who are living together and making comparable incomes, who either will not, or can not, get married, get favorable tax treatment. Heterosexual couples who are living together are a good example of the "will not" category; homosexual couples are a good example of the "can not" category. The Congressional Budget Office estimates that this tax subsidy for homosexual couples will cost the government between $200 and $400 million per year from 2005 to 2010, and from $500 to $700 million per year thereafter.[b] Do you suppose that it was intended?

2001 Legislation

In 2001, Congress addressed the marriage penalty in two ways. First, it doubled the basic standard deduction for married couples filing a joint return to twice the standard deduction for single taxpayers. See Chapter 10 at 547 for a discussion of the standard deduction. Second, it increased the size of the 15% bracket for married taxpayers filing joint returns to twice that of the single taxpayers. See Economic Growth and Tax Relief Reconciliation Act of 2001, section 301.

Of course, as shown above, it is impossible to fix the marriage penalty/marriage bonus problem, unless Congress enacts a flat tax. Note that the 2001 legislation gives a tax break not only to those who had truly experienced a marriage penalty, but also to those who had enjoyed a marriage bonus. Moreover, any provision which benefits the tax treatment of married couples necessarily exacerbates the unfairness as between marrieds and singles.

---

b. Cong. Budget Office, *The Potential Budgetary Impact of Recognizing Same–Sex* Marriages *(June 21, 2004)* available at *http://www.cbo.gov/showdoc.cfm?index=5559&sequence=0.*

3. DIVORCE

(a) Alimony—General Definition

Code: §§ 71, 215

Regulations: §§ 1.71–1T, 1.215–1T

Want to shift taxable income from one taxpayer to another? What could be easier than transferring the money, deducting it from transferor's income, and including it in transferee's income? That's exactly what §§ 71 and 215 accomplish. Of course, transferor and transferee must be separated or divorced.

Before 1984, issues concerning the taxation of divorced couples often wound up in court. The major question was the nature of alimony payments, as distinguished from property settlements. The stakes were high. Alimony, then as now, was deductible by the payor, and taxable to the payee. Property settlements were neither deductible nor taxable. Alimony payments tended to be periodic, terminating upon the death or remarriage of the payee spouse. Property settlements tended to be lump sums.

In 1984, Congress made the entire area statutory. From then on, if the taxpayers wanted alimony treatment, they needed but to follow the statutory recipe, found in § 71(b). On the other hand, if they did not want alimony treatment, they needed to make sure that the payments were not alimony under the same statute. In fact, note that § 71(b)(1)(B) provides that a payment is not alimony if the taxpayer doesn't want it to be, and says so. In effect, Congress not only eliminated a tendentious, litigated issue in 1984; it virtually invited taxpayers to consider what treatment would create the optimum tax result, and then to choose that treatment.

That said, however, it still must be noted that alimony is more rare, and perhaps more difficult to obtain, than it once was. But there's the rub. The case in which alimony is most likely is the one in which one spouse earns substantially more money than the other, such that one of the spouses can truly be called a dependent spouse. Often, poor families cannot afford to have one spouse not working outside the home. Usually, only rich families have that option. Now, which families do you think are most likely to hire lawyers for tax advice at the time of divorce?

Problems

In each instance, determine whether the payments are alimony (deductible to payor spouse, taxable to payee spouse) or not. Unless otherwise indicated, assume that payments are pursuant to a divorce decree, and the Husband and Wife are living separately.

1. Wife agrees to pay ex-Husband cash of $1,000 per month for the rest of his life, or until he remarries.

2. Husband agrees to pay ex-Wife or her estate $1,000 per month for the next 25 years.

3. Husband agrees to transfer to ex-Wife 100 shares of IBM stock each year for the rest of her life.

4. Husband agrees to transfer to ex-Wife a new Cadillac Eldorado, or a comparable car which is satisfactory to ex-Wife, every three years. Every three years, Wife picks out a new Cadillac at the dealership, and sends the bill to Husband, who pays it.

5. Wife transfers the Lexus from her name to Ex–Husband's name. Also, she agrees to make the remaining payments on the car loan, unless Ex–Husband dies or remarries before the loan is paid off. What about: a) the car? b) the payments?

6. Wife agrees that Ex–Husband can live in the house, which will remain in her name, for the rest of his life. She also agrees to continue making the mortgage payments, unless Ex–Husband dies or remarries before the loan is paid off. What about the mortgage payments?

7. Husband and Wife's marriage is over, but they continue to live in the same house, since they can't afford to maintain separate households. Husband agrees to make monthly cash payments to Wife, until her death or remarriage.

A) The payments are pursuant to a divorce decree.

B) The payments are pursuant to a written separation agreement.

(b) Negotiating Optimal Divorce and Separation Agreements in Light of the Tax Brackets of the Two Spouses

PROBLEM

Wife is in the 35% tax bracket and Husband is in the 25% tax bracket

1. Calculate the after-tax cost to Wife and the after-tax income to Husband if Wife transfers $100 to Husband as

(a) alimony; or

(b) non-alimony.

2. Wife is willing to incur $100 of after-tax costs to transfer cash to Husband. What are the two ways in which she could incur exactly $100 in after-tax costs? Which would Husband prefer?

3. What if Wife were to transfer $125 in alimony to Husband?

(c) Alimony—Front End Loading

Code: § 71(f)

As stated above, alimony tends to be periodic; property settlements tend to be lump sum. Graphically, property settlements tend to look like this:

Illustration 12

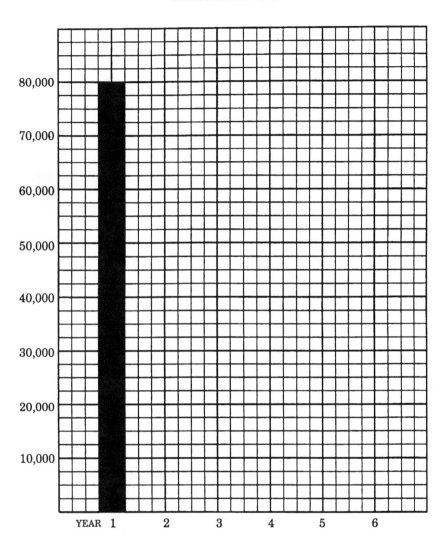

Alimony tends to look like this:

Illustration 13

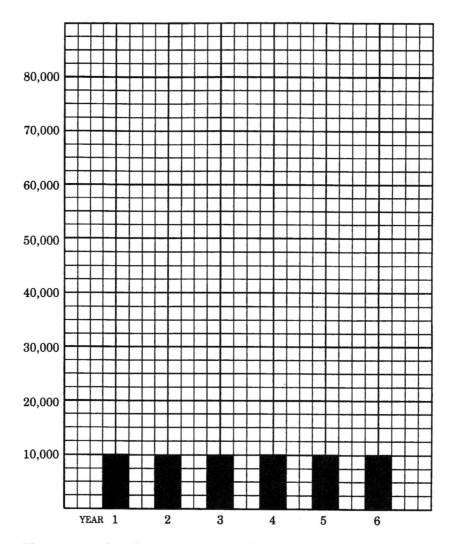

However, under the new rules, tendencies are irrelevant; either you fit the statute or you don't. Therefore, just looking at § 71(b), it would have been possible to have a series of payments which look like this:

Illustration 14

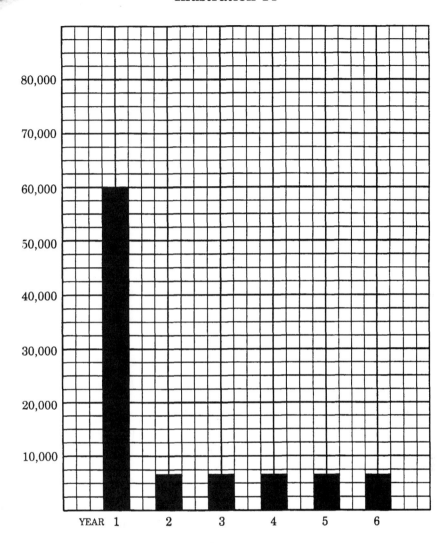

which would still be treated as alimony. Such a stream of payments is called "front-end loading."

"Front end loading" violates the Congressional scheme. It appears that you still obtain a deduction for alimony even though you've loaded a substantial lump sum payment on to the front end. However, Congress deals with the problem in § 71(f). Note as you read the statute that each general provision refers you down to a more specific one: you only need to recompute under § 71(f)(1) if there are "excess alimony payments." "Excess alimony payments" are defined in § 71(f)(2) as the sum of "excess alimony payments for the 1st post-separation year [defined in § 71(f)(3)]" and "excess alimony payments for the 2nd post-separation year" [defined in § 71(f)(4)]. You need to compute "excess alimony payments for the 2nd post-separation year" first. Can you explain why?

PROBLEMS

Analyze the following problems, and consider how well Congress addressed the situation:

1. Wife paid Husband the following amounts of alimony:

1st post-separation year:	$120,000
2nd post-separation year:	$100,000
3rd post-separation year:	$ 80,000

2. Wife paid Husband the following amounts of alimony:

1st post-separation year:	$ 80,000
2nd post-separation year:	$100,000
3rd post-separation year:	$120,000

3. Wife paid Husband $100,000 of alimony in post-separation year 1. She paid him 0 in post-separation year 2 because he died.

(d) Property Settlements and the Davis Case

Code: § 1041

Regulations: 1.1041–1T

Generally, the giving or receipt of a property settlement should not be a taxable event in and of itself. However, what if the assets transferred are not cash, and have a low basis? The Supreme Court, in United States v. Davis, 370 U.S. 65, 82 S.Ct. 1190, 8 L.Ed.2d 335 (1962) held that exchanging appreciated property for a release of marital rights is a realization event in a common law state. Congress, in part loath to create more tax differences between common law and community property states, enacted § 1041. This section effectively repealed *Davis*.

Section 1041 applies to transfers between spouses, and from a spouse to a former spouse if the transfer is incident to divorce. Generally, in such transfers:

(1) There will be no taxable event; and

(b) Transferee spouse acquires transferor spouse's basis.

You might remember § 1041 from the brief introduction in Chapter 3, *supra*.

PROBLEMS

What are the tax consequences to Husband and Wife in each of the following cases? In each case, assume that Husband resells the asset for its fair market value as soon as he receives it:

1. Wife purchases a painting for $25,000. When it is worth $100,000,

a) she transfers it to Husband as part of a divorce settlement.

b) she borrows $50,000, using the painting as collateral. She then transfers the painting, subject to the debt, to Husband, as part of the divorce settlement.

2. Wife purchases a painting for $100,000. When it is worth $25,000, she transfers it to Husband as part of a divorce settlement.

In both cases, consider whether wife would have been better off if she had sold the painting for cash and transferred the cash to Husband. Would it have mattered if she had acquired the painting as an investment?

(e) Child Support

Code: § 71(c)

Regulations: § 1.71–1T Questions 15–18

Divorce and separation effect certain changes which have significant financial consequences. Other things are left the same as they were. The tax laws which relate to divorce and separation ought to change the taxpayers' tax situation only when their financial situation changes, not when they remain the same.

What changes is the number of households. Divorce usually means maintaining two households instead of one. This change has significant financial consequences to both spouses, and it is the major justification for the tax-saving provisions of §§ 71 and 215.

What doesn't change is the obligation of child support. This obligation exists during the marriage; it remains after divorce. Since separation and divorce do not change this obligation, there should be no particular tax consequences to making child support payments. Such payments weren't deductible during the marriage; they shouldn't be deductible when the marriage has ended. Section 71(c) achieves this result.

Section 71(c)(1) speaks about that part of any payment which the terms of the instrument "fix" for child support. In Commissioner v. Lester, 366 U.S. 299, 81 S.Ct. 1343, 6 L.Ed.2d 306 (1961), a divorce instrument provided for a certain sum to transferee spouse. It then provided that, if any of the three children died, married, or became emancipated, the payment would be reduced by one sixth. Any fool could have seen that the parties intended that one sixth of the total payment would be for each child, so that one half of each payment was for the three children. However, the Supreme Court held that the instrument had not "fixed" the child support payments in specific terms. Therefore, all of the payments were includible in the income of the transferee spouse as alimony. Congress has changed the result of this case by enacting § 71(c)(2).

PROBLEMS

In each of the problems below, determine what amount, if any, is deductible to the payor spouse and includible in the income of the payee spouse.

1. Husband pays Wife $5,000 per month in alimony. Although the divorce decree is silent on how the alimony is to be used, Wife spends $1,500 per month of the alimony on child support.

2. Pursuant to the divorce decree, Husband pays Wife $3,500 per month in alimony and $1,500 per month in child support.

3. The divorce decree is the same as in Problem 2. This year, Husband did not make all of the required payments. His total payments to Wife were $30,000. See § 71(c)(3).

4. The divorce decree requires Husband to pay Wife $5,000 per month, until the couple's daughter reaches the age of eighteen. Then, the payments will be reduced to $3,500 per month. How are this year's payments of $5,000 per month treated?

(f) Breakups of Unmarried Couples

REYNOLDS v. COMMISSIONER

United States Tax Court, 1999.
T.C. Memo. 1999–62.

Laro, J.

* * * The principal issue we decide is whether payments received by petitioner under a settlement agreement are includable in her gross income. We hold they are not. * * *

Background

Petitioner and Gregg P. Kent (Mr. Kent) were involved in a close personal relationship from 1967 until 1991, and they cohabited as an unmarried couple during the last 24 years of the relationship. Mr. Kent told petitioner early in the relationship that she should not work and that he would provide for her financially. Petitioner generally was not employed during the relationship. She took care of the house and grounds in and on which she and Mr. Kent lived, and she took care of a boat that was acquired during their 25 years together. She also acted as hostess for their parties and as Mr. Kent's nurse when he was ill. Her relationship with Mr. Kent resembled that of a husband and wife, including, but not limited to, the sharing of affection and the presence of sexual relations.

Several items of real and personal property were purchased during their relationship. Each item was placed in the name of Mr. Kent or in the name of KENCOR, a California corporation in which Mr. Kent was the majority shareholder. The property included a house, an automobile, furniture, and boats. The house was purchased in 1980, and, following the purchase, Mr. Kent and petitioner lived there for the next 11 years.

Mr. Kent purchased clothing and jewelry for petitioner and gave her a weekly allowance. When Mr. Kent and petitioner traveled together, they would hold themselves out as husband and wife.

In July 1991, Mr. Kent moved out of the house and broke off the relationship. He asked petitioner to leave the house and return the vehicle she was driving (a 1987 Lincoln Town Car), which was in the name of KENCOR. Petitioner refused, and Mr. Kent and KENCOR (collectively, the plaintiffs) sued petitioner for ejectment, trespass, and conversion (the lawsuit). The plaintiffs prayed mainly for a judgment stating that petitioner had no interest in the property that was purchased during their relationship. Petitioner, in answering the plaintiffs' claim, asserted as a "First Affirmative Defense" that she had an equitable interest in the property. She stated in a "Declaration" filed in the lawsuit:

2. I met Mr. Gregg P. Kent in 1957. At that time each of us was married. * * *

3. In 1967, Mr. Kent and I had an affair that lasted for approximately a year. In 1968 Mr. Kent rented an apartment in Kent, Washington. He asked me to leave my husband and move in with him. At that time, we discussed getting married but, as I indicated, we were both already married. In connection with our discussions of marriage, Mr. Kent told me: "As my wife, Violet, you would not have to work. I am the provider, I do that job." He told me that my role in our relationship would be to provide for his needs, be the hostess and social director, and take care of the home. Relying on that agreement, I left my husband and moved into Mr. Kent's apartment in Kent, Washington with him some time in 1968. * * *

4. * * * In 1980, we purchased the property in which I presently reside * * *.

7. * * * At the time we purchased the home, he and I went looking for new homes. He told me that things were going well in the business, he wanted a new home for us and wanted me to pick out our home. He and I looked at a number of houses and selected our present home. At the time the residence was purchased, he told me it would be my home, and it was our home. * * *

11. * * * in approximately 1989, Mr. Kent acquired a new Mercedes for his personal use. At that time, he told me that he was giving me the 1987 Lincoln Town Car for my car and that car would be mine. * * *

12. From the time Mr. Kent and I moved in together to the present, he has provided for all of the needs of each of us in accordance with our prior agreement. Specifically, Mr. Kent provided everything that was needed by us to live. Mr. Kent, during the last several years, would give me between $500–$600 a week, which money was to be used by me for the normal household expenses, plus personal expenditures (hair, nails, etc.), except that approximately once a month we would go to the store together to buy major items for cleaning and household purposes. Usually at those times we would spend between $500–$600.

* * *

16. In 1987, when we purchased the present boat, Mr. Kent told me he wanted us to get a bigger and better boat so that we could do more entertaining on board. At the time the boat was purchased, Mr. Kent said that the boat was ours. On many occasions he referred to it as "our boat" which I took to mean that I had an equal interest in the boat. I believe the boat's purchase price was approximately $260,000.00. Since then Mr. Kent has spent at least another $100,000.00 in upgrades on it. He told me that the reason he paid so little for it was that he was able to buy it for us at cost.

17. In 1970 when we moved in together, Mr. Kent told me that his wife had asked him to leave and that he wanted to move ahead with his life and wanted me to be part of that life. Each of us was married at that time. He told me that he and his wife were discussing a divorce and that when his divorce situation was settled, we would then talk about getting married. Subsequently, my divorce became final in 1974 and Mr. Kent's divorce became final in 1978. At that time, we discussed getting married; however, Mr. Kent told me: "Why should you worry? Look at all the things we have acquired together. It isn't necessary to be married. Why should you worry? I will continue to take care of you just like I have taken care of you in the past." I relied upon those statements and never insisted on us getting married * * *.

* * *

21. I have seen financial statements prepared by Mr. Kent where he showed that he owned assets in excess of $18,000,000.00.

* * *

26. In 1968, Mr. Kent and I entered into an agreement whereby he was to be the provider and I was to take care of our nest. That agreement subsequently became more involved and included my taking care of him, the home, the interior of the boat, acting as a hostess for all parties and entertaining he wanted to do for personal and business reasons, doing laundry, housekeeping, ironing, cooking, shopping, supervising the service people who occassionally [sic] worked on the home and acting as nurse for Mr. Kent when he had health problems. In turn Mr. Kent agreed to provide for all of my living expenses * * *. For over 20 years we have lived according to our agreement. * * * Mr. Kent wants to throw me out with nothing to show for the many years we spent together.

In October 1991, the lawsuit was settled, Petitioner and Mr. Kent (both individually and on behalf of KENCOR) signed the Release and Settlement Agreement (settlement agreement). The settlement agreement provided in pertinent part:

WHEREAS, KENT in said case contends that REYNOLDS has no right, title, or interest, or legitimate claim in and to the real and personal property referred to therein, and further, KENT contends

REYNOLDS has no right, title, or legitimate claim to any real and personal property of KENT, whether alleged in the case or not, a further, that Kent is not liable or responsible for any sums whatsoe er; and

WHEREAS, REYNOLDS contends that she has a claim to said rea and personal property and to other property, both real and personal which may belong to or stand in the name of KENT; and

WHEREAS, each of the parties hereto disputes the other's contentions: and

WHEREAS, the parties, KENT and REYNOLDS desire to resolve their respective differences concerning their respective claims and to memorialize their agreement resolving those differences, and further, forever place the dispute behind them * * *

* * *

1. In consideration for the full and complete release by REYNOLDS of any claims of any nature, including but not limited to, any sums of money, and/or claims to any real and/or personal property of KENT, KENT agrees to pay REYNOLDS the following sums, on the following terms:

A. Cash in the sum of Fifty-seven Thousand Five Hundred Dollars ($57,500), payable after REYNOLDS has delivered all items she has removed from KENT, whether removed from the property * * * or any other items belonging to KENT whether removed from the Subject Property or any other location, and after KENT has verified all items have been returned to the Subject Property * * * and

B. The sum of Two Thousand Dollars ($2,000) per month for a period of three (3) years payable to the first day of each month commencing November 1, 1991; and

C. Thereafter, the sum of One Thousand Dollars ($1,000) per month for a period of two (2) years, payable on the first day of each month commencing November 1, 1994 to and including October 1, 1996.

2. In addition to said sums, KENT will transfer all right, title, and interest in and to the following personal property:

A. That certain 1987 Lincoln Town Car automobile * * *;

B. All clothing and jewelry in Reynolds' possession;

C. * * * miscellaneous household furniture and furnishings * * *.

In accordance with the payment plan set forth in the settlement agreement, petitioner received $22,000 in 1994. This amount was received from KENCOR, and KENCOR issued a Form 1099–MISC, Miscellaneous Income, to petitioner reporting the amount as miscellaneous income.

Petitioner did not perform services for KENCOR during that year, nor did she sell it any property during that year. Petitioner, allegedly relying on advice from her attorney and accountant, did not report this amount on her 1994 Federal income tax return.

Discussion

We must decide whether the $22,000 amount is includable in petitioner's 1994 gross income. Respondent argues it is. Petitioner argues it is not. Respondent contends that petitioner received the disputed amount as compensation for her homemaking services[c] Petitioner contends that she received the disputed amount as a gift.

We agree with petitioner that the $22,000 amount is not includable in her 1994 gross income, but we do so for a reason slightly different than she espouses. The taxability of proceeds recovered in settlement of a lawsuit rests upon the nature of the claim for which the proceeds were received and the actual basis of recovery. Ascertaining the nature of the claim is a factual determination that is generally made by reference to the settlement agreement in light of the facts and circumstances surrounding it. Key to this determination is the "intent of the payor" in making the payment. We must ask ourselves: "In lieu of what was the payment received?" See Robinson v. Commissioner. Although the payee's belief is relevant to this inquiry, the payment's ultimate character depends on the payor's dominant reason for making the payment.

The settlement agreement indicates that Mr. Kent paid the disputed amount to petitioner in surrender of her rights in most of the property purchased during their relationship. Respondent agrees with this characterization, but extrapolates therefrom that Mr. Kent paid petitioner the disputed amount to compensate her for past services that she rendered to him. We do not agree. Nothing in the record persuades us that petitioner ever sought in the lawsuit remuneration for services that she may have rendered to Mr. Kent during their relationship, let alone that Mr. Kent intended to compensate her for any such services by paying her the disputed amount. The written judgment sought by Mr. Kent and the settlement agreement both indicate that the only reason Mr. Kent commenced the lawsuit and paid the disputed amount to petitioner was to retain possession of most of the assets acquired during their relationship.

Although petitioner did refer in her Declaration to an agreement under which she would provide services to Mr. Kent in exchange for support, the facts of this case do not support an inference that she ever sought in the lawsuit to recover remuneration for these services, or, more importantly, that Mr. Kent paid her the disputed amount intending to compensate her for any services that she may have rendered to him. The payor's intent controls the characterization of settlement payments, and, as we have found, Mr. Kent intended to perfect his sole possession of most of their joint property when he paid petitioner the disputed amount. * * *

---

c.   In this regard, respondent states, petitioner's homemaking services do not include sex.

Our conclusion that Mr. Kent paid petitioner the disputed amount for her interest in the property does not end our inquiry. Petitioner's sale of her property interest to Mr. Kent is a taxable event for which she must recognize gain to the extent that the selling price exceeds her basis in the property. Sec. 1001(a). As to her basis, the record indicates that petitioner received her interest in the property by way of numerous gifts that Mr. Kent made to her throughout their relationship. Petitioner's declaration depicts a setting under which Mr. Kent repeatedly "gave" her property, and the facts of this case support the conclusion that he made these "gifts" with the "detached and disinterested generosity, * * * affection, respect, admiration, charity, or the like" required by Commissioner v. Duberstein. Given the fact that petitioner and Mr. Kent for a long period of time lived as husband and wife in most regards, but for the obvious fact that they were not legally married, we find it hard to believe that their relationship was actually akin to a business arrangement.

Our conclusion * * * is consistent with prior decisions * * *. [I]in Reis v. Commissioner, T.C. Memo. 1974–287, the taxpayer was a young female nightclub dancer who met an older man when he bought dinner and champagne for the performers in the show. The man paid each person at the table, other than the woman, $50 to leave the table so that he and she would be alone. The man gave the woman $1,200 for a mink stole and another $1,200 so that her sister could have an expensive coat too. Over the next 5 years, the woman saw the man "every Tuesday night at the [nightclub] and Wednesday afternoons from approximately 1:00 p.m. to 3:00 p.m. * * * at various places including * * * a girl friend's apartment and hotels where [he] was staying." He paid her living expenses, plus $200 a week, and he provided her with money for other things, such as investing, decorating her apartment, and buying a car. We held that none of the more than $100,000 that he gave her over the 5 years was taxable to her. We concluded that she received the money as a gift. We reached this conclusion notwithstanding the fact that the woman had stated that she "earned every penny" of the money.

Given our conclusion in this case that petitioner received her interest in the property as gifts from Mr. Kent, her basis in the property equals Mr. Kent's basis immediately before the gifts, to the extent that his basis is attributable to the gifted property. Sec. 1015(a). Although the record does not indicate with mathematical specificity the amount of Mr. Kent's basis that passed to petitioner as a result of the gifts, we are satisfied from the facts at hand that her basis equaled or exceeded the amount that she realized on the sale; i.e., $153,500. We conclude that petitioner had no gain to recognize upon receipt of the disputed payment.

* * *

Decision will be entered for petitioner.

QUESTION

How would the Reynolds have been treated on their breakup if they had been married? Is there any difference? Should there be?

(g) Innocent Spouse Rules

Code: § 6015

Assume that one spouse prepares the joint tax return, and the other spouse merely signs it, asking no questions. Under what circumstances should the "innocent" spouse be jointly and severally liable for any deficiencies in the return?

STEPHENSON v. COMMISSIONER

United States Tax Court.
T.C. Memo. 2011–16.

OPINION

VASQUEZ, JUDGE.

Pursuant to section 6015(e)(1), petitioner seeks review of respondent's determination that she is not entitled to relief from joint and several liability under section 6015(f) with respect to her Federal income tax liability for 1999.

FINDINGS OF FACT

I. *Petitioner's Relationship With Sean Stephenson*

Petitioner met Sean Stephenson (Mr. Stephenson) in 1990 when she was a freshman and he was a junior at the same high school in Phoenix. He proposed the following school year. They were married on May 12, 1991, shortly after Mr. Stephenson graduated from high school and enlisted in the U.S. Marine Corps (Marine Corps).

After the wedding Mr. Stephenson was stationed in Sacramento and petitioner remained in Phoenix to begin her junior year of high school. Three months into her junior year petitioner dropped out and moved to Sacramento to live with Mr. Stephenson. She never graduated from high school and has failed the General Education Development (GED) test three times.

During their time in Sacramento Mr. Stephenson began verbally abusing petitioner, often making fun of her lack of education and learning disabilities in front of Mr. Stephenson's family and their friends. In 1994 Mr. Stephenson completed his service in the Marine Corps, and they moved back to Phoenix. The verbal abuse turned into physical abuse, and Mr. Stephenson began throwing items at petitioner when he became angry.

* * *

II. *Mr. Stephenson's Financial Control and the 1999 Federal Income Tax Liability*

At all relevant times Mr. Stephenson managed the couple's finances. He did not allow petitioner access to the mail box or to a filing cabinet that contained the checkbook and financial documents, both of which required a key that only Mr. Stephenson possessed. When Mr. Stephenson needed petitioner to sign something, he placed it in front of her and told her where to sign. If petitioner asked what she was signing, Mr. Stephenson made threats of violence or told her she was not intelligent enough to understand.

Petitioner and Mr. Stephenson jointly filed Form 1040, U.S. Individual Income Tax Return, for 1999 (the return) showing $214,711 of taxable income and tax owed of $77,865. No payment was included with the return, and the return showed only a $915 withholding credit.

Beginning in August 2004 and continuing throughout 2006 petitioner and Mr. Stephenson made regular payments to the Internal Revenue Service (IRS), attempting to pay off the 1999 tax liability. At the direction of Mr. Stephenson petitioner wrote at least five of the checks.

Petitioner attempted to leave Mr. Stephenson in 2003. When she informed him of her decision he pushed her against a wall, grabbed his gun, pointed it at her head, and told her that he would kill her or himself if she left him. Petitioner became so frightened that she decided to remain in the relationship.

In 2005 petitioner met Mike Thomas (Mr. Thomas), a fire engineer with the City of San Diego Fire Department. Petitioner routinely walked her dog around the fire station, and one day she and Mr. Thomas began talking. Mr. Thomas immediately noticed bruises on petitioner's body. At some point within the first year of their friendship petitioner confided in Mr. Thomas that the bruises came from Mr. Stephenson and that she was in an abusive relationship.

IV. *Petitioner Files for Divorce*

On February 23, 2007, petitioner left Mr. Stephenson while he was in Flagstaff, Arizona. Mr. Thomas drove petitioner and whatever belongings she could grab to her mother's house in Phoenix. He also lent petitioner money since she had none.

When petitioner arrived in Phoenix, she contacted a divorce attorney but was told that she needed to reside in Arizona for 3 months before she could file for divorce. During the 3–month waiting period Mr. Stephenson appeared at petitioner's mother's house and an altercation ensued resulting in petitioner's obtaining an order of protection against Mr. Stephenson. In June 2007, with financial assistance from Mr. Thomas, petitioner hired an attorney to begin the divorce proceedings. The decree of dissolution of marriage (divorce decree) was finalized on June 5, 2008.

V. *Petitioner's Federal Income Tax Compliance and Request for Innocent Spouse Relief*

Petitioner lived in Phoenix from February 23 until December 7, 2007. In an attempt to take financial control of her life she timely filed her own Federal income tax return for 2006. * * *

In April 2007 petitioner called the IRS to ensure that her payment had been received. During the phone call petitioner became aware for the first time of the unpaid 1999 joint tax liability and her and Mr. Stephenson's failure to file a 2005 Federal income tax return. The IRS told petitioner about the possibility of innocent spouse relief for the 1999 tax liability and her opportunity to file a separate 2005 tax return since no previous joint return had been filed for that tax year. Petitioner filed her own 2005 tax return and requested information on innocent spouse relief. She has since timely filed her 2007, 2008, and 2009 Federal income tax returns and received refunds for 2008 and 2009.

On January 11, 2008, petitioner filed Form 8857, Request for Innocent Spouse Relief, requesting relief from joint and several liability for the 1999 and 2004 tax years. Respondent preliminarily denied petitioner's request for relief for 1999 because it was untimely. Petitioner appealed, and respondent's Appeals Office also denied petitioner's request because it was untimely.

* * *

VI. *Current Situation*

Petitioner lives in a bedroom in Mr. Thomas' basement in San Diego. She is unemployed and unable to pay the rent.

Since returning to San Diego petitioner has held four jobs and quit three of them. She is not eligible to receive unemployment benefits because she quit her most recent job, and she has not received the $500 per month of spousal maintenance that she is entitled to since August 2008.

* * *

OPINION

In general, a spouse who files a joint Federal income tax return is jointly and severally liable for the entire tax liability. Sec. 6013(d)(3). However, a spouse may be relieved from joint and several liability under section 6015(f) if: (1) Taking into account all the facts and circumstances, it would be inequitable to hold her liable for any unpaid tax; and (2) relief is not available to the spouse under section 6015(b) or (c). The Commissioner has published revenue procedures listing the factors the Commissioner normally considers in determining whether section 6015(f) relief should be granted. See Rev. Proc.2003–61, 2003–2 C.B. 296.

Threshhold Conditions for Granting Relief

In order for the Commissioner to determine that a taxpayer is eligible for section 6015(f) relief, the requesting spouse must satisfy the following threshold conditions: (1) She filed a joint return for the taxable year for which she seeks relief; (2) relief is not available to her under section 6015(b) or (c); (3) no assets were transferred between the spouses as part of a fraudulent scheme by the spouses; (4) the nonrequesting spouse did not transfer disqualified assets to her; (5) she did not file or fail to file the returns with fraudulent intent; and (6) with enumerated exceptions, the income tax liability from which she seeks relief is attributable to an item of the nonrequesting spouse.

Respondent concedes that conditions (1), (2), (3), (4), and (5) are met. As to condition (6), we presume on the basis of petitioner's testimony that a small portion of the tax liability is attributable to income she earned. We find, however, that the abuse exception in Rev. Proc.2003–61, sec. 4.01(7)(d), applies. Mr. Stephenson abused petitioner throughout their marriage, and she did not question or disobey him for fear of abuse. If we find that petitioner is entitled to relief on the basis of these circumstances, it would be inequitable to hold her liable for the amount of the tax liability attributable to the income she earned.

Accordingly, we find that petitioner has met the threshold criteria for relief as to the entire tax liability.

B. *Circumstances Under Which Relief Is Ordinarily Granted*

When the threshold conditions have been met, the Commissioner will ordinarily grant relief from an underpayment of tax if the requesting spouse meets the requirements set forth under Rev. Proc.2003–61, sec. 4.02, 2003–2 C.B. at 298: (1) On the date of the request for relief the requesting spouse is no longer married to, or is legally separated from, the nonrequesting spouse, or has not been a member of the same household as the nonrequesting spouse at any time during the 12–month period ending on the date of the request for relief; (2) on the date the requesting spouse signed the return she had no knowledge or reason to know that the nonrequesting spouse would not pay the income tax liability; and (3) the requesting spouse will suffer economic hardship if relief is not granted.

When petitioner filed her request for relief on January 11, 2008, she was still married to Mr. Stephenson; and they were not legally separated although she had moved out in February 2007. Additionally, since petitioner and Mr. Stephenson were members of the same household until February 2007, they were members of the same household during the 12–month period preceding the date she filed for relief. Thus, petitioner is not entitled to relief under the criteria set forth in Rev. Proc.2003–61, sec. 4.02.

C. *Factors Used To Determine Whether Relief Will Be Granted*

Where a requesting spouse meets the threshold conditions but fails to qualify for relief under Rev. Proc.2003–61, sec. 4.02, a determination to grant relief may nevertheless be made under the criteria set forth in Rev. Proc.2003–61: (1) Whether the requesting spouse is separated or divorced from the nonrequesting spouse (marital status factor); (2) whether the requesting spouse would suffer economic hardship if not granted relief (economic hardship factor); (3) whether, at the time she signed the joint return, the requesting spouse knew or had reason to know that the nonrequesting spouse would not pay the income tax liability (knowledge factor); (4) whether the nonrequesting spouse has a legal obligation to pay the outstanding tax liability pursuant to a divorce decree or agreement (legal obligation factor); (5) whether the requesting spouse received a significant benefit from the unpaid income tax liability (significant benefit factor); and (6) whether the requesting spouse has made a good faith effort to comply with tax laws for the taxable years following the taxable year to which the request for such relief relates (compliance factor).

The Commissioner may consider two other factors that, if present in a case, will weigh in favor of granting relief: (1) Whether the nonrequesting spouse abused the requesting spouse (abuse factor); and (2) whether the requesting spouse was in poor mental or physical health at the time she signed the return or at the time she requested relief (mental or physical health factor). The absence of either factor will not weigh against granting relief.

* * *

1. *Marital Status*

* * * Accordingly, this factor weighs in favor of granting relief.

2. *Economic Hardship*

A requesting spouse suffers economic hardship if paying the tax liability would prevent her from paying her reasonable basic living expenses. Respondent contends that petitioner failed to show that she would suffer economic hardship if not granted relief. We disagree.

Petitioner currently cannot afford to pay her basic living expenses. She is unemployed and not receiving the $500 per month of spousal maintenance that she is entitled to. Her only asset is her car, which she is currently paying off with money borrowed from Mr. Thomas, and she owes money to her divorce attorney and Mr. Thomas.

Respondent argues that we should not consider petitioner's current employment status in making our determination. He reasons that petitioner's unemployment is of her own volition and that her past job experience shows that she can find work if necessary. While we understand respondent's position, we believe that requiring petitioner, who has no assets and whose most recent job paid her $10 per hour, to pay a tax liability of more than $66,000 would cause her economic hardship.

Accordingly, the economic hardship factor weighs in favor of granting relief.

3. *Knowledge*

A third factor is whether the requesting spouse knew or had reason to know that the nonrequesting spouse would not pay the tax liability. In making the determination whether the requesting spouse had reason to know, consideration is given to, among other things: (1) The requesting spouse's level of education; (2) the requesting spouse's degree of involvement in the activity generating the income tax liability; (3) the requesting spouse's involvement in business and household financial matters; (4) the requesting spouse's business or financial expertise; and (5) any lavish or unusual expenditures compared with past spending levels. Rev. Proc. 2003–61, sec. 4.03(2)(a)(iii)(C), 2003–2 C.B. at 298. The presence of abuse by the nonrequesting spouse may mitigate the requesting spouse's knowledge or reason to know that the nonrequesting spouse would not pay the tax liability. *Id.* sec. 4.03(2)(b)(i), 2003–2 C.B. at 299.

We believe that petitioner did not know or have reason to know that Mr. Stephenson would not pay the tax liability. Mr. Stephenson controlled the couple's finances, and petitioner was not allowed access to any financial documents. Mr. Stephenson did not discuss with petitioner the filing of the return or payment of the tax owed. Finally, Mr. Stephenson earned a substantial income in 1999 from which he had adequate funds to pay the tax owed.

Additionally, the factors stated in Rev. Proc.2003–61, sec. 4.03(2)(a)(iii)(C), favor granting relief: (1) Petitioner never graduated from high school and failed the GED test three times; (2) her involvement in the activities generating the income tax liability was extremely limited; (3) she had no involvement in business and household financial matters and limited business or financial expertise; and (4) any expenditures were commensurate with Mr. Stephenson's income.

* * *

We also note that requiring petitioner to inquire into whether Mr. Stephenson reported on the return the income she earned could have put her at risk of abuse. Petitioner's efforts to become more informed of what she was signing and questions about their finances in general resulted in threats of violence or verbal abuse from Mr. Stephenson.

Accordingly, we hold that at the time petitioner signed the joint return she had no knowledge or reason to know that Mr. Stephenson would not pay the tax liability, and the knowledge factor weighs in favor of granting relief.

4. *Legal Obligation*

* * *

Accordingly, we hold that the legal obligation factor weighs in favor of granting relief.

5. *Significant Benefit*

A fifth factor is whether the requesting spouse received a significant benefit (beyond normal support) from the unpaid tax liability. "Normal" support is measured by the parties' circumstances.

Respondent contends that petitioner significantly benefited from the unpaid tax liability in the form of the car she drove and the highrise buildings and their amenities that she took advantage of. In determining whether this constitutes significant benefit (beyond normal support) we must consider that petitioner and Mr. Stephenson had net income of almost $150,000 in 1999 and Mr. Stephenson continued to be successful for a number of years.

Mr. Stephenson purchased the BMW that petitioner drove at the height of his success. We do not believe that Mr. Stephenson's purchase of the BMW and petitioner's driving of it to and from work is a benefit to petitioner that goes beyond normal support for a couple in their financial situation. Moreover, the car was not a gift to petitioner or purchased in her name.

We also do not believe that petitioner's highrise living in Dallas and San Diego amounts to a significant benefit from the unpaid tax liability. Mr. Stephenson was successful, and renting condominiums for himself and petitioner to live in does not provide petitioner with a benefit beyond normal support. The fact that the condominiums had a gym and/or swimming pool that petitioner took advantage of does not change this result.

Accordingly, the significant benefit factor weighs in favor of granting relief.

6. *Compliance*

* * * Accordingly, the compliance factor weighs in favor of granting relief.

7. *Abuse*

Abuse by the nonrequesting spouse favors relief. Rev. Proc.2003–61, sec. 4.03(2)(b)(i). Abuse need not be physical. The Court has found that mental, emotional, and verbal abuse may incapacitate a requesting spouse in the same way as physical abuse. Claims of abuse require substantiation or specificity in allegations.

Mr. Stephenson abused petitioner throughout their marriage. During trial petitioner provided specific examples of abuse, including a time when Mr. Stephenson threatened to kill her or himself if she left him and times when Mr. Stephenson threw items at her. Mr. Stephenson regularly humiliated petitioner in front of his family and their friends and demeaned her when she asked questions. Mr. Thomas corroborated some of petitioner's testimony by credibly testifying that petitioner had bruises on her body and told him that she was in an abusive relationship.

Respondent argues that petitioner's testimony is not credible because she did not document any of the abuse. We find that petitioner credibly testified to specific allegations of abuse that took place before she moved to San Diego and believe that Mr. Thomas' testimony substantiates petitioner's allegations of abuse that took place while she was living in San Diego. Accordingly, the abuse factor weighs in favor of granting relief.

8. *Mental or Physical Health*

There is no evidence that petitioner was in poor mental or physical health at any relevant time. Thus, this factor is neutral.

D. *Conclusion*

In summary, seven factors favor relief and one factor is neutral. After weighing the testimony and evidence in this fact-intensive case, we conclude that it is inequitable to hold petitioner liable for the 1999 joint tax liability. Accordingly, we relieve petitioner from joint tax liability for tax year 1999.

CHAPTER X

PERSONAL DEDUCTIONS AND CREDITS

∎ ∎ ∎

We have already explored, *supra* at 142, why business expenses are generally deductible and personal expenses are not. Why, then, are any personal expenses deductible? In a theoretically pure income tax, perhaps they would not be. Suffice it to say that they are suspect. Whenever you see a deductible personal expense, you should be looking for a reason as to why that particular one is justified.

Three types of justification come to mind. The first is structural concerns. Sometimes, personal deductions and credits are used as a way of adjusting the tax rates. Notably, the personal and dependency exemptions, the standard deduction, and the earned income tax credit function, among other things, to ensure that those who are too poor to pay taxes don't pay any.

The second is ability to pay. Remember, income is but an imperfect measure of ability to pay. Extraordinary events can make some taxpayers far less able to pay taxes than other taxpayers with comparable incomes. Fairness requires that the tax bill be adjusted in such cases. These concerns underlie the medical expense and casualty loss deductions.

The third is social engineering. We are strongly tempted to use the tax laws to encourage certain types of behavior and discourage others. That temptation has not always been resisted. The deduction for charitable contributions might be seen in this light.

A. STRUCTURAL CONCERNS

1. THE POVERTY LINE

Code: §§ 63(c)(2), 151, 152

Virtually everyone would agree that one should not pay income tax unless one already has sufficient income to provide for minimum food, clothing, and shelter for one's self and one's dependents.[a] It would follow

---

[a]. For arguments contra, see Pollock v. Farmers' Loan & Trust Company, 157 U.S. 429, 596–97, 15 S.Ct. 673, 695–696, 39 L.Ed. 759 (1894) (Field, J., concurring), arguing that everyone, no matter how poor, should pay some tax as a means of participating in government. *See also,*

that a taxpayer whose income falls below the poverty line should owe no federal income tax. This result is achieved most of the time, through a combination of factors. First, each taxpayer receives a personal exemption for herself, and one for each dependent. This exemption was $600 in 1948. It was $3,650 in Tax Year 2010. It is indexed for inflation, but, in truth, it has not kept up. To be equivalent to the $600 exemption in 1948, the exemption would have had to be $7,000 in 1991, and over $9,000 in 1996.[b]

In addition, there is the standard deduction, described in § 63(b)(2) and discussed *infra*, which, in 2010, was $11,400 for married couples filing jointly and $5,700 for singles and married filing separately. To determine whether those below the poverty line truly pay no taxes, however, one must consider three additional factors. First, there is the Earned Income Tax Credit, described *infra*. Second, there is the Social Security tax, which kicks in at the first dollar of income. Third, there is the Child Tax Credit.

As you can see in the Table below, sometimes the poverty levels and the tax thresholds match up; sometimes they don't.

TABLE 5. POVERTY LEVELS AND NET FEDERAL TAX THRESHOLDS IN 2010, FOR SELECTED HOUSEHOLDS

		Unmarried Individual	Single parent with one child	Married couple with two children	Married couple with three children
1	*Poverty levels*	$10,830	$14,570	$22,050	$25,790
2	*Single income tax threshold (before credits)*	$9,350	$15,700	$26,000	$29, 650
3	*Income tax threshold after the earned income, making work pay, and child tax credits*	$13,395	$32,380	$50,250	$60,567
4	*Employee Social Security and Medicare payroll tax threshold*	$0	$0	$0	$0
5	*Combined income and payroll tax threshold (i.e., net federal tax threshold*	$9,348	$25,717	$38,638	$43,788

From Jonathan Barry Forman, *Using Refundable Tax Credits to Help Low–Income Taxpayers: What Do We Know, and What Can We Learn From Other Countries?* 8(2) eJournal of Tax Research 128–61, Table 5 (December 2010). Reprinted with permission.

2. THE EARNED INCOME TAX CREDIT

Code: § 32

As suggested in the table above, the Earned Income Tax Credit (EITC) has a significant effect on the tax liability of low-income taxpayers. Therefore, it must be considered when determining how well we do at keeping those with incomes below the poverty line off the tax rolls.

The EITC is a refundable credit for low-income taxpayers who have earned income. It has been amended often, and, despite recent efforts to

---

Report on Japanese Taxation Submitted to the Supreme Commander for the Allied Powers 52 (1949).

b. *Reclaiming the Tax Code for American Families: Hearing Before the House Select Committee for Children, Youth and Families,* 102nd Cong., 1st Sess. 3 (1991) (statement of Rep. Patricia Schroeder); Jonathan Barry Forman, *Simplification for Low–Income Taxpayers: Some Options,* 57 Ohio St. L. J. 145, 174 (1996).

simplify it, it remains quite complex. Grounded as much in welfare policy as in tax policy, it has been associated with the following policy goals relating particularly to low income workers:

(1) offset Social Security taxes,

(2) provide income security,

(3) provide a work incentive for welfare families,

(4) subsidize special needs of children, and

(5) offset the regressive effects of other income tax proposals.

Example

Taxpayer earned wages of $15,000 in 2008. He has no other income that year. He has a six-year-old son who lives with him.

The son is a "qualifying child" according to §§ 32(c)(3) and 152(c). Since the taxpayer has a qualifying child, taxpayer is an "eligible individual" pursuant to § 32(c)(1). Therefore, he is eligible for the EITC.

Pursuant to § 32(a)(1), taxpayer is allowed a credit "equal to the credit percentage of so much of the taxpayer's earned income for the taxable year as does not exceed the earned income amount." For a taxpayer with one qualifying child, the credit percentage is 34% [§ 32(b)(1)(A)], and the "earned income amount" is $6,330 [§ 32(b)(2)(A)]. Accordingly, § 32(a)(1) allows the taxpayer a credit of:

earned income amount	$6,330
× credit percentage	× 34%
credit	$2,152.20

However, the allowable credit is limited by § 32(a)(2), which provides that the credit computed above shall not exceed the excess of:

(A) the credit percentage of the earned income amount, over

(B) the phaseout percentage of so much of the adjusted gross income (or, if greater, the earned income) of the taxpayer for the taxable year as exceeds the phaseout amount.

For a taxpayer with one child, the "phaseout percentage" is 15.98% [§ 32(b)(1)(A)], and the "phaseout amount" is $11,610 [§ 32(b)(2)(A)]. The "credit percentage of the earned income amount" as described in § 32(a)(2)(A) was already computed above for purposes of § 32(a)(1). We know that it is $2,152.20. Therefore:

credit percentage of earned income amount	$2,152.20
− the phaseout percentage of so much of the adjusted gross income . . . as exceeds the phaseout amount	− [($15,000 − $11,610) × 15.98% = $541.72]
Limitation	$1,610.48

Taxpayer's earned income credit shall not exceed $1,610.48. Therefore, the EITC will in fact be $1,610.48.

Note that the EITC is designed to give a tax break to certain types of people, with certain types of income, which income must be in certain low ranges. The types of people are targeted by the definitions of "eligible individual" and "qualifying child." The types of income are defined as "earned income." Finally, the desired low ranges of income are achieved by stating the "earned income amount" for the various categories, and the phaseout provisions.

If you think they didn't get it quite right, stay tuned. They'll probably change it again.

3. THE STANDARD DEDUCTION AND ADJUSTED GROSS INCOME

(a) Adjusted Gross Income

Code: § 62(a)

In terms of structural concerns and, specifically, wiping the lowest income taxpayers off the tax rolls, it is the standard deduction which does the significant work. However, to understand how the standard deduction functions, one must first understand adjusted gross income.

Adjusted gross income ("AGI") is defined at § 62. It is gross income minus the deductions listed in § 62. Therefore, as will be further explained in § 63, the ultimate computation looks like this:

Gross Income
− deductions listed in § 62
= AGI
− other deductions
= Taxable Income

In the above computation, think of AGI as "the line." In common tax parlance, the deductions listed in § 62 are "above the line." The "other" deductions are "below the line." Those "other deductions," except for the deductions for personal exemptions provided by § 151, are called the "itemized deductions." See § 63(d).

The "above the line" deductions listed in § 62 are essentially business deductions. Given the basic structure of our net income tax, it makes sense that the above the line, business deductions are treated somewhat better, while the below the line, itemized deductions are treated somewhat worse. The materials on the standard deduction below will confirm this discrimination in treatment.

However, it is too simplistic to say that the above the line deductions are business, while the itemized deductions are personal. The above the line deductions have a stronger business flavor, but they also include those deductions which Congress, for any number of reasons, wants to treat better. Read § 62 carefully to see the kinds of decisions Congress has made.

AGI as a Floor

AGI functions as a floor on other deductions. See § 165(h)(2), which places a 10% of AGI threshold under net personal casualty losses. In addition, medical expenses are deductible only to the extent that they exceed 7.5% of AGI. See § 213(a). Imagine two taxpayers, Sick and Sicker, both with gross income of $100,000. Sick has $90,000 in above-the line deductions, hence AGI of $10,000. Sicker has no above-the-line deductions, hence AGI of $100,000.

Sick can deduct medical expenses when they exceed 7.5% of $10,000, or $750. Sicker has to wait until his medical expenses exceed 7.5% of $100,000, or $7,500, before he can deduct any.

Another instance in which a percentage of AGI is used as a floor on other deductions is § 67, which places a 2% of AGI threshold under "miscellaneous itemized deductions," as defined in § 67(b). Section 67 has had a particularly devastating effect upon the trade or business expenses of employees. Such deductions, such as unreimbursed employee travel expenses, are excluded from the above the line category by the last clause of § 62(a)(1). Therefore, they are "itemized deductions," within the definition of § 63(d). Since they do not appear on the list set forth in § 67(b)(1) through (12), they are "miscellaneous itemized deductions," subject to the 2% floor.

However, the 2% floor can often be avoided. Suppose that employer and employee agree to recharacterize certain salary payments as travel expense reimbursements. If the reimbursements are paid pursuant to an "accountable plan," as described in Reg. § 1.62–2(c), then the reimbursements will not be included in the employee's gross income at all.[c]

ILLUSTRATIVE PROBLEM

Law school runs a summer program in Athens. Each year, they send two of their law professors to run it. This year, they send professors Tort and Tax. Each negotiates her own deal. Professor Tort negotiates a salary of $5,000, plus airfare. Out of the $5,000, she pays her meal and lodging expenses in Greece. Her meals and lodging cost her $1,000.

Professor Tax negotiates a salary of $4,000, plus airfare, plus $1,000 for meals and lodging while in Greece. It is understood that Professor Tax will only receive the $1,000 if she presents the university with receipts evidencing payment of at least US$1,000 in legitimate meals and lodging expenses while

---

c. Note that reimbursed expenses of employees are above the line deductions pursuant to § 62(a)(2)(A). Therefore, the employee travel expense deductions and the reimbursements effectively cancel out each other.

teaching on the university's behalf in Greece. Professor Tax duly tenders the receipts, and is reimbursed $1,000 on her return from Greece.

Who got the better deal? You might also want to consider the impact of § 274, especially subsections (n) and (e)(3).

AGI as a Ceiling

AGI can also be a ceiling. Charitable contributions are deductible only up to 50% of one's "contribution base." "Contribution base," it turns out, is AGI with one minor adjustment [§ 170(b)(1)(F)].

Example

Well Off has a contribution base of $100,000. Filthy Rich has a contribution base of $1,000,000. Well Off can deduct charitable contributions up to $50,000; Filthy Rich can deduct contributions up to $500,000.

(b) The Standard Deduction

Code: § 63(c)(2)

Consider § 63. You will note that you can compute taxable income in one of two ways—under § 63(a), or under § 63(b).

§ 63(a)	§ 63(b)
Gross Income	Adjusted Gross Income
− deductions allowed by this chapter (other than the standard deduction)	− standard deduction
	− deduction for personal exemptions
= Taxable Income	= Taxable Income

However, the two computations are not as different as they might appear at first. Section 63(a) starts with "gross income," while § 63(b) starts with "adjusted gross income." But you know that "adjusted gross income" is gross income minus the deductions listed in § 62. Are the deductions listed in § 62 subtracted from gross income in the § 63(a) computation? They are. Note that § 63 is part of Chapter 1 of the Code— which comprises §§ 1 through 1401. Therefore, when § 63(a) subtracts "the deductions allowed by this chapter," it is deducting all of the deductions you know about. Those deductions include the deductions listed in § 62.

But that's not all. When § 63(a) subtracts "the deductions allowed by this chapter," it is subtracting the deductions listed in § 62 (the "above the line" deductions), the deductions for personal exemptions provided in § 151, and all the other deductions (the "below the line" or "itemized" deductions).

Therefore, the two alternative computations can be restated, with a view to seeing what the real differences are:

§ 63(a) computation	§ 63(b) computation
Gross Income	Gross Income
− above the line deductions	− above the line deductions
= Adjusted Gross Income	= Adjusted Gross Income
− deductions for personal exemptions	− deductions for personal exemptions
− itemized deductions	− standard deduction
= Taxable Income	= Taxable Income

Stated this way, you can see that the only difference between §§ 63(a) and 63(b) is that in (a) you subtract the itemized deductions, while in (b) you subtract the standard deduction.

Why do we have the standard deduction? Because "itemizing" requires taxpayers to keep records of personal expenses. Most taxpayers hate to keep records. So the government gives them a choice. In effect, if a taxpayer does not want to keep the records necessary to support the itemized deductions (including records of medical expenses, charitable contributions, and the like), they don't have to. Instead, they can simply accept the government's guess as to how much their itemized deductions would have been. The standard deduction, then, is the government's guess as to how much the average person's itemized deductions would have been, had she kept the records.

The standard deduction actually does two good things for taxpayers. First, it alleviates the recordkeeping burden. Second, for many of us, it is generous. More likely than not, the standard deduction is larger than the actual itemized deductions that many taxpayers would otherwise have taken. In addition to these two good things, of course, it also plays a major role in keeping really low-income taxpayers off the tax rolls. The combination of the standard deduction and the personal and dependency exemptions are the most significant factors in keeping such taxpayers off the tax rolls, and avoiding unnecessary returns.

Of course, the standard deduction is not for everyone. For those whose itemized deductions would be greater than the standard deduction amount, the recordkeeping may well be worth the bother.

When should you itemize? When your itemized deductions exceed the standard deduction for your category. Generally, homeowners itemize; renters do not. It's the mortgage interest and real estate taxes that make the difference.

The nature of itemized deductions and the standard deduction are what affords better treatment to above the line deductions than below the line deductions.

Example

It's 2010. John and Jerry, both married, filing joint returns, are considering giving another $50 to charity. They'll do it if there's a tax break. John, a homeowner, itemizes. His itemized deductions are already well over the $11,400 standard deduction. Another $50 in charitable donations will be subtracted from his income, and lower his taxes. He makes the donation.

Jerry, an apartment renter, has expenses in the itemized deduction category of $3,000—well under the $11,400 standard deduction. If he contributed another $50 to charity, his itemized deductions would still be well under $9,700. Therefore, he'd still take the standard deduction, and the extra donation would have no effect on his tax bill. No donation.

4. DEPENDENCY EXEMPTIONS

Code: §§ 151, 152

Suppose that you, a single taxpayer, decide to share your household and your income with someone else, a "dependent" who does not work outside the home. Surely, this decision of yours will cost you, and will leave you with less ability to pay taxes than you had before. But isn't this the ultimate personal choice? Why should this lifestyle choice allow you to pay less taxes than your more hermit-like friends?

Part of the answer is that, if your income is low and you are not given a tax break, then your after-tax income may not be sufficient to provide minimum food, clothing and shelter for yourself and your dependents. This concern, however, should disappear as your income rises.

But what is a dependent anyway?

PROBLEMS, NOTES

1. Taxpayer and his spouse and two minor children live in a house. They file a joint return. How many personal and dependency exemptions?

2. Taxpayer's 23–year–old son lives at home and goes to law school. Does Taxpayer get an exemption for Son as a dependent?

3. Can taxpayer's brother be his dependent? What if his brother is a citizen and resident of Mexico? What about his sister-in-law?

4. Taxpayer's minor child was kidnapped in March. Needless to say, Taxpayer has no idea where the child has lived since March, nor who was paying for the child's support. Of course, Taxpayer has incurred considerable expense in trying to find him. May Taxpayer claim a dependency exemption? *See* § 152(f)(6).

5. H.R. 3441, introduced in July of 2005, would have extended the definition of "qualifying child" to cover a child born within nine months after the close of the taxable year. Good idea?

6. For the relation of the dependency exemption to the alternative minimum tax, *see infra* at 654.

7. In the first year after IRS required children's social security numbers before a dependency exemption could be taken, the number of children claimed went down by 7 million. Mass infanticide?

5. THE CHILD TAX CREDIT

Code: § 24

Section 24 creates a child tax credit of $1,000 per child. The credit is available for each qualifying child [within the meaning of § 152(c)] of the taxpayer under the age of 17.

The tax credit is phased out for upper-income taxpayers. The phase-out begins at $110,000 of "modified adjusted gross income"[d] for married taxpayers filing joint returns, and $75,000 for unmarried taxpayers. For incomes above those thresholds, the credit per child is reduced by $50 for each $1,000 (or fraction thereof) of the excess over the threshold. For example, in the case of a married taxpayer filing a joint return, if modified adjusted gross income is $111,000, the tax credit per child would be $950. For such a taxpayer, the credit phases out completely at modified adjusted gross incomes of $130,000 and above [§ 24(b)].

The credit is designed to be refundable in certain narrow circumstances, for families with three or more children, and to offset social security taxes as well as income taxes. See § 24(d). Good luck.

QUESTIONS

1. Why a credit and not a deduction? Consider the interaction of the credit with the dependency exemption.

2. Why stop at age 17?

3. Why phase out at high incomes? Don't rich people spend money on their children as well?

B. CHARITY

Code: § 170

Regulations: §§ 1.170A–1, A–4

Of course charitable contributions should be encouraged. And why not use the tax laws to do so?

There is, however, a more pragmatic reason to encourage some charitable contributions. They save the government money. Many of the things charities do would have to be done by government if the charities didn't exist. Therefore, perhaps it makes sense for the government to be indifferent as between a dollar in tax revenue and a dollar in charitable contributions.

You might also want to consider the charitable deduction as a sort of escape valve. Say a taxpayer disapproves of the way the government is

---

d. "Modified adjusted gross income" is adjusted gross income increased by the amount excluded from gross income by §§ 911, 931, and 933. [§ 24(b)(1)].

spending its money. Given that feeling, the taxpayer would be even less enthusiastic than usual about paying taxes. Such a lack of enthusiasm, sometimes termed "taxpayer morale," could be devastating in a system which relies as heavily as ours does on voluntary compliance by the taxpayer.

In this light, the charitable deduction lowers the stakes, and, hopefully, the anger. The disaffected taxpayer can lower her taxes by paying those dollars to a charity of her choice instead. Of course, as you will see later, there are limits on the extent to which taxpayers can substitute charitable contributions for tax payments.

Given the existence of a deduction for charitable contributions, one needs to know:

(1) What is a contribution?

(2) To whom may I contribute? and

(3) How much of a deduction will I get?

These basic questions are addressed in parts 1, 2 and 3 of this topic.

All entities to which charitable contributions are deductible are themselves largely exempt from income taxes. However, not all tax-exempt entities can receive deductible charitable contributions. Part 4 of this topic addresses the general question of tax-exempt entities, and the specific area of the unrelated business income tax. Part 5 addresses substantiation, valuation, and ethics. The topic is concluded with a policy analysis of the charitable contribution deduction in tax expenditure terms.

1. WHAT IS A CONTRIBUTION?

The definition of "contribution" for purposes of § 170 has much in common with the definition of "gift" for purposes of § 102. In both cases, there must be no quid pro quo. If you get something back, then what you give is something less than a total contribution.

In most cases, this concept is not difficult to apply. If you pay tuition to a private college, the tuition is not a charitable contribution. The private college may well be a qualified charitable donee, but you are presumed to get your money's worth in educational services in return for your tuition payments. If you attend a benefit concert, you get a charitable contribution deduction only for the amount by which what you paid exceeds the fair market value of the tickets you received. Moreover, for contributions of $250 or more, the charitable donee is required to give you a good faith estimate of the value of what you received back. See § 170(f)(8).

(a) Athletic Booster Clubs

Sometimes, it is impossible to get tickets to certain major college sports events unless:

1) Someone wills them to you;

2) You take your chances with a scalper; or

3) You join the school's athletic booster club and make a significant payment of dues.

What are these membership dues? Are they charitable contributions, or are they a back door way of purchasing hard-to-get tickets to athletic events? Should the answer depend upon the university, or should it be the same across the board?

For an early, sneaky approach, consider § 1608 of the Tax Reform Act of 1986, below:

TREATMENT OF CERTAIN AMOUNTS PAID TO OR FOR THE BENEFIT OF CERTAIN INSTITUTIONS OF HIGHER EDUCATION.

(a) IN GENERAL.—Amounts paid by a taxpayer to or for the benefit of an institution of higher education described in paragraph (1) or (2) of subsection (b) (other than amounts separately paid for tickets) which would otherwise qualify as a charitable contribution within the meaning of section 170 of the Internal Revenue Code of 1986 shall not be disqualified because such taxpayer receives the right to seating or the right to purchase seating in an athletic stadium of such institution.

(b) DESCRIBED INSTITUTIONS.—

(1) An institution is described in this paragraph, if—

    (A) such institution was mandated by a State constitution in 1876,

    (B) such institution was established by a State legislature in March 1881, and is located in a State capital pursuant to a statewide election in September 1981,

    (C) the campus of such institution formally opened on September 15, 1883, and

    (D) such institution is operated under the authority of a 9–member board of regents appointed by the governor.

(2) An institution is described in this paragraph if such institution has an athletic stadium—

    (A) the plans for renovation of which were approved by a board of supervisors in December 1984, and reaffirmed by such board in December 1985 and January 1986, and

    (B) the plans for renovation of which were approved by a State board of ethics for public employees in February 1986.

(c) EFFECTIVE DATE.—The provisions of this section shall apply to amounts paid in taxable years beginning on or after January 1, 1984.

It just so happens that the University of Texas and Louisiana State University, respectively, fit the descriptions found in §§ (b)(1) and (2) of the statute. It appears unlikely that any other institutions would qualify.

For a somewhat broader approach to the problem, consider Revenue Ruling 86–63, set forth below. This Revenue Ruling was superseded by current § 170(*l*), which takes a markedly different tack. Read the Revenue Ruling, and then read current § 170(*l*). Which approach do you like better?

REV. RUL. 86–63

1986–1 C.B. 88.

* * *

Issue

Whether payments to athletic scholarship programs are charitable contributions under section 170 of the Internal Revenue Code in situations where the payments afford the right to purchase preferred seating at football games.

Facts

Situation 1. Taxpayer A, an individual, made a payment of $300 to a particular athletic scholarship program maintained by a university, an organization described in section 170(c)(2) of the Code. A minimum payment of $300 is required to become a "member" of the program. The only benefit afforded members is that they are permitted to purchase, by paying the stated price of $120, a season ticket to the university's home football games in a designated area in the stadium. Because the games are regularly sold out well in advance, tickets to the games covered by the season ticket would not have been readily available to A if A had not made the payment to the program. The $300 membership fee is paid annually, and a member is required to make a separate $300 payment for each season ticket the member purchases. The university did not inform its donors of the fair market value of the right to purchase a season ticket in the designated area.

Situation 2. The facts are the same as in Situation 1 except that taxpayer B, an individual, made a payment of $500 to the program, even though only a $300 payment is required to become a "member" of the program. The additional $200 did not result in any benefit to B other than that afforded members paid $300.

Situation 3. Taxpayer C, an individual, made a payment of $300 to an athletic scholarship program of a university, an organization described in section 170(c)(2). This payment entitled C to become a "member" of the program and, as a member, to purchase a season ticket, for an additional payment of the stated price, in a designated area in the stadium. Tickets are offered to members before season tickets go on sale to the public.

Seating reasonably comparable to that available to C as a result of membership in the program would have been readily available to C even if C had not made the payment to the program.

Situation 4. Taxpayer D, an individual, made a payment of $300 to an athletic scholarship program of a university, an organization described in section 170(c)(2). This payment entitled D to become a "member" of the program and, as a member, to purchase a season ticket to the university's home football games, for an additional payment of the stated price, in a designated area of the stadium. The membership fee is paid annually and a member is required to make a separate $300 payment for each season ticket the member purchases. Although the games are not regularly sold out, seating reasonably comparable to that available to D as a result of membership in the program would not have been readily available to D if D had not made the payment to the program. The university reasonably estimated that the fair market value of the right to purchase a season ticket in the designated area of the stadium would be x dollars, and advised prospective members that the additional ($300—x dollars) was being solicited as a contribution. In making the estimate, the university considered the level of demand for tickets, the general availability of seats, the relative desirability of seats based on their types, locations, and views, and other relevant factors.

Law and Analysis

Section 170(a) of the Code allows. subject to certain limitations, a deduction for contributions and gifts to or for the use of organizations described in section 170(c), payment of which is made within the taxable year.

A contribution for purposes of section 170 of the code is a voluntary transfer of money or property that is made with no expectation of procuring financial benefit commensurate with the amount of the transfer. See section 1.170A–1(c)(5) of the Income Tax Regulations and H.R. Rep. No. 1337, 83d Cong., 2d Sess. A44 (1954).

Rev. Rul. 67–246, 1967–2 C.B. 104, sets forth various examples concerning the deductibility, as charitable contributions under section 170 of the Code, of payments made by taxpayers in connection with admission to or other participation in fund-raising activities for charitable organizations. The revenue ruling provides that to be deductible as a charitable contribution for federal income tax purposes under section 170, a payment to or for the use of a qualified charitable organization must be a gift. No gift exists for such purposes unless, among other requirements, there is a payment of money or transfer of property without adequate consideration. Where consideration in the form of substantial privileges or benefits is received in connection with payments by patrons of fund-raising activities, there is a presumption that the payments are not gifts. See also Rev. Rul. 76–185, 1976–1 C.B. 60.

Rev. Rul. 67–246 explains that, if a charitable contribution deduction is claimed with respect to a payment for which such consideration is received, the burden is on the taxpayer to establish that the amount paid is not the purchase price of the privileges or benefits and that part of the payment, in fact, does qualify as a gift. In showing that a gift has been made, it is essential for the taxpayer to establish that the portion of the payment that is claimed as a gift represents the excess of the total amount paid over the fair market value of any substantial privileges or benefits received in return.

Rev. Rul. 67–246 states that, if payments solicited for a charitable fund-raising activity are designed to be partly a gift and partly the purchase price of certain privileges or benefits, the organization conducting the activity should employee procedures that make clear not only that a gift is being solicited in connection with the activity, but also the amount of the gift being solicited. To do this, the amount properly attributable to the purchase of privileges or benefits and the amount solicited as a gift should be determined in advance of solicitation. In making such a determination, the fair market value of any substantial privileges or benefits attributable to the purchase must be taken into account. After making such a determination the charitable organization should notify its donors of the amounts allocable to each component of the payment.

In the four situations described above taxpayers made payments to athletic scholarship programs of organizations described in section 170(c)(2). Each taxpayer's payment entitled the taxpayer to become a member of an athletic scholarship program. The taxpayer has made a charitable contribution only if, and only to the extent that, the payment made exceeded the value of any substantial privileges or benefits afforded by membership in the program.

Holding

In Situations 1 and 2, because tickets to the games covered by the season ticket would not otherwise have been readily available to A and B, the right to purchase a season ticket in a designated area in the stadium was a substantial benefit. This substantial benefit was afforded to A and B because each paid the minimum membership fee of $300. Accordingly, a presumption arises that the $300 reflects the value of the benefit received. Unless the taxpayer can establish that $300 exceeded the value of the benefit received, no part of the $300 payment is a charitable contribution under section 170 of the Code.

In Situation 2, however, the additional $200 contributed by B resulted in no additional substantial benefit and thus, is a charitable contribution.

In Situation 3, although the taxpayer was entitled to purchase a ticket before tickets went on sale to the public and although the ticket was for seating in a designated area, reasonably comparable seating would have been readily available to C even if C had not made a payment to the program. Although C received the benefit of obtaining a ticket early and of sitting with other program members, the benefit was not substantial. Accordingly, the entire $300 is a charitable contribution.

In Situation 4, because reasonably comparable seating would not otherwise have been readily available to D, the right to purchase a season ticket in a designated area in the stadium was a substantial benefit. This substantial benefit was afforded to D because D paid the minimum membership fee of $300. Accordingly, a presumption arises that the $300 reflects the value of the benefit received. The university, however, after taking all relevant facts and circumstances into account, reasonably estimated the fair market value of the benefit as x dollars. Because the university solicited the other ($300—x dollars) as a contribution and the x dollar figure reflected the fair market value of the benefit provided, ($300—x dollars) of D's $300 payment is a charitable contribution.

(b) Intangible Religious Benefits

Some benefits which contributors receive back for their contributions are not taken into account. For example, when you contribute $50 to the United Way, you are not required either to value or to subtract the warm, fuzzy feeling you get for doing so. But how about "intangible religious benefits"? Have a look at § 170(f)(8)(B)(iii), and see if you can figure out what it means, in light of *Hernandez*.

HERNANDEZ v. COMMISSIONER

United States Supreme Court, 1989.
490 U.S. 680, 109 S.Ct. 2136, 104 L.Ed.2d 766.

JUSTICE MARSHALL delivered the opinion of the Court.

Section 170 permits a taxpayer to deduct from gross income the amount of a "charitable contribution." The Code defines that term as a "contribution or gift" to certain eligible donees, including entities organized and operated exclusively for religious purposes. We granted certiorari to determine whether taxpayers may deduct as charitable contributions payments made to branch churches of the Church of Scientology (Church) in order to receive services known as "auditing" and "training." We hold that such payments are not deductible.

I

Scientology was founded in the 1950's by L. Ron Hubbard. It is propagated today by a "mother church" in California and by numerous branch churches around the world. The mother Church instructs laity, trains and ordains ministers, and creates new congregations. Branch churches, known as "franchises" or "missions," provide Scientology services at the local level, under the supervision of the mother Church.

Scientologists believe that an immortal spiritual being exists in every person. A person becomes aware of this spiritual dimension through a process known as "auditing." Auditing involves a one-to-one encounter between a participant (known as a "preclear") and a Church official (known as an "auditor"). An electronic device, the E-meter, helps the auditor identify the preclear's areas of spiritual difficulty by measuring skin responses during a question and answer session. Although auditing sessions are conducted one on one, the content of each session is not individually tailored. The preclear gains spiritual awareness by progressing through sequential levels of auditing, provided in short blocks of time known as "intensives".

The Church also offers members doctrinal courses known as "training." Participants in these sessions study the tenets of Scientology and seek to attain the qualifications necessary to serve as auditors. Training courses, like auditing sessions, are provided in sequential levels. Scientologists are taught that spiritual gains result from participation in such courses.

The Church charges a "fixed donation," also known as a "price" or a "fixed contribution," for participants to gain access to auditing and training sessions. These charges are set forth in schedules, and prices vary with a session's length and level of sophistication. In 1972, for example, the general rates for auditing ranged from $625 for a 12 1/2–hour auditing intensive, the shortest available, to $4,250 for a 100–hour intensive, the longest available. Specialized types of auditing required higher fixed donations: a 12 1/2–hour "Integrity Processing" auditing intensive cost $750; a 12 1/2–hour "Expanded Dianetics" auditing intensive cost $950. This system of mandatory fixed charges is based on a central tenet of Scientology known as the "doctrine of exchange," according to which any time a person receives something he must pay something back. In so doing, a Scientologist maintains "inflow" and "outflow" and avoids spiritual decline.

The proceeds generated from auditing and training sessions are the Church's primary source of income. The Church promotes these sessions not only through newspaper, magazine, and radio advertisements, but also through free lectures, free personality tests, and leaflets. The Church also encourages, and indeed rewards with a 5% discount, advance payment for these sessions. The Church often refunds unused portions of prepaid auditing or training fees, less an administrative charge.

Petitioners in these consolidated cases each made payments to a branch church for auditing or training sessions. They sought to deduct these payments on their federal income tax returns as charitable contributions under § 170. Respondent Commissioner * * *, disallowed these deductions, finding that the payments were not charitable contributions within the meaning of § 170.

* * * Before trial, the Commissioner stipulated that the branch churches of Scientology are religious organizations entitled to receive tax-deductible charitable contributions under the relevant sections of the Code. This stipulation isolated as the sole statutory issue whether pay-

ments for auditing or training sessions constitute "contribution[s] or gift[s]" under § 170.

* * *

II

* * *

The legislative history of the "contribution or gift" limitation, though sparse, reveals that Congress intended to differentiate between unrequited payments to qualified recipients and payments made to such recipients in return for goods or services. Only the former were deemed deductible. The House and Senate Reports on the 1954 tax bill, for example, both define "gifts" as payments "made with no expectation of a financial return commensurate with the amount of the gift." Using payments to hospitals as an example, both Reports state that the gift characterization should not apply to "a payment by an individual to a hospital *in consideration of* a binding obligation to provide medical treatment for the individual's employees. It would apply only if there were no expectation of any quid pro quo from the hospital."

In ascertaining whether a given payment was made with "the expectation of any quid pro quo," the IRS has customarily examined the external features of the transaction in question. This practice has the advantage of obviating the need for the IRS to conduct imprecise inquiries into the motivations of individual taxpayers. * * *

In light of this understanding of § 170, it is readily apparent that petitioners' payments to the Church do not qualify as "contribution[s] or gift[s]." As the Tax Court found, these payments were part of a quintessential *quid pro quo* exchange: in return for their money, petitioners received an identifiable benefit, namely, auditing and training sessions. The Church established fixed price schedules for auditing and training sessions in each branch church; it calibrated particular prices to auditing or training sessions of particular lengths and levels of sophistication; it returned a refund if auditing and training services went unperformed; it distributed "account cards" on which persons who had paid money to the Church could monitor what prepaid services they had not yet claimed; and it categorically barred provision of auditing or training sessions for free. Each of these practices reveals the inherently reciprocal nature of the exchange.

Petitioners do not argue that such a structural analysis is inappropriate under § 170, or that the external features of the auditing and training transactions do not strongly suggest a *quid pro quo* exchange. * * * Petitioners argue instead that they are entitled to deductions because a *quid pro quo* analysis is inappropriate under § 170 when the benefit a taxpayer receives is purely religious in nature. Along the same lines, petitioners claim that payments made for the right to participate in a religious service should be automatically deductible under § 170.

We cannot accept this statutory argument for several reasons. First, it finds no support in the language of § 170. Whether or not Congress could, consistent with the Establishment Clause, provide for the automatic deductibility of a payment made to a church that either generates religious benefits or guarantees access to a religious service, that is a choice Congress has thus far declined to make. Instead, Congress has specified that a payment to an organization operated exclusively for religious (or other eleemosynary) purposes is deductible *only* if such a payment is a "contribution or gift." The Code makes no special preference for payments made in the expectation of gaining religious benefits or access to a religious service. The House and Senate Reports on § 170, and the other legislative history of that provision, offer no indication that Congress' failure to enact such a preference was an oversight.

Second, petitioners' deductibility proposal would expand the charitable contribution deduction far beyond what Congress has provided. Numerous forms of payments to eligible donees plausibly could be categorized as providing a religious benefit or as securing access to a religious service. For example, some taxpayers might regard their tuition payments to parochial schools as generating a religious benefit or as securing access to a religious service; such payments, however, have long been held not to be charitable contributions under § 170. Taxpayers might make similar claims about payments for church-sponsored counseling sessions or for medical care at church-affiliated hospitals that otherwise might not be deductible. Given that, under the First Amendment, the IRS can reject otherwise valid claims of religious benefit only on the ground that a taxpayers' alleged beliefs are not sincerely held, but not on the ground that such beliefs are inherently irreligious, the resulting tax deductions would likely expand the charitable contribution provision far beyond its present size. We are loath to effect this result in the absence of supportive congressional intent.

Finally, the deduction petitioners seek might raise problems of entanglement between church and state. If framed as a deduction for those payments generating benefits of a religious nature for the payor, petitioners' proposal would inexorably force the IRS and reviewing courts to differentiate "religious" benefits from "secular" ones. If framed as a deduction for those payments made in connection with a religious service, petitioners' proposal would force the IRS and the judiciary into differentiating "religious" services from "secular" ones. We need pass no judgment now on the constitutionality of such hypothetical inquiries, but we do note that "pervasive monitoring" for "the subtle or overt presence of religious matter" is a central danger against which we have held the Establishment Clause guards.

Accordingly, we conclude that petitioners' payments to the Church for auditing and training sessions are not "contribution[s] or gift[s]" within the meaning of that statutory expression.

[The Court's discussion of the Constitutional issues is omitted.]

JUSTICE O'CONNOR, with whom JUSTICE SCALIA joins, dissenting.

The Court today acquiesces in the decision of the Internal Revenue Service (IRS) to manufacture a singular exception to its 70–year practice of allowing fixed payments indistinguishable from those made by petitioners to be deducted as charitable contributions. Because the IRS cannot constitutionally be allowed to select which religions will receive the benefit of its past rulings, I respectfully dissent.

* * *

It must be emphasized that the IRS' position here is *not* based upon the contention that a portion of the knowledge received from auditing or training is of secular, commercial, nonreligious value. Thus, the denial of a deduction in these cases bears no resemblance to the denial of a deduction for religious-school tuition up to the market value of the secularly useful education received. Here the IRS denies deductibility solely on the basis that the exchange is a *quid pro quo,* even though the *quid* is exclusively of spiritual or religious worth. Respondent cites no instances in which this has been done before, and there are good reasons why.

When a taxpayer claims as a charitable deduction part of a fixed amount given to a charitable organization in exchange for benefits that have a commercial value, the allowable portion of that claim is computed by subtracting from the total amount paid the value of the physical benefit received. If at a charity sale one purchases for $1,000 a painting whose market value is demonstrably no more than $50, there has been a contribution of $950. The same would be true if one purchases a $1,000 seat at a charitable dinner where the food is worth $50. An identical calculation can be made where the *quid* received is not a painting or a meal, but an intangible such as entertainment, so long as that intangible has some market value established in a noncontributory context. Hence, one who purchases a ticket to a concert, at the going rate for concerts by the particular performers, makes a charitable contribution of zero even if it is announced in advance that all proceeds from the ticket sales will go to charity. The performers may have made a charitable contribution, but the audience has paid the going rate for a show.

It becomes impossible, however, to compute the "contribution" portion of a payment to a charity where what is received in return is not merely an intangible, but an intangible (or, for that matter a tangible) that is not bought and sold except in donative contexts so that the only "market" price against which it can be evaluated is a market price that always includes donations. Suppose, for example, that the charitable organization that traditionally solicits donations on Veterans Day, in exchange for which it gives the donor an imitation poppy bearing its name, were to establish a flat rule that no one gets a poppy without a donation of at least $10. One would have to say that the "market" rate for such poppies was $10, but it would assuredly not be true that everyone who "bought" a poppy for $10 made no contribution. Similarly, if one buys a $100 seat at a prayer breakfast receiving as the *quid pro quo* food for both body and soul—it would make no sense to say that no charitable contribution whatever has occurred simply because the "going rate" for all prayer breakfasts (with equivalent bodily food) is $100. The latter may well be true, but that "going rate" *includes* a contribution.

Confronted with this difficulty, and with the constitutional necessity of not making irrational distinctions among taxpayers, and with the even higher standard of equality of treatment among *religions* that the First Amendment imposes, the Government has only two practicable options with regard to distinctively religious *quids pro quo:* to disregard them all, or to tax them all. Over the years it has chosen the former course.

Congress enacted the first charitable contribution exception to income taxation in 1917. A mere two years later, the IRS gave its first blessing to the deductions of fixed payments to religious organizations as charitable contributions:

> "[T]he distinction of pew rents, assessments, church dues, and the like from basket collections is hardly warranted by the act. The act reads 'contributions' and 'gifts.' It is felt that all of these come within the two terms.

> "In substance it is believed that these are simply methods of contributing although in form they may vary. Is a basket collection given involuntarily to be distinguished from an envelope system, the latter being regarded as 'dues'? From a technical angle, the pew rents may be differentiated, but in practice the so-called 'personal accommodation' they may afford is conjectural. It is believed that the real intent is to contribute and not to hire a seat or pew for personal accommodation. In fact, basket contributors sometimes receive the same accommodation informally."

The IRS reaffirmed its position in 1970, ruling that "[p]ew rents, building fund assessments and periodic dues paid to a church ... are all methods of making contributions to the church and such payments are deductible as charitable contributions." Similarly, notwithstanding the "form" of Mass stipends as fixed payments for specific religious services, the IRS has allowed charitable deductions of such payments.

These rulings, which are "official interpretation[s] of [the tax laws] by the [IRS], flatly contradict the Solicitor General's claim that there" is no administrative practice recognizing that payments made in exchange for religious benefits are tax deductible. "Indeed, an Assistant Commissioner of the IRS recently explained in a" question and answer guidance package "to tax-exempt organizations that" [i]n contrast to tuition payments, religious observances generally are not regarded as yielding private benefits to the donor, who is viewed as receiving only incidental benefits when attending the observances. The primary beneficiaries are viewed as being the general public and members of the faith. Thus, payments for saying masses, pew rents, tithes, and other payments involving fixed donations for similar religious services, are fully deductible contributions. "Although this guidance package may not be as authoritative as IRS rulings, in the absence of any contrary indications it does reflect the continuing adherence of the IRS to its practice of allowing deductions for fixed payments for religious services.

There can be no doubt that at least some of the fixed payments which the IRS has treated as charitable deductions, or which the Court assumes the IRS would allow taxpayers to deduct, are as "inherently reciprocal," as the payments for auditing at issue here. In exchange for their payment of pew rents, Christians receive particular seats during worship services. Similarly, in some synagogues attendance at the worship services for Jewish High Holy Days is often predicated upon the purchase of a general admission ticket or a reserved seat ticket. Religious honors such as publicly reading from Scripture are purchased or auctioned periodically in some synagogues of Jews from Morocco and Syria. Mormons must tithe their income as a necessary but not sufficient condition to obtaining a "temple recommend," *i.e.,* the right to be admitted into the temple. A Mass stipend—a fixed payment given to a Catholic priest, in consideration of which he is obliged to apply the fruits of the Mass for the intention of the donor—has similar overtones of exchange. According to some Catholic theologians, the nature of the pact between a priest and a donor who pays a Mass stipend is "a bilateral contract known as *do ut facias.* One person agrees to give while the other party agrees to do something in return." A finer example of a *quid pro quo* exchange would be hard to formulate.

This is not a situation where the IRS has explicitly and affirmatively reevaluated its longstanding interpretation of § 170 and decided to analyze *all* fixed religious contributions under a *quid pro quo* standard. There is no indication whatever that the IRS has abandoned its 70–year practice with respect to payments made by those other than Scientologists. In 1978, when it ruled that payments for auditing and training were not charitable contributions under § 170, the IRS did not cite—much less try to reconcile—its previous rulings concerning the deductibility of other forms of fixed payments for religious services or practices.

Nevertheless, respondent now attempts to reconcile his previous rulings with his decision in these cases by relying on a distinction between direct and incidental benefits in exchange for payments made to a charitable organization. This distinction, adumbrated as early as the IRS' 1919 ruling, recognizes that even a deductible charitable contribution may generate certain benefits for the donor. As long as the benefits remain "incidental" and do not indicate that the payment was actually made for the "personal accommodation" of the donor, the payment will be deductible. It is respondent's view that the payments made by petitioners should not be deductible under § 170 because the "unusual facts in these cases ... demonstrate that the payments were made primarily for 'personal accommodation.'" Specifically, the Solicitor General asserts that "the rigid connection between the provision of auditing and training services and payment of the fixed price" indicates a *quid pro quo* relationship and "reflect[s] the value that petitioners expected to receive for their money."

There is no discernible reason why there is a more rigid connection between payment and services in the religious practices of Scientology than in the religious practices of the faiths described above. Neither has respondent explained why the benefit received by a Christian who obtains the pew of his or her choice by paying a rental fee, a Jew who gains entrance to High Holy Day services by purchasing a ticket, a Mormon who makes the fixed payment necessary for a temple recommend, or a Catholic who pays a Mass stipend, is incidental to the real benefit conferred on the "general public and members of the faith," while the benefit received by a Scientologist from auditing is a personal accommodation. If the perceived difference lies in the fact that Christians and Jews worship in congregations, whereas Scientologists, in a manner reminiscent of Eastern religions, gain awareness of the "immortal spiritual being" within them in one-to-one sessions with auditors, such a distinction would raise serious Establishment Clause problems. The distinction is no more legitimate if it is based on the fact that congregational worship services "would be said anyway," without the payment of a pew rental or stipend or tithe by a particular adherent. The relevant comparison between Scientology and other religions must be between the Scientologist undergoing auditing or training on one hand and the congregation on the other. For some religions the central importance of the congregation achieves legal dimensions. In Orthodox Judaism, for example, certain worship services cannot be performed and Scripture cannot be read publicly without the presence of at least 10 men. If payments for participation occurred in such a setting, would the benefit to the 10th man be only incidental while for the personal accommodation of the 11th? In the same vein, will the deductibility of a Mass stipend turn on whether there are other congregants to hear the Mass? And conversely, does the fact that the payment of a tithe by a Mormon is an absolute prerequisite to admission to the temple make that payment for admission a personal accommodation regardless of the size of the congregation?

Given the IRS' stance in these cases, it is an understatement to say that with respect to fixed payments for religious services "the line between the taxable and the immune has been drawn by an unsteady hand." This is not a situation in which a governmental regulation "happens to coincide or harmonize with the tenets of some or all religions," but does not violate the Establishment Clause because it is founded on a neutral, secular basis. Rather, it involves the differential application of a standard based on constitutionally impermissible differences drawn by the Government among religions. As such, it is best characterized as a case of the Government "put[ting] an imprimatur on [all but] one religion." That the Government may not do.

NOTE

Hernandez notwithstanding, IRS caved in to the Scientologists. In the closing agreement, both sides dropped all pending lawsuits. I have found no evidence whatsoever that Tom Cruise had anything to do with it.

PROBLEMS

Consider in each case whether or not there has been a deductible contribution:

1. The following amounts were contributed to New York University. In return, NYU named the facility after the donor, as indicated:[e]

Tisch School of the Arts	$7.5 million	1982
Leonard N. Stern School of Business	$30 million	1988
Iris and B. Gerald Cantor Film Center	$3.5 million	1995
Lillian Vernon Center for International Affairs	$1.5 million	1996

[Could it be that some of these people were simply ripped off? In 1804, Nicholas Brown managed to get an entire university named after him for a mere $5,000.]

2. If you go to Charitymall.com or iGive.com, you can buy merchandise from the listed online stores, at the regular price. The store pays the "charity mall" a referral fee of some 5% to 10%. The charity mall then makes a donation of some or all of that referral fee to the public charity designated by you.

3. In 1999, Healthy Choice foods offered 500 frequent flyer miles for every 10 Healthy Choice UPC bar codes turned in by December 31. "Early birds," who submitted bar codes by May 31, could earn 1,000 miles per 10 bar codes. David Phillips, of Davis, California, purchased 12,150 individual cups of Healthy Choice chocolate pudding at 25a cup, for a total expenditure of $3,140, plus 50 hours of his time to buy and transport the pudding. He then made a deal with some local charities. He donated the pudding to them, and, in exchange, they peeled off the bar codes for him. As a result, Mr. Phillips obtained 1.25 million miles of frequent flyer miles. Mr. Phillips would like to deduct $3,140 for the donation of pudding to qualified charities. Can he deduct? On the other hand, does he have any income?

4. Paul performs at a "benefit concert." He charges his customary $100,000, and is duly paid by the charitable organization which put on the concert. He turns around and donates the $100,000 to the charity.

Ringo performs at a "benefit concert." Although his customary fee is $100,000, he tells the charitable organization that he will perform for free.

How should Paul and Ringo be treated by IRS? *See* Reg. § 170A–1(g)

5. Taxpayer donated his house to the local fire station, so that they could burn it down as a training exercise. As it turned out, Taxpayer's wanted to demolish the house anyway. Does he get a charitable deduction? See Rolfs v. Commissioner, 135 T.C. 471 (2010).

---

e. *What's in a Name?* N.Y. TIMES, Aug. 29, 1999, at WK 5.

2. WHO IS A CHARITABLE DONEE?

INTRODUCTORY QUESTION

Mr. Green was drowning. Mr. Brown, who happened to be passing by, saved his life. Mr. Green was so grateful that he put Mr. Brown through college.

Had these events occurred in Germany, Mr. Green could have deducted the tuition payments. Why can't he do that here?

* * *

(a) General

Section 170(c) defines "charitable contribution" as "a contribution or gift to or for the use of ..." It then goes on to list the sorts of organizations which can be charitable donees. Note that § 170(c)(2)(B) would include an entity "organized and operated exclusively for religious, charitable, scientific, literary, or educational purposes ..." The Salvation Army is surely an entity organized and operated exclusively for charitable purposes. Therefore, a contribution to the Salvation Army should be fully deductible.

What if my nephew were homeless? Presumably, I could make a deductible contribution to the Salvation Army, which could, in turn, use it to defray the expenses of putting up my nephew in a homeless shelter. If that is true, then can I take a charitable contribution deduction for putting up my nephew in my own home? No. My nephew is not a qualified charitable donee, and neither am I. Doesn't that deter some very common, and very admirable, giving?

(b) What Is a Church?

A church is clearly a qualified charitable donee. What is a church, and who decides?

Private Ruling 9624001, set forth below, lays out the factors used by the Internal Revenue Service to determine whether or not a given entity is a church. Apply these factors to the facts of *United States v. Kuch*, which follows the Private Ruling. Is the Neo–American Church, as described in that case, a church for tax purposes? If not, are there some easy steps which they could take if they wanted to become one?

PRIVATE RULING 9624001
1995 PRL LEXIS 2277.

* * * [there are] 14 factors that the Service considers is helpful in determining whether a religious organization is a church. These factors include:

1.   a distinct legal existence;
2.   a recognized creed and form of worship;

3. a definite and distinct ecclesiastical government;

4. a formal code of doctrine and discipline;

5. a distinct religious history;

6. membership not associated with any other church or denomination;

7. ordained ministers;

8. selection of ministers for ordination after prescribed studies;

9. its own literature;

10. established places of worship;

11. regular congregations;

12. regular religious services;

13. "Sunday school" for instructing children; and

14. schools for preparing ministers.

UNITED STATES v. KUCH

United States District Court, District of Columbia, 1968.
288 F.Supp. 439.

[Defendant argued that her indictment for unlawfully obtaining and transferring marijuana and for the unlawful sale, delivery and possession of LSD should be dismissed, because all of the alleged violations impinged on her free exercise of religion as a member of the Neo–American Church—Ed.]

* * * The Neo–American Church was incorporated in California in 1965 as a nonprofit corporation. It claims a nationwide membership of about 20,000. At its head is a Chief Boo Hoo. Defendant Kuch is the primate of the Potomac, a position analogized to bishop. She supervises the Boo Hoos in her area. There are some 300 Boo Hoos throughout the country. In order to join the church a member must subscribe to the following principles:

"(1) Everyone has the right to expand his consciousness and stimulate visionary experience by whatever means he considers desirable and proper without interference from anyone;

"(2) The psychedelic substances, such as LSD, are the true Host of the Church, not drugs. They are sacramental foods, manifestations of the Grace of God, of the infinite imagination of the Self, and therefore belong to everyone;

"(3) We do not encourage the ingestion of psychedelics by those who are unprepared."

Building on the central thesis of the group that psychedelic substances, particularly marihuana and LSD, are the true Host, the Church specifies that "it is the Religious duty of all members to partake of the sacraments on regular occasions."

A Boo Hoo is "ordained" without any formal training. He guides members on psychedelic trips, acts as a counselor for individuals having a "spiritual crisis," administers drugs and interprets the Church to those interested. The Boo Hoo of the Georgetown area of Washington, D.C., testified that the Church was pantheistic and lacked a formal theology. Indeed, the church officially states in its so-called "Catechism and Handbook" that "it has never been our objective to add one more institutional substitute for individual virtue to the already crowded lists." In the same vein, this literature asserts "we have the right to practice our religion, even if we are a bunch of filthy, drunken bums." The members are instructed that anyone should be taken as a member "no matter what you suspect his motives to be."

* * * Reading the so-called "Catechism and Handbook" of the Church containing the pronouncements of the Chief Boo Hoo, one gains the inescapable impression that the membership is mocking established institutions, playing with words and totally irreverent in any sense of the term. Each member carries a "martyrdom record" to reflect his arrests. The Church symbol is a three-eyed toad. Its bulletin is the "Divine Toad Sweat." The Church key is, of course, the bottle opener. The official songs are "Puff, the Magic Dragon" and "Row, Row, Row Your Boat." * * *

The official seal of the Church is available on flags, pillow cases, shoulder patches, pill boxes, sweat shirts, rings, portable "communion sets" with chalice and cup, pipes for "sacramental use," and the like. The seal has the three-eyed toad in the center. The name of the Church is at the top of the seal and across the bottom is the Church motto: "Victory over Horseshit." * * *

NOTES, QUESTIONS

1. The Neo–American Church website is at okneoac.com. *The Boo Hoo Bible, The Neo–American Church Catechism and Handbook* is available from Amazon. Here is an excerpt from the author's review of his own book:

> Although major advances in Church doctrine have been made since the Boo Hoo Bible was published, and the Church itself, in contrast to the easy-going practices of the early days, has become elitist, exclusive, xenophobic, hierarchical, monarchial and doctrinaire in consequence of the unremitting religious persecution of our members by the supernaturalist Sado–Judeo–Paulinian Republicrat punishment freaks of the moronocratic American imperium, much of the contents of this book apply equally well today as when it first spronged forth and elicited from the mass media mills of the powers that were a howling shit storm of "New Age" idiocy.

2. In light of the First Amendment, how can the Internal Revenue Service, which is, after all, a government agency, possibly rule on what is, or is not, a church?

3. In 1985, Senator Jesse Helms (R., N.C.) proposed the following amendment, relating to the definition of § 501(c)(3) organizations:

No funds appropriated under this Act shall be used to grant, maintain, or allow tax exemption to any cult, organization, or any other group that has as a purpose, or that has any interest in, the promoting of satanism or witchcraft: Provided, That for the purposes of this section, 'satanism' is defined as the worship of Satan or the powers of evil and 'witchcraft' is defined as the use of powers derived from evil spirits, the use of sorcery, or the use of supernatural powers with malicious intent. 131 CONG. REC. S12168–02 (1985)

His proposal didn't make it. Necessary? Appropriate? Constitutional?

3. MECHANICS: PERCENTAGE LIMITATIONS, CONTRIBUTIONS OF APPRECIATED PROPERTY

Assume that we have managed to get past the first two hurdles. The transfer of money or property is a contribution. The recipient is a qualified charitable donee. Now, how much of a deduction do you actually get for the contribution? All contributions must be considered in light of the percentage limitations, below at (a). Contributions of appreciated property must be considered in light of the obstacle course of § 170(e), considered below at (b).

(a) Percentage Limitations

Section 170 contains two major percentage limitations, the 50% cap on contributions "to" public charities, found in § 170(b)(1)(A), and the 30% cap for contributions "for the use of" public charities, or "to or for the use of" private charities, found in § 170(b)(1)(B). It also contains a special 30% cap on certain capital gain property in § 170(b)(1)(C), discussed below at 558, and a 20% cap in § 170(b)(1)(D). All of these limitations are percentages of the taxpayer's "contribution base," defined at § 170(b)(1)(F) as, essentially, adjusted gross income. See 545 *supra* for adjusted gross income.

Example

Phil has an adjusted gross income this year of $250,000. He had no net operating loss carrybacks. He gave $175,000 this year to Mercy Hospital.

Since Phil had no net operating loss carrybacks, his contribution base is the same as his adjusted gross income of $250,000 [§ 170(b)(1)(F)]. Mercy Hospital is a public charity, described in § 170(b)(1)(A)(iii). Therefore, the percentage limitation is 50%. Fifty per cent of Phil's contribution base of $250,000 is $125,000.

Accordingly, of the $175,000 which Phil contributed to Mercy Hospital, $125,000 will be deductible this year. The remaining $50,000 will be carried over to next year pursuant to § 170(d)(1)(A).

Contributions in excess of any of these caps can be carried over to subsequent years. Note that, in each case, it will be treated as that same type of contribution in the subsequent year. For the 50% cap to public charities, the carryover is in § 170(d). For the 30% cap on private charities, the carryover is in the last sentence of § 170(b)(1)(B). For the 30% cap of certain capital gain property, the carryover is described in § 170(b)(1)(C)(ii). For the 20% cap described in § 170(b)(1)(D), the carryover provision is found at § 170(b)(1)(D)(ii).

Public charities are described in § 170(b)(1)(A) (i) through (viii). They include churches [§ 170(b)(1)(A)(i)], educational organizations [§ 170(b)(1)(A)(ii)], hospitals [§ 170(b)(1)(A)(iii)], and generally, charitable organizations which receive their contributions from the general public [§ 170(b)(1)(A)(vi)]. Private charities are, as § 170(b)(1)(B) points out, everything else. Generally, private charities receive their contributions from a small group of defined individuals. When you think of private charities, consider that they are more under the control of the donors, and therefore perhaps less deserving of tax breaks.

PROBLEMS

Read § 170(b)(1)(B) carefully and apply the inter-related percentage caps to determine the deductible charitable contributions in the following problems. In each instance, determine whether or not there is a carryover, and, if so, how much, and what kind. The contribution base is $100,000:

1. Donor gave $75,000 to the Catholic Church.

2. Donor gave $40,000 to the Catholic Church.

3. Donor gave $50,000 to the Donor Foundation, a private charity.

4. Donor gave $25,000 to the Donor Foundation, a private charity.

5. Donor gave $40,000 to the Catholic Church and $25,000 to the Donor Foundation.

(b) Contributions of Appreciated Property

Code: § 170(e)

NOTE

Imagine that you are in the 35% tax bracket. You own a first edition book with a basis of one penny and a fair market value of $1,000 (you wish). You sell it for $1,000 and contribute the cash to a public charity. Imagine that you are well within your 50% cap. You have a gain on the sale of the book of essentially $1,000, and a charitable contribution deduction of $1,000 for the cash contribution. Of course, the gain might well be taxed at a lower rate if capital, while the charitable contribution deduction will offset income which was taxed at 35%.

But here's a better deal. Give the book directly to the charity. Now, there's no sale of the book, so you don't realize the gain. Yet, it would appear that you still get a charitable contribution deduction measured by the fair market value of the asset contributed, or $1,000. So, you get a deduction of $1,000, worth $350 to you in your bracket. In addition, you don't have to pay tax on the $1,000 of appreciation on your stock.

Too good to be true? Double benefit? Congress thinks so, sometimes. Read § 170(e). Pursuant to § 170(e)(1)(A), if the contributed property was ordinary income property [i.e. would have generated ordinary income if sold], the charitable contribution deduction is limited to basis. Pursuant to § 170(e)(1)(B), if the property would have generated long term capital gain if sold, then the contribution deduction is limited to basis **if** the property is:

tangible

personal, and

if the use is unrelated to the exempt function; **or**

if the donee is that kind of private foundation described in § 170(e)(1)(B)(ii).

However

If the appreciated property generates a full charitable contribution deduction for its full fair market value, then you are subject to the special 30% cap described in § 170(b)(1)(C). **Unless** you elect out of the 30% cap pursuant to § 170(b)(1)(C)(iii).

Applying § 170(e) to the facts above, it is assumed that the book, if sold, would have generated a long term capital gain. The book is tangible, personal property. Moreover, assume that the use of the book will be unrelated to the exempt function of the charity. For an example of a use related to the exempt function, consider a donation of a painting to an art museum, which then displays the painting. See Reg. § 1.170A–4(b)(3). Therefore, the deductible contribution will be limited to the basis of one penny.

For the purposes of this introductory course, enough is enough. We will ignore charitable contributions of intangible intellectual property, addressed in § 170(e)(1)(B)(iii). Moreover, despite their obvious temptations, we will ignore certain contributions of stuffed, dead animals, addressed in § 170(e)(1)(B)(iv).

PROBLEMS

In each case, how much of a charitable contribution deduction would be possible? Assume that Taxpayer has a contribution base of $100,000. No other contributions have been made this year.

1. Taxpayer is a dealer in art. Taxpayer donated artwork, with a basis of $10,000 and a fair market value of $40,000, to an art museum, which plans to exhibit the paintings.

2. Same as 1, but the paintings are donated to a hospital, which intends to sell them and use the proceeds for its exempt purposes.

3. Taxpayer owns one painting. She bought it many years ago for $10,000; now it's worth $40,000. She donates it to an art museum, which plans to exhibit the paintings.

4.   Same as 3, but the painting is donated to a hospital, which plans to sell it.

5.   Taxpayer donated a pint of blood to the Red Cross. *See* Lary v. United States, 787 F.2d 1538 (11th Cir. 1986). What if she donated one of her organs?

Wisconsin allows a deduction against its income tax, up to $10,000, for travel expenses, lodging expenses, and lost wages incurred in donating one's organs. For the purposes of the deduction, organs are limited to the liver, pancreas, kidney, intestine, lung, or bone marrow. Good idea? See W.S.A. § 71.05(10)(i).

6.   Taxpayer owns a lumber yard. Taxpayer has in inventory 1,000 board feet of lumber, with a basis to Taxpayer of $1,000. The fair market value of the lumber is $4,000. Taxpayer conveys the lumber to Habitat for Humanity, a public charity, in a bargain sale transaction, in exchange for a payment of $3,000. What are the tax consequences to Taxpayer? See § 1011(b).

7.   Taxpayer owns depreciable property, with a basis of $10,000 and a fair market value of $40,000. If sold, the property would generate a taxable gain of $30,000, of which $5,000 would be long term capital gain, and $25,000 would be recaptured as ordinary income. Taxpayer donates the property to a public charity, which plans to sell it.

4.   TAX EXEMPTS AND UNRELATED BUSINESS INCOME

(a) Tax Exempts

"Trying to understand the various exempt organization provisions of the Internal Revenue Code is as difficult as capturing a drop of mercury under your thumb."

—Weingarden v. Commissioner, 86 T.C. 669, 675 (1986); *rev'd*, 825 F.2d 1027 (6th Cir.1987)

The entities to which charitable contributions are deductible are also themselves largely exempt from the income tax. The category of tax-exempts, however, is far larger than the category of those tax-exempts to which charitable contributions are deductible. The "deductible" entities are described in §§ 170(c) and 501(c)(3). Consider the rest of the subsections of § 501(c) to get a feel for the variety of possible tax-exempts.

If there is one dominant, common theme to all of the tax-exempts, it is that "no part of their net earnings may inure to the benefit of any private shareholder or individual." You will find this phrase sprinkled liberally throughout § 501(c). Note, however, that there does not seem to be any blanket restriction on the existence of net earnings—only on where they can go.

In fact, some tax-exempts have substantial net earnings. For example, for the fiscal year ending June 30, 1985, the Red Cross had revenues of $466 million. Its excess of revenues over expenses was $41.2 million. Such excess as a percentage of "sales" was 8.8%. Had the Red Cross been compared to for-profit corporations in 1985, its revenues would have placed it at number 473 in the Fortune 500, and its 8.8 percentage would have tied it for number 50.[f]

Two other general restrictions of note relate to discrimination and lobbying. As to discrimination, § 501(c)(i) specifically prohibits discrimination on the part of the social clubs described in § 501(c)(7) "on the basis of race, color, or religion."

More generally, in Bob Jones University v. United States, 461 U.S. 574, 103 S.Ct. 2017, 76 L.Ed.2d 157 (1983), Bob Jones University denied admission to applicants who engaged in or advocated interracial dating or marriage. Revenue Ruling 71–447, 1971–2 C.B. 230, provided that the purpose of a charitable trust could not be illegal or contrary to public policy. Pursuant to this Revenue Ruling, IRS threatened to revoke the University's tax-exempt status unless its admissions policies were changed. The University sued, and lost.

As to lobbying, § 501(c)(3), in describing the "deductible" tax-exempts, provides:

> . . . no substantial part of the activities of which is carrying on propaganda, or otherwise attempting, to influence legislation (except as otherwise provided in subsection (h)), and which does not participate in, or intervene in (including the publishing or distributing of statements), any political campaign on behalf of (or in opposition to) any candidate for public office.

As mentioned in the first parenthetical in the excerpt above, § 501(h) provides a limited exception for certain severely restricted lobbying activities. Consider these provisions in light of the discussion of § 162(e), and the discussion of the deductibility of lobbying, *supra* at 473.

In light of these restrictions, many organizations bifurcate their activities, so that there is at least one entity within their corporate family which may receive deductible contributions. For example, the American Civil Liberties Union, although tax-exempt, is not a § 501(c)(3) organization, because it engages in substantial lobbying activities. Therefore, contributions to the American Civil Liberties Union are not tax deductible. However, the American Civil Liberties Union Legal Defense Fund engages in no lobbying, and can receive tax deductible contributions.

(b) Unrelated Business Income and the Mobil Oil Cotton Bowl

In 1947, the C.F. Mueller Company ("Delaware") was incorporated in Delaware. According to its certificate of incorporation, its purpose was charitable. All profits and assets available for distribution were to be paid to New York University for the exclusive benefit of NYU Law School. Delaware then acquired the C.F. Mueller Company, a for-profit New Jersey corporation engaged in the macaroni business, and proceeded to sell pasta for the greater glory of NYU.

---

f. Andrea Rock, *Inside the Billion–Dollar Business of Blood*, Money, Mar. 1986, at 152.

NYU was delighted; other macaroni companies were outraged. How could free competition in the macaroni industry be preserved if one of the competitors was tax-exempt, and all of the others were not?

The other macaroni companies were unsuccessful in court, C.F. Mueller Co. v. Commissioner, 190 F.2d 120 (3d Cir.1951), so they took their complaint to Congress. Congress responded with the unrelated business income tax, §§ 511 through 514. Check the statutes to see how it works. Read § 513, especially, for the definition of unrelated business.

What is an unrelated business? Does it depend at all on the size of the business in relation to the size of the exempt operation? Consider museum stores. Originally, art museums established small gift shops, usually to be found close to the entrance. They sold postcards, souvenirs, prints, and art books. These museum stores afforded museum patrons an opportunity to take home copies of the paintings which they had admired in the museum, and admire them some more. Clearly, the stores helped to expose a larger audience to works of art, thus helping to carry out the museums' exempt functions.

However, currently, the gift shops of some of the larger museums are in the mail order business. Their sales volumes are huge, and they clearly compete with taxpaying retailers in the business of selling books, stationery and Christmas cards. Should the profits from these stores still be tax-exempt?

Also; consider the former Mobil Oil Cotton Bowl (now the AT & T Cotton Bowl). In 1991, Mobil Oil donated over one million dollars to the Cotton Bowl Association, a tax exempt organization. Pursuant to contract, inter alia:

(1) the name of the annual football game was changed to the "Mobil Oil Cotton Bowl;"

(2) all of the players' uniforms bore the name of Mobil Oil;

(3) "Mobil Oil" was prominently displayed on both end zones; and

(4) The name "Mobil Oil" had to be mentioned at least four times during the broadcasts.

Was the money donated by Mobil Oil a tax-free contribution, or was the Cotton Bowl Association in the unrelated business of advertising, in which case the Mobil Oil contribution should have been treated as taxable advertising revenues? It is appropriate for a charity to acknowledge the name of a substantial contributor. However, where does one draw the line between acknowledgment and advertising?

The IRS opined that the Mobil Oil donation was unrelated business income. Private Letter Ruling 9147007 (August 16, 1991); Announcement 92–15, 1992–5 I.R.B. 51 (February 3, 1992). Predictably, there was a firestorm of criticism from the tax exempts and their powerful friends. H.R. 5645, which would have excluded corporate sponsorship payments from UBIT, was introduced, and passed in the House of Representatives.

"One prominent attorney was heard to say that as long as there were three Texans on the House Ways and Means Committee, the Cotton Bowl would never be taxed."[g]

IRS retreated, and promulgated new proposed regulations. See Taxation of Tax–Exempt Organizations' Income from Corporate Sponsorship, 58 Fed. Reg. 5687 (proposed Jan. 22. 1993) [Proposed Treasury Regulations sections 1.512(a)–1(e), 1.513–4] at § 1.513–4(g) (Example 4).

However, IRS no longer has to feel guilty about wimping out. Have a look at § 513(i), added by the Taxpayer Relief Act of 1997. As you can see, IRS is no longer alone.

For other hot UBIT issues, consider affinity credit cards. The credit card company agrees with the charitable organization that a percentage of all charges on the credit card will be paid to the charity. Part of the money paid to the charity is for the rental of its mailing list of members. That rental income was held to be royalties, and therefore not UBIT, in Sierra Club, Inc. v. Commissioner, 86 F.3d 1526 (9th Cir.1996). However, the 9th Circuit remanded on the broader question of affinity credit cards, noting that more information was needed on whether or not the charity rendered any services in return for the payments.

5. SUBSTANTIATION, VALUATION, ETHICS

Client intends to claim a $50 charitable contribution deduction on his tax return. However, he tells Lawyer, in confidence, that he has made no charitable contributions whatsoever. Client asks about his chances of getting away with his planned tax fraud. Lawyer knows that the IRS audit rate has always been well under 2%. Therefore, there is a better than 98% chance that the IRS will not audit the return. Should Lawyer tell Client?

What if, rather than out and out tax fraud, Client merely contemplates taking a controversial position on his tax return. Lawyer knows that, if the IRS audited and litigated, Client would probably lose in court. Now, may Lawyer tell Client that there is a 98% chance that IRS won't audit the return? See Joel S. Newman, *The Audit Lottery: Don't Ask, Don't Tell?* 86 Tax Notes 1438 (March 6, 2000).

Never mind the lawyer. What about the charitable organization? Let's say that an important person (or one who thinks he is) wants to donate his papers to a university library. He puts a value of $1 million on them, due to their historical significance, and takes a charitable deduction in that amount. The university library is pleased to receive the donation, as they have some value. Furthermore, the library really doesn't care if the donor defrauds the government a little bit. In fact, it's happy to help, by agreeing to whatever valuation the donor claims.

The same game can be played with works of art, whose value is far from objective. Then there was the scandalous case in which the Smithso-

g. Paul Streckfus, *News Analysis: IRS' Pre–Inaugural Gift for Charities*, 58 Tax Notes 384, 385 (Jan. 25, 1993).

nian Institution allegedly accepted donations of precious gems, and went along with the donors' claims that they were worth up to twenty times their actual value.

In response, there is the IRS Art Advisory Panel, which second guesses the valuations which donors put on works of art. More recently, Congress has added §§ 170(f)(8) and (f)(12), and 6115, which make life, and record keeping, considerably more burdensome for the charities.

6. CHARITABLE DEDUCTIONS AS A TAX EXPENDITURE

Is the charitable contribution deduction more efficient than a direct expenditure? First, it should be noted that the charitable contribution deduction can accomplish some things which a direct expenditure cannot. A direct transfer of government funds to a religious organization would violate the First Amendment. Arguments that indirect tax expenditures were equally unconstitutional have been put to rest in Walz v. Tax Commission of the City of New York, 397 U.S. 664, 90 S.Ct. 1409, 25 L.Ed.2d 697 (1970).

Beyond the problem of religious organizations, are these indirect tax expenditures as efficient as direct subsidies? To do a cost-benefit analysis, one must define the cost, and the benefit. First, one must quantify the cost. How much tax revenue does the federal government lose as a result of the charitable contribution deduction? That figure is available, but it does not quite answer the question. To put a better question, how much more tax revenue would the government receive if the charitable contribution deduction were eliminated? Perhaps a lot, perhaps none. If § 170 were repealed, would charitable donors keep behaving as they had before, or would they shift to some other tax-favored activity, such as investing in tax-exempt bonds, thus generating no new additional tax revenue for the government? This behavior shift, known as the secondary effect of a tax change, is very difficult to measure.

The benefit must also be measured. One cannot point to annual charitable giving as the benefit. That is too simplistic. Many would contribute to charity even if there were no tax advantage in doing so. The relevant benefit, then, is the amount of increased charitable contributions caused solely by the tax incentive. This figure is, of course, not available.

However, we can speculate. We know that the level of charitable contributions went down after 1986, when the highest marginal rates went from 50% to 28%. That fact suggests that some amount of charitable contributions are, indeed, tax-driven, and that the tax-driven contributions tend to come from the higher bracket taxpayers. We also know that contributions to religious organizations, especially tithing, would probably occur even with no tax incentive. Contributions to educational institutions, museums, symphony orchestras and the like are more likely to be tax-driven. First, they are not religious organizations. Second, they tend to be the charities of choice for the higher bracket, more tax-driven donors.

Difficulties notwithstanding, some attempts have been made to gauge the efficiency of the charitable contribution deduction. They go both ways. *Compare,* Michael K. Taussig, *Economic Aspects of the Personal Income Tax Treatment of Charitable Contributions,* 20 Nat'l Tax J. 1 (1967); with Martin Feldstein, *The Income Tax and Charitable Contributions,* 28 Nat'l Tax J. 81 and 209 (1975).

The above discussion also suggests that looking at § 170 as an upside-down subsidy might be worthwhile. First of all, high bracket taxpayers are given 35¢ for every $1 they give to charity. Low bracket taxpayers are given only 10¢. Given the nature of charitable giving, that means that the government subsidizes private support of art museums and universities more than it subsidizes private support of churches and social welfare organizations. Do you suppose that anyone intended that result? *See generally,* Alice Gresham Bullock, *Taxes, Social Policy and Philanthropy: The Untapped Potential of Middle–and Low–Income Generosity,* 6 Cornell J. L. & Pub. Pol'y 325 (1997).

C. CASUALTY AND THEFT LOSSES

Code: §§ 165(c)(3), 165(h)

The deduction for personal casualty and theft losses is a hardship deduction. Normally, if two taxpayers have the same adjusted gross income, they have the same ability to pay taxes. However, if one has suffered a significant casualty loss, then his ability to pay will not be comparable. Accordingly, an adjustment must be made.

But what is a significant casualty loss? Surely, accidentally breaking one's pencil will not affect anyone's ability to pay taxes. Moreover, even as to larger losses, what is significant will not be the same for everyone. The same dollar loss might be huge for a poor man, and insignificant for a rich man.

The first concern, that some losses are simply too small to be significant for anyone, is addressed in § 165(h)(1). That section provides that a loss must exceed $100 to be considered at all. Even then, only the excess will be considered. The second concern, that the same loss can have a different impact, depending upon the taxpayer's income level, is addressed in § 165(h)(2), which provides a 10% of AGI floor under all casualty loss deductions.[h]

---

h. The 10% threshold can be explained in part on ability to pay grounds. However, there are other reasons. In 1982, Congress noted that about 35% of claims for casualty loss deductions were improper (there was no breakdown as to how many were honest mistakes and how many were fraudulent). By inserting a 10% threshold under the deduction, fewer deductions would be taken, and fewer ''mistakes'' would be made.

1. DEFINITION OF CASUALTY

(a) Physical Harm

CHAMALES v. COMMISSIONER

United States Tax Court, 2000.
T.C. Memo. 2000–33.

Nims, J.

Findings of Fact

Gerald and Kathleen Chamales (petitioners) are married and resided in Los Angeles, California, at the time of filing their petition in this case. In the spring of 1994, petitioners became interested in purchasing a residence in Brentwood Park, an exclusive Los Angeles neighborhood. They were attracted to the beautiful, parklike setting and the quiet peacefulness of the area. Subsequently, on June 2, 1994, petitioners opened escrow on property located in Brentwood Park, at 359 North Bristol Avenue. * * *

At the time petitioners opened escrow, O.J. Simpson (Simpson) owned and resided at the property located directly west of and adjacent to that being purchased by petitioners. Simpson's address was 360 North Rockingham Avenue. Both parcels were corner lots, bounded on the north by Ashford Street. The rear or westerly side of petitioners' land abutted the rear or easterly side of the Simpson property.

During the escrow period, on June 12, 1994, Nicole Brown Simpson and Ronald Goldman were murdered at Ms. Brown Simpson's condominium in West Los Angeles. Simpson was arrested for these murders shortly thereafter. Following the homicides and arrest, the Brentwood Park neighborhood surrounding the Simpson property became inundated with media personnel and equipment and with individuals drawn by the area's connection to the horrific events. The media and looky-loos[1] blocked streets, trespassed on neighboring residential property, and flew overhead in helicopters in their attempts to get close to the Simpson home. Police were summoned to the area for purposes of controlling the crowds, and barricades were installed at various Brentwood Park intersections to restrict traffic. This police presence, however, had little practical effect. Significant media and public attention continued throughout 1994 and 1995. Although Simpson was acquitted on October 4, 1995, civil proceedings in 1996 reignited public interest.

Petitioners closed escrow on June 29, 1994, purchasing the residence on North Bristol Avenue for $2,849,000. Petitioners had considered can-

---

1. As explained by petitioners' counsel, "looky-loo" is a term developed in Hollywood to describe individuals who gather at places and events in hopes of glimpsing celebrities. The phrase is apparently used in California to denote those who frequent a location not because of its status as a conventional tourist sight but because of its association with a famous or notorious person. We adopt the terminology and spelling as used in petitioners' briefs and by the witnesses at trial.

celing the escrow and had discussed this possibility with their attorney, but upon being advised that liability would result from a cancellation, they decided to go through with the transaction. Later that summer, as the crowds and disruption persisted, Gerald Chamales (petitioner) inquired of his broker Solton whether the value of his property had declined. Solton indicated that she estimated a decrease in value of 20 to 30 percent.

Petitioners' 1994 tax return was prepared by Ruben Kitay (Kitay), a certified public accountant. In the course of preparing this return, Kitay and petitioner discussed the possibility of claiming a deduction for casualty loss. After preliminary research in the regulations addressing casualty loss, Kitay spoke with two area real estate agents regarding the amount by which petitioners' property had decreased in value. The agents estimated the decline at 30 to 40 percent. Kitay and petitioner decided to use the more conservative 30 percent figure in calculating the deduction to be taken on petitioners' return. An expert appraisal was not obtained at this time, as Kitay felt that a typical appraisal based on values throughout the Brentwood Park area would be inconclusive as to the loss suffered by the few properties closest to the Simpson home.

Kitay and petitioner also recognized and discussed the fact that there existed a substantial likelihood of an audit focusing on petitioners' 1994 return. Hence, to clarify the position being taken and the reasons underlying petitioners' deduction, an explanatory supplemental statement labeled "Casualty Loss" was attached to the return. After indicating the location of petitioners' property in relation to that of Simpson, it stated that the casualty loss was premised on "the calamity of the murder & trial, which was sudden & unavoidable & which resulted in a permanent loss to value of property." A table enumerating instances of minor physical damage to petitioners' property, such as damage to lawn and sprinklers, was also attached to the return, but no valuation was placed upon the harm caused thereby.

* * *

As of early 1999, the area surrounding the former Simpson home was no longer inundated with media personnel or equipment. The police barricades restricting traffic in the immediate vicinity of petitioners' property had been removed. Looky-loos, however, continued to frequent the neighborhood, often advised of the location of Simpson's former residence by its inclusion on "star maps" published for the Los Angeles area. Anniversaries of the murders were also typically accompanied by periods of increased media and public attention.

Opinion

* * *

Petitioners contend that the media and onlooker attention following the murders and focusing on Simpson's home has decreased the value of their adjacent property. They argue that because the homicides were a

sudden, unexpected, and 1   cts of the public
interest precipitated thereby continued at least to the time of trial in this
case, they have suffered a permanent casualty loss. Petitioners further
allege that the proximity of their residence to that of Simpson has
stigmatized their property and rendered it subject to permanent buyer
resistance.

Conversely, respondent asserts that public attention over the course
of a lengthy murder trial is not the type of sudden and unexpected event
that will qualify as a casualty within the meaning of the Code. Respondent
additionally contends that the Court of Appeals for the Ninth Circuit, to
which appeal in this case would normally lie, has limited the amount that
may be claimed as a casualty loss deduction to the loss suffered as a result
of physical damage to property. According to respondent, since petitioners
have failed to substantiate any such damage, they are entitled to no
deduction. In respondent's view, any decline in market value represents
merely a temporary fluctuation and not a permanent, cognizable loss.

We agree with respondent that petitioners have not established their
entitlement to a casualty loss deduction. The difficulties suffered by
petitioners as a consequence of their proximity to the Simpson residence
do not constitute the type of damage contemplated by section 165(c)(3).
However, because we find that petitioners acted reasonably and in good
faith in the preparation of their tax return, no additional liability for the
section 6662(a) accuracy-related penalty will be imposed.

Issue 1. *Casualty Loss*

Section 165 * * * reads in relevant part * * *

Regulations promulgated under section 165 additionally provide that,
to be allowable as a deduction, a loss must be both "evidenced by closed
and completed transactions" and "fixed by identifiable events".

As interpreted by case law, a casualty loss within the meaning of
section 165(c)(3) arises when two circumstances are present. First, the
nature of the occurrence precipitating the damage to property must
qualify as a casualty. At issue here then are whether the events surrounding the alleged Simpson murders and affecting petitioners' property can
properly be termed a casualty and whether the type of loss suffered by
petitioners as a consequence of these events is recognized as deductible.
We conclude that both inquiries must be answered in the negative.

A. *Nature of Occurrence Constituting a Casualty*

The word "casualty" as used in section 165(c)(3) has been defined,
through application of the principle of ejusdem generis, by analyzing the
shared characteristics of the specifically enumerated casualties of fire,
storm, and shipwreck. As explained by this Court:

> wherever unexpected, accidental force is exerted on property and the
> taxpayer is powerless to prevent application of the force because of
> the suddenness thereof or some disability, the resulting direct and

proximate damage causes a loss which is like or similar to losses arising from the causes specifically enumerated in section 165(c)(3).

Hence, casualty for purposes of the Code denotes "an undesigned, sudden and unexpected event", or "an event due to some sudden, unexpected or unusual cause." Conversely, the term " 'excludes the progressive deterioration of property through a steadily operating cause." The sudden and unexpected occurrence, however, is not limited to those events flowing from forces of nature and may be a product of human agency.

Here, we cannot conclude that the asserted devaluation of petitioners' property was the direct and proximate result of the type of casualty contemplated by section 165(c)(3). While the stabbing of Nicole Brown Simpson and Ronald Goldman was a sudden and unexpected exertion of force, this force was not exerted upon and did not damage petitioners' property. Similarly, the initial influx of onlookers, although perhaps sudden, was not a force exerted on petitioners' property and was not, in and of itself, the source of the asserted decrease in the home's market value. Rather, petitioners base their claim of loss on months, or even years, of ongoing public attention. If neither media personnel nor looky-loos had chosen to frequent the Brentwood Park area after the murders, or if the period of interest and visitation had been brief, petitioners would have lacked grounds for alleging a permanent and devaluing change in the character of their neighborhood. Hence, the source of their difficulties would appear to be more akin to a steadily operating cause than to a casualty. Press and media attention extending for months bears little similarity to a fire, storm, or shipwreck and is not properly classified therewith as an "other casualty".

B. Nature of Damage Recognized as Deductible

With respect to the requisite nature of the damage itself, this Court has traditionally held that only physical damage to or permanent abandonment of property will be recognized as deductible under section 165. In contrast, the Court has refused to permit deductions based upon a temporary decline in market value.

For example, in *Citizens Bank v. Commissioner*, 252 F. 2d 425 (4th Cir. 1958), the Court stated that "physical damage or destruction of property is an inherent prerequisite in showing a casualty loss." When again faced with taxpayers seeking a deduction premised upon a decrease in market value, the Court further explained in *Pulvers v. Commissioner*, 407 F. 2d 838 (9th Cir.). "The scheme of our tax laws does not, however, contemplate such a series of adjustments to reflect the vicissitudes of the market, or the wavering values occasioned by a succession of adverse or favorable developments." Such a decline was termed "a hypothetical loss or a mere fluctuation in value." The Court likewise emphasized that "Not all reductions in market value resulting from casualty-type occurrences are deductible under section 165; only those losses are deductible which are the result of actual physical damage to the property." This rule was reiterated yet again when the Court observed:

In the instant case there was likewise relatively small physical damage to petitioner's property and the primary drop in value was due to buyer resistance to purchasing property in an area which had suffered a landslide. If there had been no physical damage to the property, petitioner would be entitled to no casualty loss deduction because of the decrease in market value resulting from the slide.

* * *

In *Caan v. United States*, 99–1 U.S.Tax Cas. (CCH) ¶ 50 (C.D.Cal. 1999), the District Court dismissed for failure to state a claim the complaint of taxpayers alleging facts nearly identical to those at issue here. The Caans, residents of Brentwood Park, argued that they were entitled to a section 165(c)(3) casualty loss deduction for the decline in market value and permanent buyer resistance to which they asserted their property became subject as a result of the "O.J. Simpson double murders". The court, however, reiterated that "the Ninth Circuit only recognizes casualty losses arising from physical damage caused by enumerated or other similar casualties" and held that "Because the Caans have not alleged any physical damage to their property due to the murders and subsequent media frenzy, they have not alleged a casualty loss that is a proper basis for a deduction."

Given the above decisions, we conclude that petitioners here have failed to establish that their claimed casualty loss is of a type recognized as deductible for purposes of section 165(c)(3). They have not proven the extent to which their property suffered physical damage, and their attempt to base a deduction on market devaluation is contrary to existing law.

With respect to physical damage and assuming arguendo that petitioners' loss stemmed from an occurrence that could properly be deemed a casualty, they would be entitled to a deduction for physical harm to their property. Nonetheless, although petitioners attached to their return a list of minor instances of physical damage and mentioned several other items at trial, they have neither offered evidence of the monetary value of nor provided any substantiation for such losses. We therefore have no basis for determining what, if any, portion of the claimed deduction might be allowable, and we cannot sustain a $751,427 deduction on the grounds of damage to a lawn or a sprinkler system.

* * *

Moreover, we further note that petitioners' circumstances do not reflect the type of permanent devaluation or buyer resistance which would be analogous to that held deductible in *Finkbohner v. United States*, 788 F.2d 723 (11th Cir. Ala. 1986). The evidence in the instant case reveals that media and onlooker attention has in fact lessened significantly over the years following the murders. Access to petitioners' property is no longer restricted by media equipment or police barricades. Residents of Brentwood Park have continued to invest substantial funds in remodeling and upgrading their homes. Hence, petitioners' difficulties are more akin to a temporary fluctuation in value, which no court has found to support a deduction under section 165(c)(3). We therefore hold that petitioners have failed to establish their entitlement to a casualty loss deduction. Respondent's determination of a deficiency is sustained.

haiku

Buy next to OJ

Put up with those Looky Loos

What did you expect?

(b) Sudden and Unexpected

CORBALEY v. COMMISSIONER

United States Tax Court, 1984.
T.C. Memo. 1984–201.

Memorandum Opinion

FEATHERSTON, JUDGE:

* * * In April 1978, petitioner purchased a 1946 Stinson 108–1 airplane which contained a Franklin 6A4–150–B3 engine. At the time of purchase, the airplane's engine was a replacement engine, not its original one. Apparently, there exist records which show the age of the replacement engine at the time petitioner purchased the airplane; such records, however, have not been submitted in evidence. Thus, the age of the replacement engine is unknown. Petitioner used the airplane for personal transportation and recreational purposes only.

In a letter dated August 20, 1980, addressed to "Audit Officer, Department of Treasury, Internal Revenue Service" and signed by petitioner, petitioner set forth a statement with respect to his claimed 1978 casualty loss which, he stated, "should clarify the events." In relevant part, petitioner stated that on July 28, 1978, at approximately 2:00 p.m., while en route on a flight from San Diego to Oroville, California, he experienced an airplane engine failure which forced him to land at Hanford Municipal Airport, the nearest airport he could safely reach.

After landing the airplane, and upon initial inspection and troubleshooting of the engine, petitioner found that the exhaust valve in the No. 1 cylinder had broken off inside the No. 1 cylinder. Later disassembly and thorough examination of the engine showed extensive internal damage beyond serviceable or overhaul limits.

Petitioner further stated that the engine had approximately 500 operating hours since complete major overhaul, approximately 100 operating hours since complete top overhaul, and had been thoroughly inspected and tested by an authorized inspector of the Federal Aviation Administration (FAA) some 3 months and approximately 25 operating hours prior to its failure.

In a letter to "Jon" dated April 4, 1983, apparently written to his tax preparer, Jon Nichols, in response to questions posed by respondent's counsel with respect to the casualty loss, petitioner stated that the weather conditions at the time of the engine failure were "clear, daylight, VFR—beautiful day for engine failure!"[2] He described the cause of engine failure and the extent of damage as follows—#1 cylinder exhaust valve broke off it's [sic] stem inside the cylinder cruise power. * * * rapid disintigration [sic] of #1 cylinder and piston caused massive metalic [sic] contamination of the oil system which in turn caused extensive wear on all moving parts as well as the engine case.

Petitioner further stated that the purchase price of the airplane was $6,200. With respect to the fair market value of the engine before its failure, petitioner stated that he "could only guess"; after the engine failure, petitioner stated: "No one wants a 'blown' engine," thus, the engine had no fair market value. Petitioner stated that he had no insurance to cover the engine. In February 1979, petitioner ultimately purchased, at a price of $3,600, an overhauled replacement engine of unknown age for the airplane.

On his 1978 Federal income tax return, petitioner deducted $4,345 as a casualty loss for the loss of his airplane engine. Respondent disallowed the deduction in full.

Section 165(c)(3) allows an individual a deduction for "losses of property not connected with a trade or business, if such losses arise from fire, storm, shipwreck, or other casualty, or from theft." The issue of whether petitioner is entitled to a deduction for the loss of his airplane engine turns on whether the failure of and the resultant damage sustained to the engine arose from a "casualty" within the meaning of the statute. With respect to this issue, petitioner bears the burden of proving that respondent's disallowance of the casualty deduction was erroneous.

After careful consideration of the fully stipulated record, we hold that petitioner has failed to demonstrate that the damage to his airplane engine arose from a casualty, and, therefore, we sustain respondent's determination.

The term "casualty" has been defined as—an accident, a mishap, some sudden invasion by a hostile agency; it excludes the progressive deterioration of property through a steadily operating cause. In White v. Commissioner, this Court stated that a casualty occurs: wherever unexpected, accidental force is exerted on property and the taxpayer is powerless to prevent application of the force because of the suddenness thereof or some disability, the resulting direct and proximate damage causes a loss which is like or similar to losses arising from the causes specifically enumerated in § 165(c)(3). * * *

As stated above, petitioner purchased the airplane in April 1978. At the time of purchase, this 32–year–old airplane contained a replacement

---

2. VFR—Visual Flight Rule: The weather was sufficiently clear so that the pilot could operate by visual references and without instrumentation.

engine of unknown age. The flight conditions on the day of engine failure were "clear, daylight, VFR." The engine failure, thus, was not due to adverse weather conditions, i.e., a storm. Instead, the engine failed when an exhaust valve stem broke off in the No. 1 cylinder, causing rapid disintegration of the No. 1 cylinder and piston. This resulted in massive metallic contamination of the oil system and extensive wear on all moving parts and the engine encasement beyond serviceable or overhaul limits, i.e., a "blown engine." The evidence does, not, therefore, demonstrate that the engine failure was due to an accident, a mishap, or a sudden invasion by a hostile agency, or the exertion of an "unexpected, accidental force" similar in nature to a fire, storm, or shipwreck.

While the engine's failure was concededly unexpected by petitioner, we think it is more likely, and petitioner has failed to prove otherwise, that the damage was caused by the gradual, progressive deterioration of the exhaust valve stem which finally snapped and destroyed the No. 1 cylinder. The age of the replacement engine, and of the exhaust valve itself, are unknown. Absent a showing by petitioner that the damage was caused by some external force, rather than progressive deterioration of the exhaust valve stem, we conclude that the failure was not the result of a casualty within the meaning of § 165(c)(3). Petitioner, therefore, is not entitled to the claimed casualty deduction.

To reflect the foregoing,

Decision will be entered for the respondent.

QUESTIONS

1. Why are casualties limited to "sudden, unexpected" occurrences? Could it be that only those losses are deserving of sympathy? Perhaps taxpayers should be careful enough to avoid "gradual, expected" losses on their own. If, however, we are trying to limit the deduction to unavoidable casualties, then why does Reg. § 1.165–7(a)(3)(i) allow a casualty loss deduction for an automobile accident caused by the driver's negligence?

2. What about casualty insurance? Imagine one taxpayer who buys casualty insurance to cover a personal asset. The premiums over 10 years equal $1,000. A casualty in fact occurs, but it is fully compensated by insurance. A second taxpayer declines to buy casualty insurance. During the same 10 years, a casualty occurs, which costs $1,000. Both taxpayers have incurred an expense of $1,000. However, the insurance premiums are nondeductible, while the uninsured casualty loss is deductible. Are we trying to encourage people to be negligent and uninsured?

3. You own a tree just inside your property. A wind blows the tree toward your house, and through your roof. Casualty loss?

The wind blows the tree away from your house, through your neighbor's roof. He sues, you pay. Casualty loss to you?

4. Your kindly great aunt has given you a diamond brooch, worth $10,000. Everyone in the family knows it's an heirloom. You would never sell

it. What's more, you plan to will it to your daughter. She already knows that it's an heirloom, never to be sold. Both you and your daughter think that the brooch is painfully ugly. You wear it only when your great aunt comes to visit. The brooch is stolen. Is this really a loss to you?

2. PRELIMINARY ARITHMETIC

There are personal casualty losses, and personal casualty gains. The losses will be discussed further below. Personal casualty gains occur when the casualty is compensated either by insurance coverage, damage awards, or the like. If the compensation exceeds the taxpayer's adjusted basis in the personal asset subject to the casualty, then there is a personal casualty gain.

Personal casualty losses are generally measured by the diminution in value of the asset. Repair costs are an acceptable substitute for diminution in value. To compute the casualty loss deduction, first subtract $100 from each casualty loss, and consider only the excess. Then, net out any remaining losses against any casualty gains. Finally, subtract 10% of AGI from the resulting net amount.

Example

Taxpayer has an adjusted gross income of $20,000. She owns a painting, which she purchased for $100 and is now worth $500.[i] She also owns a Plymouth Neon. Neither is a business asset.

The painting is destroyed in a fire. Her insurance pays $500.

The Neon is in a wreck. The repairs cost $4,100. Insurance pays $1,000.

The painting is a "casualty gain."

Amount Realized	$500
Less: Basis	− $100
Casualty Gain	$400

The wreck is a casualty loss.

Repairs	($4,100)
Less: Insurance	− $1,000
Less: § 165(h)(1)	− $ 100
Total Personal Casualty Loss	($3,000)

The $3,000 personal casualty loss exceeds the $400 personal casualty gain, by $2,600. Therefore, pursuant to § 165(h)(2)(A), the personal casualty loss shall be allowed to the extent of the the sum of:

---

i. The painting is neither property used in the trade or business nor held in connection with a transaction entered into for profit. Therefore, you need not worry about § 1231.

(i) the personal casualty gain of $400, plus

(ii) so much of such excess ($2,600) as exceeds 10% of AGI.

So, such excess	$2,600
Minus 10% AGI	-$2,000
	$600

3. MEASURING THE LOSS

Regulations: § 1.165–7

HELVERING v. OWENS ET AL.

United States Supreme Court, 1939.
305 U.S. 468, 59 S.Ct. 260, 83 L.Ed. 292.

MR. JUSTICE ROBERTS delivered the opinion of the Court.

* * * In No. 180 the facts are that the respondent Donald H. Owens purchased an automobile at a date subsequent to March 1, 1913, and prior to 1934, for $1,825, and used it for pleasure until June 1934 when it was damaged in a collision. The car was not insured. Prior to the accident its fair market value was $225; after that event the fair market value was $190. The respondents filed a joint income tax return for the calendar year 1934 in which they claimed a deduction of $1635, the difference between cost and fair market value after the casualty. The Commissioner reduced the deduction to $35, the difference in market value before and after the collision. The Board of Tax Appeals sustained the taxpayers' claim and the Circuit Court of Appeals affirmed its ruling.

In No. 318 it appears that the taxpayers acquired a boat, boathouse, and pier in 1926 at a cost of $5,325. In August 1933 the property, which had been used solely for pleasure, and was uninsured, was totally destroyed by a storm. Its actual value immediately prior to destruction was $3,905. The taxpayers claimed the right to deduct cost in the computation of taxable income. The Commissioner allowed only value at date of destruction. The Board of Tax Appeals held with the taxpayers but the Circuit Court of Appeals reversed the Board's ruling.

* * * The income tax acts have consistently allowed deduction for exhaustion, wear and tear, or obsolescence only in the case of "property used in the trade or business." The taxpayers in these cases could not, therefore, have claimed any deduction on this account for years prior to that in which the casualty occurred. For this reason they claim they may deduct upon the unadjusted basis,—that is,—cost. As the income tax laws call for accounting on an annual basis; as they provide for deductions for "losses sustained during the taxable year"; as the taxpayer is not allowed annual deductions for depreciation of non-business property; as section

23(h) [current § 165] requires that the deduction shall be on "the adjusted basis provided in section 113(b)" [current § 1016], thus contemplating an adjustment of value consequent on depreciation; and as the property involved was subject to depreciation and of less value in the taxable year, than its original cost, we think [§ 1016] must be read as a limitation upon the amount of the deduction so that it may not exceed cost, and in the case of depreciable non-business property may not exceed the amount of the loss actually sustained in the taxable year, measured by the then depreciated value of the property. The Treasury rulings have not been consistent, but this construction is the one which has finally been adopted.

In No. 180 judgment reversed.

In No. 318 judgment affirmed.

PROBLEMS

1. You purchase a Honda Accord as your personal car for $20,000. A few years later, when the car is worth $15,000, you are involved in an accident. The fair market value of the car immediately after the accident is $11,000. Your insurance, after your deductible, pays you $1,000. Compute the casualty loss (before considering your AGI threshold, etc.).

2. You purchase a Ford Crown Victoria for $18,000 for your personal use. After a year, when the automobile is worth $15,000, you convert it to business use. You then take $2,000 in depreciation deductions, before you are involved in an accident. You have no idea what the value of the car was before or after the accident. However, you take the car to two mechanics. The lower repair estimate is $2,500. Since you are only using the car to haul things from your business to the dump, and it still runs, you don't see why you should fix it. The other driver, concerned about his insurance premiums, offers you $1,000 if you will forget about the whole thing. You accept. Compute the casualty loss. See Reg. §§ 1.165–7(a)(5) and 1.165–7(b).

3. You purchase an Infiniti for $40,000. You use it as your personal automobile for two years. Then, when it is worth $30,000, you convert it to business use. Over the next year, you take $5,000 in depreciation deductions on the automobile. At that point, when its fair market value is $20,000, it is totally destroyed in an accident. Compute the casualty loss. See Reg. § 1.165–7(b). Pay particular attention to the sentence following Reg. § 1.165–7(b)(ii).

4. THEFT

SCHONHOFF v. COMMISSIONER

United States Tax Court, 1963.
T.C. Memo. 1963–213.

MULRONEY, JUDGE:

* * * [Petitioner's] claim that he suffered a casualty loss in 1960, presumably under section 165(c)(3) of the Internal Revenue Code of 1954, is based upon his payment in 1957 of a sum of money to a dancing studio in St. Louis for dancing lessons, which payment was allegedly induced by 'implied' misrepresentations, and only partially refunded in 1960.

Petitioner appeared pro se and he testified that in November 1957, being dissatisfied with his status as a bachelor, he enrolled in a dancing studio for 15 hours of dancing lessons in order to meet girls with a view toward marriage. He paid $184.80 under this first contract. Later that month or the next month he signed a contract with the studio for 1,000 hours of lessons and paid the studio $8,825.20. It was his contention that he signed the second contract and paid the money because of the implied representation of the studio manager that he would be able to date the girl instructors, whereas the policy of the studio was that the instructors could not have dates with students. He did not testify the manager told him he could date the instructors. It was his testimony that when he told the manager he was enrolling in order to meet girls with a view to changing his bachelor status the manager replied to the effect that he could meet pretty girls at the studio and pointed to two instructors who were then present. Almost immediately thereafter petitioner learned he could not date the instructors.

Petitioner continued with his dancing lessons in 1957, 1958 and 1959 taking, in all, about 221 hours of lessons. He tried to have dates with instructors but was unsuccessful, at least while they remained studio employees. Becoming dissatisfied in about the middle of 1959 he demanded his $8,825.20 from the studio. The studio, in 1960, refunded to him $5,500 and canceled the contract for future lessons and petitioner agreed to the cancellation and signed a release to the studio of any and all claims. Petitioner paid an attorney $600 to represent him in the matter of his claim against the studio. In his 1960 income tax return under the heading 'Other Deductions' petitioner computed loss deduction by reason of the above transaction with the dancing studio, as follows:

Loss by theft discovered in 1960	
Total original loss	$8,825.20
Recovery (less $600 attorney fee)	4,900.00
Net loss	$3,925.20

Respondent was right in disallowing the claimed theft loss. Petitioner's own version of his transactions with the dancing studio is sufficient to demonstrate he was not entitled to the claimed 1960 theft loss deduction.

In order to sustain his claimed theft loss petitioner's evidence would have to show the studio did 'steal * * * ($3,925.20) by means of deceit' within the provisions of 1955 Revised Statutes of Missouri, section 560.156. Petitioner's own evidence of his transactions with the dancing studio falls far short of establishing the substantive elements of such a crime. Petitioner failed in his burden of proof to substantiate the deduction.

Haiku

dancing to steal love
dance school steals money instead
but it is not theft

D. MEDICAL EXPENSES

Code: § 213

Regulations: § 1.213–1

1. THRESHOLDS

Like the casualty loss deduction, the medical expense deduction is a hardship deduction, targeted at those who have extraordinary medical expenses in a given taxable year. However, like the casualty loss, what is an "extraordinary" medical expense is a function of income level. Just as personal casualty losses are not deductible until they exceed 10% of AGI, medical expenses are not deductible until they exceed 7½% of AGI.

The medical expense deduction was first enacted in 1942. At that time, the threshold was 5% of AGI. Bureau of Labor Statistics figures showed that the average family spent 5% of income on medical care. Therefore, expenditures in excess of 5% were considered to be extraordinary.

When the tax laws were recodified in 1954, it had become apparent that the 5% threshold was too high, and that some with extraordinary medical expenditures were being denied a deduction. Accordingly, the threshold was lowered to 3%.

By the 1970's, there was considerable evidence that the 3% threshold was too low. In 1970, consumer expenditures on medical care averaged 5.9% of personal income. In 1978, the Treasury Department estimated that they were 8%.

In 1974, the House Ways and Means Committee tentatively agreed to raising the threshold to 5%, but the change was not enacted into law. In 1978, President Carter recommended a floor of 10% for combined medical expenses and casualty loss deductions, but the proposal got nowhere. Had the medical expense deduction evolved from a hardship provision for extraordinary expenses to a government subsidy for average medical expenses? Perhaps, alternatively, Congress just wasn't going to do anything suggested by President Carter in 1978.

In 1986, the House wanted the threshold to be 10%; the Senate wanted 5%. They compromised at 7.5%.

2. WHAT IS A DEDUCTIBLE MEDICAL EXPENSE?

FERRIS v. COMMISSIONER

United States Court of Appeals, Seventh Circuit, 1978.
582 F.2d 1112.

Before PELL, SPRECHER, and WOOD, CIRCUIT JUDGES.

PELL, CIRCUIT JUDGE.

In 1971, taxpayers Collins and Bonnie Ferris spent $194,660 to construct a swimming pool addition to their home in Maple Bluff, Wisconsin. The question in this litigation is how much of that sum may be deducted from the couple's 1971 income as a medical expense in computing their federal tax liability for that year.

Certain background facts are not disputed. Mrs. Ferris suffers from a degenerative spinal disorder which was, in 1970, causing her serious difficulty in walking or sitting. Her physician recommended that the Ferrises install a swimming pool at their residence and that Mrs. Ferris use it twice a day for the rest of her life to prevent the onset of permanent paralysis.

The Ferris residence was fairly described by Sherman Geib, taxpayers' expert appraiser, as "a luxury residence with highest quality materials and workmanship. Numerous special features and meticulous attention to details." The residence is a two and one-half story English Tudor style home, constructed of hand-cut, hand-laid stone, with servants' quarters, pantries, and other amenities befitting a home of its type. Geib estimated the market value of the home prior to the construction of the pool addition at $275,000, including therein the $160,000 value of the 3.8 acres on which the house is built.

The Ferrises, responding to the physician's suggestion, retained an architect to design an addition to their home to enclose a swimming pool. He designed a 20 by 40 foot pool with a hand-cut stone edge, Tudor style semi-circular ends, and a fountain. He recommended that the housing structure and the interior areas ought to be designed so as to use materials architecturally compatible with the main residence and of the same quality construction. The Ferrises agreed, and the exterior of the addition was constructed of hand-cut, hand-laid stone, with an expensive roof to match that of the residence. The interior featured more hand-cut stone for some walls, exposed cedar paneling for others, a cathedral ceiling with exposed wood paneling, and a ceramic tile pool deck area. All of these features, needless to say, were costly. The architect also proposed, and the Ferrises accepted, inclusion in the structure of a number of recreational entertainment facilities, such as a bar and cooking area, a sauna bath, an open terrace, a raised dining area, an indoor sunning area, and two dressing rooms. Geib, the appraiser, estimated that the swimming pool addition increased the value of the Ferris home by $97,330.

On their joint federal tax return for 1971, taxpayers claimed that $172,160 of the $194,660 spent on the pool addition were expenses for medical care within the meaning of § 213. Taxpayers had reduced the cost of the pool by the amount of money estimated to have been spent for some of the entertainment and recreational features included in the addition. Based on Geib's appraisal that the increase in the value of the residence would be roughly 50% of the cost of the addition, taxpayers claimed as deductible uncompensated expenses for medical care $86,000. The Commissioner of Internal Revenue took a different view, determining that the entire cost of a building to house the pool was not incurred primarily for medical purposes, and, using taxpayers' appraiser's 50% value added factor, allowing only a deduction of $6,500, roughly one-half of the $13,074 cost of the pool itself.

In the proceedings in the Tax Court, the Commissioner conceded that some sort of enclosure was medically necessary if Mrs. Ferris was to take twice-daily swims during the winter, and the battle shifted to the question of how much of the costs of the luxurious addition constructed by the Ferrises was properly deductible. The Commissioner contended that the expensive construction materials used were not medically necessary, and that a cost reduction should be made to account for the fact that the non-medical features built into the addition necessarily increased its size above what would have been medically necessary. He argued that an adequate pool with enclosure could have been built for $70,000 that would have increased the value of taxpayers' residence by $31,000, and thus that only $39,000 should be considered a medical expense.

The Tax Court found as a fact that "no doubt ... a large portion of the total cost of the ... addition was attributable to the need of having the structure architecturally and aesthetically compatible with petitioner's residence which is clearly a personal motivation." The court rejected the Commissioner's argument that the degree to which the addition's costs could be considered medical expenses should be accordingly reduced, however, because it was aware of "no case limiting a medical expense within the meaning of section 213 to the cheapest form of treatment." The court did agree with the Commissioner that a reduction to account for the enlarged size of the building due to the clearly nonessential features of the addition was appropriate, and reduced taxpayers' claimed medical expense by $4,000 (50% of the $8,000 it found allocable to the space for nonessentials). The court reasoned, alternatively, that the Commissioner's hypothetical $70,000 addition (with $10,000 of extra costs the court thought were medically necessary but which were not included in the Commissioner's hypothetical figures) would have added nothing to the value of taxpayers' residence, thus yielding virtually the same result the court had reached by its preferred approach. The Commissioner appeals.

As we have indicated, the Commissioner does not dispute that the reasonable costs of a swimming pool and enclosure, to the degree they are uncompensated by increased value in taxpayers' residence, are properly deductible as a medical expense within the meaning of § 213 in the circumstances of this case. It no doubt would startle the average taxpayer that the cost of an enclosed swimming pool facility, which would typically be erected for other than medical purposes and which, even given a medical motive for its construction, could receive substantial nonmedical use once built and could be deducted for federal income tax purposes.[2] Even those with passing familiarity with federal tax principles might well be surprised that an expense like this, which is clearly capital in nature, could possibly be deducted in its entirety in the year in which incurred.

Nonetheless, this is the approach Congress has chosen. Section 213 contains no ceiling limitation on the amount of deductible medical expenses, although all earlier formulations of the deduction did contain such a limitation. When the ceiling limitations were removed by the Social Security Amendments of 1965, Congress was responding to the hardship imposed when a taxpayer incurred extraordinary medical expenses but was obliged to pay income taxes on funds used to defray them. It nonetheless recognized that its choice would allow deductibility of expenses "for facilities, devices, services, and transportation which are of the types customarily used, or taken, primarily for other than medical purposes," and expressed its concern over the possibilities of abuse in such areas, swimming pools being specifically cited. We believe the history of ceiling limitations on medical deductions and Congress' expressed concern over the abuse potential inherent in removing that limitation counsel against loose construction of § 213, but it does seem clear that even capital expenditures, to the extent they are uncompensated by increases in property value, may be considered medical expenses to the degree they are incurred "for medical care" within the meaning of § 213.

The central question here is the degree to which the cost of taxpayers' swimming pool addition was an expense "for medical care." The Secretary of the Treasury has promulgated regulations on this point which taxpayers do not attack and which we find wholly consistent with § 213. § 1.213–1(e) (1)(ii) provides, in part:

> Deductions for expenditures for medical care allowable under section 213 will be confined strictly to expenses incurred primarily for the prevention or alleviation of a physical or mental defect or illness.

§ 1.213–1(e)(1)(iii) is more specific:

> Capital expenditures are generally not deductible for Federal income tax purposes.... However, an expenditure which otherwise qualifies as a medical expense under section 213 shall not be disqualified merely because it is a capital expenditure. For purposes of section 213 and this paragraph, a capital expenditure made by the taxpayer may qualify as a medical expense, If it has as its primary purpose the medical care ... of the taxpayer, his spouse, or his dependent.... (A)

---

2. We note that the tax reform proposals recently submitted by the President to the Congress would eliminate deductions for "non-medical equipment like air-conditioners and swimming pools even if purchased for medical reasons...." 9 1978 P–H Fed. Taxes P 60,062 at 60,093–94 (Jan. 26, 1978).

capital expenditure for permanent improvement or betterment of property which would not ordinarily be for the purpose of medical care ... may, nevertheless, qualify as a medical expense to the extent that the expenditure exceeds the increase in the value of the related property, if the particular expenditure is related directly to medical care.

We believe, in the light of the legislative history of § 213 and the Secretary's regulations, that the Tax Court erred as a matter of law in rejecting the Commissioner's argument that the substantial expense attributable to architectural and aesthetic compatibility was not incurred with the "primary purpose" of and "related directly to" the medical care of Mrs. Ferris. Section 213, by allowing complete deduction of capital expenditures even though they may receive substantial nonmedical use, is already quite generous in providing for medical expense deductions. We have no doubt that the 89th Congress which removed the ceiling on medical expenses, not to mention the average taxpayer, would be astounded to learn that this generosity allows deduction not only of a swimming pool and a building to house it, but also of a pool addition constructed in the grand and luxurious style employed here. This is not the law. Where a taxpayer makes a capital expenditure that would qualify as being "for medical care," but does so in a manner creating additional costs attributable to such personal motivations as architectural or aesthetic compatibility with the related property, the additional costs incurred are not expenses for medical care.

It is no answer to say, as the Tax Court did, that taxpayers are not limited to choosing the cheapest form of medical treatment available to them. A taxpayer with the means and the inclination to patronize a relatively expensive physician or to select a private room for his stay in a hospital will undoubtedly deduct more from his taxable income than a taxpayer with lesser means or more frugal tastes, but the fact remains that both taxpayers are incurring costs unquestionably directly related to medical care. That cannot be said here.

The task in cases like this one is to determine the minimum reasonable cost of a functionally adequate pool and housing structure. Taxpayers may well decide to exceed that cost and construct a facility more in keeping with their tastes, but any costs above those necessary to produce a functionally adequate facility are not incurred "for medical care." Assessing the minimum cost will not always be an easy matter, but we think evidence could support reasonably certain findings in either of two ways, both of which the Commissioner attempted to use in the Tax Court. It may be possible to deduct from a taxpayer's actual costs a sum appropriate to account for unnecessarily expensive building materials and methods and for a building size larger than needed to accommodate the therapeutic pool. Alternatively, evidence of actual costs of other taxpayers who have constructed therapeutic facilities in the same geographic area (adjusted, if necessary, for inflation) may be introduced.

Unfortunately from the point of view of judicial economy, the Tax Court did not perform the close analysis necessary to determine the minimum reasonable cost, being of the opinion that taxpayers were not limited to choosing such a facility. Much as we might like to resolve the matter without additional litigation, that is impossible on the record before us. The Commissioner's expert, Engineer Agent Frank Hanrahan, attempted to estimate deductions of luxury materials from taxpayers' actual costs, but he expressed no real confidence in his conclusions using this method because of the speculativeness of the figures with which he was working. The costs of such items as hand-cut stone, ceramic tile, exposed wood paneling, and a cathedral ceiling, relative to less expensive but adequate materials, simply do not appear in the record. Nor is there any solid evidence on which we might base a conclusion as to the amount that could have been saved had the Ferris addition been of the smaller size necessary to house the pool without additional recreational facilities.

Hanrahan also testified that other taxpayers had constructed therapeutic facilities in the general area, and that based on his examination of two of them and their actual costs, he estimated that an adequate pool and housing facility could have been constructed for $70,000, all costs included. The Tax Court found, however, that even if this approach were a proper one, there were several items necessary to the operation of a therapeutic pool that Hanrahan had not included in his hypothetical facility. At least some of the factors mentioned by the court, however, e.g., vapor barriers and water temperature, were expressly stated by Hanrahan to have been considered in his analysis. Moreover, the court's estimate that $10,000 would be necessary to cover the cost of omitted necessities was, as the court recognized, based on no real cost evidence. In these circumstances, and because, as will be seen shortly, no final resolution of the hypothetical facility's deductibility can be made now in any event, we think the soundest course is to remand the whole issue to the Tax Court in the hope that the parties' evidence will be more to the point the second time around.

As we mentioned earlier, the Tax Court ultimately rejected the Commissioner's hypothetical cost approach because an addition constructed at minimum functional cost would add nothing to the value of the Ferris residence. This finding was clearly erroneous. The only evidence to support it was that given by Geib, the appraiser, who specifically declined to estimate what if any value would be added by the hypothetical enclosure and pool because there were too many variables undefined, but who did indicate that an unattractive or shoddy facility could in fact detract from the total property value. The point, of course, is that no specific reference to the hypothetical $70,000 facility was made. On remand, the parties will no doubt want to do a better job of adducing evidence of exactly what a hypothetical adequate facility would involve, and of precisely what effect such a facility would have on the Ferris' property value.[3]

---

3. We also decline the Commissioner's invitation to apply Geib's 50% rule of thumb for value enhancement to the $70,000 facility. Geib expressly stated that the 50% factor was a maximum,

We emphasize in this regard that the degree to which a minimum adequate facility would increase property value, while relevant to the Tax Court's analysis, is not relevant in deciding whether or not the luxury elements of a facility are undertaken "for medical care." We have already determined that they are not. They fit into the analysis after the proper medical expense is determined, in order to decide the degree to which the expense would be "compensated" for within the meaning of section 213 by an increase in property value. A deduction for medical expenses should not in any circumstance exceed the cost of a functionally adequate facility, although we do not foreclose the possibility, if the evidence on remand should support it, that in the market of potential buyers of luxury residences, a facility of mere functional adequacy would add nothing to the property value of the related property and, thus, that the whole cost thereof should be deductible. On the other hand, we do have some difficulty in conceiving that a functional indoor swimming pool sufficient for therapeutic purposes, even though not encased in and constructed with expensive architectural and building materials, would not add with some reasonable substantiality to the fair market value of the residence, willing purchasers presumably realizing that the costs of the basic component of a more splendid recreational natatorium had already been incurred, and that the basic structure could be the beginning point of a structure more desirable to them.

For the reasons stated herein, the judgment of the Tax Court is reversed and the cause is remanded for further proceedings consistent herewith.

QUESTIONS, NOTES

1. What, exactly, was the holding of the case?

2. What happens, on remand, if the appraiser determines that a minimally adequate $70,000 pool, presumably with a corrugated iron roof, would actually lower the value of the house by $50,000?

3. Collins Ferris was once General Patton's personal pilot during the North African campaign in World War II. He spent 30 years in the Air Force, retiring as a major general. He then went to law school, and ended up a bank president. The house in question was once owned by Glenn Frank, president of the University of Wisconsin.

COMMISSIONER v. BILDER

United States Supreme Court, 1962.
369 U.S. 499, 82 S.Ct. 881, 8 L.Ed.2d 65.

MR. JUSTICE HARLAN delivered the opinion of the Court.

This case concerns the deductibility as an expense for "medical care," under § 213 of the International Revenue Code of 1954, § 213, of rent

---

subject to reduction in various circumstances, including very possibly those that would be involved in erecting a "merely" adequate $70,000 facility beside a high priced luxury residence.

paid by a taxpayer for an apartment in Florida, where he was ordered by his physician, as part of a regimen of medical treatment to spend the winter months.

The taxpayer, now deceased, was an attorney practicing law in Newark, New Jersey. In December 1953, when he was 43 years of age and had suffered four heart attacks during the previous eight years, he was advised by a heart specialist to spend the winter season in a warm climate. The taxpayer, his wife and his three-year-old daughter proceeded immediately to Fort Lauderdale, Florida, where they resided for the ensuing three months in an apartment rented for $1,500. Two months of the succeeding winter were also spent in Fort Lauderdale in an apartment rented for $829.

The taxpayer claimed the two rental payments as deductible medical expenses in his 1954 and 1955 income tax returns. These deductions were disallowed in their entirety by the Commissioner.[4] The Tax Court reversed the Commissioner's determination to the extent of one-third of the deductions, finding that proportion of the total claimed attributable to the taxpayer's own living accommodations. The remaining two-thirds it attributed to the accommodations of his wife and child, whose presence, the Tax Court concluded, had not been shown to be necessary to the medical treatment of the taxpayer's illness.

On cross-appeals from the decision of the Tax Court, the Court of Appeals held, by a divided vote, that the full rental payments were deductible as expenses for "medical care" within the meaning of § 213. Because of a subsequent contrary holding by the Court of Appeals for the Second Circuit, and the need for a uniform rule on the point, we granted certiorari to resolve the conflict.

The Commissioner concedes that prior to the enactment of the International Revenue Code of 1954 rental payments of the sort made by the taxpayer were recognized as deductible medical expenses. This was because § 23(x) of the International Revenue Code of 1939, though expressly authorizing deductions only for "amounts paid for the diagnosis, cure, mitigation, treatment, or prevention of disease," had been construed to include "travel primarily for and essential to * * * the prevention or alleviation of a physical or mental defect or illness," and the cost of meals and lodging during such travel.

The Commissioner maintains, however, that it was the purpose of Congress, in enacting § 213(e)(1)(A) of the 1954 Code, albeit in language identical to that used in § 23(x) of the 1939 Code to deny deductions for all personal or living expenses incidental to medical treatment other than the cost of transportation of the patient alone, that exception having been

---

4. The Commissioner concedes that the taxpayer's sojourn in Florida was not for vacation purposes but was "a medical necessity and * * * a primary part of necessary medical treatment of a disease" from which the taxpayer was suffering, i.e., atherosclerosis. The taxpayer also claimed in each of his tax returns a $250 deduction for his transportation between Newark and Fort Lauderdale. Although the Commissioner initially disallowed this deduction, he thereafter acquiesced in its allowance by the Tax Court.

expressly added by subdivision (B) to the definition of "medical care" in § 213(e)(1).

We consider the Commissioner's position unassailable in light of the congressional purpose explicitly revealed in the House and Senate Committee Reports on the bill. These reports, anticipating the precise situation now before us, state: "Subsection (e) defines medical care to mean amounts paid for the diagnosis, cure, mitigation, treatment, or prevention of diseases or for the purpose of affecting any structure or function of the body (including amounts paid for accident or health insurance), or for transportation primarily for and essential to medical care. The deduction permitted for 'transportation primarily for and essential to medical care' clarifies existing law in that it specifically excludes deduction of any meals and lodging while away from home receiving medical treatment. For example, if a doctor prescribes that a patient must go to Florida in order to alleviate specific chronic ailments and to escape unfavorable climatic conditions which have proven injurious to the health of the taxpayer, and the travel is prescribed for reasons other than the general improvement of a patient's health, the cost of the patient's transportation to Florida would be deductible but not his living expenses while there. However, if a doctor prescribed an appendectomy and the taxpayer chose to go to Florida for the operation not even his transportation costs would be deductible. The subsection is not intended otherwise to change the existing definitions of medical care, to deny the cost of ordinary ambulance transportation nor to deny the cost of food or lodging provided as part of a hospital bill."[4]

Since under the predecessor statute, as it had been construed, expenses for meals and lodging were deductible as expenses for "medical care," it may well be true that the Committee Reports spoke in part inartistically when they referred to subsection (e) as a mere clarification of "existing law," although it will be noted that the report also referred to what was being done as a pro tanto "change" in "the existing definitions of medical care." Yet Congress' purpose to exclude such expenses as medical deductions under the new bill is unmistakable in these authoritative pronouncements. It is that factor which is of controlling importance here.[5]

---

4. The substance of the rule set forth in both Reports has been embodied in the Treasury Regulations interpreting § 213: "(iv) Expenses paid for transportation primarily for and essential to the rendition of the medical care are expenses paid for medical care. However, an amount allowable as a deduction for 'transportation primarily for and essential to medical care' shall not include the cost of any meals and lodging while away from home receiving medical treatment. For example, if a doctor prescribes that a taxpayer go to a warm climate in order to alleviate a specific chronic ailment, the cost of meals and lodging while there would not be deductible. On the other hand, if the travel is undertaken merely for the general improvement of a taxpayer's health, neither the cost of transportation nor the cost of meals and lodging would be deductible. If a doctor prescribes an operation or other medical care, and the taxpayer chooses for purely personal considerations to travel to another locality (such as a resort area) for the operation or the other medical care, neither the cost of transportation nor the cost of meals and lodging (except where paid as part of a hospital bill) is deductible." Treasury Regulations on Income Tax (1954 Code) § 1.213–1(e)(1)(iv).

5. The explicitness of the Committee Reports renders it unnecessary to consider the Commissioner's alternative argument that the statute on its face precludes these deductions because (1)

We need not consider whether we would be warranted in disregarding these unequivocal expressions of legislative intent if the statute were so written as to permit no reasonable construction other than that urged on behalf of the taxpayer. Even the initial decision of the Tax Court under the 1939 Code respecting the deductibility of similar expenses under § 23(x) recognized that the language of that statute was "susceptible to a variety of conflicting interpretations," The Tax Court's conclusion as to the meaning of § 23(x) of the earlier statute which was affirmed by the Court of Appeals, and acquiesced in by the Commissioner, necessarily rested on what emerged from a study of the legislative history of that enactment. So too the conclusion in this case, which turns on the construction of the identical words re-enacted as part of § 213, must be based on an examination of the legislative history of this provision of the 1954 Code. The Committee Reports foreclose any reading of that provision which would permit this taxpayer to take the rental payments for his Florida apartment as "medical care" deductions.

Reversed.

MR. JUSTICE DOUGLAS would affirm the judgment below for the reasons given by JUDGE KALODNER, 289 F.2d 291.

MR. JUSTICE FRANKFURTER took no part in the decision of this case.

MR. JUSTICE WHITE took no part in the consideration or decision of this case.

FINZER v. UNITED STATES

United States District Court, N.D. Illinois, Eastern Division, 2007.
496 F. Supp.2d 954.

Memorandum Opinion and Order

KENNELLY, DISTRICT JUDGE.

* * *.

In 2002, John and Elizabeth Finzer entered into a residency agreement with CC–Lake, Inc., which owns and operates Classic Residence by Hyatt at the Glen, a lifetime care facility located in Glenview, Illinois (collectively, Hyatt). Classic Residence is a continuing care community * * * that provides life care services to individuals aged sixty-two years and older. Under the agreement, the Finzers receive residential accommodations, meals, upscale amenities, and assisted living and skilled nursing services if needed. The agreement will remain in effect for the rest of their lives unless terminated by the Finzers upon sixty days notice, or by Hyatt for one of the causes enumerated in the agreement.

---

§ 262 of the 1954 Code, 26 U.S.C. § 262, 26 U.S.C.A. § 262, allows no deductions for "personal, living, or family expenses" "(e)xcept as otherwise expressly provided in this chapter," and (2) apart from the medical "transportation" expense provided in § 213(e)(1)(B), no other express exception can be found in the statute. And the equitable considerations which the respondent brings to bear in support of her construction of § 213 are of course beside the point in this Court, since we must give the statute effect in accordance with the purpose so clearly manifested by Congress.

The agreement requires all residents to pay an entrance fee, which varies based upon the living unit selected by the resident. The Finzers selected a 2,021 square foot, two-bedroom, two-and-a-half bath villa that required an entrance fee of $723,800. Other models required a significantly smaller entrance fee. * * * It is undisputed that all residents receive the same access to assisted living and nursing care regardless of the size of their residential unit or the entrance fee they pay.

The residency agreement provides that when the agreement is terminated for any reason, including the death of the resident, the resident (or his estate) is entitled to a refund equal to the greater of 90% of the entrance fee, or the entrance fee less a fee of 2% for each month the resident was at Classic Residence. In other words, if a resident dies or terminates the agreement after being at Classic Residence for only one month, he or his estate will be entitled to a refund of 98% of the entrance fee. After a resident has been at Classic Residence for five months, he is entitled to a refund of 90% of the entrance fee. Hyatt places no conditions on a resident's entitlement to a refund, other than that Hyatt has one hundred twenty days after termination to give a former resident (or his estate) the money. The Finzers' agreement includes as an appendix a promissory note made by Hyatt in favor of the Finzers for the full amount of the entrance fee. The note states that the entrance fee "is intended to be a loan." It further states that upon termination of the residency agreement, Hyatt will repay the entrance fee, less a charge of 2% of the entrance fee for each month of occupancy up to a maximum charge of 10%. The note does not bear interest except in the case of Hyatt's default. Hyatt's chief financial officer, Gary Smith, testified that the entrance fee is intended to be a loan.

The residency agreement also requires the Finzers to make monthly payments for as long as they live at Classic Residence. The monthly payment, currently $4,665, may be increased or decreased by Hyatt upon sixty days written notice. The Finzers' agreement states that all costs of operating Classic Residence, including the cost of assisted living and skilled nursing care, are intended to be paid from the monthly fees, not including the proceeds of the residents' entrance fees. Smith testified that the agreement accurately states how Classic Residence's operating costs are paid. He also testified that Hyatt does not make a profit from the monthly fees but hopes to make a profit from the entrance fees.

* * *

Hyatt sent [the Finzers] another letter regarding the potential deductibility of their entrance fee. * * *[The letter was] based upon actuarial information and statistics. * * * [The letter claimed that in] 2002, 41% of the entrance fee could have been claimed as a medical deduction * * *. Hyatt based the 41% figure on an analysis completed by its outside consultants, Milliman USA. Hyatt retained Milliman to calculate Hyatt's obligation to provide future services to Classic Residence residents. Hyatt's chief financial officer testified that Hyatt did not take into account depreciation, selling, administrative and general expenses in determining that 41% of the entrance fees are attributable to medical expenses. Hyatt's letter to the Finzers providing the 41% figure stated that they should contact their tax advisor and that Hyatt was taking no position on potential tax deductibility.

The Finzers' accountant, Marshall Weller, testified that he relied on the 41% figure in the letter from Hyatt to prepare an amended 2002 return for the Finzers. He testified that he simply relied on the letter from Hyatt and did no separate analysis or research but nonetheless believed that it was appropriate to use Hyatt's 41% figure. (Weller did not explain this, and the Finzers offered no evidence to explain why Weller appropriately could rely on Hyatt's letter given its hedging regarding deductibility.) Using the 41% figure, the Finzers' submitted an amended return showing a $159,960 increase in their total itemized deductions. They therefore sought a $43,178 refund, which the IRS denied.

In a tax refund case, the taxpayer bears the burden of proving that the IRS's assessment of taxes was erroneous and of showing the correct amount he is entitled to recover. * * * To do so, they must show that the 41% medical expense ratio Hyatt provided them was proper.

There are several reasons why the Finzers have not met their burden. First and foremost, the testimony was undisputed that residents at Classic Residence pay different entrance fees based on the size of the residential unit they select. Though the Finzers paid $723,800, they would have received the same access to medical care had they selected a smaller unit that required an entrance fee of only $275,000. The Finzers presented no evidence to support a finding that any part of their entrance fee over $275,000 can be properly attributable to medical care. Indeed, their attorney conceded in response to a question by the Court that "this is a difficult question at best." The evidence shows beyond any doubt that the portion of the entrance fee over $275,000 relates solely to the quality of the housing unit selected and has no relation to the Finzers' medical costs. Assuming for purposes of discussion that 41% of $275,000 properly could be deducted as a medical expense, the Finzers would be entitled to a deduction of $112,750, which is less than the $136,798 the Finzers claimed as a deduction on their original 2002 return.

Even if the entrance fees did not vary based on the size of the residential units, the Finzers still would be unable to prevail, because they have not met their burden of showing that 41% of *any* entrance fee is properly attributable to medical expenses. The unrebutted testimony of Hyatt's executives shows that the monthly fees are what Hyatt uses to pay for all medical expenses incurred by residents. Moreover, the residency agreement states that the proceeds of the entrance fees are not used to provide services to the residents. Gary Smith testified that the entrance fees collected from the first occupants at Classic Residence were used to repay the construction loan for the facility and that the remainder of the entrance fee proceeds were distributable to Hyatt's owners. There is no evidence that any portion of the Finzers' entrance fee was used to pay medical expenses.

Even if some portion of the entrance fees is properly deductible as a medical expense, the Finzers have not carried their burden of proving that 41% is an appropriate percentage. To the contrary, the unrefuted evidence shows that Hyatt arrived at that figure without taking into account significant components of its cost structure. Gary Smith testified that Hyatt did not take into account depreciation, the cost of acquiring new residency contracts, sales, general, or administrative expenses. Without the inclusion of these costs, Hyatt (and, therefore, the Finzers), cannot justify their position that 41% of the entrance fee is attributable to medical costs. The Finzers' argument that their accountant was entitled to simply rely on the information provided by Hyatt is not enough to carry the day.

The government also contends that 90% of the entrance fee cannot be deducted as a medical expense because it was a loan from the Finzers to Hyatt. They point out that, under the tax law, issuance or receipt of a loan is not a taxable event. * * * Examination of the substance of the transaction in this case reveals that the entrance fee was structured as a loan. The Finzers ignore the fact that the entrance agreement includes a promissory note issued for their benefit that specifically describes the entrance fee as a loan. Moreover, Hyatt always ends up returning 90% of the entrance fee to its residents. That *is* a loan.

[The Court distinguishes prior Revenue Rulings that supported the deductibility of a portion of somewhat similar fees—Ed.]

* * *

Conclusion

For the foregoing reasons, the Court directs the Clerk to enter judgment in favor of the United States.

QUESTION

Which nursing home or assisted living facility payments should qualify for the medical expense deduction?

3. MEDICAL EXPENSE REIMBURSEMENT PLANS

PRIVATE LETTER RULING 9409006

November 12, 1993

Issues

(1) Whether A, a sole proprietor, is entitled to deduct under section 162(a) of the Internal Revenue Code amounts paid to B, A's spouse and employee, as reimbursement of medical expenses under an employer-provided accident or health plan.

(2) Whether amounts B receives as reimbursement of expenses that B incurs on behalf of B, A, and their dependents are excluded from B's gross income under section 105(b).

Facts

A operates a consulting business as a sole proprietor and employs B, A's spouse, to perform certain services in connection with the business. B receives compensation for the services B performs and includes the compensation in gross income on the couple's jointly-filed federal income tax return. A adopted a written employer-provided accident and health plan that, by its terms, covers all employees of A's business. During the year in question, A reimbursed B, pursuant to the plan, for the expenses of medical care that B incurred on behalf of B, A, and their dependents. You agreed that there is a bona fide employer-employee relationship between A and B.

Law

Section 162(a) of the Code allows a deduction for all the ordinary and necessary expenses paid or incurred during the taxable year in carrying on a trade or business, including reasonable salaries and other compensation for services rendered.

Section 213(a) of the Code allows a deduction for the expenses paid during the taxable year, not compensated by insurance or otherwise, for medical care of the taxpayer, the taxpayer's spouse, or a dependent, to the extent that such expenses exceed 7.5 percent of the taxpayer's adjusted gross income. The term "medical care" is defined in section 213(d).

Section 105(b) of the Code generally allows an employee to exclude from gross income employer-paid reimbursements for the expenses of medical care (as defined in section 213(d)) of the employee and the employee's spouse and dependents.

Rev.Rul. 71–588, 1971–2 C.B. 91, holds that amounts paid by a sole proprietor to his spouse, a bona fide employee of the business, under an accident and health plan covering all employees are (1) excludable from the employee-spouse's gross income under section 105(b) of the Code and (2) deductible by the employer-spouse as a business expense under section 162(a).

Conclusion

Applying the law to the facts of the present case, the amounts paid to B under the plan as reimbursement for medical expenses are deductible by A as a business expense under section 162(a) of the Code. Further, B may exclude these amounts from gross income under section 105(b).

QUESTION

Alice receives salary of $100,000. She incurs $5,000 in medical expenses this year, within the meaning of § 213.

Betty receives salary of $95,000. In addition to her salary, her employer reimburses her medical expenses of $5,000 this year.

Assume that Alice and Betty's adjusted gross incomes are pretty comparable. Who has a better deal?

4. OTHER MEDICAL EXPENSES

Dancing lessons cannot be deductible as medical expenses, J.J. Thoene, 33 T.C. 62 (1959), not even ballet, N. Ende, T.C. Memo. 1975–256. Other expenses held nondeductible as medical expenses include:

Teeth whitening	Rev. Rul. 2003–57
Paid Lawn Mowing Service	Taylor v. Commissioner, T.C. Memo. 1987–399 [Even though taxpayer's allergies preventing him from mowing himself.]
Cult deprogramming	Letter Ruling 8021004
Ear piercing	Rev. Rul. 82–111, 1982–1 C.B. 48
Marriage Counselling	Rev. Rul. 75–319, 1975–2 C.B. 88
Pilgrimage to the Shrine of Our Lady of Lourdes	Ring v. Commissioner, 23 T.C. 950 (1955).
Veterinary Expenses	L.J. Schoen, T.C. Memo. 1975–167 [Held: the pet was not a dependent. However, in Van Dusen v. Commissioner, 136 T.C. No. 25 (2011), taxpayer incurred out-of-pocket veterinary expenses in neutering wild cats on behalf of Fix Our Ferals, a § 501(c)(3) organization. Those expenses were held deductible.]
Fathering children through unrelated gestational carriers via in vitro fertilization	Magdalin v. Commissioner, T.C. Memo. 2008–293.
Cost of infant formula after double mastectomy makes breastfeeding impossible	PRL 200941003. BUT breast pumps are deductible. Announcement 2011–14.

In Frank M. Rabb, T.C. Memo. 1972–119, the expenses of "milieu therapy" prescribed by taxpayer's psychiatrist, including shopping excursions and home remodeling, were held to be nondeductible.

However, the following expenditures were held to be deductible medical expenses:

Smoking cessation programs	Rev. Rul. 99–28
Treatment of Obesity	Rev. Rul. 2002–19
Clarinet lessons (recommended by orthodontist)	Rev. Rul. 62–210, 1962–2 C.B. 89

Acupuncture   Rev. Rul. 72–593, 1972–2 C.B. 180

Navajo "sing"   R.H. Tso, T.C. Memo 1980–399

Vasectomy   Rev. Rul. 97–9, 1997–1 C.B. 77.

[But the deduction was reduced due to taxpayer's failure to produce adequate substantiating records.]

Sex change [deductible in part]   O'Donnabhain v. Commissioner, 134 T. C. 34 (2010)

CHAPTER XI

DEFERRED PAYMENT SALES

■ ■ ■

Code: §§ 453, 453A

Regulations: §§ 1.453–1, 4, 6 and 9; 15a.453–1

A. INTRODUCTION

Review the cash method, the accrual method, and the cash equivalency doctrine, *supra* at 265.

You have all seen advertisements for automobiles and major appliances that promise, "No money down!" These advertisements are offering to sell you something today, with the purchase price not due until tomorrow, or even next year. Of course, you sign a contract to pay in the future, and interest is charged.

Consider the effect of the cash equivalency doctrine on these installment sales. If the installment obligations are deemed to be the equivalent of cash, and the sale produced a gain, then the seller will have to pay tax on the entire gain in the year of sale. This tax treatment will follow even though she determines income by the cash method,[a] and receives no actual payment until the next year.

This harshness (tax due on a transaction that produced no cash) has been addressed by the mechanism of installment reporting. Treasury began allowing installment reporting as early as 1918[b], and Congress confirmed the treatment by statute in 1926.[c] The operation of installment reporting has remained remarkably consistent from 1918 to the present.

---

a. If the seller is on the accrual method, the same result occurs automatically, without regard to the cash equivalency doctrine.

b. Treas. Reg. 33, art. 120 (1918).

c. § 212(d) Revenue Act of 1926, 44 Stat. 23. This legislation was in response to B.B. Todd, Inc., 1 B.T.A. 762 (1925). In Todd, the installment reporting regulation was held invalid as inconsistent with the then current statute, which authorized only cash or accrual reporting.

Since the regulation was promulgated by the government and favorable to the taxpayer, one might well ask who challenged the regulation. Actually, neither party to the case challenged the

B. HOW IT OPERATES

1. GENERAL

Installment reporting does two things. First, it allows the taxpayer to report income as the cash comes in. Second, it prorates the total income generated by a sale among the cash receipts.

Illustrative Example

After four years of lessons, Xavier Yuppie has bowed to the increasingly strident demands of his entire family. Reluctantly, he has abandoned his quest to become a concert pianist. Now, he must get rid of the baby grand.

He bought it from a famous pianist for $15,000, and he's selling it for $30,000. The buyer will pay him $5,000 down, and sign a contract to pay $10,000 next year, and the remaining $15,000 the year after that. Appropriate interest will be paid along with the second and final payments.

Section 453(c) provides that Yuppie will recognize as income each year:

> ... that proportion of the payments received in that year which the gross profit ... bears to the total contract price.

Yuppie's total contract price is $30,000. His gross profit is:

Amount Realized	$30,000
Basis	$-15,000
Gross Profit	$15,000

The ratio of gross profit to contract price is

$$\frac{\text{gross profit}}{\text{contract price}} \quad = \quad \frac{\$15,000}{\$30,000} \quad = \quad \frac{1}{2}$$

Therefore, every time Yuppie receives $1 of sales proceeds, 50 cents will be recognized as income. In the year of the sale, Yuppie receives a down payment of $5,000, of which $2,500 will be taxable income.

Compute Yuppie's taxable income from the second and third installments.

2. DEALERS AND FACTORING

What if Yuppie simply sells (factors) his installment contract? (See Chapter 6, *supra*, at 274) Indeed, if the contract provides for sufficient interest to cover the risk of nonpayment and the time value of money, it

---

regulation. The government claimed the taxpayer failed to maintain adequate records to qualify for installment reporting. The Board of Tax Appeals seized the opportunity to consider the validity of the regulation and struck it down.

might be factorable for at or near its face value. If so, the seller would receive $30,000 in cash in the year of sale, and installment reporting would be unnecessary.

Although dealers factor their installment contracts all the time, nondealers like Yuppie don't. They wouldn't know where to turn to find a buyer. In 1987, Congress recognized this difference between dealers and nondealers. Subject to minor exceptions, the Omnibus Budget Reconciliation Act of 1987 repealed installment reporting for dealer sales of personal and real property. See § 453(b)(2).

QUESTION

What result to Yuppie (a nondealer) if he sells the contract in the year following the year of sale, but before receiving the $10,000 payment due that year? See § 453B (a), (b).

3. THE TREATMENT OF INTEREST

Installment reporting affects only gain realized on the sale of property. It has no impact on when interest on the deferred payments must be reported. See Rev. Rul. 75–171, 1975–1 CB 140 (accrual basis taxpayer reporting profit on deferred payment sales of property under the installment method, must accrue interest income on the sales). If the deferred payment contract fails to provide for adequate interest there will be "unstated interest" under section 483 or 1274, depending upon which provision applies. The selling price (and gain reported on the installment method) is reduced by the unstated interest, and the unstated interest is reported as interest income under the taxpayer's regular accounting method. See Reg. § 15a.453–1(b)(2)(ii) ("Neither interest, whether stated or unstated, nor original issue discount, is considered to be part of the selling price."). In general, unstated interest will arise only if the deferred payment contract fails to provide for interest at or above the applicable federal rate under section 1274(d)(1). The applicable federal rate is set each month by the Treasury, and is based on market rates of interest.

PROBLEM

In Year 1 Fred purchased Greenacre for $50,000. In Year 2 Fred sold Greenacre for $200,000; $50,000 was paid at closing, and the buyer signed a note calling for three equal annual installment payments of $50,000 each in Years 3, 4 and 5. The note provided for adequate interest on the deferred payments. If Fred uses the installment method available under section 453, how much income must he report in Years 2, 3, 4 and 5? Does it matter whether Fred determines income from other sources using the cash or accrual method?

1.   FOR A FIXED PRICE

Suppose Freu,   ...ceuing problem, made a timely election to have section 453 *not* a~~p~~ y to his sale? Assuming Fred is an accrual basis taxpayer, how much income would he report for Years 2, 3, 4 and 5?

Can you think of any reason why Fred, as an accrual basis taxpayer, might choose to avoid installment reporting? Remember *Stranahan, supra* at 286.

Suppose Fred, like most individuals, is a cash basis taxpayer. How much income would he report in Years 2, 3, 4 and 5, if he elected not to use installment reporting under section 453? Before you answer this question, consider the next case.

WARREN JONES COMPANY v. COMMISSIONER

United States Court of Appeals, Ninth Circuit, 1975.
524 F.2d 788.

Before ELY and HUFSTEDLER, CIRCUIT JUDGES, and TAYLOR, SENIOR DISTRICT JUDGE.

ELY, CIRCUIT JUDGE:

During its taxable year ending on October 31, 1968, the Warren Jones Company, a cash basis taxpayer, sold an apartment building for $153,000. In return, the taxpayer received a cash downpayment of $20,000 and the buyer's promise in a standard form real estate contract, to pay $133,000, plus interest, over the following fifteen years. The Tax Court held, with three judges dissenting, that the fair market value of the real estate contract did not constitute an "amount realized" by the taxpayer in the taxable year of sale under section 1001(b) of the Internal Revenue Code. The Commissioner of Internal Revenue has appealed, and we reverse.

I.   Background

On May 27, 1968, the taxpayer, a family-held corporation chartered by the State of Washington, entered into a real estate contract for the sale of one of its Seattle apartment buildings, the Wallingford Court Apartments, to Bernard and Jo Ann Storey for $153,000. When the sale closed on June 15, 1968, the Storeys paid $20,000 in cash and took possession of the apartments. The Storeys were then obligated by the contract to pay the taxpayer $1,000 per month, plus 8 percent interest on the declining balance, for a period of fifteen years. The balance due at the end of fifteen years is to be payable in a lump sum. The contract was the only evidence of the Storeys' indebtedness, since no notes or other such instruments passed between the parties. Upon receipt of the full purchase price, the taxpayer is obligated by the contract to deed the Wallingford Apartments to the Storeys.

The Tax Court found, as facts, that the transaction between the taxpayer and the Storeys was a completed sale in the taxable year ending on October 31, 1968, and that in that year, the Storeys were solvent obligors. The court also found that real estate contracts such as that between the taxpayer and the Storeys were regularly bought and sold in the Seattle area. The court concluded, from the testimony before it, that in the taxable year of sale, the taxpayer could have sold its contract, which had a face value of $133,000, to a savings and loan association or a similar institutional buyer for approximately $117,980. The court found, however, that in accordance with prevailing business practices, any potential buyer for the contract would likely have required the taxpayer to deposit $41,000 of the proceeds from the sale of the contract in a savings account, assigned to the buyer, for the purpose of securing the first $41,000 of the Storeys' payments. Consequently, the court found that in the taxable year of sale, the contract had a fair market value of only $76,980 (the contract's selling price minus the amount deposited in the assigned savings account.)

On the sale's closing date, the taxpayer had an adjusted basis of $61,913 in the Wallingford Apartments. In determining the amount it had realized from the sale, the taxpayer added only the $20,000 downpayment and the portion of the $4,000 in monthly payments it had received that was allocable to principal. Consequently, on its federal income tax return for the taxable year ending October 31, 1968, the taxpayer reported no gain from the apartment sale. The taxpayer's return explained that the corporation reported on the cash basis and that under the Tax Court's holding in Nina J. Ennis, 17 T.C. 465 (1951), it was not required to report gain on the sale until it had recovered its basis. The return also stated, however, that in the event the taxpayer was required to report gain in the taxable year of the sale, it elected to do so on the installment basis (I.R.C. § 453).

The Commissioner disagreed with the taxpayer's assertion that it had realized no gain on the sale, but he conceded that the sale qualified as an installment sale. Consequently, the Commissioner recalculated the taxpayer's gain in accordance with section 453 and notified the taxpayer that it had recognized an additional $12,098 in long term capital gain. The taxpayer then petitioned the Tax Court for a redetermination of its liability.

Section 1001 provides, in pertinent part, as follows:

(a) COMPUTATION OF GAIN OR LOSS. The gain from the sale or other disposition of property shall be the excess of the amount realized therefrom over the adjusted basis....

(b) AMOUNT REALIZED. The amount realized from the sale or other disposition of property shall be the sum of any money received plus the fair market value of the property (other than money) received.

The question presented is whether section 1001(b) requires the taxpayer to include the fair market value of its real estate contract with the Storeys in determining the "amount realized" during the taxable year of the sale.

Holding that the fair market value of the contract was not includable in the amount realized from the sale, the Tax Court majority relied on the doctrine of "cash equivalency." Under that doctrine, the cash basis taxpayer must report income received in the form of property only if the property is the "equivalent of cash."

The Tax Court majority adopted the following as its definition of the phrase, "equivalent of cash":

> ... if the promise to pay of a solvent obligor is unconditional and assignable, not subject to set-offs, and is of a kind that is frequently transferred to lenders or investors at a discount not substantially greater than the generally prevailing premium for the use of money, such promise is the equivalent of cash ...

Applying the quoted definition, the Tax Court held that the taxpayer's contract, which had a face value of $133,000, was not the "equivalent of cash" since it had a fair market value of only $76,980. Had the taxpayer sold the contract, the discount from the face value, approximately 42 percent, would have been "substantially greater than the generally prevailing premium for the use of money."

The Tax Court observed that requiring the taxpayer to realize the fair market value of the contract in the year of the sale could subject the taxpayer to substantial hardships. The taxpayer would be taxed in the initial year on a substantial portion of its gain from the sale of the property, even though it had received, in cash, only a small fraction of the purchase price. To raise funds to pay its taxes, the taxpayer might be forced to sell the contract at the contract's fair market value, even though such a sale might not otherwise be necessary or advantageous. Most importantly in the Tax Court's view, if the taxpayer were required to realize the fair market value of the contract in the year of the sale, the sale transaction would be closed for tax purposes in that year; hence, the taxpayer's capital gain on the transaction would be permanently limited to the difference between its adjusted basis and the contract's fair market value plus the cash payments received in the year of sale. If the taxpayer did retain the contract, so as to collect its face value, the amounts received in excess of the contract's fair market value would constitute ordinary income. The Tax Court also noted that requiring the cash basis taxpayer to realize the fair market value of the real estate contract would tend to obscure the differences between the cash and accrual methods of reporting.

The Commissioner does not dispute the Tax Court's conclusion that the taxpayer's contract with the Storeys had a fair market value of $76,980, or any other of the court's findings of fact. Rather, the Commissioner contends that since, as found by the Tax Court, the contract had a fair market value, section 1001(b) requires the taxpayer to include the amount of that fair market value in determining the amount realized.[6]

II. Statutory Analysis

The first statutory predecessor of section 1001(b) was section 202(b) of the Revenue Act of February 24, 1919, which stated:

> When property is exchanged for other property, the property received in exchange shall for the purpose of determining gain or loss be treated as the equivalent of cash to the amount of its fair market value, if any. . . .

We have no doubt that under that statute, the taxpayer would have been required to include the fair market value of its real estate contract as an amount realized during the taxable year of sale.

Only three years later, however, in the Revenue Act of November 23, 1921, Congress replaced the language of the statute enacted in 1919 with the following:

> On an exchange of property, real, personal or mixed, for any other such property, no gain or loss shall be recognized unless the property received in exchange has a readily realizable market value. . . .

The original statute had created "a presumption in favor of taxation." In the 1921 Act, Congress doubtless intended a policy more favorable to the taxpayer. Interpreting the 1921 statute, the Treasury Regulations provided that:

> [p]roperty has a readily realizable market value if it can be readily converted into an amount of cash or its equivalent substantially equal to the fair value of the property.

The law established in 1921 appears to have been substantially in accord with the position taken in this case by the Tax Court majority.

Notwithstanding the foregoing, in the Revenue Act of 1924, Congress again changed the law, replacing the 1921 statute with the language that now appears in section 1001(b) of the current Code. Of the 1921 statute, and its requirement of a "readily realizable market value," the Senate Finance Committee wrote in 1924:

> The question whether, in a given case, the property received in exchange has a readily realizable market value is a most difficult one, and the rulings on this question in given cases have been far from satisfactory. * * * The provision can not be applied with accuracy or consistency.

---

6. The Commissioner's theoretical approach to the result for which he contends is not altogether clear. He may be rejecting the doctrine of cash equivalency altogether, * * * or he may be contending that any property with a fair market value is the equivalent of cash in the amount of its fair market value. Since as to a cash basis taxpayer, with which we are here concerned, both theories would achieve the same result, we need not distinguish between them.

Under the 1924 statute, "where income is realized in the form of property, the measure of the income is the fair market value of the property at the date of its receipt."

There is no indication whatsoever that Congress intended to retain the "readily realizable market value" test from the 1921 statute as an unstated element of the 1924 Act. Indeed, as noted above, Congress sharply criticized that test. We cannot avoid the conclusion that in 1924 Congress intended to establish the more definite rule for which the Commissioner here contends and that consequently, if the fair market value of property received in an exchange can be ascertained, that fair market value must be reported as an amount realized.

Congress clearly understood that the 1924 statute might subject some taxpayers to the hardships discussed by the Tax Court majority. In the Revenue Act of 1926, Congress enacted the installment basis for reporting gain that is now reflected in section 453 of the current Code. * * *

By providing the installment basis, Congress intended "... to relieve taxpayers who adopted it from having to pay an income tax in the year of sale based on the full amount of anticipated profits when in fact they had received in cash only a small portion of the sales price." * * * [T]he installment basis also eliminates the other potential disadvantages to which the Tax Court referred. Since taxation in the year of the sale is based on the value of the payments actually received, the taxpayer should not be required to sell his obligation in order to meet his tax liabilities. Furthermore, the installment basis does not change the character of the gain received. If gain on an exchange would otherwise be capital, it remains capital under section 453. Finally, the installment basis treats cash and accrual basis taxpayers equally.

We view section 453 as persuasive evidence in support of the interpretation of section 1001(b) for which the Commissioner contends. The installment basis is Congress's method of providing relief from the rigors of section 1001(b). In its report on the Revenue Act of 1926, the Senate Finance Committee expressly noted that in sales or exchanges not qualifying for the installment basis, "deferred-payment contracts ... are to be regarded as the equivalent of cash if such obligations have a fair market value. In consequence, that portion of the initial payment and of the fair market value of such obligations which represents profit is to be returned as income as of the taxable year of the sale."

III. Case Law

The prior decisions of our own court support the conclusion we have reached.

* * *

There are, of course, "rare and extraordinary" situations in which it is impossible to ascertain the fair market value of a deferred payment obligation in the year of sale. The total amount payable under an obligation may be so speculative, or the right to receive any payments at all so contingent, that the fair market value of the obligation cannot be fixed. See Burnet v. Logan. If an obligation is not marketable, it may be impossible to establish its fair market value.

The Tax Court found, as a fact, that the taxpayer's real estate contract with the Storeys had a fair market value of $76,980 in the taxable year of sale. Consequently, the taxpayer must include $76,980 in determining the amount realized under section 1001(b). As previously noted, however, the Commissioner has conceded that the taxpayer is eligible to report on the installment basis and has calculated the taxpayer's deficiency accordingly.

The decision of the Tax Court is reversed, and on remand, the Tax Court will enter judgment for the Commissioner. Reversed and remanded, with directions.

NOTES AND QUESTIONS

1. When *Warren Jones* was decided, taxpayers wishing to report gain by the installment method had to make an affirmative election under § 453. Currently, installment reporting applies automatically, unless the taxpayer elects out of § 453. See § 453(d). The taxpayer in *Warren Jones* did not elect § 453, and took the position that it had no realized gain from the sale until the cash received exceeded the basis of the property sold.

This treatment, which was disallowed by the Court of Appeals, is commonly referred to as the open transaction method. Do you see why? Why was the open transaction method preferable to reporting gain under the installment method of § 453? Why was the installment method the taxpayer's second choice? Consider what the result would have been had the taxpayer not been allowed to use either the open transaction method or the installment method.

Under the Court of Appeals' decision, the taxpayer was limited to choosing between reporting gain under the installment method, or closing the transaction and reporting the fair market value of the contract as part of the amount realized on the sale.

2. Section 446 gives taxpayers a choice between cash and accrual accounting. The taxpayer in *Warren Jones* choose cash accounting. Regulation § 1.446–1(c)(1)(i) provides that under the cash method items of income "whether in the form of cash, property, or services" are taken into account when received. Similarly, § 1001(b) includes in the amount realized from a sale the "money received plus the fair market value of the property" received. Clearly, the taxpayer did not receive money in the amount of $76,980 when it received the installment obligation. Rather it received the right to future cash payments totalling $133,000, and that right had a fair market value of $76,980. The question was whether the right to receive money in the future should be viewed as either "money" or "property."

This question, which can arise under both Reg. § 1.446–1(c)(1)(i) and § 1001(b), presents a very tricky problem. Suppose, for example, that we focus on the term "property," and conclude that all rights to future payments are property under the statute and the regulation, so long as they have an ascertainable market value. Such an approach would mean that a cash basis taxpayer, like an accrual basis taxpayer, normally would recognize income when the right to income arises, rather than when it is received in cash.

Do you think that's what Congress intended when it adopted § 446, giving taxpayers the right to choose between cash and accrual reporting?

One view of the cash equivalency doctrine might be that it separates those rights to future cash payments that constitute property (and must be recognized by a cash basis taxpayer when received), from those that do not constitute property (and are not taken into account until converted into cash). This view is consistent with the holding of *Warren Jones*. So long as the right to future payments has an ascertainable fair market value it is equivalent to cash in an amount equal to that value, and (like any in-kind receipt) must be taken into account as property received. Note that under this view the cash equivalency doctrine doesn't really contribute to the analysis. One could just as well say that so long as a right to future payments has an ascertainable fair market value, it is property and must be taken into account accordingly.

Alternatively, the Court of Appeals may have simply disregarded the cash equivalency doctrine, either on the theory it applies only under § 446, or never applies. *See Warren Jones*, note 6, *supra* at 611. Since the court did not attempt to reconcile its view with the cash equivalency doctrine, we are left to speculate.

The important point is that the Court of Appeals focused on the term "property" in § 1001(b). Since the installment obligation had an ascertainable fair market value, it was treated as "property" received under that statute. The court did not indicate what, if any, role the cash equivalency doctrine should have in this analysis. So, that doctrine was not important to the analysis.

The Tax Court's approach was fundamentally different. It apparently assumed that the right to future payments of money was not "property" under § 1001(b), and focused on the term "money." With that focus, the question was whether the right to future payments was so close to money itself, that it ought to be treated as money. The cash equivalency doctrine addresses this question by looking to whether the right to receive future payments totaling $133,000 is the economic equivalent of receiving $133,000 in cash. If the answer is no, the taxpayer has received neither money nor its equivalent, and need not report the item until the money comes in. In *Warren Jones*, the Tax Court held that before a right to future payments can be characterized as a cash equivalent, it must be determined that it can be readily converted into cash approximately equal to its face value ($133,000). Since that was not the case, the taxpayer did not receive a cash equivalent. Therefore, it received neither money nor property, and was not required to take the installment obligation into account when it was received.

So, the Tax Court and the Court of Appeals not only disagreed on the answer to the question raised by the case, they disagreed on what the question was. To the Court of Appeals, the question was whether the taxpayer's right to future cash constituted property (with a measurable value). If the cash equivalency doctrine was considered at all, it was used to answer that question. To the Tax Court, the question was whether the taxpayer's right to future cash constituted the economic equivalent of money. Which court reached the correct result probably depends on which court correctly framed the issue. Considering § 446(a), Reg. § 1.446–1(c)(1)(i), and § 1001(b); what do you think?

As *Warren Jones* demonstrates, the courts have had great difficulty in grappling with this problem. Is it true, as the Tax Court claimed, that the Court of Appeals' approach "would tend to obscure the differences between the cash and accrual methods of reporting?"

If so, why do both § 1001(b) and Reg. § 1.446–1(c)(1)(i) treat property received by a cash basis taxpayer as income at the time of receipt? Consider the appropriate treatment if the taxpayer in *Warren Jones* had exchanged its apartment building for G.M. stock or an airplane worth $76,000. When Congress used the term "property" in § 1001(b), and when the Treasury used it in Reg. § 1.446–1(c)(1)(i), did they have in mind in-kind receipts such as G.M. stock or an airplane, rights to future payments of money, or both?

3. See Temporary Regulation § 15a.453–1(d)(2). It adopts the *Warren Jones* approach to reporting gain realized by a cash basis taxpayer on a deferred payment sale, when the taxpayer elects not to report gain on the installment method. In fact, it goes further than did the Court of Appeals in limiting open transaction reporting. It provides, "Under no circumstances will an installment sale for a fixed amount obligation be considered an 'open' transaction." Furthermore, it doesn't matter whether the installment obligation is a written obligation or an oral promise. See § 453(j). Exactly what provision of § 453 does this regulation "carry out?" Is it a valid regulation? Note that the question of how much is realized when the taxpayer elects out of § 453 arises under § 1001, not § 453.

In 1994, the Treasury adopted Reg. § 1.1001–1(g). It provides that when a debt instrument is issued in exchange for property, the amount realized is equal to the issue price under Reg. § 1.1273–2 or Reg. § 1.1274–2. In general, if the instrument provides for adequate interest, the issue price is its face value, that is, the principal amount due at maturity. Applied to the facts of *Warren Jones*, this means the amount realized was the face value of $133,000. Is this consistent with the plain meaning of § 1001(b)? Certainly the note did not constitute "money" in the amount of $133,000. Could it plausibly be viewed as "property" with a fair market value of $133,000?

Note that Reg. § 1.1001–1(g) conflicts with Temp. Reg. § 15a.453–1(d)(2)(ii). The latter regulation, like the Court of Appeals decision in *Warren Jones*, provides that a cash basis taxpayer electing out of § 453 "shall treat as an amount realized in the year of sale the fair market value of the installment obligation." So, one regulation would require Warren Jones to report $133,000 (face value), the other $76,980 (fair market value). In 1996, Reg. § 1.1001–1(g) was amended to provide that it overrides Temp. Reg. § 15a.453–1(d)(2). For an argument that Temp. Reg. § 15a. 453–1(d)(2)(ii) is invalid, despite drawing some support from the legislative history of section 453, see Shores, *Closing the Open Transaction Loophole: Mandatory Installment Reporting*, 10 Va. Tax Rev. 311, 344–350 (1990).

4.   If the Tax Court had found that the deferred payment contract had no ascertainable value, would the Court of Appeals have upheld the Tax Court's decision allowing open transaction reporting? In McShain v. Commissioner, 71 T.C. 998, 1005 (1979), the Tax Court held that a note for $3,000,000 received in exchange for an inn had no ascertainable value. The taxpayer was therefore allowed to report gain under the open transaction method. Since the note had no ascertainable value, the Tax Court stated: "we need not deal with, and we express no opinion regarding the issues presented in *Warren Jones*."

Did the Tax Court in *McShain* cleverly sidestep a Court of Appeals decision with which it disagreed? Should it be allowed to do so?

5.   Temporary Reg. § 15a.453–1(d)(2)(ii)(A) provides:

Under no circumstances will an installment sale for a fixed amount obligation be considered an "open transaction."

Does the regulation block any opportunity for sidestepping the *Warren Jones* holding? Is it a valid regulation? Consider this question in light of the next case which was the first to recognize the open transaction method.

2.   INSTALLMENT SALES FOR A CONTINGENT PRICE

BURNET v. LOGAN

United States Supreme Court, 1931.
283 U.S. 404, 51 S.Ct. 550, 75 L.Ed. 1143.

Mr. Justice McReynolds delivered the opinion of the Court. * * *

Prior to March, 1913, and until March 11, 1916, respondent, Mrs. Logan, owned 250 of the 4,000 capital shares issued by the Andrews & Hitchcock Iron Company. It held 12 percent of the stock of the Mahoning Ore & Steel Company, an operating concern. In 1895 the latter corporation procured a lease for 97 years upon the "Mahoning" mine and since then has regularly taken therefrom large, but varying, quantities of iron ore—in 1913, 1,515,428 tons; in 1914, 1,212,287 tons; in 1915, 2,311,940 tons; in 1919, 1,217,167 tons; in 1921, 303,020 tons; in 1923, 3,029,865 tons. The lease contract did not require production of either maximum or minimum tonnage or any definite payments. Through an agreement of stockholders (steel manufacturers), the Mahoning Company is obligated to apportion extracted ore among them according to their holdings.

On March 11, 1916, the owners of all the shares in Andrews & Hitchcock Company sold them to Youngstown Sheet & Tube Company, which thus acquired, among other things, 12 percent of the Mahoning Company's stock and the right to receive the same percentage of ore thereafter taken from the leased mine.

For the shares so acquired, the Youngstown Company paid the holders $2,200,000 in money, and agreed to pay annually thereafter for distribution among them 60 cents for each ton of ore apportioned to it. Of this cash Mrs. Logan received 250/4000—$137,500; and she became entitled to the same fraction of any annual payment thereafter made by the purchaser under the terms of sale.

Mrs. Logan's mother had long owned 1,100 shares of the Andrews & Hitchcock Company. She died in 1917, leaving to the daughter one-half of her interest in payments thereafter made by the Youngstown Company. This bequest was appraised for federal estate tax purposes at $277,164.50.

During 1917, 1918, 1919, and 1920 the Youngstown Company paid large sums under the agreement. Out of these respondent received on account of her 250 shares $9,900 in 1917; $11,250 in 1918; $8,995.50 in 1919; $5,444.30 in 1920—$35,589.80. By reason of the interest from her mother's estate, she received $19,790.10 in 1919, and $11,977.49 in 1920.

Reports of income for 1918, 1919, and 1920 were made by Mrs. Logan upon the basis of cash receipts and disbursements. They included no part of what she had obtained from annual payments by the Youngstown Company. She maintains that until the total amount actually received by her from the sale of her shares equals their value on March 1, 1913, no taxable income will arise from the transaction. Also that, until she actually receives by reason of the right bequeathed to her a sum equal to its appraised value, there will be no taxable income therefrom.

On March 1, 1913, the value of the 250 shares then held by Mrs. Logan exceeded $173,089.80—the total of all sums actually received by her prior to 1921 from their sale ($137,500 cash in 1916, plus four annual payments amounting to $35,589.80). That value also exceeded original cost of the shares. The amount received on the interest devised by her mother was less than its valuation for estate taxation; also less than the value when acquired by Mrs. Logan.

The Commissioner ruled that the obligation of the Youngstown Company to pay 60 cents per ton has a fair market value of $1,942,111.46 on March 11, 1916; that this value should be treated as so much cash, and the sale of the stock regarded as a closed transaction with no profit in 1916. He also used this valuation as the basis for apportioning subsequent annual receipts between income and return of capital. His calculations, based upon estimates and assumptions, are too intricate for brief statement. He made deficiency assessments according to the view just stated, and the Board of Tax Appeals approved the result.

In the brief for petitioner the following appears:

The fair market value of the Youngstown contract on March 11, 1916, was found by the Commissioner to be $1,942,111.46. This was based upon an estimate that the ore reserves at the Mahoning mine amounted to 82,858,535 tons; that all such ore would be mined; that 12 per cent. (or 9,942,564.2 tons) would be delivered to the Youngstown Company. The total amount to be received by all the vendors of stock would then be $5,965,814.52 at the rate of 60 cents per ton. The Commissioner's figure for the fair market value on March 11, 1916, was the then worth of

$5,965,814.52, upon the assumption that the amount was to be received in equal annual installments during 45 years, discounted at 6 per cent., with a provision for a sinking fund at 4 per cent. For lack of evidence to the contrary, this value was approved by the Board. The value of the 550/4000 interest which each acquired by bequest was fixed at $277,164.50 for purposes of federal estate tax at the time of the mother's death.

During the years here involved, the Youngstown Company made payments in accordance with the terms of the contract, and respondents respectively received sums proportionate to the interests in the contract which they acquired by exchange of property and by bequest.

The Board held that respondents' receipts from the contract, during the years in question, represented "gross income"; that respondents should be allowed to deduct from said gross income a reasonable allowance for exhaustion of their contract interests; and that the balance of the receipts should be regarded as taxable income.

The Circuit Court of Appeals held that, in the circumstances, it was impossible to determine with fair certainty the market value of the agreement by the Youngstown Company to pay 60 cents per ton. Also that respondent was entitled to the return of her capital—the value of 250 shares on March 1, 1913, and the assessed value of the interest derived from her mother—before she could be charged with any taxable income. As this had not in fact been returned, there was no taxable income.

We agree with the result reached by the Circuit Court of Appeals.

The 1916 transaction was a sale of stock—not an exchange of property. We are not dealing with royalties or deductions from gross income because of depletion of mining property. Nor does the situation demand that an effort be made to place according to the best available data some approximate value upon the contract for future payments. This probably was necessary in order to assess the mother's estate. As annual payments on account of extracted ore come in, they can be readily apportioned first as return of capital and later as profit. The liability for income tax ultimately can be fairly determined without resort to mere estimates, assumptions, and speculation. When the profit, if any, is actually realized, the taxpayer will be required to respond. The consideration for the sale was $2,200,000 in cash and the promise of future money payments wholly contingent upon facts and circumstances not possible to foretell with anything like fair certainty. The promise was in no proper sense equivalent to cash. It had no ascertainable fair market value. The transaction was not a closed one. Respondent might never recoup her capital investment from payments only conditionally promised. Prior to 1921, all receipts from the sale of her shares amounted to less than their value on March 1, 1913. She properly demanded the return of her capital investment before assessment of any taxable profit based on conjecture.

"In order to determine whether there has been gain or loss, and the amount of the gain if any, we must withdraw from the gross proceeds an amount sufficient to restore the capital value that existed at the commencement of the period under consideration." Ordinarily, at least, a taxpayer may not deduct from gross receipts a supposed loss which in fact is represented by his outstanding note. And, conversely, a promise to pay indeterminate sums of money in not necessarily taxable income. "Generally speaking, the income tax law is concerned only with realized losses, as with realized gains."

From her mother's estate, Mrs. Logan obtained the right to share in possible proceeds of a contract thereafter to pay indefinite sums. The value of this was assumed to be $277,164.50, and its transfer was so taxed. Some valuation—speculative or otherwise—was necessary in order to close the estate. It may never yield as much, it may yield more. If a sum equal to the value thus ascertained had been invested in an annuity contract, payments thereunder would have been free from income tax until the owner had recouped his capital investment. We think a like rule should be applied here. The statute definitely excepts bequests from receipts which go to make up taxable income. The judgments below are affirmed.

NOTES AND QUESTIONS

1. Consider again the questions posed in note 5, preceding *Burnet v. Logan*. The holding of *Burnet v. Logan* doesn't control the treatment of fixed amount obligations, such as that involved in *Warren Jones*. But, does its rationale apply? Which of the following five factors was most important to the Supreme Court's holding in *Burnet v. Logan*?

(1) The amount realized could not be determined without resort to estimates, assumptions and speculation.

(2) The contract did not provide for fixed payments.

(3) The contract was not a cash equivalent.

(4) The contract had no ascertainable fair market value.

(5) The transaction was not a closed one.

2. The issue in *Warren Jones* can be viewed as whether the taxpayer was entitled to open transaction treatment on the authority of *Burnet v. Logan*. Do you see why the lower courts might disagree on the answer to that question?

3. Would Mrs. Logan qualify for open transaction treatment today under Temp. Reg. § 15a.453–1(d)(2)(iii)? Prior to the Installment Sales Revision Act of 1980, installment reporting was not available for contingent payment sales, such as Mrs. Logan's. Thus, she had to choose between open transaction treatment (as upheld by the Supreme Court), and closing the transaction (as urged by the Commissioner). The 1980 Act made clear that installment reporting is available for contingent payment sales. See § 453(f)(8)(B). Consider what, if any, additional choices Mrs. Logan would have today under Temp. Reg. § 15a.453–1(c), which implements the 1980 legislation.

4. Should the courts view the 1980 legislation as narrowing the scope of *Burnet v. Logan*? Senate Report No. 96–1000 on the 1980 Act states:

[T]he effect of the new rules is to reduce substantially the justification for treating transactions as "open" and permitting the use of the cost recovery method sanctioned by Burnet v. Logan. Accordingly, it is the Committee's intent that the cost recovery method not be available in the case of sales for a fixed price ..., and that its use be limited to those rare and extraordinary cases involving sales for a contingent price where the fair market value of the purchaser's obligation cannot reasonably be ascertained.

The most interesting aspect of the Senate Report is what it says about sales for a fixed price: They should never qualify for open transaction treatment. The Treasury took the hint and adopted Temp. Reg. § 15a.453–1(d)(2)(ii) discussed in note 3, following *Warren Jones*. It flatly denies open transaction reporting for such sales. Is this a proper way to overrule a body of case law. Remember, both the Tax Court and the Court of Appeals in *Warren Jones* (and courts in numerous other cases) allowed open transaction treatment for fixed amount contracts. They disagreed only on whether such treatment depended on the cash equivalency test (Tax Court view) or the fair market value test (Ninth Circuit view). Congress could easily have adopted a rule in § 453 providing that any taxpayer electing out of § 453 shall treat as an amount realized in the year of sale the fair market value (or the face value), of any fixed amount obligation. Should the Treasury, supported only by a Senate Report, be permitted to adopt such a rule and thereby jettison a body of case law?

Consider again the exchange between Senators Armstrong and Dole, *supra* at 113, concerning the significance of committee reports, especially:

[F]or any jurist, administrator, bureaucrat, tax practitioner, or others who might chance upon the written record of this proceeding, let me just make the point that this (a Senate Finance Committee report) is not the law, it was not voted on (by either the Committee or the Senate), it is not subject to amendment, and we should discipline ourselves to the task of expressing congressional intent in the statute.

CHAPTER XII

NON-RECOGNITION TRANSACTIONS

■ ■ ■

A. INTRODUCTION

One of the first concepts addressed in Chapter 2 was realization. The concept was introduced with the following hypothetical:

In 1990, Joe purchases Blackacre for $25,000. By 1994, the value of Blackacre has increased to $100,000.

The increase in the value of Joe's property rights is economic income. However, it will not be recognized as income for tax purposes until realization occurs. The simplest case of realization would be a sale of Blackacre for $100,000 in cash.

Before the cash sale, taxing Joe's unrealized appreciation would have led to problems of valuation and liquidity. After the sale:

(1) the agreement between Joe and his arm's length buyer fixes the fair market value of the parcel, so Joe's income of $75,000 is easily measured; and

(2) Joe has cash with which to pay the tax bill.

But what if Joe traded Blackacre, now worth $100,000, for Greenacre, also worth $100,000, in an arm's length exchange? Joe has a realized gain. See section 1001 (a), (b). However, the question remains whether the gain should be recognized. If so, there would still be problems.

(1) As to valuation, the arm's length exchange would imply that Blackacre and Greenacre were of equal value. However, the exchange event would not, in and of itself, support any inference as to the fair market value of either parcel. Unless the value of Greenacre is known, Joe's gain cannot be determined.

(2) As to liquidity, Joe would emerge from the transaction, not with cash, but with real property, not necessarily any more liquid than the property he started with.

Perhaps property exchanges should not lead to a recognition of gain or loss. Instead, recognition could be deferred until the replacement property is sold for cash. However, imagine what would happen if the government taxed only cash sales. If cash sales were taxed, while property exchanges were deferred, people would go to extraordinary lengths to avoid cash sales. See 40 *supra* for a discussion of similar problems with barter sales.

Property exchanges are problematic for the income tax. Yet, we cannot afford a blanket provision that defers income until cash is received. As a compromise, Congress has carved out certain limited categories of property exchanges for nonrecognition treatment. As indicated by § 1001(c), these nonrecognition provisions are exceptions to the general rule that exchanges, like sales, are taxable events.

This chapter will address two of these nonrecognition provisions— § 1031, dealing with like-kind exchanges of the type described in the introductory problem, and § 1033, dealing with involuntary conversions. Both provisions share a common feature—the properties exchanged must be quite similar to each other. Under § 1031, they must be "of like kind." Under § 1033, they must be "similar or related in service or use." Prior to the adoption of the Taxpayer Relief Act of 1997, old § 1034 provided similar nonrecognition treatment for gain on the sale of a principal residence, if a replacement residence was purchased within 2 years of the sale. That provision has now been replaced with § 121, also considered in this chapter.

Consider again the initial facts. In 1990, Joe invested cash in Blackacre; in 1994, he traded Blackacre for Greenacre. In 1990, Joe started with cash, but he invested it in real estate. After the trade in 1994, he still had no cash, and he still had real estate. There was no "disinvestment"; there has merely been an exchange of one real estate parcel for another.

Joe has continued his investment. Before and after the trade, his money is tied up in more or less the same thing. Both sections 1031 and 1033 require continuity of investment as a condition for nonrecognition. Continuity of investment furnishes a policy justification for special treatment.

Common Attributes of Nonrecognition Provisions

Each of the nonrecognition regimes that we'll examine has its own, individual quirks. However, each has two common attributes aside from the continuity of investment requirement. The first relates to the treatment of boot, and the second is deferral of the taxable event rather than exemption. Indeed, all nonrecognition provisions share these attributes.

Boot

In the real world, when property is exchanged for property, the two assets are rarely of equal value. What if, for example, Blackacre was worth $100,000, while Greenacre was worth only $95,000? The owner of Greenacre would have to pay an additional $5,000 to make the exchange come out even.

Usually, the $5,000 would be cash. However, it could be anything—a used car, a collectible postage stamp, a diamond ring. Cash, or other property not of like-kind, used to even out the value of the exchange is usually referred to as "boot," although that is not a term used in the Code.

When boot is involved, it can no longer be said that the recipient of the boot has full continuity of investment. The recipient of Greenacre, in the example above, has continuity of investment only with respect to $95,000. The other $5,000 is now held in cash, a used car, or whatever.

Moreover, if lack of liquidity is one of the justifications for nonrecognition treatment, it does not apply with the same force when cash boot is involved. Boot usually takes the form of cash. In that event, the recipient of Greenacre does indeed have $5,000 in cash with which to pay any tax that might be levied. For these reasons, the presence of boot will lead to some recognition of income.

Deferral vs. Exclusion

A second characteristic common to nonrecognition provisions is that gain not recognized is merely deferred, to be taxed at a later time. Deferral is accomplished by reducing the basis of the property received. The mechanics of the basis adjustment may differ from one provision to another, but the idea is always the same. The basis of the property received must be adjusted to reflect the deferred gain, so that it will be taxed when that property is sold.

As a mechanical matter, it is easy to arrange for deferral of the gain realized on an exchange. For example, if Joe purchased Blackacre for $25,000, and later exchanged it for Greenacre worth $100,000, the gain not recognized (taxed) can be preserved for taxation at a later time by simply giving Joe a basis in Greenacre equal to that of Blackacre ($25,-000). Greenacre then has an "exchanged basis." See § 7701(44). The gain realized (but not recognized) on the exchange will be recognized when Greenacre is sold.[a]

It is this deferral characteristic that distinguishes nonrecognition provisions from exclusionary provisions such as §§ 102 (gifts and bequests) and 104 (compensation for personal injuries) considered earlier, and § 121 (sale of a principal residence), considered below. When an exclusionary provision applies, the realized gain is never taxed.

---

a. Of course, Greenacre could decline in value prior to its sale, in which case the gain realized on the exchange would never be recognized. But if the exchange had not occurred, Blackacre could have declined in value prior to its sale, in which case the accession to wealth represented by the appreciation of its fair market value to $100,000 would never have been recognized. Nonrecognition of the exchange does not increase the likelihood of the accession to wealth escaping taxation over what that likelihood would have been absent the exchange. Furthermore, without nonrecognition the exchange is less likely to occur. So, the possibility that deferred gain realized on the exchange will never be taxed does not seem a strong reason to deny nonrecognition.

B. LIKE–KIND EXCHANGES OF PROPERTY

Code: § 1031

1. INTRODUCTORY QUESTIONS

Read § 1031(a)(1). What are the three requirements for nonrecognition? Would the hypothetical discussed in the introduction (Joe purchased Blackacre for $25,000 and later exchanged it for Greenacre worth $100,000) meet the requirements if:

(1) Blackacre were an undeveloped city lot with good potential for commercial development, and Greenacre were a lot on the seashore with a nice cottage? See Reg. § 1.1031(a)–1(b),(c). See also Reg. § 1.1031(a)–2(b)(2)(i) (office furniture, fixtures, and equipment are of like-kind).

(2) Joe held Blackacre as an investment, but plans to use Greenacre as a vacation cottage?

2. PROBLEMS

Assume that the above exchange in which Joe transferred Blackacre and received Greenacre qualifies for nonrecognition under § 1031. Determine Joe's recognized gain (if any), his basis in Greenacre, and his basis in any boot received in each of the following situations:

1. The parcels are of equal value, so no boot changes hands.

2. The parcels are of unequal value, so Joe receives Greenacre plus cash of $5,000. See §§ 1031(b),(d).

3. The parcels are of unequal value, so Joe receives Greenacre, plus GM stock worth $5,000.

4. The parcels are of unequal value, so Joe transfers $5,000 cash along with Blackacre. Hint: It will be useful to think of Joe as acquiring Greenacre in two portions. One portion is received in exchange for Blackacre, and the basis of that portion is determined under § 1031(d). The other portion is received in exchange for cash, and the basis of that portion is determined under § 1012. *Cf.* Reg. § 1.1031(d)–1(e) Ex.

5. The parcels are of unequal value, so Joe transfers GM stock worth $5,000 with a basis of $500 along with Blackacre.

6. Reconsider 1–5 above with the assumption that the basis of Blackacre in Joe's hands is $125,000 rather than $25,000.

3. THE EXCHANGE REQUIREMENT

In simple transactions like those considered above the exchange requirement is not problematic. Sometimes one party might want to exchange properties, but the other wishes to sell for cash. For example, suppose Ann holds Ranch #1 worth $1,000 with a basis of $100, and would like to exchange it for a larger ranch, paying the difference in cash. To achieve her goal, Ann must locate a larger ranch suitable to her needs, owned by someone who wants to sell, and who is willing to take a smaller ranch in trade. It might be difficult for Ann to locate another ranch meeting all three criteria.

Multi-party Exchanges

Suppose Ann finds Bill, who is interested in purchasing Ranch #1 for cash of $1,000. If Ann sold to Bill, she could then go shopping for a larger ranch, without worrying about whether the owner is willing to trade, but she would have a recognized gain of $900 on the sale. To avoid this, Ann enters into an agreement to sell Bill Ranch #1 for $1,000. The agreement also commits Bill to cooperate with Ann to effectuate an exchange, if Ann locates suitable property prior to closing the sale of Ranch #1. Thereafter, Ann locates Ranch #2 owned by Charlie, and available for sale at a price of $1,800. Bill purchases Ranch #2 with cash of $1,800. Immediately after purchasing Ranch #2, Bill exchanges it for Ranch #1 plus $800.

The transfers look like this:

Illustration 15

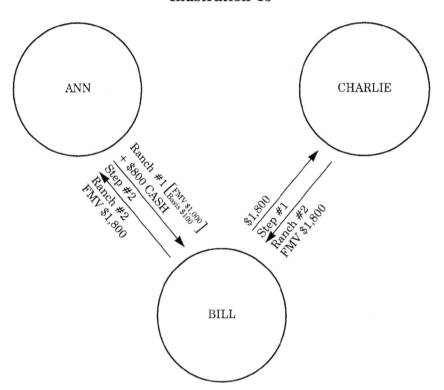

Should § 1031 apply to Ann?

Courts frequently announce that federal taxation is a matter of substance, not form. If Ann had simply sold Ranch #1 to Bill for $1,000, and then purchased Ranch #2, for $1,800, gain on the sale would have been taxed. Is there a substantive difference between such a sale and purchase by Ann, and the "exchange" described above? If not, was there really an exchange?

Suppose in order to save local transfer taxes and title recording fees, Charlie, at the direction of Bill, transfers title to Ranch #2 directly to Ann? Suppose Bill has only $1,000 in cash and doesn't want to borrow the additional $800 needed to purchase Ranch #2. So Ann pays $800 directly to Charlie, and Bill pays $1,000. Would it be better for Ann to pay the $800 to Bill, with Bill then paying Charlie $1,800? Should tax consequences turn on such distinctions?

The Tax Court considered these questions in Barker v. Commissioner, 74 T.C. 555 (1980):

* * *

This case involves another variant of the multiple-party, like-kind exchange by which the taxpayer, as in this case, seeks to terminate one real estate investment and acquire another real estate investment without recognizing gain. The statutory provision for nonrecognition treatment is section 1031. The touchstone of section 1031, at least in this context, is the requirement that there be an exchange of like-kind business or investment properties, as distinguished from a cash sale of property by the taxpayer and a reinvestment of the proceeds in other property.

The "exchange" requirement poses an analytical problem because it runs headlong into the familiar tax law maxim that the substance of a transaction controls over form. In a sense, the substance of a transaction in which the taxpayer sells property and immediately reinvests the proceeds in like-kind property is not much different from the substance of a transaction in which two parcels are exchanged without cash. Yet, if the exchange requirement is to have any significance at all, the perhaps formalistic difference between the two types of transactions must, at least on occasion, engender different results.

The line between an exchange on the one hand and a nonqualifying sale and reinvestment on the other becomes even less distinct when the person who owns the property sought by the taxpayer is not the same person who wants to acquire the taxpayer's property. This means that multiple parties must be involved in the transaction. In that type of case, a like-kind exchange can be effected only if the person with whom the taxpayer exchanges the property first purchases the property wanted by the taxpayer. This interjection of cash, especially when the person who purchases the property desired by the taxpayer either uses money advanced by the taxpayer or appears to be acting as his agent, or both, makes the analysis that much more difficult.

* * *

We begin by observing that there is nothing inherent in a multiple-party exchange that necessarily acts as a bar to section 1031 treatment. Thus, it is not a bar to section 1031 treatment that the person who desires the taxpayer's property acquires and holds another piece of property only temporarily before exchanging it with the taxpayer. Similarly, it is not fatal to section 1031 treatment that the person with whom the taxpayer exchanges his property immediately sells the newly acquired property.

Difficulties arise, however, when the transaction falls short of the paradigm in which transitory ownership is the only feature distinguishing the transaction from two-party exchanges. Still, the courts (and by and large the Commissioner), in reviewing these transactions, have evinced awareness of business and economic exigencies.

Often the taxpayer and a prospective purchaser will enter into an exchange agreement before acceptable like-kind property has been located. In *Alderson v. Comm'r, supra*, as in *Biggs v. Comm'r*, 69 T.C. 905 (1978), on appeal (5th Cir., Oct. 23, 1978), the court approved tax-free exchange treatment since the properties were designated before the date set for transfer of taxpayer's property even though the to-be-received properties had not been identified as of the date of the agreement. This aspect of *Alderson* was approved in Rev. Rul. 77–297, 1977–2 C.B. 304, in which the Commissioner also allowed the taxpayer to search for and select the property to be received by him in the exchange....

In *W. D. Haden Co. v. Comm'r*, 165 F.2d 588 (5th Cir.1948), an individual purchased property from a third party with the intent of exchanging this property for property held by the taxpayer, but the individual never acquired legal title to the property. Despite this, the court sanctioned tax-free exchange treatment, holding that the buyer may direct the third party to deed this property directly to the taxpayer so long as the cash paid to the third party is transferred directly from the buyer to the third party and not through the taxpayer. *See also Biggs v. Comm'r*, 69 T.C. 905 (1978), where this Court sustained tax-free exchange treatment, again notwithstanding the fact that the exchanging party did not obtain legal title to the property to be exchanged.

* * *

Notwithstanding those deviations from the standard multiple-party exchanges which have received judicial approval, at some point the confluence of some sufficient number of deviations will bring about a taxable result. Whether the cause be economic and business reality or poor tax planning, prior cases make clear that taxpayers who stray too far run the risk of having their transactions characterized as a sale and reinvestment.

For example, in *Carlton v. United States*, 385 F.2d 238 (5th Cir.1967), the parties intended to enter into an *Alderson* like-kind exchange (*i.e.*, the person who wanted the taxpayer's property was to temporarily acquire and hold the property wanted by the taxpayer), but to avoid unnecessary duplication in the transfer of money and titles, the third party conveyed his property directly to the taxpayer, and the buyer paid money to the taxpayer, intending that the taxpayer pay this money to the third party. Focusing on the taxpayer's receipt of cash rather than real property, the court held that the transaction was a sale.

* * *

NOTE

The court in *Barker* held that § 1031 applied to a four party transaction. The parties were: A, who wished to make a like-kind exchange; B, who held property of like-kind to A's property and wanted to sell for cash; C, who wanted to purchase A's property for cash; and D, who served to facilitate the transaction. D arranged to purchase B's property, exchange it for A's property, and then sell A's property to C.

Commenting on the fact that D's ownership of both properties was transitory, the court noted: "To the complaint that . . . (§ 1031) treatment places undue emphasis on a formalistic step of no substance, we repeat what we have already said: that the conceptual distinction between an exchange qualifying for section 1031 on the one hand and a sale and reinvestment on the other is largely one of form." 74 T.C. at 565–66.

A party (such as D) whose ownership of property is transitory does not hold the property for use in a trade or business or for investment. Therefore, section 1031 will not apply to that party. Application of section 1031 is seldom a concern, however, since a transitory owner will not have a realized gain on the exchange. For example, in the Barker case D had a basis in the property acquired from B equal to its fair market value. No gain was realized by D when he exchanged that property for A's property.

The difference between a multi-party exchange (sometimes called a three-cornered exchange) and a sale may well be more a matter of form than substance. But in this context the statute focuses on form. So form is critical. Perhaps it could be said that formal distinctions become substantive when the statute makes them so.

Deferred Exchanges

Returning to the ranch hypothetical, suppose Ann had been unable to locate suitable property prior to closing on the sale of Ranch #1. At closing, Ann conveyed Ranch #1 to Bill, but, instead of cash, received a promise from Bill to acquire property designated by Ann and to transfer such property to Ann within 5 years. If no property is designated within 5 years, Bill is to pay Ann $1,000 plus a growth factor of 8 percent per year.

One year after closing, Ann designates Ranch #2 which Bill acquires for cash of $1,000 plus a note of $800. Bill then transfers Ranch #2 to Ann, and Ann assumes the note. An exchange?

In Starker v. United States, 602 F.2d 1341 (9th Cir.1979), the government unsuccessfully argued that transfers must be simultaneous to constitute an exchange. The court allowed nonrecognition treatment on facts similar to those described above, but held the "growth factor" taxable as interest. *Cf.* § 1031(a)(3), the so-called anti-*Starker* amendment.

Considering the policy reasons for nonrecognition discussed in the Introduction, do any provide support for the anti-*Starker* amendment? Can you think of any other reason for requiring that an exchange involve simultaneous, or nearly simultaneous transfers?

Debt Problems

1.   A holds Ranch #1 with a basis of $100. B holds Ranch #2 with a basis of $500. The ranches are exchanged with A paying boot (cash) of $800 to B. Both parties qualify for nonrecognition under § 1031.

What is the basis of Ranch #2 to A and Ranch #1 to B following the exchange? See § 1031(d). Hint: A is similarly situated to Joe in variation (4) of the problem on page 624 above. Also, to determine the basis of Ranch #1 to

B, you might have to determine its fair market value. If so, you should assume Ranch #1 is worth $1,000.

2. What result in problem 1 if instead of paying cash of $800, A gave B a $800 note with reasonable interest? Should the fact $800 will be paid in the future rather than immediately affect the tax treatment of either party? See § 453(f)(6); Reg. § 1.453–1(f).

3. What result in problem 1 if instead of paying cash of $800, A assumed a liability of B in the amount of $800? See § 1031(d) (last sentence); Reg. § 1.1031(b)–1(c).

4. Finally, what result in problem 1 if instead of paying cash of $800, A assumed a liability of B in the amount of $1,000, and B assumed a liability of A in the amount of $200? See Reg. § 1.1031(b)–1(c) (last sentence).

C. INVOLUNTARY CONVERSIONS

INTRODUCTORY PROBLEM

Last year, Dan purchased a 1969 Mercedes Benz SL230 for $20,000. The car appreciated to $25,000, but was then destroyed in an accident. Dan collected $25,000 under an insurance policy as compensation for his loss. What must Dan do to avoid recognition of his $5,000 gain? See § 1033(a)(2).

If Dan purchases a replacement automobile costing $28,000, and § 1033 applies, what will be his basis in the new car? See § 1033(b) (last sentence). Suppose the replacement car cost $23,000.

1. SECTIONS 1031 AND 1033 COMPARED

Sections 1031 and 1033 have some obvious common features. Both provide for deferral (not exemption) of gain realized when one item of property is replaced with another item of property, if certain conditions are met. They also have some significant differences. Section 1031 applies to loss as well as gain, and is never elective. Section 1033 applies only to gain, and usually *is* elective.[b] Also, unlike § 1031, § 1033 allows the receipt of cash and applies without regard to whether the property is held for profit. These differences are rooted in the different nature of the transactions to which the two provisions apply: voluntary exchanges in the case of § 1031, and involuntary conversions in the case of § 1033. For example, as a practical matter many involuntary conversions will necessarily involve the receipt of money. It would be awkward if Dan had to receive a replacement car from the insurance company in order to avoid recognition in the introductory problem.

---

b. Involuntary conversions occur when property is damaged, stolen or condemned and the owner receives compensation. Usually compensation will be paid in cash, in which case nonrecognition of gain is elective. Section 1033(b)(2). If property other than cash is received as compensation, and it meets the requirements of § 1033, nonrecognition of gain is automatic. § 1033(a)(1).

2. SIMILAR OR RELATED IN SERVICE OR USE

In some instances the reason for differences in the two provisions is less obvious. For an exchange to qualify under § 1031 the properties exchanged must be of "like kind." For § 1033 to apply the properties must be "similar or related in service or use." "Similar or related in service or use" is a narrower concept than "like-kind." For example, if Dan held the Mercedes for pleasure, and replaced it with a Ford used in his business as a traveling salesman, the Ford would not meet the similar or related in service or use test. However, a Ford and a Mercedes are of like-kind (a notion that some purist might resist), at least for purposes of § 1031. Note, however, if Dan had exchanged the Mercedes for a Ford, § 1031 would not apply, since the Mercedes was held for pleasure.

Perhaps a reason behind this difference is suggested by § 1033(g). It provides that if real property held for profit is condemned, property of a like-kind to be held for profit will be treated as similar or related in service or use. So, the idea seems to be that the more flexible like-kind test should apply to some involuntary conversions, so long as the properties are held for profit. But why should this special rule apply to real property and not personal property? And why condemnations but not other forms of involuntary conversions?

(a) Property Used by the Owner

SANTUCCI v. COMMISSIONER

United States Tax Court, 1973.
T.C. Memo 1973–178.

IRWIN, JUDGE:

From May 1963 to October 1968, petitioners operated a car wash on leased land in Richmond, Calif. On October 27, 1965, the San Francisco Bay Area Rapid Transit District filed a complaint in eminent domain to condemn the property upon which petitioners conducted their business. As a result of condemnation proceedings petitioners' business was closed in October 1968.

The property of petitioners which was condemned consisted of tangible personal property upon which depreciation had been claimed and allowed from 1963 through 1968 in the amount of $42,700. Petitioners received a net award, after payment of attorney fees, of $53,461.11 for their condemned property. The adjusted basis of the property was $43,398.51. Petitioners realized a gain upon this involuntary conversion of their property in the amount of $10,062.60.

Following the receipt of these proceeds petitioners reinvested the funds in a printing company. No evidence was presented as to the exact nature of this investment (i.e., whether stock purchase, partnership interest, proprietorship, etc.); nor was any evidence presented indicating exactly when the investment occurred or exactly how much of the award was in fact reinvested. In deference to petitioners, however, it does appear that the total award was reinvested and that at least a part of the investment was in depreciable personal property (printing presses and some related equipment).

On their 1968 joint individual income tax return petitioners reported the gain realized on the involuntary conversion as long-term capital gain. In his statutory notice of deficiency respondent determined that the gain realized on the involuntary conversion should be includable as ordinary income under section 1245(a)(1). Petitioners now contend that the gain should not be recognized by reason of section 1033. . . .

Section 1033(a)(3) [current § 1033(a)(2)] provides in part that if property is involuntarily converted into money as a result of condemnation proceedings the gain, if any, shall be recognized at the election of the taxpayer only to the extent the amount realized on such conversion exceeds the cost of other property purchased by the taxpayer which is "similar or related in service or use" to the property so converted. Section 1033(a)(3)(A) [current § 1033 (a)(2)(A)]. This "similar or related in service or use" test is a much narrower test than the "like-kind" test of section 1031. The "like-kind" test is also applied in the case of condemnation of real property held for productive use in trade or business or for investment. Section 1033(g). Here, however, the property condemned was personal rather than real. Petitioners seem to have confused the two tests since they speak only in terms of "like-kind."

In this instance petitioners have replaced the converted property, a car wash, with a printing company. In determining whether the replacement property is "similar or related in service or use" to the property replaced, the burden is on petitioners to show the requisite relationship. As to the proper test to apply in making this determination, the issue has been litigated often. . . . Suffice it to say that in a situation involving an owner-operator of property, as we have here, this Court in the past has applied a "functional use" test whereby the end use of the replacement property had to be substantially similar to the replaced property. A different test is applied in the investor-lessor situation. Here petitioners have failed to show that the replacement was "similar or related in service or use" to the replaced property. Since petitioners have made no attempt to show the requisite relationship other than by way of conclusionary statements, we are not compelled to go into the merits of the test applied. . . .

It is clear from the foregoing that petitioners cannot prevail.

NOTE

For purposes of § 1033, property is divided into two broad categories:

(1) that which is used or operated by the owner; as in *Santucci* and

(2) that which is not used or operated by the owner (usually because it is leased to another).

The functional use test applies only to the first category. It focuses on the actual use of the properties, and asks whether the replacement property serves the same function as the converted property.

The Tax Court held that the taxpayers failed to demonstrate that equipment used in their printing business served the same function as equipment used in their car wash business. Can you imagine any evidence the taxpayers might have used to satisfy the functional use test? Or, was the case a lost cause once it was determined that the functional use test applied, rather than (as the taxpayers apparently assumed) the like-kind test? Consider the following IRS rulings.

PRIVATE LETTER RULING 8127089

April 10, 1981.

Dear * * *:

This is in response to your letter dated * * * In that correspondence you requested a determination letter stating that no gain will be recognized under section 1033 of the Internal Revenue Code if insurance proceeds from the loss of works of art are reinvested in other works of art. . . .

On * * *, a fire occurred in the residence then occupied by the taxpayers. There was damage to an art collection consisting of approximately 3,000 lithographs, representing the works of approximately 200 different artists and having an approximate value of * * * The art collection damage also included some oil paintings, pencil drawings, sculptures, masks, wood carvings and block prints. There was smoke and water damage to this collection slightly in excess of * * * Insurance proceeds were paid to the taxpayers in the amount of the damage in * * * The bulk of the insurance proceeds were paid for the damage to and loss in value of the print collection; 1 percent or less was attributable to the loss in value of art objects other than the lithographs. Some portion of the insurance proceeds represents gain.

The taxpayers are currently experiencing difficulty in having the lithographs restored within a reasonable period of time. They are offering to buy other works of art. The proceeds would be used to purchase replacement property which would consist of approximately 63 percent lithographs and 37 percent art works in other artistic media, such as oil paintings, watercolors, sculptures or other graphic forms of art. . . .

Under the provisions of section 1033(a) of the Code, when property is involuntarily converted into money, the taxpayer must purchase property similar or related in service or use to the property converted in order to avoid recognizing gain. The facts presented have established that you are proposing to replace approximately 99 percent of the lithographs and approximately 1 percent of art works in other artistic media that were partially destroyed with approximately 63 percent lithographs and 37 percent art works in other artistic media. The internal Revenue Service will not consider as property similar or related in service or use, art work in one medium, destroyed in whole or in part, replaced with art work in another medium. Therefore, in order to qualify for complete nonrecognition of gain under section 1033(a), you must purchase the same percentage of lithographs as were destroyed in whole or in part and the same percentage of art works in other artistic media as were destroyed in whole or in part.

Accordingly, gain will be recognized under section 1033(a) of the Code if proceeds of insurance derived from the partial destruction of approximately 99 percent lithographs and approximately 1 percent art works in other art media are reinvested in approximately 63 percent lithographs and approximately 37 percent art works in other art media. Gain would be recognized to the extent that 36 percent of the proceeds were reinvested in art works in other artistic media.

(b) Property Not Used by the Owner

JOHNSON v. COMMISSIONER

United States Tax Court, 1965.
43 T.C. 736.

* * *

Dawson, Judge:

The only issue presented is whether the petitioner, Helene C. Johnson, reinvested the proceeds she received from farm property, which was taken by the Cleveland & Pittsburgh Railroad Co. pursuant to condemnation proceedings, in other property "similar or related in service or use" to the converted property within the meaning of section 1033(a)(3)(A) [current § 1033(a)(2)(A)]. [The farm property (33 acres) was leased to a riding club and used as a place for its members to ride horses and socialize. The replacement property was a half acre triangular parcel in downtown Cleveland, Ohio. It was subject to a 10 year lease to Standard Oil Company, and was used for the operation of a service station.] ...

[P]etitioner held the farm property, subsequently condemned, primarily as rental income-producing property, (and) ... held the urban gasoline station property primarily as rental income-producing property....

Again we must consider an issue which has been litigated often, and with varying results and rationale....

The following comments of the Court of Appeals for the Ninth Circuit In Filippini v. United States, 318 F.2d 841 (9th Cir. Cal. 1963) are pertinent:

> The purpose of the statute is to relieve the taxpayer of unanticipated tax liability arising from involuntary condemnation of his property, by freeing him from such liability to the extent that he reestablishes his prior commitment of capital within the period provided by the statute.

The statute is to be liberally construed to accomplish this purpose.
* * *

It would be fatuous to suggest that the recent decisions applying this standard to taxpayer-lessors are wholly consistent in approach or result. All of them except McCaffrey agree that since the statute is intended to relieve the taxpayer, the question of whether the condemned and replacement investments are similar must be determined from the taxpayer's relationship to each.

The amount and kind of services rendered by the petitioners here to the tenants of the converted and replacement properties were negligible. As to both, they paid the taxes and insurance and collected the rent. They had no control over the business operations of the riding club, the racehorse owners, or the filling station. We are satisfied that both properties were held for investment purposes, even though respondent advances the unconvincing argument that petitioners were owner-users of the farm property and operated it as a business. As our findings of fact indicate, these were rental income-producing properties. Here, as in Ponticos, there is no substantial difference between the relationship and responsibilities of the petitioner as lessor of the converted property and as lessor of the replacement property. Under these circumstances we think the replacement property represents a reasonably similar continuation of the petitioner's prior commitment of capital and not a departure from it. . . .

We hold for the petitioners. . . .

DRENNEN, J., dissenting: (Dissenting opinion in which RAUN, TRAIN, and HOYT, J.J. concurred, omitted).

QUESTION, NOTE

How would *Johnson* be decided today? See § 1033(g). Note that prior to the adoption of § 1033(g), if the taxpayer in *Johnson* had operated the riding club and the service station, § 1033 would not have applied, since the properties would fail the functional use test. The distinction between owner-users and owner-lessors remains important in contexts to which § 1033(g) does not apply.

The Internal Revenue Service has adopted the approach of the Tax Court in *Johnson*. See Rev. Rul. 80–184, 1980–2 C.B. 232 ("In the owner-lessor situation the important factor is the similarity of the taxpayer's relationship to the original and replacement properties. The relationship can be sufficiently similar even though the use by the respective tenants changes.").

(c) What Constitutes Involuntary Conversion?

WILLAMETTE INDUSTRIES, INC. v. COMMISSIONER

United States Tax Court, 2002.
118 T.C. 126.

GERBER, J.

Background

* * * Petitioner operates a vertically integrated forest products manufacturing business, which includes the ownership and processing of trees (raw materials) at various types of manufacturing plants, including lumber mills, plywood plants, and paper mills. The raw materials used in the manufacturing process are derived from petitioner's trees and from trees grown by others. Approximately 40 percent of petitioner's timber needs is acquired from petitioner's timberland, which comprises 1,253,000 acres of forested land.

Petitioner suffered damage to some of its standing trees during each of the years in issue, 1992–95. The damage was caused by wind, ice storms, wildfires, or insect infestations. The damage left part of petitioner's damaged trees standing and part of them fallen. The intended use of the trees was continued growth and cultivation until maturity, at which time the trees would have been systematically and efficiently harvested. The damage occurred prior to the intended time for harvest.

Petitioner salvaged its damaged trees to avoid further loss (from decay, insects, etc.) by means of the following steps: (1) Taking down damaged trees that remained standing; (2) cutting damaged trees into standard length logs; (3) stripping the branches from the logs; (4) dragging the logs to a pickup point; (5) grading and sorting the logs; (6) stacking the logs at a landing point; and (7) loading the logs onto trucks for further use or processing.

Petitioner chose to take the seven steps described in the preceding paragraph, rather than attempting to sell the damaged trees in place to a third party. Once it performed the seven steps, its options were to (1) attempt to sell the partially processed damaged trees to a third party; or (2) complete the processing of the damaged trees in its own plants in the ordinary course of its business. Petitioner chose the latter and completed the processing itself.

Petitioner relies on section 1033 for involuntary conversion treatment (deferral of gain). Petitioner did not realize income from harvesting and processing the damaged trees until it sold the products it manufactured from the damaged trees. Petitioner is seeking to defer only that portion of the gain attributable to the difference between its basis and the fair market value of the damaged trees as of the time its salvage of them began; that is, the value petitioner contends would have been recognized if it had sold the damaged trees on the open market instead of further processing and/or milling the damaged trees into finished products. Petitioner further contends that it is not attempting to defer any portion of the gain attributable to the processing, milling, or finishing of products.[5] Respondent determined that petitioner understated income by improperly deferring gain from the sale of the end product of the damaged trees, as follows: 1992—$647,953; 1993—$2,276,282; 1994—$3,592,035; and 1995—$4,831,462.

Discussion

The specific question we consider is whether petitioner is disqualified from electing deferral of gain under section 1033 because it processed damaged trees into end or finished products rather than being compelled simply to sell the damaged trees.

Respondent contends that under section 1033 the realization of gain must stem directly or solely from the damage and the involuntary conversion. More particularly, respondent asserts that petitioner's conversion was not "involuntary" because damaged trees were processed into end products in the ordinary course of its business. Respondent points out that section 1033 is a relief provision which does not or should not include petitioner's situation; i.e., where the damaged trees are processed in the same manner as undamaged trees. Finally, respondent contends that section 1033 was not intended for the long-term deferral of profits from petitioner's timber processing and manufacturing business.

Petitioner argues that its factual situation complies literally with the requirements of section 1033 allowing deferral of gain realized from salvaging its damaged trees. Specifically, petitioner contends that it was compelled (in order to avoid further damage or loss) to salvage (process) the damaged trees resulting in an involuntary conversion within the meaning of section 1033. Petitioner also points out that the conversion was "involuntary" because the damaged trees were not scheduled for harvest at the time of the damage. In response to respondent's argument, petitioner contends that its choices for salvaging the damaged trees should not preclude deferral of the portion of the gain that it was compelled to realize on account of the damage to its trees. Petitioner emphasizes that it is not attempting to defer gain from processing and/or milling the damaged trees. Petitioner seeks to defer only that portion of the gain attribut-

---

5. Based on a hypothetical example presented by petitioner, the majority of the gain deferred would appear to be attributable to the difference between the fair market value of the damaged trees and petitioner's basis. Petitioner posed a hypothetical example which included the premises that the damaged trees had a $100 basis and a $475 selling price if sold in place. If the damaged trees were processed into logs, the processing cost would be $25 resulting in a $500 selling price. Petitioner further posits that the cost of milling timber is $100 and that a finished product would have a $610 selling price, resulting in $10 of gain from milling. Petitioner argues that, under this hypothetical, respondent would have allowed a deferral of the $375 gain if petitioner had sold the damaged trees in place. Petitioner contends that respondent has denied any deferral whatsoever, even though the milling of timber into a final product adds only $10 of additional gain in the context of petitioner's hypothetical. We consider here only whether petitioner is entitled to use sec. 1033. The parties have left to another day the question of the amount of gain to be deferred if petitioner's motion for partial summary judgment is granted.

able to the difference between its basis in the damaged trees and their fair market value at the time the process of salvaging the trees began.

Section 1033 provides, under certain prescribed circumstances, for relief from taxpayer's gains realized from involuntary conversion of property. The relief provided for under section 1033 is deferral of the gain from involuntary conversion, so long as the proceeds are used to acquire qualified replacement property.

The purpose of section 1033 was described, as follows:

> The purpose of the statute is to relieve the taxpayer of unanticipated tax liability arising from involuntary * * * [conversion] of his property, by freeing him from such liability to the extent that he re-establishes his prior commitment of capital within the period provided by the statute. The statute is to be liberally construed to accomplish this purpose. On the other hand, it was not intended to confer a gratuitous benefit upon the taxpayer by permitting him to utilize the involuntary interruption in the continuity of his investment to alter the nature of that investment tax free. * * *

Only a limited amount of legislative history has accompanied the enactment of the various involuntary conversion relief provisions since 1921. The House and Senate reports issued in connection with section 214(a)(12) of the 1921 Act explained that the relief "permits the taxpayer to omit or deduct the gains involuntarily realized, when he proceeds forthwith in good faith to invest the proceeds of such conversion in the acquisition of similar property or in establishment of a replacement fund therefor."

From that limited legislative history, it can be gleaned that Congress intended relief from involuntary conversions only to the extent of the "proceeds of such conversion", and expected taxpayers to acquire replacement property within a reasonable time. Obviously, relief was intended only where the conversion was involuntary. Although Congress was concerned about the timeliness and "good faith" of efforts in seeking replacement property, there was no explanation or particular focus upon the use of damaged assets in the taxpayer's business.

Where the complete destruction or loss of property has occurred, there has been only a limited amount of litigation about whether a taxpayer should be allowed to defer the attendant gain. Where the destruction or loss to property is partial, however, additional questions have arisen.

In *C.G. Willis, Inc. v. Commissioner*, 342 F.2d 996 (3d Cir. 1965), the taxpayer's ship was damaged in a 1957 collision, and the insurance company paid $100,000 to the taxpayer. The insurance payment was approximately $9,000 less than the taxpayer's basis in the ship, and, accordingly, no gain was realized for 1957. In 1958, however, the taxpayer sold the damaged, but unrepaired, ship for an amount which exceeded the remaining basis by approximately $86,000. Under those circumstances, it was held that the 1958 sale was not an "involuntary conversion" within the meaning of section 1033 so that the gain had to be recognized and could not be deferred. In so holding, it was explained that the damage to the taxpayer's ship was insufficient to compel the taxpayer to sell and, accordingly, the sale was not involuntary. In that setting, "involuntary conversion" under section 1033 was defined to mean "that the taxpayer's property, through some outside force or agency beyond his control, is no longer useful or available to him for his purposes."

* * *

Those cases reveal two general elements as being necessary to qualify for deferral of gain under section 1033. First, a taxpayer's property must be involuntarily damaged, and second the property must no longer be available for the taxpayer's intended business purposes for the property.

* * *

* * * Rev. Rul. 80–175, 1980–2 C.B. 230, * * * permitted deferral of gain from the sale of damaged trees. The factual predicate * * * was as follows:

the taxpayer was the owner of timberland. As a result of a hurricane, a considerable number of trees were uprooted. The timber was not insured, and once downed, was subject to decay or being rendered totally worthless by insects within a relatively short period of time. The taxpayer was, however, able to sell the damaged timber and realized a gain from such sale. The proceeds of the sale were used to purchase other standing timber.

The rationale articulated in Rev. Rul. 80–175, *supra*, is that gain is "postponed on the theory that the taxpayer was compelled to dispose of property and had no economic choice in the matter" and that the taxpayer "was compelled by the destruction of the timber to sell it for whatever the taxpayer could or suffer a total loss." Accordingly, the taxpayer in the 1980 ruling was found to have met the two part test; i.e., that the damage was involuntary and the timber was no longer available for the taxpayer's intended business purpose. Most significantly, the 1980 ruling eliminated the requirement that the damage-causing event convert the property directly into cash or other property.

The 1980 ruling also contained a comparison with the holding in *C.G. Willis, Inc. v. Commissioner, supra,* as follows:

In the present case, the downed timber was not repairable and was generally no longer useful to the taxpayer in the context of its original objective. The destruction caused by the hurricane forced the taxpayer to sell the downed timber for whatever price it could get. Unlike the situation in *Willis,* the sale of the downed timber was dictated by the damage caused by the hurricane.

The taxpayer in the 1980 ruling apparently intended to grow trees and/or hold timberland for sale at a particular maturity. The hurricane caused the taxpayer to involuntarily sell/use the trees prior to the time intended for harvest or sale. The taxpayer's intended purpose or use was only affected as to timing, and the sale was prior to the time the taxpayer intended to sell or harvest.

Returning to the disagreement here, petitioner contends that, at the time of the damage, it did not intend to harvest the damaged trees, so that the conversion was involuntary and within the meaning of the statute. Petitioner argues that a taxpayer may not have a choice as to *whether* to dispose of damaged property, but a taxpayer may have a choice as to *how* to dispose of damaged property.

Respondent contends that petitioner should not be entitled to such deferral because of its choice to further process the trees into logs or finished products, its original intention. Respondent's position in this case is a reversion to the requirement of the 1972 ruling that the sale (conversion to cash) be the direct result of the damage-causing event. For more than 21 years, the Commissioner's ruling position has permitted section 1033 deferral even though the conversion is not directly into cash.

* * *

The critical factor is that petitioner was compelled to harvest the damaged trees prior to the time it had intended. The possibility that the partial damage to petitioner's trees might have been relatively small or resulted in a nominal amount of reduction in gain is not a reason to deny relief. In addition, if petitioner's salvage efforts were more successful than other taxpayers that is not a reason for denial of relief under section 1033.

Petitioner's circumstances fulfill the statutory purpose and intent. There was unanticipated tax liability due to various casualties that damaged the trees. Petitioner seeks to defer the gain that was occasioned by the damage and which it had reinvested in like property. Petitioner had not planned to harvest the damaged trees. Identical to the taxpayer's situation in the 1980 ruling, petitioner's trees were damaged by forces without its control, and petitioner was compelled to salvage its damaged trees prior to the intended date for harvest, sale, and/or processing into end products. Unlike the taxpayer in *C.G. Willis v. Commissioner, supra,* petitioner was forced to salvage (process or sell) the damaged trees or suffer a total loss.

Respondent's attempt to distinguish petitioner's situation from the ruling does not reconcile with the rationale of the 1980 ruling, the underlying statute, and case law. The taxpayer in the ruling and petitioner were both forced to salvage the damaged trees or suffer the imminent and total loss of the damaged trees. The taxpayer in the ruling and petitioner were prematurely forced to salvage (sell or use) the damaged trees. The damaged trees were used in their businesses, but not in the same manner as they would normally have done. In the 1980 ruling, the taxpayer was forced to sell the trees under unintended business conditions. Likewise, petitioner was forced to use the damaged trees, albeit in its manufacturing process, under unintended business conditions; i.e. before maturity and/or before the time at which the trees would normally be ready for efficient harvest.

Respondent also argues that petitioner is not entitled to defer gain because "there were no actual sales of damaged timber." Respondent argues that section 1033 requires a sale or conversion of the damaged property into money or property similar in use to the damaged property. Section 1033 simply requires that property be involuntarily converted into money or property. There is no requirement, as argued by respondent, that the deferred gain be derived in a particular manner; i.e., only from a distress sale. Based on the holding of Rev. Rul. 80–175, it is unlikely that respondent would have questioned the deferral of gain if petitioner had been forced to sell the damaged trees in place.

Finally, respondent contends that section 1033 was intended to provide relief for taxpayers who experience "destruction [of property] in whole or in part". Although respondent agrees that petitioner had a casualty, damage to the trees, and petitioner was compelled to salvage them, respondent infers that petitioner's situation is somehow not directly affected by the destruction. Respondent contends that petitioner's gain is voluntary or not caused by the damage because petitioner is able to process the logs into finished products.

Admittedly, petitioner's circumstances may appear more favorable than might have been expected after a "casualty", but the statute does not have a quantitative threshold. Petitioner is not seeking a windfall in the form of the deferral of gain from processing and/or making the finished products. Nor is petitioner attempting to "utilize the involuntary interruption in the continuity of his investment to alter the nature of that investment tax free." Petitioner is seeking to defer the unexpected gain that resided in trees that it had not, at the time of the damage, intended to harvest and to reinvest that gain in trees that will fulfill petitioner's intended purpose. Such deferral was the intended purpose for the enactment of section 1033.

Respondent argues that the purpose of section 1033 may be better served where a taxpayer is unable to process damaged property into the taxpayer's usual product(s). But that disability is not a threshold for relief or a requirement of the statute. Section 1033 is a relief provision, and we are to construe it liberally to effect its purpose.

Respondent would have this Court impose its own judgment as to which taxpayer deserves relief. So, for example, if a taxpayer, like the one in the 1980 ruling, was growing trees for eventual sale, relief is available even though the taxpayer sells the damaged trees to its usual customers. Under respondent's suggested approach, petitioner would not be entitled to relief because it had choices other than sale; i.e., to further process the damaged trees. Petitioner, under respondent's approach, would be deprived of relief from involuntarily generated gain merely because of happenstance. Under that type of reasoning, petitioner would be denied relief merely because it was a grower of trees and also a manufacturer of products using trees, whereas a similarly situated grower of trees without the ability to use the damaged trees to make products would be entitled to relief, even though its damaged trees might ultimately be manufactured into products by others. The line respondent asks us to draw would be illusive and a matter of conjecture.

Petitioner was growing its trees for harvest when they reached a certain maturity. The damage occurred outside of petitioner's control and forced petitioner to salvage its trees earlier than intended. That situation is indistinguishable from the circumstances set forth in Rev. Rul. 80–175, where the taxpayer's trees were felled by a hurricane. The fact that the damage was sufficiently partial so as to result in a substantial amount of deferral is not a reason, under the statute, to deny relief.

We read the statute in light of respondent's Rev. Rul. 80–175, *supra,* which has been outstanding for 22 years.

haiku

Trees fall in empty woods

Willamette processes

Will IRS hear?

D. EXCLUSION OF GAIN FROM SALE OF PRINCIPAL RESIDENCE

Code: § 121

1. GAIN OR LOSS REALIZED ON THE SALE OF A PRINCIPAL RESIDENCE

When Congress considered the Taxpayer Relief Act of 1997, it was pointed out that gain on the sale of a principal residence is subject to taxation, while a loss is never deductible. Some members of Congress felt this treatment was unfair to homeowners. Do you agree?

Congress did not allow a deduction for such losses. However, it repealed old § 121 which, as described below, provided a limited exclusion for gain on the sale of a principal residence; and replaced it with current § 121, which, for most (but not all) taxpayers, exempts from taxation all gain realized on the sale of a principal residence. Unlike §§ 1031 and 1033, which merely defer recognition of gain, § 121 provides an exclusion from income. Gain qualifying for the exclusion is completely exempt from taxation. It is never taxed.

The amount of gain excluded under § 121 is limited to $250,000 ($500,000 on a joint return) for any one sale [§ 121 (b) (1), (2)]. Although the exclusion can be used repeatedly over the taxpayer's lifetime, it is limited to only one sale every 2 years [§ 121 (b) (3)]. If the conditions of § 121 are met, it applies automatically; but a taxpayer may elect not to have the section apply. It seems unlikely many taxpayers will choose to elect out of § 121. In rare cases, the 2–year limitation might make such an election desirable.

The only requirement for the exclusion (aside from meeting the 2–year limitation) is that the property sold have been owned and used by the taxpayer as his principal residence for periods aggregating 2 years or more, during the 5 year period ending on the date of sale [§ 121 (a)]. Let's call this the 2–year rule, to distinguish it from the 2–year limitation described above.

Neither the 2–year limitation, nor the 2–year rule, applies if a taxpayer fails to meet them by reason of a change in place of employment, health, or other unforeseen circumstances specified in the regulations. However, in such cases the amount excluded is proportionately reduced. For example, if a single taxpayer owned and used a house as his principal residence for 1 year prior to relocating due to a change in his place of employment, and otherwise qualified for the exclusion under § 121, the exclusion for gain realized on sale of the house would be limited to $125,000 (one-half of the usual $250,000 exclusion). See § 121 (c).

PRIVATE LETTER RULING 200820016

* * *

FACTS

On Date 1, Taxpayer purchased and moved into the Residence to be used as her primary residence for herself and her two daughters. In Month 1, one of the daughters, while riding the school bus, was subjected to unruly behavior, verbal abuse, and sexual assault. After the traumatic nature of the crimes, the daughter suffered from persistent fear, and her performance at school started to deteriorate dramatically. The daughter's behavioral change was noticed by the faculty at the school and Taxpayer. Taxpayer tried to work with the school district to resolve these problems, but finally sold the Residence on Date 2 to move her daughter away from the problems.

On Date 2, Taxpayer had not owned and used the Residence as Taxpayer's principal residence for two years during the five-year period preceding the sale. However, Taxpayer requests that she be entitled to exclude the gain from the sale of the Residence under the reduced maximum exclusion provisions of § 121(c).

LAW AND ANALYSIS

Section 121(a) provides that gain from the sale or exchange of property is not included in gross income if, during the 5–year period ending on the date of the sale or exchange, the taxpayer has owned and used the property as the taxpayer's principal residence for periods aggregating two years or more.

* * *

Section 121(c) provides for a reduced maximum exclusion when a taxpayer fails to satisfy the ownership and use requirements of subsection (a) if the primary reason for the sale is the occurrence of employment, health, or unforeseen circumstances.

The reduced maximum exclusion is computed by multiplying the applicable maximum exclusion by a fraction. The numerator of the fraction is the shortest of the following periods:(1) the period of time that the taxpayer owned the property during the 5–year period ending on the date of the sale; (2) the period of time that the taxpayer used the property as the taxpayer's principal residence during the 5–year period ending on the date of the sale; or (3) the period of time between the date of a prior sale or exchange of property for which the taxpayer excluded gain under section 121 and the date of the current sale. The numerator of the fraction may be expressed in days or months. The denominator of the fraction is 730 days or 24 months (depending on the measure of time used in the numerator).

Section 1.121–3(b) of the Income Tax Regulations provides that all the facts and circumstances of a sale will determine whether the primary reason for the sale is the occurrence of unforeseen circumstances. Factors that may be relevant in determining the primary reason for a sale include the following:(1) the sale and the circumstances giving rise to the sale are proximate in time; (2) the suitability of the property as the taxpayer's residence materially changes; (3) the taxpayer's financial ability to maintain the property is materially impaired; (4) the taxpayer uses the property as the taxpayer's residence during the period of the taxpayer's ownership of the property; (5) the circumstances giving rise to the sale are not reasonably foreseeable when the taxpayer begins using the property as the taxpayer's principal residence; and (6) the circumstances giving rise to the sale occur during the period of the taxpayer's ownership and use of the property as the taxpayer's principal residence.

Section 1.121–3(e)(1) provides that a sale is by reason of unforeseen circumstances if the primary reason for the sale is the occurrence of an event that the taxpayer could not reasonably have anticipated before purchasing and occupying the residence. Section 1.121–3(e)(3)states that the Commissioner may issue rulings addressed to specific taxpayers identifying events or situations as unforeseen circumstances with regard to those taxpayers.

Based on the facts, representations, and the relevant law, we conclude that Taxpayer's primary reason for the sale was the occurrence of unforeseen circumstances. Consequently, even though Taxpayer sold the Residence before Taxpayer had owned and used it as Taxpayer's principal residence for two of the preceding five years, Taxpayer is granted permission to exclude gain up to the reduced maximum exclusion amount under § 121(c).

* * *

PROBLEM

On January 1, Year 1, Jean, a single individual, purchased House I costing $55,000. After using the house as her principal residence for 1 year, she moved to another location on January 1, Year 2, where she purchased House II, costing $75,000 (she did not sell House I). On January 1, Year 5, after using House II as her principal residence for 3 years, Jean sold it for $125,000, and returned to House I. After living in House I for 6 months, Jean sold it on June 30, Year 5, for $150,000.

During the 3 years she lived in House II, Jean rented House I. During the rental period Jean properly claimed depreciation deductions on House I totalling $5,000.

1. What is the amount of taxable gain, if any, that Jean must report on sale of the 2 houses? See § 121(a), (b), (d) (6).

2. How would your answer to question 1 change if the reason Jean sold House I after living in it for only 6 months following her return, was that she had a new place of employment? See § 121(c)(2)(B).

3. Harriet purchased a home on January 1, 1999, and lived in it for one year. On January 1, 2000, she, a member of the United States Army, began serving "qualified official extended duty" within the meaning of § 121(d)(9)(c). This tour of qualified official extended duty lasted for six years. On January 1, 2006, she returned to her home. She sold her home on June 30, 2007, having lived there for the previous year and a half. Can she take advantage of § 121?

Internal Revenue Service Notice 2002–60

Notice

REDUCED MAXIMUM EXCLUSION OF GAIN FROM SALE OR EXCHANGE OF PRINCIPAL

RESIDENCE FOR TAXPAYERS AFFECTED BY THE SEPTEMBER 11, 2001, TERRORIST ATTACKS

* * *

Recently, the Service has been asked whether taxpayers affected by the September 11, 2001, terrorist attacks are entitled to exclude the gain from the sale of a principal residence in a reduced maximum amount by reason of unforeseen circumstances. In response, the Commissioner has determined that taxpayers affected by the September 11, 2001, terrorist attacks are entitled to the reduced maximum exclusion. Therefore, a taxpayer may claim a reduced maximum exclusion of gain on a sale or exchange of the taxpayer's principal residence by reason of unforeseen circumstances if the taxpayer sells or exchanges the residence as a result of being affected by the attacks in one or more of the following ways:

(1) A qualified individual (as defined below) was killed,

(2) The taxpayer's principal residence was damaged (without regard to whether, under the taxpayer's circumstances, the taxpayer is entitled to a casualty loss deduction under § 165(h)),

(3) A qualified individual (as defined below) lost employment and became eligible for unemployment compensation (as defined in § 85(b)), or

(4) A qualified individual (as defined below) experienced a change in employment or self-employment that resulted in the taxpayer's inability to pay reasonable basic living expenses for the taxpayer's household (including amounts for food, clothing, housing and related expenses, medical expenses, taxes, transportation, court-ordered payments, and expenses reasonably necessary to production of income, but not for the maintenance of an affluent or luxurious standard of living).

For purposes of the preceding sentence, the term "qualified individual" means, as of September 11, 2001, (1) the taxpayer, (2) the taxpayer's spouse, (3) a co-owner of the residence, or (4) a person whose principal place of abode is in the same household as the taxpayer.

Taxpayers who qualify to claim a reduced maximum exclusion under this notice and have filed their returns for taxable year 2001 may file amended returns to claim the exclusion.

Computation of the Reduced Maximum Exclusion

The reduced maximum exclusion is computed by multiplying the maximum dollar limitation of $250,000 ($500,000 for certain joint filers) by a fraction. The numerator of the fraction is the shortest of the following periods: (1) the period of time that the taxpayer owned the property during the 5–year period ending on the date of the sale or exchange, (2) the period of time that the taxpayer used the property as the taxpayer's principal residence during the 5–year period ending on the date of the sale or exchange, or (3) the period of time between the date of a prior sale or exchange of property for which the taxpayer excluded gain under § 121 and the date of the current sale or exchange. The numerator of the fraction may be expressed in days or months. The denominator of the fraction is 730 days or 24 months (depending on the measure of time used in the numerator).

CHAPTER XIII

TAX SHELTERS, THEIR CAUSE AND CURE

■ ■ ■

Tax shelters are virtually dead, so why do we still bother with them? We do so, first, because they furnish an excellent case study on how the income tax lent itself to manipulation, and how the government managed, after a number of fits and starts, to shut it down. Second, the statutory and caselaw mechanisms developed in the war against tax shelters are still with us. If you are to deal with them effectively, you must know where they came from. Third, reading tax shelter cases are excellent exercises for the beginning tax student. If you can understand what happened in *Frank Lyon* and *United Parcel Service*, and why, then there are few worlds left for you to conquer.

To understand what a tax shelter is, we turn to an excellent description by the Joint Committee on Taxation staff. Then, with some notion of what tax shelters are, we will walk through some of the major congressional attempts to control them, §§ 465 and 469. Then, we will consider what the tax shelter provisions have done to penalties, and to the legal ethics of the tax practice in general. At this point, we will be sufficiently equipped to attack *Frank Lyon* and *United Parcel Service*.

A. GENERAL

JOINT COMMITTEE STAFF PAMPHLET ON TAX SHELTERS (1983)

Overview

Tax-shelter investments enable taxpayers to reduce their tax liabilities by use of tax benefits generated by the investments. There are three selling points that are common to most tax-shelter investments: (1) the ability to defer tax liability to a later year; (2) the opportunity to convert ordinary income to tax-favored income (such as capital gains); and (3) the use of borrowed funds to finance the investment (leverage). * * *

Elements of a Tax–Shelter Investment

In general, a tax shelter is an investment in which a significant portion of the investor's return is derived from the realization of tax

647

savings on other income, as well as the receipt of tax-favored (or, effectively, tax-exempt) income from the investment itself. Tax shelters are typically characterized as abusive if they are formed primarily to obtain tax benefits, without regard to the economic viability of the investment.

In some instances, tax shelters are used to take advantage of specific incentives, such as the accelerated cost recovery system, the deduction for intangible drilling costs, or the deduction for research and experimental expenses, which Congress has legislated. Other shelters use devices in the tax law to achieve tax savings which were never specifically intended by Congress, and some shelters attempt to inflate certain deductions, credits, etc. beyond the properly allowable amount.

Although tax-shelter investments take a variety of forms, there are several elements that are common to most tax shelters. The first of these is the "deferral" of tax liability to future years, resulting, in effect, in an interest-free loan from the Federal Government. The second element of a tax shelter is the "conversion" of ordinary income (subject to tax at a maximum rate of 50 percent)[a] to tax-favored income (such as capital gains subject to tax at a maximum rate of 20 percent). Finally, many tax shelters permit a taxpayer to leverage his investment (i.e., to use borrowed funds to pay deductible expenditures), thereby maximizing the tax benefit of deductibility. What follows is a general description of the elements of a tax shelter.

Deferral

Deferral generally involves the acceleration of deductions, resulting in the reduction of a taxpayer's tax liability in the early years of an investment, instead of matching the deductions against the income that is eventually generated by the investment. Deferral also occurs when, for example, taxpayers funnel U.S. investments through a foreign corporation the earnings of which are not subject to current U.S. tax.

The effect of deferral is that the taxpayer grants himself an interest-free loan from the Federal Government, which loan is repayable when, and as, the tax-shelter investment either produces taxable income or is disposed of at a gain. For example, consider the case of a taxpayer who, at the end of year one, realizes that he or she requires a $1,000 loan for use in year two. If this taxpayer obtained a one-year loan when the prevailing rate of interest is 15 percent (compounded annually), he or she would repay $1,150 at the end of year two. If, instead of obtaining a loan, the taxpayer were to invest in a tax shelter that generated a current deduction of $2,000 in year one, and the underlying investment were not expected to generate $2,000 of income until the following year, the taxpayer would have a $1,000 tax savings (at the 50–percent maximum rate of tax). In the latter case, at the end of year two, instead of repaying a lender $1,150, the taxpayer would incur a Federal income tax of $1,000 on the $2,000 of income generated by the investment. Obviously, the longer the deferral

---

a. Now 35%.

period, the greater the benefit obtained by the taxpayer. Alternatively, the taxpayer could invest the $2,000 of income in another tax shelter to provide a "rollover" or further deferral of the tax.

In some cases, deferral is obtained by the use of legislatively sanctioned tax benefits, such as, for example, the Accelerated Cost Recovery System (ACRS) or the expensing of intangible drilling costs. Other benefits associated with deferral reflect the tax law's treatment of the time value of money. * * *

Conversion

The second aspect of most tax-shelter investments is the "conversion" of ordinary income to tax-favored income (such as capital gains or income that is otherwise subject to a reduced rate of tax). Conversion is achieved where, for example, a taxpayer takes an accelerated deduction against ordinary income, and the income that is eventually generated by the investment is taxed at the 20–percent capital gains rate. Also, if the taxpayer is in a lower tax bracket in the year when the investment generates income, he or she effectively "converts" the tax rate.

In the case of certain deductions (e.g., depreciation deductions), * * * Congress has dealt with conversion by requiring a portion of the gain on disposition of an investment to be treated as ordinary income (rather than capital gains). However, the current "recapture" rules apply only to prevent the conversion of some ordinary income to capital gains, and do not apply to all tax shelters.

Leverage

The use of borrowed money to fund a tax-shelter investment may result in an economic benefit, as well as a tax benefit. Generally, a taxpayer will borrow an amount of money that equals or exceeds his or her equity investment. From an economic viewpoint, to the extent that a taxpayer can use borrowed money to fund a tax-shelter investment, he or she can use his or her own money for other purposes (such as other investments), resulting in an increase in earnings if the investments are profitable. From a tax viewpoint, borrowed funds generally are treated in the same manner as a taxpayer's own money that he or she puts up as equity in the investment. Because a taxpayer is allowed deductions for expenditures paid with borrowed funds, the tax benefits of deductibility (e.g., deferral) are maximized.

Because interest payments on indebtedness are themselves deductible, a debt-financed investment provides an additional tax advantage relative to an equity-financed investment. This is so because the deductibility of interest payments lowers the effective tax rate on the income generated by the investment.

The benefits of leveraging a tax-shelter investment can be illustrated by a simple example. Assume that a 50–percent bracket taxpayer invests $10,000 of his or her own money, and borrows $90,000 to fund a $100,000 investment. If the investment generates a "tax loss" of $30,000 in the first year by reason of accelerated deductions, the taxpayer will save taxes of $15,000 on his or her investment of $10,000.

The significance of leverage increases where a taxpayer obtains a nonrecourse loan (i.e., where there is no personal liability to repay the loan). The benefits associated with the use of nonrecourse loans are discussed below in connection with the partnership rules.

Scope of tax shelter cases

Tax shelter cases require substantial resources of the Internal Revenue Service and the Tax Court. As of September 30, 1982, 284,282 returns with tax shelter issues were in the Internal Revenue Service examination process, an increase of 36,000 returns over the prior year. During 1982, 71,793 returns were closed after examination, with recommended tax and penalties totaling $954.2 million.

On January 1, 1982, the Tax Court had 10,522 tax-shelter cases docketed. At the end of 1982, that number had increased to 15,693. During the 10–month period beginning March 1, 1982, 6,780 tax shelter cases were received by the Tax Court and 2,362 cases were disposed of.

According to a private register of tax shelters, taxpayers invested $8 billion in "tax-advantaged investments" (excluding IRAs and municipal bonds) in 1981 and $9 billion in 1982, and will invest an estimated $11 billion in 1983. According to a related newsletter, investments in public tax shelters (i.e., limited partnerships registered with the Securities and Exchange Commission) for the first quarter of 1983 were 53 percent higher than they were one year ago. This increase appears partially attributable to the improvement in the oil and real estate markets, two major tax shelter areas.

B.   EARLY ATTEMPTS TO ATTACK TAX SHELTERS

1.   CRANE AND TUFTS

As you already know, *Crane* and *Tufts* both helped tax shelters and hindered them. They helped them because they allowed the taxpayer to use someone else's money, and someone else's risk, to create a high basis for the taxpayer's investments. Yet, *Crane* and *Tufts* hindered tax shelters on the amount realized side. When tax shelters terminated, application of the *Crane* and *Tufts* doctrines often left the taxpayer with real losses, but tax gains. *See* Chapter 2.

2. SHAM

Substance over form

Many things about tax shelters were not what they appeared to be. Remember that, in the typical tax shelter, the taxpayer was a wealthy, sophisticated investor, who had always seemed to make money effortlessly in the past. Yet, all of a sudden, he seemed to be losing his shirt.[b]

The sudden "problems" ranged from subtle mischaracterizations to outright fraud. Often, such fudging and beyond were attacked directly. For starters, one could argue that mere labels shouldn't change one type of transaction into another. To quote an old colloquy attributed to Lincoln:

"How many legs does a dog have?"

"Four."

"How many legs does a dog have if you call the tail a leg."

"Four. Calling a tail a leg doesn't make it a leg."

To put the matter more formally, the substance of a transaction must win out over its form. See Gregory v. Helvering, 293 U.S. 465, 55 S.Ct. 266, 79 L.Ed. 596 (1935).

When is a loan not a loan?

Remember that nonrecourse financing was very popular in tax shelters, for it allowed the investor to use someone else's money, with very little risk. But why would a rational "lending" institution have accepted the risk of nonrecourse debt? Perhaps they accepted it because they didn't really view the transaction as a loan in the first place. Instead, they viewed the transaction as one in which they, as agent, create a tax-saving opportunity in exchange for a fee. Perhaps, if the lending institution does not view the transaction as a loan, it really isn't a loan, and the claimed, deductible interest payments are actually something else—something non-deductible.

Another possibility was that the loan was real, but the taxpayer didn't owe nearly as much money as she claimed. Consider, for example, Agro Science Company v. Commissioner, 934 F.2d 573 (5th Cir.1991). Each of the taxpayer partnerships signed notes for $600,000 to pay research fees, and took deductions accordingly. However, the notes were denominated in Brazilian cruzeiros, and were not indexed to inflation, as was commonly done in Brazil. In fact, the value of the Brazilian cruzeiros declined precipitously. Five years later, each of the $600,000 notes could have been satisfied by purchasing cruzeiros then worth US$184.

---

b. "... tax shelter economics were so bad that nineteen out of twenty investments could only be sold to groups of doctors. The twentieth scheme was awful beyond belief and could only be sold to dentists." Martin D. Ginsburg, *Teaching Tax Law After Tax Reform*, 65 Wash. L. Rev. 595 (1990).

Valuation

With real loans, collateral is crucial, and accurate valuation of the collateral is important. When the loans are not real, however, there is no reason to value the collateral correctly. In fact, the higher the valuation, the better. Over-valuation leads to higher basis and higher depreciation deductions. Therefore, many tax shelters were attacked on their valuations. See the statutory definition of "gross valuation overstatement," *infra*.

Example of Overvaluation and Nonrecourse Loans

Taxpayer purchases a limited partnership interest in a jojoba plantation from Promoter. The limited partnership interest is actually worth $1,000. However, Taxpayer agrees to purchase it from Promoter for $100,000. According to the Purchase Agreement, Taxpayer will pay $1,000 down. The remaining $99,000 will be a nonrecourse liability. Only nominal interest payments will be made by Taxpayer during the term of the note. At the end of the term, the remaining principal amount, plus accrued interest, will be due in one balloon payment.

Neither Promoter nor Taxpayer expects Taxpayer to make that final balloon payment. When Taxpayer defaults, Promoter will simply reacquire the limited partnership interest. In the meantime, Taxpayer has a high basis in the partnership interest. Whatever interest payments Taxpayer makes will be deductible. Moreover, the limited partnership agreement will provide that a disproportionate share of partnership deductions will be allocated to Taxpayer. At least, that's how Taxpayer and Promoter hope the scheme will work.

Definitions of Tax Shelters

Perhaps, some thought, if we only could define tax shelters, then we could outlaw them. In Rose v. Commissioner, 88 T. C. 386 (1987) [tax years 1979 and 1980] the Tax Court suggested the following elements of a "generic tax shelter":

1) Tax benefits were the focus of promotional materials;

2) the investors accepted the terms of purchase without price negotiation;

3) the assets in question consist of packages of purported rights, difficult to value in the abstract and substantially overvalued in relation to tangible property included as part of the package;

4) the tangible assets were acquired or created at a relatively small cost shortly prior to the transactions in question; and

5) the bulk of the consideration was deferred by promissory notes, nonrecourse in form or in substance. 88 T.C. at 412.

On appeal, the Sixth Circuit affirmed. However, they did not approve of the Tax Court's suggested definition. Instead, it seemed that the Sixth

Circuit knew a lack of economic substance when it saw it. Rose v. Commissioner, 868 F.2d 851 (6th Cir.1989).

For a more recent, statutory definition, see § 6700, which penalizes the promoters of "abusive tax shelters." The promoter can run afoul of this section in either of two ways. First, the promoter can make:

a statement with respect to the allowability of any deduction or credit, the excludability of any income, or the securing of any other tax benefit by reason of holding an interest in the entity or participating in the plan or arrangement which the person knows or has reason to know is false or fraudulent as to any material matter . . .

§ 6700(a)(2)(A).

Second, the promoter can make a "gross valuation overstatement," which is defined as:

. . . any statement as to the value of any property or services if—

(A) the value so stated exceeds 200 percent of the amount determined to be the correct valuation, and

(B) the value of such property or services is directly related to the amount of any deduction or credit allowable under chapter 1 to any participant.

§ 6700(b)(1).

Other suggested definitions of tax shelters include:

1) Any investment whose promotional materials are printed on glossy paper in at least four colors.

2) Any investment in which early deductions will be at least five times the amount of the cash investment.

C. STATUTORY SOLUTIONS

1. ALTERNATIVE MINIMUM TAX

Code: §§ 55–58

(a) The Basic Scheme

As you have learned, Congress has seen fit to lard the Code with all sorts of tax-saving provisions—some designed to achieve fairness in individual cases, some to provide tax incentives to promote various types of behavior. If a given taxpayer took advantage of one or two of these tax-saving provisions, that would be fine. But what if one taxpayer took advantage of all of them?

In 1969, Treasury Secretary Joseph Barr reported that 154 taxpayers had adjusted gross incomes of $200,000 or more, but taxable incomes of zero. Surely, these taxpayers were not being taxed in accordance with their ability to pay. Congress reacted with the first alternative minimum tax scheme. The notion of the alternative minimum tax is that, even if a given taxpayer qualifies for any number of tax-saving provisions, she should still pay a certain minimum level of tax on her income.

Pursuant to § 55(b)(2), one computes alternative minimum taxable income by starting with one's normal taxable income, and then making appropriate adjustments. The adjustments include, inter alia:

- adding back excessive depreciation pursuant to § 56(a)(1),

- taking away some of the medical expense deduction [§ 56(b)(1)(B)]

- reversing tax preferences such as depletion [§ 57(a)(1)]

- denying tax shelter farm activity losses [§ 58 (a)(1)(A)]

Having computed alternative minimum taxable income, one then subtracts the exemption amount [e.g., $70,950 for married filing joint returns—§ 55(d)(1)(A)]. The resulting "taxable excess" [§ 55(b)(1)(A)(ii)] is multiplied by 26% or 28% [§ 55(b)(1)(A)(i)]. If the resulting "tentative minimum tax" [§ 55(b)] exceeds the regular tax for the taxable year, then such excess is imposed as alternative minimum tax.

So much for simplification.

(b) AMT Runs Amok

KLAASSEN v. COMMISSIONER

United States Tax Court, 1998.
T.C. Memo. 1998–241, *affirmed in an unpublished
opinion*, 182 F.3d 932 (10th Cir. 1999).

Findings of Fact

Petitioners are husband and wife. Petitioners are also members of the Reformed Presbyterian Church of North America (the Church). Members of the Church are taught that the production of many offspring is a blessing. Accordingly, petitioners are opposed to birth control and abortion.

Petitioners have a large family. In 1994, the taxable year in issue, petitioners had 10 children. Shortly before trial, their 13th child was born. All of petitioners' children qualify as petitioners' dependents within the meaning of section 151(c).

Petitioners timely filed a joint Federal income tax return, Form 1040, for 1994. On their return, petitioners properly claimed a total of 12 exemptions; i.e., two for themselves and 10 for their children. Petitioners reduced their income by the aggregate value of the 12 exemptions, or $29,400.

For 1994, petitioners itemized their deductions on Schedule A. Included on Schedule A were deductions for medical and dental expenses in the amount of $4,767.13 and state and local taxes in the amount of $3,263.56.

Petitioners neither completed nor attached Form 6251 (Alternative Minimum Tax—Individuals) to their 1994 income tax return, nor did petitioners report any liability for the alternative minimum tax on line 48 of Form 1040.

[Petitioners reported net taxable income of $34,092.47, and paid tax of $5,111. IRS determined that they owed an additional $1,085.43 in AMT. Ed.] * * *

Opinion

* * *

Petitioners do not challenge the mechanics of the foregoing computation. Rather, petitioners contend that they are not liable for the alternative minimum tax for two independent reasons. First, petitioners contend that the elimination of personal exemptions under the alternative minimum tax adversely affects large families and results in an application of the alternative minimum tax that is contrary to congressional intent. In this regard, petitioners argue that legislative history demonstrates that the alternative minimum tax was intended to limit items of tax preference, not personal exemptions.

Second, petitioners argue that the alternative minimum tax violates various constitutional rights, particularly the right to religious freedom.

A. Congressional Intent

* * *

Accordingly, where, as here, a statute appears to be clear on its face, unequivocal evidence of a contrary purpose must be demonstrable if we are to construe the statute so as to override the plain meaning of the words used therein.

If Congress had intended to tax only tax preferences, it would have defined "alternative minimum taxable income" differently, for example, solely by reference to items of tax preference. Instead, Congress provided for a tax measured by a broader base, namely, alternative minimum taxable income, in which tax preferences are merely included as potential components.

* * *

B. Constitutional Considerations

Having thus decided that the alternative minimum tax is otherwise applicable on the facts of this case, we turn now to petitioners' contention that such tax unconstitutionally inhibits the free exercise of religion.

Cases have held that the usual presumption of constitutionality is particularly strong in the case of a revenue measure. The constitutionality of the alternative minimum tax has previously been upheld by the courts.

Absent clear evidence to the contrary, we are reluctant to hold that the alternative minimum tax infringes on a taxpayer's personal religious beliefs. "The fact that a law with a secular purpose may have the effect of making the observance of some religious beliefs more expensive does not render the statute unconstitutional under the First Amendment." Moreover, we conclude, as in Black, that "religious beliefs have consistently been held not to furnish a basis for complaint about our tax system, at least where the statutory provision attacked is not specifically based, or cannot be shown to be based, upon a classification grounded on religion."

In the present case, the alternative minimum tax is not based upon "a classification grounded on religion." Rather, the statute demonstrates that such tax is triggered by the value of deductions and exemptions claimed, the disallowance of which is unrelated to a taxpayer's religious beliefs. Consequently, we do not agree that the alternative minimum tax unconstitutionally inhibits the free exercise of petitioners' religion.

C. *Conclusion*

In view of the foregoing, we hold that petitioners are liable for the alternative minimum tax. Accordingly, we sustain respondent's determination of the deficiency in income tax.

* * *

Nᴏᴛᴇ

The AMT was intended to address the problem of high income taxpayers who abused the system. However, as *Klaassen* shows, it has led to some unintended consequences. In fact, due to the failure of Congress to make inflation adjustments to the exemption amounts in § 55(d), the Joint Committee on Taxation projects that the number of taxpayers subject to the AMT will grow from the current 1 million to approximately 17 million by the year 2010.

Everyone knows that AMT needs fixing. However, Congress is reluctant to do so. Fixing AMT would lead to a significant decrease in tax revenues. In light of the major cuts in tax revenues since 2001, perhaps the government cannot afford to do the right thing by AMT.

2. A WORD ABOUT BASKETS

One of the common mechanisms of tax shelter legislation is to require the taxpayer to put various categories of income and deductions into separate baskets. In this manner, deductions can only be used to offset income which is in the same basket. No longer may the deductions be used to "shelter" unrelated income.

Suppose you owned a farm and a restaurant, and operated each as a trade or business. Last year, the farm lost money:

Income	$100,000
– Expenses	– $125,000
= Profit (Loss)	(Loss of $25,000)

However, the restaurant made a profit:

Income	$125,000
− Expenses	− $100,000
= Profit (Loss)	Profit of $25,000

If you combine the two operations, you broke even:

Combined Income	$225,000
− Combined Expenses	− $225,000
= Combined Profit (Loss)	0

If you want financial information, with a view toward planning your future (expand the restaurant? sell the farm?), it makes sense to keep separate accounts for the two operations. However, one would think that, for tax purposes, the only relevant figures are the combined figures, which show that your income was wiped out by your deductions.

Note, however, that, when the results of the two operations are combined, the restaurant income is wiped out (dare we say "sheltered"?) by the farm losses. If both are legitimate businesses, and if all of the income and expense figures are real, then there is no cause for complaint. However, possibilities for tax manipulation abound. What if the farm were a "hobby farm"? See Chapter 8, *supra*. To keep the scheming at a minimum, perhaps it is better to keep the restaurant and the "hobby farm" in separate baskets. In that way, farm expenses only affect farm income, and restaurant expenses only affect restaurant income.

3. AT RISK RULES

Code: § 465

As noted above, tax shelters are much more fun when you use nonrecourse financing. Congress attacked nonrecourse financing directly with the enactment of § 465—the at risk rules.[c] Section 465(a)(1) provides that losses from an activity will only be allowed to the extent that the taxpayer is at risk for such activity. Section 465(b)(2) provides that a taxpayer is at risk with respect to borrowed amounts to the extent he:

(A) is personally liable for the repayment of such amounts; or

(B) has pledged property, other than property used in such activity, as security for such borrowed amount (to the extent of the net fair market value of the taxpayer's interest in such property).

Assume that taxpayer borrows $500,000 in a nonrecourse loan. She immediately uses the $500,000 to purchase the rights to a movie. The

---

c. Remember *Higgins*, *supra* in Chapter 8. The taxpayer's real estate activities were considered to be a trade or business, while his other investments were not. Perhaps it was the greater risk associated with the direct ownership of real estate that prompted the court to give those investments preferential treatment. The same bias appears in § 465.

creditor's only recourse for nonpayment of the debt is to foreclose on the movie rights.

Taxpayer takes interest and depreciation deductions in the first year. There is no income. May taxpayer actually deduct anything?

No. Taxpayer's losses due to the activity are limited to the amount which taxpayer has at risk. Taxpayer's loan, being nonrecourse, is not considered to be an amount at risk. Therefore, taxpayer has risked zero, and may deduct zero.

Note, however, that § 465 disallows **losses,** not deductions. Therefore, expenses from such activities will be deductible, as long as there is income from the activities to be offset. Only after the income from the activities has been totally wiped out by deductions, will there be a disallowed loss. In fact, a loss disallowed this year will be carried over, to see if there is any income from the activity next year. The basket approach strikes again.

Section 465 did, indeed, crimp the style of tax shelter promoters, but there were huge chinks in the section's armor. One of them was real estate. Section 465 as originally enacted did not apply to real estate. The reaction was predictable. Investment dollars flowed from other, now suspect tax shelters, into real estate. Banks were happy to lend money for such projects, whether or not there was any market demand for the construction. The loose regulation of savings and loans made things even easier.

The result was see-through office buildings—office buildings which had no tenants, and often not even interior walls. If one looked through the windows on one side, one would "see right through" to the other. The city of Houston was particularly famous for its see-through office buildings.

In 1986, Congress closed the loophole. The § 465 change, as well as the enactment of § 469 described *infra*, had much to do with the collapse in the real estate market. In addition, these two statutory changes were a significant cause of the collapse of many savings and loan associations, particularly in Texas.

4. 1986 CHANGES

Passive activity losses
Code: § 469

Section 469 is yet another attempt to distinguish the real from the sham. This time, the premise is that taxpayers who are genuinely motivated to make money will be actively involved in their transactions. By contrast, those whose true motives relate to tax savings rather than profit will not be actively involved.

Section 469 creates, you guessed it, a separate basket for "passive activities." If your aggregate losses from all passive activities for a taxable year exceed the aggregate income from all passive activities for such year, then you have a "passive activity loss." Such a passive activity loss will not be allowed. However, the disallowed loss will be carried over to the next taxable year. During the next taxable year, the disallowed loss will again be placed in the passive activity basket, and the whole thing starts all over again. If the passive activity loss is not ultimately used in this carryover process, then it will be taken into account upon final disposition of the passive activity.

Note that these provisions neither prohibit nor permanently deny deductions from passive activities. Instead, they defer the deductions until there is sufficient income to be offset in the passive activity basket. Therefore, the statute ultimately creates deferral of deductions, not denial. Its ultimate effect is to prevent passive activity losses to be used to shelter income from other sources.

The crucial term in the whole scheme is "passive activity." Pursuant to § 469(c)(1), the term generally means any activity—

(A) which involves the conduct of any trade or business, and

(B) in which the taxpayer does not materially participate.

"Material participation" has the honor of a regulatory section all to itself—Reg. § 1.469–5T. There are seven ways to show material participation:

1) The individual participates in the activity for more than 500 hours during such year;

2) The individual's participation in the activity for the taxable year constitutes substantially all of the participation in such activity of all individuals (including individuals who are not owners of interests in the activity) for such year;

3) The individual participates in the activity for more than 100 hours during the taxable year, and such individual's participation in the activity is not less than the participation in the activity of any other individual (including individuals who are not owners of interests in the activity) for such year;

4) The activity is a significant participation activity (within the meaning of paragraph (c) of this section) for the taxable year, and the individual's aggregate participation in all significant participation activities during such year exceeds 500 hours;

5) The individual materially participated in the activity (determined without regard to this paragraph (a)(5)) for any five taxable years (whether or not consecutive) during the ten taxable years that immediately precede the taxable year;

6) The activity is a personal service activity (within the meaning of paragraph (d) of this section), and the individual materially participated in the activity for any three taxable years (whether or not consecutive) preceding the taxable year; or

7) Based on all of the facts and circumstances (taking into account the rules in paragraph (b) of this section), the individual participates in the activity on a regular, continuous, and substantial basis during such year.

Does this regulation remind you of the Byzantine Empire?

PROBLEM

Charles is an orthopedic surgeon. His income from the practice of medicine is $300,000 this year. In addition, he earned interest income of $25,000 and dividend income of $35,000.

Charles owns two coin-operated laundromats. Each are totally self-service, providing only standard washers and dryers. Charles pays a management company to see to the business, making sure that the facilities are clean, that the machines are maintained and repaired, that customer complaints are handled, and that the money is collected. None of the management company employees spends more than 100 hours per year performing these duties at Charles' laundromats.

Charles's income and expenses from the two businesses are:

	Laundromat #1	Laundromat #2
gross receipts	$11,000	$20,000
management fee	$3,000	$3,000
depreciation	$2,000	$2,500
interest on loan	$5,500	$5,000
cost of goods sold (sales detergent, bleach)	$4,000	$8,000
Profit Loss	($3,500)	$1,500

Given the management contract, Charles spends no time at all on such things as cleaning, maintenance, normal customer relations, or even collecting the coins deposited in the machines. However, Charles does spend considerable time at each location. Charles is a single parent, and his six-year-old daughter loves to do artwork. Accordingly, Charles and his daughter have decorated each laundromat for each and every holiday that Charles could think of. Charles has spent 55 hours this year (in the company of his daughter) at each location doing these decorating projects, or a total of 110 hours at the two locations. Charles' regular customers generally have found his daughter's holiday decorations to be charming. However, one or two, who are in a distinct minority, have been heard to mutter "Bah, humbug!"

How is Charles treated if the two laundromats are deemed separate businesses? How is he treated if they are deemed to be one business?

What result to Charles if he sells both businesses? Aggregate basis is $30,000; aggregate amount realized is $40,000.

What result if instead of laundromats, the two businesses were parking lots?

Other 1986 changes

Granted, the mortal blow to tax shelters in 1986 was the new passive activity loss section. However, other 1986 changes should be noted. First, by lowering the highest marginal rate from 50% to 28% (even though it has crept back up since), Congress lowered the stakes for the entire game. Second, by taxing capital gains just like ordinary income (albeit briefly) Congress eroded considerably the ability of tax shelters to arrange for the eventual income to be taxed at lower rates.

In addition, the time value of money rules make it more difficult for tax shelters to accelerate deductions into the early years of an investment, unless the investors actually shell out the money. See §§ 461(h) and especially 461(i).

5. ECONOMIC SUBSTANCE

Code: § 7701(*o*)

Section 7701(*o*) was added in 2010. It provides, in part:

In the case of any transaction to which the economic substance doctrine is relevant, such transaction shall be treated as having economic substance only if—

(A) The transaction changes in a meaningful way (apart from Federal income tax effects) the taxpayer's economic position; and

(B) The taxpayer has a substantial purpose (apart from Federal income tax effects) for entering into such transaction.

The lack of economic substance will have an impact on various penalties, as provided in §§ 6662(b)(6), 6662(i) and 6664(c)(2).

Economic substance has been around as a caselaw doctrine for a long time. You will see mention of it in both *Frank Lyon* and *UPS, infra.* In codifying the doctrine, Congress did not intend to change the underlying caselaw. We will just have to see what actual changes Section 7701(*o*) makes.

D. PENALTIES

This chapter is as good a place as any to describe penalties. Although penalties are by no means limited to tax shelter cases, they tend to become considerably more harsh when tax shelters are involved. Moreover, beefed up penalties are a part of the government's broad-ranging attack against tax shelters.

1. TAXPAYER PENALTIES

Code: §§ 6662 and 6702

Start with § 6662, the accuracy-related penalty. Note that the penalty for substantial understatement of income tax in § 6662(d) can be reduced if there was substantial authority for the taxpayer's treatment § 6662(d)(2)(B)(i), or if there was:

(I) adequate disclosure of the relevant facts, and

(II) a reasonable basis for the tax treatment.

See Regulation § 1.6664–4 for what constitutes "reasonable basis."

Pursuant to § 6702, if a tax return either

A) does not contain information on which the substantial correctness of the self-assessment can be judged; or

B) contains information that on its face indicates that the self-assessment is incorrect,

and that conduct is due either to

A) a position which is frivolous; or

B) a desire to delay or impede the administration of the tax laws,

then there are additional civil penalties. Do we detect some overkill?

2. PREPARER PENALTIES

Code: §§ 6694 and 6701

The penalties described above are levied against the taxpayer. However, the tax preparer can also be penalized. Listen up. The preparer might be you. Have a look at §§ 6694 and 6701.

Note that the penalties of § 6694 only apply if there is an understatement of liability due to an unreasonable position. A position is not unreasonable if it is "more likely than tan to be sustained on the merits" Reg. § 1.6694–2(b)(1). However, if there is, or was, substantial authority for your position, then you are okay.

Even if you do not reach the exalted status of a tax return preparer (defined in Reg. § 301.7701–15), you might still have aided and abetted in the preparation of a document which understates a tax liability. If so, you will be liable pursuant to § 6701.

So far, we have considered penalties against the taxpayer, and against the lawyer as tax return preparer, both in terms of monetary penalties and disbarment from practice before the IRS. However, one must not forget the penalties against the lawyer as tax shelter promoter, as set forth in § 6700.

3. CIRCULAR 230

Circular 230, 31 C.F.R. Part 10, governs practice before the Internal Revenue Service by attorneys, certified public accountants, enrolled agents, actuaries, and appraisers. Violation of Circular 230 can get a lawyer disbarred from practice before the Internal Revenue Service.

4. THE LAWS OF PROFESSIONAL RESPONSIBILITY

All of these rules, of course, must be considered in conjunction with the laws governing the professional responsibility of lawyers generally. To muddy the waters still further, consider ABA Formal Opinion 85–352:

> A lawyer may advise reporting a position on a tax return so long as the lawyer believes in good faith that the position is warranted in existing law or can be supported by a good faith argument for an extension, modification or reversal of existing law if there is some realistic possibility of success if the matter is litigated.

The ABA Section of Taxation interpreted Opinion 85–352 as follows:

If the lawyer does not have the requisite good faith belief in the position, he may not ethically advise its being taken. If the client nevertheless takes the position, the lawyer must withdraw.

* * *

> The standard adopted by Opinion 85–352 does not permit taking into account the likelihood of audit or detection in determining whether the ethical standard is met. Whether the return will be audited or not is simply of no consequence to the application of the new standard. The determination of whether there is a realistic possibility of success is made without regard to the reality of the audit lottery, and assumes that the issue is in court and to be decided.

Report of the Special Task Force on Formal Opinion 85–352, 39 Tax Lawyer 635 (1986).

NOTE

Lawyers are often asked to give opinions on proposed tax shelters. These opinions are then used to market the shelters. Circular 230 addresses issues involving tax shelter opinions, and has generated substantial controversy in the tax bar. See especially, Circular 230, § 10.35.

E. FRANK LYON

Frank Lyon is, as you can see, a relatively early case. See if you can trace the dollars, and the ownership. What do you think really happened?

FRANK LYON COMPANY v. UNITED STATES

United States Supreme Court, 1978.
435 U.S. 561, 98 S.Ct. 1291, 55 L.Ed.2d 550.

MR. JUSTICE BLACKMUN delivered the opinion of the Court.

This case concerns the federal income tax consequences of a sale-and-leaseback in which petitioner Frank Lyon Company (Lyon) took title to a building under construction by Worthen Bank & Trust Company (Worthen) of Little Rock, Ark., and simultaneously leased the building back to Worthen for long-term use as its headquarters and principal banking facility.

I

* * *

A

Lyon is a closely held Arkansas corporation engaged in the distribution of home furnishings, primarily Whirlpool and RCA electrical products. Worthen in 1965 was an Arkansas-chartered bank and a member of the Federal Reserve System. Frank Lyon was Lyon's majority shareholder and board chairman; he also served on Worthen's board. Worthen at that time began to plan the construction of a multistory bank and office building to replace its existing facility in Little Rock. About the same time Worthen's competitor, Union National Bank of Little Rock, also began to plan a new bank and office building. Adjacent sites on Capitol Avenue, separated only by Spring Street, were acquired by the two banks. It became a matter of competition, for both banking business and tenants, and prestige as to which bank would start and complete its building first.

Worthen initially hoped to finance, to build, and to own the proposed facility at a total cost of $9 million for the site, building, and adjoining parking deck. This was to be accomplished by selling $4 million in debentures and using the proceeds in the acquisition of the capital stock of a wholly owned real estate subsidiary. This subsidiary would have formal title and would raise the remaining $5 million by a conventional mortgage loan on the new premises. Worthen's plan, however, had to be abandoned for two significant reasons:

1. As a bank chartered under Arkansas law, Worthen legally could not pay more interest on any debentures it might issue than that then specified by Arkansas law. But the proposed obligations would not be marketable at that rate.

2. Applicable statutes or regulations of the Arkansas State Bank Department and the Federal Reserve System required Worthen, as a state bank subject to their supervision, to obtain prior permission for the investment in banking premises of any amount (including that placed in a real estate subsidiary) in excess of the bank's capital stock or of 40% of its

capital stock and surplus.[5] Worthen, accordingly, was advised by staff employees of the federal reserve system that they would not recommend approval of the plan by the system's board of governors.

Worthen therefore was forced to seek an alternative solution that would provide it with the use of the building, satisfy the state and federal regulators, and attract the necessary capital. In September 1967 it proposed a sale-and-leaseback arrangement. The State Bank Department and the Federal Reserve System approved this approach, but the Department required that Worthen possess an option to purchase the leased property at the end of the 15th year of the lease at a set price, and the federal regulator required that the building be owned by an independent third party.

Detailed negotiations ensued with investors that had indicated interest, namely, Goldman, Sachs & Company; White, Weld & Co.; Eastman Dillon, Union Securities & Company; and Stephens, Inc. Certain of these firms made specific proposals.

Worthen then obtained a commitment from New York Life Insurance Company to provide $7,140,000 in permanent mortgage financing on the building, conditioned upon its approval of the titleholder. At this point Lyon entered the negotiations and it, too, made a proposal.

Worthen submitted a counterproposal that incorporated the best features, from its point of view, of the several offers. Lyon accepted the counterproposal, suggesting, by way of further inducement, a $21,000 reduction in the annual rent for the first five years of the building lease. Worthen selected Lyon as the investor. After further negotiations, resulting in the elimination of that rent reduction (offset, however, by higher interest Lyon was to pay Worthen on a subsequent unrelated loan), Lyon in November 1967 was approved as an acceptable borrower by First National City Bank for the construction financing, and by New York Life, as the permanent lender. In April 1968 the approvals of the state and federal regulators were received.

In the meantime, on September 15, before Lyon was selected, Worthen itself began construction.

B

In May 1968 Worthen, Lyon, City Bank, and New York Life executed complementary and interlocking agreements under which the building was sold by Worthen to Lyon as it was constructed, and Worthen leased the completed building back from Lyon:

1. Agreements between Worthen and Lyon. Worthen and Lyon executed a ground lease, a sales agreement, and a building lease.

---

5. Worthen, as of June 30, 1967, had capital stock of $4 million and surplus of $5 million. During the period the building was under construction Worthen became a national bank subject to the supervision and control of the Comptroller of the Currency.

Under the ground lease dated May 1, 1968, Worthen leased the site to Lyon for 76 years and 7 months through November 30, 2044. The first 19 months were the estimated construction period. The ground rents payable by Lyon to Worthen were $50 for the first 26 years and 7 months and thereafter in quarterly payments:

12/1/94 through 11/30/99 (5 years)—$100,000 annually

12/1/99 through 11/30/04 (5 years)—$150,000 annually

12/1/04 through 11/30/09 (5 years)—$200,000 annually

12/1/09 through 11/30/34 (25 years)—$250,000 annually

12/1/34 through 11/30/44 (10 years)—$10,000 annually.

Under the sales agreement dated May 19, 1968, Worthen agreed to sell the building to Lyon, and Lyon agreed to buy it, piece by piece as it was constructed, for a total price not to exceed $7,640,000, in reimbursements to Worthen for its expenditures for the construction of the building.[6]

Under the building lease dated May 1, 1968, Lyon leased the building back to Worthen for a primary term of 25 years from December 1, 1969, with options in Worthen to extend the lease for eight additional 5–year terms, a total of 65 years. During the period between the expiration of the building lease (at the latest, November 30, 2034, if fully extended) and the end of the ground lease on November 30, 2044, full ownership, use, and control of the building were Lyon's, unless, of course, the building had been repurchased by Worthen. Worthen was not obligated to pay rent under the building lease until completion of the building. For the first 11 years of the lease, that is, until November 30, 1980, the stated quarterly rent was $145,581.03 ($582,324.12 for the year). For the next 14 years, the quarterly rent was $153,289.32 ($613,157.28 for the year), and for the option periods the rent was $300,000 a year, payable quarterly. The total rent for the building over the 25–year primary term of the lease thus was $14,989,767.24. That rent equaled the principal and interest payments that would amortize the $7,140,000 New York Life mortgage loan over the same period. When the mortgage was paid off at the end of the primary term, the annual building rent, if Worthen extended the lease, came down to the stated $300,000. Lyon's net rentals from the building would be further reduced by the increase in ground rent Worthen would receive from Lyon during the extension.[7]

---

6. This arrangement appeared advisable and was made because purchases of materials by Worthen (which then had become a national bank) were not subject to Arkansas sales tax. See Ark.Stat.Ann. § 84–1904(*l*) (1960); First Agricultural Nat. Bank v. Tax Comm'n, 392 U.S. 339, 88 S.Ct. 2173, 20 L.Ed.2d 1138 (1968). Sales of the building elements to Lyon also were not subject to state sales tax, since they were sales of real estate.

7. This, of course, is on the assumption that Worthen exercises its option to extend the building lease. If it does not, Lyon remains liable for the substantial rents prescribed by the ground lease. This possibility brings into sharp focus the fact that Lyon, in a very practical sense, is at least the ultimate owner of the building. If Worthen does not extend, the building lease expires and Lyon may do with the building as it chooses. The Government would point out, however, that the net amounts payable by Worthen to Lyon during the building lease's extended

The building lease was a "net lease," under which Worthen was responsible for all expenses usually associated with the maintenance of an office building, including repairs, taxes, utility charges, and insurance, and was to keep the premises in good condition, excluding, however, reasonable wear and tear.

Finally, under the lease, Worthen had the option to repurchase the building at the following times and prices:

11/30/80 (after 11 years)—$6,325,169.85

11/30/84 (after 15 years)—$5,432,607.32

11/30/89 (after 20 years)—$4,187,328.04

11/30/94 (after 25 years)—$2,145,935.00

These repurchase option prices were the sum of the unpaid balance of the New York Life mortgage, Lyon's $500,000 investment, and 6% interest compounded on that investment.

2. Construction financing agreement. By agreement dated May 14, 1968, id., at 462, City Bank agreed to lend Lyon $7,000,000 for the construction of the building. This loan was secured by a mortgage on the building and the parking deck, executed by Worthen as well as by Lyon, and an assignment by Lyon of its interests in the building lease and in the ground lease.

3. Permanent financing agreement. By Note Purchase Agreement dated May 1, 1968, New York Life agreed to purchase Lyon's $7,140,000 6 3/4 25–year secured note to be issued upon completion of the building. Under this agreement Lyon warranted that it would lease the building to Worthen for a noncancelable term of at least 25 years under a net lease at a rent at least equal to the mortgage payments on the note. Lyon agreed to make quarterly payments of principal and interest equal to the rentals payable by Worthen during the corresponding primary term of the lease. The security for the note was a first deed of trust and Lyon's assignment of its interests in the building lease and in the ground lease. Worthen joined in the deed of trust as the owner of the fee and the parking deck.

In December 1969 the building was completed and Worthen took possession. At that time Lyon received the permanent loan from New York Life, and it discharged the interim loan from City Bank. The actual cost of constructing the office building and parking complex (excluding the cost of the land) exceeded $10,000,000.

C

Lyon filed its federal income tax returns on the accrual and calendar year basis. On its 1969 return, Lyon accrued rent from Worthen for December. It asserted as deductions one month's interest to New York Life; one month's depreciation on the building; interest on the construc-

---

terms, if all are claimed, would approximate the amount required to repay Lyon's $500,000 investment at 6% compound interest.

tion loan from City Bank; and sums for legal and other expenses incurred in connection with the transaction.

On audit of Lyon's 1969 return, the Commissioner of Internal Revenue determined that Lyon was "not the owner for tax purposes of any portion of the Worthen Building," and ruled that "the income and expenses related to this building are not allowable . . . for Federal income tax purposes." He also added $2,298.15 to Lyon's 1969 income as "accrued interest income." This was the computed 1969 portion of a gain, considered the equivalent of interest income, the realization of which was based on the assumption that Worthen would exercise its option to buy the building after 11 years, on November 30, 1980, at the price stated in the lease, and on the additional determination that Lyon had "loaned" $500,000 to Worthen. In other words, the Commissioner determined that the sale-and-leaseback arrangement was a financing transaction in which Lyon loaned Worthen $500,000 and acted as a conduit for the transmission of principal and interest from Worthen to New York Life.

All this resulted in a total increase of $497,219.18 over Lyon's reported income for 1969, and a deficiency in Lyon's federal income tax for that year in the amount of $236,596.36. The Commissioner assessed that amount, together with interest of $43,790.84, for a total of $280,387.20.

Lyon paid the assessment and filed a timely claim for its refund. The claim was denied, and this suit, to recover the amount so paid, was instituted in the United States District Court for the Eastern District of Arkansas within the time allowed by 26 U.S.C. § 6532(a)(1).

After trial without a jury, the District Court, in a memorandum letter-opinion setting forth findings and conclusions, ruled in Lyon's favor and held that its claimed deductions were allowable. It concluded that the legal intent of the parties had been to create a bona fide sale-and-leaseback in accordance with the form and language of the documents evidencing the transactions. It rejected the argument that Worthen was acquiring an equity in the building through its rental payments. It found that the rents were unchallenged and were reasonable throughout the period of the lease, and that the option prices, negotiated at arm's length between the parties, represented fair estimates of market value on the applicable dates. It rejected any negative inference from the fact that the rentals, combined with the options, were sufficient to amortize the New York Life loan and to pay Lyon a 6% return on its equity investment. It found that Worthen would acquire an equity in the building only if it exercised one of its options to purchase, and that it was highly unlikely, as a practical matter, that any purchase option would ever be exercised. It rejected any inference to be drawn from the fact that the lease was a "net lease." It found that Lyon had mixed motivations for entering into the transaction, including the need to diversify as well as the desire to have the benefits of a "tax shelter."

The United States Court of Appeals for the Eighth Circuit reversed. It held that the Commissioner correctly determined that Lyon was not the true owner of the building and therefore was not entitled to the claimed deductions. It likened ownership for tax purposes to a "bundle of sticks" and undertook its own evaluation of the facts. It concluded, in agreement with the Government's contention, that Lyon "totes an empty bundle" of ownership sticks. It stressed the following:

(a) The lease agreements circumscribed Lyon's right to profit from its investment in the building by giving Worthen the option to purchase for an amount equal to Lyon's $500,000 equity plus 6% compound interest and the assumption of the unpaid balance of the New York Life mortgage.[8]

(b) The option prices did not take into account possible appreciation of the value of the building or inflation.[9]

(c) Any award realized as a result of destruction or condemnation of the building in excess of the mortgage balance and the $500,000 would be paid to Worthen and not Lyon.[10]

(d) The building rental payments during the primary term were exactly equal to the mortgage payments.[11]

(e) Worthen retained control over the ultimate disposition of the building through its various options to repurchase and to renew the lease plus its ownership of the site.[12]

(f) Worthen enjoyed all benefits and bore all burdens incident to the operation and ownership of the building so that, in the Court of Appeals' view, the only economic advantages accruing to Lyon, in the event it were considered to be the true owner of the property, were

8. Lyon here challenges this assertion on the grounds that it had the right and opportunities to sell the building at a greater profit at any time; the return to Lyon was not insubstantial and was attractive to a true investor in real estate; the 6% return was the minimum Lyon would realize if Worthen exercised one of its options, an event the District Court found highly unlikely; and Lyon would own the building and realize a greater return than 6% if Worthen did not exercise an option to purchase.

9. Lyon challenges this observation by pointing out that the District Court found the option prices to be the negotiated estimate of the parties of the fair market value of the building on the option dates and to be reasonable.

10. Lyon asserts that this statement is true only with respect to the total destruction or taking of the building on or after December 1, 1980. Lyon asserts that it, not Worthen, would receive the excess above the mortgage balance in the event of total destruction or taking before December 1, 1980, or in the event of partial damage or taking at any time.

11. Lyon concedes the accuracy of this statement, but asserts that it does not justify the conclusion that Lyon served merely as a conduit by which mortgage payments would be transmitted to New York Life. It asserts that Lyon was the sole obligor on the New York Life note and would remain liable in the event of default by Worthen. It also asserts that the fact the rent was sufficient to amortize the loan during the primary term of the lease was a requirement imposed by New York Life, and is a usual requirement in most long-term loans secured by a long-term lease.

12. As to this statement, Lyon asserts that the Court of Appeals ignored Lyon's right to sell the building to another at any time; the District Court's finding that the options to purchase were not likely to be exercised; the uncertainty that Worthen would renew the lease for 40 years; Lyon's right to lease to anyone at any price during the last 10 years of the ground lease; and Lyon's continuing ownership of the building after the expiration of the ground lease.

income tax savings of approximately $1.5 million during the first 11 years of the arrangement.[13]

The court concluded that the transaction was "closely akin" to that in Helvering v. Lazarus & Co., 308 U.S. 252 (1939). "In sum, the benefits, risks, and burdens which [Lyon] has incurred with respect to the Worthen building are simply too insubstantial to establish a claim to the status of owner for tax purposes.... The vice of the present lease is that all of [its] features have been employed in the same transaction with the cumulative effect of depriving [Lyon] of any significant ownership interest."

We granted certiorari because of an indicated conflict with American Realty Trust v. United States, 498 F.2d 1194 (4th Cir. Va. 1974).

II

This Court, almost 50 years ago, observed that "taxation is not so much concerned with the refinements of title as it is with actual command over the property taxed—the actual benefit for which the tax is paid." In a number of cases, the Court has refused to permit the transfer of formal legal title to shift the incidence of taxation attributable to ownership of property where the transferor continues to retain significant control over the property transferred. In applying this doctrine of substance over form, the Court has looked to the objective economic realities of a transaction rather than to the particular form the parties employed. The Court has never regarded "the simple expedient of drawing up papers," as controlling for tax purposes when the objective economic realities are to the contrary. Nor is the parties' desire to achieve a particular tax result necessarily relevant.

In the light of these general and established principles, the Government takes the position that the Worthen–Lyon transaction in its entirety should be regarded as a sham. The agreement as a whole, it is said, was only an elaborate financing scheme designed to provide economic benefits to Worthen and a guaranteed return to Lyon. The latter was but a conduit used to forward the mortgage payments, made under the guise of rent paid by Worthen to Lyon, on to New York Life as mortgagee. This, the Government claims, is the true substance of the transaction as viewed under the microscope of the tax laws. Although the arrangement was cast in sale-and-leaseback form, in substance it was only a financing transaction, and the terms of the repurchase options and lease renewals so indicate. It is said that Worthen could reacquire the building simply by satisfying the mortgage debt and paying Lyon its $500,000 advance plus interest, regardless of the fair market value of the building at the time; similarly, when the mortgage was paid off, Worthen could extend the lease at drastically reduced bargain rentals that likewise bore no relation to fair rental value but were simply calculated to pay Lyon its $500,000 plus interest over the extended term. Lyon's return on the arrangement in no

---

13. In response to this, Lyon asserts that the District Court found that the benefits of occupancy Worthen will enjoy are common in most long-term real estate leases, and that the District Court found that Lyon had motives other than tax savings in entering into the transaction. It also asserts that the net cash after-tax benefit would be $312,220, not $1.5 million.

event could exceed 6% compound interest (although the Government conceded it might well be less). Furthermore, the favorable option and lease renewal terms made it highly unlikely that Worthen would abandon the building after it in effect had "paid off" the mortgage. The Government implies that the arrangement was one of convenience which, if accepted on its face, would enable Worthen to deduct its payments to Lyon as rent and would allow Lyon to claim a deduction for depreciation, based on the cost of construction ultimately borne by Worthen, which Lyon could offset against other income, and to deduct mortgage interest that roughly would offset the inclusion of Worthen's rental payments in Lyon's income. If, however, the Government argues, the arrangement was only a financing transaction under which Worthen was the owner of the building, Worthen's payments would be deductible only to the extent that they represented mortgage interest, and Worthen would be entitled to claim depreciation; Lyon would not be entitled to deductions for either mortgage interest or depreciation and it would not have to include Worthen's "rent" payments in its income because its function with respect to those payments was that of a conduit between Worthen and New York Life.

The Government places great reliance on Helvering v. Lazarus & Co., supra, and claims it to be precedent that controls this case. The taxpayer there was a department store. The legal title of its three buildings was in a bank as trustee for land-trust certificate holders. When the transfer to the trustee was made, the trustee at the same time leased the buildings back to the taxpayer for 99 years, with option to renew and purchase. The Commissioner, in stark contrast to his posture in the present case, took the position that the statutory right to depreciation followed legal title. The Board of Tax Appeals, however, concluded that the transaction between the taxpayer and the bank in reality was a mortgage loan and allowed the taxpayer depreciation on the buildings. This Court, as had the Court of Appeals, agreed with that conclusion and affirmed. It regarded the "rent" stipulated in the leaseback as a promise to pay interest on the loan, and a "depreciation fund" required by the lease as an amortization fund designed to pay off the loan in the stated period. Thus, said the Court, the Board justifiably concluded that the transaction, although in written form a transfer of ownership with a leaseback, was actually a loan secured by the property involved.

The Lazarus case, we feel, is to be distinguished from the present one and is not controlling here. Its transaction was one involving only two (and not multiple) parties, the taxpayer-department store and the trustee-bank. The Court looked closely at the substance of the agreement between those two parties and rightly concluded that depreciation was deductible by the taxpayer despite the nomenclature of the instrument of conveyance and the leaseback.

The present case, in contrast, involves three parties, Worthen, Lyon, and the finance agency. The usual simple two-party arrangement was legally unavailable to Worthen. Independent investors were interested in participating in the alternative available to Worthen, and Lyon itself (also independent from Worthen) won the privilege. Despite Frank Lyon's presence on Worthen's board of directors, the transaction, as it ultimately developed, was not a familial one arranged by Worthen, but one compelled by the realities of the restrictions imposed upon the bank. Had Lyon not appeared, another interested investor would have been selected. The ultimate solution would have been essentially the same. Thus, the presence of the third party, in our view, significantly distinguishes this case from Lazarus and removes the latter as controlling authority.

III

It is true, of course, that the transaction took shape according to Worthen's needs. As the Government points out, Worthen throughout the negotiations regarded the respective proposals of the independent investors in terms of its own cost of funds. It is also true that both Worthen and the prospective investors compared the various proposals in terms of the return anticipated on the investor's equity. But all this is natural for parties contemplating entering into a transaction of this kind. Worthen needed a building for its banking operations and other purposes and necessarily had to know what its cost would be. The investors were in business to employ their funds in the most remunerative way possible. And, as the Court has said in the past, a transaction must be given its effect in accord with what actually occurred and not in accord with what might have occurred.

There is no simple device available to peel away the form of this transaction and to reveal its substance. The effects of the transaction on all the parties were obviously different from those that would have resulted had Worthen been able simply to make a mortgage agreement with New York Life and to receive a $500,000 loan from Lyon. Then Lazarus would apply. Here, however, and most significantly, it was Lyon alone, and not Worthen, who was liable on the notes, first to City Bank, and then to New York Life. Despite the facts that Worthen had agreed to pay rent and that this rent equaled the amounts due from Lyon to New York Life, should anything go awry in the later years of the lease, Lyon was primarily liable.[14] No matter how the transaction could have been devised otherwise, it remains a fact that as the agreements were placed in final form, the obligation on the notes fell squarely on Lyon.[15] Lyon, an ongoing enterprise, exposed its very business well-being to this real and substantial risk.

The effect of this liability on Lyon is not just the abstract possibility that something will go wrong and that Worthen will not be able to make its payments. Lyon has disclosed this liability on its balance sheet for all the world to see. Its financial position was affected substantially by the presence of this long-term debt, despite the offsetting presence of the

---

14. New York Life required Lyon, not Worthen, to submit financial statements periodically.

15. It may well be that the remedies available to New York Life against Lyon would be far greater than any remedy available to it against Worthen, which, as lessee, is liable to New York Life only through Lyon's assignment of its interest as lessor.

building as an asset. To the extent that Lyon has used its capital in this transaction, it is less able to obtain financing for other business needs.

In concluding that there is this distinct element of economic reality in Lyon's assumption of liability, we are mindful that the characterization of a transaction for financial accounting purposes, on the one hand, and for tax purposes, on the other, need not necessarily be the same. Accounting methods or descriptions, without more, do not lend substance to that which has no substance. But in this case accepted accounting methods, as understood by the several parties to the respective agreements and as applied to the transaction by others, gave the transaction a meaningful character consonant with the form it was given. Worthen was not allowed to enter into the type of transaction which the Government now urges to be the true substance of the arrangement. Lyon and Worthen cannot be said to have entered into the transaction intending that the interests involved were allocated in a way other than that associated with a sale-and-leaseback.

Other factors also reveal that the transaction cannot be viewed as anything more than a mortgage agreement between Worthen and New York Life and a loan from Lyon to Worthen. There is no legal obligation between Lyon and Worthen representing the $500,000 "loan" extended under the Government's theory. And the assumed 6% return on this putative loan—required by the audit to be recognized in the taxable year in question—will be realized only when and if Worthen exercises its options.

The Court of Appeals acknowledged that the rents alone, due after the primary term of the lease and after the mortgage has been paid, do not provide the simple 6% return which, the Government urges, Lyon is guaranteed. Thus, if Worthen chooses not to exercise its options, Lyon is gambling that the rental value of the building during the last 10 years of the ground lease, during which the ground rent is minimal, will be sufficient to recoup its investment before it must negotiate again with Worthen regarding the ground lease. There are simply too many contingencies, including variations in the value of real estate, in the cost of money, and in the capital structure of Worthen, to permit the conclusion that the parties intended to enter into the transaction as structured in the audit and according to which the Government now urges they be taxed.

It is not inappropriate to note that the Government is likely to lose little revenue, if any, as a result of the shape given the transaction by the parties. No deduction was created that is not either matched by an item of income or that would not have been available to one of the parties if the transaction had been arranged differently. While it is true that Worthen paid Lyon less to induce it to enter into the transaction because Lyon anticipated the benefit of the depreciation deductions it would have as the owner of the building, those deductions would have been equally available to Worthen had it retained title to the building. The Government so concedes. The fact that favorable tax consequences were taken into account by Lyon on entering into the transaction is no reason for disallowing those consequences.[15] We cannot ignore the reality that the tax laws affect the shape of nearly every business transaction. Lyon is not a corporation with no purpose other than to hold title to the bank building. It was not created by Worthen or even financed to any degree by Worthen.

The conclusion that the transaction is not a simple sham to be ignored does not, of course, automatically compel the further conclusion that Lyon is entitled to the items claimed as deductions. Nevertheless, on the facts, this readily follows. As has been noted, the obligations on which Lyon paid interest were its obligations alone, and it is entitled to claim deductions therefor under § 163(a) of the 1954 Code.

As is clear from the facts, none of the parties to this sale-and-leaseback was the owner of the building in any simple sense. But it is equally clear that the facts focus upon Lyon as the one whose capital was committed to the building and as the party, therefore, that was entitled to claim depreciation for the consumption of that capital. The Government has based its contention that Worthen should be treated as the owner on the assumption that throughout the term of the lease Worthen was acquiring an equity in the property. In order to establish the presence of that growing equity, however, the Government is forced to speculate that one of the options will be exercised and that, if it is not, this is only because the rentals for the extended term are a bargain. We cannot indulge in such speculation in view of the District Court's clear finding to the contrary. We therefore conclude that it is Lyon's capital that is invested in the building according to the agreement of the parties, and it is Lyon that is entitled to depreciation deductions, under § 167 of the 1954 Code.

IV

We recognize that the Government's position, and that taken by the Court of Appeals, is not without superficial appeal. One, indeed, may theorize that Frank Lyon's presence on the Worthen board of directors; Lyon's departure from its principal corporate activity into this unusual venture; the parallel between the payments under the building lease and the amounts due from Lyon on the New York Life mortgage; the provisions relating to condemnation or destruction of the property; the nature and presence of the several options available to Worthen; and the tax benefits, such as the use of double declining balance depreciation, that accrue to Lyon during the initial years of the arrangement, form the basis of an argument that Worthen should be regarded as the owner of the building and as the recipient of nothing more from Lyon than a $500,000 loan.

---

15. Indeed, it is not inevitable that the transaction, as treated by Lyon and Worthen, will not result in more revenues to the Government rather than less. Lyon is gambling that in the first 11 years of the lease it will have income that will be sheltered by the depreciation deductions, and that it will be able to make sufficiently good use of the tax dollars preserved thereby to make up for the income it will recognize and pay taxes on during the last 14 years of the initial term of the lease and against which it will enjoy no sheltering deduction.

We however, as did the District Court, find this theorizing incompatible with the substance and economic realities of the transaction: the competitive situation as it existed between Worthen and Union National Bank in 1965 and the years immediately following; Worthen's undercapitalization; Worthen's consequent inability, as a matter of legal restraint, to carry its building plans into effect by a conventional mortgage and other borrowing; the additional barriers imposed by the state and federal regulators; the suggestion, forthcoming from the state regulator, that Worthen possess an option to purchase; the requirement, from the federal regulator, that the building be owned by an independent third party; the presence of several finance organizations seriously interested in participating in the transaction and in the resolution of Worthen's problem; the submission of formal proposals by several of those organizations; the bargaining process and period that ensued; the competitiveness of the bidding; the bona fide character of the negotiations; the three-party aspect of the transaction; Lyon's substantiality[17] and its independence from Worthen; the fact that diversification was Lyon's principal motivation; Lyon's being liable alone on the successive notes to City Bank and New York Life; the reasonableness, as the District Court found, of the rentals and of the option prices; the substantiality of the purchase prices; Lyon's not being engaged generally in the business of financing; the presence of all building depreciation risks on Lyon; the risk borne by Lyon, that Worthen might default or fail, as other banks have failed; the facts that Worthen could "walk away" from the relationship at the end of the 25–year primary term, and probably would do so if the option price were more than the then-current worth of the building to Worthen; the inescapable fact that if the building lease were not extended, Lyon would be the full owner of the building, free to do with it as it chose; Lyon's liability for the substantial ground rent if Worthen decides not to exercise any of its options to extend; the absence of any understanding between Lyon and Worthen that Worthen would exercise any of the purchase options; the nonfamily and nonprivate nature of the entire transaction; and the absence of any differential in tax rates and of special tax circumstances for one of the parties—all convince us that Lyon has far the better of the case.[18]

In so concluding, we emphasize that we are not condoning manipulation by a taxpayer through arbitrary labels and dealings that have no economic significance. Such, however, has not happened in this case.

In short, we hold that where, as here, there is a genuine multiple-party transaction with economic substance which is compelled or encour-

---

17. Lyon's consolidated balance sheet on December 31, 1968, showed assets of $12,225,612, and total stockholders' equity of $3,818,671. Of the assets, the sum of $2,674,290 represented its then investment in the Worthen building.

18. Thus, the facts of this case stand in contrast to many others in which the form of the transaction actually created tax advantages that, for one reason or another, could not have been enjoyed had the transaction taken another form. Indeed, the arrangements in this case can hardly be labeled as tax-avoidance techniques in light of the other arrangements being promoted at the time.

aged by business or regulatory realities, is imbued with tax-independent considerations, and is not shaped solely by tax-avoidance features that have meaningless labels attached, the Government should honor the allocation of rights and duties effectuated by the parties. Expressed another way, so long as the lessor retains significant and genuine attributes of the traditional lessor status, the form of the transaction adopted by the parties governs for tax purposes. What those attributes are in any particular case will necessarily depend upon its facts. It suffices to say that, as here, a sale-and-leaseback, in and of itself, does not necessarily operate to deny a taxpayer's claim for deductions.

The judgment of the Court of Appeals, accordingly, is reversed.

It is so ordered.

Mr. Justice White dissents and would affirm the judgment substantially for the reasons stated in the opinion in the Court of Appeals for the Eighth Circuit.

Mr. Justice Stevens, dissenting.

In my judgment the controlling issue in this case is the economic relationship between Worthen and petitioner, and matters such as the number of parties, their reasons for structuring the transaction in a particular way, and the tax benefits which may result, are largely irrelevant. The question whether a leasehold has been created should be answered by examining the character and value of the purported lessor's reversionary estate.

For a 25–year period Worthen has the power to acquire full ownership of the bank building by simply repaying the amounts, plus interest, advanced by the New York Life Insurance Company and petitioner. During that period, the economic relationship among the parties parallels exactly the normal relationship between an owner and two lenders, one secured by a first mortgage and the other by a second mortgage.[1] If Worthen repays both loans, it will have unencumbered ownership of the property. What the character of this relationship suggests is confirmed by the economic value that the parties themselves have placed on the reversionary interest.

All rental payments made during the original 25–year term are credited against the option repurchase price, which is exactly equal to the unamortized cost of the financing. The value of the repurchase option is thus limited to the cost of the financing, and Worthen's power to exercise the option is cost free. Conversely, petitioner, the nominal owner of the reversionary estate, is not entitled to receive any value for the surrender of its supposed rights of ownership.[2] Nor does it have any power to control Worthen's exercise of the option.

---

1. "[W]here a fixed price, as in Frank Lyon Company, is designed merely to provide the lessor with a predetermined fixed return, the substantive bargain is more akin to the relationship between a debtor and creditor than between a lessor and lessee."

2. It is worth noting that the proposals submitted by two other potential investors in the building did contemplate that Worthen would pay a price above the financing costs for acquisition

"It is fundamental that 'depreciation is not predicated upon ownership of property but rather upon an investment in property.' No such
investment exists when payments of the purchase price in accordance with
the design of the parties yield no equity to the purchaser." Here, the
petitioner has, in effect, been guaranteed that it will receive its original
$500,000 plus accrued interest. But that is all. It incurs neither the risk of
depreciation,[4] nor the benefit of possible appreciation. Under the terms of
the sale-leaseback, it will stand in no better or worse position after the
11th year of the lease—when Worthen can first exercise its option to
repurchase—whether the property has appreciated or depreciated.[5] And
this remains true throughout the rest of the 25–year period.

Petitioner has assumed only two significant risks. First, like any other
lender, it assumed the risk of Worthen's insolvency. Second, it assumed
the risk that Worthen might not exercise its option to purchase at or
before the end of the original 25–year term.[6] If Worthen should exercise
that right not to repay, perhaps it would then be appropriate to characterize petitioner as the owner and Worthen as the lessee. But speculation as
to what might happen in 25 years cannot justify the present characterization of petitioner as the owner of the building. Until Worthen has made a
commitment either to exercise or not to exercise its option,[7] I think the
Government is correct in its view that petitioner is not the owner of the
building for tax purposes. At present, since Worthen has the unrestricted
right to control the residual value of the property for a price which does

of the leasehold interest. For instance, Goldman, Sachs & Company proposed that, at the end of
the lease's primary term, Worthen would have the option to repurchase the property for either its
fair market value or 20% of its original cost, whichever was the greater. A repurchase option
based on fair market value, since it acknowledges the lessor's equity interest in the property, is
consistent with a lessor-lessee relationship.

4. Petitioner argues that it bears the risk of depreciation during the primary term of the
lease, because the option price decreases over time. This is clearly incorrect. Petitioner will
receive $500,000 plus interest, and no more or less, whether the option is exercised as soon as
possible or only at the end of 25 years. Worthen, on the other hand, does bear the risk of
depreciation, since its opportunity to make a profit from the exercise of its repurchase option
hinges on the value of the building at the time.

5. After the 11th year of the lease, there are three ways that the lease might be terminated.
The property might be condemned, the building might be destroyed by act of God, or Worthen
might exercise its option to purchase. In any such event, if the property had increased in value,
the entire benefit would be received by Worthen and petitioner would receive only its $500,000
plus interest.

6. The possibility that Worthen might not exercise its option is a risk for petitioner because in
that event petitioner's advance would be amortized during the ensuing renewal lease terms,
totaling 40 years. Yet there is a possibility that Worthen would choose not to renew for the full 40
years or that the burdens of owning a building and paying a ground rental of $10,000 during the
years 2034 through 2044 would exceed the benefits of ownership. Ante, at 1301.

7. In this case, the lessee is not "economically compelled" to exercise its option. Indeed, it
may be more advantageous for Worthen to let its option lapse since the present value of the
renewal leases is somewhat less than the price of the option to repurchase. See Brief for United
States 40 n. 26. But whether or not Worthen is likely to exercise the option, as long as it retains
its unrestricted cost-free power to do so, it must be considered the owner of the building. In
effect, Worthen has an option to "put" the building to petitioner if it drops in value below
$500,000 plus interest. Even if the "put" appears likely because of bargain lease rates after the
primary terms, that would not justify the present characterization of petitioner as the owner of
the building.

not exceed the cost of its unamortized financing, I would hold, as a matter of law, that it is the owner.

I therefore respectfully dissent.

QUESTION

Does it really matter if there were two parties to the transaction or three?

See Bernard Wolfman, *The Supreme Court in the Lyons Den: A Failure of Judicial Process,* 66 Cornell L. Rev. 1075 (1981).

F. SUBSTANCE OVER FORM REVISITED

In its war against abusive tax shelters, much depends upon the government's ability to elevate substance over form. If the government is forced to accept the form—to accept a transaction as documented and characterized by the taxpayer and her lawyers—the government will probably lose. How would you assess the government's chances in the 11th Circuit, after the case below?

UNITED PARCEL SERVICE OF AMERICA, INC. v. COMMISSIONER

United States Court of Appeals, Eleventh Circuit, 2001.
254 F.3d 1014.

COX, CIRCUIT JUDGE:

The tax court held United Parcel Service of America, Inc. (UPS) liable for additional taxes and penalties for the tax year 1984. UPS appeals, and we reverse and remand.

I. Background

UPS, whose main business is shipping packages, had a practice in the early 1980s of reimbursing customers for lost or damaged parcels up to $100 in declared value. Above that level, UPS would assume liability up to the parcel's declared value if the customer paid 25per additional $100 in declared value, the "excess-value charge." If a parcel were lost or damaged, UPS would process and pay the resulting claim. UPS turned a large profit on excess-value charges because it never came close to paying as much in claims as it collected in charges, in part because of efforts it made to safeguard and track excess-value shipments. This profit was taxed; UPS declared its revenue from excess-value charges as income on its 1983 return, and it deducted as expenses the claims paid on damaged or lost excess-value parcels.

UPS's insurance broker suggested that UPS could avoid paying taxes on the lucrative excess-value business if it restructured the program as insurance provided by an overseas affiliate. UPS implemented this plan in 1983 by first forming and capitalizing a Bermuda subsidiary [Can you spell Tax Haven? Ed.], Overseas Partners, Ltd. (OPL), almost all of whose shares were distributed as a taxable dividend to UPS shareholders (most of whom were employees; UPS stock was not publicly traded). UPS then purchased an insurance policy, for the benefit of UPS customers, from National Union Fire Insurance Company. By this policy, National Union assumed the risk of damage to or loss of excess-value shipments. The premiums for the policy were the excess-value charges that UPS collected. UPS, not National Union, was responsible for administering claims brought under the policy. National Union in turn entered a reinsurance treaty with OPL. Under the treaty, OPL assumed risk commensurate with National Union's, in exchange for premiums that equal the excess-value payments National Union got from UPS, less commissions, fees, and excise taxes.

Under this plan, UPS thus continued to collect 25per $100 of excess value from its customers, process and pay claims, and take special measures to safeguard valuable packages. But UPS now remitted monthly the excess-value payments, less claims paid, to National Union as premiums on the policy. National Union then collected its commission, excise taxes, and fees from the charges before sending the rest on to OPL as payments under the reinsurance contract. UPS reported neither revenue from excess-value charges nor claim expenses on its 1984 return, although it did deduct the fees and commissions that National Union charged.

The IRS determined a deficiency in the amount of the excess-value charges collected in 1984, concluding that the excess-value payment remitted ultimately to OPL had to be treated as gross income to UPS. UPS petitioned for a redetermination. Following a hearing, the tax court agreed with the IRS.

It is not perfectly clear on what judicial doctrine the holding rests. The court started its analysis by expounding on the assignment-of-income doctrine, a source rule that ensures that income is attributed to the person who earned it regardless of efforts to deflect it elsewhere. The court did not, however, discuss at all the touchstone of an ineffective assignment of income, which would be UPS's control over the excess-value charges once UPS had turned them over as premiums to National Union. The court's analysis proceeded rather under the substantive-sham or economic-substance doctrines, the assignment-of-income doctrine's kissing cousins. The conclusion was that UPS's redesign of its excess-value business warranted no respect. Three core reasons support this result, according to the court: the plan had no defensible business purpose, as the business realities were identical before and after; the premiums paid for the National Union policy were well above industry norms; and contemporary memoranda and documents show that UPS's sole motivation was tax avoidance. The revenue from the excess-value program was thus properly deemed to be income to UPS rather than to OPL or National Union. The court also imposed penalties.

UPS now appeals, attacking the tax court's economic-substance analysis and its imposition of penalties. The refrain of UPS's lead argument is that the excess-value plan had economic substance, and thus was not a sham, because it comprised genuine exchanges of reciprocal obligations among real, independent entities. The IRS answers with a before-and-after analysis, pointing out that whatever the reality and enforceability of the contracts that composed the excess-value plan, UPS's postplan practice equated to its preplan, in that it collected excess-value charges, administered claims, and generated substantial profits. The issue presented to this court, therefore, is whether the excess-value plan had the kind of economic substance that removes it from "shamhood," even if the business continued as it had before. The question of the effect of a transaction on tax liability, to the extent it does not concern the accuracy of the tax court's fact-finding, is subject to de novo review. We agree with UPS that this was not a sham transaction, and we therefore do not reach UPS's challenges to the tax penalties.

II.   Discussion

* * * This economic-substance doctrine, also called the sham-transaction doctrine, provides that a transaction ceases to merit tax respect when it has no "economic effects other than the creation of tax benefits." Even if the transaction has economic effects, it must be disregarded if it has no business purpose and its motive is tax avoidance.

The kind of "economic effects" required to entitle a transaction to respect in taxation include the creation of genuine obligations enforceable by an unrelated party. See Frank Lyon Co. The restructuring of UPS's excess-value business generated just such obligations. There was a real insurance policy between UPS and National Union that gave National Union the right to receive the excess-value charges that UPS collected. And even if the odds of losing money on the policy were slim, National Union had assumed liability for the losses of UPS's excess-value shippers, again a genuine obligation. A history of not losing money on a policy is no guarantee of such a future. Insurance companies indeed do not make a habit of issuing policies whose premiums do not exceed the claims anticipated, but that fact does not imply that insurance companies do not bear risk. Nor did the reinsurance treaty with OPL, while certainly reducing the odds of loss, completely foreclose the risk of loss because reinsurance treaties, like all agreements, are susceptible to default.

The tax court dismissed these obligations because National Union, given the reinsurance treaty, was no more than a "front" in what was a transfer of revenue from UPS to OPL. As we have said, that conclusion ignores the real risk that National Union assumed. But even if we overlook the reality of the risk and treat National Union as a conduit for transmission of the excess-value payments from UPS to OPL, there remains the fact that OPL is an independently taxable entity that is not under UPS's control. UPS really did lose the stream of income it had earlier reaped from excess-value charges. UPS genuinely could not apply that money to any use other than paying a premium to National Union; the money could not be used for other purposes, such as capital improvement, salaries, dividends, or investment. These circumstances distinguish UPS's case from the paradigmatic sham transfers of income, in which the taxpayer retains the benefits of the income it has ostensibly forgone. Here that benefit ended up with OPL. There were, therefore, real economic effects from this transaction on all of its parties.

The conclusion that UPS's excess-value plan had real economic effects means * * * that it is not per se a sham. But it could still be one if tax avoidance displaced any business purpose. The tax court saw no business purpose here because the excess-value business continued to operate after its reconfiguration much as before. This lack of change in how the business operated at the retail level, according to the court, betrayed the restructuring as pointless.

It may be true that there was little change over time in how the excess-value program appeared to customers. But the tax court's narrow notion of "business purpose"—which is admittedly implied by the phrase's plain language—stretches the economic-substance doctrine farther than it has been stretched. A "business purpose" does not mean a reason for a transaction that is free of tax considerations. Rather, a transaction has a "business purpose," when we are talking about a going concern like UPS, as long as it figures in a bona fide, profit-seeking business. This concept of "business purpose" is a necessary corollary to the venerable axiom that tax-planning is permissible. The Code treats lots of categories of economically similar behavior differently. For instance, two ways to infuse capital into a corporation, borrowing and sale of equity, have different tax consequences; interest is usually deductible and distributions to equity-holders are not. There may be no tax-independent reason for a taxpayer to choose between these different ways of financing the business, but it does not mean that the taxpayer lacks a "business purpose." To conclude otherwise would prohibit tax-planning.

The transaction under challenge here simply altered the form of an existing, bona fide business, and this case therefore falls in with those that find an adequate business purpose to neutralize any tax-avoidance motive. True, UPS's restructuring was more sophisticated and complex than the usual tax-influenced form-of-business election or a choice of debt over equity financing. But its sophistication does not change the fact that there was a real business that served the genuine need for customers to enjoy loss coverage and for UPS to lower its liability exposure.

We therefore conclude that UPS's restructuring of its excess-value business had both real economic effects and a business purpose, and it therefore under our precedent had sufficient economic substance to merit respect in taxation. * * *

REVERSED AND REMANDED.

RYSKAMP, DISTRICT JUDGE, dissenting:

I respectfully dissent. Although I agree with the majority's recitation of the facts as well as its interpretation of the applicable legal standard, I find that its reversal of the tax court is contrary to the great weight of the evidence that was before the lower court. The majority, as well as the tax court below, correctly finds that the question before the Court is whether UPS's insurance arrangements with NUF and OPL are valid under the sham-transaction doctrine. Under the sham-transaction doctrine, UPS's transaction ceases to merit tax respect when it has no "economic effects other than the creation of tax benefits," or has no business purpose and its sole motive is tax avoidance. Thus the question before the Court is not strictly whether UPS had a tax avoidance motive when it formulated the scheme in question, but rather whether there was some legitimate, substantive business reason for the transaction as well. There clearly was not.

As the tax court articulated in great detail in its well-reasoned 114–page opinion, the evidence in this case overwhelmingly demonstrates that UPS's reinsurance arrangement with NUF and OPL had no economic significance or business purpose outside of UPS's desire to avoid federal income tax, and was therefore a sham transaction. First, the tax court based its decision upon evidence that the scheme in question was subjectively motivated by tax avoidance. For example, the evidence showed that tax avoidance was the initial and sole reason for the scheme in question, that UPS held off on the plan for some time to analyze tax legislation on the floor of the United States House of Representatives, and that a letter sent to AIG Insurance from UPS detailing the scheme claimed that AIG would serve in merely a "fronting" capacity and would bear little or no actual risk. The evidence thus showed that this scheme was hatched with only tax avoidance in mind.

Second, the tax court based its decision on overwhelming evidence that UPS's scheme had no real economic or business purpose outside of tax avoidance. For example, the evidence showed that NUF's exposure to loss under the plan (except in the very unlikely event of extreme catastrophe) was infinitesimal, and that UPS nevertheless continued to fully bear the administrative costs of the EVC program. NUF was only liable for losses not covered by another insurance policy held by UPS, yet UPS still collected the EVC's and deposited the money into UPS bank accounts, still processed EVC claims, and continued to pay all EVC claims out of UPS bank accounts (while collecting the accrued interest for itself). All NUF really did in the scheme was collect over $1 million in fees and expenses before passing the EVC income on to OPL, which was of course wholly owned by UPS shareholders. In essence, NUF received an enormous fee from UPS in exchange for nothing.

Moreover, the tax court systematically rejected every explanation of the scheme put forth by UPS. UPS claimed that the scheme was meant to avoid violation of state insurance laws, yet the evidence showed no real concern for such laws and that in fact UPS was well aware that federal preemption of these state laws likely made its old EVC plan legal. UPS claimed that it intended OPL to become a full-line insurer someday, yet the evidence showed that it was nevertheless unnecessary to specifically use EVC income for such a capital investment. UPS claimed that elimination of the EVC income allowed it to increase its rates, yet one of its own board members testified that this explanation was untrue. I also note that UPS's claim that OPL was a legitimate insurance company fails in light of the fact that OPL was charging a substantially inflated rate for EVCs. Evidence in the tax court showed that in an arms-length transaction with a legitimate insurance company, EVC rates would have been approximately half those charged by UPS (and in turn passed on to OPL), providing further evidence that the transaction was a sham. In sum, UPS failed to show any legitimate business reason for giving up nearly $100 million in EVC income in 1984.

For these reasons, I would affirm the holding of the tax court and find that UPS's arrangement with NUF and OPL was a sham transaction subject to federal tax liability.

APPENDIX

PRESENT VALUE TABLES

■ ■ ■

Suppose that you were given a choice of receiving one dollar on January 1, Year 1, or one dollar on December 31, Year 1. Which would you choose? You would take the dollar on January 1.

A dollar received on January 1 could be put in a savings account. If your savings earn 4% interest, that account will have grown to a value of $1.04 by December 31. If you choose to receive one dollar on December 31, then all you get is the dollar. Surely, you would rather have $1.04 on December 31 than $1 on December 31.

Say you have a right to receive $1 on December 31, Year 1. What amount would you accept on January 1, Year 1, instead? You can't answer that question without assuming an interest rate. Let us assume 4%.

At a 4% interest rate, you would be indifferent between 96¢ January 1 and $1 on December 31. Why? Because in one year, at 4% interest, that 96¢ in a savings account will grow to a value of $1.

$$\begin{array}{r} \$\ .96 \\ \times 1.04 \\ \hline \$1.00 \end{array}$$

Now assume that you have a right to receive one dollar at the end of two years. What amount would you accept today, instead? At 4% interest, you would accept 92½¢ That amount, invested for two years at 4%, will grow to one dollar.

$$\begin{array}{r} \$.925 \\ \times 1.04 \\ \times 1.04 \\ \hline \$1.00 \end{array}$$

The computations are present value computations. The present value of one dollar in one year at 4% is $.96; the present value of one dollar in two years at 4% is $.92. Below is a portion of a present value table.

685

Value of the Right to Receive One Dollar in the Future After n Years

Year	4%	5%	6%	7%	8%	10%
1	.962	.952	.943	.935	.926	.909
2	.925	.907	.890	.873	.857	.826
3	.890	.864	.839	.816	.794	.751
4	.855	.823	.792	.763	.735	.683
5	.823	.784	.747	.713	.681	.620
6	.790	.746	.705	.666	.630	.564
7	.760	.711	.665	.623	.583	.513
8	.731	.677	.627	.582	.540	.466
9	.703	.645	.591	.544	.500	.424
10	.676	.614	.558	.508	.463	.385
11	.650	.585	.526	.475	.429	.350
12	.625	.557	.497	.444	.397	.318
13	.601	.530	.468	.415	.368	.289
14	.577	.505	.442	.388	.340	.263
15	.555	.481	.417	.362	.315	.239

Present value computations have many applications in tax planning. Below are two of such applications.

1. Tax planner has devised a way for Taxpayer to defer realization and recognition of an income item so that, instead of paying $1,000 in taxes this year, Taxpayer will pay that $1,000 in taxes next year. The plan which tax planner has constructed has some costs. It is important to weigh the costs against the benefits.

The benefit is the difference between paying $1,000 now and paying $1,000 one year from now. The cost, today, of paying $1,000 today is $1,000. The cost, today, of paying $1,000 one year from today is the present value of $1,000 one year from now. At 4%, such present value is $962. Taxpayer could fund next year's tax liability of $1,000 by investing $962 today, at 4%. In one year, that $962 will have grown to $1,000. Therefore, the benefit of the one-year deferral is worth

$$\begin{array}{r} \$1,000 \\ -\,\$962 \\ \hline \$38 \end{array}$$

The costs, properly, should be computed in the same way, discounting any future payments to present value. Then, costs and benefits can be compared to evaluate the plan.

2. Section 7872 is considered *supra* at 409. However, in those materials, consideration was confined to the simpler cases, involving gift loans and demand loans, addressed in § 7872(a). A demand loan is one which has no set term. Rather, the lender can demand repayment whenever he wishes.

Section 7872(b) addresses other loans. For example, imagine that lender loans borrower $1,000, to be paid back in one year. There is no interest stated. If § 7872(b)(1) applies, then the lender shall be treated as having transferred, and the borrower shall be treated as having received, cash equal to the excess of:

(A) the amount loaned, over

(B) the present value of all payments which are required to be made under the terms of the loan.

There is only one payment which is required to be made under the terms of the loan. That is a repayment of the principal amount of $1,000, payable in one year. Assuming an interest rate of 4%, the present value of that payment is $962. Thus:

amount loaned	$1,000
– present value of required payments	– $ 962
amount deemed transferred from lender to borrower	$ 38

Annuity Tables

What if, instead of having the right to receive only **one dollar** in the future, you had the right to receive **one dollar a year**, for some given number of years. Suppose, for example, that you had the right to receive one dollar a year for two years. What would be the present value of that right?

That right can be separated into its two component parts:

1) the right to receive one dollar after one year; and

2) the right to receive another dollar after two years.

The total value of your right can be computed by adding up the values of its component parts. You can value the component parts by referring to the present value tables above. Again, you need to posit an interest rate. At 4%, the present value of the right to receive one dollar after one year is $.962. The present value of the right to receive another dollar after two years is $.925. Thus, the value of your two-year annuity is

$.962
+ $.925
$1.87

You could, if you had to, compute all annuities that way. However, there are tables which will do the job for you.

Present Value of One Dollar Per Year

For a Term of n Years at r%

Year	4%	5%	6%	7%	8%	10%
1	.9615	.9524	.9434	.9346	.9259	.9091
2	1.8861	1.8594	1.8334	1.8080	1.7833	1.7355
3	2.7751	2.7232	2.6730	2.6243	2.5771	2.4868
4	3.6299	3.5459	3.4651	3.3872	3.3121	3.1699
5	4.4518	4.3295	4.2123	4.1002	3.9927	3.7908
6	5.2421	5.0757	4.9173	4.7665	4.6229	4.3553
7	6.0020	5.7863	5.5824	5.3893	5.2064	4.8684
8	6.7327	6.4632	6.2098	5.9713	5.7466	5.3349
9	7.4353	7.1078	6.8017	6.5152	6.2469	5.7590
10	8.1109	7.7217	7.3601	7.0236	6.7101	6.1446
11	8.7604	8.3064	7.8868	7.4987	7.1389	6.4951
12	9.3850	8.8632	8.3838	7.9427	7.5361	6.8137
13	9.9856	9.3935	8.8527	8.3576	7.9038	7.1034
14	10.5631	9.8986	9.2950	8.7454	8.2442	7.3667
15	11.9379	10.3796	9.7122	9.1079	8.5595	7.6061

Perhaps this table will give you a better sense for how annuity companies work. All of the numbers in the table above can be multiplied by the appropriate annual payment. Thus, for example, if the present value of a right to receive one dollar a year for 10 years at 4% is $8.11, then the present value of the right to receive $50 per year for 10 years at 4% is $50 \times \$8.11 = \$405.50$.

Assume that an annuitant with a life expectancy of 10 years would like to purchase an annuity yielding payments of $50 per year for the rest of her life. If the annuity company is willing to give her a return on her investment of 4%, it will charge her $405.50 for the annuity. Of course, the annuity company will hope to invest the $405.50 at a rate of return higher than 4%. Assuming that the annuitant lives exactly her life expectancy, the annuity company's profit will be the difference between its rate of return on its investment, and 4%.

TOPICAL INDEX FIFTH EDITION

References are to Pages